THE SMALL HOUSE
IN EIGHTEENTH-CENTURY LONDON

THE SMALL HOUSE
IN EIGHTEENTH-
CENTURY LONDON

A Social and Architectural History

PETER GUILLERY

Drawings by

ANDREW DONALD

New Photographs by

DEREK KENDALL

Published for
THE PAUL MELLON CENTRE FOR STUDIES IN BRITISH ART
by
YALE UNIVERSITY PRESS
NEW HAVEN AND LONDON
in association with
ENGLISH HERITAGE

Designed by Gillian Malpass

Printed in Singapore

Library of Congress Cataloging-in-Publication Data

Guillery, Peter.

The small house in eighteenth-century London

/ Peter Guillery.—1st ed.

p. cm. Includes bibliographical references and index.

ISBN 0-300-10238-0 (cl : alk. paper)

1. Vernacular architecture—England—London.

2. Workingclass—Dwellings—Great Britain—History—18th century.

3. Architecture, Domestic—England—London.

4. London (England)—Buildings, structures, etc.

I. Title.

NA7552.G85 2004

728'.37'0942109033—D22

2003018895

A catalogue record for this book is available from

The British Library

Frontispiece

Three-room timber houses of *c.*1690 on Ewer Street, Southwark.

Detail from a watercolour by Thomas Hosmer Shepherd, 1852

(see fig. 109) (LMA)

Contents

Acknowledgements

This book has come about through collective effort, institutional support, public involvement and, most importantly, shared enthusiasm.

From its beginnings in the Royal Commission on the Historical Monuments of England, and since 1999 from within English Heritage, the work presented here had its home at No. 55 Blandford Street, in a frequently redesignated group of people engaged in buildings investigation. Andrew Donald was a lynchpin of that group, and that is more than ever true here. Without his drawings these houses would be unintelligible. In producing the drawings for this book Andy has maintained his usual excellence as an illustrator with great perseverance, for which I am deeply grateful. Another colleague, Joanna Smith, has been substantially involved with the project. Much of chapter 4 is based on her survey and research, as drawn together in her report 'Georgian Bermondsey', and, beyond that, she has contributed to other field surveys. Throughout, Jo has been a perceptive critic to whom I am greatly indebted. June Warrington has been hugely supportive, in particular in drawing together illustrations, and Jonathan Clarke also assisted with some survey and research. Most of the recent photographs are by Derek Kendall, who, as always, has brought much more to fieldwork than just estimable photographic skills. Other photographic contributions have been made by Sid Barker and James O. Davies, aided by Mike Seaforth, Amanda Polito and Charles Walker. Others in English Heritage have also been instrumental. Martin Cherry, Colum Giles, Paul Barnwell and Humphrey Welfare have all had managerial responsibility for the project and have all been unstintingly supportive, in Colum's and Paul's cases also commenting closely on the text. From the Survey of London Alan Cox, Malcolm Dickson, John Greenacombe, Stephen Porter, Harriet Richardson, Philip Temple, Colin Thom and George Wilson have generously provided information from their own current or past work and/or commented on the text. Karen Dorn has navigated the book through to publication, and Susie Barson, Richard Bond, Roger Bowdler, Paul Calvocoressi, John Cattell, Ian Goodall, Richard Hewlings, Robert Hook, Delcia Keate, Richard Lea, Ian Leith, Adam Menuge, Kathryn Morrison, Cathy Philpotts, Steven Robb, Simon Taylor, Anne Woodward and Nicola Wray have helped in different ways. It is sad to note, and rather more than a reflection of a lengthy gestation period, that a number of those to whom thanks are owed fall into the category of being former staff of the Royal Commission or English Heritage, specifically John Bold, Mike Clements, Nicholas Cooper, Roger Leech, Chris Miele, Sarah Pearson, Ann Robey and the late Catherine Steeves. To John, Nicholas and Sarah, in particular, an intellectual debt rooted in the Royal Commission is immeasurable. As students on placements Colin Burgess, Emily Gee, Mia Jüngskar, Susanne Larsen, Neville Stankley and Jacky Taylor have also contributed.

Many people wholly outside the institutional base have provided help along the way. Foremost among these is Bernard Herman, whose fizzing excitement when confronted with the then undocumented eighteenth-century buildings of Deptford High Street provided inspiration out of which much, not least this book, has followed. Bernie's contribution has also been concrete, as a partner in the survey of Deptford that forms the basis of much of chapter 6, and through further help with the analysis and measured survey of other buildings. Beyond this, from his base in Delaware he has provided a valuably different North American view of eighteenth-century London, as well as specific information about places and buildings outside London. So, to Bernie, enormous thanks. Andrew Byrne, then of the Spitalfields Trust, introduced me to the neglected eighteenth-century weavers' houses of Bethnal Green, and Dan Cruickshank shared his views on these buildings and wider aspects of Spitalfields. Elizabeth McKellar helped open up avenues of enquiry, especially regarding London's periphery, and has been much more widely supportive. Neil Burton and Frank Kelsall have both shared freely and extensively their knowledge of eighteenth-century London and its domestic architecture. I am grateful to all these people, as I am, for diverse information, insights and support, to Malcolm Airs, Anthony Baggs, Simon Bradley, Ann Coats, David Dewing, Charles Edwards, Brian Gill, Gareth Harris, Matthew Hillier, James Howett, Eleanor John, Carl Lounsbury, William Marshall, Derek Morris, Charles O'Brien, Will Palin, Philip Roys, Wendy de Silva, Christopher B. Smith, Jess Steele, Chris Thomas and Isobel Watson. All this help notwithstanding, mistakes have no doubt been made. For these responsibility is entirely my own.

A number of archive-holding institutions are mentioned in the list of abbreviations and in the illustration credits. Additional mention should be made here of the help provided by staff at these places, especially by Bob Aspinall, John Coulter, Gwynydd Gosling, Chris Lloyd, David Mander, Leonard Reilly, Marion Roe, Julian Watson and all their colleagues. The London Borough of Lewisham made a financial contribution to the survey of houses in Deptford, and numerous local authority conservation and planning staff have provided information and support, notably Phil Ashford, Steve Crow, Mark Dykes, Rachel Ferry, Alec Forshaw, Steve Gould, John Hardy, Mark Hutton, Aine McDonagh, Jan Mondrzejewski, Jonathan Nicholls, Anne-Marie O'Hara, Kay Owen and Lance Penman.

The publication of the book by Yale University Press has been made possible through the support of the Paul Mellon Centre for Studies in British Art and, most particularly, by the interest and commitment of Gillian Malpass. Ruth Thackeray has been a sympathetic and incisive text editor.

This is a book about houses, and most of the buildings considered in it remain homes or small shops. It could not have been written without the co-operation, sometimes initially tinged with scepticism – 'English Heritage? here? why?' – of owners and occupiers who have often been both informative and enthusiastic. With so many people associated with so many buildings it is difficult to be confident of listing them all here. Indeed some, at their own wish, remained anonymous even while co-operating. I hope that they and any others inadvertently omitted will accept collective but no less heartfelt thanks for their part in making this work possible. I am thus grateful to Mr Amini, Mrs Ash, G. Asher, Mr Bandak of Champers Footwear, Benham & Reeves, Rachel Berry, Peter Bloor, M. A. Boshor, Bruno of Blue Audio-Visual, Café Rouge, Cards Galore, Beatrice Carolan, Chambers and Partners, Alan Chandler, Sidney Charles, Dave Collett, John Curtis of the South London Press, Dr Dattani, Nicholas Dawe, Tony Dayton, Mrs Depena, Peter Desbois, Dimestore Ltd, Rashid Diwan of Tronseal Ltd, Reverend Peter Fellows, Jean Field, Denis Flinn, Mr Francis of Juicy Fruits, Tiffany Fraser-Steele, Furlong Homes, Gary's Carpets, Delia Gaze, George and Michael Goddard and Clive Mellor of Goddard's Pie Shop, Jane Greenwood, Yvonne Gregory, Catherine Grimshaw, Hair Dome, Mrs Harrison, Jane Holbury, Hoxton Takeaway, Mark Husband of Keabeach Amusements, Jackets, Andrew Jackson, Stuart Jago, Neville Johnny, Margaret Jones, Steve Jones, Andrew Kennedy, Keith, Cardale & Groves, Martin King, Margaret Kinsley of Kentish Foods, A. P. Kirby, Tim Knox, Mrs Krieger, The Lady Florence Trust, Gwendolin Leick, Grace Lewis of the Adun Society and the African Design Centre, Todd Longstaffe-Gowan, Moosa and Hanif Loonat, Adam Lowe, Sanjay Luthra, Robert Maitland, Chris Mansfield of Readysnacks Café, David Morgan of Angel Flowers, J. A. Patel, R. Patel of Kim's Newsagents, John Price, Mohammed Rajani, Norris Raymond, Mr Reed, Rococo Frames, Gundi Royle, Joe Santos of Tojo Children's Wear, John Senter of the Dulwich Estate, Barry Shelton, Andreas Solomon and his tenants, Phillipa Suarez, Mr Tam, S. K. Thakrar, Dick Turpin, Mrs Vagjiani, William Wellbeloved, Rupert Wheeler, Duncan Wilson, Witches Hut and Ernie Witcomb.

Author's Note

Textual reference to size is given in imperial feet, as this is how the buildings were conceived and built, and how an admittedly declining but significant proportion of an English-speaking readership still quantifies its own living spaces. Square footage is important but its enumeration can be baffling and so it is generally avoided; 12 ft square is preferred to 144 square feet. The term 'storey' refers, as is usual, to each of the three-dimensional vertical divisions of a house, though these same divisions are often referred to, as is also conventional, as 'floors', taking in more than simply the lower plane that is walked on or shown on a plan. Reference to storeys and floors follows British usage, that is the first storey or floor coming above the ground storey or floor.

Introduction

We know little of the artisans and labourers, the shopkeepers and clerks and street-
sellers, who made up the mass of the population. The houses they lived in have been
swept away or transformed out of recognition.

M. Dorothy George[1]

On London's smaller eighteenth-century houses, that, by and large, has been that. The aim of this book is not just to show that some of these houses do still exist and remain capable of recognition, it also sets out to show that they matter. Despite fragmentary survival and the unprepossessing nature of the buildings, they cast new light on eighteenth-century London and its people. Studying them is one of relatively few routes into understanding how life was lived by a large part of the population of a great metropolis, western Europe's biggest city, its principal centre of manufacturing and commerce, and the hub of transformations often characterised as the dawning of modernity.

Reasons for the lack of knowledge about London's smaller eighteenth-century houses are readily grasped. Dorothy George was broadly right; most of the houses lived in by the city's artisans *et al.* have been swept away. Architectural historians and, following their lead, social historians have inevitably concentrated on the more widely surviving larger and higher-status houses of eighteenth-century London. A great deal is known about domestic architecture built for the wealthiest quarter of the population, while next to nothing has been written about that provided for the others. As Raphael Samuel has said, 'Despite, or perhaps because of its apparently solid location, the built environment, as historical evidence, conceals far more than it reveals. [. . .] As with any other form of historical record, the built environment is apt to give a privileged place to the powerful, and indeed very often to leave them as the only presence in the field. [. . .] Differential survival sets up its own biases.'[2] In other spheres it is understood that eighteenth-century London was a place of huge variety and

dissonance, multicultural in the sense that across the social classes there was not a single shared culture. Historical research and literary evocations have begun to draw out the strength of the local and the traditional, but they have lacked evidential bases in buildings. Without the necessary architectural history, lower-status houses remain absent as a material presence in accounts of eighteenth-century London. Many refer in passing to courts, alleys and tenements, usually with noxious adjectives, but rarely with any concrete specificity. In so far as documentation relating to smaller houses has been used by historians, it has generally been abstracted for the purposes of quantitative lines of enquiry relating to 'housing'. From such and other evidence it is probably fair to conclude that, for the poorest half of eighteenth-century London's population, there was either no purpose-built architecture or that its material history has irretrievably escaped study. Much of this book focuses on the second quarter, the bottom half of the top half, broadly definable as made up of artisans, that is skilled tradespeople and their families. Lest this seem a slice of the pie not warranting fuss, these people alone were about as numerous as the combined total populations of Manchester, Liverpool and Birmingham around 1800.

So any notion that the houses of eighteenth-century London constitute a well-understood architectural entity is at best premature. It is not just that smaller houses have not been investigated. There are also problems with the way buildings have been interpreted. The architectural history of eighteenth-century London has retained a tendency to rely on aesthetic valuations of artefacts as stylistically progressive or otherwise, on Whiggish top-down models that stress the spread of the polite. Clas-

facing page Sclater Street in the Spitalfields silk district, where workshop tenements were first built *c.*1719 (see fig. 66). Photographed in the early twentieth century and showing the bird market. These buildings have been demolished, but a market endures (THLHL).

sical ideals of urban space have been pervasive and their deep influence has steered the gaze away from diversity and tradition in eighteenth-century London. 'Improvement' has been taken at face value, without interest in what it was that was being improved. But, as Fernand Braudel put it, in housebuilding 'more than anywhere else the strength of precedent makes itself felt', a house 'bears perpetual witness to the slowness of civilizations, of cultures bent on preserving, maintaining and repeating.'[3] Johan Huizinga went further, turning progressivist views of *Zeitgeist* around by suggesting that 'Traditional forms may contain the spirit of the coming age.'[4] These perceptions have not been applied to houses in London, in part because in England architectural history and the study of vernacular architecture have remained separate and scarcely communicating disciplines.[5]

Sir John Summerson (1904–1992) is a larger than life presence looming over any attempt at a revisionist history of houses in eighteenth-century London, his influence so great that Summersonian historiography is a growing field of scholarship in itself.[6] *Georgian London* was, and remains, a commanding synthesis; first published in 1946 and revised by Summerson himself through seven editions to 1988, it has been re-edited by Howard Colvin for publication in 2003. However, it does not claim, and need not be granted, omniscience; indeed Summerson's modest explanation that the book was a series of essays that 'fell into the shape of a plausible historical perspective'[7] can not be outflanked by postmodern relativism. Summerson took 'taste' and 'wealth' as the twin 'foundation stones' for his analysis. That speaks for itself. Other stories were not the ones that he was telling; 'The nature of Summerson's interest, and of his sources, were such that for the most part his is necessarily a history of the building of aristocratic London, with much less attention given to the "other Londons" in the south and east.'[8] Even so, for much of the architectural history of eighteenth-century London, Summerson said what needed to be said, succinctly and nearly sixty years ago. For any work addressing architecture in eighteenth-century London his authority and clarity continue to light the way.

There has been, of course, much advance on Summerson in terms of particular research, with the Survey of London to the fore, leading to a much more developed understanding of how higher-status or polite houses were built and used. Recently, new emphasis has been given to the complex interplay of the traditional, or vernacular, with the innovative, or polite, in the rise of standardised speculative building.[9] But the focus has continued to be on the central and western districts, where wealth was concentrated, and, even when there have been forays to the poorer and more industrial east and south, on higher-status houses. Whether stress has been on the emulative spread of the polite, or on the standardising impact of market forces, the subject has remained in thrall to a familiar and linear story. Concentration on what was new has obscured what was not, and the degree to which unstandardised urban-vernacular building traditions endured through the eighteenth century in parts of London has not been addressed. Established emphases on vernacular precedent in the years up to 1720 and on 'improvements' after 1760 do provide abutments for an attempt to bridge these themes across the century as a whole. However, the bridge-crossing metaphor should not be extended; lower-status housing in eighteenth-century London does not provide a single alternative linear story, rather it gives evidence of variety across a wide spectrum.

Houses similar to those presented in this book survive better in places outside London. Concentration on the metropolis might therefore be thought perverse. Against that perception it must be stressed that this is a book about London, not one about a class of houses *per se*. Eighteenth-century London has enormous importance as a crucible of modernity, so the presence in it of vernacular architecture carries particular significance. Modernity, an attribute that characterises a whole historical period, while much debated and given many nuances, is widely and increasingly understood as referring not just to those aspects of recent times that have been new, but rather, in a translation of Walter Benjamin, to 'the new in the context of what has always already been there.'[10] The perceptual and necessarily oppositional separation of new and old, an awareness that the present is unlike the past, must underpin any idea of modernity. The perpetuation of tradition was itself a part of modernity in so much as it was sometimes a reaction to what was new. A rounded understanding of the phenomenon must embrace counter-currents, in an eighteenth-century context those that flowed underneath the Enlightenment and the Industrial Revolution, not parallel or unconnected forces, but the conflicting and underlying. Miles Ogborn has offered a rich new historical geography for multi-faceted modernity in eighteenth-century London, providing a foundation onto which the architectural historian can place buildings in 'a fractured and heterogeneous city',[11] a hybrid of diverse localities, characterised by continuity as much as by change. Viewed in this way, the deliberately novel – estate development in London's West End, for example – can be understood as having been anachronistic, because consciously creating something new, while more traditional and local approaches to housebuilding would have been seen as being in and of the present rooted in the past. It is only with the hindsight of a modern society that tradition is read as on the wane and so obliterated from progressivist historical awareness, which sees only the new as being 'of its time'. In an introduction to an account of an architectural dog that didn't bark, this brief epistemological diversion is vital if it is to be accepted that the dog might have had something to say.

Before going any further it is necessary to define some terms. First is that difficult word – vernacular, from *vernaculus* as meaning native, indigenous or autochthonous, also carrying undertones of the domestic and low status.[12] The vast and heterogeneous *Encyclopaedia of Vernacular Architecture of the World* defines vernacular architecture as 'the term most widely used to denote indigenous, tribal, folk, peasant and traditional architecture.'[13] A more *de haut en bas* view comes from Jill Lever's and John Harris's *Illustrated Dictionary of Architecture*, vernacular architecture being 'Designed by one without any training in design guided by a tradition based on local needs, materials and construction methods. Unconcerned with national or international styles, vernacular architecture is essentially local and conservative.'[14] The word 'design' here should perhaps be capitalised, to avoid the implication that the guidance described can not constitute training, but emphasis on the 'local and conservative' is important and unexceptionable. These are contextual words; vernacular buildings can rise only out of their own places and precedents. The relativity of the vernacular was emphasised by Eric Mercer, who paraphrased prevalent understandings of domestic vernacular architecture as indicating traditional form and construction, and relative commonness, smallness and meanness in any local context.[15]

The *Encyclopaedia* cited above lacks an index entry for London. Does London lack historic architecture that can be classified as indigenous, traditional, or even tribal? In England, the world's first predominantly urban-dwelling country, but also home to William Morris and a powerful prelapsarian myth, the word 'vernacular' has been allowed to become separate from both the urban and the recent, resulting in a substantial barrier to the integrated study of social and architectural (building) history. Perhaps 'vernacular' should be dispensed with as worn out, vague and too susceptible to misunderstanding. In sticking with it here, the hope is that it will encourage awareness that there are always local and conservative contexts at the interface of social and architectural history, and that, as Mercer was at pains to stress, what is or is not vernacular changes over time. There is a danger, of course, that 'vernacular' will be spun round until black becomes white, or both become grey.

'Metropolis' is less problematic. It is used here to mean London as a whole, beyond the City, including not only Westminster and Southwark, but also contiguous suburbs, tentacles beyond, and the margins and hinterland that are more obscurely traced. It is intended to emphasise London's especial importance, as not just a large city, or a national capital, but as a cultural parent.

'Small' is a slippery word, but one that can not be avoided without adopting alternatives that carry unwanted baggage. Obviously relative, it has in the past been used to denote eighteenth-century houses much larger than those discussed here, where the frame of reference has excluded anything of lower status.[16] On the other hand, small should not be understood here as embracing the smallest. London had smaller dwellings than those discussed, too ephemeral to have left any evidence for empirical study. The simple absence of evidence for the smallest houses is a problem for the study of historic vernacular architecture generally.[17] Smallness exists only in relation to bigness, an opposition that disguises a continuum. The small-big opposition in houses is broadly translatable as lower- and higher-status, an equally false duality, all the more so as there can be no simple equation of house size with status. Clearly people lived only in houses they could afford, but it should not be assumed that people always lived in the largest house that they might have done. Without other information house size can only be a general guide to status. House form and the use of domestic space, infinitely variable, are even less straightforwardly legible. The opposition of polite and vernacular is also, of course, a retrospective construct that conceals another continuum along which there are many hybrids. That said, the cusp where the vernacular meets the polite is a compass needle pointing to defining areas of social change.

To round off this semantic apologia, 'house' is used in preference to less neutral alternatives. The subject is urban houses built by and for those of modest means. Houses of a rural nature that happen to have been embraced by London's growth are not discussed. The terms 'town house' and 'housing' are sometimes used in the text, but are avoided in the title because in a London context 'town house' tends to mean a large house for a wealthy person who might also have a country house, and 'housing' tends to connote large-scale provision by one group for another.

The origins of this book are in a series of thematic area surveys initiated by the Royal Commission on the Historical Monuments of England in 1997, and, following institutional merger, continued by English Heritage from 1999. These area surveys, as well as numerous topically related single-building surveys, came about because, one after another, regeneration and conservation initiatives in what are now inner London districts threw up evidence of humble eighteenth-century houses for which any interpretative framework was lacking. Methodologically the area surveys were a blend of established Royal Commission and Survey of London approaches, taking the investigation of surviving buildings as a starting-point, combining this with topographical study and documentary research, and setting findings within economic, social and cultural contexts. The institutional roots extend further. Given a subject where survival is relatively sparse, much has been gained from the earlier investigation and recording of buildings long since demolished, using material generated by the Royal Commission, by the Survey of London, and by the London County Council and Greater London Council, most of which is now held by English Heritage in the National Monuments Record. A number of previously unpublished early twentieth-century Royal Commission investigators' 'snaps' are reproduced here. They are not always high-quality photography, but aside from their intrinsic value as records of buildings of which one would otherwise have no knowledge, they have, with the passage of time, gained an added value, being reminiscent of Eugène Atget's Paris, casual documents of the ordinary, all the more precious for the absence of self-conscious composition or site preparation.

The core evidence of this study derives from the analysis of buildings, but it attempts to steer away from what Mercer characterised as 'Formalism' in vernacular architecture studies wherein the documentation of structure and form becomes an end in itself. It is, instead, an attempt to use the empirical study of buildings as the basis for a history that is not at bottom about buildings but rather about people, and a place – London. This makes relatively extensive expositions of historical contexts for the buildings necessary. It also means the suppression of much detail, both in terms of the archaeological description of the buildings as recorded, and in relation to data arising from building-specific documentary research. The plans published here are interpretative reconstructions, not surveys, and observations about the fabric, builders and occupants of the buildings are limited to those that lead towards broader, more or less speculative conclusions. For those desiring more specific information such as site reports, survey drawings or photographs, there is an appendix listing the buildings investigated that have files in the National Monuments Record, a public archive. Access to interiors was through the goodwill of owners and occupiers. Sometimes access was limited, and other buildings that it would have been valuable to investigate have remained wholly inaccessible. In what is not a short book the separation of evidence and synthesis is essentially pragmatic. It is to be hoped that, alongside as yet undiscovered and unresearched buildings and documents, the archived material from this study will help to support other syntheses. As in any field of historical study, it hardly needs saying, there are only flawed and partial accounts, and there are always alternative narratives. One of the main reasons for avoiding 'Formalism' is that these inescapable limitations apply as much to individual building records as they do to synthetic overviews.[18]

This is also a deliberately unbalanced account. Or rather, it is critically counterbalanced, tipping towards London's east and south, to artisans and labourers, with little to say about the west or the wealthy. The core of the book is a series of case studies based on particular localities, arising from the separately undertaken area surveys. This topographical approach and deliberately discontinuous structure have been preferred because they direct attention to the local and to cross-typological comparisons and contexts. There is nothing innovative here; it is the kind of narrative structure that has become widespread in the broader study of domestic architecture, in works 'that take for granted the interdependence of architecture and social life'.[19]

The first two chapters are not case studies, but rather general surveys intended to provide a grounding. They treat eighteenth-century London as a whole, looking at its social make-up, its topography, and the general circumstances of domestic architecture, concentrating on aspects of continuity. The first case study in chapter 3 examines London's silk district, which spread from Spitalfields into Bethnal Green, and the workshop tenements built there to house weavers. Southwark and Bermondsey were more various architecturally, providing evidence of great conservatism, and of what happened when this met 'improvement'. From Mile End Road and Kingsland Road there are accounts of ribbon development on major arteries, illustrating the intersection of the vernacular and the polite at the city's margins through the course of the eighteenth century. Houses associated with the military-industrial satellite that stretched along the south bank of the Thames from Deptford to Woolwich provide a different perspective, emphasising artisan autonomy.

The last of the case study chapters takes the form of a tour round London's hinterland, focusing on smaller buildings to consider how vernacular architecture was connected with polite architecture in sub-metropolitan places where different kinds of house often stood side by side. After quick comparative visits to the rest of England and to the Atlantic coast of North America, chapter 9 returns to London to look at what happened to its vernacular architecture at the end of the eighteenth century. Finally, the nature of the inheritance is considered in chapter 10.

Perceiving it a duty to unearth the histories of those whose viewpoints were not in the ascendant, not least because they might inform understanding of latter-day outlooks, this is an attempt to listen to quiet voices, to address tentatively questions of identity and agency in domestic architecture, without losing awareness that voices from the past speak in languages that are no longer spoken fluently. However much it may be possible to gain new insights, it always has to be remembered that the underlying mentalities, purposes and values of those by whom and for whom the houses considered here were built can not be reliably reconstructed.[20]

Though scattered, fragmentary and ultimately inscrutable, these houses are valuable historical evidence. They are remarkable, simply for having physically endured. But they are also alarmingly ephemeral; once recognised, they have called for urgent documentation. This, in turn, has opened up a new view on eighteenth-century London, a diverse and dynamic city that was not entirely dominated by taste and wealth, but was also a place of production, strongly informed by custom. The houses have their own significance, but they also cast more familiar buildings in new lights, drawing out the interdependence of high and low cultures, of the vernacular and the polite.

1   An impecunious journeyman faces having to find about half of his week's wages to pay for a joint of meat.
Engraving by James Gillray, *The British Butcher*, 1795 (BM).

Chapter 1

THE VERNACULAR METROPOLIS:
LOOKING ACROSS EIGHTEENTH-CENTURY LONDON

One end of London is like a different country from the other in look and in manners.
James Boswell[1]

So James Boswell concluded on 19 January 1763, having walked with two friends across London, from west to east, from Hyde Park Corner through the City to Mile End. The purpose of this chapter is to explore Boswell's perception by providing a survey of aspects of difference in eighteenth-century London, taking into account its extent, economy, social structure, topography and housing conditions. Many such overviews have been written before, but it is necessary to attempt another here, to open the way to interpreting eighteenth-century London's humbler domestic architecture, a 'different' material presence that undoubtedly informed Boswell's observation.

Writing a sweeping account of the city and its wider history to permit a fresh take on its houses involves taking some liberties. There are, of course, debates about the relative importance of numerous trends, but complexities are here suppressed for the sake of brevity and clarity. This is not to say that problems are elided. The objective is simply to set out some building blocks from mainstream history to provide foundations for the architectural history to follow.

London's Size and Population

Before London can be taken apart it needs to be grasped as a whole. Set against sprawling Greater London or many other cities at the beginning of the twenty-first century, eighteenth-century London was tiny and compact − just a few square miles, it could readily be traversed on foot. But in eighteenth-century terms it was vast. Since Daniel Defoe, for whom London was 'such a prodigy of buildings, that nothing in the world does, or

ever did, equal it, except old Rome in Trajan's time',[2] every writer on eighteenth-century London has had to start by emphasising its sheer bigness.

Within its still small geographical compass the city was full of people, with an overall population density about three times that of London's inner boroughs in the 1990s. There had been enormous growth through immigration since the sixteenth century, the number of Londoners all but trebling in the seventeenth century, rising from about 200,000 in 1600 to about 400,000 in 1650, then to about 575,000 in 1700, making London western Europe's largest city, for the first time more populous than less rapidly growing Paris. Growth slowed in the eighteenth century, but population increase to about 675,000 around 1750 made London larger than Constantinople, and further growth to about 959,000 by 1800 put it in touch with Peking (Beijing) and Edo (Tokyo), the even more populous great cities of Asia.[3]

London's size set it firmly apart in England, as it still does. Yet, after the nineteenth-century growth of other towns and all the standardising and urbanising developments of the twentieth century, it is difficult to appreciate just how transcendently big, and therefore different, eighteenth-century London was in English terms. England's next biggest towns around 1670 were Norwich and Bristol with about 20,000 people each, that is each about 4 per cent the size of London, the capital then having about 70 per cent of England's urban population. Bristol had more than doubled its size by 1750 to about 50,000, while relatively stagnant London added 'only' 200,000 in the same period. It has been estimated that in the century 1650 to 1750 one adult in six in England experienced life in London. Even in 1801, by when Manchester, Liverpool and Birmingham were each approaching 100,000 people, these towns remained less than a tenth the size of London. Despite widespread late eighteenth-century urbanisation, London still had more people than the aggregate population of England's twenty-six next biggest towns.[4]

London's rate of population growth was slower in the eighteenth century than it had been in the seventeenth, but each century saw a population increase of a similar order, that is 300,000 plus. Each increase demanded tens of thousands of new houses. Estimates of London's housing stock suggest a rise from about 60,000 to 70,000 houses in 1700 to about 120,000 in 1800.[5] What is easily overlooked in assessments of growth is that during the eighteenth century much of the widespread short-life housing of the seventeenth century had to be replaced. This applies even to parts of the City, largely redeveloped after the Great Fire of 1666. It can be deduced that something in the order of 80,000 or more houses were built in eighteenth-century London.[6] Nowhere else in eighteenth-century Europe, not even St Petersburg, rising from marsh to become a city of more than 200,000 people, generated a comparable demand for new housing. The overwhelmingly huge numbers that apply to London in the eighteenth century make it reasonable to expect that housing provision would have been broad-based, various and untrammelled, certainly innovative in terms of the scale of production, but also opportunistic and inclusive, following old patterns as well as new ones, simply to cope with demand.

Economy

MANUFACTURING AND COMMERCE

The economic realities of London's size had huge ramifications. The capital and its growth were at the heart of the complex web of forces that has often been understood as the Industrial Revolution. The relevant and oft-used metaphor is that London was an engine, driving change in England before and into the eighteenth century.

If London was an engine then it was not, *pace* Braudel, essentially parasitic.[7] In the eighteenth century and into the nineteenth London was Europe's, if not the world's, biggest centre of industrial output. By 1700 manufacturing engaged around half the city's total workforce, production having grown increasingly capitalistic in its organisation since the sixteenth century. Even so, eighteenth-century manufacturing remained small scale, diverse, fragmented and specialised. It was concentrated in the finishing trades where skilled labour was most

important. Being in London meant proximity to a vast, concentrated and fickle market, as well as to the country's largest port. Around 1700 the biggest industry, clothing, incorporating most notably the silk trade, employed perhaps 40,000 to 50,000, or about 20 per cent of the labour force. Other large industries were leather- and metal-working, each employing about 10,000, and shipbuilding, furniture making, coach making and hat making each employed some fewer thousands. There were innumerable smaller trades. The dependent victualling, building and distribution sectors together accounted for about 25–30 per cent of the workforce. Great breweries grew to be the largest concentrations of private capital in eighteenth-century London, and housebuilding alone accounted for about 20 per cent of capital formation nationally in the late eighteenth century, likely more in the populous metropolis.[8]

The whole notion of an eighteenth-century industrial revolution as fundamental economic change has been repeatedly questioned. Without going into this argument, it can be said that by the eighteenth century London had already undergone a kind of industrial revolution without factories. The highly developed 'putting-out' or 'domestic' subcontracting system used the household as the unit of production wherever possible. In such a densely populated city with expensive land (high rents) and plentiful labour, this made sense in a way that factories would not have done. Given the significance of this industrialisation, it is the more surprising that so little attempt has been made to understand the houses within which it took place.

Industrialisation elsewhere did, of course, have an impact on London, but it was limited. Labour costs caused framework knitting to move to Nottingham, with some shoe and hat making also leaving. Yet, despite similarly high labour costs, silk weaving (though not silk throwing), watch making, tanning, shipbuilding and other manufacturing trades all endured in London into the nineteenth century, concentrated in suburbs to the east, south and north, silk weaving in Spitalfields, watch making in Clerkenwell. Further afield where land was cheaper were industries that could not be run on a purely domestic basis: tanning in Bermondsey; and shipbuilding to the east on both sides of the Thames. There was increasing concentration on finished products, leaving primary or intermediate production to be carried out elsewhere.[9]

In London's complex social economy particular trades were highly concentrated in particular localities, but manufacturing inevitably mingled with other commerce all across London. Indeed, notwithstanding its primacy in comparisons with other places, manufacturing was not the capital's most important economic sector. Services and trade were even more significant. In the City there was a concentration of finance and commerce, reflecting the adjoining presence of the nation's prime port. In Westminster there was commercial activity pursuant to its being the national centre of government growing out of the presence of the Royal Court. Attendant courtiers provided a great deal of employment, not least for the building trades. There was much work for women, through domestic and other support services, including prostitution. About 8 per cent of all Londoners were employed in domestic service, of which number about four-fifths were women. Some 10 per cent of London's whole working population were shopkeepers, running more than 20,000 shops in the 1750s. It has been estimated that of some 30,000 businesses engaging in 754 separate trades in London in the 1770s almost half were in wholesale or retail distribution, with about a quarter in manufacturing, and about 5 to 10 per cent in construction. About one in every twenty-six of London's inhabitants was then running a business. This gains comparative resonance when set against a ratio of one in thirty-eight for the United Kingdom in the 1990s. The prevalence of shopkeeping is evident in the equivalent figures for retail businesses – one in thirty in London in 1759, as against one in 240 for the UK in the 1990s.[10]

Everywhere employment was contingent, casual and seasonal. Both the port and the court, prime generators of work in trade and services, had their 'seasons', as did many manufacturing trades. This had greater impact than the broader trade cycles, though the long depression of the second quarter of the eighteenth century was a pronounced phenomenon in London, and wars were frequently disruptive, though not fundamentally so before the 1790s. Valerie Pearl has stressed the remarkable stability amid vast change of seventeenth-century London, and Leonard Schwarz has emphasised that over the long run, the eighteenth century in London was a period of economic equilibrium without fundamental structural change.[11] For many London people there was great continuity.

CONSUMPTION

London was not, of course, only, or even primarily, a place of production or supply. Its special character in the eighteenth century has largely to do with cultural dynamism driven by consumption or demand. For consumers London had it all. It was the place to come to find anything, and visitors were unfailingly astonished. Recent historians have been no less struck. 'Material culture' in relation to the spread of prosperity, fashion and emulative behaviour from eighteenth-century London outwards, and from the top of the social scale downwards, has been much emphasised.[12]

The 'pre-industrial home was marked for most men and women by a simplicity, an austerity, a sheer lack of possessions.'[13] But this changed; the goldfish was 'an aristocratic marvel in the 1730s which had become a plebeian decoration' by 1800.[14] In London the spread of luxury household goods (books, looking glasses, window curtains, knives and forks) was significantly wider than elsewhere in England in the years around 1700. The rapid spread of possessions in the first quarter of the eighteenth century in some cases clearly reflects changing consumption patterns fuelled by fashion or the availability of novelties. The percentage of inventoried London households recorded as having utensils for hot drinks rose from 2 to 57 between 1695 and 1725.[15] Clearly, housing provision had to adjust to accommodate increasing amounts of clutter, even for artisans and labourers. In the late eighteenth century Josiah Tucker assessed such people in England as possessing household goods worth three times as much as those of their French counterparts, including more and better furniture, and 'Carpets, Screens, Window Curtains, Chamber Bells, polished Brass Locks, Fenders, etc. (Things Hardly known abroad among persons of such Rank)'.[16] But there are important underlying complexities. Indeed the acquisition of a wider range of goods was in some measure itself the result of the changing nature of the household in what has been called the 'industrious revolution'. People worked harder at their trades, households releasing labour reserves to the market, thereby becoming more dependent on consumption.[17]

Consumption reflects wealth, one of Summerson's 'foundation stones'. The other, taste, was, in so far as it was perceived, very much dictated from above.[18] London was the prime nexus of the establishment of a high culture based in new institutions. Significantly for the spread of the polite, this culture was not inaccessibly 'high'. It was within reach of the 'middling sort'. Analyses of the English-speaking world away from London in the late seventeenth and eighteenth centuries have stressed emulation as explaining the spread of polite, that is classical, architecture in place of vernacular traditions. Classicism has been understood as a tool in defining the gap in identity between the cultural 'haves' and 'have nots'.[19] However, too great a linkage between wealth and taste takes agency away from the 'have nots', implying that they invariably would have emulated the rich if they could have, and that the absence of emulation just means poverty and a void in the place of taste.

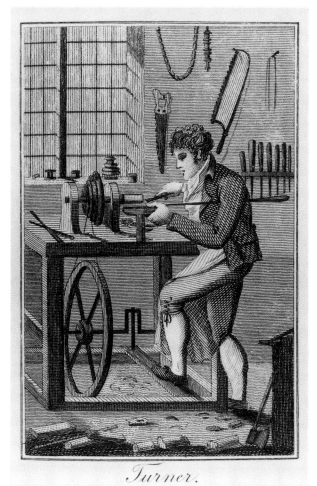

Turner.

Published July 7 1804 by Richard Phillips 71 S.t Pauls Church Yard

Taylor.

'ublishd July 7 1804 by Richard Phillips . 71. St Pauls Church Yard.

2a–h (*above and following pages*)   Turner, tailor, laundress, weaver; jeweller, shipwright, currier, tallow-chandler – some of Georgian London's working trades. From Anon., *The Book of Trades*, 1804 (By permission of the British Library, 1042.a.18 and 19, and 012806.de.11).

The importance and meaning of emulative consumption have been questioned, and distinctions do need to be made between emulation as an end in itself and the acquisition of previously unaffordable comforts.[20] Problems with who was consuming what, and the pervasiveness of emulation, will be revisited. In the context of an introductory overview it can be said without equivocation that London's extraordinary overall growth was significantly fuelled by consumption, conspicuous, emulative or otherwise. There were ever more shops, and more and more goods were readily available. However, there can be no simple transferral of this or any other

single or even dual cultural dynamic to being prime cause of the full range of developments in London's eighteenth-century domestic architecture.

Society

A grounding in great economic forces, productive or consumptive, should inform an understanding of housing, but perhaps not so much as an awareness of people. 'Formalism' notwithstanding, houses are principally interesting because people live in them. It is necessary, therefore, to look at eighteenth-century Londoners. Who made up this unprecedentedly huge urban population, and how was the society structured and divided?

No one has answered this better than Dorothy George. Her magisterial *London Life in the Eighteenth Century* (1925), quoted in the epigraph to the introduc-

Laundress.

Published July 7th 1804 by Richard Phillips, 71 St Pauls ChurchYard

Weaver.

London, Publish'd by Tabart & Cᵒ Aug. 11-1804.

tion of this book, remains unsurpassed as a characterisation of London's people in the eighteenth century. More than any other single work, her account is an inspiration for any attempt to bridge the gulf between architectural and social histories of the eighteenth-century metropolis. For the early part of the period Peter Earle has provided a great deal more to work with in trying to understand who inhabited London, with particular focus on the crucial 'middle', whether it is called a 'sort', a 'class' or a 'rank', or split into sub-categories. As to social class, nothing is straightforward, David Cannadine having described three basic models for society's structure as having coexisted in the minds of eighteenth-century Britons, that is the hierarchical or ordained, the triadic or upper/middle/lower, and the dichotomous or oppositional high/low.[21]

Class separation was, of course, perceived rather than real, but some statistical underpinning derived from Schwarz will help. At the end of the eighteenth century the 'upper income group' (those with an average annual income of over £200) comprised only 2–3 per cent of London's adult male population. The 'middling sort' (those with average incomes over £80) accounted for another 16–21 per cent. The rest, about 75 per cent, was made up of the working population, a very disparate group. Of this group about two-thirds (50 per cent of the whole) were unskilled or semi-skilled labourers. The other third (25 per cent of the whole) were artisans or skilled workers. This means that at the end of the eighteenth century there were something in the order of 100,000 artisans in London, the equivalent *without dependents* of more than the total population of any other English town.[22] It is the houses of these people with which this book is principally concerned. Such quantification is only broadly indicative, and for earlier periods it is perhaps not even possible, though it is unlikely that the percentages would be radically different for the beginning of the century. At that time

A Jeweller.

Pub. Jan 1 1806, by Tabart & C°.

Shipwright.

Published July 7 1804, by Richard Phillips, 71 S.t Paul: Church Yard.

Defoe famously divided British society into seven classes: 'the great, who live profusely', 'the rich, who live very plentifully', 'the middle sort who live well', 'the working trades who labour hard, but feel no want', 'the country people, farmers, &c., who fare indifferently', 'the poor, that fare hard' and 'the miserable, that really pinch and suffer want'.[23] Artisans are identifiable as Defoe's 'working trades' (fig. 2). They were rarely of the 'middle sort', in that they did not generally 'live well', but they were better off than the half of the population that fared 'hard' and felt 'want'. 'The great', 'the rich' and 'the country people' do not figure large in this book. The 'middle sort' is an omnipresent foil. For present outline purposes it is enough to know that a small sector of society was extremely well off, their primary demographic impact being as employers of others, and perhaps also that many Londoners had begun their lives as 'country people'. Indeed, immigration in the sixteenth

and seventeenth centuries sewed the seeds for the rise of both London's 'working trades' and its 'middle sort'. But the capital was 'a powerful solvent of the customs, prejudices and modes of action of traditional, rural England'.[24]

ARTISANS

Crudely then, artisans were a second quartile, but the eighteenth century 'was an age of minute social distinctions. Lines were drawn between the artisan and the labourer, the master and the journeyman [. . .]. They were, however, drawn with difficulty.'[25] The homogenising term 'working class' is here generally avoided as being anachronistic before about 1800. George Rudé distinguished four groups within the 'lower orders': first, the master craftsmen, small shopkeepers and petty tradesmen who bordered on the 'middle sort'; second,

Currier.

Published July 7 1804, by Richard Phillips, 71 S.t Pauls Church Yard.

Tallow-chandler.

Published July 7.th 1804 by Richard Phillips 71 S.t Pauls Church Yard.

skilled journeymen and apprentices; third, semi-skilled and unskilled labourers; and fourth, the vagrant and destitute.[26] At the points where the 'middle sort' and the 'lower orders' met there was a high degree of vagueness, if not of actual social mobility. As ever, perceptions counted. Gentility had more to do with independence than with wealth *per se*, and the term 'gentleman' was loosely used. Many independent artisans therefore clung on to a status that has been called 'precarious gentility'.[27] For a lucky few there was no precariousness. Defoe cites 'topping workmen' who, though 'only journeymen under manufacturers, are yet very substantial fellows'.[28] So affluence did not invariably mean abandonment of artisan identity. Wealth spread across numerous occupations, but industrial production became increasingly hierarchical as the scale of operations rose, and truly independent artisans were an elite. Most, as many as 90 per cent, were employed rather than employing. Shop-

keepers, depending on what they kept, varied widely in status. They were generally not poor, though frequently unskilled. What constituted a 'shop' is never clear, the word extending *inter alia* to refer to workshops. At or beyond the margins of the 'retail sector' *per se* there would have been many small back-street shops where 'petty-parlour shopkeepers', out-of-work artisans or widows, sold daily necessities from their homes.[29]

Artisans were fiercely proud and defensive of their often ephemeral independence, and of an identity through work that placed them squarely in the realm of respectability if only precariously in that of gentility. There was a centuries-long tradition of maintaining distinctions between artisans and labourers, as in an early eighteenth-century dictionary that differentiated the 'mechanic arts' of building craftsmen from the 'drudgery work' of labourers.[30] Artisans possessed highly developed skills that were crucial to the prosperity of London and

Britain. From silk weavers to shipwrights, skill was power. Across many more trades skill was also identity, the source of independence and respectability, dignity and status. For Pierre-Jean Grosley in 1772, 'Mechanics of the lowest sort, even journeymen themselves, carry English independence still farther; nothing but want of money, can compel them to work. [. . .] The perfection of handicraft and the love of liberty in the lowest class of artificers, contribute equally to render English manufactures very dear.'[31]

Artisan status and mentality were transmitted through a seven-year apprenticeship leading to work as a journeyman, subsequently leading on, for some, to the higher status of a master. Through the eighteenth century trade guilds continued to have influence, and the artisan class remained largely closed and self-perpetuating; to obtain an apprenticeship substantial fees (£20 or more, more than a year's income for most labourers) had to be paid. There were 'higher class' and 'lower class' trades, the status of a trade being gauged by the level of the apprentice fee. Apprenticeship was thus structured to protect against downward mobility more than it was able to permit upward mobility. This was increasingly so through the century as London felt the impact of competition from the provinces and the overall number of apprenticeships declined. The control of employment through apprenticeship broke down and a growing proportion of artisans spent their whole working lives as journeymen. As Adam Smith related, 'almost all journeymen artificers are liable to be called upon and dismissed by masters from day to day and from week to week, in the same manner as day-labourers in other places.'[32] London thus had what has been described as a de facto 'proletariat'.[33]

For most artisans prosperity was a dream; few were able even to rely on a steady income. Continuing immigration meant surplus labour. For many carpenters, joiners, bricklayers, plasterers, house painters, bookbinders, upholsterers, milliners, tanners, shoe makers, hatters, coopers, wheelwrights and others, everyday reality was too little work for too little money. Tailors were 'as numerous as Locusts, [. . .] and generally as poor as Rats.'[34] There was a fluid mass of semi-skilled workers, multiple occupations being common, particularly in relation to the seasonality of much work. The picture of general upward mobility that arises from an emphasis on consumption and emulation is misleading. Inequality of wealth was growing. It was more and more difficult for even a prosperous artisan to rise into 'the middling sort', faced with 'diminishing prospects, the entrenchment of economic and social oligarchy, the decline of traditional institutions, and the growth of cultural differentiation.'[35]

Artisans were invariably male, but much of the wider workforce was female. Many unmarried women were employed through domestic service, and not only by the well-to-do. Most wives of working men were expected to, indeed needed to, earn money through shopkeeping, laundry, needlework, charring or street-selling. Women might have been 'helpmeets', that is worked at the same trade as their husband, but this was not a bon vieux temps of 'family industry', all labouring happily together under one roof. Even under the 'domestic' system of home-working, custom and law kept women from undertaking 'men's work'. Women generally had to take disagreeable, unskilled and poorly paid work, opportunities increasingly squeezed by male competition. Many women who were widows, deserted wives or unmarried mothers could not depend on male support. About half of all women heading households around 1700 were widows; others were concentrated in riverside areas where many men, being sailors, were away for long periods.[36]

THE POOR

Any night found 'One Third of the Inhabitants of London, Westminster and Southwark, fast a-sleep, and almost Pennyless.'[37] Defoe's 'poor' and 'miserable' were the unskilled labourers and the destitute unemployed. There were innumerable labouring jobs for porters, chairmen, servants, coal-heavers, street-sellers, building or general labourers, but in a world of casual and plentiful labour most were underemployed. As many again were uninterested or unemployable. There is relatively little to be said here about the labouring poor because, except at the archaeologically irretrievable margins, this population neither provided nor had provided for it purpose-built housing other than of an institutional nature. Around 1700 perhaps as much as 10 per cent of London's population was itinerant or homeless.[38] As is always the case, housing mobility was greater among the poor, in a sliding scale from the frequently shifting lodgings of journeymen to life on the street. There was dirt, noise, prostitution, crime, mental illness and drunkenness. From Ned Ward to Defoe and Hogarth and beyond there are plentiful portrayals of poverty, squalor, vice and degradation in eighteenth-century London – latterly too often romanticised in a picturesque postmodern and ironic urban variant of the prelapsarian myth.

The Plague did not return to London after 1665, but subsequent outbreaks of serious disease, especially smallpox, were frequent, deadly, and not, of course, confined to the poor. In the early eighteenth century more than half the children born in London did not survive into adulthood, and many more died as young adults. London's population was stagnant in the second quarter of the century, with burials exceeding baptisms by 65 per cent, but the capital was never depopulated by disease. The difference was made up by immigration, proportionally lower in the eighteenth century than it had been in the seventeenth, but new populations did continue to arrive, and not only from the English countryside. By the late eighteenth century there were significant minorities (that is populations numbering between 10,000 and 25,000 each) of Irish, Jews and black Africans, many newly free, alongside northern European (Netherlandish and north German) groups and the descendants of the largely assimilated late seventeenth-century Huguenot immigrants. Whether poor or not, new immigrants were like children in lacking the immunities of adult Londoners, and so suffered disproportionately from disease.[39]

'One half of the world knows not how the other half live' is the revealing subtitle of the anonymous publication *Low-life*, of around 1750. It reflects growing segregation of the classes in an ever more unencompassable city. Yet, however much the 'precarious gentility' of some artisans might have desired it, the 'poor' can not be hived off as an entirely separate class. There was downward mobility and apprentices are prominent among the statistics of criminality. There were trade-based, geographical and wider cultural interdependencies between skilled workers and those less well placed. The latter are now even more voiceless than contemporary artisans, but the 'poor' were far from endlessly tractable, and relative historical silence should not be mistaken for meek acquiescence. Neither should the outside-looking-in views of contemporary social reformers be taken at face value. In the 1790s scaremongering from the magistrate Patrick Colquhoun, based in imaginative and utilitarian number crunching, was highly successful in criminalising the poor, particularly the large numbers of riverside labourers, tending to define these people as a species apart needing regulation in places apart. This was more a way of shaping the future than it was reliable documentation of the present.[40]

LIVING STANDARDS

Difficult though it is to draw lines, there are important distinctions to be made between the poor and the not-so-poor in relation to housing. To aid in this it is necessary to know about incomes and standards of living. London's wages were historically relatively high, thus did it attract immigrants. They were also broadly constant through the eighteenth century. Skilled and successfully

established artisans could earn 3 shillings a day or £1 or more in a week, which, taking into account variable employment, would have produced annual incomes of about £25 to £50. Journeymen and labourers earned less, perhaps somewhat more or less than two shillings a day or 10 shillings a week, which, allowing for seasonality, means that for many people annual incomes were below £20 a year.[41] Real wage rates (reflecting the cost of living) were more volatile, rising erratically in the early eighteenth century, declining significantly from around 1750 and plummeting after 1793 as a result of massive wartime inflation (figs 1 and 3). Wages were not the only income, but the value of perquisites has been notoriously difficult to gauge, historians disagreeing about both their ubiquity and their impact. It is clear, however, that for many trades there were important customary payments in kind, notably waste materials or offcuts, ranging from shipbuilding 'chips' to tailors' 'cabbage'.[42]

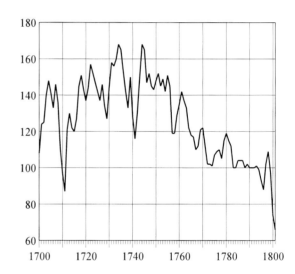

3 Real wage rates of London bricklayers in the eighteenth century (1790 = 100, adapted from Schwarz, 1992).

Most households below the 'middling sort' depended on more than one income to make ends meet; for many, savings would have been impossible. Pawning, often of clothes, and borrowing were widespread means of bridging shortfalls in income. Household budgets are elusive, but there was much day-to-day consumption to be paid for. The 'industrious revolution' meant that in London 'spinning, weaving, baking, brewing and candle-making were no longer done by housewives. [. . .] even cooking was not a necessary part of domestic economy.'[43] For a journeyman or a labourer perhaps a quarter to a half of earnings was spent on bread, and rent might have averaged about another eighth (see below). Dining at cook shops that served 'Measly Pork, rusty Bacon, stinking Lamb, rotten Mutton, slinked Veal, and coddled Cow, with yellow Greens, sooty Pottage, and greasy Pudding'[44] was no luxury. Other outlays that might be identified with affluence were perhaps more a reflection of the gap between those who were managing and those who were desperate: 'we have to go very far down the social scale to find the woman who did not employ some other woman or child to help her in washing and scouring or in the "minding" of children.'[45] Secondhand books and cheap prints were affordable for artisans, and even labourers sometimes possessed luxury items of silver or silk. At the same time numerous others died of starvation.

Full-blown emulative behaviour was beyond all but the wealthiest of artisans, but some imitative consumption at the margins of everyday life – owning books, prints or silver objects; wearing silk or taking hot drinks – was widespread. This does imply an escape from poverty, but it does not mean a loss of identity or the abandonment of tradition. Imitating is not the same as emulating, most obviously so if applied to comfort, foodstuffs or literacy, where the copied behaviour brings its own rewards. London, where a degree of literacy can be regarded as the norm in the eighteenth century, had far higher literacy rates than elsewhere in England, but this bald fact says nothing about what was being read or about underlying attitudes. The masquerades of Vauxhall Gardens were a notorious solvent of rank, and apprentices and journeymen were prominent among those availing themselves, emulatively and otherwise, of other metropolitan pleasure gardens and peripheral retreats like the Cold Bath, the Spa Fields Pantheon, Bagnigge Wells and Sadler's Wells, all just north of Clerkenwell towards Islington, as well as of other 'resorts' across the Thames (fig. 4) or further afield, as in Hampstead or Greenwich Park. Alongside involvement with 'high culture', traditional entertainments and celebrations persisted, from bull-baiting, duck-hunting and dog-fighting to May Day masquerades. The inevitable accompaniment of drunk-

4   Dancing outside a public house on Lambeth Marsh, *c.*1770, in a watercolour view by Paul Sandby looking towards the City (Lambeth Archives).

enness gave reformers an excuse for censure. Selfconscious group identity being something of great import for most artisans, the retention of ceremony, ritual and 'brotherhood' (much of this was exclusively male) mattered. Old trade-based drinking customs and 'fines' endured. For many reasons, both obvious and obscure, traditional culture was not simply relinquished.[46]

POLITICAL INVOLVEMENT AND AGITATION

Dorothy George stressed the paradox that eighteenth-century London combined turbulence with fundamental orderliness. Too much emphasis on underlying stability and continuity belies the period's conflicts. Politics was not purely the realm of the elite. There was a tradition of widespread participation in local administration. The City of London was, and long had been, a rate-payers' democracy. Alongside it eighteenth-century Westminster was the country's most open parliamentary constituency, giving the vote to every householder. More than a third of Westminster's eighteenth-century electors are broadly identifiable as artisans (fig. 5).[47] For those without the vote strikes and riots were regular means of political engagement. Eighteenth-century London's riots were not about food, and its frequent labour disputes were often about matters of custom and legitimacy rather than simply about pay. Various causes espoused by journeymen, apprentices and labourers through the whole century tended to become confrontational; 'popular political attitudes in London were essentially oppositionist and critical.'[48] Certain trades, most notably the weavers, staged frequent insurrections to defend their livelihoods. In 1768–9 a huge wave of unrest spread across numerous trade groups. This coincided and overlapped with the defence of 'liberty' and revival of seventeenth-century egalitarian principles that crystallised in the explicitly political Wilkite rebellion. John Wilkes was all things to all men, uniting disparate groups behind the ill-defined notions of 'liberty' and 'independence'. His quintessential supporters were small merchants and master artisans, with strong following from all sectors of the 'working classes', much of it in the near suburbs to the east and south. Similarly, those who took part in the Gordon Riots in 1780, 'the most violent and the most savagely repressed of all the riots in London's history', were 'a fair cross-section of London's working population'.[49] Throughout the century 'mob' violence was defensive rather than assertive, but it was not indiscriminate. It was orchestrated and directed against the rich, not by the poorest but by those in 'respectable' artisan districts. It is small wonder that after events in France in 1789 dissent was assiduously suppressed.[50]

5   In a satire on the open-ness of Westminster's electorate, Charles James Fox is shown here in the artisan district of Peter (latterly Great Peter) Street, Westminster, canvassing votes for the election of 1784. With the Duchess of Devonshire on his knee patronising shoemakers in their shop, Fox gives his hand to an apparently destitute man to whom Sam House, Fox's 'publican and republican' ally, is holding up a tankard. Thomas Rowlandson, *Wit's Last Stake*, 1784 (GL).

ARTISAN IDENTITY, DECLINE AND RESISTANCE

These points are made here to indicate the powerful oppositional forces that were flowing within the upper and middle, that is housebuilding, strata of society. Artisan identity has already been addressed, but it needs more attention, particularly in relation to decline, real or perceived, resistance thereto, and questions of cultural impact or agency that are relevant to domestic architecture.

While many of London's poor probably remained indifferent to religion, wide support for the established Church did not displace a long-standing tradition of religious Dissent, strongly rooted among artisans, that was an inheritance from the turmoil of the English Revolution. There were said to be over 100,000 Dissenters in London in the late seventeenth century, bolstered by the arrival of thousands of Huguenots and the abolition of legislative restrictions in the 1680s. From the broadly based groupings of Quakers, Baptists and others, to the Unitarians, Muggletonians and other small sects, through to the indicatively eccentric William Blake, religion, radicalism and artisan identity remained closely intertwined through the eighteenth century. Methodism was separately influential, John Wesley putting much effort into finding the soul of London's artisan districts, though he was often received with hostility. Irish immigrants, overwhelmingly poor, were London's largest Roman

Catholic community. There were frequent clashes, as in 1736 when local labourers rioted against Irish workmen taking low wages in building the Church of St Leonard, Shoreditch. It was an upsurge of anti-Catholic feeling mixed with class envy that culminated in the Gordon Riots. Beneath the radical and libertarian face of artisan Dissent were the illiberal and defensively xenophobic attitudes that were a fundamental part of the mentality of London's eighteenth-century 'mob'. Rudé has provided the necessary corrective to any anachronistic notions of inclusivity or inter-ethnic multiculturalism: 'The ordinary Londoner was easily given to religious intoleration, had a considerable contempt for foreigners (including the Scots and Irish) and felt a passionate concern to defend his "Englishman's liberties" against both "tyranny" at home and despotism (particularly when linked with Popery) abroad.'[51]

From machine-breaking to anti-Popery much rioting was resistance to change. It was conservative in nature, upholding tradition. Artisans 'were engaged in a ceaseless quest for stability. [. . .] journeymen knew that from instability they would probably emerge the losers.'[52] Defensiveness against pressures such as the undermining of apprenticeship restrictions kept the artisan world determinedly male. Any acceptance of competition from women and children, or of low rates of pay, was regarded as betrayal of collective ownership of the property of skill. Some of the new ideas of enlightened elites were absorbed, and adapted to conservative ends. Traditional attempts to enforce standards of workmanship through guild control were abandoned and translated into new forms of collective action designed to maintain status – machine-breaking, friendly societies, savings clubs, combinations and early trade unions, 'An older language of defence of traditional collective rights thus gave way to a discourse of utility based on the rights of the individual.'[53] The essentially retrospective 'leave-us-alone' nature of the artisan position was not nostalgia for a pre-industrial or pre-urban world, but a harking back to an imagined seventeenth-century 'golden age' when 'independent' and 'respectable' artisan status more than material well-being was seen as having been at the heart of an urban and industrial existence. Resistance to trade dilution, lower pay, the criminalisation of customary perquisites, in short to industrial capitalism and proletarianisation, became ever more ordered, if largely futile, in the late eighteenth and early nineteenth centuries.[54]

Improvement, 'the most over-used word' in eighteenth-century England,[55] was widely deployed as a shorthand term for the implementation of the rational and utilitarian ideas of the English Enlightenment, its applicability ranging from agriculture to street lighting.

As such 'improvement' was, in social terms, infiltrated if not imposed from above, and, however beneficial in its broad effects, it tended to be perceived as representing a threat to the continuity and stability of the social order that many artisans sought to preserve. There was genuine improvement in late eighteenth-century London, in reduced mortality and other advances in living conditions, notably to do with medicine and sanitation. Improvement in London's physical fabric was also real, through new bridges, roads and stronger building control (see chapter 9). However, any positive impact on artisans as a group was limited in the late eighteenth century. The rhetoric of 'improvement' would have been understood as parallel to and reflective of other negative forces, declining living standards and the sense of a loss of cultural control or agency. What Roy Porter termed 'elite cultural cleansing' was not, as he stressed, a conspiracy aiming at social control. But it did happen. On top of this the severe financial and economic crisis of the 1790s precipitated collapse for many, not least those in the building trades. The terms 'middle class' and 'working class' first appeared early in the nineteenth century, when artisans fought harder than ever to separate themselves from the poor. The decline thereafter of many trades into poverty was most famously documented by Henry Mayhew.[56]

This analysis is not new – it is largely made up from old saws of the period's social history. They are revisited here, however, because their implications have not been investigated in relation to London's domestic architecture. In other fields there has been much emphasis on straining to hear voices from below, but with a strong focus on words, and too little attention to material culture.

The Different Londons: A Tour

Thus far, and despite having started out with Boswell's differentiation of its ends, London has been characterised as a unity. It is time to begin to think about it as made up of parts, and to address who lived where (figs 6 and 7).

PARTS OR ENDS?

Boswell was not alone among eighteenth-century Londoners in characterising the city as heterogeneous or, to use that anachronistic term, 'multicultural'. Fifty years before him Joseph Addison had written in *The Spectator* that 'When I consider this great city in its several quarters and divisions, I look upon it as an aggregate of various nations distinguished from each other by their respective customs, manners and interests.'[57] In the 1770s John Fielding, the magistrate, social reformer and blind half-brother of Henry Fielding, averred that 'When one goes into Rotherhithe or Wapping, which places are inhabited chiefly by sailors, but that somewhat of the same language is spoken, a man would be apt to suspect himself in another country. Their manner of living, speaking, acting, dressing, and behaving are so very peculiar to themselves.'[58] Visitors from overseas also registered differences within London. The Prussian Johann Wilhelm von Archenholz found the contrast between the eastern and western parts of London in the 1780s 'astonishing',[59] and, a century after Addison, the Swiss-American Louis Simond concluded that 'every minute of longitude east is equal to as many degrees of gentility *minus*, or towards west, *plus*.'[60]

The increasingly oppositional east–west specificity of these remarks mark the emergence of a hierarchical construct through which, by 1800, it came to be accepted by those whose comments have endured – commentators who were invariably more at home in the West End – that London was essentially divided between its east and west ends. In this consensual, stereotyping or 'othering' geography the south was tacitly lumped with the east. It is important to understand that what is being referred to here is a construct, the perception not the reality. Much less emphasised, but no less real, were the social and economic differences and barriers between the north and south sides of the river. Right through the eighteenth century London continued, in fact, to be distinguished by great diversity between its neighbourhoods, by its fractured or patchwork character. People of many sorts tended to live together within small compasses in a mosaic of neighbourhoods in an administratively fragmented city. Local identity endured and neighbourhood bonds were perhaps stronger than any of class or trade. There was gradually decreasing mingling of the rich with the poor, but few real separations into neighbourhoods that could be defined by class. For most occupations there were no particular local concentrations, and affluent areas were often hard by much poorer enclaves. Matthew Bramble, the Welsh squire in Tobias Smollett's final novel, observes on his visit to London that 'The different departments of life are jumbled together – the hod-carrier, the low mechanic, the tapster, the publican, the shop-keeper, the pettifogger, the citizen, and courtier, *all tread upon the kibes of one another*.'[61]

But the perceived east–west divide was not all imagined. By the end of the century there was considerably more social segregation, wealth, if not middling incomes,

concentrating to the west.[62] At the same time there had been a loss of physical distinctiveness between localities, brought about in some measure by 'improvement' through both urban renewal (regeneration) and outward growth. Boswell returned to east London in 1792, only to be disappointed to find in Wapping 'that uniformity which has in modern times, in a great degree, spread through every part of the Metropolis'.[63] Local differences were being smoothed out, and in this physically more homogeneous city it became all the more important for commentators to differentiate hierarchically between east and west, to provide geographical anchorage for the growing social opposition and segregation.

In the years around 1800, as seen retrospectively from the 1850s,

> The inhabitants of the extreme east of London knew nothing of the western localities but from hearsay and report and vice versa. [. . .] There was little communication or sympathy between the respective classes by which the two ends of London were occupied. They differed in external appearance, in the fashion of their clothes, in their pleasures and in their wits. [. . .] Each district was comparatively isolated, the state of isolation produced peculiarities and the peculiarities corroborated the isolation, and thus the householders of Westminster, whether noblemen, gentlemen, tradesmen [. . .] or of any other grade of society, were as distinct from the householders of every sort of Bishopsgate Without, Shoreditch and all those localities [. . .] as in these days they are from the inhabitants of Holland or Belgium.[64]

An understanding of the differing dynamics of physical geography, from general variability towards uniformity, and social geography, from perceived local isolation to hierarchical bipolarity, requires a highly tuned topographical awareness. Some account of the differing characteristics of various neighbourhoods is therefore needed, briefly tracking major developments over time, though, as J. P. Malcolm observed, it is 'a labour of little less difficulty to attempt to describe the varying form of a summer cloud, than to trace from year to year the outline of London.'[65]

GROWTH AND CHURCHES

Before describing the vast changes that had occurred in his lifetime, Defoe divided London into three: 'The city is the centre of its commerce and wealth. The Court of its gallantry and splendour. The out-parts of its numbers and mechanics; and in all these, no city in the world can equal it.'[66] The rebuilding of the City after the Great Fire of 1666 was accompanied and succeeded by huge building activity beyond. By the 1670s the City of London, the 'Square Mile' that is the ancient heart of the metropolis, had already been outstripped by its own suburbs, its topographical and demographic predominance gone. After a period of very rapid growth London's built environment at the end of the seventeenth century was what has been characterised as 'low-density sprawl',[67] unconstrained by fortifications, such as existed in many other European cities (figs 6 and 7).

London's growth up to the middle of the eighteenth century can be introduced through reference to the formation of new parishes and the building of churches. Of eighteen new parishes formed from 1660 to 1743, seven were in the eastern suburbs (Tower Hamlets), five in the west (from Covent Garden round to St John Smith Square), three in the north (from Bloomsbury to Old Street) and three in the south. The siting of the churches built under the Act of 1711 that created the Commission for Building Fifty New Churches is also revealing of London's growth, or how it was perceived. Of the twelve new churches completed, three were in the eastern suburbs (Christ Church, Spitalfields, St George in the East and St Anne, Limehouse), three in the southern suburbs (St John, Horselydown, St Paul, Deptford, and, beyond, St Alfege, Greenwich), two to the north (St George, Bloomsbury, and St Luke, Old Street) and two to the west (St John, Smith Square, and St George, Hanover Square), the total being made up by St Mary le Strand and the rebuilding of St Mary Woolnoth in the City. Many factors determined where these churches were built, but it is notable that, with the exception of the last three, they were sited in the burgeoning suburbs that had predominantly artisan and labourer populations. This was a large part of the point, to counter Dissent, irreligion and more dangerous disaffection with an impressive show of the State's pious munificence. These big Baroque churches were deliberately scaled and sited so as to be intimidating symbols of power, to appear 'enormous when compared to the neighbouring diminutive houses'.[68] It is also worth noting that these artisan suburbs had not been dependent on central benefaction for their ecclesiastical architecture, many having in the seventeenth century provided themselves with humbler churches with simple, but sophisticated and chastely classical, interiors for auditory Protestant worship.[69]

WESTWARDS GROWTH

'The Court', that is Westminster, had long since been linked to the City along the intervening riverside, via the Strand and environs, but seventeenth-century development of Covent Garden, St Giles in the Fields, Soho and St James, and the impact of the Fire in the City, brought about a significant westwards shift in the balance of prosperity.[70] The situation of the Court and the willingness of aristocratic landowners to grant building leases stimulated rip-roaring development to the west, with additional impetus provided by the sanitising effects of the prevailing winds, which kept away the 'fumes, steams and stinks of the whole easterly pyle'.[71] This deliberate separation of the rich from the poor was new. The social cachet of the newly built-over areas provided a basis for the entrenchment of the east–west split in social standing that henceforth allowed western parts of the metropolis to be defined as 'polite' to the exclusion of other parts. The deliberate provision of open spaces such as squares between regularly laid-out large brick houses has long been recognised as an important departure, and has fired recent scholarly discussion about the nature of modernity in early modern London. Most notably in the present context, the speculative development that extended London, principally westwards, in the period 1660 to 1720 has been re-characterised, emphasising the profit motive and the anarchy of market forces as underlying the great growth. This analysis of London's speculative housebuilding has great relevance to the material presented here, not least in that it links the modernity of the period's housing for an affluent market to earlier traditions, that is to the vernacular (see chapter 2).[72]

By the early eighteenth century, development further west into Mayfair and further north between Bloomsbury and Holborn was taking fashion and the well-to-do away from more central areas, leaving St Giles and Soho behind to house poorer populations. By 1720, when the Grosvenor Estate began to develop its land in Mayfair, St Giles was already 'filled with abundance of Poor'.[73] However, it should not be thought that the gentry had ever formed a majority of the West End's inhabitants; servants aside, tradesmen, labourers and paupers had always been more numerous. Parts of Soho had been modestly developed initially, given the presence of noxious industries and a pesthouse, and the early fringes of Mayfair were also relatively humble. More fundamentally countering the growing east–west, fashionable–unfashionable divide was the parish of St Margaret, Westminster, south of St James's Park extending towards Tothill Fields, which had undergone dense small-scale development for a population of artisans and labourers in the seventeenth century, becoming and remaining an insalubrious suburb (fig. 5). Across the river, Lambeth was separate and much more sparsely developed (fig. 4).[74]

There was more to London than the City and West-minster. It has been calculated that in the 1690s about 30 per cent of London's people lived in the City (within and without the walls), about 19 per cent in the 'West End' (excluding St Margaret, Westminster, which had about 4 per cent), about 22 per cent in the eastern suburbs, another 15 per cent south of the river, and about 10 per cent in northern suburbs.[75] This puts just over half the city's people in Defoe's 'out-parts', those working suburbs for many of which domestic industry was of the essence. It was to these places that work was put *out*, to evade City regulation. Classically, early modern suburbs housed the poor and transient; 'to reach the suburbs was always to take a step downwards'.[76] Elsewhere this did change during the eighteenth century, but London's West End was still unusual. The drama of its growth has tended to occlude the stories of other less unusual outer districts, to the extent that eighteenth-century London has been misunderstood as somehow excluding the poor – 'through the half-urban spaces of manufactures [*sic*], vegetable gardens and stable yards the poor trudged miles to work in the city.'[77] In fact, those of the poor who had work were likely to be working at home, or nearby, in districts that were every bit as 'urban' as were the peripheral aristocratic quarters.

There had been substantial growth in London's eastern suburbs before the Fire, particularly near the river. At the turn of the seventeenth century John Stow, who notoriously rued London's growth, made many dis-paraging references to east London's numerous small houses.[78] Much of the housebuilding was illicit and ram-shackle, poor short-life housing going up in defiance of late sixteenth- and early seventeenth-century proclama-tions against new development, vain attempts to keep poor immigrants away from London (see chapter 2). The growth continued, principally dependent on manufac-turing and port activities. Ribbons of development along the river and roads gradually grew together, with popu-lations that were overwhelmingly made up of artisans and labourers. In a marshy area land was poor and much development was unplanned. However, from the 1630s onwards, growth was along increasingly regular, neat and orderly streets. By 1700 the riverside districts of Wapping, Shadwell, Ratcliff and Limehouse were densely built over with small houses, though not exces-sively crowded (figs 6 and 7). The preponderance of mariners and shipbuilding near the river meant that, unusually in relation to London's other artisan districts, few worked from home, that the houses were just houses. Many men were away at sea, many others walked

to work in local yards. There were also other factory employments, from breweries and distilleries, through foundries, glasshouses, sugar houses and dye houses, to white lead works and copperas works, some of the sources of the 'fumes, steams and stinks'.[79]

Mid-seventeenth century Shadwell was almost entirely populated by artisans and labourers. Over 70 per cent of the population owed its livelihood to the river, whether as mariners, watermen, or in shipbuilding. The overwhelmingly working population had few posses-sions, and workplace and domestic accommodation were closely interwoven. Later in the century Sir Thomas Neale (d. *c*.1699), better known for his development of Seven Dials in St Giles in the 1690s, was also active in Shadwell, improving a Commonwealth church and other civic amenities to give a shapeless 'edge city' greater coherence. This was not the vicious slum or shanty town that might be imagined from post-1800 outlooks, but a respectable industrial centre, with housing that was probably superior to much that was available elsewhere.[80]

During the late seventeenth century there was also much growth to the north-east, especially in and around Spitalfields, across Whitechapel to Mile End New Town, and more sparsely around Shoreditch.[81] Outlying stray ribbon development all but linked Mile End Old Town (Stepney) and Poplar to London, but these still then remained places apart. The inland silk district that centred on Spitalfields was very different to the riverside (see chapters 3 and 5). Comparably dominated by industry, it was the place of domestic labour *par excel-lence*. There was greater coherence to development, with some substantial housing amid much that was small and poorly built. In the early eighteenth century any one of twelve of the Tower Hamlets was by non-metropolitan standards a large town, each 'hamlet' having a population in the range of 5,000 to 22,000, for a total of 140,000 plus (at a time when Bristol was booming to its mid-century population of 50,000).[82]

SOUTH LONDON

South of the river the ancient transpontine suburb of Southwark was growing prodigiously in the seventeenth century, back from and along the arms of a T that met at London Bridge. The already substantial core on and around Borough High Street was rebuilt after South-wark's own fires in 1676 and 1689. Bermondsey and Rotherhithe were linked by ribbon development, but inland growth was inhibited by marshy conditions and the use of open land for tanning (see chapter 4). Devel-opment further west on the south bank was sparse in the

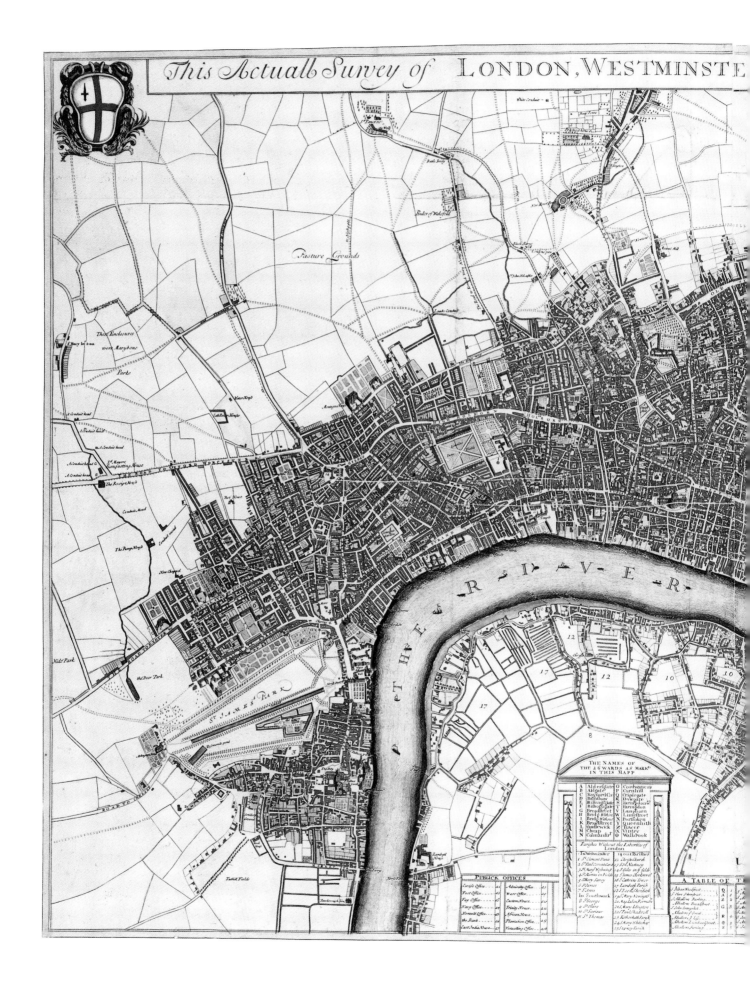

This Actuall Survey of LONDON, WESTMINSTE

PUBLICK OFFICES

THE NAMES OF
THE 26 WARDS AS MARKᵈ
IN THIS MAPP

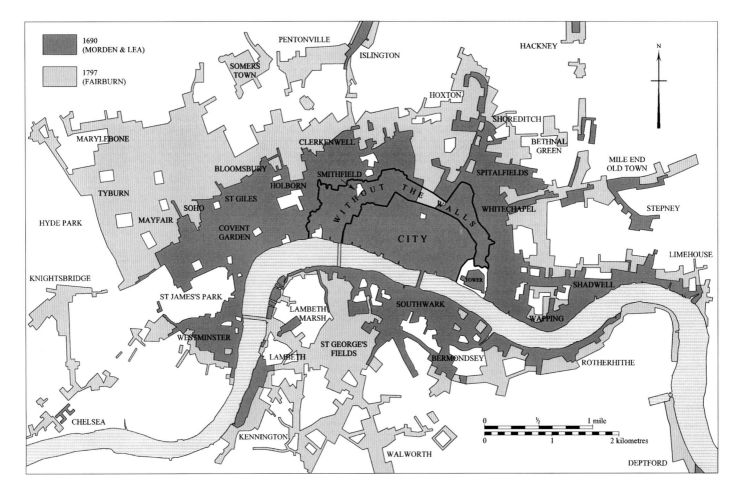

7　The growth of London in the eighteenth century, taking the maps shown in figs 6 and 9 as bases, and indicating the principal districts discussed in this book.

absence of both port activity and alternative river crossings (figs 6 and 7). Early eighteenth-century Southwark's 60,000 people were thus densely packed, and subjected to irony: 'The principal beauty of the borough of Southwark, consists in the prodigious number of its inhabitants.'[83] There were many small houses, and much was 'meanly built' and 'poorly inhabited'.[84]

Downriver from Rotherhithe, and 'effectually joined',[85] was Deptford, a large and densely populated town of about 10,000 people in 1700. Through ship-building centred on a royal dockyard Deptford was an industrial satellite without being strictly metropolitan. Deptford combined further downstream with Greenwich, the former royal palace of which was being transformed into a naval hospital from 1694, and Woolwich, which had another royal dockyard and a growing official presence on Woolwich Warren (from 1805 the Royal Arsenal), to form a great conurbation, a semi-governmental military-industrial outpost. This was over-

whelmingly populated by artisans, labourers and mariners, highly dependent on wage labour, and far larger and more densely built up than any other London 'suburbs' that had not been wholly absorbed into the metropolis (see chapter 6).

NORTH LONDON AND OUTLYING SETTLEMENTS

North London presents greater ambiguities in terms of defining what was or was not metropolitan in the early eighteenth century. It does seem that the term 'urban' can be rapidly disapplied for areas away from the river. South of its Green and Spa Fields, Clerkenwell was much built over and had been absorbed into London, but other districts had more ambiguous identities. Hoxton saw some concerted estate development in the 1680s that was contiguous with Shoreditch and the route north from the City. However, this push fizzled and Hoxton remained a sparsely populated 'semi-rural location'.[86] Many other districts can be characterised as simultaneously rural, urban and intermediate in the early Georgian period, as being not in but of London. Islington and Hackney remained substantial outlying settlements, long since retreats for the well-to-do, the linear disposition of the former bringing it close to London at Sadler's Wells (figs 6 and 7), while the latter was a more distant and amorphous aggregation of hamlets. Further north, Hampstead and Highgate were distant though estimable hilltop resorts, favoured for their spa waters, clean air and elevated positions (see chapter 7). Much further afield, beyond Stoke Newington, but linear and suburban to an extent that reflected London's proximity, was Tottenham, all these places 'generally belonging to the middle sort of mankind, grown wealthy by trade, and who still taste of London'.[87]

To the south, Peckham was a pleasure resort, as was Greenwich away from the river, 'rather a town for pleasure than trade'.[88] More remotely, Clapham, Dulwich, Sydenham Wells and Streatham Wells were all modest fashionable retreats and spas. To the west, from Chelsea, through 'royal' Kensington, to Fulham, then Hammersmith, and on to Chiswick, Brentford, Richmond and Twickenham, there were scattered settlements many of which embraced fashionable retreats, but none of which can be properly characterised as either integral parts of London or as substantial urban satellites (see chapter 7). These were not suburbs in any latter-day sense, except as 'the suburbia of prosperity, of the townsman's search for a country foothold'.[89] These settlements lacked the scale, self-sufficiency or nucleation of industrial places like Shadwell, Deptford or Woolwich, where the best housing was for local elites rather than for London escapees. In more distant places, such as Brentford or Richmond, there were notable outcroppings of high-status housing of urban form in the early eighteenth century, but these were manifestations of London fashion in outposts rather than reflections of any real density. None of these outlying places was anything like as populous or built up as the inner suburbs to the east and south.

STASIS AT MID–CENTURY AND THE
DISTRIBUTION OF TRADES

London's outward growth slowed in the second quarter of the eighteenth century, as economic stagnation stifled the boom in speculative housebuilding.[90] Mayfair was taken up to Hyde Park, where westwards expansion was forced to stop. Fashionable Westminster's concerted westwards march had great consequence for the rest of London. It sucked money away from the somewhat less westerly suburbs which went into rapid decline, and heightened the contrast between east and west. What wealth there had been in artisan districts in the early eighteenth century had largely fled by the late eighteenth century.

A re-presentation of a frequently used schematic rendering of the *dominant* occupations and occupancies of London's various districts at mid-century shows the basic distribution of trades (fig. 8). While useful as a broad guide, this diagram risks underplaying the intricacies of social integration and overplaying topographical segregation. Nevertheless, it shows that around the City, where many small tradesmen still operated alongside great commerce, there were three main industrial sectors. To the north, west of Moorfields and across Clerkenwell, there was a concentration of the 'metal trades', ranging from the highly skilled making of clocks and jewellery to lower-grade work like wire-drawing. East of Moorfields from Shoreditch to Whitechapel and extending out towards Bethnal Green and Stepney was the silk-weaving district centred on Spitalfields. South of the river in and around Bermondsey was the leather industry or tanning district. Southwark also had much hat making, dyeing, brewing and glass making. The riversides, extending quite far inland on the north side, were dominated by maritime and port-based activity, with shipbuilding and numerous factories, as well as much unskilled labour. On the south bank wharfage, docks and associated housing extended from close to Lambeth east to Rotherhithe.

LATE EIGHTEENTH–CENTURY GROWTH

There was renewed growth in the late eighteenth century (figs 7 and 9), housebuilding picking up sharply in the 1760s.[91] In the West End estate development marched on as a relatively coherent process, the primary direction of growth shifting northwards across Oxford Street to St Marylebone. As before, the wealthier people who undertook, underwrote and consumed this development laid out squares and other designed spaces between the large new houses. Westminster was still not, however, monoculturally affluent despite intended appearances. Interstitial and marginal spaces were, and needed to be, occupied by those thousands of artisans and tradesmen in the service sector who maintained the rich. The sheer acreage (perhaps 600 plus) covered by eighteenth-century estate development in the West End reinforces Summerson's emphases in seeming to suggest that in terms of housebuilding this was the only show in town. On maps, expansion to the west seems

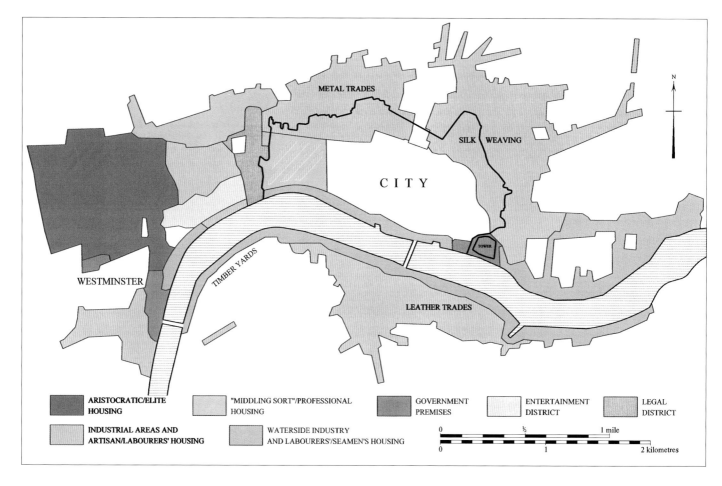

8 Dominant occupations and occupancies in mid-eighteenth-century London (based on Spate, in Darby, ed., 1936).

overwhelmingly dominant (fig. 7). But maps are two-dimensional and this is misleading. It would be a major mistake to assume that the period hatching of a map says everything about where housebuilding occurred. Above all it fails to represent the widespread and intensive replacement of earlier houses in already fully built-up areas.

Westminster's population grew from about 70,000 in 1700 to more than 150,000 in 1801, great increase certainly, but only about 20 per cent of London's overall growth. Some of the additional population was squeezed into the already densely populated central areas, but there was also continuing growth, piecemeal, sometimes ribbon-like, and generally incoherent, on the peripheries to the north, east and south (fig. 7). Small houses built in small groups produced few dramatic changes on the map, but through the eighteenth century thousands of houses were built in the southern and eastern suburbs, many of them always destined for occupation by artisans and labourers.

East London did not grow through large-scale green-field development in the late eighteenth century, in part because there was little economic impetus in districts that could not easily be marketed as fashionable, and where concerted speculative development to house artisans and labourers would not have paid good returns. There were other reasons why east London 'grew obscurely',[92] though the often repeated assumption that the prevalence of manorial copyhold tenures worked against coherent development is open to question.

To a lesser degree these limitations also applied south of the river, though circumstances did change following the building of Westminster Bridge and Blackfriars Bridge, opened in 1750 and 1769 respectively. These new bridges and associated road building opened up St George's Fields, Lambeth, Kennington and Walworth (see chapter 4). Much development there was for a commuting clientele of the 'middling sort', but these marginal areas retained pronounced social ambiguities. The same was true to the north and east, where road-

26

side wastes and commons were built on, coming to meet London through ribbon development, as on Kingsland Road and at Mile End (see chapter 5). The New Road of 1756–63 (latterly Marylebone, Euston, Pentonville and City Roads) opened up the northern margins and Islington to estate development. This was by no means all of a high standard. Marginality still carried with it connotations of undesirability, as became evident in Somers Town at the end of the century (see chapter 9). However, improved transport and the great extent of London's growth was bringing a new kind of social indeterminacy to the urban fringes. Terraces, crescents and villas were scattered amid brick-pits and market gardens for the growing 'middling' market that wanted a more spacious and genteel way of living, but was obliged to live at a distance from the workplace to get it. In 1800 brickmaking still encircled the built-over area, with market gardens beyond, in concentrations to the south, the near north-east, and close to the Thames to the west as far as Richmond. A great deal of land to the north was meadow and pasture.[93]

SEGREGATION

Transport had improved, but, as contemporaries noted, London's parts, excepting those along the river, still had little intercommunication at the end of the eighteenth century. In the meantime, and notwithstanding new developments at the margins, social segregation had increased, the 'comfortable' middle classes having become significantly more concentrated, residing either in the western suburbs or in the City. The eastern and southern suburbs were more than before home to people on lower incomes, with few 'middling sort' residents left in densely built-up areas. That is not to say that these areas were the poorest. The worst areas were those resettled areas between the City and Westminster such as St Giles in the Fields, a 'nest of banditti'.[94] Lower 'middling' groups, notably shopkeepers, remained more evenly spread. In the predominantly larger houses to the west, shopkeepers and others were more often obliged to sublet to lodgers, and there were always large numbers of working people in the wealthier West End districts.[95]

East London, with about 190,000 people, still had about 21 per cent of the city's population in 1801, of which perhaps only 4 per cent were middle or upper class. In and around Spitalfields, silk remained overwhelmingly dominant. In the riverside parishes, mariners and shipbuilding were still comparably prevalent, and Whitechapel had a concentration of Jewish immigrants. In the innermost and outermost eastern parishes there was marginally more gentility, and more mixed employ-ment.[96] In the crisis years of the 1790s, at the same time as there was a campaign to reform the port through the building of new enclosed docks in east London, the area's riverside parishes were being stigmatised as undesirable. As if in collaboration, a huge fire swept through wooden Ratcliff in 1794. Increased segregation had created the conditions for Colquhoun's demonisation of the riverside poor, and for the all but complete alienation of the rest of London from its 'East End'. In 1807 J. P. Malcolm articulated the new outlook and the shutting of the door in his description of Shadwell: 'we search in vain on the surface for antiquity or modern objects of interest. Thousands of useful tradesmen, artizans, and mechanicks, and numerous watermen inhabit it, but their houses and workshops will not bear description; nor are the streets, courts, lanes, and alleys, by any means inviting.'[97] Their houses have indeed not borne description.

Housing Conditions

The next chapter will look at the nature of eighteenth-century London's houses, but before that something needs to be said about housing conditions, as a way of distinguishing between the different kinds of houses that existed in different parts of London.

OVERCROWDING

For many in eighteenth-century London, housing options ranged from wretched to non-existent. In addressing the causes of crime in the parish of St Giles in the Fields, Henry Fielding wrote in 1751:

There are great numbers of houses set aside for the reception of idle persons and vagabonds who have their lodgings there for two-pence a night; that in the above parish, and in St George, Bloomsbury, one woman alone occupies seven of these houses, all properly accommodated with miserable beds from the cellar to the garret. [. . .] in these beds men and women, often strangers to each other, lie promiscuously.[98]

Hogarth's 'Idle Prentice' was portrayed in what is as close as there is to a contemporary view of such conditions (fig. 10).

Historians have vividly described London's eighteenth-century 'Alsatias', its no-go areas where a dis-possessed and casually lawless 'yahoo proletariat' found sanctuary amid decrepit built environments, the conditions and dangers of which kept outsiders away. These were small local pockets, as in St Giles, Saffron Hill

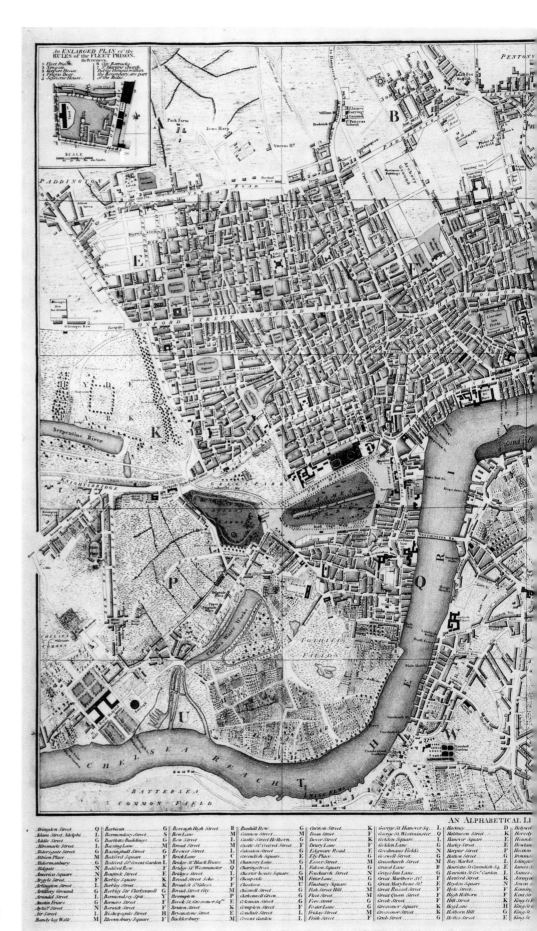

9   John Fairburn, *London and Westminster*, 1797 (GL).

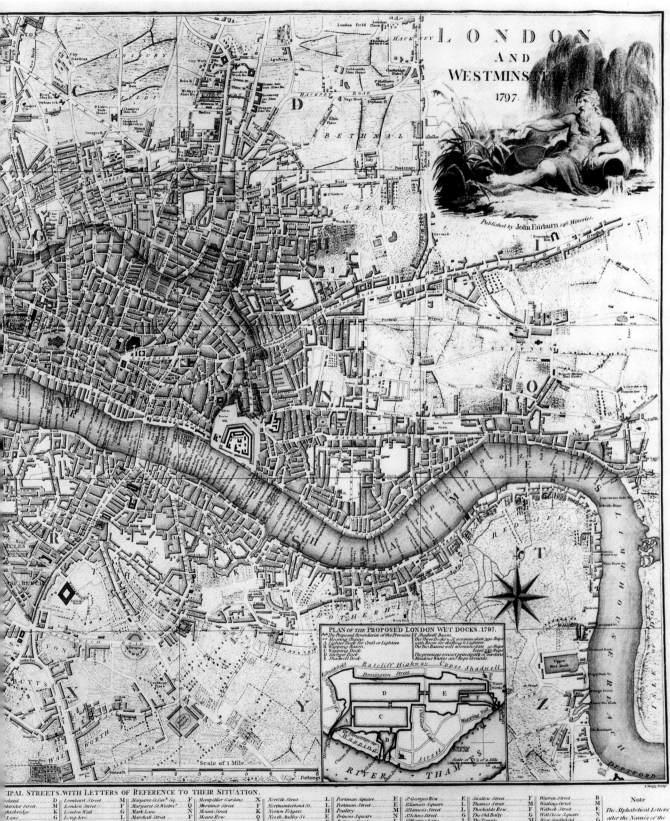

10 William Hogarth, 'The Idle 'Prentice return'd from Sea, & in a Garret with a common Prostitute', from *Industry and Idleness*, 1747 (GL).

(Holborn), Whitefriars, Rosemary Lane and Rag Fair (East Smithfield), around Great Peter Street in Westminster and across the river in parts of Southwark.[99] In 1800 it was reported that in St Giles, Holborn, Clerkenwell and across to Cripplegate, in 'Liquor Pond Street, Hog Island, Turnmill Street, Old Street, Whitecross Street, Grub Street, Golden Lane', as well as in 'Rosemary Lane, Petticoat Lane, Lower East Smithfield, some parts of Upper Westminster, and several streets of Rotherhithe', housing conditions were such that 'from three to eight individuals, of different ages, often sleep in the same bed; there being in general but one room and one bed for each family', and that 'in many instances idleness, in others the cumbrous furniture, or utensils of trade with which the apartments are clogged, prevents the salutary operation of the broom and white-washing brush, and favour the accumulation of a heterogenous, fermenting filth' (fig. 12).[100]

Even among the relatively law-abiding and industrious populations of less squalid districts, many families occupied a single room. 'In a large proportion of the dwellings of the poor, a house contains as many families as rooms [. . .] of a size scarcely more than sufficient to admit of a bed, with space for a person to pass it, and so much as is necessary for a fire-place.'[101] These rooms often had also to serve as a workshop. By contrast the 'middling sort' family of the early eighteenth century typically had five to eight rooms, in effect a whole house. However, cramped living conditions were not exclusive to the poor. A great many 'middling' people who were single or making their way in society had only one or two rooms. Limited domestic space meant that even the relatively affluent had to spend time in taverns and coffee houses. 'Conveniences of all kinds are nowhere so much wanted as in London houses, nor is there anywhere so little room for them.'[102] That even some better-off Londoners lived with little space is evident in the ingenuity that was devoted to high-quality folding furniture. Such solutions were not restricted to the genteel. Tradesmen's homes and lodging houses had 'turned-up bedsteads, and beds inclosed in resemblances of chests of drawers and bookcases'.[103] For meals the less well-to-do resorted to cook shops, and much of life was conducted in the street. There was great mobility, with a large floating population changing lodgings frequently, midnight finding 'Pawn-brokers' Shops very full of Men and Women, who are bringing Cloaths to a new Lodging, and fetching them from their Last Week's Habitation.'[104] As ever,

> eternal removals indicate that discontent and alterca-tion exist but too frequently between the landlord's family and the lodger. Kitchens used in common by both parties are sources of discord; the cleansing of stairs ascended by all the inhabitants of the house is another; and the late hours of the latter a third. It is therefore common to see the streets almost obstructed every quarter-day with cart-loads of furniture.[105]

Garrets, draughty, low-ceilinged and often unheated, were notoriously undesirable, but they were not the worst part of many buildings. Damp and gloomy cellars were considered worse. The intervening storeys were much to be preferred, with front rooms, often larger, being better than back rooms. The housekeeper's family generally took the ground floor, the distinction between tax-paying housekeepers and lodgers being of some importance in terms of status.[106]

Worse than lodgings in a house were the lodging houses (fig. 13). Many large seventeenth-century build-ings in the more densely populated central districts were decaying tenement blocks, and these areas also had numerous smaller houses in 'courts within courts and alleys behind alleys forming perfect labyrinths'.[107] Poor construction was rife, and collapsing buildings were not at all unusual. Between the housed and the wholly homeless were those who lived or at least slept in stalls and sheds. 'A Cobler there was and he lived in a Stall which served him for Parlour and Kitchen and Hall.'[108] But the shanty-town picture should not be overdone. Continental visitors found London exceptionally clean. 'Even in lodging-houses, the middle of the stairs is often covered with carpeting, to prevent them from being soiled. All the apartments in the house have mats or carpets.'[109]

There was indoor relief for the poor, that is the work-house or 'pauper farms', with a number of new institu-tions in London parishes following the Workhouse Test Act of 1722. This might have had some limited impact in reducing the numbers of the poor needing to find housing on the open market, but efforts to avoid the workhouse should not be underestimated.[110]

★   ★   ★

MORTALITY

Perhaps the most important subject to address in squar-ing the social structures of working people with an understanding of differences in housing in relation to localities is mortality. The reasons for eighteenth-century London's high mortality rates have been much debated, but important emphasis has recently been placed on housing.[111] The exceptionally high mortality rates of the 1730s and 1740s have traditionally been blamed on gin, the effects of which were famously and powerfully depicted by Hogarth (fig. 11). However, exposure to infection and poor housing may have been more signif-icant as the root causes of high mortality. The worst death rates were in what has been identified as a 'high-instability belt' across the centre-north suburbs, centred on St Giles in the Fields, Covent Garden, and Holborn, where Hogarth located 'Gin Lane', just north of which the Foundling Hospital was established in the 1740s to attempt to stem the tide of infant deaths, and where many new immigrants, particularly the Irish, lived. These areas were characterised by the convergence of a certain kind of housing stock and slack estate management, that is by large houses built as much as a century or as little

11   Human and architectural collapse in central London's mid-eighteenth-century 'high-instability belt'. William Hogarth, *Gin Lane*, 1751 (GL).

12 The Fleet Ditch, Saffron Hill, showing long decrepit, probably seventeenth-century housing in one of eighteenth-century London's 'Alsatias' shortly before clearance for the making of Farringdon Road over the malarial Fleet. Watercolour by Thomas Hosmer Shepherd, 1844 (LMA).

as a generation earlier for a wealthy market that had migrated further west. There were also other types of housing, but great overcrowding in tall, densely packed and decaying buildings was the norm. Hogarth's St Giles is a scene of both human and architectural collapse, presided over by a pawnbroker.[112]

London faced a crisis in the supply of living space after 1730 as economic stagnation caused speculative house-building to stop, bringing ever-greater overcrowding in the lodging houses at the bottom end of the trickle-down housing market, leading in turn to greater infec-tivity and higher mortality. It is important to register that this kind of housing stock, elite houses subdivided into

lodging houses, was not found in such concentration elsewhere. In the manufacturing suburbs to the east and south there were generally smaller houses, purpose-built for occupation by artisans and labourers. There was also less disease, though in the worst years dreadful mor-tality waves did spread out from the 'high-instability belt', much as had happened in the Great Plague in 1665. The differences in mortality and the related differences in the nature of houses between the 'unhealthy' centre-north suburbs and the apparently healthier suburbs to the east and south are crucial to an understanding of London's housing options. It is also important to note that mortality in London was significantly lower in the

13 A 'thieves' lodging house', Blackboy Alley, near the Fleet, another apparently seventeenth-century building recorded before clearance in the 1840s. Watercolour by Thomas Hosmer Shepherd (LMA).

late eighteenth century. Many factors have been adduced to explain this, not least improvements in nutrition and hygiene, but among them would have been improved housing supply following the revival in housebuilding after 1760.

HOUSE SIZE AND OCCUPANCY

Emphasis on the worst housing, which does not survive, is an important counterweight to awareness of the large houses of the wealthy, numbers of which do survive. However, attention to the two extremes obscures what came in between: 'the great majority of Londoners had

a roof over their heads and lived in a house or part of a house.'[113] But these houses were not everywhere from the same mould.

Differences in mortality light a path away from the treatment of eighteenth-century London's housing as uniform, both topographically and through time. Housing was highly variable and, in the broad sweep, the manufacturing suburbs to the east and south were not the worst areas. The characterisation of mid-seventeenth-century maritime Shadwell as a relatively decent and socially homogeneous working place has already been mentioned. With a few exceptions the houses were small. Hearth-tax returns show that in the

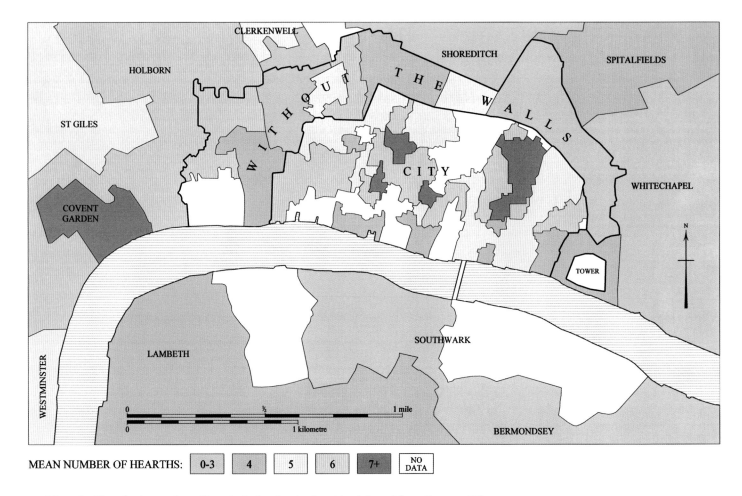

MEAN NUMBER OF HEARTHS: | 0-3 | 4 | 5 | 6 | 7+ | NO DATA |

14   Mean dwelling size by number of hearths in London in the 1660s (adapted from Power, 1986).

1660s there were marked differences in the average sizes of houses in the different parts of London (fig. 14). Suburbs to the north, east and south, sweeping round from Clerkenwell clockwise through Shoreditch and the Tower Hamlets across to Southwark, Bermondsey and Lambeth, had mean dwelling sizes of four or fewer hearths. Suburbs to the west from Holborn anticlockwise to Westminster, taking in St Giles, all had mean dwelling sizes of four or more hearths. Crudely, east London houses, averaging 2.7 hearths, were half as big as those of west London, averaging 5.5 hearths (though only 4.2 in St Margaret, Westminster). The City was very mixed. These data have been analysed in relation to social class, revealing that for skilled artisans an average house had about four hearths, semi-skilled workers had closer to three, and professionals and merchants about six. In the 1660s suburbs with concentrations of artisans had, on the whole, smaller houses, many of which must have been singly occupied rather than divided.[114]

House occupancy, single or multiple, is a highly problematic area about which there is more detailed discus-

sion in later chapters. So far, the general picture has the larger houses of St Giles and other 'high-instability-belt' suburbs declining into overcrowded multiple occupation, with the smaller houses of manufacturing suburbs being rather less crowded. It has been estimated that only 15 per cent of London's houses were divided in the early seventeenth century. Multiple occupation was seemingly exceptional in seventeenth-century east London, but more common in the West End, perhaps occurring in about one in four houses. Most of the divided houses in seventeenth-century London were probably in the poorest central areas around the fringes of the City, many of them adapted single-family houses, perhaps with some purpose-built tenements alongside (see chapters 2 and 3). Smaller houses in other districts were evidently built for single occupation, though sometimes later divided, multiple occupation being more often the result of decline than of design. As in St Giles, so in Shadwell: multiple occupation was rare there in the 1650s, when the area was newly developed, but much more prevalent in the 1690s, when it occurred in about one in four houses. It was not only, nor even primarily, big houses that were divided. In Shadwell the least desirable properties were those most readily subdivided. The spread of divided houses may also reflect the age of housing stock. Craig Spence has found that in the 1690s the buildings of the northern and eastern suburban parishes were comparatively newer than those of the West End, with about two-thirds to three-quarters of the houses to the north and east being no older than thirty years, while only about a third of the West End's buildings were then new, perhaps also a reflection of differentials in the durability of developments before 1670 (see chapter 2). So, it seems, artisan districts in the late seventeenth century had numerous relatively new small singly occupied houses, perhaps crowded and overfurnished, but not squalid.[115]

In 1708 Edward Hatton reckoned that only 10 per cent of London's houses were divided.[116] Separately derived estimates – that around 1700 London's average household size was about six to eight people, higher than elsewhere in the country, and that there were about eight people per house[117] – suggest that Hatton was not far wrong and that multiple-household or multi-occupied houses were still in a clear minority, while still varying in prevalence a great deal from district to district.

Throughout eighteenth-century London houses tended to be in single ownership, though some old houses in the City had different freeholders on different floors. The leasehold system conventionally worked so that whole new houses were in single ownership and sublet, shopkeepers and other small landlords typically occupying the ground floor and letting off the other rooms. As Adam Smith related in 1776:

> A dwelling-house in England means everything that is contained under the same roof. In France, Scotland, and, many other parts of Europe, it frequently means no more than a single story. A tradesman in London [. . .] expects to maintain his family by his trade, and not by his lodgers. Whereas at Paris and Edinburgh, the people who let lodgings have commonly no other means of subsistence.[118]

Households in central London were on average larger than elsewhere, because more complex, comprehending to a greater degree lodgers, servants and apprentices. The smaller houses in some outer districts accommodated smaller households, and the ratio of people to houses in 1801 remained greater in central-suburban parishes.[119] If multiple occupation did become more widespread through the eighteenth century, it remained something to be avoided where possible. It was certainly associated with poverty at the beginning of the nineteenth century,

when Louis Simond claimed of London that 'Each family occupy a whole house, unless very poor.'[120] Though divided houses were not rare, the association made here may have been essentially true. It implies that there were still then many small singly occupied houses, since forgotten.

AFFORDABILITY

Significantly, and in keeping with the evidence so far adduced, it has been argued that 'the upper end of the mechanick class' (artisans) could afford newly built small houses in the late seventeenth century, even in the post-Fire City where rents were high, perhaps £6 to £9 a year for the smallest three- or four-room houses.[121] Such rents were widespread, affordable and relatively constant through the eighteenth century. In most places £10 a year would rent a respectable small house; in 1739 London's lowest house rents were in East Smithfield, averaging £4 8s 7d a year. It has been calculated that in the 1690s 50 per cent of all London rents were £11 or less a year, and about 20–25 per cent were £5 or less (fig. 15). In the eastern suburbs, however, more than 40 per cent of rents were £5 or less, and only about 10 per cent were above £20. In the West End this was reversed, with only about 10 per cent of rents being below £5 and more than 40 per cent being £20 or more. Henry Fielding stated that a bed in a lodging house in St Giles in 1751 cost tuppence a night, about a shilling a week, or £3 a year.[122] There were worse beds to be had for a penny a night, but even so the gap in affordability between space in a lodging house and a small house was not all that great. It has been estimated that eighteenth-century rents were paid at about one-eighth of income, and that the 'standard' rent of a working London artisan before 1795 earning about £1 a week would have been 2s 6d, enough for a small house at £6 a year. Many earned less than £1 a week on a regular basis. Nevertheless, the size of the artisan population was such that it is credible that London's smaller houses in its eastern and southern suburbs were being built for an essentially artisan market, and that a significant number of working artisans were able to pay as much as £10 a year in rent.[123]

Larger houses, that is those of five rooms or more, were out of reach of all but the wealthiest quarter of the population. When it was being developed in the 1690s, the Seven Dials area in St Giles had a mean household annual rent of £15 10s, and the 'middling sort' had to pay rents of £20 to £30 a year for houses, even in 'meaner areas'. For journeymen and labourers earning around £20 a year rooms, garrets or tenements were widely rentable for about £2 a year.[124]

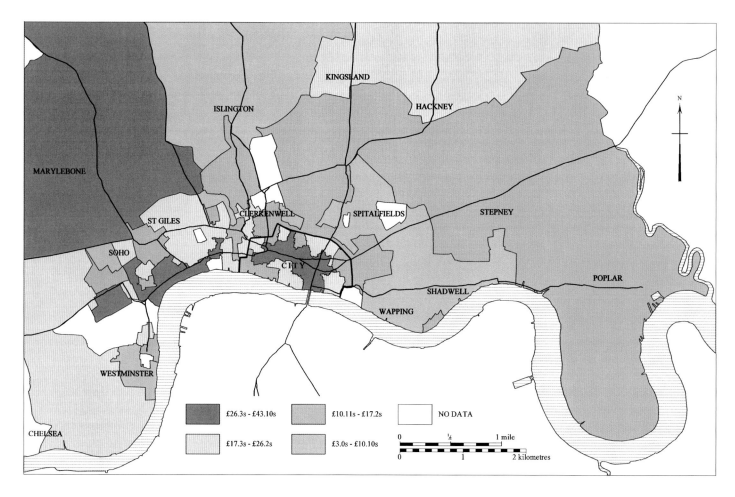

£26.3s - £43.10s   £10.11s - £17.2s   NO DATA

£17.3s - £26.2s   £3.0s - £10.10s

0   ¼   1 mile

0   1   2 kilometres

15   Mean household rent value per annum in London north of the Thames in the 1690s (based upon the Four Shilling Aid assessments of 1693–4 and adapted from Spence, 2000, p. 71, fig. 4.4).

Conclusion

At the beginning of the eighteenth century there was a strong tradition of building small but respectable houses for an artisan market concentrated in east and south London. Occupancy of a whole house was, it seems, not beyond modest aspiration. Living conditions in the small houses in the artisan suburbs remained substantially better than in the overcrowded bigger houses and subsidiary courts of the central 'high-instability-belt' suburbs, though there were pockets of abject poverty and overcrowding from St Margaret's, Westminster, to Rotherhithe. There were greatly different population mixes in the central and outer districts, on one hand poor immigrants and the dispossessed concentrated to the centre, on the other skilled artisans were localised in suburbs. It is known that the latter were more politically engaged: 'the most riotous parts of London were not the crowded quarters of St Giles in the Fields or the shadier

alleys of Holborn but the more solid and respectable popular districts of the City, the Strand, Southwark, Shoreditch and Spitalfields.'[125] It is hardly surprising that the politicised parts of the 'lower orders' should have had housing that made it possible to look above the threshold of survival. A mental leap away from stereotypes of noisome squalor is needed. Artisan suburbs were in parts relatively new, clean, comfortable and orderly, not by latter-day standards perhaps, but by those then operative.

Statistically based analyses show only those crude dualistic contrasts between smaller and bigger houses, ironing out variety within localities and revealing nothing about house form or about other architectural subtleties. It also remains unclear how things changed through the eighteenth century. As London continued to grow, did multiple occupancy become more usual? Did small houses continue to be built for single occupation by artisans and labourers? What did they look like? How were they different? Where were they concentrated? How did emulative consumption, artisan decline and 'improvement' affect the traditions of artisan housing? These are questions addressed in subsequent chapters.

This chapter has explored eighteenth-century London, focusing on a range of its characteristics to which Boswell's phrase 'like a different country' might be applied. First of all it has stressed that London, a vast megalopolis without parallel or precedent, was set apart from the rest of England. It has emphasised the range of the city's social groupings, cultural heterogeneity, and the question of identity in relation to London's artisan class.

It has addressed Boswell's basic meaning, the pointed cultural, physical and perceptual contrast between the city's eastern and western parts, which disguised more local particularities. Finally, it has looked at housing conditions, to adumbrate differences between overcrowded multi-occupied large buildings in central areas and less densely populated, singly occupied small houses in industrial suburbs. Throughout it has attempted to show that in relation to the eighteenth-century London that architectural historians have tended to describe there was another, a vernacular metropolis that was 'like a different country'.

16   Nos 13 and 13A Poplar High Street, a small brick house of *c.*1700 with a later and smaller timber house adjoining. Photographed *c.*1890. Demolished (EH, CC76/568).

Chapter 2

'THE MULTIPLICITY OF HUMAN HABITATIONS': UNDERSTANDING EIGHTEENTH-CENTURY LONDON'S SMALLER-HOUSE ARCHITECTURE

> Sir, if you wish to have a just notion of the magnitude of this city you must not be satisfied with seeing its great streets and squares, but must survey the innumerable little lanes and courts. It is not in the showy evolutions of buildings, but in the multiplicity of human habitations which are crouded [*sic*] together, that the wonderful immensity of London consists.
>
> Samuel Johnson[1]

Six months after Boswell's differentiating walk across London, this advice from Dr Johnson sharpened his focus. This chapter also takes heed and so begins to survey that 'multiplicity of human habitations'. Given the 'immensity' of the subject, it is necessarily another overview, this time of London's smaller-scale domestic architecture. It tracks developments chronologically through the seventeenth and eighteenth centuries, using examples from central districts and some inner, particularly eastern, suburbs that are not accounted for in the local case studies that make up subsequent chapters. Intended as a background for the case studies, much of this chapter is devoted to seventeenth-century forerunners, to provide a basis for the investigation of eighteenth-century buildings. It is a survey rather than an argument, drawing out threads of change and continuity over time and across a large area, aiming to introduce themes that run through the case studies: the nature of small-scale speculative development; the impact of legislation; plan forms in relation to circulation patterns, room use and occupancy; materials used in house construction, especially timber versus brick; functionality and aesthetics, traditional design or classicism in elevations and internal finishes; and, in embryo at least, questions of distinctiveness and variability in relation to differing local contexts.

No more than an introduction to such a broad range of issues can be provided from smaller houses in London's central districts, that is the City across to West-minster, for want of evidence. Towns have always had small houses, and London is no exception. The older ones, however, tend not to survive, especially where, as in London, there have been strong susceptibilities to loss through fire, and the wealth to enable redevelopment. The richer a place, the greater the attrition rate of old houses; and the further back in time one looks, the thinner the evidence becomes.[2] Where they survived fire and consistently strong development pressures, London's smaller houses tended to become bad housing, that is 'slums', a nineteenth-century coinage, and thereby subject to clearance schemes. This arose in part from 'impermanent' construction and poor maintenance, but also from changing standards as to what constituted adequate domestic space, to do with growth in personal possessions and improving hygiene, as well as to Victorian views on decency, that is sex, that judged whole families sharing one bedroom to be intolerable. In central London few small early houses survived long enough even to be recorded. Many of the buildings that were recorded in the nineteenth and twentieth centuries have since been demolished. It is not possible to build a discussion on the basis of field survey in London's most central districts, as it is in somewhat more outlying places.

Looking back at earlier records of smaller early houses with the benefit of detailed study of comparable material, it becomes clear that previous estimates of build dates are often suspect. At the lower end of the architectural spectrum, conventional stylistic typologies based in high art are of little use. Where there are embellishments at all, they have tended to suggest dates that are too early because insufficient account has been taken of conservatism below the threshold of the fashionable. This is not to imply any fundamental divide. Passing comparative reference will be made to the period's better-known, better-surviving and larger 'middling sort' houses, but their no more than shadowy presence here should not give rise to a rigid dichotomy. As has been pointed out in relation to use of the term 'small', there were not large houses and small houses, but houses of all sizes along a continuum, on the whole thoroughly jumbled together, the humble and the grand often cheek by jowl. The focus here is simply on one part of this spectrum, and that part not even the smallest, rather the smaller to middling, the smallest houses having left no traces.

Size was not the only determinant of status, but size does matter, so a grasp of relative dimensions is crucial to this subject. For this reason the house plans illustrated here are presented as compilations, all with a common scale, reconstructed and simplified to show interpretations of basic original form. Rear outshuts, for which evidence is rare, are generally omitted from these plans, though single-storey back rooms, for wash-house, storage or other service purposes, were probably much more widespread than it is possible to document. In seventeenth- and eighteenth-century London linear frontage was the primary determinant of house size. A house with a frontage of 20 ft (6.1 m) or more is not here considered to be 'small'.

Some Early Houses

In late medieval and Tudor London most houses were timber built, their fronts often jettied and gabled. The best surviving evidence for the size and layouts of London's sixteenth-century and earlier houses is the collection of plans made by Ralph Treswell in 1607–12. These show that many houses then standing in London were only one room in plan, often about 12 ft square, not infrequently smaller. By this date such houses in and around the densely populated City were generally three or more storeys tall, with winder staircases in one or other corner. Multiple occupation was widespread and there would have been many one-room tenancies, with smaller houses frequently facing narrow and insalubrious courts, alleys or yards. Two-room layouts were also widespread through the late medieval period, generally having the essentially urban front-room/back-room

'double-pile' disposition that is a reflection of narrow plots, that is of population density and the value of street frontages. There was no established standard plan form and the internal layouts of these larger houses were highly variable, perhaps in part a reflection of accretive development. Spaces for commercial and domestic use were increasingly differentiated by the sixteenth century. Ground floors often had shops and warehouses, with kitchens sometimes placed at the back on the first floor. Many rooms remained without fireplaces. In bigger, that is polite or gentry houses, both urban and rural, diversity of room use spread in the sixteenth century, growing specialisation in the use of space permitting not only the separation of living from working, but greater privacy in general. In early seventeenth-century London large and small houses mingled indiscriminately, the smaller houses remaining highly irregular, wholly unstandardised, and defiant of typological rigidities.[3]

There were legal restrictions on building, but these were notoriously ineffective, and confused. Numerous royal proclamations and Acts of Parliament, from 1580 up to an Act of 1657 'for preventing the multiplicity of Buildings in and about the Suburbs of London and within ten miles of the same', were promulgated in attempts to curb immigration and suburban growth, in effect outlawing housebuilding for the poor. Outright bans on new building did admit exceptions and licences, and many of the preventive proclamations simultaneously attempted to promote better building and uniformity, directing that what new building there was should be of brick rather than cheaper and more combustible timber. But the restrictions were blatantly defied, unsurprisingly given the huge demand for housing arising from enormous population growth. The Crown, while sweeping away some illegal developments, generally those of the poorest sort, allowed many more, opportunistically using the system to generate income, from fines as well as from licences. Leases of thirty-one years were usual, and houses were not generally built with a view to their lasting longer than the lease. If anything, the restrictions encouraged a lower standard of building, as speculators covered themselves for running the additional risks of having developments cleared or of paying a fine. Most building 'craftsmen' operating in the suburbs were not members of London companies, and were not therefore subject to trade regulation. A great deal of low-grade short-life housing was built.[4]

It would be misleading to imply that as London did grow it grew any old how, that the economic factors that underpin later standardisation were wholly absent. Houses had been speculatively built in uniform rows, or 'rents', for centuries. In a notable instance of a coherent large-scale speculative development on the extramural margins of the City, the fairground at St Bartholomew, Smithfield, was laid out in the years 1598 to 1616 with about 175 new houses, evidently largely occupied by artisans and shopkeepers from the outset.[5] Of the Bartholomew Fair houses, about 140 were of a more or less standard type. They had one room on each floor, with frontages of about 12 ft and varying depths of up to as much as about 23 ft. They rose three full storeys, with shops on the ground floor (used as booths during the fair), cellars below, and chambers and garrets above. There were party-wall chimneystacks, and staircases in back corners were directly accessible from back doors. Most of the houses were of timber, jettied and gable fronted in keeping with traditional practice. Remarkably, some of these buildings survive, though with inevitably extensive alteration. No. 74 Long Lane still has a jettied timber front (figs 17, 18 and 21). From around 1610 brick was used at Bartholomew Fair in what may have been a novel departure, possibly reflecting two new proclamations of 1611 against timber building and jetties, but also perhaps symptomatic of a concern for amenity and urban improvement that is otherwise evident in the wider development. At least twenty-eight of the houses were originally wholly brick built, many seemingly with simple flat elevations, segmental window heads and plat bands. A few smaller houses were built back to back, as at No. 20 Middle Street and No. 5 East Passage of around 1612, one of which pair was already multi-occupied in 1616. As recorded in 1911, these had winder staircases at the front lit by small windows, an arrangement discussed below (figs 17 and 19).[6] The brick front to No. 20 Middle Street that was then photographed may have been from a rebuilding in the late seventeenth or early eighteenth century, but an early seventeenth-century date can not be ruled out. The houses of Bartholomew Fair are an important link, both growing out of medieval practice and informing later developments.

Little is known about other early to mid-seventeenth-century houses in central London away from the high-profile and high-status departures of the 1630s and 1640s at Covent Garden and Lincoln's Inn Fields, the regular open spaces and uniform brick ungabled 'trim discipline' of which were Summerson's points of departure for his account of Georgian London. Undoubtedly consequential, these developments need not be understood as either entirely innovative or universally influential.[7] 'The Old Curiosity Shop', just south of Lincoln's Inn Fields, survives to represent a humbler idiom, and houses more closely comparable with those of Bartholomew Fair continued to be built in and around the City, if not in such large speculations. Away from the fashionable pull

of Westminster, even substantial buildings continued to be built of timber, as on Peter's Lane, linking Cowcross Street and St John's Street in Clerkenwell (fig. 20), where a group of three houses, each about 15 ft square on plan and thus probably only one room on each storey, stood into the nineteenth century.[8] On Aldgate High Street two mid-seventeenth-century timber buildings survive at Nos 46 and 47 (the Hoop and Grapes), and on Winchester Street, just south of London Wall, a large and regular group of gabled timber houses was built in the 1650s.[9]

Royal proclamations notwithstanding, small-scale timber housing spread in London's suburbs through the seventeenth century. The status of an area could increasingly be defined in terms of whether its houses were of brick or of stick. Unlicensed development in 'outer' Covent Garden from around 1612 into the 1630s was predominantly timber and small, contrasting sharply with the licensed and truly radical development of Covent Garden's 'inner' precinct after 1630, where big brick houses on the estate of Francis Russell, 4th Earl of Bedford, were aimed at a genteel market. In 1650 about two-thirds of the houses in High Holborn, Long Acre and Piccadilly were brick, compared to only 9 per cent in the Tower Liberty and Shadwell, to the east, and New Palace Yard in Westminster, to the south-west.[10]

Emphasis on what was innovative in London house-building has obscured underlying continuity to the point that the occurrence of vernacular architectural features in the late seventeenth century and the eighteenth has, when noticed at all, been traced to rural precedent. It is far more likely that London had, over the centuries, generated its own templates. This is an assertion that, in the absence of much archaeological or documentary research into the forms of central London's vanished humbler sixteenth- and early to mid-seventeenth-century houses, lacks detailed evidential support. However, neither is there much specific basis for the notion of rural-to-urban transfers in ordinary house design. This argument will resurface periodically, with particular reference to plan form.[11]

Away from the centre the small but decent timber houses and riverine working population of mid-seventeenth-century Shadwell have already been mentioned (see chapter 1). The district was developed in the 1630s and 1640s with about seven hundred houses, built piecemeal, at first in small speculations of two or three houses, with some larger developments following, along increasingly regular street layouts. Local entrepreneurs involved in shipbuilding owned much property, though direct involvement in housebuilding has not been shown. Frontages of 12–15 ft were typical, but this and other

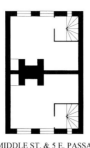
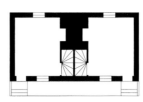
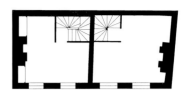

74 LONG LANE
SMITHFIELD
FIRST FLOOR
c.1598 and c.1700

20 MIDDLE ST. & 5 E. PASSAGE
SMITHFIELD
FIRST FLOOR
c.1612 and c.1700 (dem.)

75-77 CAMBRIDGE HEATH ROAD
BETHNAL GREEN
GROUND FLOOR
mid to late 17th century (dem.)

19-20 COCK LANE
CITY OF LONDON
FIRST FLOOR   SECOND FLOOR
c.1670 (dem.)

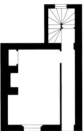
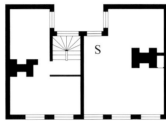
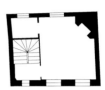

8 BRAHAM STREET
WHITECHAPEL
GROUND FLOOR
1680s (dem.)

21-22 NEWPORT COURT
SOHO
SECOND FLOOR
c.1688

4 LOWER JOHN STREET
ST JAMES
FIRST FLOOR
c.1685 and c.1770

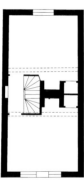
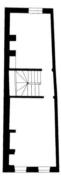

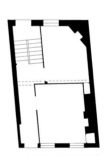

92 NARROW STREET
LIMEHOUSE
FIRST FLOOR
c.1700

22 ST JOHN STREET
CLERKENWELL
FIRST FLOOR
c.1700

227 SHOREDITCH HIGH ST.
SHOREDITCH
SECOND FLOOR
c.1700

30 BRITTON STREET
CLERKENWELL
GROUND FLOOR
1719-1723

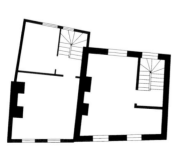

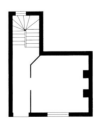

5-6 AVERY ROW
MAYFAIR
FIRST FLOOR
c.1725

2 DERBY STREET
MAYFAIR
FIRST FLOOR
1745 enlarged 1761

7 NOTTINGHAM PLACE
MARYLEBONE
GROUND FLOOR
c.1800

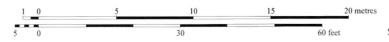

1 0   5   10   15   20 metres

5 0   30   60 feet

S = FORMER STAIR POSITION

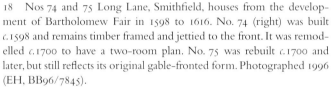

18 Nos 74 and 75 Long Lane, Smithfield, houses from the development of Bartholomew Fair in 1598 to 1616. No. 74 (right) was built
c.1598 and remains timber framed and jettied to the front. It was remodelled c.1700 to have a two-room plan. No. 75 was rebuilt c.1700 and
later, but still reflects its original gable-fronted form. Photographed 1996
(EH, BB96/7845).

19 No. 20 Middle Street, Smithfield. This one-room-plan house
with origins of c.1612 was one of an always multi-occupied back-
to-back pair in Bartholomew Fair. It was perhaps rebuilt c.1700.
Photographed 1911. Demolished (EH, AP 102).

aspects of house form were highly variable. About two-
thirds of the houses had two full storeys, with only about
5 per cent being taller. More than half had one room
per storey, and about 70 per cent had three or fewer
rooms altogether, with many garret rooms probably
remaining unheated. As has already been noted, there
was not great overcrowding, most of the houses starting
in single occupation. Ground-floor rooms were used as
combined living, dining and cooking spaces. There were
beds in most rooms, even in kitchens, and shop or workshop use within the houses was widespread.[12] The occupation of a whole three-room house in Shadwell would
have been within reach of working artisans; one that was
14 ft square cost £50 to build in the 1650s, suggesting an
annual rent of £6 or less.[13]

Not a splinter of seventeenth-century Shadwell survives, the heart of the early district having been displaced
by nineteenth-century extension of the London Docks
and by the north end of the Rotherhithe Tunnel in
1904–8, by when slight timber construction, fire and
decline associated with poverty had already taken their
toll. There is little visual evidence by which to judge the
early houses. Some in the wider district did stand long
enough to be recorded, but in most cases building dates
can not be determined. In east and south London small
timber houses were rebuilt when leases expired, more
or less like for like, up to the mid-eighteenth century.
On St John's Hill, just off The Highway, in an area to
the west of Shadwell that was first developed in the late
seventeenth century, a two-storey timber house was

17 (facing page) Reconstructed plans of seventeenth- and eighteenth-century houses in central and other London districts.

20 Peter's Lane, Clerkenwell, timber one-room-plan houses, probably built in the early seventeenth century. Photographed by William Strudwick, c.1867. Demolished (EH, BB99/06769).

21   Nos 19–22 Cloth Fair, Smithfield, timber-framed, jetty-fronted, one-room-plan houses of *c*.1600 from the development of Bartholomew Fair. Photographed by Henry Dixon, 1910. Demolished 1917 (EH, DD57/17).

22 A timber house on St John's Hill, Wapping, recorded as having been built in 1753, presumably replacing a late seventeenth-century predecessor. Photographed in the early twentieth century. Demolished (MiD).

Poplar, sometimes wider, sometimes taller, if of timber invariably long gone, and perhaps anyway rebuilt in the eighteenth century (fig. 24). Complex aspects of the piecemeal short-lease seventeenth- and eighteenth-century development of Poplar, where carpenters and shipwrights were prominent among those responsible for small developments of houses along the High Street,

23 Lower Turning and Star Street, Shadwell (latterly the corner of Milk Yard and Monza Street by the Shadwell Basin). In an area first developed soon after 1650 the house on the left is like the St John's Hill house (fig. 22) in indicating the nature and scale of most of the area's seventeenth-century houses, though it too may have been rebuilt in the eighteenth century. Pencil drawing by J. P. Emslie, c.1877. Demolished (MiD).

24 Nos 39 and 41 Limehouse Causeway, timber houses of the mid- to late seventeenth century, perhaps also rebuilt in the eighteenth century. Pencil drawing by J. P. Emslie, 1877. Demolished (MiD).

photographed and noted as bearing the information that it had been built in 1753 (fig. 22).[14] This points to the difficulty of dating buildings in other views, such as that of a corner in a part of Shadwell first developed soon after 1650 which shows a long timber building in the foreground, perhaps built as two houses, with what was probably a more typical three-room timber dwelling beyond an obviously rebuilt or refronted house (fig. 23). Many of Shadwell's relatively few larger houses, often jettied and gable fronted, stood along the High Street (latterly The Highway), the main road that was the district's northern boundary (fig. 25).[15]

Housing in neighbouring districts was not very different, modest but not without neatness and order. The fire of 1794 in neighbouring Ratcliff destroyed 453 houses, most of them small, but remarkably evenly spread in a rectilinear distribution, perhaps reflecting late seventeenth-century second-generation upgrading more than what would probably have been cruder first development.[16] Many mid- to late seventeenth-century buildings were built in ones and twos, across Limehouse to

25   A view along Ratcliff Highway showing some of Shadwell's larger timber houses of the 1630s and 1640s. Pencil drawing by J. P. Emslie, 1877. Demolished (MiD).

26   'Dog Row', Nos 65–77 (odd) Cambridge Heath Road (between Headlam Street and Darling Row), Bethnal Green, mid- to late seventeenth-century brick houses from the urban margins. With raised ground floors and cellars, these approximately 14 ft-square houses comprised four rooms each, with unlit front staircases. The fronts combined discontinuous plat bands and a continuous eaves cornice. The low stuccoed projections were said to have been blocked-up dog kennels, part of the area's dog-breeding past, from which the row's name derives. Photographed in the early twentieth century. Demolished (EH, BB60/1202).

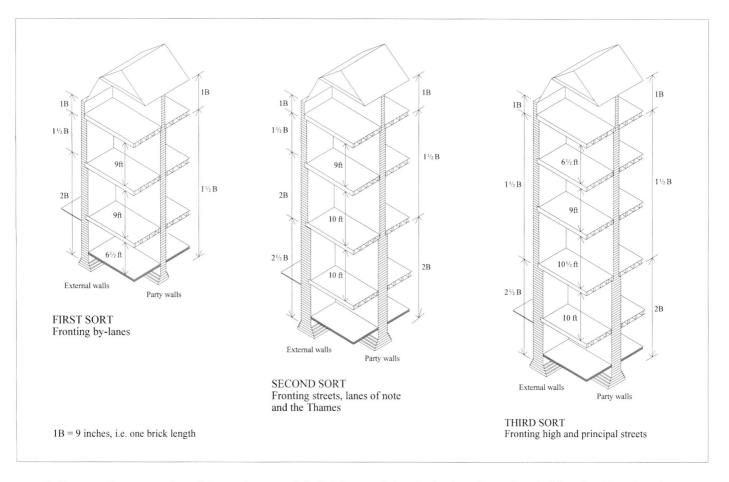

FIRST SORT
Fronting by-lanes

1B = 9 inches, i.e. one brick length

SECOND SORT
Fronting streets, lanes of note
and the Thames

THIRD SORT
Fronting high and principal streets

27   A diagrammatic representation of the requirements of the building regulations in the Act of 1667 for rebuilding the City of London, as applied to the three smaller 'sorts' of houses. The fourth 'sort' ('mansion houses') was not to exceed four storeys, with no wall thicknesses or room heights prescribed (Mike Clements).

have been unravelled. Many of these houses were timber, irregular in profile, and small in scale. They too are now entirely vanished.[17]

Across the sprawling eastern suburbs further inland there were some larger speculations during the seventeenth century, and regular rows of uniform houses did go up where land ownership allowed, most notably in Spitalfields and Mile End New Town, where there was some grid-like regularity from the 1650s onwards. There was more widespread use of brick in these places away from the river where brickearth was locally available, bricks being expensive to transport (see chapter 3). Away to the north-east was Dog Row, latterly the southern part of Cambridge Heath Road, isolated and marginal ribbon development of the late sixteenth century onwards, on waste linking the outlying settlements of Mile End Old Town and Bethnal Green (see chapter 5). Dog Row was a mix of small timber and brick houses that included a group of seven brick houses of the mid-

to late seventeenth century that survived to be recorded in the early twentieth (figs 17 and 26).[18]

After the Great Fire

This detour to the margins has served to set out the architectural range of London's seventeenth-century vernacular houses, incidentally hinting at continuity in eighteenth-century rebuilds. Before re-entering the eighteenth century through the front door, a return to the later seventeenth century will give due weight to pivotal events at the centre. In September 1666 the Great Fire destroyed about 13,000 houses in the City and extramural areas just to the west, about a quarter of the capital's housing stock. A year earlier the Great Plague had killed tens of thousands of Londoners. Densely packed timber buildings had permitted both fire and disease to spread easily. Ambitious and hasty projections for a fresh start with formal grid-based street layouts, drawn up by Christopher Wren, Robert Hooke, John Evelyn and others, were passed over as impracticable. The existing street pattern, alleys and all, was retained, although with many streets widened and paved. Rebuilding was remarkably quick and efficient. By 1672, 8,000 replacement houses had been built, a number that was not greatly exceeded thereafter, some sites remaining open, and many others taking larger houses than previously.[19]

The Act of 1667 that enabled the rebuilding of the City was drawn up by a commission of six 'surveyors', Wren, Hooke, Roger Pratt, Hugh May, Peter Mills and Edward Jerman. It was a significant departure from earlier building control legislation, introducing to England the rational notion that ordinary domestic architecture might be controlled via stratification into standard categories. It also followed earlier legislation in attempting to impose uniformity of appearance in what Jules Lubbock has characterised as an instance of 'the tyranny of taste' that had long-lasting influence.[20] The Act classified houses into four 'sorts', controlling heights so as to dictate regularity of streetscape. Widened high streets would not have low buildings and tall buildings would not be built on narrow lanes. Smaller two-storey and garret houses were to be 'The first or least sort of house fronting by-lanes'. The Act also specified for the first time that outside and party walls were to be of brick or stone, specifying thicknesses for the brick walls and scantlings for timber floors and roofs (fig. 27).[21] As it applied only to the square mile of the City of London, and there was immediate and unprecedented occasion for its implementation there under specially appointed surveyors, this range of specific regulations was relatively successfully enforced.[22]

The rebuilding Act helped give the City a significantly new aspect, but it did not mean that the rebuilt City was a phoenix of rational modernity, or that there had been a clean break with the past. The classification of houses into four sorts was not the product of a popular architectural tide. It was a paper exercise on the part of a professional elite given statutory force, more effective than the comparably motivated visionary ideas for replanning the City as a whole, but not wholly decisive. Legislation does not *ipso facto* alter behaviour, and London's house-builders had for decades been accustomed to ignoring building regulations. Speedy reconstruction had been possible only because, for the first time, suburban unaffiliated builders (non-freemen) had been allowed into the City. There was much poor workmanship. In his old age in 1707 John Evelyn lamented that 'Vulgar Workmen, who for want of some more solid Directions,

Faithful and easy Rules in this Nature, fill as well whole Cities as Private Dwellings with Rubbish and a thousand Infirmities.'[23] Nicholas Hawksmoor was comparably bitter about the missed opportunity, grumbling that 'we have noe city, nor Streets, nor Houses, but a Chaos of Dirty Rotten Sheds, allways Tumbling or takeing fire.'[24] Allowance has to be made for hyperbole, but it was certainly the case that elevations were far from uniform, fenestration patterns remained asymmetrical, and other unevenness including inconsistent heights endured. To some degree what has been seen as new building practice arising from the Act of 1667 had been on its way anyway. Brick was already fashionable in the mid-seventeenth century, and earlier regulation had encouraged its use, as well as the shift to flat fronts through the banning of jetties and bays. In any case building anything other than a flat front in brick becomes complex and costly in a way that is not true with timber. There had been important changes, but post-Fire housebuilding in the City had strong elements of continuity with what had come before.[25]

The City has seen much rebuilding since the late seventeenth century, and there are no good surviving examples of the 'first sort' of post-Fire house. Nos 124–6 Cheapside have a stone tablet in their back wall that commemorates a build date of 1687, but no other seventeenth-century fabric appears to survive and, given their position on a 'high and principal street', the seventeenth-century buildings were certainly taller (fig. 28). Even so, they are a remarkable survival, two-room buildings that show the scale if not the reality of the smallest 'first sort' of post-Fire houses, each property being about 15 ft square. They are illustrated here to show how shockingly small such buildings now seem in central London. The Cheshire Cheese at No. 145 Fleet Street, famed for its associations with Dr Johnson, is more genuine though still fragmentary evidence. Its late seventeenth-century origins are as a mirrored pair of three-storey houses facing a narrow court. Originally there was a single approximately 20 ft-square room on each floor of each house, with staircases in the inner back corners and fireplaces on the outer party walls.[26] Better evidence of similar 'second sort' houses came from Nos 19 and 20 Cock Lane (*c*.1670), a pair that stood just outside the City walls near Newgate, at the margins of the extent of the Fire (figs 17 and 29).[27] These houses were each about 16 ft square, each comprising five rooms in three storeys with garrets and cellars. The stairs were again cased to the rear, comprising only winders at top and bottom for economy of space. Other sorts of staircase 'take up more room than those with a single solid Newel; because the Stairs of a solid Newel spread only

upon one small Newel, as the several Foulds of the Fans Woman use spread about their Center.'[28] Remains of a row of six comparable and contemporary brick houses on Black Raven Alley, near the north end of London Bridge just west of Fishmongers' Hall, were excavated in 1974. These differed in having their stairs behind the party-wall chimneystacks.[29] A building agreement of 1671 by which the Society of Apothecaries allocated ground behind its hall to John Rogers, a weaver, and Lyonell Weage, a bricklayer, provides evidence for a group of four houses more like those built in Bartholomew Fair seventy years earlier. These were to have 15 ft fronts with depths of 22 ft, to comprise a single room on each of three storeys, cellars and garrets, with ground-floor shops. The stairs were to rise at the back behind party-wall stacks and beside small unheated partitioned spaces on the first and second floors, perhaps closets or bed enclosures.[30] Houses with analogous layouts and dimensions continued to be built for some time, as at Nos 3–5 Wardrobe Place, dated to around 1714.[31]

The one-room plan was widespread in the late seventeenth- and early eighteenth-century City, and houses of three to five rooms were not unusual. Post-Fire builders' pricing handbooks show that these 'first and second sort' houses would have cost £50 to £100 to build, generating annual rents of £6 to £13. The examples for which there is evidence were from the upper end of this spectrum, but even these houses might not have been beyond the reach of an ordinary artisan in work, people in the building trades, tailors or shoe-makers, for example. The houses would have been all the more affordable if one or two rooms were sublet. With 200 or more square feet of living space, any of these rooms would have represented relatively commodious housing for many people.[32]

In so far as there was greater standardisation of house design in London beyond the City in the late seventeenth and early eighteenth century, it arose more from economic than from legislative or aesthetic exigencies. The increasingly capitalistic nature of building activity has been ably explored.[33] Moves towards standardisation in the design of larger houses for the 'middling sort', for the most part in and around the West End, arose from

28 (*above left*)   Nos 124–6 Cheapside, City of London, two-storey buildings bearing the date 1687, wholly rebuilt since, but demonstrating the scale of the smallest 'first sort' of post-Fire houses in the City. Photographed 2002 (EH, AA033082).

29 (*left*)   Nos 19 and 20 Cock Lane, City of London, a pair of one-room-plan 'second sort' houses of *c.*1670. Photographed by Frank Kelsall, *c.*1974, shortly before demolition.

larger-scale speculations, most famously those of Dr Nicholas Barbon, whose extensive and unscrupulous activities generated such opposition that he was prompted to write *An Apology for the Builder* in 1685. Barbon produced streets of houses that were externally regular in appearance and internally regular in layout because he was operating on a large scale. Regularity suits large-scale development because it facilitates measuring and pricing, even perhaps price-fixing. Standardisation was driven by economies of scale for the producers, not by consumer demand. Barbon was, like Henry Ford, offering 'any colour you like so long as it's black'. A degree of standardisation was not entirely new, as the Bartholomew Fair houses show. Yet, a century on, Barbon remained more an exception than the rule. There were a few other big operators, but most housebuilding in London was still in the hands of much smaller speculators. They were not in principle any less capitalistic, but their smaller scale of operations meant aggregate patchy irregularity rather than uniform standardisation.

There is no need to revisit here in any depth the complexities of the building process, the nature of building agreements, and the various paths that led from landowner to housebuilder.[34] Restated simply, remote landowners often leased small parcels to speculative builders who put up a few houses at a time, usually selling an unfinished carcass for the occupier to fit out. In the early eighteenth century intermediaries were common and small speculators from a wide range of backgrounds both in and beyond the building trades could set up with little if any ready money, raising capital on a building agreement, or via a mortgage. Being a 'builder' meant acting as designer, surveyor, contractor and construction manager. There was no need for, or prospect of, the involvement of 'architects' below the highest levels. This system brought about *ad hoc* partnerships or informal co-operatives of independent artisans. In what have been termed 'work-for-work' arrangements, the lead tradesman, who generally and increasingly came from a building trade, frequently being a carpenter, subcontracted to or bartered with others from different trades to get the houses built. So undertaken piecemeal leasehold development was fragmentary and disjointed, sometimes arising from haphazard encroachment onto common land or waste. It often concluded in abortive failure as entrepreneurs overstretched themselves. As Summerson put it, 'any clown of a bricklayer with some spare cash in hand could plunge into the speculative business.'[35] Small houses were unlikely to yield great profits and were therefore relatively unattractive to ambitious speculators. New small houses

designed for occupation by artisans or labourers were unlikely to arise other than from small speculations of anything up to about six houses originating from within a traditional artisan milieu. The period's changes in the scale of output and operating procedures left the building industry in flux. 'For some the changes were bewildering and threatening and they hung on desperately to the business and craft ethos, as embodied in the guilds, with which they were familiar. For others it was a period of liberation, which provided them with once undreamt of business horizons and opportunities.'[36]

Functioning in a system that worked increasingly through contracting and complex webs of finance demanded literacy and numeracy. The rebuilding of the City stimulated private attempts to encode building practice through the publication of books aimed as much at wary clients as at builders. The titles of Stephen Primatt's *The City and Country Purchaser and Builder*, of 1667, and William Leybourne's *A Platform for Purchasers, Guide for Builders, Mate for Measurers*, of 1668, reflect the economic rather than aesthetic basis of these publications. These books were not concerned with architectural form, but with computation, that is measuring and pricing. Pattern books as design advice did not catch on until after 1720. Pierre Le Muet's *Manière de bastir pour touttes sortes de personnes*, translated and published in London by Robert Pricke in 1670 as *The Art of Fair Building*, warrants mention as an exception, an interesting but alien early attempt at prescription. This book was about architectural form and, distinctively and remarkably, it opens with a handful of models for the building of small town houses, an approach neglected by subsequent English architectural writers. The book was a folio publication, not a pocket book, and was largely devoted to the design of mansion houses. It is unlikely to have found its way into the hands of many artisans engaged in building small houses, and with a few exceptions, its models for smaller houses do not seem to relate closely to what is known to have been built in London. The published elevations are distinctly polite, French in appearance with the smallest 12 ft-front house given a round pediment. Well into the eighteenth century the design of even relatively large London houses continued to be determined less by books than by traditional practice, structurally and formally indebted to timber predecessors, asymmetrical, unproportional and largely unaffected by the dictates of classicism.[37] The smaller the housebuilding enterprise, the more this was so.

The almost universal adoption of brick in better West End developments was not due to legislation, though the rebuilding Act of 1667 was sometimes cited in building agreements, but to economics and fashion. Structural timber endured, as bonding within brick walls, for whole back or side walls, and more universally beyond the West End. Similarly, land value in wealthier districts tended to militate against low buildings, few street frontages taking buildings of less than three storeys. Even fashion was not uniform. There were distinctive variations between what was fashionable in the City, in the West End, and in the better developments of Spitalfields. Suburban growth continued to mix house types within localities, and large-scale standardisation was only rarely achieved. It is important to emphasise these realities in considering smaller houses, but none of this should obscure the degree to which in central areas there was a genuine transformation in the architecture of London's larger 'middling sort' houses in the decades around 1700. The evidently significant degree to which it was influenced by Netherlandish practice remains an unexplored subject of considerable interest.

Some Houses from around 1700

Examples and discussions of what was new in the period's larger houses can be found elsewhere. To return to smaller houses, an anti-clockwise sweep from Shadwell to Westminster will pick up disparate bits of evidence to provide an indication of some of what would have been the hugely varied range of 'small' house 'types' being built and rebuilt at the lower end, even at the heart of London in the years around 1700. The purpose of this piecemeal reportage is to emphasise that much that was old or traditional endured in houses designed for relatively humble occupation. It is evidence of the lower end, but, it must again be stressed, not the lowest. There is a significant difference between surviving and recorded lower-status housing and the lowest-grade poor housing, single room shacks, that has long not been extant at all. What is described here, and through most of this book, is a formerly widespread intermediate class of house that artisans and some better-off labourers might have hoped to occupy.

Ogilby's and Morgan's map of London in 1676 delineates a great deal of small-scale housing, especially around the extramural peripheries of the City, much of which would then have been newly built.[38] Numerous modest speculations were placed off main roads flanking courts. Speculative courts can be compared with charitable almshouses, the best surviving and most accessible reflection of the scale and internal layout of small-scale early-modern domestic architecture. The formal origins of these development types are medieval. From the fifteenth century onwards almshouses provided multiple-

occupation housing, each room being a distinct dwelling, usually grouped in short low ranges. Comparably scaled non-charitable speculative development occurred as 'rents'. Where street frontages were built up or costly, especially in the City and Southwark, small developments frequently took the form of two ranges behind the street facing each other across a confined space, a narrow open 'court'. Houses in such courts were not necessarily hovels. They could be respectable; indeed, some late seventeenth-century courts in the City had large and prestigious houses.

More typical of east London was Angel Court, off New Gravel Lane, in Shadwell, where twelve modest, early eighteenth-century brick houses, each about 15 ft square on plan, were given an elegant profile through classical finish that suggests concern for amenity (fig. 30). This finish is not as spectacular as that of the Trinity Almshouses of 1695, but the scale of the units of accommodation in facing ranges was not dissimilar (fig. 31). There were many similar but humbler groups of almshouses, for example the single-storey opposed ranges of three rooms each laid out in 1686 as Esther Hawes Almshouses in Poplar.[39] The paucity of visual evidence for early speculative courts has tended to leave early nineteenth-century courts dominant in historical awareness of what became 'slums'. The latter were often extremely mean, 10–12 ft square, rarely possessing even the most cursory gesture towards amenity, and those that survived into the twentieth century had inevitably declined into squalor by that time (see chapter 9). Some seventeenth- and eighteenth-century court developments would have been mean, particularly in more central districts, but many others did provide good housing when new.

East London had some larger speculations in brick, with echoes of the incipient standardisation that was characterising central districts, but house form remained closer to local antecedents. Pennington Street in Wapping, laid out on the north edge of a marsh in 1678–80 following the granting of sixty-year building leases by a major landowner, John Pennington, was an unusually large development of small houses, each evidently comprising three rooms, the scale of the speculation being remarkable given that the houses can have been intended for occupation only by artisans or labourers (figs 32 and 33). A degree of uniformity in these rows reflected the scale of the development and the freeholder's attempt to impose a minimum standard, as had been the case at Bartholomew Fair, and as would be the case in many subsequent developments of rows of larger houses that have been retrospectively and artificially unified with the designation 'terrace'. It is notable that

30 Angel Court (later Sarah's Court), New Gravel Lane (Garnet Street), Shadwell, an early eighteenth-century court, small houses showing attention to outward amenity through classical finish. Pencil drawing by J. P. Emslie, late nineteenth century. Demolished early twentieth century (MiD).

31 Trinity Almshouses, Mile End Road, built to designs by William Ogborne in 1695. Drawing of 1896 for the Committee for the Survey of the Memorials of Greater London (EH, BB84/3672).

Pennington's leases of 17 ft frontages to John Skermer, a local carpenter, and others stipulated not brick houses, but brick front walls, suggesting concern not for fire prevention, but for the perceived amenity of streetscape, here only remotely classical. About forty of Pennington Street's hundred or more houses survived on the north side of the road to be recorded in the 1920s, the south side having gone for the construction of the London Docks in 1800–05.[40]

In nearby Whitechapel tall but shallow timber houses of seventeenth-century origin lined the larger roads,[41] and to the north of Goodman's Fields there were clusters of modest late seventeenth- and early eighteenth-century courts, sometimes in what were mapped as back-to-back groups. In the 1680s the area north-east of Goodman's Fields and south of Whitechapel High Street was laid out with a substantial new grid of streets. On Braham Street (previously Colchester Street) a number of 16 ft-square five-room houses were recorded in the 1920s and 1940s (figs 6, 17 and 35).[42] They went one better than the Cock Lane houses in taking the staircases back into discrete rear blocks. External stairs were current in sixteenth- and seventeenth-century London, and this is a simply developed variant from the Cock Lane type, but it should be noted that this layout is also that

of Le Muet's smallest house models.[43] With such a simple form this may, of course, be coincidence. Lines between the vernacular and the polite, the customary and the externally introduced, are not easily drawn. This was also evident inside these houses, where there were fine mouldings on the staircases, but rooms with exposed ceiling beams. The speculation may have been aimed at a modestly genteel market; at this period gentility did not necessarily require horizontal circulation within a house.

Further west in Clerkenwell and Covent Garden there were numerous courts, with more back-to-back groups, as off Cowcross Street and Turnmill Street or Drury Lane. Clerkenwell's smaller houses are known to have been highly industrialised, with numerous workshops in upper-storey rooms as well as in back yards.[44] But, as in the City and east London, court developments were not always as mean as might be imagined. Bishop's Court, ten two-room-plan houses of 1726–8 to the east of Clerkenwell Green, was not unusual (fig. 272).[45] The late seventeenth-century houses that faced Hand Court off High Holborn, near Barbon's Red Lion Square and Bedford Row developments, had plain brick fronts that were, as at Braham Street, wide enough to permit entrance passages and staircases beside single rooms, such separation seeming to be a nod towards privacy, whether

32 (*above*) Nos 134–43 Pennington Street, Wapping, three-room houses from a large speculation of *c*.1680. As at Dog Row (fig. 26) plat bands stepped up and down over doorways, some of which had later pedimental hoods. The small upper-storey windows below the modillioned eaves cornice indicate that the staircases were to the front. Photographed 1928. Demolished (EH, BB71/1000).

33 (*right*) No. 109 Pennington Street, Wapping, a three-room house of *c*.1680 with a round staircase window, and a Royal Commission on Historical Monuments investigator at the doorstep. Photographed 1928. Demolished (EH, AP 189).

indicative of gentility or of multiple occupation; the back walls were timber framed.[46] Just to the north in Ormond Mews (later Great Ormond Yard) off Great Ormond Street, designedly galleried houses were still being built around 1700, further evidence of the absence of standardisation, even under Barbon's nose. To the west of Covent Garden, on the north side of New Row, there are still some one-room-deep houses with late seventeenth-century origins. Goodwin's Court, off St Martin's Lane, has a row of eight three-room-and-basement houses, each about 16 ft square, which were first built around 1690 and evidently rebuilt with bowed shop-fronts around 1800.[47]

Parts of Soho were humbly developed. Nos 21–4 Newport Court are a fascinating survival from around 1688, part of a 'messy little development'[48] initiated by

34 (*above*)   Nos 13 and 14 Archer Street, Soho, two brick houses of *c*.1700. The building was seemingly only one room deep with stacks on the back wall. There may always have been large ground-floor windows, suggesting shop use. Photographed by Henry Dixon, 1910. Demolished 1912 (EH, DD57/36).

35   Nos 6–10 Braham Street, Whitechapel, one-room-plan brick houses of the 1680s. Photographed 1928. Demolished (EH, AP 155).

36 (*left*)   View to the nine-bay front of Nos 21–4 Newport Court, Soho, three superficially regular but inwardly uneven houses of *c*.1688 in what has become London's Chinatown, shown here at Chinese New Year, 2003 (EH, AA033436).

Barbon, and of the tightly knit warren of streets that has become London's Chinatown (figs 17 and 36). From early on this was an area characterised by immigrants and artisans. In 1720 Newport Court was 'for the Generality inhabited by French; as indeed are most of these Streets and Alleys, which are ordinarily built, and the Rents cheap.'[49] Goldsmiths, a plateworker and a jeweller were among the residents. Nos 21–4 were built as three unequal houses, subdivided before 1741, with a depth of only about 22 ft as they virtually backed on to other houses to the south. Behind a unified if irregular brick front the houses were differently and unusually laid out.[50] A more outwardly vernacular pair of around 1700 survived until 1912 on Archer Street, between Rupert Street and Great Windmill Street, on a site now behind the Apollo Theatre (fig. 34).[51]

Further west some small houses were more closely informed by the City's post-Fire development and legislation. No. 4 Lower John Street, just off the initially distinctly well-to-do Golden Square, survives as a one-room-plan house with origins of around 1685. Perhaps originally one of a group of four comparable houses, this one was possibly first occupied by tenants of a Captain Betherland (figs 17, 39, 41 and 52). It was raised a storey and altered internally around 1770, but the fenestration and internal panelling, plain but with an early dado rail, suggest that the front-staircase layout is unchanged.[52] Nearby No. 40B Greek Street, also originally late seventeenth century and recast in the eighteenth century, but since demolished, was similarly laid out in a 16 ft square.[53] There would once have been many more houses like this in St Giles, Soho and St James, in small and interstitial speculations, but there was widespread rebuilding towards the end of leases that ran for sixty-one years or less. This rebuilding would often have been conservative in terms of form. Even where the Survey of London has blazed the trail, it is rarely known whom the builders or first occupants of these modest houses were, but their size is evidence of the likely status of their occupants.

At London's south-west extremity part of the parish of St Margaret, Westminster, was like the eastern suburbs in the scale of its houses, in the predominance of timber, and in its population of artisans and labourers. The timber houses escaped documentation, but views of modest early brick rows from an enclave of streets first developed in the 1680s and 1690s show the similarities (figs 5, 37 and 38). By the early nineteenth century this area had acquired a reputation for extreme poverty and criminality; Dickens labelled it the Devil's Acre. Victoria Street was pushed through in 1845–51, and early Peabody Estate housing replaced some of the once decent but then decrepit late seventeenth-century buildings in the 1860s. The rest has since been wholly redeveloped, though some of the early street layout with its narrow lanes does remain.[54]

Evidence of front staircases, and of small windows suggestive of front staircases, has recurred through many of these examples. The sixteenth-century spread in London of discrete stair blocks or external staircases has been linked to the growth of multiple occupation, as such staircases provided access to upper spaces that was not dependent on walking through the ground-floor space. Similar functional logic is evident in the multi-occupied

37 Nos 22–5 Old Pye Street, late seventeenth-century houses from the poorer end of Westminster, analogous to Angel Court or Pennington Street in elevation, but seemingly two rooms deep. Pencil drawing by J. P. Emslie, 1877. Demolished (WA).

38 Duck Lane, Westminster (latterly St Matthew Street, and partially obliterated by Victoria Street in the nineteenth century). Another late seventeenth-century block of houses, again with stepped plat bands and small windows, probably lighting front staircases. Pencil and wash by T. C. Dibdin, 1851. Demolished (WA).

fifteenth- to seventeenth-century residential buildings of English universities and in the 'chambers' of London's seventeenth-century Inns of Court, where there are or frequently were entrances linked to 'front' staircases, which were sometimes lit by small windows, as in the west range of the Chapel Quadrangle at Lincoln College, Oxford, of 1608–31, or in the courtyard and

39   No. 4 Lower John Street, St James, showing the much disguised front of this one-room-plan house of the late seventeenth century. Photographed 2001 (EH, AA009770).

40   Furnival's Inn, Holborn, showing the courtyard elevation of the front range of 'chambers' of 1638, with the entrances onto staircases as befits multiple occupation. Engraving from a drawing by Robert Blemmell Schnebbelie (published in Wilkinson, ii, 1825).

entrance elevation of the front range of 1638 at Furnival's Inn, Holborn (fig. 40). On a more modest scale, Trinity Almshouses (fig. 31), Morden College, Blackheath, of 1695–1702, and the Geffrye Almshouses, Kingsland Road, of 1712–14 (fig. 152), were all laid out with their staircases towards the entrance front of each housing range. When high-status, lettable residential 'chambers' or flats do appear in London, at Nos 1 and 2 Robert Street in 1768–74 – part of the Adam brothers' Adelphi development – they, too, have front-staircase layouts, though no small windows.[55]

Purpose-built multiple occupation has been understood as having been otherwise absent from seventeenth- and eighteenth-century London. Given that divided houses were a well-established reality, it would be odd if this had been so, and it is unlikely that the builders of chambers and almshouses would have been divorced from the practice of domestic architecture more generally. In larger if not the largest London houses, staircases were conventionally placed to the centre or rear, beyond at least one room, mediating access to the upper storeys. Staircases appear to have been sited directly off entrances at the front of houses in large speculations only in districts where artisan or labourer occupancy might have been expected. This seems to have occurred across London, from the seventeenth century and into the eighteenth, from Bartholomew Fair and the Fleet, to Dog Row and Pennington Street in the east, and Lower John Street and Duck Lane in Westminster (figs 12, 19, 26, 32, 33, 38, 39 and 41). The parallels with other building types indicate that it is suggestive of design for multiple occupation, that is it seems to show that these buildings were purposely designed to function as tenements,[56] the front staircases permitting immediate access to the upper storeys without compromising separate use of the ground-floor space. This building type may have been unusual away from the centre before the 1680s, perhaps spreading as population pressures increased. Still, typological distinctions would have been fluid. As much as buildings designed with single occupation in mind could be used as tenements, small buildings designed with multiple occupation in mind could be used as houses. Indeterminate flexibility may have been foremost in the minds of speculating builders.

41 No. 4 Lower John Street, St James, perspective view reconstructing the house of *c.*1685, as raised a storey and altered internally *c.*1770. In a 17 ft frontage there is a single 12 ft-deep room on each level, alongside which a staircase lit by narrow windows rises in front of closets.

Again, and surprisingly, Le Muet can be invoked. One of his model designs, published in England in 1670, shows a 15 ft-wide two-room-deep house with a front staircase, forcing an asymmetrical façade. However, the layout seems to have unsettled Le Muet as the elevation and the plan disagree, the upper levels of the staircase being fenestrated in the latter, but not in the former. This mistake may have been made because front stair-cases were rare in Paris; where they did occur they were not articulated in façades. Seventeenth- and eighteenth-century Parisian tenements were typically tall and two rooms deep, with stairs at the back alongside a court-yard, that is they were deeper versions of the Braham Street layout (fig. 17).[57] In depicting a front-staircase layout, Le Muet seems to have been illustrating a theo-retical possibility rather than a known house type. As in other instances where his models exhibit general simi-larities to London houses, there is no close correlation and no good reason to suppose any direct link between housebuilding in London and Paris. The same holds true for eighteenth-century Amsterdam, where workers' houses were divided, but typically given multiple ground-floor entrances. Such differences need not be wondered at. The adoption of foreign or published models for the speculative building of houses for humble occupation seems inherently unlikely.

The epithet foreign may not, in this case, apply to Scotland. In Edinburgh tall tenement blocks or 'lands' were standard by the mid-seventeenth century and into the eighteenth, sometimes with front staircases lit by small windows.[58] Whether in relation to London this reflects linkage or convergence is unclear. Nevertheless, the use of the front-staircase-plan form in London's smaller seventeenth-century houses appears to have been a functional development or perpetuation of British urban vernacular building practice, probably associated with multiple occupation. It can be expected that the design of houses for occupation by artisans or labourers would be conservative rather than innovative, and limited in its receptivity to alien cultural traditions. This subject is considered in more detail in the context of Bethnal Green's weavers' houses (see chapter 3).

Plans

The one-room plan is a plan in two senses; it is not just a representation of a building on a horizontal plane, it is also a premeditated scheme. It is an architectural or design choice that, as the suggestion that it may some-times relate to divided occupation suggests, has implica-tions for living arrangements. Though basic, it generates a varied array of layouts. In most of the instances of one-room-plan houses that have been investigated in London, the absence of a back room can not be explained by plot density or land prices. Why were these houses not deeper? What Summerson characterised as London's 'vertical-living idiom' was remarked upon by overseas visitors, most famously by Louis Simond, who likened Londoners to birds perching in cages. At various social levels houses may have been built for single occu-pation, but with the knowledge that subdivision would often ensue, though only when the district's or an indi-vidual's straitened circumstances made it necessary (see chapter 1). The choice of a vertical layout might reflect ambivalence in the face of this likelihood; verticality could derive from a general awareness that nearly all houses in London were provisional divided housing. A more direct explanation for verticality is light. The deeper the house the darker its innermost parts; as the architect John Gwynn commented, 'Another error which contributes towards making rooms dark, is the making them too deep.'[59] The one-room layout might reflect the need for good interior lighting, particularly where upper-storey rooms might have been expected to be used all day long as workshops (see chapter 3).

But artisan occupancy and the endurance of vernac-ular housebuilding practice were not confined to houses with only one room per storey. Much more variable, of course, is the two-room layout. In densely built areas where frontages were expensive, double-fronted houses mean conspicuous wealth. However, if an artisan could perhaps afford a five-room house laid out vertically, then a six-room house laid out less vertically, on three levels with front and back rooms, might have been attainable, especially allowing for subletting. Ownership and occu-pation of whole such houses would have been beyond the reach of any but successful artisan masters, but the boundaries between single and multiple occupation were blurred in a range of less than neat domestic arrangements. A closer look at some of the ways of ordering modest double-pile two-room-plan houses will further illustrate variety in the laying out of houses, the strength of tradition and the limits of standardisation and emulation.

Plan form is an arcane subject, but it is a crucial mirror of the functional and cultural determinants of domestic architecture. As Primatt put it in his pragmatic primer of 1667: 'The Art of Architecture to be used in any sort of Building in High Streets or Lanes, consists only in the placing of Chimneys and Stair-cases.'[60] He illustrated eight different single-fronted two-room layouts, not pre-scriptively, but to show existing practice, to represent 'those sorts which are most in use for City Buildings';[61]

two with chimneys and staircases across the middle between the rooms, the other six with chimneys in the outer walls, four having central staircases between the rooms, two with staircases at the back. Fireplaces are often omitted for the ground-floor front rooms on the assumption that these would be shops (fig. 42).[62] For the sake of simplicity and brevity, and in keeping with convention, these possibilities can be introduced as three broad 'types': the central-chimneystack plan; the central-staircase plan; and the rear-staircase plan. It must be stressed that this is an artificial and latter-day typology, not one used by contemporary commentators. Emphasis on larger houses and a view of the percolation of the polite as a linear progress or transition has brought about an understanding wherein these types are seen to have been successively dominant through the seventeenth century until the rear-staircase plan achieved universal acceptance in London's speculative housing after 1720. This is questionable even in relation to 'middling sort' houses. Once smaller houses are taken into account, the need for a more layered interpretation as well as for a longer view of what constituted transition becomes much greater. This will be made clearer through the case studies in subsequent chapters. All that is needed here is to introduce the plan types.

The two-room plan that has the rooms separated by back-to-back chimneys alongside a staircase (fig. 42a) was widespread in London by 1500. It made structural and economic sense in a timber context, minimising the loss of light caused by the presence of large brick chimneystacks, as well as the likelihood of fire spreading to party walls. This layout should probably not be understood as a derivation at right angles from the post-medieval, rural, double-fronted, lobby-entry-plan type. Rather, the process of 'closure' that has been described in the essentially seventeenth-century adoption of the lobby-entry-plan house in a rural context seems to reflect the spread of the more inward-looking and urban concerns of genteel architecture in the period.[63] Innovation tends to move from town to country. In the early seventeenth century John Thorpe drew the plan of a house with a 24 ft front, showing front and back rooms separated by back-to-back fireplaces flanked by a closet and staircase, this being one of three conjoined houses 'for the cytty or for a country howse'.[64] The back-to-back or central-chimneystack plan continued to be widely used in late sixteenth- and early seventeenth-century London. It has been documented around what were then the outskirts, from the Gray's Inn Road to Bishopsgate and Borough High Street (fig. 124), in small speculations of two to six timber houses of five to ten rooms each with frontages of as little as 10 ft. Ground

floors often had shops, perhaps unheated, in front of kitchens. The layout made the jump to brick building, and the remains of a group of the 1670s with fronts of about 14 ft were recorded at Harrow Yard off Aldgate, where there was evidence for humble artisan occupancy. A variant of the central-chimneystack plan that suits narrower frontages, where the staircase is sandwiched between the separated halves of the central chimneystack, was illustrated by Primatt in 1667, and can be seen in the extant and then outlying group of four substantial brick houses of 1658 at Nos 52–5 Newington Green (fig. 209). Another variant, where the plan was turned through 90 degrees to give an entrance onto the staircase in front of the central chimneystack in a double-fronted layout, was used for the good-sized houses of around 1680 in Racquet Court, off Fleet Street, demolished in the 1970s.[65] Another peculiar variant of the 1680s has been described at No. 21 Newport Court (fig. 17), where the shallow plot is turned to advantage to allow natural lighting of the staircase, one of the principal difficulties with a central stair position.

In its various guises the central-chimneystack plan was not only widely extant, but also still being built in houses large and small all round London up to about 1720. It has been recorded in and around the City, and it was also widespread in the eastern suburbs; an impressive standing group of riverside houses of around 1700 and 1720 on Narrow Street, Limehouse, incorporated central-chimneystack plans (figs 17 and 43). The plan appears to have become unusual north of the Thames after 1720, but south of the river it remained popular right through the eighteenth century (see chapters 4–7).[66] It rarely survives, perhaps largely because of its incompatibility with later patterns of use; the chimneys got in the way, especially where there were shops.

It has been stressed that architectural design at this level was transmitted by precedent rather than by pattern book. The central-chimneystack plans published by Primatt in 1667 were presented simply by way of setting out comparative costs. His comparison of large ('third sort' and 20 ft front) designs found that the use of a central chimneystack in lieu of timber partitions saved money (fig. 42a and b). In houses with fireplaces in all rooms, the savings in a total cost of £426 would have been about £17 or 4 per cent. It is unclear whether comparable savings would have been made in groups of two or more houses where stacks could be built into party walls, or in smaller houses, and such calculations were, of course, subject to changes in the relative prices of timber and brick. Whatever the reality of costs, it may be that the central-chimneystack plan was *perceived* to be cheaper, something of obvious significance at the lower

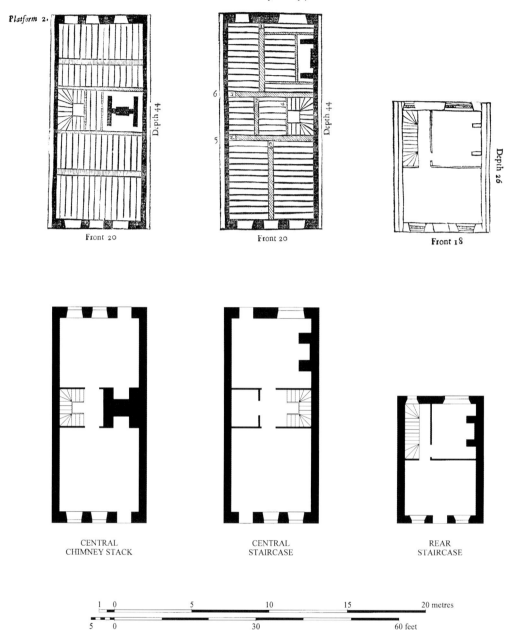

Platform the firſt.

Depth 44

Depth 44

Depth 26

Front 20

Front 20

Front 18

CENTRAL
CHIMNEY STACK

CENTRAL
STAIRCASE

REAR
STAIRCASE

| 1 | 0 | | 5 | 10 | 15 | 20 metres |
| 5 | 0 | | | 30 | | 60 feet |

42   Three house plans from Stephen Primatt's *The City and Country Purchaser and Builder* [1667], as reissued by William Leybourne (3/1680; by permission of the British Library, 10443.k.2), with supplementary diagrams of each type to the same scale as figure 17 and other plan compilations: (a) 'Platform 2', showing a central chimneystack and stairs; (b) 'Platform the first', showing a central staircase and side-wall chimney; (c) an undesignated 'platform', showing a rear staircase and side-wall chimney. (Primatt's delineation of floor timbers reflects the book's intended use as a pricing manual.)

43 (*above*) Thames-side houses at Nos 76–92 Narrow Street, Limehouse. Nos 88 and 92 (to the centre right), probably built *c*.1700, the latter with a shaped gable, have central-chimneystack plans. The six houses adjoining at Nos 76–86 were built *c*.1720 and No. 86 (at least) also had a central stack. Photographed by Henry Taunt, *c*.1885 (EH, BB76/8960).

end of the market.[67] However, economically based arguments can not easily explain local differentials. The plan seems also to have carried cultural associations.

The central-chimneystack plan was again published in 1700 by James Moxon in an addition for the third edition of his father Joseph Moxon's *Mechanick Exercises: Or, The doctrine of handy-works* (fig. 44). This was not a pricing guide, nor was it a pattern book, more an empiricist's encyclopaedia. It was a part-work series of hand-

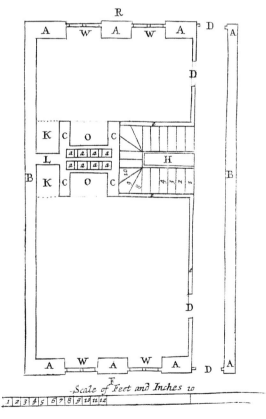

44 (*right*) Plan for a central-chimneystack-plan house, from James Moxon's *Mechanick Exercises: Or, The doctrine of handy-works applied to the art of bricklayers-works* of 1700, an addition to his father Joseph Moxon's part-work, showing two rooms separated by a chimney stack (O) flanked by 'clossets' (cupboards) (K), and an open-well staircase (H), with a side passage running front to back (by permission of the British Library, 538.i.5).

books, speculatively printed as a guide to existing artisan ('mechanick') practice, that is precedent, in the building and other trades. Following Francis Bacon, 'Philosophy would be improv'd, by having the Secrets of all Trades lye open; not only because much Experimental Philosophy, is coutcht amongst them; but also that the Trades themselves might, by a Philosopher, be Improv'd.'[68] Begun in 1677–80 and revised in 1693–4, Moxon's first editions included house carpentry and much discussion of how to build a timber house for a shopkeeper; there was nothing on building with brick until 1700, indicating a lack of interest in latest 'best practice' in the City and West End. *Mechanick Exercises* is significant and unusual as an essentially retrospective publication that was not attempting to present anything new. It contains straightforward accounts of how to build, from setting out to the making of small fittings.

The publication in 1700 of the central-chimneystack plan fits into this framework. The plan for a large (25 ft front) brick house was accompanied by an asymmetrically fenestrated and gabled front elevation, conservative codification of what by this date were well-trodden and unfashionable forms. The interest of the book is not so much the degree to which it may have been influential; indeed in terms of sales it was not a great success. Its importance lies in the fact that it reflects otherwise undocumented and long-lived practice. It was assumed that house carpenters would be 'master-Workmen' with responsibility for house design, but readers were not asked to think about architecture, 'a Mathematical Science, and therefore different from my present undertakings',[69] and were reminded that 'a Gentleman's house must not be divided as a Shop-keeper's'.[70] Moxon's awareness that differences in scale demanded a different architectural vocabulary was even more explicit in reference to rules as to the spacing of steps in staircases, as imposed by 'Several Writers of Architecture [. . .]. But here we must understand they mean these Measures should be observed in large and sumptuous Buildings: But we have here proposed an ordinary private House, which will admit of no such Measures, for want of room.'[71] Cultural differentiation and the limits to emulation were clearly understood. Even Barbon recognised that 'as men differ in Estates so they differ in their manner of living.'[72]

The second two-room plan 'type' can be dealt with more briefly. The central-staircase layout, where there are party-wall chimneystacks and the front and back rooms are separated by a stair across the middle of the building (fig. 42b), was widespread in the late seventeenth century and particularly popular at the top end of the speculative house market in the 1660s and 1670s. The form may derive from earlier houses with distinct stair blocks between separate main builds and rear annexes, as in one of the mid-seventeenth-century timber houses that is the Hoop and Grapes (No. 47 Aldgate High Street). The layout is also present in multi-occupied chambers in the Inns of Court, from both before and after the Fire. Where there was not space for a top-lit open well, the staircase could be lit by a narrow lightwell between the stairs and the party wall, as it is in the other part of the Hoop and Grapes (No. 46 Aldgate High Street). Such lightwells were deployed in narrower buildings such as No. 22 St John Street, Clerkenwell (*c.*1700, fig. 17), the last survivor of a short row, occupied in the early eighteenth century by Jane Cart, the wealthy widow of a City merchant. This layout was used in St Martin's Lane, Westminster, in both 1690 and 1739. In other narrow fronts an unlit winder staircase was made to suffice, as at No. 227 Shoreditch High Street (*c.*1700, fig. 17), a once gable-fronted house that was largely rebuilt in 1999. This variant can be linked with seventeenth-century houses in the Jordaan, then Amsterdam's main working district, though in Amsterdam's narrow houses stairs and fireplaces tend to be on opposite walls.[73]

The central-staircase layout endured at lower social levels into and through the eighteenth century. It often occurs in commercial properties or 'shophouses', but there is no obvious functional or cultural reason for such a link. It may simply be that the plan remained popular in, because suited to, houses with narrow frontages (see below). Such frontages occur on high streets, and shopkeepers would have been numerous among the occupants of these smaller houses. In collections of house plans from the City and its margins in the late seventeenth century and the eighteenth, those houses where the ground-floor front room was given over to shop use do frequently have central-staircase plans, but the same collections also show that the layout of the shophouse was highly variable. A row of four two-room-plan shophouses at Nos 1–4 Carthusian Street, Clerkenwell, perhaps datable to around 1700, had rear-staircase layouts, but with winder staircases, in frontages of 15 ft to 19 ft. Domestic commerce was ephemeral in nature, and any link with house layout in eighteenth-century London remains elusive, without clarity as to cause and effect. It would, in any case, be anachronistic to isolate the shophouse as an architectural type. The inevitable wholesale renewal of ground-floor spaces for modern shop use in surviving buildings makes tracing early shops all the more difficult.[74]

The rear-staircase plan that was illustrated by Summerson in 1945 as the 'Plan of a typical London house of the period after the Great Fire',[75] which phrase was revised in his edition of 1988 to the more cautious and more accurate 'plan of a house of the type built by Nicholas Barbon',[76] did achieve dominance in speculatively built rows of houses with frontages of about 20 ft or more. In essence, that is with the stair framed against the back part of one party wall, lit from the back and opposite a party-wall fireplace, it was among the plans illustrated by Primatt in 1667 (fig. 42c), though without the entrance passage from which it was conventionally approached in a house that did not include a shop. This layout was in use by the 1670s, and was widespread in Barbon speculations, as on Denmark Street in the 1680s, and elsewhere in Soho and St James. By the 1690s Roger North was able to refer to it as 'the comon forme of all late built houses'.[77] The cultural relativity of this remark is evident in that, in 1700, James Moxon ignored the possibility.[78] By 1720 the rear-staircase plan had become standard in houses marketed for 'middling sort' habitation, its dominance formalised in pattern books after about 1730. The great estates in the West End were the most effective agents of standardisation, entrenching the rear-staircase plan behind increasingly regular fronts.[79]

Examples from Clerkenwell illustrate the degree to which the rear-staircase plan had percolated through to relatively small houses by 1720; other localities, St Giles or Soho, could equally well be chosen. Britton Street was laid out in 1719 just behind the densely developed courts and alleys that ran off notoriously insalubrious Turnmill Street. At the less desirable southerly end of the street, the houses had frontages of about 17 ft and two-room layouts in three storeys, basements and garrets (fig. 17). With ten rooms each these were not small houses, and by local standards this was a high-quality development. Yet the fronts were fairly narrow and the interiors were divided by no more than plain panelled partitions, the back rooms alongside the stairs being very cramped. First occupants may have included prospering artisans; the houses later came to incorporate clockmakers' workshops. Somewhat more marginally, development of the Baynes-Warner Estate through the first half of the century was in many respects typical of the degree to which standardisation had spread. Streets were laid out around Cold Bath Square and Mount Pleasant, the ironic designation for what had been a rubbish tip. Few of the houses had frontages wider than about 18 ft or heights above three storeys. Early occupants were predominantly tradesmen, ranging from merchants to small manufacturers and shopkeepers. Yet many houses had two rooms on each level, laid out with rear staircases, moulded panelling and three regularly arrayed windows squeezed into narrow fronts (fig. 45).[80]

45   No. 55 Mount Pleasant, Clerkenwell, the first-floor interior, looking from front to back in a 'standard' rear-staircase layout house of 1720. Photographed 1996 (EH, BB96/577).

Summerson said further of the rear-staircase plan: 'There is no escape from it. Mariners' humble cottages in the East End have this plan; and so have the fashionable houses on the Grosvenor Estate.'[81] It was remarkably widespread, but this was deliberate over-simplification, projecting back a generalisation based in the early nineteenth century. Through the eighteenth century there were, in fact, many escapes. The rear-staircase plan was far from universal, and it was certainly not standard for smaller houses such as tended to be built in smaller speculations. It was uncommon in east and south London before the 1790s, and even on the Baynes-Warner Estate in Clerkenwell other houses had only one room per floor. It has been argued that the underlying reason for its spread was economy of construction, and it is true that a two-room plan with a rear staircase can be laid out with about 10 per cent less overall depth than a central-staircase plan with equivalent floor space. However, this overlooks the space for closets next to the landing that the central-staircase plan often permitted, and the fact that a small closet wing soon became a popular addition to the rear-staircase plan, cancelling out theoretical savings. Perhaps other factors contributed to the spread of the plan. For the consumer the principal advantage of having the staircase at the back is that it can be directly lit. The larger the house (below the truly grand level where a big, top-lit open-well stair becomes possible), the gloomier the lower flights of a central staircase. The main disadvantage of the rear-staircase plan was the sacrifice of width in the back rooms. In a wide frontage this was perhaps acceptable. However, with fronts of anything less than about 18 ft a loss of about 6 ft to the staircase renders the back room inconveniently narrow, especially taking into account the fact that a fireplace had to project into the room at some point, as is evident in Britton Street (fig. 17).

The unsuitability of the rear-staircase layout to narrow houses was highlighted by a correspondent to *The Builder* in 1843, when the plan really was ubiquitous in London. The writer pointed out that in a 15 ft front this layout made 'it quite impossible to place the bedstead across the room without (which frequently happens) setting fire to the bedding.'[82] Further, in a smaller house a central staircase would not be so dark, as borrowed light would more readily penetrate from the front and back walls. Perhaps these are reasons why the rear-staircase plan did not catch on at the cheaper (narrower and shallower) end of the market. It is not closely paralleled in Amsterdam, where frontages tended to be narrow, rarely more than 20 ft. Nor was the plan widely used in Paris, where rear stairs tend to rise alongside open courts, though the 'London' rear-staircase plan was illustrated by Le Muet in 1623, but for a substantial house with a 30 ft front.[83]

The rear-staircase layout seems to be neither an import nor an ideal. It is probably best understood as an indigenous rationalisation of pre-existing practice, devised for a combination of reasons based on cost and convenience. This is not to rule out the possibility that there may also have been less material factors in play in the marketing and consumption of a 'standard' house form, extending to perceptions of status and emulation. The sense of formal entry, display and of *en suite* flow between linked spaces that is gained from the entrance hall or upper-storey landing in a rear-staircase-plan house is absent in alternative one-room or central-chimney layouts. The open circulation that the rear-staircase layout offered might have gained connotations of gentility that would have had little purchase at lower social levels, where there would have been a greater expectation that a house was anyway destined for multiple occupation. Separation of spaces does seem to have remained an essential quality of the layouts that remained more typical of artisan than of 'middling sort' housing, but there is no compelling evidence that plan form in and of itself carried intimations of identity.

Attempts to link variations in domestic architecture with distinct patterns of use and sentiment must be handled carefully. Recent emphasis on the spread of privacy in the eighteenth century has elicited a useful cautionary note.[84] Links that have been made between architectural innovation and cultural change have been questioned, as has the premise that subtle changes in how people lived in eighteenth-century London are susceptible to being read straight from the fabric of houses. Readings of domestic space in London's eighteenth-century houses have constantly run up against ambiguities of room use, even where inventories are available. Most houses had in-built flexibility, and there was a great deal of the *ad hoc* about room use; in smaller houses few rooms did not contain a bed. Vast numbers of houses were divided or incorporated shops, yet in the 'middling sort' range of the spectrum that has dominated the architectural history of London's sub-elite eighteenth-century houses there are few departures from the singly occupied house type. The eighteenth-century house in London has been misunderstood as a more or less uniform entity, and emphasis on architectural innovation has tended to downplay the underlying reality of continuity. By addressing the heretofore unacknowledged variability of house form in eighteenth-century London, it is possible to look at continuity alongside innovation and pose, if not answer, questions about relationships between architecture, use and sentiment, while still acknowledging that there are limits to the usefulness of houses as evidence for social history. Architecture does not invariably or reliably reflect use of space, but it does hold clues.

Architectural Innovation and Continuity to 1760

Accounts of houses in eighteenth-century London have overlooked smaller buildings, and this has tended to reinforce an emphasis on the fashionable, the innovative and the newly standardised as being straightforward and uncomplicated embodiments of the modernity for which eighteenth-century London is continually re-examined, whether the focus is the aesthetic or the economic, 'taste' or 'wealth'. But it was London's variety rather than its uniformity that was celebrated by many contemporary commentators, and the myth that Georgian London was dominated by the decorous needs no more debunking. As has been emphasised, eighteenth-century London's modernity also needs to be understood in terms of continuity and diversity.

The 'London terrace house' as conventionally understood was not a revolutionary invention, but the product of an evolving interplay between tradition, the profit motive, legislation and fashion. London's growth was prodigious and change was radical, but the relative strength of the factors affecting house design varied greatly from place to place. 'Uniform' is a word that needs to be used sparingly in relation to London's early and mid-eighteenth-century domestic architecture. It can justly be applied to certain terraces of big houses, Great James Street perhaps, or to great charitable bequests such as the Geffrye Almshouses (fig. 152), but these were atypical. Much attention has been devoted to these exceptional elements, but London's topography was everywhere variable. Once one acknowledges the southern and eastern parts of the city and the in-between spaces that existed in other localities, eighteenth-century London's urban environment emerges as not simply lacking in uniformity, but as dominated by many of the vernacular qualities that had governed its appearance for centuries. It is only after 1760 that this came to be seen and acted upon as a problem (see chapter 9).[85]

At the beginning of the century further legislation, the London Building Acts of 1707 and 1709, had extended from the City to cover Westminster and all other parishes within the bills of mortality, that is suburbs and beyond, including Stepney, Hackney, Islington, Westminster, Lambeth and Rotherhithe, earlier attempts to limit expansion being abandoned. Another Act in 1724 embraced Marylebone, Paddington, St Pancras and Chelsea. Unlike the rebuilding Act of 1667, these Acts were not fundamentally standardising in intent, limiting their provisions to fire prevention. Timber building, wooden eaves cornices, and flush-frame doors and windows were all banned. Party-wall parapets were made mandatory. However, no effective means of enforcement was introduced, and these Acts were widely ignored.[86]

The heterogeneous growth of the great building boom slowed down after 1720, winding up with no real standardisation of house style or form. Rather less was built in the second quarter of the century, and up to and beyond mid-century the lower down the social scale one looks the more vernacular variability remained the norm. The prolonged downturn in the building cycle reflected a wider economic malaise. It lasted until around 1760, carrying with it important consequences in over-crowding, crime, mortality and the spread of perceptions about the need for positive action to bring about 'improvement' in the urban environment (see chapters 1 and 9).

At the highest social levels, Palladianism had an impact on speculative town-house design from the 1720s, but this was narrowly limited in its spread. The Palladian architect Isaac Ware attempted to up the game in his *A Complete Body of Architecture* of 1756, advocating an ideal for 'common houses in London', which he described as costing £600 to £700 to build and having two rooms on each of five floors.[87] His, of course, was a particular understanding of 'common', one that posited a typical

family as being two or three people rattling around in ten rooms with the company of three or four servants. Even Peter Earle's 'middling sort' sample of late seventeenth- and early eighteenth-century inventories averaged only seven rooms to each household.[88] Most people had very much less living space. But smaller houses were not of interest to Ware or his readership. As they were not written about, and as so few survive, the perceptions of Ware and others concerned with high-status architecture have been unduly influential in understanding the period's housing. In a leaflet of 1996 titled 'London terrace houses 1660–1860', English Heritage followed Ware, illustrating a 'typical early eighteenth-century terrace house' as having ten rooms (fig. 47). For Ware these 'common houses' needed improvement. The layout, with stairs set to one side at the back beyond an entrance passage, forced an asym-

46   The ideal 'common house' in London, as envisioned by Isaac Ware, from *A Complete Body of Architecture*, 1756.

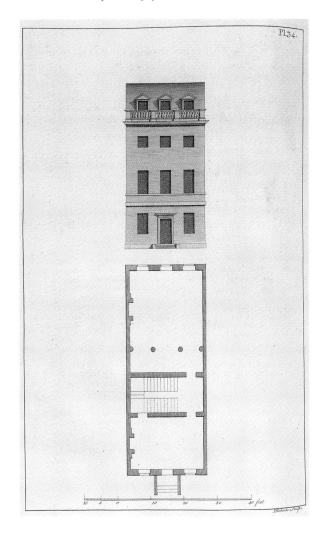

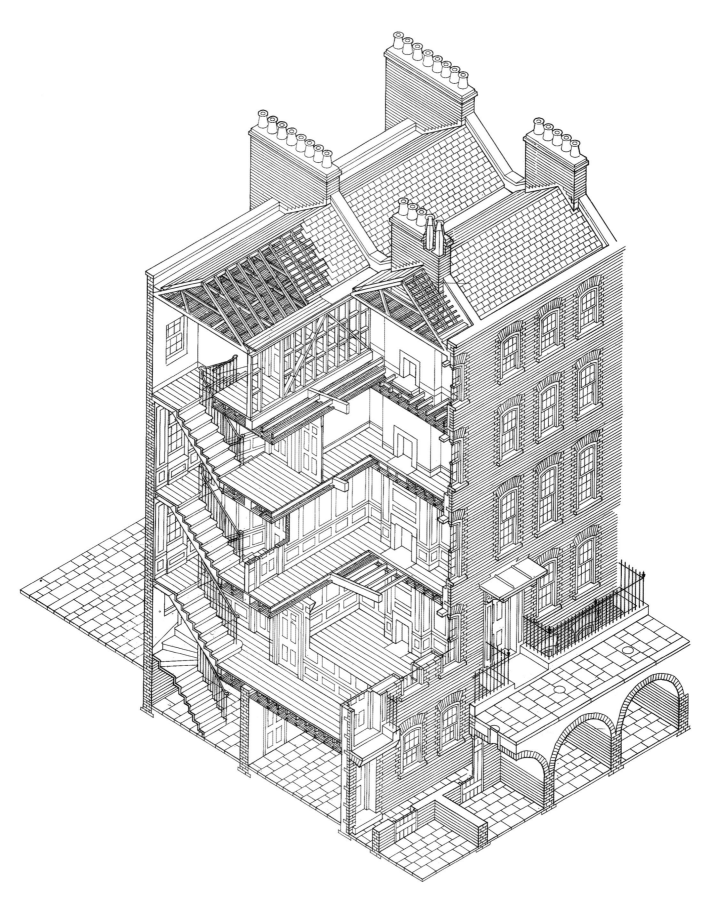

47   Cutaway isometric view of a pair of ten-room buildings, representing the prevailing image of 'typical' early eighteenth-century London terrace houses (EH, drawing by Keith Garner for Alan Baxter and Associates, 1996).

metrical front. He envisioned a more classically satisfying, if impractical, façade with a central entrance, meaning that the whole ground-floor front room had to be given over to use as an entrance hall (fig. 46). His concern for elevational symmetry extended to the rear, so the house had to be given a central-staircase layout. Ware's classically inspired idealism was thus out of step with fashionable modernity as it was manifest around him. Tellingly, it found little response. Even in the bigger houses that are not the subject of this book there remained great architectural pragmatism; flexibility and adaptability transcended aesthetic ideals.

Ware's failure notwithstanding, 'Books were the most important single factor in establishing the dictatorship of Palladian taste throughout the building world.'[89] Pattern books intended as design advice, sometimes produced in pocket format, were increasingly aimed at and used by builders. James Gibbs published *The Rules for Drawing the Several Parts of Architecture* in 1732, its subtitle, *in a More Exact and Easy Manner than has been heretofore practised*, indicative of a new idiot's guide approach to the dissemination of classicism. However, this process was by no means all *de haut en bas*, with William Halfpenny (*The Builder's Pocket-Companion*, 1728, and *The Modern Builder's Assistant*, 1757), Batty Langley (*The Builder's Jewel: Or, The Youth's Instructor, and Workman's Remembrancer*, 1741) and others mediating as self-improved artisans speaking to (and sometimes as passionate defenders of) other artisans desirous of self-improvement, if not salvation, as their position at the top of the housebuilding tree came increasingly under threat from speculators and professionals. At the same time other works, most notably *The Builder's Dictionary* of 1734, carrying a prefatory puff from Nicholas Hawksmoor, John James and James Gibbs, followed Moxon and others in demystifying and thereby appropriating the skills of the building trades for a more genteel readership.[90]

These building trades were numerous and diverse, and, with the quality control systems of the City Companies ever weakening, people moved freely between trades. Those artisans who became 'builders', or what might rather be considered contractors, were most commonly carpenters, the elite among the building trades. Even in brick houses 'the Carpenter, by the Strength of Wood, contributes more to the standing of the House than all the Bricklayer's Labour.'[91] Many eighteenth-century books on building were therefore addressed to the carpenter, who was expected not only to be able to read, write and handle geometry, but also to 'know how to Design his Work'.[92] As basic trade skills were learned through apprenticeship, most of these books were essentially to do with the additional knowledge needed for

moving into speculative building, both the practical, that is mensuration and pricing, and the aspirational, that is classicism, for those aiming to be surveyors or architects. For an intelligent builder, a keen eye was probably as valuable as pattern books in adapting to changing fashions in better houses. But building was expensive, and most builders were small operators, developing small parcels on piecemeal leases. A brick house cost £100 or more to build, that is more than two years' wages for a reasonably well-paid artisan. In small developments of modest houses, books with information about pricing and classicism would not have been without interest, but precedent remained an overwhelmingly dominant design source.[93]

Already by 1700 capitalisation of the building industry was such as to have divorced many building tradesmen from design, but the master builder if not the journeyman continued to be an important agent of building design through the eighteenth century. For speculative houses design, which often took place on site, was not divorced from production. For the design of lesser houses artisan manufacture remained the rule, and the role of prescription or drawings of any kind remained insignificant.[94] 'Bricklayers, Carpenters, &c. all commence Architects; especially in and about *London*, where there go but few Rules to the building of a City-House.'[95]

In London's best houses this was a period of superb craftsmanship.[96] However, a tendency to generalise from the top down has perpetuated an emphasis on craft and implied that high-quality work was pervasive. In such a huge and dynamic city this was, inevitably, not the case. London's early Georgian houses were no more the product of unwaveringly fine craftsmanship than they were all cast from a prescribed mould. In a trade that was rooted in speculation poor building was endemic. 'It has ever been the practice of the London builders to erect houses at the least possible expence, because their tenures are almost exclusively leasehold.'[97] In some cases this meant cheaply enough to bring profits from the rents of the relatively poor. As Pierre-Jean Grosley attested, 'the agreement made, the solidity of the building is measured by the duration of the lease, as the shoe by the foot.'[98] There was no incentive to build houses that would outlast their leases. These were tending to be granted for longer periods, typically sixty-one years in the early eighteenth century and ninety-nine years in the later part of the century, but this did not alter the expectation of rebuilding at the end of the lease. In-built obsolescence was not, of course, against the collective interests of the building trades, and, away from the large estates, there was little to counter jerrybuilding. Where the lease was short and the occupancy likely to be humble, houses were built with poorly made bricks:

the wall consists only of a single row of bricks, these being made of the first earth that comes to hand, and only just warmed at the fire [. . .] in strength scarce equal to those square tiles or pieces of earth, dried in the sun, which in certain countries, are used to build houses, [. . .] the excrements taken out of necessary-houses [are] entered into the composition of bricks of this sort.[99]

The collapse of a building due to defective bricks was a common occurrence; it is not to be wondered at that the less well-made buildings have tended not to survive across centuries.

Bricks were made round the margins of London, and often on the spot for large developments, to minimise transport costs. London's bricks were made from a mix of clay with 'Spanish', that is soil (excrement), ash (a high proportion of the waste generated by a city dependent on burning coal for heat) or domestic rubbish; they were clamp fired, that is not in kilns, but in the open air. Highly variable in quality, those more adulterated and less well fired were irregular in size, surface and hardness; many were indeed unusable.[100] Eighteenth-century bricks seen in the twenty-first century tend to be the better ones that have proved durable, generally regularly laid to Flemish bond. In better houses poorer bricks were concealed behind the outer wall face as 'place' bricks, often in snapped-header inner faces. Otherwise, the poor and weak bricks scorned by Grosley are seldom still seen, but they were there, no doubt as irregularly laid as made. As has always been the case, many small vernacular buildings were designedly 'impermanent'.[101]

The spread of brick building was in part dictated by legislation, but it also reflected fashion, wooden buildings being widely regarded as infra dig. However, where compliance with legislation could be dodged and fashion was of small or no concern, brick building was avoided unless it made economic sense. The requirements of shipbuilding meant that native hardwood was increasingly scarce and little used other than in the best buildings, though the re-use of older oak house timbers was entirely usual. For London housebuilders from the Great Fire onwards there had been a dramatic shift to dependency on imported softwood timber, mainly from the Baltic and Scandinavia. The price of indigenous timber increased rapidly, not simply because of shortages, but also because of the resistance of English sawyers to mechanised sawing. In London proximity to the port

kept the transport costs of the imported wood low. Additionally, at the lower end of the market and on the urban margins, much housebuilding timber would have been inferior local wood.[102] It probably remained cheaper to build in timber until the end of the eighteenth century, the margin perhaps shrinking until the 1780s, fluctuating as wars affected imports. Comparative figures for London are not available, but in Norfolk, like London in that there was local brick, a cottage that cost £116 to build in timber in 1775 cost £132 in brick. Norfolk's 'brick threshold', when brick became more likely than timber at a vernacular level, has been found to be around 1760.[103] London's was evidently roughly contemporary. The cost factor joined more effective legislation and the percolation of fashion to see off timber building in favour of brick, though not decisively before the Building Act of 1774.

In spite of the widespread acceptance of brick and the architectural vocabulary that went with it, the building of wholly timber houses continued, in defiance of legislation. An east London field between Wapping and Whitechapel, known as Wells Close, lying near Pennington Street, had begun in the 1680s to undergo a gradual transformation into Wellclose Square in a Barbon development. The eastern location made this a risky speculation, and the square was only gradually and incoherently completed. Situated near the port, it was also known as Marine Square; the area came to be settled by Scandinavians connected with the timber trade, and a Danish church was built in 1694–6 to designs by Caius Gabriel Cibber, himself a Dane and best known as a sculptor.[104] Up to the mid-eighteenth century houses in and around the square were built or rebuilt in timber (figs 48 and 49). These were not modest houses, and they incorporated fashionable classical embellishments, like the ground-floor Serliana. The Scandinavian link here should not be allowed to imply that these houses were an exotic import. Nearby, across The Highway, much smaller houses were being rebuilt in timber in what had been the local vernacular idiom for more than a century, as on St John's Hill in 1753 (fig. 22). Indeed, many illustrations of what might ostensibly be seventeenth-century timber houses in London may well depict eighteenth-century rebuildings (figs 23 and 24). Further afield, in less central locations, but within the reach of the London Building Acts, from Bermondsey to Poplar, Mile End to Islington, timber building remained common for smaller houses (fig. 16) (see chapters 3–7). Even in Mayfair timber continued to be used: the boarded Waverton Street elevation of No. 27A Charles Street – said to have been built in 1754 by John Phillips,

48 (facing page)   Wellclose Square (No. 26 in the foreground), mid-eighteenth-century timber houses in east London. Photographed by Henry Dixon, 1913. Demolished (EH, BB70/1068A).

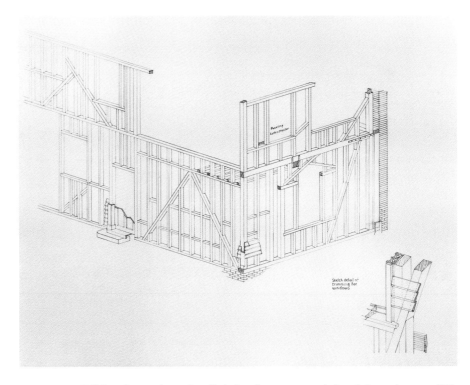

49   No. 26 Wellclose Square, its stud-wall timber frame as recorded and drawn in 1953 (EH, GLC Drawings Collection, 96/1393).

a master carpenter, for use as his workshop – is prominent surviving evidence.[105]

No. 26 Wellclose Square illustrates that the design of elevations remained, as ever, an improvised balance of the functional with the aesthetic. The smaller the building the less room, literally, for the latter. Much of the outward appearance of the surfaces of houses derived from tested techniques of economical building, tempered by the dictates of legislation. Design imperatives of a canonical nature, that is classicism, were a weak follower, and it was rare that form did not follow function. The external elevations of smaller houses often had no classical embellishment, or perhaps no more than a bracketed hood. The systematic application of rational Palladian principles of proportion to fronts rarely occurred outside the elite of larger buildings where amplitude of frontage enabled such treatment. The narrower the front, the more difficult it is to realise a regular array of openings, let alone symmetry. Avoidance of the window tax may also have had some small influence on the design of humbler elevations. This should not be taken to imply that classicism was tried and found to be inappropriate. More likely in this context it was simply not understood as an architectural language, but rather as a pick-and-mix collection of words – or at best phrases – that might, if convenient, be inserted into the vernac-

ular language, the syntax of which remained unaffected.

It is to be expected that rising standards of comfort and amenity, whether in relation to heating or lighting, or to the spread of material possessions through all but the poorest groups (see chapter 1), will have affected approaches to domestic interiors at all levels, vernacular or polite. Fewer rooms were left without fireplaces and windows tended to become bigger. However, comfort and fashion are not the same thing. Confined spaces, not least winder staircases, gave even less scope for proportionality and ornament than did house fronts. Even where stairs were more spacious, a few turned balusters were introduced more as gestures of conspicuous consumption – 'Look, there is space for this' – than as any kind of commitment to classicism or politeness more widely defined. A simple cyma cornice in the best room or over the best fireplace served a similar purpose. Where it does occur, classical ornament is invariably a signal of status, its presence in one room only of a humble house indicating a degree of internal hierarchy that does not necessarily favour the most public or accessible space, perhaps harking back to the medieval hall/parlour relationship rather than referring to a more fashionable or emulative front/back distinction (see chapter 6). In many rooms ceiling beams incongruously interrupted contemporary cornices, though joists were generally under-drawn. Panelling or wainscot was a long-standing tradition of interior finish by the eighteenth century, and its disposition and terminology in better houses had come to be conditioned by an understanding of the classical orders. However, plain painted-deal panelling was used widely in all but the poorest houses, being generally 'the thinnest that can possibly be found. This makes the rooms wider and contributes to lessen the expense.'[106] Panelled as opposed to framed partitions were often all that separated rooms in smaller houses (figs 17, 45 and 47). Full-height panelling became unfashionable from around 1720, but in humbler houses it endured, not least because it was a customary and cheap means of forming a partition. Whether double-sided or otherwise, vernacular plain panelling contrasted with better usage through the eighteenth century in having panel faces that were visibly feathered. If classically embellished at all, this panelling might have a moulded dado rail, itself not without functional justification as a chair rail. Plank-and-muntin partitions and plank doors also continued to be used, even in large houses in the garrets or basements.

In addressing the general character of such internal features, a rider about dating should follow. Dating by means of stylistic typologies is unreliable at any time, all the more so if no account is taken of differential take-up across the social spectrum. Many houses remained wholly unornamented, for which there are obvious economic explanations, but among those smaller houses that were decorated moulding profiles tend to be *retardataire*, perhaps saying more about mentality than about economics. As J. P. Malcolm put it in describing artisan houses in the parish of St George in the East in 1803: 'Their houses are examples for neatness and cleanliness; but the elegances of internal decoration have not yet universally travelled so far to the East.'[107]

There is an assumption there that taste would eventually trickle down. Yet the spread of the polite through the eighteenth century derived its potency from contrast with the vernacular: 'Since popular society lacked the means to dabble in the new fashions, and often the literate skills to understand them, then the rise of classicism further widened the cultural gap.'[108] Both these viewpoints ignore the possibility that adherence to custom might in some measure have been a positive choice in favour of continuity, intentional rather than innate. Through the seventeenth century sumptuary laws and the 'luxury debate' had been a part of a public discourse that included London's artisans. Many of those who were not upwardly mobile, and not just those of a puritanical disposition, would have joined City merchants and aristocrats in defending stability and the status quo through the control of conspicuous consumption,

in opposition to 'bourgeois' exponents of the market, as epitomised by Barbon. In many spheres the maintenance of traditional values and social differentiation did extend to acceptance of the vernacular and a sense of stylistic decorum or fitness to purpose – a 'taste' that, as much as classicism, might have had its own potency and trickled, whether down or up (see chapters 6, 7 and 9).[109]

Some Later Houses

To draw this overview to a close, a few more examples of smaller houses from 1720 onwards will show that the grounding supplied in this chapter has continuing relevance across all of London, not only in the eastern, southern and marginal districts to which attention will turn hereafter. In areas where larger houses were prevalent, it must be repeated, there can be no clean lines of demarcation between small houses and large ones. In attempting to draw attention to the smaller end of a spectrum there are dangers, both of setting up a false opposition and of suggesting that small houses were somehow physically apart from larger ones when they were generally intermixed. To reiterate, the houses presented here are representative of a much wider group from which little survives.

For the City there is little more to say. Following the comprehensive and relatively durable post-Fire redevelopment, most subsequent rebuilding for which evidence survives is of larger houses. It is important to add with regard to the City in the eighteenth century that this does not necessarily mean fashionable. The Whiggish and mercantile City stayed stubbornly conservative in its architectural tastes. To the east Spitalfields had its own distinctive architectural qualities, latterly much fêted in relation to the area's better houses. Among the most modest of the 'middling sort' houses that have been studied are pairs from the 1720s on Elder Street, which had one-room plans, about 18 ft square, and winder stairs. Less well-known and lower-status aspects of Spitalfields' smaller houses are considered in chapter 3. From Whitechapel to Bethnal Green and Hoxton modest developments of a few houses at a time remained various, irregular and distinctly vernacular. Examples from Clerkenwell (figs 17 and 45) have already shown how standardisation that tied in with emulation rubbed awkwardly with smallness of scale.

Even in the West End there was conservatism, as well as a good deal of improvisation. Standardisation is retrospectively detectable in the spread of the rear-staircase plan, but the non-standard remained widespread and streetscapes were varied. Many houses were unusually

50 No. 9 Lancashire Court, Mayfair, the ground-floor interior of c.1720, showing rich ornamental mouldings in a small house on a back street that housed artisans and shopkeepers. Photographed 1990 (EH, B905351).

streets retain a heterogeneous mix of small-scale irregular early buildings on a part of the Conduit Mead estate that was laid out around 1720 and completely built up by 1733. No. 9 Lancashire Court (c.1720) is little more than 20 ft square, but has a two-room rear-staircase plan, and surprisingly extensive and elaborate internal joinery for a house of this size (fig. 50). Yet the front is unevenly, indeed eccentrically, fenestrated, with the flush frames that contravened legislation. No. 5 Avery Row (c.1725) is rather less than 20 ft square and laid out with a single room on each floor. Next door No. 6 Avery Row is a timber-framed building with a front of about 14 ft and a rear-staircase plan with unheated back rooms (figs 17 and 51). Its framing and the presence of a stylistically early fireplace have led to it being ascribed to the late seventeenth century, but given what is known about local development and the fact that it seems to be built round No. 5 it is likely that it too is of the 1720s. These and neighbouring buildings housed artisans, shopkeepers and other tradesmen whose livelihoods would have been gained servicing the wealthy. Around 1790, when No. 9 Lancashire Court was occupied by a bookbinder, a survey of householders along Avery Row listed a dairyman, a chandler, a glazier and painter, a baker, a carpenter, a barber, a trunkmaker, a japanner, a victualler, a servant, a bookseller and another carpenter.[113]

The Grosvenor Estate in Mayfair was developed from 1720. Grosvenor Square excepted, there was no strict segregation of the gentry and tradespeople, though certain areas were clearly less sought after. North of Brook Street and Grosvenor Square, development up to Oxford Street in the 1720s and 1730s was low rent, even insalubrious, especially along and around Duke Street. The north-west margin near Tyburn (Marble Arch), the notorious site of public hangings until 1783, remained undesirable. The mid-century population here consisted predominantly of tradespeople, about two-thirds in the building and victualling trades, and this did not change greatly later in the century.[114]

In the 1740s the part of Mayfair south of the Grosvenor Estate remained sparsely built, inchoate and marginal. Curzon Street ran through to Hyde Park, with little on its north side until Chesterfield House was built in 1748–9, to designs by Isaac Ware. The south side of Curzon Street had a miscellany of mews, courts, market gardens and, at the park end, a block of guards' stables. Facing the east side of these stables three small houses were built in 1745–6, one of which survives as No. 2 Derby Street (fig. 17). Among the smallest houses in the area, these appear to have been only one room in plan originally, about 16 ft wide by only 12 ft deep. The devel-

laid out, in particular at corners and in other places where building plots were awkward. Property boundaries forced a row of houses of around 1720 on the east side of Bond Street (Nos 6–16 New Bond Street) to be no more than 20 ft deep, some of the houses initially being of comparable width, and each one different in layout.[110]

Behind the larger regularity of streets laid out in grids there were still yards and courts with smaller houses. There were also, of course, mews, with small buildings for coaches and horses in rows behind genteel town houses, very much part of the West End scene, but not treated here for not being built as houses. However, by the early nineteenth century many mews were already 'more generally occupied by poor families carrying on little trades, and by profligate persons, than as stables.'[111] As has been pointed out, artisans and shopkeepers made up a substantial proportion of the population even in the wealthiest districts (see chapter 1).[112] On the fringe of Mayfair, just west of Bond Street, Lancashire Court and Avery Row lie behind what were built to be prestigious houses, including No. 25 Brook Street, home to George Frideric Handel from 1723. Exceptionally, these back

51 Nos 5 and 6 Avery Row, Mayfair, houses of c.1725 in the same district as shown in figure 50, that to the left (No. 6) being largely timber framed. Photographed 2003 (EH, AA033434).

52 No. 4 Lower John Street, St James, the first-floor interior in the one-room-plan house of *c*.1685 with its plain panelling and early dado rail, as remodelled *c*.1770 with a cyma cornice and window architraves. Photographed 2001 (EH, BB009773).

opment and desirability of the area picked up sharply from about 1760, and No. 2 Derby Street was seemingly extended in 1760–61 with a narrower staircase and back-room wing. The upgrading perhaps introduced imposing and out-scale classical ornament on the first floor, at the same time deploying plank-and-muntin partitions on the top floor.[115]

The extended form of this house has a version of the central-staircase plan. This continued to be used in new houses, and not only at a humble level. It had been Ware's ideal in 1756 (fig. 46), and in many grander single-fronted town houses the layout had continued to be preferred over the perhaps more cost-effective rear-staircase plan. Where the central staircase could be made big enough to be toplit, it carried no disadvantage, and its use meant less compromise in the proportioning of rooms. Examples from the 1720s and 1730s have been recorded in Mayfair and St Martin's Lane (see above).[116] No. 8 Argyll Street and No. 5 Savile Row are other houses of the late 1730s with central-staircase layouts and frontages of about 20 ft.[117] Against the run of pattern-book plan advice, William and John Halfpenny published the central-staircase plan in *The Modern Builder's Assistant* of 1757, at about which time Robert Taylor was laying it out in John Street, Holborn. The Adam brothers used

it at the Adelphi in the early 1770s, when it also occurred in houses at Queen Anne's Gate, all in frontages of about 20 ft. A decade later it appeared in genteel suburban speculations, as at Surrey Place, Old Kent Road, of 1784, or Nos 122 and 124 Kennington Park Road of 1788, designed to incorporate full-width bay or bow windows at the back.[118] In house planning, heterogeneity, that is freedom, endured at the top and bottom ends of the housebuilding market, less so between.

The apparent early form of the Derby Street house illustrates the continuing use of the one-room plan, as do surviving houses of about 1730 at Nos 18 and 19 Crown Passage, St James, just off Pall Mall. It was by no means always the poorest option, but continued to occur in association with relative respectability of finish, as in No. 4 Lower John Street (figs 17, 39, 41 and 52), the house of around 1685 that was raised a storey and upgraded internally around 1770. It is notable that its earlier one-room layout was retained, without substantial rear addition, though this would have been possible. The first-floor room, given a simple cyma cornice and new door and window architraves, still evidently carried distinction despite the small size of the house.[119]

At the end of the eighteenth century the house type that had been built in Braham Street in the 1680s, that is one room with an external rear-staircase wing, was built again, across London and a world away, at No. 7 Nottingham Place, Marylebone (figs 17 and 53). Just south of the Marylebone Road, this was close to the St Marylebone Workhouse. There was a good deal of modest housing in the area, much of which would have been smaller, though nothing else of this scale seems to survive. Given that the house comprised four rooms, each about 200 square feet in area, an interesting comparative survival that puts the 'smallness' of this house into perspective is a servant's room of less than 100 square feet inserted in the roofspace of No. 5 Meard Street, a late Georgian alteration in a house of around 1732.[120]

These later examples are jumping ahead of the narrative. The years after 1760 brought immense change. Population increase gained pace and housebuilding boomed again. New Building Acts in 1764, 1772 and 1774 proved much more effective controls, taking London-wide standardisation of housebuilding beyond market forces and making it firm state policy. These Acts were accompanied by road and other infrastructural improvements in the 1760s and 1770s that took a grip on what were perceived by reformers to be some of London's more alarmingly disorderly aspects, channelling later growth towards regularity. Ambitious carpenters and others styling them-

53 Nottingham Place, Marylebone. The right-hand bay (No. 7) was built *c.*1800 as a four-room house, near the Marylebone Work-house; there were then many even smaller houses nearby. Photographed 1991 (EH, BB91/28023).

selves 'builders' increasingly undertook the building of whole streets in suburban areas, committing themselves to the significant additional costs of paving and drainage. In the 1790s inflation and a squeeze on credit caused numerous small builders to fail. Artisan engagement in housebuilding followed the increasingly dependent and downwards path of artisan culture more widely. This story is taken up after the case studies, which build on the generalities set out so far (see chapter 9). The case studies move away from Mayfair and Marylebone and redirect attention to the eastern and southern parts of eighteenth-century London. It has been important to

dwell a while on the 'wrong' end of town in this chapter, to establish that even in the West End housing was not uniform or monocultural, and that vernacular aspects of domestic architecture continued to ramify across the whole metropolis. The vernacular, however, is essentially local. A sharper focus on a few localities will draw out particularities and permit a deeper look into some of the complex issues surrounding small-scale domestic architecture. This should prepare the way for a return to investigation of the wider forces that affected vernacular housebuilding in London as a whole in the late eighteenth century.

Cor. Sclater-st & Brick la.
Spitalfields, 1914.

E.A.Phipson.

Chapter 3

ANOTHER GEORGIAN SPITALFIELDS: WORKSHOP TENEMENTS IN LONDON'S SILK DISTRICT

> And may no treacherous, base, designing men
> E'er make encroachments on our rights again;
> May upright masters still augment their treasure,
> And journeymen pursue their work with pleasure.
>
> Anonymous Spitalfields journeymen weavers[1]

A half century ago, in 1951, Millicent Rose wrote that 'In the history of Spitalfields, the poor journeymen, makers of plain silks, of ribbons and handkerchiefs, the immigrant Irish and all who failed to attain any high degree of skill, have been forgotten with the hovels in which they lived. It is the craftsmen who specialized in figured silks and fine velvets, the professional designers of patterns, the master-weavers and middle-men, who survive in memory as their houses have survived in fact.'[2] Much has happened in Spitalfields since that was written, with the area's history being extensively explored and celebrated. A ground-breaking study of the district was published by the Survey of London in 1957,[3] and subsequent conservation battles led to the forma-tion of the Spitalfields Historic Buildings Trust in 1977.[4] Since then historical engagement has been diverse, ranging from explorations of the archaeology of mor-tality to imaginative reincarnations of eighteenth-century domestic life at No. 18 Folgate Street, and of immigrant experience at No. 19 Princelet Street. Beyond Spitalfields, social historians have, of course, set out to rescue eighteenth-century weavers and other

working people from 'the enormous condescension of posterity'.[5] It remains essentially true, however, that the Spitalfields journeymen and their 'hovels' have been for-gotten. It is usual to see only what is known, and to notice only what is sought. So it is not altogether sur-prising that once the journeymen's 'hovels' are looked for, it emerges that they too 'have survived in fact', if in limited measure. They are to be found in the northern part of the Spitalfields silk district that lies in the parish of Bethnal Green, an area that was designedly developed in the 'long eighteenth century' as an industrial suburb for habitation by the poor, its housing comprising mul-tiple-occupation workshop tenements. This chapter looks at the distinctive domestic-industrial urban-vernacular architecture of this area, the intelligibility of which depends on an understanding of local circum-stances; discussion of the buildings follows an examina-tion of the place.[6]

Bethnal Green and Silk

London's silk district grew outwards to the east and north from its heart in Spitalfields, extending into the western part of the hamlet of Bethnal Green. In 1703 this corner of the hamlet was largely open fields and market gardens. By the 1740s it had been much built over (figs 55–7). The transformation was remembered by Defoe who reflected in 1725 that 'Brick-Lane, which is now a long well-paved street, was a deep dirty road,

54 (*facing page*)   No. 125 Brick Lane, on the corner with Sclater Street, facing which is a street-name plaque (figs 82 and 92). This building was a lettable, mixed-use block, incorporating a ground-level shop and upper-storey workshop tenements. It was proba-bly built in 1778, along with the adjoining house at No. 127, for Daniel Delacourt, a distiller. Watercolour by E. A. Phipson, 1914 (LMA).

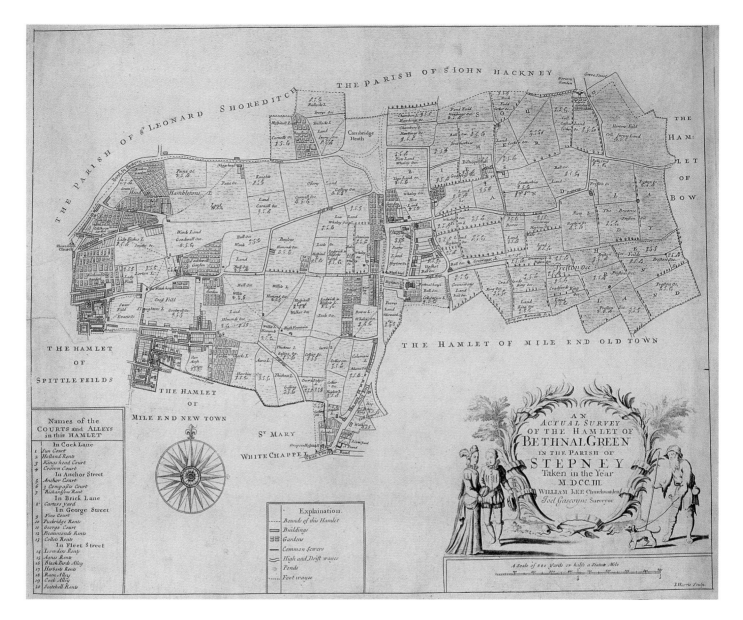

55   The entire hamlet of Bethnal Green in 1703, the silk district lying to the west (from Joel Gascoyne, *An Actual Survey of the Hamlet of Bethnal Green*, 1703).

frequented by carts fetching bricks that way into White-Chapel from Brick-Kilns in those fields.'[7]

The number of houses in Bethnal Green had risen from 215 in 1664 to 1,800 in 1743. The vast majority of these were concentrated in the south-west part of the hamlet bordering Spitalfields. The area's development was simply growth outwards from Spitalfields, part of which it was understood as being at the time. Bethnal Green's population was estimated as being about 8,500 in 1711 and more than 15,000 in 1743, when parish status was granted, making it equivalent to one of England's larger provincial towns, though only peripheral overspill in London.[8]

The story of the area's growth in terms of estate development needs only to be touched upon here (fig. 59).[9] Shoreditch High Street was part of the main route north from Roman London, and a major road throughout the medieval period. Brick Lane was the first large road to run through land to the east, brick earth being dug in the fields around by 1550. These fields were sufficiently close to London that their attractions for speculative development were obvious. As happened in Spitalfields the land was parcelled up into estates. Sales of sequestered demesne lands in the 1650s created several large freeholds, the larger properties being purchased by London merchants and lawyers. This created the conditions for

56   (*facing page*)   The Spitalfields silk-weaving district in 1703 (from Joel Gascoyne, *Survey of the Parish of St Dunstan, Stepney*, 1703).

THE PAR...

The Road to Hackney

Borders Garden

Hambletons L.

Naggshead

Head land

Hambletons L.

THE

THE

H

Knight...

Godwells Garden

Lar...

Crabtree Lane

Browns Garden

Thoreditch Church

Virginia Row

Wards Land

Wards

Austin street

Castle street

Coll Sharps

Land

Kemps Garden

Lady Fitches L.

Satchwells Garden

Cocklane

Richardsons Garden

Lortons

Willits Land

Lady Fitch

Nicolls street

Satchwells Rents

cook Lane

the Watch house

Austins Garden

Club Row

Slaughters Land

Cross Field

Silver Street

Willits Land

York Street

Swan Field

Anchor st.

Patience st.

7

Hare Street

5

King street

S. John street

18

19

Phenix street

George street

Hambletons Garden

3

16

13

Fleet Str

Clarks Land

14

22 23

12

17

Carters L.

Acres

Wentbur...st

Quaker st.

51

14 18

20

Land

15 18

Spicer

19

Monmouth street

Pearl

32

Carters Rents

9

33 25

Pelham st.

White Lyon Yard

Wheeler

Black Eagle street

Black Eagle

79

THE

12

SPITTLE

Lamb str.

Browns Lane

Montague

HAMLET OF

52

78

MILE END

FEILDS

Brick Lane

Booth Str

NEWTOWNE

39

North Str.

Thomas Str.

Red Lyon Str.

HAMLET

Tenters

53

High Street

Kings Str.

Duke Str.

Prince street

White street

Spittle street

Church Str.

Crispin...

Tatt Pater noster

Dorset street

40 42 43 44 45 46 47 48 49

54

Halston street

50

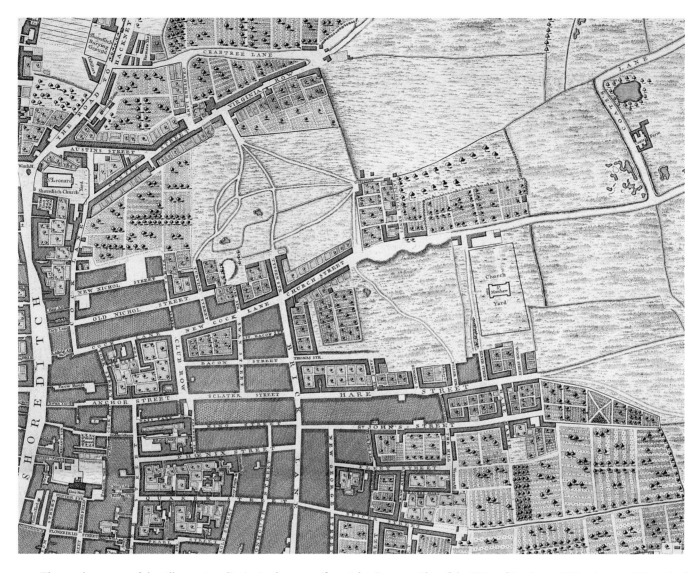

57 The northern part of the silk-weaving district in the 1740s (from John Rocque, *Plan of the Cities of London and Westminster and Borough of Southwark*, 1746).

coherent development, spreading broadly and in small steps from the south and west to the north and east, but following the vagaries of estate boundaries and road frontages in its topographical lines, and the ups and downs of building cycles in its temporal lines. By 1708 Hare Street (latterly Cheshire Street) had become 'a considerable, pleasant street' (fig. 58).[10] There were peaks in building activity around 1680 and 1720 as there were all round London. About two hundred houses were built in Bethnal Green in the years 1719–24, most of them on the Red Cow Estate across the top end of Brick Lane (fig. 59). Advances onto the Tyssen Estate in the 1730s were more desultory. Relative inactivity thereafter until the mid-1760s was also consistent with London-wide building patterns, as were sporadic revivals in the build-

ing of new houses from the 1760s to the 1780s, slowly spreading development eastwards (fig. 63). Few of the area's eighteenth-century houses are still standing, but there is more left than is obvious from the street, as what does survive has been refronted, raised or otherwise rebuilt (fig. 64).

Silkworking was one of London's largest industries in the eighteenth century, accounting for about 10 per cent of the capital's working people.[11] The scale of the industry put it on a par with that of the more long-standing French silk industry of Lyons. Silkworking dominated Spitalfields, and with it Bethnal Green. Weavers were far and away the largest group in the industry, more so later in the century, but, particularly in the early decades, there were related trades, notably

82

silk throwsters or silkwinders (those who twisted raw silk into thread, often women) and dyers. Imported raw silk was thrown, then dyed, bought by a master weaver and 'put out' to journeymen for weaving in houses. The silk masters sold the woven silk to mercers, much of it as elaborate brocaded taffetas, satins and damasks. The industry was capitalistic in its organisation, increasingly so through the century, with numerous masters paying wages to very much more numerous artisan weavers – nominally mostly men, as women who were not widows were not permitted to use looms under Weavers' Company ordinances.[12]

58 (*right*) No. 57 Hare Street (later Nos 74 and 76 Cheshire Street), a pair of one-room-deep houses, probably of the late seventeenth century, when this south side of the road was solidly built up. Later refronting retained small front-staircase and upper-storey workshop windows. Photographed *c.*1925. Demolished (LMA).

59 (*below*) Bethnal Green's eighteenth-century silk-weaving district, indicating eighteenth-century estates.

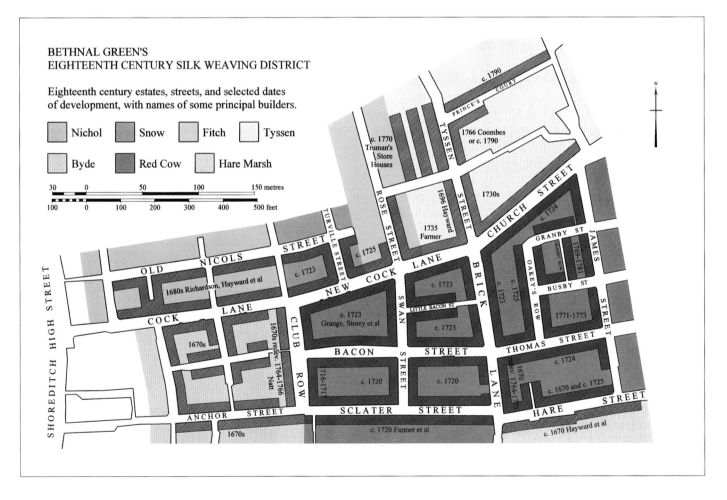

**BETHNAL GREEN'S
EIGHTEENTH CENTURY SILK WEAVING DISTRICT**

Eighteenth century estates, streets, and selected dates of development, with names of some principal builders.

Nichol   Snow   Fitch   Tyssen

Byde   Red Cow   Hare Marsh

60   Weaving in a Spitalfields house in 1894 (THLHL).

After the Revocation of the Edict of Nantes in 1685 Huguenot immigration was an important factor in Bethnal Green's growth and demography. About 15–20 per cent of the names in the land tax assessments for the streets considered here appear to be of French origin, a figure that is consistent with other estimates for Spitalfields more generally. Overwhelmingly dependent on the silk trade, local Huguenots appear to have mixed with the English, their addresses perhaps determined principally by wealth or by trade speciality rather than by ethnicity. By the 1730s Irish immigration had become another important factor in the area's demography.[13]

The silk industry was domestic, the norm where possible for manufacturing in London; premises solely dedicated to industrial production (factories) would have imposed a substantial additional cost. Weaving was carried out in houses in areas that were first developed in association with the growth of the industry. Houses were built largely for occupation by weavers whose home lives were dominated by work (fig. 60). It is important to grasp this circumstance. In few (if any) other London districts would the provision of new housing have been so clearly and directly associated with the needs of a single industry. New buildings were

61 (*right*) The idle and industrious apprentices (Tom Idle and Francis Goodchild) and a master in a poorly lit Spitalfields workshop. From William Hogarth, *Industry and Idleness*, 1747 (GL).

needed for weaving as much as for housing, and in a world of domestic industry these needs were resolved together. These 'houses' should therefore be considered not simply as domestic architecture, but should equally be understood as industrial buildings.

In 1743 it was reported that the inhabitants of Bethnal Green 'consist chiefly of Journeymen Weavers, and other inferior Artificers, belonging to the Weaving Trade, who, by hard Labour and Industry can scarcely, in the most frugal Way of Life, maintain themselves and Families.'[14] The population was almost entirely working people, the upper class and 'middling sort' of Bethnal Green in 1770 accounting for only about 3 per cent of adult males.[15] As 'inferior artificers' the weavers were an intermediate group, with a status below that of artisans and above that of labourers. But this disguises the great variability of status within the trade that Millicent Rose noted. At the top, leaving aside the silk masters who co-ordinated pro-

duction, most of whom were living away from the district by mid-century, there were highly skilled artisans, literate and self-improving, with strong traditions of horticulture and bird fancying, 'to cheer their quiet hours

62   Weaving in a Spitalfields house, 1853 (*The Builder*).

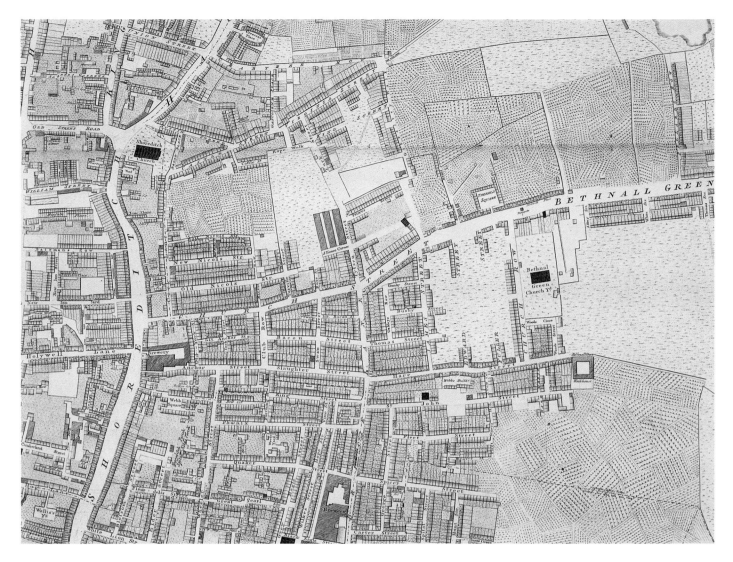

63   Bethnal Green's silk-weaving district in the 1790s (Richard Horwood, *Plan of London*, 1799).

when at the loom'.[16] These weavers, who probably owned their own looms and kept their own stable households, 'formed an intensely orthodox community, intelligent, skilled and enlightened within limits but, on the whole, generally anxious to be accepted as "gentlemen".'[17] Gentlemen, that is, with what has been described as 'precarious gentility' (see chapter 1), a commitment to solid and retrospective artisan respectability, rather than aspirational gentility rooted in entrepreneurship. The Spitalfields Mathematical Society, founded in 1717, flourished, and many other societies (historical, floricultural, entomological and musical) grew up out of the weaving monoculture. This intriguing mix of civilised pursuits on the part of those whose life was otherwise a loom-bound drudge has been explained: 'Patience, intricacy, concentration were alike the quali-

ties of their labour and their idleness.'[18] This artisan respectability has been much emphasised, documented by Henry Mayhew, among others.[19] Dorothy George long ago provided a corrective. Beside the elite there were many others of whom less is known, not just the poor journeymen, but also the women and children, skilled only in filling quills, throwing a shuttle or drawing thread, and others, illiterate, vagrant and desperately poor. For many bullock hunting would have been preferred to flower tending.[20] While remembering this mix, it is also worth recalling the glaring contrast between the silk producer of whatever level and the consumer, the former eking out a subsistence living, the latter devoted to conspicuous consumption. Materials for a silk dress might cost about £50 – more than two years' earnings for many weavers.[21]

86

Along with poverty Bethnal Green was characterised by religious Dissent and social unrest, the latter ebbing and flowing with the fluctuations of the silk industry. When the silk boom of 1715 fell away, weavers starved of work and income led the calico riots of 1719–20, and successfully gained protective legislation.[22] The housing boom of 1719–24 did not coincide with prosperity in the silk industry. Depression in the silk trade may actually have encouraged investment in building – one of the few alternative local outlets for what capital there was in the hands of those with some wealth. Despite general poverty, population growth meant that there was a constant demand for housing, and when there was no work for weavers cheap labour was available to builders. Peaks in London's building cycles in 1720, 1735 and 1766 were all reflected by housebuilding activity in Bethnal Green, all at times of depression in the silk trade.[23]

The downturn of the 1760s was serious, the workforce being reduced by 50 per cent, bringing impoverishment that again took people to the point of starvation.

Riots and sabotage achieved a prohibition on the importation of French silks in 1766, reducing competition. However, there followed further confrontation and 'combination', the word generally used in the eighteenth century (before trade unions) to describe, from the outside looking in, trade association for mutual benefit. Journeymen organised themselves with unparalleled rigour and carried out further sabotage, of both cloth and machines, reacting against the breakdown of established piece-work rates.[24] A memorandum to William Petty, Lord Shelburne, documents the view of the situation in 1768 from within the government:

The Workmen have united into Combinations of a very dangerous & alarming Nature, they have form'd a Plan of greater Extent and More Singularity than ever has been yet done in Cases of Combinations of this kind. They amount to several thousands and are reduc'd to the most exact Discipline under their Leaders, they plant Centinels in all ye Neighbour-

64   Bethnal Green's eighteenth-century silk-weaving district, indicating sites with surviving evidence of early buildings as identified in 2000.

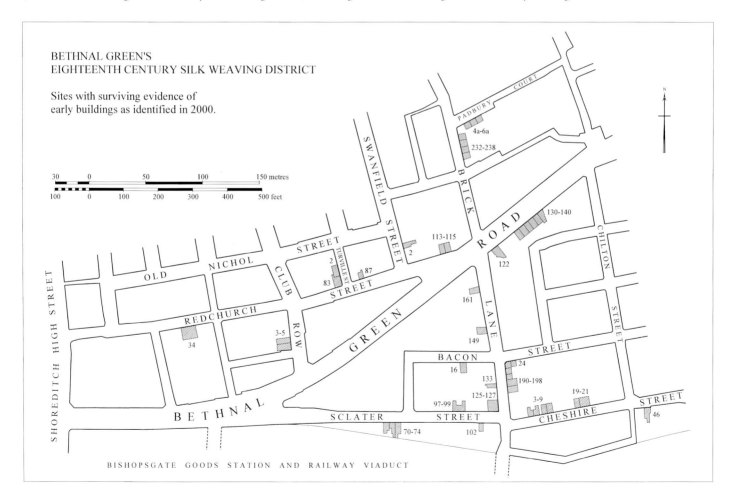

BETHNAL GREEN'S
EIGHTEENTH CENTURY SILK WEAVING DISTRICT

Sites with surviving evidence of
early buildings as identified in 2000.

hoods of Spital Fields and are ready to collect themselves upon any Alarm. They disguise themselves with Crapes and are arm'd with Cutlasses and other Weapons. They write threatening Letters in the form of humble Petitions to the Master Manufacturers and they deter by Threats those labourers from working at an under Price who would be otherwise glad to be employ'd. They enter in the Night such Houses where they have Intelligence any Work is carried on at an under Price and cut and destroy the Looms to the Damage often of several hundred pounds. It is said they are learning the discipline of regular Troops. . . . The few Persons who have occasionally been taken up and confin'd for Disorders and Assaults in the Streets have been immediately rescued. They have their Watch Words and a cant Language understood only by themselves.[25]

John Doyle and John Valloine, leaders of what was termed 'Bold Defiance', were arrested in 1769 at its headquarters in New Cock Lane (Redchurch Street). They were executed, not – exceptionally – at Tyburn, but in Bethnal Green, in order, as was said, 'to strike Terror into the Rioters'. This was ineffective. In 1771 Daniel Clarke, who had been a witness against Doyle and Valloine, was stoned to death in a brick field by a mob said to be two thousand strong. For this two more men were hung in Hare Street, 'the very heart of the residence of the perpetrators'.[26]

An alliance of weavers with coal heavers in Shadwell pushed for lower food prices, bringing affairs closer to a revolutionary edge in 1773, and thence to a denouement through the passage of the first Spitalfields Act. This introduced wage regulation to London's silk industry through a system for negotiating agreed piece rates. The Spitalfields Act was long recognised as a monument to the power the weavers had managed to wield, though it also outlawed combination. Silk masters could not easily escape the Act by moving out of London. Highly developed weaving skills were not simply relocated. Further, proximity to the port, where raw materials arrived, and, more critically, to the famously fickle market for silk, did matter. Finally, the Act forbade masters resident in London from employing those resident outside. The Act of 1773 brought stability to the silk trade, which, this time, coincided with a housing boom in the late 1770s.[27]

Stability did not mean wealth. Average incomes declined, and poverty and radicalism endured. Further Acts extended protective regulations and riots subsided. In the early years of the nineteenth century the London silk industry had its last boom. There were still no factories and the household remained the unit of industrial production. Many new streets of weavers' houses were built in Bethnal Green in the first decades of the century, extending the silk district further north and east. For some living conditions improved for a time.[28]

However, the Spitalfields Acts were becoming a factor in the gradual decline of local industry, as the silk trade's regulated wages did tend to drive production out of London, to many centres, from Essex to Macclesfield (fig. 258), Coventry and Paisley. Parts of the trade, notably silk throwing, had already long since moved out of London and into factories, but the shift accelerated in the early nineteenth century when the view that the Acts were anti-competitive spread. In a significant experiment Stephen Wilson, a leading silk master, built a large silk factory in Streatham in 1820, just beyond the reach of the Acts, aiming to reduce labour costs through the introduction to Britain of the Jacquard loom, too tall to be installed in the houses of the silk district. In evidence to Parliament in 1818 Wilson had said that the Acts encouraged a 'spirit of combination' among the journeymen, who were, he also said, 'after a little talking to, very tractable.'[29] To David Ricardo and other liberal reformers, the Spitalfields Acts were a disgrace, limiting, as they did, free and open competition, and the exploitation of tractability. Theirs was the day, and the Acts were repealed in 1824. Crucially, foreign silks could again be imported. Legislation had a more immediately negative impact on Spitalfields than did the re-mechanisation of weaving in factories, which did not take hold until the 1840s. By then poverty had spread, unrest had resurfaced, and the 'distress' of the Spitalfields' weavers caught the nation's attention, becoming a focus for investigating reformers who published descriptions of unending filth and misery (fig. 62).[30]

Bethnal Green was physically severed from Spitalfields when the viaduct of the Eastern Counties Railway was put through in 1839–42. Further transformation was wrought in 1878–9 when the Metropolitan Board of Works rerouted Bethnal Green Road diagonally across the existing grid of streets north of Sclater Street. Then, in the 1890s, the reforming zeal of the London County Council was made manifest in the Boundary Street Estate, an important early municipal housing scheme that followed clearance of a large area to the north of what is now Redchurch Street, which had been the notoriously poor and lawless 'Old Nichol' or 'Jago' slum.[31]

As silk receded, the clothing and furniture industries grew to dominate the area, use by tailors serving to preserve some of the weavers' houses. Immigration of Jewish refugees from eastern Europe at the end of the nineteenth century changed the area's population mix. Amid

65 'Club Row in ye Olden Time', sentimental commemoration of the Bethnal Green silk district's fame as London's songbird and pet market, which reputedly traced its origins to the silk weavers' passion for birdkeeping. A tile panel of the 1890s from the porch of the Well and Bucket Public House, No. 143 Bethnal Green Road (demolished), made by W. B. Simpson and Company. Photographed *c*.1980. (THLHL).

continuing desperate poverty and ill-health, street markets thrived, on Club Row, Sclater Street, Hare Street and Brick Lane, the last already in 1871 'sacred to costers' barrows and street stalls'.[32] Until the 1970s the area was famous as London's songbird and pet market, the trade's origins said to lie in the silk weavers' passion for bird-keeping (fig. 65).[33] Through another wave of immigration, this time Bengali, poverty and dependence on domestic textile industry have remained constants in the area.

Builders

To shift the focus from the place to its buildings, the transition can be constructively made via people, those who built and lived in the area's houses. The Bethnal Green part of the silk district was like the rest of London in that late seventeenth- and early eighteenth-century housebuilding was most commonly piecemeal leasehold development, that is the leasing by remote landowners of relatively small parcels to speculative builders who put up a few houses at a time (see chapter 2). Given local circumstances, the area was probably never seen as having the potential to be a polite suburb, and it never attracted major freehold development. Even so, London's greatest speculator, Nicholas Barbon, did own some property on Hare Street in the 1670s,[34] and Jon Richardson, a City mason, acquired the whole Nichol Estate in 1680 (figs 56 and 59), converting garden ground into brickfields and gradually leasing plots for the building of small three- to five-room houses, typical frontages being 15 ft.[35] Others were smaller operators, though some enjoyed modest success. One of the main builders on the Nichol Estate was John Hayward (d. 1719), a bricklayer who was also active on Hare Street and at the north end of Brick Lane, being responsible for several parcels of up to eight small houses, generally with 15 ft fronts and of brick. He ended his days prosperously with a leasehold estate of sixty-four houses. His probate inventory indi-

66   Nos 71–9 Sclater Street, one-room-deep houses, first built *c.*1719, perhaps by William Farmer and Richard Storey, carpenters. Small windows for front staircases and large workshop windows indicate origins as weavers' tenements. Photographed in the early twentieth century and showing the bird market. Demolished (THLHL).

cates that he lived in Bethnal Green in a six-room house, large in local terms, with two parlours, in which a clock and a spice box were among the furnishings, and three bedchambers, each with pictures and looking glasses.[36]

One of the next wave of leading local builders in the 1720s and 1730s was William Farmer (d. 1742), a carpenter. Probably born locally, he completed his apprenticeship in 1712. By 1718 he was taking sixty-one-year leases of small parcels on both sides of Sclater Street and building or having built three-storey brick houses that were about 17 ft square on plan, one room per storey, with cellars and one-room back buildings (figs 66, 73, 76, 77 and 78). Farmer himself lived on the corner of

Sclater Street and Brick Lane, in one of these five-room houses.[37] His influence over the development of the Red Cow Estate extended to Edward Grange, another carpenter and an immigrant from Yorkshire who had been Farmer's apprentice until 1720, and who was immediately thereafter leasing multiple 17 ft-wide plots on the south side of Bacon Street. Farmer was also working on the Tyssen Estate, probably building a group of five houses in or soon after 1735, from which Nos 113 and 115 Bethnal Green Road survive (figs 67, 71, 73 and 78).[38] Grange remained locally active as a builder into the 1740s, also working in Spitalfields, and holding property in Mile End New Town.[39]

67 Nos 113 and 115 Bethnal Green Road, five-room houses of *c.*1735, probably built by William Farmer, carpenter. Photographed 2000 (EH, AA004726).

Hayward, Farmer and other local builders were 'citizens', that is freemen of the City of London, the status acquired through the guilds after apprenticeship or work in the City. By the end of the seventeenth century many citizens were living and trading in suburbs, and company membership soon become an irrelevance. Yet the trade companies did not entirely give up their supervisory and standard-setting roles. Proximity to the City may have been a factor in the predominance of citizens in the development of Bethnal Green. In addition the area's City-based freeholders may have been keen to consolidate their investment in land by ensuring a relatively good standard of building. They seem to have seen to it that the builders to whom they gave leases were, if not master carpenters, at least traditionally qualified rather than suburban 'cowboys' such as those non-affiliated tradesmen who were responsible for much housebuilding in less coherently developed parts of east London. This degree of quality control is notable, given that much of the building would have been knowingly destined for habitation by 'inferior artificers'.[40]

There is little evidence that these builders were active elsewhere, even in adjoining Spitalfields. They seem to have lived locally, and in this impoverished weaving district they would have been among the area's wealthier inhabitants. Yet some of them inhabited houses similar to those they built for others. Further insight into the nature of their own houses is a guide in attempting to assess the status and occupancy of the area's houses as a whole.

Samuel Vevers, a bricklayer who in 1732 had taken a small development plot on the north side of Bethnal Green Road from the Tyssen Estate, died in 1737. His probate inventory describes him as being of St Leonard, Shoreditch, but he had previously lived in one of a row of 15ft-front houses that John Hayward had leased and perhaps built at the top end of Brick Lane in 1696. Vevers's inventory indicates that his house at the time of his death was alike in scale to those in the Brick Lane row, which were in turn comparable with those adjoining at Nos 113 and 115 Bethnal Green Road (figs 67, 71, 73 and 78). Vevers's inventoried house comprised five rooms, the main block apparently having only two storeys under a garret; behind there was a wash-house with a room above. There was no designated parlour, but the ground-floor kitchen had a clock, and the bed-chamber above had a mirror and five small pictures. The garret contained another bed and two birdcages, and the room over the wash-house also had a bed. Vevers's house-hold goods, including timber and other building equip-ment on two sites in Bethnal Green, were altogether worth only about £50. However, he too owned other property, two houses in Shoreditch High Street and land in Camberwell, and his whole estate was valued at £716 8s 6d.[41] Vevers was neither poor, narrowly based, nor poorly housed, occupying all of a five-room house in an area where few can have been so amply accommodated.

Building leases sometimes went to local merchants or 'gentlemen', who took them on as speculations with the intention of subcontracting. John Oakey, a wealthy silk throwster and justice, after whom a street was named (later renamed Granby Street), provides an example of this from the 1720s.[42] Conversely, some of the same people encountered as speculating carpenters are else-where identified as weavers, more likely reflecting involvement in the co-ordination of silk production than actual weaving. This was true of Farmer, as it was of Richard Storey, who was also involved in building on the Red Cow Estate.[43] There were ambiguities in and loose boundaries among trade designations. By the same token that building would have been one of the prin-cipal alternative economic activities to weaving in the area when the silk industry was depressed, the reverse would have been true. These builders were businessmen, involved in building not simply or even primarily as 'craftsmen', but for profit. As artisan entrepreneurs they needed to, and evidently knew how to, sustain credit, a difficult trick in this period. Farmer was wealthy enough to protect his investments, taking out insurance policies on some of the houses he built. Substantial operators in a local context, they nevertheless remained locally based and modestly housed, generally possessing trade back-grounds appropriate to housebuilding.[44]

As time went on, the building process seems gradu-ally to have come to be dominated by more ambitious entrepreneurship based in property, still local but branch-ing out. Anthony Natt (d. 1756), a successful carpenter, acquired the Byde Estate in 1736 (fig. 59). This had been first developed in the 1670s and, with leases falling in, would have been ripe for rebuilding. The son of a car-penter from Bexley in Kent, Natt had grown up in the silk district, completing his apprenticeship with Richard Storey in 1705. He rose to high status in the Carpenters'

Company, becoming warden in 1747. He had continued to live locally, in Anchor Street, and was active on the Nichol and Hare Marsh estates in the 1720s and 1730s.[45] Around 1748 he retired to the greener purlieu of Bethnal Green proper (fig. 55), building a row of substantial but strikingly conservative suburban houses, one for himself that survives as No. 19 Old Ford Road (figs 212 and 213). His son, also Anthony, rose out of the family trade into a profession, becoming a clergyman, and moved further east into rural Essex. He kept his property interests in Bethnal Green, being responsible for redeveloping the west side of Club Row with eleven new houses in 1764–6, from when Nos 3 and 5 Club Row survive (figs 68 and 74).[46]

David Wilmot 'Esquire' was Bethnal Green's parish treasurer and a magistrate who made the arrests that led to the public hangings on Hare Street in 1771, going on to help with the framing of the Act of 1773. As a mag-istrate he not only helped fix weaving wage rates through that Act, but also gained significantly greater control over local building works through the London Building Act of 1774. Wilmot had begun locally as a labourer, and rose through property dealings and specu-lative building in the 1760s, working with Thomas

68　Nos 3 and 5 Club Row, two survivors from a row of six four-room houses built in 1764–6, the front staircases here being without natural light. Photographed 2000 (EH, AA004729).

69 Early nineteenth-century two-room weavers' 'cottages', in the 'Old Nichol' or 'Jago' (latterly the site of the Boundary Street Estate). Designed as houses, with living space below workshops. Photographed *c*.1890. Demolished (LMA).

Munday, an East Smithfield pewterer, and John Wilmot, probably his son and a bricklayer. Also linked to this group was John Price, a Petticoat Lane plasterer, who was building on the Red Cow estate around what had become Granby Street in the 1770s. On land owned by David Wilmot, these people speculatively created a new residential enclave well to the east, amid open fields and away from the weaving district, laying out Wilmot Street in 1766–72 and Wilmot Square from 1777. Wilmot's own large house, Wilmot's Folly, stood at the north end of this 'suburban' island.[47]

Others probably aspired to Wilmot's levels of enterprise. James and Ann Merceron, who may have started as Huguenot weavers, were by the 1760s Brick Lane pawnbrokers, the ultimate intermediate trade and a flourishing line in a poor area so subject to dramatic fluctuations in prosperity. On Sunday evenings, 'Jour-

neymen-Weavers, Taylors, Shoemakers, and other impoverished Tradesmen, [took] off their wearing Apparel, as holding it by no longer Tenure, than the opening of Pawnbrokers Shops, the ensuing Morning.'[48] The Mercerons were also active as builders. By the 1770s they had become major local landlords, using housing demand and the elusiveness of property for the poor as routes to wealth. In a parish with an open vestry managed by about two thousand householders, Joseph Merceron (1764–1839), probably the son of James and Ann, displaced Wilmot as Bethnal Green's treasurer and became the leading local politician by the 1790s. Despite being notoriously corrupt, he held on to his power base and local popularity until he was jailed in 1818 for misappropriation of funds and the licensing of public houses used for debauchery, most in the weaving district. Though a magistrate, he refused to conform to notions

93

70 Fournier Street, Spitalfields. These large houses of the 1720s were built for single occupation by wealthy silk merchants or masters, and comprised ten or more rooms. The fenestration of the attic for weaving is probably an early alteration. Photographed 1993 (EH, AA93/5603).

of law-abiding respectability. He was imprisoned again for organising bullock hunting in the parish churchyard. Again he returned and still retained his popularity.[49] Thomas Green, a Petticoat Lane baker, and Peter Mansell, a local tallow chandler, were others involved in property speculation in the 1760s and 1770s, the latter as another major landlord.[50]

After 1800 the need for speculators to develop sites intensively to find even small profit from housebuilding brought a marked lowering of standards at the bottom end of the market, a shift that occurred across London

(see chapter 9). This debasement of the building process can be represented in Bethnal Green by Saunderson Turner Sturtevant, a tallow chandler who in 1804 bought a large plot for large-scale freehold development, much of it on the Fitch Estate (fig. 59). By 1819 this land had been built over with very poor quality housing, instant slums, by what were soon after termed 'speculative builders of the most scampy class' (fig. 69).[51] It was later redeveloped as part of the Boundary Street Estate. Not all early nineteenth-century housing in the area was so mean, but the ability to build had been concentrated, and alienated from its local and trade-based roots. Bethnal Green housed the poor throughout, but the areas that needed clearance at the end of the nineteenth century were those that had been developed more recently. Already in 1842 the area's worst sanitation problems were in its newer houses, 'which may be called more huts than houses, built in swamps, at a cheap rent, for the purpose of being let out to weekly tenants at as much money as they can get for them.'[52] The eighteenth-century houses were not necessarily superior; of the smallest and worst no evidence survives. By the nineteenth century they had certainly become overcrowded, but the greater part were not so poorly made nor so small. The survival of a handful of these eighteenth-century buildings, as compared with the utter disappearance of the early nineteenth-century 'huts', is significant.

Occupants

Most of those who lived in the eighteenth-century houses of the Bethnal Green part of the silk district were weavers, not builders. What were their living spaces? The domestic topography of Spitalfields up to the early eighteenth century has been characterised as 'small scale and paternalistic', masters and journeymen living together in the masters' houses, set among smaller houses inhabited by other journeymen. While there was such a mix of small houses around big houses in Spitalfields proper, this description does not fit more peripheral development in Bethnal Green.[53] From about 1716 into the 1730s larger streets on estates at the heart of the silk district in Spitalfields were being built up with big merchant's or master's houses, with fronts of 20 ft plus and at least two rooms to each storey (fig. 70). In Bethnal Green little apart from narrow one-room-plan houses was being built. There were small houses in Spitalfields, though few are still extant, while there were never many big houses in Bethnal Green. Many silk masters were probably small operators employing only two or three journeymen at a time. Perhaps some of the early eighteenth-century occupants of Sclater Street and environs were such small masters holding whole houses for themselves, with adjoining houses of comparable size subdivided for the journeymen they employed; this, however, is neither the co-habitational 'weavers-in-the-garret' nor the big house/little house relationship that has been understood as having held in parts of Spitalfields. Silk masters were already moving away from Spitalfields to more salubrious surroundings in the 1720s. By the 1740s many large Spitalfields houses were being divided into lodgings, and those few masters that there might have been in Bethnal Green had probably also emigrated. With a domestic-industrial weaving monoculture Bethnal Green's silk district was not closely comparable with Spitalfields, nor to any other localities in the metropolis. A different model is needed to make sense of a place populated by 'inferior artificers' where there were not great variations in house size.

This means returning to the ambiguities of multiple occupation. It is clear, and perhaps self-evident, that on the whole London's speculative builders sought optimum letting potential, designing buildings to accommodate aspirations towards single occupancy, even in the knowledge that multiple occupation might quickly arise. However, scattered circumstantial evidence has been invoked to suggest that some humble housing across seventeenth-century London that was characterised by the placing of staircases directly inside the front door may have been so designed with a view to multiple occupation (see chapters 1 and 2, and figs 19, 33, 38, 39 and 40).

Hector Gavin noted in his *Sanitary Ramblings* in the 1840s that Bethnal Green's eighteenth-century houses were 'constructed in the French fashion, – flat upon flat',[54] and there is straightforward evidence of multiple occupation in a petition of 1743: 'by far the greatest Part of the Houses in the said Hamlet are lett at Ten Pounds *per Annum*, and under; and are mostly lett out by the Owners of such Houses, in Two or Three distinct Parts or Tenements, by reason of the Great Poverty of the Inhabitants, who are unable to take a whole House upon themselves.'[55] This can be confirmed. Allowing anything around usually accepted measures of an average of about four to six people per household (that is distinct domestic establishments, whether of families, however extended, or individuals), it is evident that in the 1740s Bethnal Green had many more households (about 2,500–3,750 for about 15,000 people) than houses (about 1,800).[56] This is not exceptional in relation to other parts of London, but in Bethnal Green there were no large old houses to be divided. Single-family occupation of

the small houses built since about 1670 could not have been the rule in the 1740s. Some late seventeenth-century houses might have been designed for single-family occupation and converted to multiple occupation following population growth. However, such a pattern seems unlikely to apply to the many houses built in Bethnal Green after 1700. There were already many more households than houses in 1711, so multiple occupation must already then have been widespread.[57] With this as the status quo, about two hundred new houses were built in the years following 1719, in the face of what would have been obvious and intensifying local poverty. It may be inferred that houses built in Bethnal Green after 1700 were designed knowing that many were certainly destined for multiple occupation.

Further insight into who might have lived in what space and when may be gained through comparison of rents and incomes. Sales of houses in and around Sclater Street suggest annual rents for whole houses of £7 to £9 from the 1720s to the 1770s, confirming the claim made in the petition of 1743.[58] These were three- or four-room houses, so a typical room rental of £2 to £3 a year, or about a shilling a week, can be deduced, rather less than was typical elsewhere in London, as is to be expected (see chapter 1). As late as 1853 Bethnal Green weavers still typically paid 1s 6d per week room rent.[59] Loom rents were supplementary, but not significant; wooden looms were crudely and cheaply made.[60]

What does this mean in relation to incomes? Journeymen weavers earned up to 15 shillings a week in the 1760s, but there were often long periods of unemployment, so this is not translatable as an income of £39 a year. Women and children did work, but under severe restrictions, and for very low pay. Household incomes of £20 a year and less were not unusual.[61] Calculating an average expenditure of about an eighth of income on rent (see chapter 1), a room in a Sclater Street house would have been affordable with an income of £20 a year and thus within reach of typical journeymen weavers. Two rooms would have been possible only for prospering fully employed artisans or those families with substantial supplementary incomes. Whole three-room houses would have called for an annual income of about £60, unimaginable to all but a few in Bethnal Green.

Bethnal Green's housebuilders of the 1720s and 1730s would have been aware that there was not a substantial local market for single-family houses. They would have designed and built the area's houses in the knowledge that many if not most would be used for multiple occupation, as workshop homes for a floating population of short-term tenant journeymen weavers. Those who

71 Nos 113 and 115 Bethnal Green Road, perspective reconstruction of the one-room-deep houses as built *c*.1735, showing part of one of the front winder staircases and the partly surviving full-width workshop windows in the timber-framed back wall.

could have afforded long-term tenancies of whole houses were few, would have been likely to have preferred to live elsewhere, and were anyway decreasing in their numbers.

Later in the eighteenth century new building did not keep pace with population growth and single-family occupation became progressively more exceptional. Contemporary testimony relates that in 1763 about one in three houses was controlled by a local oligarchy of landlords, building tradesmen and others, the Wilmots, Mercerons *et al.*, who let properties out as lodgings for journeymen weavers.[62] Towards the end of the century growing distress in the silk industry meant that there was generally a family in every room.[63] Daniel Lysons reported on Bethnal Green in 1795 that: 'The town part of this parish is extremely populous; being inhabited principally by journeymen weavers, who live three or four families in a house, and work at their looms and reels for the master weavers in Spitalfields.'[64] During the early nineteenth century the number of people per house declined with the appearance of the numerous new streets of low 'cottages'.[65] The older houses remained multi-occupied, and it was still usual that 'among the weavers of Spitalfields a man has a loom in his room and sleeps in it with all his family.'[66]

Evidence as to what the eighteenth-century weavers' rooms were like as homes is elusive. Unsurprisingly, contemporary pictorial representations of the interiors of weavers' homes are lacking. The first plate from

Hogarth's *Industry and Idleness* of 1747 (fig. 61) famously shows the industrious and idle apprentices, Francis Goodchild and Tom Idle, in an improbably poorly fenestrated room into which the master has entered. It is not evident that this is anyone's living space. Written accounts can be evocative. In 1803 J. P. Malcolm wrote of the weavers' homes: 'The houses occupied by those industrious and useful tradesmen are generally decayed and wretched, the streets dirty and melancholy, and the eternal hum of their looms conveys a confusing effect to the passenger, by no means pleasant.'[67] More than a century later Dorothy George described how 'The work was done in small, crowded rooms in horribly insanitary dwellings, and the air was carefully excluded by paper pasted over the cracks of the windows, to prevent the silk from losing weight and so making the weaver liable to deductions from his earnings.'[68] Such latter-day images of squalor (fig. 62) need to be offset by an awareness that cleanliness would have been paramount in the handling of such a precious commodity as silk (fig. 2).[69]

72   Houses of the 1670s on Castle Street (latterly the site of Nos 5–17 Virginia Road), with small windows in the entrance bays indicating front-staircase layouts, and the spire of the Church of St Leonard, Shoreditch, rising in the background. Watercolour by J. Appleton, 1890, shortly before the houses were demolished (HAD).

73 *(following page)*   Reconstructed plans of late seventeenth- and early eighteenth-century houses in Bethnal Green.

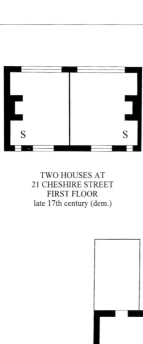

TWO HOUSES AT
21 CHESHIRE STREET
FIRST FLOOR
late 17th century (dem.)

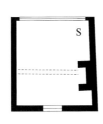

46 CHESHIRE STREET
SECOND FLOOR
1670s

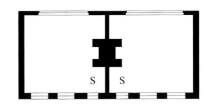

97-99 SCLATER STREET
FIRST FLOOR
c.1720

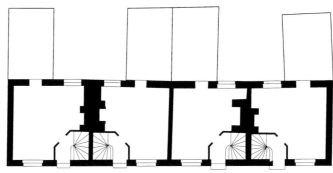

70-76 SCLATER STREET
GROUND FLOOR
c.1719

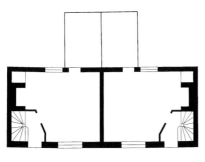

7-9 GRANBY STREET
GROUND FLOOR
c.1725 (dem.)

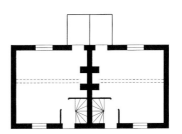

3-4 HARE COURT
BETHNAL GREEN
GROUND FLOOR
c.1725 (dem.)

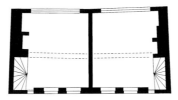

113-115 BETHNAL GREEN ROAD
FIRST FLOOR
c.1735

1   0   5   10   15   20 metres

5   0   30   60 feet   S = FORMER STAIR POSITION

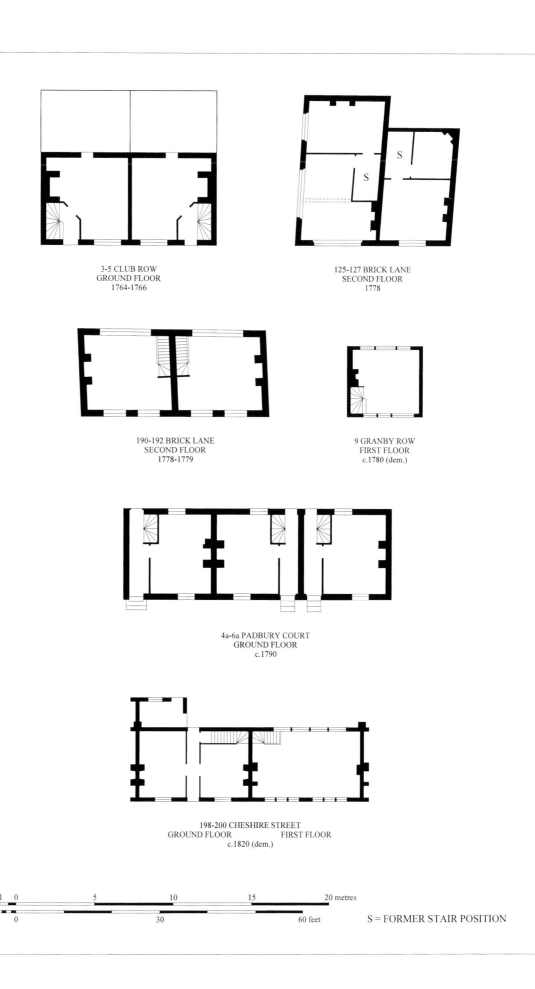

3-5 CLUB ROW
GROUND FLOOR
1764-1766

125-127 BRICK LANE
SECOND FLOOR
1778

190-192 BRICK LANE
SECOND FLOOR
1778-1779

9 GRANBY ROW
FIRST FLOOR
c.1780 (dem.)

4a-6a PADBURY COURT
GROUND FLOOR
c.1790

198-200 CHESHIRE STREET
GROUND FLOOR   FIRST FLOOR
c.1820 (dem.)

1   0   5   10   15   20 metres

5   0   30   60 feet   S = FORMER STAIR POSITION

Direct evidence for the occupation of particular buildings by people firmly identifiable as weavers in the eighteenth century is also difficult to find, and it is important always to bear in mind that even those names listed in official records compiled for taxation purposes need to be handled with caution. The poor did not pay tax, and there would have been subletting, often informal. Probate inventories rarely make it possible to place people at particular addresses, but, as those of John Hayward and Samuel Vevers show, they have value in depicting how houses were occupied and, something for which there is little other evidence below the highest social levels, how rooms were furnished and used. However, inventories tend to exclude the poor, so no exhaustive inventory research has been attempted; any quantitative evidence derived therefrom would be likely to be misleading in this social milieu. Nonetheless, for an evocation of house interiors in the late seventeenth century and the early eighteenth, probate inventories are unrivalled, so it is worth relating the details of a few from the upper range of house occupancy in early to mid-eighteenth-century Bethnal Green.[70]

Luke Miller, an affluent weaver who died in 1735, was evidently a master, doing well enough not to have looms in his own house. He was apparently in single occupation of his house, which comprised five rooms described as one above another from a garret to a cellar, implying a building like some of those built in Sclater Street around 1720 or Bethnal Green Road around 1735 (figs 66 and 71). The ground-floor or 'lower' room was the kitchen, and the cellar was no more than a coal store. The first-floor room contained a bed, with some silver, including a watch, silk clothing and wigs. The second-floor room had two beds and some books, and the garret no beds, but unspecified 'working tools' and two spice boxes. Miller's household goods were worth £48 8s 0d, with the goods of his weaving trade worth another £126 15s 0d.[71] Susannah Lermigne was a silk windstress and widow who lived simply in two rooms, the contents of which were valued at only £1 16s 8d when she died in 1740. Both rooms contained 'engines' as well as beds, one room also serving for cooking, with kettles, pans and bottles stowed away in a closet.[72] Tenancy of a single room did not necessarily mean poverty, as is shown in the inventory of the room occupied by Anne Minier, another Bethnal Green widow, who died in 1752. She was not evidently a weaver, though the inventory gives no obvious indication of trade. Her room had two windows, two beds, a looking glass, an easy chair and a tea table. Her cooking equipment included a tea kettle and a coffee pot; by the 1750s tea and coffee drinking

were spreading through all levels of society. Her goods were worth £18 2s 9d.[73]

The index to some of the Sun Fire Insurance policy registers helps put particular weavers into particular houses in the 1770s and 1780s: Mary Emms and Isaac Stevens as tenants of Peter Mansell on the south side of Sclater Street in 1777 and 1780 (figs 73 and 76); James Prouteaux and John Levesque in Nos 143 and 145 Brick Lane in 1776–7; and Paul Batteux and Ann Cobbeal, a loom broker and silk windster, in two of the houses of the 1760s on the west side of Club Row (figs 68 and 74), their valuations of household goods, stock and apparel ranging from £100 to £500.[74] Nearby houses of comparable size could accommodate head tenants with widely divergent levels of insurable assets, demonstrating that there are limitations as to what house size reveals about the status of occupants. Even the most modest of the houses for which records have emerged were not necessarily for the very poor. John Willock, a weaver who lived in one of the then new two-room houses in Granby Row in 1776 (fig. 74), was himself the owner of a small tenanted house in Ratcliff.[75] A small two-room house was perhaps considered an improvement on the local standard of one larger room in a divided house.

The census of 1841 confirms the continuing use of many eighteenth-century buildings for the silk trade even at that late date. The three- to five-room early eighteenth-century houses on Sclater Street all then had at least two households, many three or four. Of 230 tradespeople identified as living on Sclater Street in 1841, 130 were still in the silk trade, mostly weavers, with some winders; many of the others were shopkeepers. On Club Row the equivalent figures were 145 tradespeople of whom fifty-four were in the silk trade.[76]

Domestic–Industrial Urban–Vernacular Architecture

The lack of contemporary views or descriptions of ordinary housing in the eighteenth-century silk district makes the evidence of surviving buildings all the more important. In so far as there have been accepted 'images' of the architecture of London's weavers' housing they tend to have their roots in two places – the attics of early eighteenth-century merchants' houses in Spitalfields proper (fig. 70), or the no longer extant rows of two-storey early nineteenth-century 'cottages' in Bethnal Green (fig. 69).[77] But this is too simple. An entire class of eighteenth-century weavers' houses has been forgotten (figs 58, 66–8 and 71, 73–6).

74 (*previous page*)   Reconstructed plans of late eighteenth- and early nineteenth-century houses in Bethnal Green.

75   Nos 194–8 Brick Lane, a four-storey mixed-use tenement block built in 1763–5 for Peter Mansell, a tallow chandler and major local landlord. The block comprised fifteen rooms in three one-room-deep stacks, each room being about 15 ft square. It probably always incorporated ground-level shops, with associated first-floor domestic space, and at least five intercommunicating upper-storey workshop tenements. Photographed 1956 (LMA).

76 Nos 78–88 Sclater Street, one-room-deep weavers' houses of *c*.1720, the functional staircase and workshop fenestration largely retained through refrontings. Photographed 1955. Demolished (LMA).

The eighteenth-century streets of the weaving district in Bethnal Green bore little resemblance to anything of the period that is familiar. Spitalfields, while then being more varied than it is now, corresponded more closely to notions of regular and classical development, reflecting higher-status occupation. The irregular and functional elevations of Bethnal Green's houses are alien to prevailing understandings of London's Georgian domestic architecture.

The absence of classical proportionality that is such an arresting quality of the fronts of these weavers' houses needs to be understood in functional terms, both in relation to multiple occupation by journeymen, and in terms of the exigencies of industrial use. Fenestration patterns are key, most obviously through the wide windows variously known as weavers' windows, loom lights or long lights. Good light was crucial for the intricate skill of silk weaving, for the joining of fine threads should they break, and for colour matching. The maximising of light in rooms used for silk weaving was an architectural priority from at least the seventeenth century, more perhaps than for other kinds of weaving. Broad windows in the main body of the house, as opposed to in attics, are clear indicators that the houses were designed for, rather than altered to, workshop use. Brick front walls made segmentally arched heads to wide windows structurally advisable, flat-arched heads to such

openings being technically difficult. Alternatively, full-width windows were readily achieved just below the eaves to the front, where many houses had mullioned casements, sometimes seen below the parapets of remade front walls. In London the fully fenestrated full upper storey in lieu of a garret in the roofspace was not peculiar to the weaving district in the early eighteenth century, having occurred more than a century earlier in Smithfield (fig. 21). Wide top-storey windows were not unusual across the Georgian city as a whole, but whole streets dominated by long lights were distinctively characteristic of Bethnal Green. It is significant that this was so before the end of the eighteenth century when such streetscapes began to appear in other parts of England where domestic industry was important (see chapter 8).

The long light is only one part of the peculiar fenestration, the other being the small staircase window. These invariably occur in entrance bays, lighting winder staircases in the front corners of one-room-plan houses. The surviving houses at Nos 70–74 and 97–9 Sclater Street, with origins of around 1720, largely but conservatively rebuilt, show this particularly clearly (figs 73 and 77).[78] As has been discussed in relation to similar seventeenth-century buildings from across London, the placing of a staircase at the front of a building just inside the front door appears to have been a long-standing vernacular practice associated with design for multiple

77 Nos 70–74 Sclater Street, three houses built for weavers with origins of *c*.1719; No. 70 refronted *c*.1777, Nos 72 and 74 largely rebuilt in the early to mid-nineteenth century retaining their original shape and layout. Photographed 2000 (EH, AA004718).

occupation (see chapter 2). Front staircases are rare in multi-storey homes where mediation of private circulation between the levels is desirable, but they are suited to multiple occupation, allowing the upper-storey tenants to come and go without intruding into the ground-floor tenant's space. The form is also efficient in relation to the comings and goings of industrial use; eighteenth-century warehouses frequently had front staircases lit by small windows.[79] It would also have been advantageous in permitting better lighting from the rear. Most of the weavers' houses were brick fronted, in conformity with the Building Acts, but many seemingly had illegal and concealed timber back walls. Trabeated timber construction enabled full-width fenestration to the rear below the upper storey, as at Nos 113 and 115 Bethnal Green Road (fig. 71). This potential would have been compromised if the staircases had been framed against the back walls, and it is sounder construction to frame a stair into a brick wall than into one of slight timber. So the front-staircase layout was probably favoured for a range of functional reasons. The staircases were some-

times unlit, as at Nos 3 and 5 Club Row (figs 68 and 74), but this was unusual. More often they were given the distinctive small windows, so indicative of indifference to classical proportion. Even in humble dwellings it would have been important to light the staircases, if only because the valuable silk, which needed to be kept clean, was carried up and down them; these were industrial buildings.

The front-staircase window occurs consistently in Bethnal Green from the later seventeenth century until at least the 1760s, often persisting through later refrontings, as at Nos 70–74 Sclater Street (fig. 77). The tell-tale small openings were present on Castle Street (now Virginia Road), in the north-west corner of Bethnal Green, in a row probably built in the 1670s (fig. 72).[80] From nearly a century later there was, until 2003, another such window at Nos 194–8 Brick Lane (fig. 75), put up in 1763–5 in redevelopment by one of the area's landlord oligarchs, Peter Mansell, to provide what is best understood as a large mixed-use tenement block rather than as three separate houses.[81]

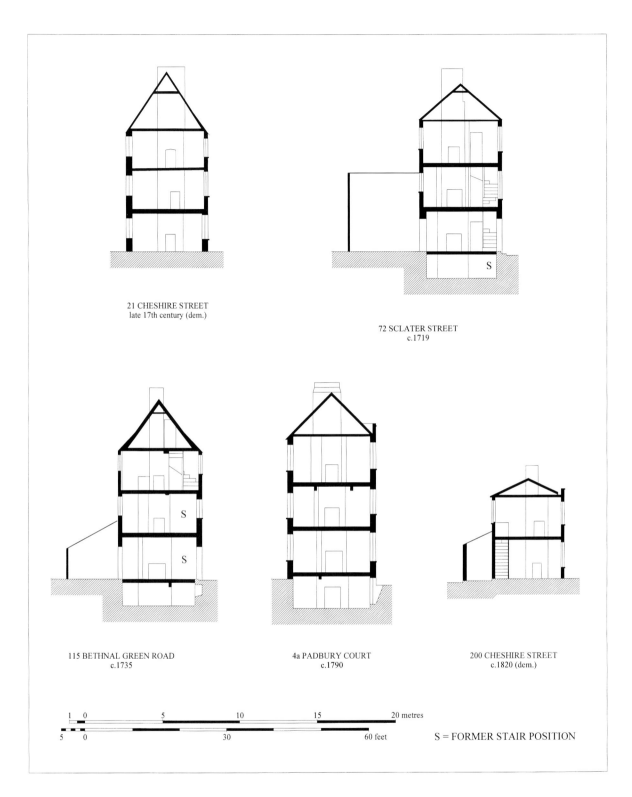

21 CHESHIRE STREET
late 17th century (dem.)

72 SCLATER STREET
c.1719

115 BETHNAL GREEN ROAD
c.1735

4a PADBURY COURT
c.1790

200 CHESHIRE STREET
c.1820 (dem.)

S = FORMER STAIR POSITION

78   Reconstructed sections of houses in Bethnal Green.

Front-staircase windows occurred in and around the weaving district outside Bethnal Green in the late seventeenth century and the early eighteenth, as in one-room-plan houses at No. 45 Crispin Street, Spitalfields,[82] and No. 12 Hunton Street, Mile End New Town,[83] as well as in a bigger mid-eighteenth-century house at No. 19 Redmans Road, Mile End Old Town (see chapter 5). Nowhere, however, did the feature occur as consistently as it did in Bethnal Green. No. 28 Elder Street, Spitalfields (c.1724), provides a telling instance of its absence. The house has a winder staircase just inside its front door, but it lacks the small windows.[84] Like a number of Elder Street's houses it has one-room-plan origins, broadly comparable in scale and form with houses of similar date in Bethnal Green, but Elder Street was a relatively high-status development.[85] Significantly, only No. 28 appears to have been given a front-staircase layout. In a street where the houses were intended for well-to-do single occupation, front stairs were not needed and a degree of elevational proportionality perhaps mattered. Where there is a front staircase, at No. 28, it was probably not intended for industrial use, and so remained unlit.[86]

The origins and spread of the front-staircase layout in London need further research, but it does seem clear that builders in the silk district were picking up on an established seventeenth-century form that occurred across London (figs 19, 33, 38 and 39) and beyond, particularly in small late seventeenth-century houses in densely built areas characterised by artisan and labourer populations (see chapter 8). The front-staircase layout was a vernacular building habit that endured because it was functionally appropriate to divided occupation and industrial use. Gavin's association of the weavers' houses with French flats is interesting, but not necessarily historically accurate (see chapter 2). Lyons, the centre of French silk weaving, had workshop tenements for its silkworkers and others, but of different character and layout.[87] Scarcity of evidence makes it difficult to gauge the extent to which the domestic architecture of the early eighteenth-century silk district followed long-standing and long-lost practice from London's industrial margins.

The one-room plan was all but universal in eighteenth-century Bethnal Green (figs 73, 74 and 78). Gavin noticed that eighteenth-century Bethnal Green differed from areas developed since:

The chief peculiarity of this district consists in its comparatively small number of courts and alleys, and the total absence of gardens. This part of the parish is about the oldest. The houses then built were chiefly to accommodate the weavers, and the practice fol-

lowed was, to build a street of several stories, not, as is the present custom, to plant on the damp, undrained soil, two rooms on a ground floor.[88]

This is explicable in relation to multiple occupation and one-room tenancies, but it is probably above all a function of the need for good light in the room interiors, deriving from the silk industry and workshop use of most of the rooms. Any double pile or front-back two-room layout in a narrow-fronted town house leaves the inner parts of the rooms without good natural light. A single-room depth, however, permits through light from front and back. The size of looms must have dictated the minimum dimensions for the rooms. Frontages of about 14–15 ft were usual in the late seventeenth century, as on Hare Street and Castle Street (figs 72 and 73). These rooms would have accommodated a loom and a home, but probably left precious little space for circulation. The early eighteenth-century houses tend to have 17–18 ft frontages, which would have allowed for a loom or two and rather more living space, perhaps reflecting spreading provision for the use of single rooms as family

79   The scar of No. 77 Redchurch Street, first built c.1723 (demolished and replaced by space for two cars to park), showing the verticality of the area's one-room-deep eighteenth-century weavers' houses. Photographed 2000 (EH, BB99/09163).

homes. Industrial use would have been a leading determinant of architectural form, but rentability would
have made domestic use an important consideration
for speculative builders and landlords. In Spitalfields
the one-room-plan house was not a rarity, though
disproportionately few survive.[89] Examples on Elder
Street and Crispin Street have already been cited, and
there are others at Nos 4–7 Puma Court, refronted and

80 (*left*)   Nos 188–98 Brick Lane. Nos 190 and 192 in the foreground, weavers' houses of 1778–9, were built by James Laverdure
(alias Green), a Spitalfields carpenter, to have regular two-bay
fronts with rear-staircase layouts, the always taller tenement building at Nos 194–8 of 1763–5 (fig. 75) having a much less regular
front and a front staircase. Photographed 1993 (EH, AA93/05196).

81 (*below*)   'Cottrell's Buildings', Nos 84–96 Cheshire Street,
weavers' houses of *c*.1780, named after their builder. Photographed
1952. Demolished (LMA).

82   Nos 125 and 127 Brick Lane, as restored in 2001, without the long-lost upper storey (see fig. 54). Photographed 2002 (EH, AA033056).

enlarged houses of around 1730, originally about 15 ft by 18 ft, on the last of Spitalfields' eighteenth-century alleys.[90]

The consistently tall, shallow proportions of many of Bethnal Green's eighteenth-century houses are evident in sections (figs 78 and 79). The three- or four-storey one-room-deep main block was the local standard, often accompanied by a single-storey outshut or back building, wash-houses, kitchens or additional workshops, of which evidence is even more fragmentary. In terms of seventeenth-century antecedents the houses are closer in form to those of Bartholomew Fair than they are to those of Shadwell or other riverine suburbs (figs 18–25),

a reflection of urban density. In these tall houses there was no obvious hierarchy of storey heights, neither the ground nor first floors being given emphasis. While the vertical separation of three or four undifferentiated spaces may reflect deliberate provision for multiple occupation, there was sufficient flexibility to allow for the possibility of single occupation. The house form reflects the likelihood of division without making it a necessity. Ground-floor rooms might have been used as shops or warehouses if not sufficiently light for weaving. Adaptability would have been important and room use in adjoining and architecturally identical buildings probably differed and varied through time. Design for weaving

83 Nos 4A–6A Padbury Court, three four-room houses, probably built *c*.1790. Photographed 2000 (EH, BB99/09160).

84 Nos 7–12 Padbury Court of *c*.1790, and houses beyond on the north side of the road, evidently laid out with front staircases. Photographed 1954. Demolished (LMA).

would not, of course, have prevented use of what it is convenient to call weavers' houses by some who were not weavers. The likelihood of great flexibility of use within the same architectural form can be recognised without implying that the form is thereby robbed of functional meaning.

From the 1770s onwards weavers' houses were generally given more regular elevations, in both new houses and refrontings, often without long lights, but usually retaining large windows, vertically aligned in single bays under parapets (figs 80, 81 and 278). Nos 190 and 192 Brick Lane were built in 1778–9 by James Laverdure, a Spitalfields carpenter, elsewhere known to have anglicised his name to Green.[91] The front wall of the one-room-deep main block was subsequently stuccoed to conceal small reductions in the width of the window openings. The relatively regular fronts were possible as the lower flights of stairs were in low back buildings, the upper flights rising from the back in the main block (fig. 74). There was upper-storey workshop fenestration to the rear. In these and other late eighteenth-century houses the small staircase windows were generally absent and frontages were sometimes back down to about 15ft, though the main blocks were still always one room deep. The regular fenestration and back-stair position of a surviving group of three houses on Padbury Court (figs 74, 83 and 85), probably of around 1790,[92] indicate that their builder aspired to a modicum of politeness, perhaps aiming for single occupation by non-weavers; by 1775 Truman's Brewery had a depot around the corner (figs 59 and 63). Too linear a view of developments should be resisted; houses on the other side of the road of the same date do appear to have had front staircases (fig. 84).

Late eighteenth-century changes in local architecture were anything but a straightforward transformation, as is more amply witnessed by No. 125 Brick Lane (figs 54, 74 and 82), a large and formerly four-storey corner building. The site of No. 125 was first developed in 1720 with Pierre Fromaget, a Huguenot weaver, as the earliest occupant. His house was evidently wholly rebuilt in 1778 for Daniel Delacourt, a distiller and Fromaget's grandson, as a mixed-use block incorporating a shop and lettable workshop tenements, the staircase at the back because the corner property could be lit only from the fronts. No. 127, the subsequently refronted adjoining house, may have been built at the same time; it is itself exceptional in the locality for having London's 'standard' rear-staircase plan (see chapter 2).[93]

The Spitalfields silk industry's last hurrah in the early nineteenth century was associated with a more distinct change in housing form. So long as legislation kept it

85   Nos 4A–6A Padbury Court, perspective reconstruction of three houses probably built *c.*1790, with rear winder staircases and without workshop fenestration.

in London, the industry remained domestically based because, daylight being crucial, independent loomshops or factories that would have stood empty at night would have made no economic sense in a densely populated city with expensive land. It was better to continue to build weaving space that also housed a captive market of workers who needed homes for which they had to pay rent as much as they needed work to pay the rent. Along the new streets to the north and east the new weavers' houses were more horizontally laid out, in long uniform rows, entirely brick and rising only two storeys (fig. 69). Better examples had two rooms on the ground floor, with rear-staircase layouts, single-storey wash-houses to the rear, and amply fenestrated first-floor workshops,

often only with ladder access and trapdoors to maximise the workshop floor space (figs 74, 78 and 86). Less good housing comprised two rooms or, in fewer cases, single-room dwellings, most with some kind of front or back yard. Many two-room houses measured 12 ft square or less, providing no more total floor area than a single 17 ft-square room. These were all built as single-family houses, not as divided tenements.[94] The domestic, industrial and constructional rationales for the front staircase and verticality were all no longer operative.

To turn to materials and surfaces, it is clear that brick building was already widespread in the late seventeenth-century silk district, more than in other parts of east London nearer the river, where timber house construc-

86 Nos 34 and 36 Florida Street, weavers' houses of *c*.1815 with two-room rear-staircase layouts on the ground floor and workshops on the upper storey. Recorded by the LCC in 1935. Demolished (EH, GLC Drawings Collection 96/2095).

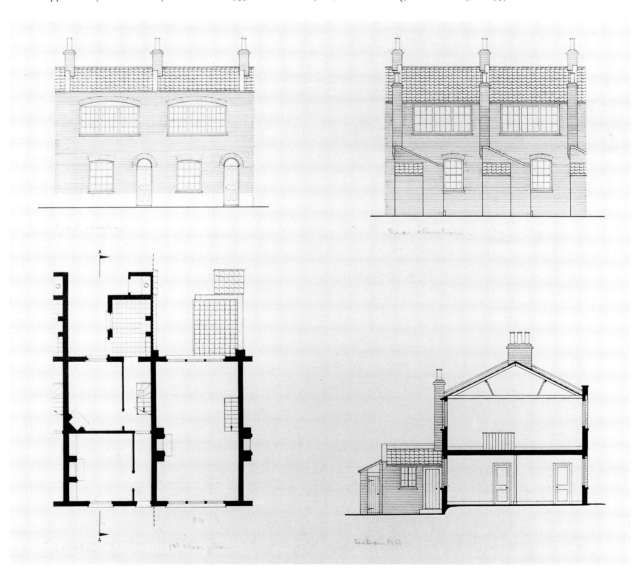

87 Hare Court, behind and probably developed with Nos 3–9 Hare Street (fig. 88), *c*.1725. It comprised two facing pairs of weavers' houses, also one room deep with front-staircase layouts. Photographed 1928. Demolished (EH, AP 247).

88 Nos 3–9 Hare (Cheshire) Street, weavers' houses of *c*.1725, one room deep with front-staircase layouts. Nos 7 and 9 appear to have retained an eaves cornice and simple bracketed hoods. A passage opening between Nos 5 and 7 led to Hare Court (fig. 87). Photographed 1928. Demolished (EH, AP 248).

tion remained the norm well into the eighteenth century (see chapter 2). But even in Bethnal Green, where there was a good supply of brickearth, there were houses with timber external walls; *The Builder* reported that 'old weather-boarded houses on the front, and half-timbered ones, are numerous in the district.'[95] The dates of first development in the area that was being described mean that many of these can only have been built well after the Building Act of 1707 outlawed such construction. It is worth noting in this context that open eaves and party walls without parapets, also forbidden by the 1707 Act, continued to be built up to the 1760s, when legislation was tightened. It is not at all surprising that

the Acts were not observed in Bethnal Green, as they were poorly enforced and blatantly disregarded through much of London (see chapters 2, 4 and 5).

Few of Bethnal Green's early houses survive because, in common with London's speculatively built houses everywhere, they were not built to last. This was all the more true at the lower end of the market, and rebuilding at the end of the first lease was common (see chapter 2). The building of new fronts was clearly not motivated by fashion, as is often the case in other contexts. Refronting might rather have been a minimum necessity, especially after 1760 when a new Building Act imposed a public duty of repair on private property,

empowering local justices to force owners to rebuild where passers by were endangered; this provision and other legislation were more effectively enforced from 1774 (see chapter 9).[96] Where rebuilding was not complete, it was often extensive, but sufficiently conservative to preserve original overall form, that is scale, plan form, massing and fenestration patterns.

Poor-quality bricks and brickwork would have been widespread, especially as the price of bricks rose during building booms. Naturally, little of this remains evident. Where it does, it can be seen that there are failures to close brickwork up to openings the jambs, of which sometimes do not align vertically from storey to storey. Bonding and brick colour are irregular, window heads ungauged, and 'place', ½ and ¾ bricks, that is those normally kept out of sight, are out in the open. The existence of such workmanship in humble buildings such as this is not surprising, but seeing such exceptional survivals, and recognising that they were not unusual when new, heightens an awareness that the absence of information about lower-status housing has led to skewed representations of the housebuilding world of eighteenth-century London. These buildings are important evidence of an all but 'craft'-less vernacular building tradition in the metropolis.[97]

In alluding to craftsmanship it should be emphasised that in none of the early Bethnal Green houses for which there are records is there evidence pointing to internal use of even the meanest classical vocabulary. Eaves cornices or simple bracketed hoods may have been the extent of classicism on the outside of Bethnal Green's houses, as at Nos 3–9 Hare (Cheshire) Street of around 1725 (fig. 88). This group is of additional interest for having fronted one of the area's few eighteenth-century courts, Hare Court, four more three-storey houses, each about 17 ft square (figs 57, 59, 73 and 87).[98] In surviving buildings interiors are invariably refinished, little more than a few lengths of plain panelling and a few flights of winder staircases enduring (figs 89–91). Given the scarcity of survivors and of early views, this absence of evidence is not, of course, sufficient proof that weavers' houses did not have ornamentally wrought surfaces, but it is suggestive. Had well-finished interiors existed, their quality might have given them a better chance

89, 90 and 91   No. 113 Bethnal Green Road, interiors, showing (bottom to top) the blocked first-floor fireplace with the front staircase beyond; the panelled first-floor back room that was added c.1773 with part of a six-light 'weavers window'; and the garret looking to the head of the stair and chimneystack. Photographed 2000 (EH, BB99/09148, 09150 and 09152).

of survival. Perhaps classical architecture was an alien irrelevance to the builders and journeymen weavers of eighteenth-century Bethnal Green. This makes a stark contrast to Spitalfields, where there is much surviving evidence of high-quality craftsmanship, especially internal joinery. The street-name plaque on No. 125 Brick Lane which greets those travelling from Spitalfields into Bethnal Green seems a decisive exception to this generalisation (fig. 92). It appears to read, 'THIS IS SCLATER Street 1778', making it all the more intriguing for the stylistic conservatism of its classicism.[99]

The differences between the houses of Bethnal Green and Spitalfields cast the houses of Spitalfields in a new light. Vernacular elements in Spitalfields houses that have heretofore seemed odd when compared with the West End or other fashionable metropolitan districts may usefully be related to housebuilding practices in adjoining Bethnal Green. Similarly, small late Georgian houses, in Spitalfields or further afield, that do not exhibit classical finish, need not be understood as the decline of a craft tradition, but simply as examples from above the 'vernacular threshold', the earlier correspondents of which have disappeared without record.

The houses of Bethnal Green's eighteenth-century weaving district seem exceptional in a wider context. They stand apart not just from Spitalfields, but from other areas as well. The absence of classicism in Bethnal Green contrasts markedly with evidence of its presence in smaller-scale housing in other eighteenth-century artisan suburbs, from other parts of east London and south of the river from Southwark to Deptford (see chapters 2, 4 and 6). In these places three- or four-room artisans' houses of the late seventeenth and eighteenth centuries, often timber built, do engage with classicism in doorcases, chimneypiece mantels, door architraves and so on. Bethnal Green seems to retain evidence of a distinctive and lower-status class of housing that was perhaps peculiar to the silk trade and not built much more widely. Further, the Bethnal Green buildings were larger than their more decorated counterparts in other artisan districts, comparative confirmation that they were indeed built for multiple occupation by the poor.

Conclusions

The history of housing in the Bethnal Green silk-weaving district in the period 1660 to 1820 falls into four broad phases. The earliest houses, of which least is known, appear to have been small, often only three square rooms in two storeys and garrets, perhaps being local variants of a once widespread central suburban and

92   The street-name plaque on No. 125 Brick Lane, inscribed 'THIS IS SCLATER Street 1778'. Photographed 2002 (EH, AA33057).

east London house type of which relatively little evidence survives (see chapter 2 and figs 72, 73 and 78). By 1720 larger houses that derived from these smaller antecedents had become dominant, to meet the need for housing a growing industry and its workforce as cheaply as possible (figs 66, 67, 71, 73, 76–80, 87 and 88). These houses had bigger frontages and were at least three full storeys tall, but they were not deeper, with one room on each storey, good light remaining crucial. The vertical layout, the front staircases, and much other evidence all tend to indicate that they were designed for dense multiple occupation by poor journeymen weavers who would have used the rooms as both workshops and homes. These tenements continued to be built into the 1770s, sometimes as large blocks (figs 54, 68 and 75). From the 1760s until about 1800 there was greater architectural discontinuity, with a shift away from high-density tall tenements towards a more horizontal distribution of workshop homes that brought with it greater external regularity, but which remained inchoate and highly variable in its architecture (figs 74, 80, 81 and 83–5). This transition resolved itself in the early years of the nineteenth century in a standard small single-occupation house type that was widely adopted and debased in a revival of high-density development in a low-rise form (figs 69, 86 and 93).

This crude typology prompts two main questions: why did the 'vertical' tenements appear when they did?;

93 Seabright Street, Bethnal Green, weavers' houses of *c.*1820 with workshops over living spaces. Photographed 1958. Demolished (LMA).

and why were they succeeded by 'horizontal' single-occupation houses when they were? The first thing that can be said about the determinants of the architecture of this housing is that aspirational emulation can, unusually, be dismissed as insignificant. Population growth, the small-scale nature of building enterprise and widespread poverty among weavers were all important local factors in the early eighteenth century. Poor weavers needed to be housed locally, and, in the absence both of existing houses available for conversion and of other local routes to prosperity for those who could engage in house-building, it was worthwhile building for this market, but in an economic manner, that is with high densities. Workshop tenements were a local solution to a local problem.

The decade from 1763 was a turbulent and traumatic time in the silk district, dominated by increased poverty and riots, leading up to the cathartic settlement of the first Spitalfields Act in 1773, which fixed prices but forbade combination. A revival in housebuilding in the 1760s that included much rebuilding brought displacement, immigration and loss of tenure, upheavals that would have exacerbated a climate of insecurity, underpinning the trade-based fears that caused rioting. Local economic circumstances still favoured high-density housing and Bethnal Green's new houses of the 1760s remained traditional if uncertain in form (figs 68 and 75), seeming to reflect the tumult amid which they were built.

It has been argued in the context of eighteenth-century Paris that the density and permeability of tenement living effaced privacy and built solidarity.[100] Distinctions between 'open' and 'closed' space were impossible, and neighbourhood life, 'that intimidating shadow',[101] was fundamental to identity. In London's silk district dense and vertical living conditions might have had similar consequences, reinforcing the unusually strong tendency to combination that characterised the weavers. Such domestic environments perhaps emphasised common status as mutually interdependent cells within an exploited economic group, rather than separate status as atomised, counterposed and competing families.

After 1770 new approaches to house architecture were being explored; compare Nos 190–92 Brick Lane of 1778–9 to their neighbour of 1763–5 at Nos 194–8 (fig. 80). Enforcement of the Building Act of 1774 was probably a significant factor in the move away from the building of tall tenements. Builders could no longer get away with timber construction, so full-width windows were no longer possible to the rear other than on the upper storey. This would have meant less good light than heretofore on the intermediate levels of buildings of three or more storeys, and that stair placement would no longer have been influenced by lighting considerations. Further, new rates based on ground-floor footprints and value imposed progressively greater party-wall thicknesses and administrative fees, and thus additional building costs. Anything below about 18 ft square on plan could be the cheapest or fourth rate, but if of high value it might fall into a higher rate. This might have tended to reduce the profitability of a tall four-room tenement, perhaps third rate by virtue of its value, as against a low two- or three-room house that might be fourth rate because less valuable (see chapter 9).

The nature of speculative development was changing at more fundamental levels. After 1773 there was a small building boom, perhaps enabled by the new-found stability of the silk trade, with some lower-density development for those just able to begin to climb out of poverty. This would have diminished the speculative appeal of high-density housing, particularly for those larger building operators who had risen out of the locality and become responsible for containing its volatility. David Wilmot, the magistrate who helped hang rioting weavers in 1771 and draft legislation in 1773, and who had experimented with 'suburban' development away from the weaving district, also became involved in extending the old district eastwards from 1771 in rows of smaller houses intended for single occupation, as on Granby Row (fig. 74). This move away from established local housebuilding practice came at precisely the time when the oppositional nature of local social relationships had become alarmingly manifest.

Yet it is neither the impact of legislation nor that of speculative innovation that is most striking about Bethnal Green's late eighteenth-century houses, but the extent to which externally derived standardisation was slow to take hold. There was no more than a gradual move away from traditional practices, the local architectural vocabulary enduring through tenement building, vertical living and elevational irregularity (figs 54, 74, 78, 81 and 84). Rebuilds were regularising to a limited degree, but more remarkable for the way that they perpetuated earlier form. The functional necessity of the 'weavers' window' meant that a prominent element of the local vernacular remained present in the area's more standardised domestic architecture well into the nineteenth century, long after housebuilding elsewhere around London had been wrestled away from local roots.

Most of the area's housebuilding in the late eighteenth century continued to be controlled by local artisans. Wilmot, though himself of humble local origins, was perhaps not as representative of the area as his successor, Joseph Merceron, who was evidently never seduced by

the emulative possibilities of upward mobility. For many, any ideas of such mobility would have been obviously chimerical; local roots and artisan identity would have been far more valued, and likely to have instilled politically radical and culturally conservative attitudes in line with those of the riotous weavers. The street-name plaque of 1778 at No. 125 Brick Lane is a proud affirmation of place, but so 'old fashioned' as to seem to reflect resistance to rather than ignorance of 'taste'. For the inhabitants of Bethnal Green, legislative or emulative 'improvements' represented at best alien priorities, at worst a threat.

After 1800 classical regularity, perhaps more accurately capitalist standardisation, had accompanied intensive speculative development in penetrating to the bottom of the social scale to supply a proletarianised working class with housing, high-density but low-rise, sometimes providing more living space, but in many cases mean and densely overbuilt. It is no coincidence that those who at this time had choices were yearning for the 'picturesque' (see chapter 7). Uniform classical architecture had come to connote a kind of domestic repression. In Bethnal Green this new housing perhaps helped to bring the riot-prone area a measure of calm, offering improved conditions in what were intended as small single-family homes, firmly separated by brick walls, with workshops distinct from living spaces (fig. 93). These succeeded the tenements that had provided indoor lives of work and sleep in the same room, among peers up and down stairs whose equivalent lives would have been intimately – probably too – familiar. There is resonance here with improvements to rural housing, as promoted from 1797 by the Board of Agriculture in a reaction to the French Revolution that sought to reduce the likelihood of sedition among peasants and increase social stability,[102] but this was not a premeditated or concerted programme of social control or housing reform, and there were not major clearances of the existing tenements. It was not Haussmannisation *avant la lettre*, but, in the context of London-wide improvements, a gradual unpicking of the local vernacular architecture, accompanied by a halting introduction of housing forms of external if not polite derivation. A move away from the purpose-built tenements that had typified local domestic architecture from the 1720s to the 1770s paralleled the Spitalfields Acts, both changes offering better living conditions and undermining combination, and thus working in harmony to loosen the bonds of weaver identity. Legislative and architectural reform brought relative tranquillity in the short term, but extreme hardship in the longer run.

Chapter 4

ACROSS LONDON BRIDGE:
TANNING, TIMBER AND TRADITION
IN SOUTHWARK AND BERMONDSEY

A Rich Man took up his residence next door to a Tanner, and found the smell of the
tan-yard so extremely unpleasant that he told him he must go. The Tanner delayed his
departure, and the Rich Man had to speak to him several times about it; and every
time the Tanner said he was making arrangements to move very shortly. This went on
for some time, till at last the Rich Man got so used to the smell that he ceased to
mind it, and troubled the Tanner with his objections no more.

Aesop[1]

In 1766 John Gwynn, writing *London and Westminster Improved*, looked at Southwark and found it 'entirely destitute of that useful regularity, convenience and utility, so very desirable in commercial cities'.[2] Irregular as Southwark was, commerce thrived; perceptions of convenience and utility depend on the ends desired. In turning to this historically complex district, this chapter focuses particularly on its eastwards adjunct, Bermondsey, where a number of eighteenth-century houses survive and where the leather or tanning industry was concentrated. These houses, together with comparative evidence from demolished buildings, show that important aspects of the area's eighteenth-century domestic architecture, particularly the persistence of timber construction and the continuing use of a range of traditional house plans, were more strongly based in local precedent than in what was happening elsewhere in London. With regularity absent it is important to draw out variety. This makes for a narrative structure unlike that of the preceding chapter. Again there is a need for introductory scene-setting sections on the particular histories of Southwark and Bermondsey up to the middle of the eighteenth century. Thereafter a large number of buildings are briefly discussed, approached via constructional materials and plan form, emphasising variability. The chapter concludes with an account of the late eighteenth-century transformation of St George's Fields on the west side of

Southwark, and its ripples across to Bermondsey, bringing in some later buildings. This opens up the question of the impact on vernacular variety of those who came after Gwynn, permitting an oblique view of the degree to which they either got rid of the tanner or grew used to the smell.

Southwark

South London was, and, many would say, still is, a place apart. The Thames forms the clearest possible boundary, differentiating London's growth south of the river from less discrete expansion to the north, east and west. Situated on the south side of London Bridge, medieval Southwark was *the* City suburb. At the same time it had a clear identity as a separate and coherent 'town', though lacking formal status as such.[3] During the late sixteenth century and the seventeenth there was enormous growth in this substantial settlement (fig. 95). In 1678 Southwark had a population of about 30,000 in its four core parishes, making it, if separated from London, England's second largest town; as Defoe put it, 'A royal city were not London by.'[4] The early eighteenth-century population of a somewhat wider area (including Bermondsey and Rotherhithe) was about 60,000, rising to more than 90,000 by 1800, figures that at each date are larger than

94 (*facing page*)   No. 74 Bermondsey Street, boarding on the timber-framed former back wall on the second floor of a house of 1755–8 (see figs 113, 115 and 116). Exposed and photographed during refurbishment in 2000 (EH, BB000104).

95 Southwark, *c.*1690 (from Richard Morden and Philip Lea, *London, Westminster and Southwark*, ed. 1700). This map extract is edited to obscure the City of London (see fig. 6), to emphasise that Southwark was a major settlement in its own right, not simply suburban spread or a transpontine appendage (GL).

the contemporary populations of any English towns other than London.[5]

But this is misleading. Southwark emphatically was a part of the metropolis. However populous and however much across the water, it was not an independent town. In many real senses it was, after all, an appendage to the City. It was a repository of that which the City wished to expel, and of those who wished to avoid the City's jurisdiction. By the sixteenth century Southwark was 'London's scrap-heap, the refuge of its excluded occupations and its rejected residents.'[6] Its long-standing reputation for the unsavoury embraced prisons and sanctuaries from arrest, brothels and bear-pits, playhouses and noxious industries. All was not disreputable. Proximity to the only southerly road access to the capital meant a proliferation of inns, as well as a number of large town houses and bishops' palaces. The 'outside' status of the place helped to make it a centre of radicalism and religious Dissent, and many immigrants (especially Flemings) settled in Southwark.

Inns, from the Tabard (gone, but immortalised by Chaucer) to the George (surviving, and immortalised by the National Trust), combined with other forms of 'catering' or victualling to make up Southwark's biggest early-modern industry. Large-scale brewing was a major employer by the seventeenth century, by when other polluting or dangerous trades – tanning, fulling, glass

making, saltpetre making and lime burning, had been pushed into Southwark. There were also river-based occupations, many watermen settling upstream from the bridge on Bankside. Inland there was much manufacturing that was small in scale and domestic in its organisation. Textile-based work employed many, and by the eighteenth century London's hat making was concentrated in Southwark, felt being a byproduct of tanning, which, of course, generated much leatherworking. Southwark was not like Spitalfields; it had a broad-based and varied economy. There was no segregation of trade groups, but a great mix, something that fragmentation of property ownership did nothing to reduce. As in other parts of London, though perhaps with more opportunity here, people often had multiple occupations or jobs, to avoid dependence on a single source of income. It was of long-standing significance that Southwark was beyond the controls and restrictions of the City companies, though many who settled in the district were 'citizens'.[7]

Southwark's development pattern was largely determined by the marshy terrain that lay south of the river. The main roads derived from the causeways through low-lying ground that were the Roman approaches to the first bridge over the Thames. Early development was in ribbons along these roads. Southwark was not walled or otherwise nucleated, and there was neither the inchoate sprawl of east London nor the coherent estate development of west London. The main road was what is now Borough High Street, the thoroughfare that linked with London Bridge, perhaps already continuously built up as far south as the Church of St George (near Borough Underground Station) in the twelfth century. Its frontages were valuable, with plots sometimes as narrow as 8ft, and its houses tended to be tall and deep, relatively high-status premises that invariably incorporated shops. Tooley Street ran eastwards from near the bridge, and Bankside extended to the west along the riverside, these roads together forming the 'T' that was the skeleton for Southwark's early development, the eastern arm linking to Bermondsey or Barnaby Street, the ancient route to Bermondsey Abbey.[8]

The physical limitations to Southwark's growth forced great density of habitation. Huge population increase could not be accommodated on marshland, so growth was squeezed onto a proliferation of short alleys off existing roads in the late fifteenth century and the early sixteenth, many of the poor living in single rooms in tenements. Until the early seventeenth century there continued to be scope for the formation of more alleys or yards off the main roads. Thereafter further population pressures had to be contained either through the subdivision of existing houses, many households taking lodgers, or by building out into the marsh. The best addresses tended to be on the main roads, the worst on the relatively inaccessible alleys. The area's few rich inhabitants were concentrated near the bridgehead; the poor were more peripheral. But this dichotomy obscures the intermediate. It has been estimated that in the early seventeenth century only 31 per cent of householders in Boroughside (near the bridge) were wealthy enough to pay rates, but that 43 per cent or nearly two-thirds of the rest were not 'poor', being rather an in-between group that was getting by on 'adequate income'.[9]

Some seventeenth-century housing development arose from change in Bankside's Clink manor. This had been the London base of the Bishops of Winchester since the twelfth century, but had become a centre of prostitution, theatre and other entertainments by the sixteenth century. Lancelot Andrewes, the last of the bishops to live in Southwark, died in 1626, and the localities' playhouses and bear gardens were closed down later in the century. Industry, notably glass making, moved into the area, and new houses were scattered through the hinterland, some along existing meandering paths, others on newly laid-out roads, most being short-lease low-grade properties for humble occupation. Further west was the manor of Paris Garden, sold in 1660 and made the Parish of Christ Church in 1671. That difficult ground condi-

tions constrained building away from the main roads is confirmed by the fate of the new parish church, which succumbed to subsidence and had to be rebuilt in 1738–41.[10]

Most seventeenth-century housebuilding would have been initiated locally, much of it by appropriately skilled tradesmen, that is carpenters or bricklayers. Alleys and yards were generally held as single blocks, with few larger landholdings. Though many alley developments were mean and poor, they were not without diversity. There were some good alley properties, and there would have been much intermediate housing for the large numbers of artisans engaged in domestic industry, notably hatters and leatherworkers ranging from saddlers to shoe makers. Alley tenements were typically held on short leases; there was much subletting and great mobility within the locality, as always security of tenure rising in proportion to wealth. Parliamentary surveys made in 1646 show that three- and four-room timber houses in Southwark then fetched annual rents of £2 to £5, those that were more valuable often incorporating cellars and shops. Multiple occupation was widespread, and even some new-built houses were divided. Alley tenements could be had for £2 a year or less. Such rents probably remained broadly typical in the eighteenth century.[11]

In 1676 a fire destroyed 624 houses in the north part of the 'town'. This prompted an Act to control rebuilding, modelled on that used in the City a decade earlier. Along and behind Borough High Street there are some brick-built survivals from the post-1676 reconstruction, not least the George Inn. There was another major fire in 1689, necessitating rebuilding further south. These fires evidently brought about comprehensive rebuilding along Borough High Street, but little change to either the street pattern, or to building practice in Southwark's hinterland.[12]

Bankside's backways harboured Protestant Nonconformity in the late seventeenth century. In an area previously renowned for licentiousness, several substantial timber meeting houses were built amid modest new dwellings. There is early nineteenth-century documentation of what then remained of two of these meeting houses, one just off what is now Park Street. The other, on what became Zoar Street just south of Bankside Power Station (Tate Modern), incorporated a school in a long barn-like structure adjoining a tenter ground, and was said to have been built in 1687–8. Though timber buildings in a poor district, these large meeting houses were not without sophistication, both having had three galleries and massive Tuscan columns. The use of the Tuscan Order had associations with Protestant primitivism in seventeenth-century London, and in this

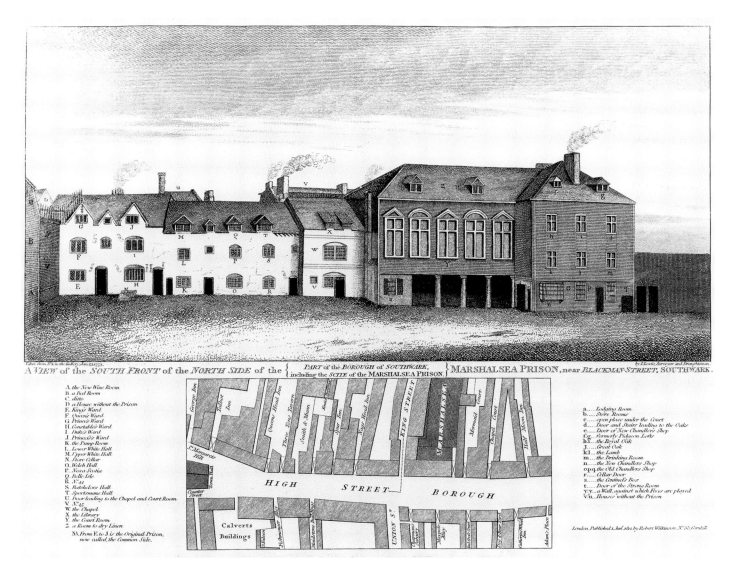

96   The Marshalsea Prison, behind Borough High Street, as recorded in 1773, the accompanying map showing the density of development off Borough High Street (from Wilkinson, ii, 1825).

respect these chapels appear to have resembled contemporary brick parish churches in the area: Christ Church (1670–71) and the rather more coherently classical St Mary Magdalene, Bermondsey (1675–9), built to designs by the local carpenter Charley Stanton that were closely based on earlier seventeenth-century London models.[13]

By 1700 London's expansion as a port and the growth of dependent facilities had brought about all but continuous riverside development to the east all the way to Rotherhithe and beyond (fig. 95). Land to the north and south of Tooley Street had been built on, extending almost into Bermondsey. Ribbon development ran south along Blackman Street (now the southern part of Borough High Street) and Kent Street (now Tabard

Street). To the west the land south of Bankside up to Gravel Lane (Great Suffolk Street) remained sparsely built, and houses were even more scattered in Christ Church. Beyond there was an inland settlement at Lambeth Marsh (now Lower Marsh, just south of Waterloo Station; fig. 4), but little else north or east of Lambeth Palace.[14]

Southwark was perceived to be London's most densely populated neighbourhood in the early eighteenth century, an impression that would have been reinforced by the presence of several horribly congested prisons, hard by the inns and the alleys off the High Street (fig. 96).[15] The area still contained a good deal of poor and overcrowded housing. Until mid-century new

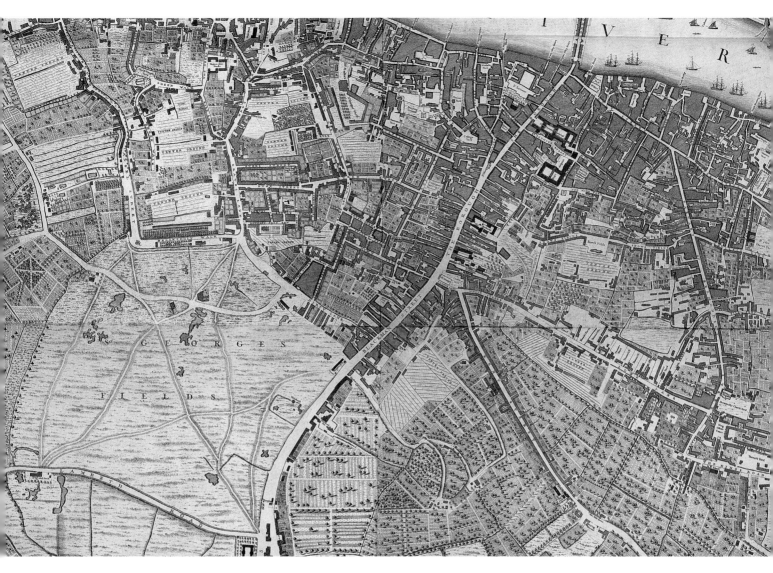

97   Southwark and Bermondsey in the 1740s (from John Rocque, *Plan of the Cities of London and Westminster and Borough of Southwark*, 1746).

development continued to be marginal, modest and unco-ordinated, pushing the extent of the built-up area further out to the south-east and the south-west, but only slowly (fig. 97). In terms of the volume of construction activity and the location of new houses, the replacement of earlier buildings was as significant a factor as green-field development. Guy's Hospital, founded in 1721 on a site east of Borough High Street, backed onto largely open ground to the south when new. On Bankside the Anchor Brewery grew greatly to become a major presence, where Samuel Johnson became a long-term intimate and house guest of Mrs Thrale, the wife of the brewery's owner.[16] Beyond and into Christ Church there was little physical change, with tenter

grounds and gardens still occupying much of the land at mid-century. In the late eighteenth century significant transformation did come in the shape of a concerted push to urbanise the hinterland. This new approach to development depended on the formation of new bridges and roads (see below).

Southwark's lack of formal or administrative identity was the result of the City having consistently thwarted the rise of an independent civic entity from the fourteenth century onwards. However, the City was not in control. Southwark had diffuse administrative independence, the lack of a single outlet for which perhaps served only to strengthen informal identities. Martha Carlin has concluded that sixteenth-century Southwark had a 'communal spirit' despite huge recent growth.[17] Thereafter, Jeremy Boulton has shown, there was great continuity in the local economy, Southwark society being underpinned by constancy in its industrial base of innkeeping, leathermaking, brewing and a mix of other trades. Local bonds remained strong in the seventeenth century, subdistricts having their own distinctive and mutually interdependent identities. The local social system cohered informally through economic improvisation and resilience in a flexible milieu, as well as formally through the structures of local administration. Despite increasing population density, the enduring intermingling of trade groups, and tenurial transience, there was stability and attachment to the place or 'neighbourhood'. As was the case in other parts of London, localism was deeply rooted; few people knew areas beyond their own neighbourhood and social horizons were narrowly restricted. This does not mean that Southwark was inward-looking or self-enclosed, simply that it was locally cohesive, and that it brought a strongly traditional or vernacular society into the eighteenth century. It was entirely urban, but it had much in common with conventional understandings of rural society. Any perceptions of urban anomie would be anachronistic.[18]

Bermondsey

Immediately south-east of Southwark is Bermondsey, a district and parish that has its own history and its own characteristics. However, awareness of local distinctiveness should not overwhelm consciousness of affinities and interdependence between adjoining areas. Some boundaries are more sharply defined than others. Bermondsey's growth in the eighteenth century was part of the expansion of London, and more particularly of that of Southwark, into which it merged. In so far as eighteenth-century Bermondsey was London it was London mediated through Southwark. Bermondsey warrants attention here because, more than in other parts of Southwark, some ordinary eighteenth-century housing survives, in the western or inner parts of the parish (fig. 98).[19] However, there is not much. Understanding the domestic architecture of eighteenth-century Bermondsey depends on comparative evidence of demolished buildings from Southwark as well as from Rotherhithe, the riverside district beyond Bermondsey. With the core that was Southwark briefly accounted for, a general exploration of Bermondsey, touching briefly on Rotherhithe, is needed to prepare the way for the examination of particular buildings in all these districts.

Eighteenth-century Bermondsey was neither urban nor rural, but marginal (figs 95, 97 and 98). Settlement in the parish was in two concentrations, then differentiated as the 'water side' and the 'land side'. By 1700 the riverfront was built up on both sides of St Saviour's Dock, the inlet that was the mouth of the River Neckinger and part of the parish boundary. There were mansions and tenements, as well as mills and wharves. To the east seventeenth-century streets followed the diverted channels of the Neckinger in a water-bound area that had come to be known as Jacob's Island. Other streets were being laid out further east near the river in Rotherhithe, which had been a place of docks and shipbuilding since the sixteenth century.[20] Inland, Bermondsey Abbey had stood on high ground near what is now the junction of Tower Bridge Road and Abbey Street. Bermondsey Street existed by the early thirteenth century as a causeway to what had then been a Cluniac Priory. Commercial and residential development of the street ensued, and by the sixteenth century there were numerous inns and taverns. By the beginning of the eighteenth century it had long been 'furnished with Buildings on both sides',[21] and back alleys or courts were being built. Long Lane was a medieval track linking the abbey to the southern end of Southwark; it had attracted less concentrated development.[22]

The suppression of the abbey in the sixteenth century took the independent heart out of Bermondsey. Thereafter the district came increasingly to be understood as an amorphous extension of Southwark, not least because industry, much of it spilling out from Southwark, had become the focus for growth in the locality. The open land around the 'island' on which the abbey had been built was largely low-lying marsh divided by a network of tidal streams. This suited the tanning industry, the processes of which were both water intensive and dependent on open space for large yards with open pits. Tanning, the conversion of animal hides into leather through steeping in infusions of oak bark, was already present in the area during the medieval period, by when its noxiousness had made it unwelcome in the City. Those fleeing the Great Plague in 1665 were allegedly attracted to the tanning pits of south London, in the desperate hope that there were medicinal virtues in the nauseating smells.[23]

The Bermondsey leather industry was thriving by 1703, when it was granted a royal charter. It was concentrated around Bermondsey Street and Long Lane, with the north side of the latter becoming a serried rank of tanyards. There was much early eighteenth-century expansion, including onto parts of the former abbey's grange lands to the south-east. An estate-management

98 (*facing page*)   West Bermondsey, indicating sites with surviving eighteenth-century houses, as identified in 2000.

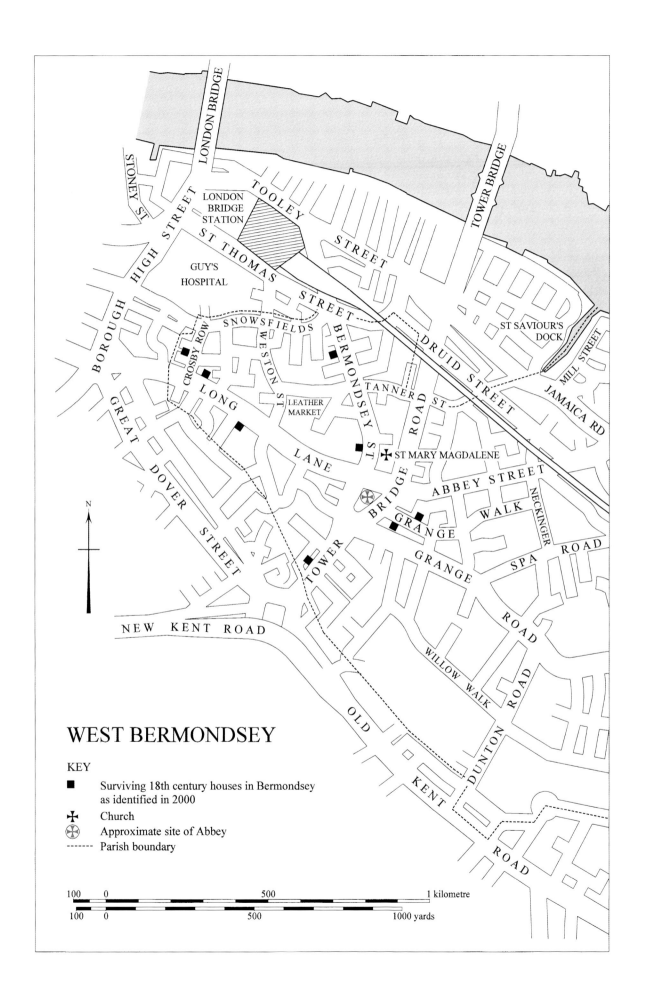

STONEY ST

LONDON BRIDGE

TOOLEY STREET

TOWER BRIDGE

HIGH STREET

LONDON BRIDGE STATION

GUY'S HOSPITAL

ST THOMAS STREET

BOROUGH

CROSBY ROW

SNOWSFIELDS

WESTON ST

BERMONDSEY

DRUID STREET

ST SAVIOUR'S DOCK

MILL STREET

JAMAICA RD

LONG

LEATHER MARKET

TANNER ST

BRIDGE ROAD

GREAT DOVER STREET

LANE

BERMONDSEY ST

✝ ST MARY MAGDALENE

⊕

ABBEY STREET

NECKINGER

GRANGE

WALK

TOWER

GRANGE

SPA ROAD

NEW KENT ROAD

ROAD

WILLOW WALK

DUNTON ROAD

OLD KENT ROAD

N

WEST BERMONDSEY

KEY

■   Surviving 18th century houses in Bermondsey as identified in 2000

✝   Church

⊕   Approximate site of Abbey

------   Parish boundary

| 100 | 0 | 500 | 1 kilometre |

| 100 | 0 | 500 | 1000 yards |

letter of about 1755 observed that: 'from Whiteing grounds, wash grounds, tenter grounds, orchards and gardens is now made tanyards, felmongers yards, and glew yards.'[24] Growth of the industry continued, and in 1792 Lysons recorded that 'Bermondsey is a place of very great trade. The tanners [. . .] are very numerous. And carry on that business to a greater extent than is known in any other part of the kingdom. From a natural connection between the several trades, there are also many woolstaplers, fellmongers, curriers, and leather-dressers, and some parchment makers.'[25] In 1805 there were 1,500 tanners in the wider district.[26] The trade prospered and endured because of the topographical conditions (access to water and land), the availability of raw materials (hides coming from animals brought to London for slaughter), and, most crucially, the proximity to London's huge market for leather goods, principally shoes.

The leather trade was much less susceptible to fluctuation than was the silk trade, on both the supply and demand sides, and work was steady. This constancy and the nature of the work, at best semi-skilled, meant that tanning workers were not like weavers (fig. 99). They were not notably educated, organised for the defence of their mutual interests or otherwise radicalised. Rather, and perhaps harshly, they were said to have been 'miserable, illiberal, sluggish, illiterate bigots'.[27] Bermondsey's tanneries and associated industrial premises were small-scale operations in the eighteenth century, and rents in

the area were comparatively low. In the 1680s Henry Howkins, a Bermondsey Street fellmonger, paid only £8 a year for a new six-room house with a yard containing one- and two-storey sheds and a stable with a hayloft.[28] In 1710 a tanyard with a house, barn, drying shed, kilnhouse, stable, hayloft, ash-hole, beamhouse and forty-one pits fetched an annual rent of only £10.[29] Many Bermondsey tanners lived in houses in front of their yards. One of these was Ralph Burdon, who had few non-essential items among the goods inventoried in 1721 in his four-room two-storey dwelling. Another tanner's inventory, from 1739, indicates that Richard Christopher and his family lived more comfortably, though not lavishly, in six well-furnished rooms in a house of two storeys with garrets. The kitchen and counting house were linked spaces.[30] The tanning work-force would have been more humbly housed nearby, in alleys and courts off Bermondsey Street and Long Lane. Even in 1813 there were few large operators, tanners then employing an average of seven to eight men. Eighteenth-century tanning has not left monumental trace, the processes having required little more than makeshift timber sheds, both as cover for wet processes and as drying lofts; the innumerable wood-lined tanning pits were open to the elements. Mechanisation was introduced slowly in the early nineteenth century, but Henry Mayhew's description of 1850 can be applied retrospectively as an evocation of eighteenth-century Bermondsey:

99a and b   The defleshing of animal hides and the rolling and hanging of tanned hides, as depicted in terracotta roundels from Bermondsey's Leather Hide and Wool Exchange, 1878. Photographed 2001 (EH, AA020705–6).

What may be styled the *architecture* of the district is that rendered necessary by the demands of its chief commerce. Long, and sometimes high, and always black wooden structures, without glass windows, but with boards that can be closed or opened to admit air at pleasure, irregularly surround a series of closely-adjacent pits, filled to the brink with a dark, chocolate-coloured, thick liquid.[31]

As Lysons noted, there were many related trades in the area. Along Bermondsey Street there had been woolstaplers since at least the sixteenth century, some in substantial houses, with wool warehouses in yards behind. In 1791 Thomas Pennant commented that 'Bermondsey-street may at present be called the great Wool-Staple of our kingdom. Here reside numbers of merchants who supply Rochdale, Leicester, Derby, Exeter, and most other weaving countries in this kingdom, with that commodity.'[32] The use of felt made hat making a more directly dependent spin-off from the tanning industry. Hatters were numerous in Bermondsey from around 1660 or earlier, this skilled and workshop-based trade having a reputation for activism that the tanners lacked.[33] An inventory of 1735 shows John Dobson, a Bermondsey feltmaker and hatter, as having lived in three rooms, a kitchen, chamber and garret, with an additional 'stuff room' and workshop. Domestic and working space intersected, with seventy-five hats and 28 lb of camel hair in the chamber being worth £34, as valuable as all the other goods in the house.[34]

Reliable figures for the housing stock of eighteenth-century Bermondsey are lacking, but the nineteenth-century sources that Dorothy George used are broadly indicative. They suggest a doubling in the overall number of houses in the parish through the eighteenth century, rising from about 1,500 to about 3,000.[35] The prevalence of short leases and poor timber construction would have meant that many houses existing in 1700 needed rebuilding by 1800; of those eighteenth-century houses that do survive, several are on sites that had been first developed earlier. It is reasonable to conclude that something in the order of 2,000 or more houses were built in Bermondsey during the eighteenth century. Of these only a tiny handful survive. Land ownership was fragmented, not least because of the parcelling off in the late seventeenth century of what had been the abbey lands. The only substantial estate was largely made up of open land in the outer parts of the parish, south of Long Lane and east of the former abbey site. This was pulled together with built-up riverside property to form what, from 1759, was the estate of James West.[36] Development in inner parts of the parish was incremental and inter-

stitial. In front of, between, and across the road from the tanyards, Long Lane was built up with houses, of varying but largely modest quality (figs 97 and 100). The land to the north that was known as Snow's Fields came to be lined on its north side by piecemeal development along a road of the same name (Snowsfields), linked through to Borough High Street as King Street (latterly Newcomen Street) between 1759 and 1774.[37]

Like Southwark, Bermondsey was a stronghold of Dissent, home to numerous Nonconformist sects, some gathering in their own modest meeting houses, some in makeshift adaptations of other premises, some as conventicles in public houses or individual members' homes, as was the case with the Muggletonians, active on Bermondsey Street in the mid-eighteenth century.[38] A meeting house built by Sayer Rudd in 1736 next to a tenter ground in Snow's Fields passed to John Wesley in 1743 (fig. 97). Following a schism, Wesley was excluded from the building and so built another meeting house nearby in 1763–5. This preceded and perhaps encouraged the formation of Crosby Row, running north-south between Snowsfields and Long Lane, with the meeting house on its west side (figs 98 and 100).[39]

In concentrating on tanning and the 'land side', the 'water side' of Bermondsey has been left behind. This area was different, effectively part of continuous riverside development from Southwark through to Rotherhithe and beyond (fig. 95). Strong economic, social and cultural links between riverside districts gave them a supra-local identity that was not shared with inland localities (see chapter 6). In the seventeenth century and the early eighteenth, riverside development boomed with London's expansion as a great international port. Behind and alongside timber wharves, mills, rope walks and ship- and boat-building yards, there were houses, varying greatly in size and quality. Many seventeenth-century developments, particularly those on Jacob's Island (fig. 101), may always have housed numbers of the poor, those who eked out livings from lighterage (plying barges) or casual labour on the wharves or in the yards. Even here, however, there were better houses for river-dependent merchants and sea captains. On East Lane, just east of Jacob's Island, John Warner, a horticulturist, kept a noted garden in the mid-eighteenth century.[40] Beyond there were rope walks, then numerous streets newly laid out in the late seventeenth century and the early eighteenth, in quasi-grid-pattern development extending back from the riverfront west of the church of St Mary, Rotherhithe, itself rebuilt gradually from 1714 to 1747. Large, durable and relatively regular rows of brick houses were built on these streets, local residents including Thomas Coram, the great timber importer and founder

100   Southwark and Bermondsey in the 1790s (from Richard Horwood, *Plan of London*, 1799).

of the Foundling Hospital.[41] The making of Jamaica Row (now Old Jamaica Road) along the landside of some of these streets in the 1750s stimulated limited subsequent development. At the end of the eighteenth century, as was the pattern elsewhere, some much smaller dwellings were inserted in courts or alleys amid the bigger early eighteenth-century Rotherhithe houses, two- and three-room houses, some no more than about 10ft square on plan.[42]

The 'water side' does have to be held apart as a place with its own coherence, not least in its architecture. As to the 'land side', the dependence on the watercourses and open yards of tanning made Bermondsey a particularly inchoate part of eighteenth-century London's industrial fringe, a highly varied and unstructured semi-urban environment. Much of the land between Long Lane and Snowsfields stayed open, not for agriculture, but for tanning and other industrial purposes (fig. 100). To the south and east Bermondsey was more conventionally rural, even remote, most of the West Estate staying undeveloped and waterlogged well into the nineteenth century. Behind and beyond buildings at the west ends of Grange Road and Grange Walk, among which there were several large broad-fronted houses, there remained market gardens and meadows.[43] The enduringly pastoral nature of this part of Bermondsey is reflected in the story of Bermondsey Spa. Thomas Keyse, an artist, formed a pleasure ground and tea garden on waste ground around 1765. With the discovery of a chalybeate spring this became a spa in 1770, adding the further attractions of musical performance and pyrotechnical displays from 1784. This improbable resort survived until 1806, its existence now commemorated through Spa Road and Spa Gardens (fig. 98).[44] Bermondsey's peripheral nature is further reflected in that, despite the formation of Abbey Street in 1806, the structure of Bermondsey Abbey was still in 1841 thought by the antiquary G. W. Phillips to survive better than any comparable 'religious edifice in or near London, owing to its remote situation'.[45]

The perception on the part of an early Victorian antiquary that Bermondsey was 'remote' arose from the late Georgian east–west conceptual division of London. Bermondsey Abbey was as close to St Paul's cathedral as was Westminster Abbey, and the growth of eighteenth-century Bermondsey was as much part of London's suburban expansion as was development in Mayfair. Yet it is not just West-End-based prejudice that makes it difficult to reconcile Bermondsey with prevailing understandings of the burgeoning metropolis. Despite the presence of a mix of skilled urban trades, from hatters to shipwrights, numerous Dissenting congregations and *ad hoc* urbani-

sation, Bermondsey did retain a shapeless semi-rural and marginal character through the eighteenth century. As in Southwark there was great economic and social continuity. Growth was significant, but incremental and traditional. This was not a place that would have felt itself to have been undergoing radical change, though change there was, perhaps less discernible for being incoherent in its nature.

Timber Houses

Timber housebuilding was the norm in Southwark and Bermondsey well into the eighteenth century, continuing widely after the Building Act of 1707 made it illegal. Wood was readily available, not least through local timber wharves, and there was not good brickearth in the immediate locality. Where conspicuous consumption was either impossible or unsought, timber would have been the building material of choice. Perhaps it was also understood that relatively lightweight timber building made sense on poor ground.

As discussed in chapter 2, timber housebuilding occurred in eighteenth-century London well above the bottom of the scale, but little survives so it is forgotten. Nineteenth-century condemnation of the timber houses of the earlier period as 'slums' has provided another barrier to understanding. The *locus classicus* for such deprecation is the description in *Oliver Twist* of Jacob's Island, where seventeenth-century streets were woven into the meanders of the Neckinger, which became significantly more polluted in the years around 1800 as industry encroached and the watercourses ceased to be tidal (figs 95 and 101). For Dickens this was 'the filthiest, the strangest, the most extraordinary of the many localities that are hidden in London.'[46] His account made the area notorious. It is often quoted, but it is worth revisiting to illustrate how, in the noble cause of progressive reform, awareness of the former decency of much humble seventeenth- and eighteenth-century housing was lost (fig. 103). Jacob's Island of the 1830s was said to be

> Jostling with unemployed labourers of the lowest class, ballast-heavers, coal-whippers, brazen women, ragged children, and the very raff and refuse of the river.' There were 'Crazy wooden galleries common to the backs of half-a-dozen houses, with holes from which to look down upon the slime beneath; windows, broken and patched, with poles thrust out, on which to dry the linen that is never there; rooms so small, so filthy, so confined, that the air would seem too tainted even for the dirt and squalor which they shelter;

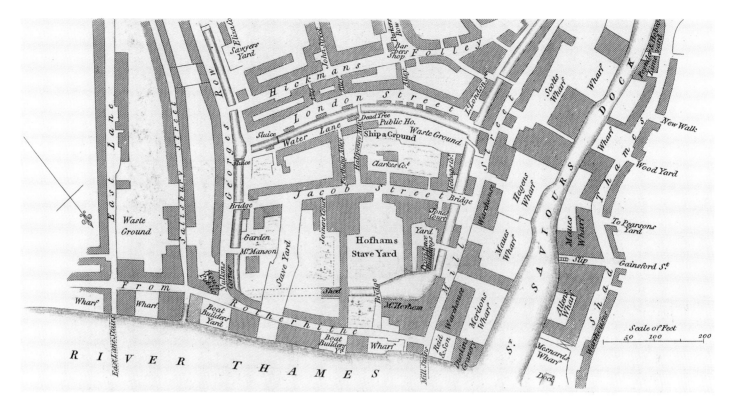

101   Jacob's Island in 1813, with south at the top (from Wilkinson, ii, 1825).

wooden chambers thrusting themselves out above the mud, and threatening to fall into it – as some have done; dirt-besmirched walls and decaying foundations; every repulsive lineament of poverty, every loathsome indication of filth, rot and garbage; all these ornament the banks of Folly Ditch.[47]

To look more closely at some of the buildings of Jacob's Island, and to suggest that they might at one time have been representative of something other than degradation and decay, is not to impugn Dickens or his motives, nor to deny the desperate character of the area by the 1840s when the watercourses had become muddy ditches rife with cholera. An earlier and somewhat less architecturally polemical depiction shows London Street (latterly Wolseley Street) behind the Neckinger (figs 101 and 102). Beyond the skinny-dipping child and the ramshackle privies, sufficient explanation for cholera, there is a long row of houses, the west end of a street of about forty.[48] Seemingly of the seventeenth century, and possibly post-1660, timber built and with little depth on maps, each house probably comprised three rooms in two storeys and a garret. Small windows over doors indicate front-staircase layouts, and raise the possibility that

the houses were designed for multiple occupation. There were also what appear to be first-floor oriel windows on most of the houses. This north-facing feature might reflect design for workshop use, but given that local employment seems always to have been largely river-based, perhaps it simply indicates awareness of amenity in the presence of what would have been a pleasant watercourse. Comparable timber housing on Jacob Street, without the oriels, continued to be built in the eighteenth century and survived into the era of photography (figs 104 and 105).[49]

Whether new-built or decrepit, such houses offered limited living space. On Hickman's Folly (later Dockhead then Jamaica Road) there were rows of eighteenth-century two-room timber houses, some of which survived up to the middle of the twentieth century (fig. 107). A late nineteenth-century account of the interior of one of these houses gives a rare if sardonic insight into how they were experienced. Upon entering:

you were straightaway in the combined reception-drawing-living-scullery-kitchen-and-extra-bedroom. A very convenient arrangement which saved a lot of

103 *(facing page bottom)*   The backs of seventeenth-century timber houses on Mill Street, Jacob's Island, with a gallery alongside 'Folly Ditch'. Dickens described the banks of this watercourse and former millstream in *Oliver Twist*. The drawing illustrated an article campaigning for improved housing (*The Builder*, 1855).

102 (*above*) Seventeenth-century timber houses on London Street, Jacob's Island, 1813. Each house in the long row probably comprised no more than three rooms, with first-floor oriel and staircase windows. Engraving from a drawing by Robert Blemnell Schnebbelie (from Wilkinson, ii, 1825).

104   A row of three-room timber houses, probably with late seventeenth-century origins, on Jacob Street, Jacob's Island. Photographed 1927. Demolished (EH, AP23).

105   Nos 24 and 26 Jacob Street, Jacob's Island. Note the central chimney positions and the Sun Fire Insurance marker of 1773. Photographed shortly before their demolition in 1934 (LMA).

106 (*above*) A timber-built block, perhaps eighteenth-century tenements, at Birdcage Alley, The Mint, near Borough High Street, Southwark. Watercolour by Thomas Hosmer Shepherd, 1840 (BM).

107 (*left*) An eighteenth-century two-room timber house on Dockhead (previously Hickman's Folly and latterly Jamaica Road). Photographed 1950. Demolished (LMA).

walking and housework. Opposite the fireplace you opened what appeared to be a cupboard door and ascended the stairs to the remaining room overhead.

The steps rising in front of your nose were placed conveniently for putting one's hands on in order to assist the assent, rendering handrails unnecessary. In the room itself the floor space still remaining was very sensitive to touch, and care was necessary in treading lest the vibrations displaced the cups from their nails in the room below.[50]

Some of the timber buildings in eighteenth-century Southwark and Bermondsey had considerably more than two rooms. On Birdcage Alley, just north of Mint Street (near present-day Borough Underground Station), there was a large timber building (fig. 106). The Mint had been a refuge for debtors and was notorious for lodging houses. These were inhabited by those committed to the King's Bench Prison who were wealthy enough to buy conditional liberty within a limited adjoining area known as 'the Rules', also by those taking advantage of this area to claim sanctuary from arrest, as well as by those formerly imprisoned who chose to stay. The status of the locality as a sanctuary was removed by statute in 1724, but notoriety persisted. People paid high rents for their refuge in the early eighteenth century, 2s 6d a week (more than £6 a year) for a room.[51] The large building of three full storeys with garrets looks like four houses, but perhaps, given the character of the area, it was built as a block of tenements. The proportions of the front and the pitch of the roof suggest a build date in the eighteenth century. The area had numerous other wooden houses that were certainly tenements by the nineteenth century.[52] On Bermondsey Street (opposite Lamb Walk) there was an impressive run of gable fronts to comparably large buildings (fig. 108). Used in the late nineteenth

108   A late seventeenth-century timber row on Bermondsey Street. Laid out with central chimneystacks, the row was perhaps built as shops and tenements, though here converted to curriers' and leather-dressers' premises. Photographed by Henry Dixon in 1881 for the Society for Protecting the Relics of Old London. Demolished c.1900 (EH, DD 65/8).

109 Timber houses of *c*.1690 on Ewer Street, Southwark, showing the south side looking south-west. The small windows over the entrances of these three-room houses presumably lit stairs, suggesting design for multiple occupation. Watercolour by Thomas Hosmer Shepherd, 1852. Demolished (LMA).

century as curriers' and leather-dressers' premises, with louvred leather-drying lofts, this jettied timber range probably had origins in the late seventeenth century as houses, perhaps always subdivided and incorporating shops. A similar though less extensive group stood on the other side of Bermondsey Street opposite Crucifix Lane in 1820.[53]

This much gives little more than a vague impression of the range of Southwark and Bermondsey's timber houses. Well-documented buildings are scarce, but a few instances will help to build a more complete picture. In the Bankside hinterland off the east side of Gravel Lane (Great Suffolk Street) was Ewer Street (figs 95 and 97), its main section now obliterated by railway lines. In existence by 1682 but not fully built up until after 1690, this peripheral and flood-prone street was lined with small timber houses, evidently built in short rows that probably represent distinct speculations (fig. 109). By the

1850s, when occupants included hat makers, leather-workers, shoe makers and many Irish labourers, the street was a verminous and cholera-ridden slum.[54] However, despite fenestration that seems to indicate design for multiple occupation, the eaves had modillioned cornices, an ornamental gesture that suggests respectable origins. Such are confirmed by Strype who, in 1720, described Ewer Street as 'a clean handsome street pretty well built and inhabited'.[55] This is another reminder that nineteenth-century perceptions of then dilapidated houses are anachronistic in the eighteenth century. So strongly and unquestioningly has the nineteenth-century repudiation of the small houses of seventeenth- and eighteenth-century London been inherited that no less an historian than Peter Earle, unaware of what Ewer Street actually looked like, interpreted Strype's description as indicating that Southwark was not unlike Westminster in having 'fine town houses', assuming, one

134

110 A timber row of *c*.1700 built opposite Christ Church, Southwark. Photographed as Nos 72–8 Colombo Street in 1927, No. 72 being in the foreground. Demolished 1948 (EH, AP).

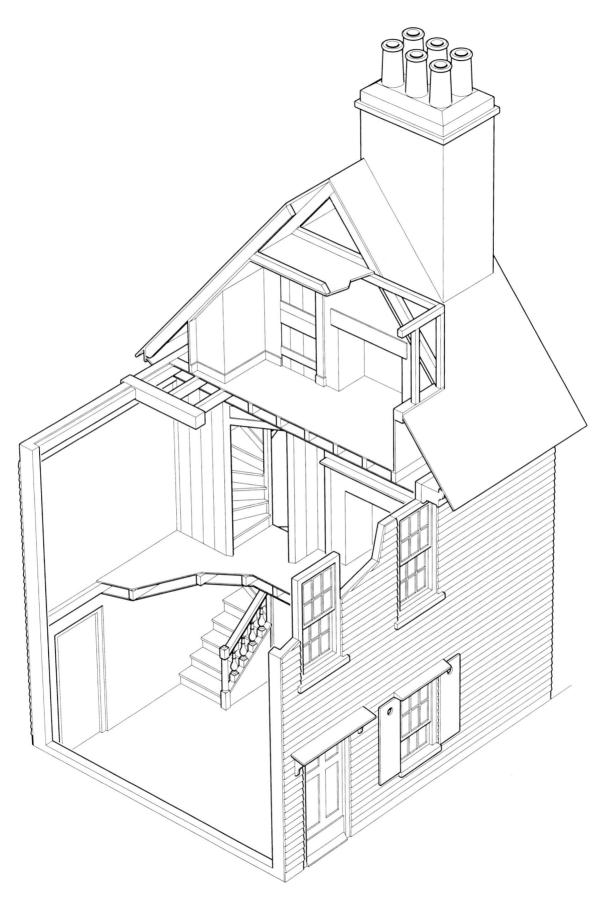

111   No. 78 Colombo Street, Southwark, a perspective reconstruction of one of the three-room timber houses of *c.*1700, showing the presence of classical amenity even in such humble buildings.

112 Nos 86–90 Snowsfields, Bermondsey, showing early eighteenth-century timber houses at Nos 87 and 88. Photographed in the late nineteenth century. Demolished (EH, BB016853).

suspects, that such words could not have been applied to anything so modest as three-room timber houses.[56]

Further west a similar row survived until 1948, long enough to be recorded by both the Royal Commission and the Survey of London, and thus to provide firmer evidence that Southwark's timber houses of this scale were not mean, that, in its own manner, artisan housing partook of amenity if not of gentility. Just across from Christ Church, Southwark, on Colombo Street (previously Green Walk, then Collingwood Street) a row of five timber houses faced the churchyard (figs 95, 97, 110, 111 and 123). The row might have been built in the late seventeenth century, perhaps following the opening of the church in 1671, but to judge from its appearance it might equally well have been of the early eighteenth. As the early name of the street indicates, the houses stood

in open fields until the late eighteenth century. Tradesmen and artisans occupied them thereafter, as they most likely had done previously. Each house was about 16ft square and originally comprised three rooms. There were winder staircases behind the chimneystacks, but across the backs of the ground-floor rooms there were single prominent straight flights of stairs, embellished with vase balusters of striking quality given the size of the houses. The first-floor fireplaces had moulded mantel shelves, in rooms which also had plank doors and exposed ceiling beams.[57] There were many outwardly similar groups of houses all through these southern districts, some with external aspects that indicate eighteenth-century build dates, as near Shad Thames, on Long Lane in Bermondsey, or across to Rotherhithe.[58] On the south side of Snowsfields just east of Crosby Row, there was a timber

113 Nos 70–78 Bermondsey Street. The stuccoed brick fronts at Nos 74 and 76 disguise eighteenth-century timber-framed buildings, while No. 78 in the foreground has seventeenth-century origins. Photographed 2003 (EH, AA03341).

114 No. 76 Bermondsey Street, an eight-room timber-framed house of c.1730 with a central-staircase plan. The second-floor back-room interior, photographed during refurbishment, shows light softwood timber framing in the flank and back walls, with straight angle braces and rough studwork. Photographed 2000 (EH, BB000120).

115 No. 74 Bermondsey Street, the surviving house of 1755–8, showing the second-floor internal partition with triple doorways to, from left to right, a former bed enclosure, a closet and the staircase. Photographed 2000 (EH, BB000101).

116   Nos 72 and 74 Bermondsey Street, a perspective reconstruction of a pair of timber-framed four-room houses of 1755–8, shown as having been brick fronted.

pair on a fringe site that was open ground until the early eighteenth century (figs 95, 97 and 112).

All these buildings have gone. At Nos 74 and 76 Bermondsey Street two eighteenth-century timber houses survive, behind brick front walls (fig. 113).[59] The taller house at No. 76 was present by 1744 when, despite a frontage of only about 14ft, it was one of the more highly rated houses in the vicinity. To judge from the visible fabric it was then fairly new, probably no earlier

119 (*facing page*) No. 61 Hopton Street, a two-room, cellar and garret house of 1699–1703. Blind openings create a regular four-bay elevation, the projecting porch appearing to be an addition to permit independent access to the upper storeys. Photographed *c*.1900 (EH, BB001525).

117 (*left*) No. 80 East Lane on Bermondsey's 'waterside', a six-room early eighteenth-century brick house with a central-chimneystack plan. Photographed 1949. Demolished (LMA).

118 (*below*) Nos 26–34 Mayflower (formerly Prince's) Street, Rotherhithe, built 1721–6 on a gated street as an outwardly regular 'terrace' of 'sea-captain's houses' with Doric doorcases. The houses mixed central-chimneystack and rear-staircase plans. Photographed by S. W. Newbery, 1953. Demolished (EH, BB54/1758)

tion continued in Bermondsey into the second half of the eighteenth century (fig. 105), even up to 1774 when London's new Building Act made more effective provision for the enforcement of the long-standing ban on timber housebuilding (see chapter 9). Southwark and Bermondsey show why this was then necessary.

The prevalence of timber housing in and around early to mid-eighteenth-century Southwark is emphasised here because it goes against expectations. However, timber was far from universal. The area's better housing had long since been brick built, in part as a result of the legislation relating to rebuilding along Borough High Street after the fires of 1676 and 1689. Naturally, brick buildings have had a better survival rate. Branching off

120 No. 89 Long Lane, much rebuilt, but the last of a row of eight three- or four-room houses of *c*.1700. Photographed 2000 (EH, AA004706).

121 Nos 17 and 18 Lower Marsh, Lambeth, two early eighteenth-century brick houses viewed from the back, the London Eye beyond. Photographed 2002 (EH, AA03070).

than around 1720, as redevelopment of an already long-inhabited site (figs 114 and 123).[60] In a deep central-staircase layout eight rooms were disposed around a spacious dogleg staircase with turned balusters. No. 74 is a very different building, about 16 ft by 18 ft on plan, probably built in 1755–8, and originally comprising only four rooms with ancillary spaces (figs 94, 114, 115 and 123). There is no evidence of early decorative finish beyond cyma-moulded door architraves, but the house retains its timber frame in the flank wall abutting No. 76 and to the rear where, astonishingly, there is still early boarding. The position of the chimneystack astride the north flank wall suggests that No. 74 was originally half of a pair with No. 72, which was rebuilt in the nineteenth century. Ratebooks seem to confirm that Nos 72 and 74 were built together in 1755–8, perhaps always incorporating shops. In 1778 Robert Atkinson, a cheesemonger and dealer in coals and earthenware, took out an insurance policy on his dwelling at No. 74, then described as 'brick and timber', perhaps indicating that the front wall has always been brick.[61] Whether originally brick fronted or not, No. 74 Bermondsey Street provides standing evidence that timber house construc-

the High Street was Counter Lane (now Stoney Street), a road of some width and a good address, described by Strype as 'a street of pretty good account, indifferent large and square with well built and inhabited houses having trees before the doors, which renders it pleasant.'[62] Things have changed, but No. 5 Stoney Street is a surviving early eighteenth-century brick building with a front of rather more than 20ft, a substantial house in local terms and a brandy and hop merchant's home in the late eighteenth century. It is telling that in relation to most surviving eighteenth-century houses in the West End it looks small (figs 122 and 123).[63]

Far away at the semi-rural periphery, the predominance of industry did not prevent the building of some even larger brick houses of a 'suburban' nature, more likely for prospering local industrialists than for commuters. Nos 142–8 Long Lane, a semi-detached pair of around 1732, faced the tanneries, a step away on the south side of the road. It incorporates a Corinthian doorcase and internal embellishment that included a distinctive depiction of a tanyard.[64] There was also larger-scale gentility on Grange Walk, east of the site of the abbey, in the shape of regularly proportioned and ornamentally finished two-storey brick houses, inserted into gaps between pre-existing timber houses in the years around 1700. Three single-fronted double-pile houses (Nos 9–11) were added to the reconstituted and gable-fronted remnants of the abbey gatehouse, and two double-fronted (five-bay) single-pile houses went up beyond and opposite (Nos 67 and 68).[65] Even on Jacob's Island there was something of a mix, as on George Row, where Bridge House (marked 'Mr Manson' on fig. 101) was an unusual and finely finished brick building bearing the date 1706, with shaped gables, ornamental overdoors and well-appointed interiors. It was not a single house but a mirrored or semi-detached pair with a service range.[66] A bit further out on East Lane there was a mixed row of simpler two- and three-storey early eighteenth-century brick houses (fig. 117) leading south to the larger East House.[67]

Close to the river, where transport costs were lower, bricks would have been less of an extravagance. This is not, however, sufficient explanation for Rotherhithe's many early eighteenth-century brick terraces, which were closer in scale and appearance to the Barbon model of high-status speculative development than anything in Southwark or Bermondsey. Adequately firm ground and a market in the shape of those living well from maritime enterprise were probably more important factors. Mayflower (formerly Prince's) Street was developed by Richard Wright in 1721–6 with a distinctly regular and fashionable three-storey row that would latterly be

122   No. 5 Stoney Street, one of Southwark's better early eighteenth-century houses, brick built and laid out with a rear-staircase plan. Photographed 2002 (EH, AA033071).

termed a 'terrace' (figs 118 and 123).[68] Comparable rows extended inland as far as Jamaica Road (formerly New Paradise Street, then Paradise Row), and stood into the 1960s.[69]

Across the whole area most brick houses until about 1760 were those at the better end of the market, comprising six or more rooms. However, in many districts some smaller houses were brick built, providing further evidence that habitations of three or four rooms were entirely respectable. No. 61 Hopton Street, Bankside, the last and much photographed survivor of a row of five approximately 20ft-square buildings of 1699–1703 is one instance, and not, in fact, all that small (figs 119 and 123).[70] No. 89 Long Lane, though much rebuilt, is

123a and b (following pages)   Reconstructed plans of houses in Southwark, Bermondsey and Rotherhithe.

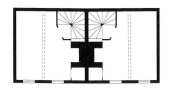

72-74 COLOMBO STREET
SOUTHWARK
FIRST FLOOR
c.1700 (dem.)

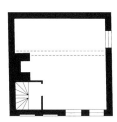

61 HOPTON STREET
BANKSIDE
FIRST FLOOR
1699-1703

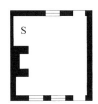

89 LONG LANE
BERMONDSEY
GROUND FLOOR
c 1700

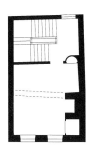

91 BOROUGH HIGH STREET
SOUTHWARK
FIRST FLOOR
early 18th century

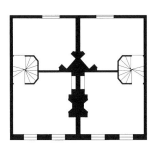

32-34 SUMNER STREET
BANKSIDE
FIRST FLOOR
c 1700 (dem.)

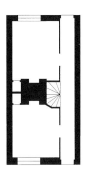

72 EAST LANE
BERMONDSEY
GROUND FLOOR
early 18th century (dem.)

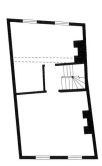

210 BERMONDSEY STREET
BERMONDSEY
FIRST FLOOR
early 18th century

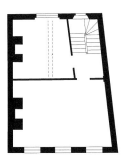

5 STONEY STREET
SOUTHWARK
SECOND FLOOR
early 18th century

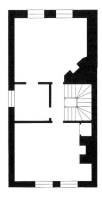

100 BERMONDSEY WALL
BERMONDSEY
FIRST FLOOR
early 18th century (dem.)

1 0   5   10   15   20 metres

5 0   30   60 feet

S = FORMER STAIR POSITION

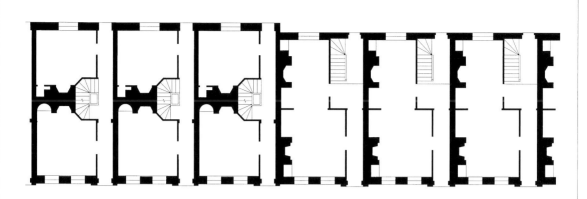

28-33 MAYFLOWER STREET
ROTHERHITHE
GROUND FLOOR
1721 to 1726 (dem.)

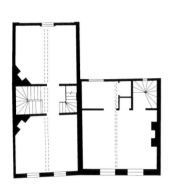

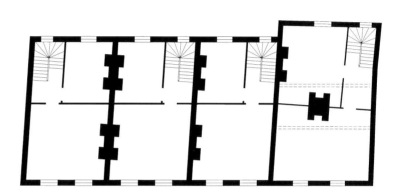

74-76 BERMONDSEY STREET
BERMONDSEY
SECOND FLOOR
No 76: c.1730   No 74: 1755 to 1758

21-27 CROSBY ROW
BERMONDSEY
FIRST FLOOR
1770-1773

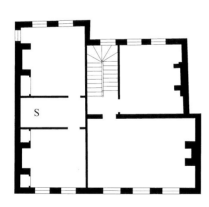

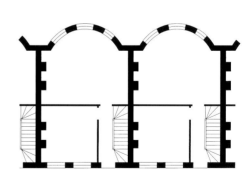

17-18 LOWER MARSH
LAMBETH
FIRST FLOOR
early 18th century

162-164 NEW KENT ROAD
SOUTHWARK
GROUND FLOOR
c.1790

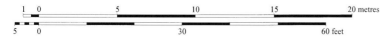

S = FORMER STAIR POSITION

another isolated survivor, coming from a row built some time between 1680 and 1740 (figs 120 and 123). Away to the west, Nos 17 and 18 Lower Marsh are early eighteenth-century survivals from the marginal hamlet of Lambeth Marsh, No. 17 being a spacious house comparable with No. 5 Stoney Street, and No. 18 a more modest 15ft-wide building (figs 121 and 123).[71]

All these examples have been invoked to draw out the nature of the housing stock in Southwark, Bermondsey and Rotherhithe during the early to mid-eighteenth century, that is diversity through a spectrum of options that would have accommodated all but the poorest people, housing artisans, tradesmen and entrepreneurs of widely varying means. Small timber houses were widespread, but larger brick ones were interspersed, and sometimes timber houses were large and brick ones small. Houses were not susceptible to straightforward stratification based on material, size or finish. Anything was possible; standardisation was absent. This indeterminacy is also evident in plans.

Tradition and Diversity in House Planning

The subject of plan form has already been addressed (see chapter 2), introduced through a rough-and-ready typology distinguishing four basic arrangements – the one-room plan and three two-room plans: the central-chimneystack, central-staircase and rear-staircase layouts. This framework continues to serve in looking at the houses of Southwark and environs, but its artificiality becomes more apparent as variation is encountered (fig. 123).

The one-room plan varied in ways already seen. From Colombo Street, Hopton Street and Long Lane there are smaller and larger examples, in brick or timber, with stairs before or behind the stack. There are other instances where the one-room plan becomes something rather more. No. 91 Borough High Street is a well-appointed early eighteenth-century brick house of four storeys and as many rooms, behind which rooms there rises a generously proportioned open-well staircase with Doric newel posts. A finely detailed first-floor niche cupboard is further evidence, if such is needed, that one-room-plan living did not preclude fashionable finish and should not be associated with poverty.[72]

No. 74 Bermondsey Street (figs 94, 113, 115, 116 and 123), the house of 1755–8, has a fascinating layout, a rational variant of the simple one-room square that has not been recorded elsewhere in London. Given the poor rate of survival of houses of this type, it is unlikely that it was unique. The first- and second-floor interiors indicate that

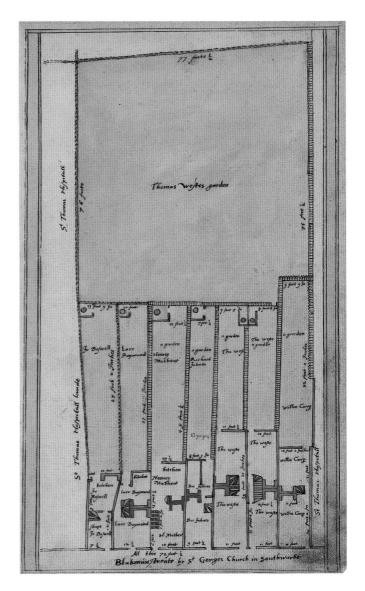

124 A plan of 1611 showing timber houses on Blackman Street (the site of Nos 291–9 Borough High Street), Southwark, with back-to-back chimneystacks alongside staircases separating front and back rooms (GL, with permission from Christ's Hospital, Horsham).

the rear third of the house was subdivided behind partitions with triple doorways, to provide for the winder staircase, unheated enclosures into which beds may have been squeezed, and two intervening closets. The bed enclosures would have given the house greater privacy and flexibility, without compromising its economy of construction. Unheated bed enclosures have medieval origins, but they remained common in the eighteenth century and are more usually encountered in higher-status houses as bed alcoves.[73] So perhaps this was conservatism and ingenuity in tandem. Further inventiveness in the pursuit of maximum usable space is evident in the

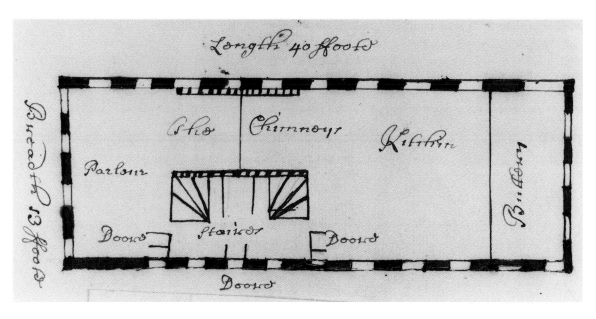

125 A plan from a Bermondsey building agreement of 1684, projecting a timber-framed house with a 'lobby-entry' layout (By permission of the British Library, MS Egerton Charter 325).

garret, where interrupted collars are pegged into posts, to create continuous headroom (fig. 116).

The origins of the central-chimneystack plan are discussed in chapter 2. Southwark, Bermondsey and Rotherhithe provide evidence for closer consideration, leading into the eighteenth century. In Southwark this layout was present by the late sixteenth century. At the town's southernmost extremity near St George's Fields it was used in all but one of a row of seven narrow two-room-deep houses on Blackman Street. A building lease of 1585 specifies that one of these houses was to rise two-and-a-half storeys and be built of oak (fig. 124).[74] As has been argued, this layout does not need to be understood as deriving from the rural lobby-entry plan, given its early occurrence in London and its constructional and functional logic where timber houses with brick chimneys were being built on narrow urban plots.

The large and distinctly urban late seventeenth-century group opposite Lamb Walk on Bermondsey Street (fig. 108), perhaps built as shops and tenements, also appears to have had central-chimneystack layouts.[75] It is striking to find that as late as 1684 an apparently rural (broad-fronted) lobby-entry house was being built on the other side of the road (fig. 125). A building agreement and lease of that date show that a house and yard backing onto Bermondsey Street tenanted by Henry Howkins, a fellmonger, and owned by Thomas Markam, a 'citizen' fishmonger, were redeveloped by Henry Barrett, a 'citizen' carpenter, for £95. Barrett agreed to build the house with two storeys and garrets, plastered

and plain tiled to the front, boarded and pantiled to the rear. The layout suggests that the house was built away from the road, unless it adjoined a passage permitting side entry. The plan shows it as being entered via a lobby in front of the stairs, with a stack beyond heating the parlour to the left and the kitchen to the right. Beyond the kitchen there is an unheated buttery.[76] The building of a timber lobby-entry house within 2 miles of London Bridge in the 1680s, when Nicholas Barbon was in his pomp, gives an arresting measure of London's heterogeneity.

The central-chimneystack plan was widely used in the better-quality early eighteenth-century brick houses of Bermondsey and Rotherhithe. Around 1720, at about which time this layout seems to have fallen out of favour north of the river, it was flourishing south of the Thames, where any house with two rooms per floor would have been relatively high in status. The form generally followed that published by Moxon in 1700 (fig. 44), at differing scales, as on East Lane and Mayflower Street (figs 117–18 and 123). This similarity should be understood not as practice following Moxon, but as practice and Moxon both following long-standing precedent. Mayflower Street had four central-chimneystack-plan houses immediately adjoining and continuous with a run of rear-staircase-plan houses in an outwardly undifferentiated and notably regular terrace. Despite this external regularity, ample open-well staircases in the central-chimneystack houses were allowed to disrupt the geometry of the rooms, indicating that spacious circulation was more desirable than regularity of room shape. There were various other ways that this traditional plan met gentility. At Nos 284–90 Jamaica Road (formerly Paradise Row) the plan was adapted to larger houses with a three-room layout and four-bay fronts.[77] At the end of Bermondsey Street where it met Grange Road (formerly the junction of Star Corner and the King's Road) two 16ft-front 'Moxon'-plan houses were built some time after 1737, as infill between two pre-existing double-fronted houses in front of a tanyard.[78] The differential popularity of this plan across London can not be explained by constructional economics. Its endurance as a south London vernacular form seems to reflect cultural difference, remoteness from the West End meaning relatively weak influence from emulative gentility. The continuing strength of precedent met and was reconciled with fashion.

Central-staircase-plan houses were also common in late seventeenth- and eighteenth-century Southwark, often where narrow frontages made alternatives difficult. This layout is thus found on Borough High Street. Nos 35 and 37, late seventeenth-century buildings that had been substantially rebuilt in the early nineteenth century, and which were demolished in the 1990s for the Jubilee Line Extension, retained central-staircase layouts, as do other large but narrow late seventeenth- or early eighteenth-century buildings at Nos 53, 146–8 and 164 Borough High Street.[79] On Bankside No. 49 (Cardinal's Wharf) is a comparably scaled early eighteenth-century house, only 15 ft wide, but very deep. An open-well stair rises between the front and back rooms.[80] More humbly, Nos 32 and 34 Sumner Street (formerly Maid Lane) survived into the 1960s on a site that is now opposite Tate Modern (figs 123 and 127). This mirrored pair was empirically attributed to the late seventeenth century in the 1950s, but it might have been built any time up to about 1760. The layout with winder staircases away from the chimneystacks was unusual in London, and more typical of seventeenth-century Amsterdam.[81] From early eighteenth-century Bermondsey Nos 9–11 Grange Walk are of comparable width, but wholly brick built and more comfortably finished with full-width dogleg stairs.[82] The timber house of around 1730 at No. 76 Bermondsey Street (figs 113, 114 and 123) is no wider, though deeper and taller, with regular room shapes and a secondary stair rising to the garrets. No. 18 Lower Marsh was probably comparable before partial rebuilding. Finally, Nos 241–5 Long Lane are three 11ft-wide three-storey houses, early nineteenth-century replacements of what were probably timber predecessors. Even after 1800 limited width forced central-staircase layouts. Constrained frontage made the rear-staircase layout,

where stairs and back rooms share the plot width, impracticable.

The central-staircase plan was sometimes used in wider early eighteenth-century houses where a closet or bed alcove could be gained in the space beside the staircase, as at No. 100 Bermondsey Wall, near Cherry Garden Pier, where there was space for an open-well stair,[83] or No. 210 Bermondsey Street (figs 123 and 126). It was also adopted, as it was in other districts, in large free-standing mirrored (semi-detached) pairs. Such houses could be lit and entered from the side, such access being either the only entrance, as at Bridge House on Jacob's Island (1706), or secondary and linked to a coach-house, as may have been the case at Nos 142–8 Long Lane (c.1732). These houses were thus, in effect, double 'fronted' and one room deep.

The last of the plan types to be considered is the rear-staircase plan that had become the norm in central and West End speculative development by about 1720 (see chapter 2). There is little to be said in relation to Southwark and Bermondsey before about 1770; evidence for this layout is notably absent, No. 5 Stoney Street and No. 17 Lower Marsh being exceptions. In Rotherhithe

126 No. 210 Bermondsey Street, an early eighteenth-century timber-framed house, raised and refronted in the early nineteenth century. Photographed 2001 (EH, AA020702).

127   Nos 32 and 34 Sumner Street, Bankside, late seventeenth- or early eighteenth-century brick-fronted timber-framed houses. Photographed 1928. Demolished (EH, AP13).

128 Nos 25 and 27 Crosby Row, two of four houses of 1770–73 that were built together with a unified façade, but mixing central-chimneystack and rear-staircase plans. Photographed 2000 (EH, BB000539).

it was more widely used, but not consistently, as has been shown (figs 118, 121, 122 and 123).[84]

Mayflower Street was only one of many developments to mix plan types promiscuously. Builders working contiguously were seemingly free to diverge even where there was co-ordination of the streetscape, design and production being interwoven. Even where it most closely approached standardisation, development in the area was never large in its scale, and small undertakings permitted continuing artisan control of the building process. This tended to mean the survival of earlier practices, but it also left scope for improvisation and experimentation. It certainly permitted difference and an architectural environment that reflected the area's socio-economic mix and physical shapelessness.

In some cases a single builder may have used different plans in adjoining buildings. This possibility, the continuing diversity of plan form into the late eighteenth century, the late adoption of the rear-staircase layout and incipient standardisation, are all illustrated by the surviving buildings at Nos 21–7 Crosby Row (figs 123 and 128). These houses were built on an as yet nameless road in 1770–73, when Wesley's new Meeting House was just to the north, Marshalsea Prison was a stone's throw to

the west, and there were views across garden ground to the east. The four three-storey brick houses had a unified front with continuous plat bands and parapets, and flush-frame sash windows in line, former unity having been compromised by some twentieth-century rebuilding. However, Nos 21–5 are each only about 16 ft wide with two closely spaced window bays. No. 27 is 22 ft wide, its two windows being much more widely spaced. The narrower houses all have rear-staircase layouts. The wider house has its identical close-string staircase similarly positioned to the rear, but it had a central chimneystack, latterly truncated. There are simple classical mouldings throughout, although on the second floor of No. 27 there are plank-and-muntin partitions, a surprisingly humble feature in a London house of this size and date.[85]

St George's Fields

Housebuilding and much more changed in Southwark and neighbouring districts in the late eighteenth century. St George's Fields was where Southwark was transformed into south London, where the vernacular

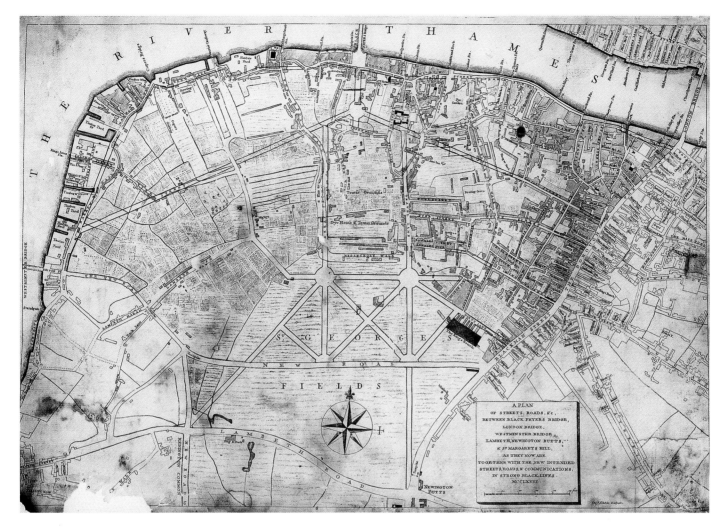

129 St George's Fields, showing an unexecuted scheme of 1768 for new roads running south from Blackfriars Bridge. Engraving by Thomas Kitchin (CLRO, Comptroller's City Land Plan 124).

met the polite, and the tanner met the rich man. In the eighteenth century St George's Fields, empty land south-west of Southwark extending across beyond Lambeth Marsh to Lambeth itself (fig. 95), represented different things to different people. The place was a swamp, a place of popular recreation, and a modest spa, waters being taken at the Dog and Duck on the road between Lambeth and Newington Butts (Elephant and Castle). It was also a traditional gathering place for 'rebels, rioters and apprentices'.[86] From early on its proximity to London meant that it was eyed for development, Defoe referring in the 1720s to an intention that 'St George's Fields should be built squares and streets.'[87] While the fields remained marshy and without good roads, this did not happen. They survived remarkably long as unenclosed open land. Meanwhile, the fringes of Bermondsey and Rotherhithe grew gently and incoherently, and

Southwark became more than ever congested, a circumstance exacerbated by the prisons in the district. Following an inquiry into cruelty and other irregularities, the King's Bench Prison was judged unsafe and dangerous. It moved to a new building in 1755–8, away from the built-up area to a site just west of Blackman Street on the edge of St George's Fields, wealthier prisoners retaining the freedom of the newly defined 'Rules'. Here John Wilkes was imprisoned. The outspoken critic of government and hugely popular defender of free speech had, for the second time, been convicted of libel in 1764. He avoided imprisonment through exile in France until returning to London in 1768. Within days of his being gaoled, 20,000 Wilkites had gathered on the fields before going to the new prison to demand their hero's release. They were met by gunfire in what came to be known as the St George's Field Massacre.[88]

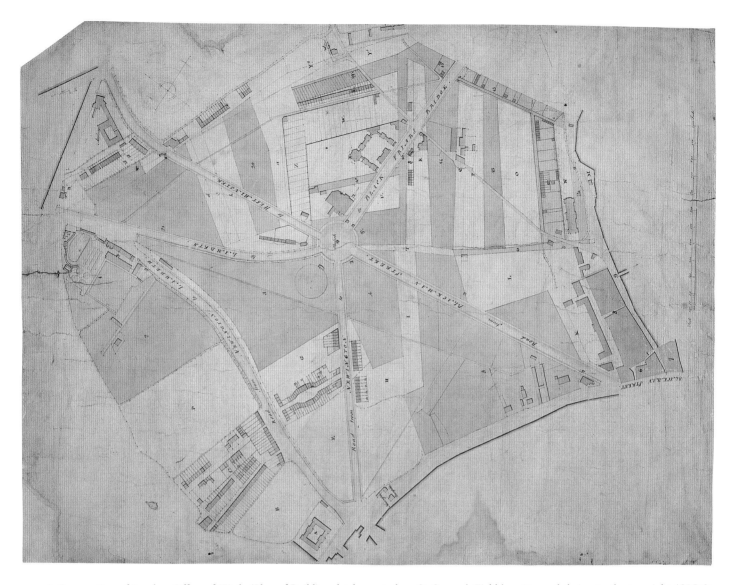

130   A Corporation of London Office of Works 'Plan of Buildings lately erected on St George's Fields', 1786, north being to the top right (CLRO, Comptroller's Bridge House Plan 103A).

To John Gwynn in 1766 St George's Fields was 'the only spot now left about London, which has not yet fallen a sacrifice to the depraved taste of modern builders, [. . .] the bridge now building at Black-Friars will undoubtedly be the means of entirely altering the face of that part of the city.'[89] It was, but not as Gwynn would have hoped. The making of bridges across the Thames, with attendant roads, certainly brought a transformation, improved transport and new building opportunities, though no clear reduction in the depravity of the built environment. After the opening of Westminster Bridge in 1750 an Act of 1751 prescribed new east–west roads to link the bridge to Borough High Street (which roads have become Westminster Bridge Road and

Borough Road), and the extension of an existing route from Lambeth to Newington Butts and on to the Old Kent Road near the site of Bermondsey abbey (New Kent Road). These roads were complete by 1760 when Blackfriars Bridge was projected. This next new bridge opened in 1769, and a new Act provided for further road building on St George's Fields, though rather less than some envisaged (fig. 129). A year later 'a handsome avenue'[90] (Blackfriars Road, formerly Great Surrey Street) had been pushed through to meet the Westminster Bridge–Borough High Street road at what became St George's Circus. In the middle of this nexus of urban improvement an obelisk was raised in 1771, and further new roads were extended south-west to the Dog and

152

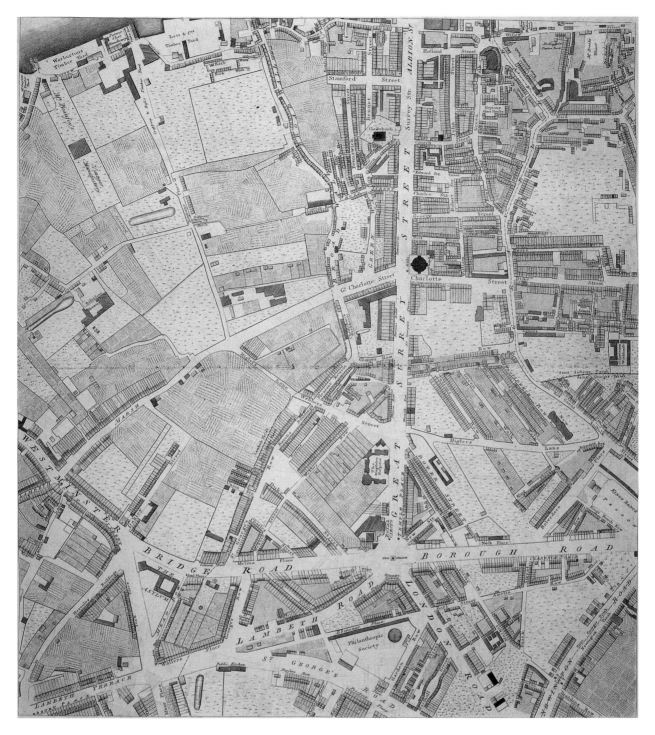

131　St George's Circus and environs in the 1790s (from Richard Horwood, *Plan of London*, 1799).

Duck (Lambeth Road) and south-east to Newington Butts (London Road) (fig. 130).[91] The driving force behind the building of Blackfriars Bridge and these roads was the City of London, through its Bridge House Committee, which owned much of the land on St George's Fields. The motivation was not simply the improvement of communications, though that was certainly important, these works being a crucial part of a wider campaign to boost commerce through the free flow of traffic into, through and out of the City. Blackfriars Bridge and associated roads need also to be understood as an episode in the City's centuries-long campaign to control and profit from its southern flank. The obelisk bore the City arms and the name of Brass Crosby, then Lord Mayor.[92]

These were major planned improvements, linking the City and Westminster with Southwark and Lambeth, and opening up large tracts of land south of the Thames to suburban development. In keeping with the improving spirit of Gwynn, this development was meant to be carefully controlled. The Act of 1769 specified that houses on the new roads had to be set back and that their fronts had to be 'Conformable to the General Design'.[93] George Dance, junior (1741–1825), Clerk of the City Works from 1768 in succession to his father, was responsible for the letting, enclosure and development of Bridge House property.[94] Through the 1770s there appears to have been little interest or activity. Southwark's long-standing reputation as a 'scrap heap' for London's 'rejected residents'[95] may have been a deterrent factor. Indeed, the 'scrap-heap' function was being reinvigorated, manifest in new ways that reflected London-wide attempts to transform the public sphere through new kinds of social intervention. On the west side of St George's Fields the Lambeth Asylum for Girls (House of Refuge or Female Orphan Society), founded by the magistrate John Fielding (see chapter 1), had used the Hercules Inn on the Westminster Bridge Road since 1758, establishing a larger presence in new buildings in 1764 (figs 130 and 131).[96] In 1769–72 the Magdalen Hospital for Penitent Prostitutes, established in 1758 by Robert Dingley and Jonas Hanway to reform prostitutes through a kind of isolation therapy, moved from Whitechapel to unsullied surrounds on the west side of Blackfriars Road and a large new quadrangular building designed by Joel Johnson, a carpenter become an architect.[97] To the east Southwark's House of Correction moved to a new building in 1772–3, alongside the previously resited King's Bench Prison. Otherwise the fields were still largely open when, on 2 June 1780, they were the starting-point for the Gordon Riots. A crowd of 60,000 mobilised and formed into divisions that branched out along the new roads and bridges into London, Westminster and Southwark. The release of prisoners and destruction of prisons was a major objective, and among those premises fired were the House of Correction and King's Bench Prison nearby, as well as Dance's architecturally radical Newgate Prison of 1768–75 in the City.[98]

There were other ways in which the planning of the 1760s went awry. The City put off decisions about what to do with its lands on St George's Fields, granting short-term leases of the greater part to the Hedger family, proprietors of the Dog and Duck, which had become a disreputable resort, soon to lose its licence. James Hedger and his son, also James, gained interests in other parts of the fields, and their tenancy of City lands was made formal in 1785, secure until 1810. Taking advantage of legal chaos, ignoring common rights and covenants against building, as well as a high-minded scheme from Dance for a huge crescent to be named after John Howard, the prison reformer, the Hedgers and others began intensive speculative development on a scale unprecedented in the area. They gradually peppered the fields with haphazard groups of small, densely packed and poorly built houses, put up during the London-wide building boom of the late 1780s and into the 1790s. Perhaps the most distinctive early development was on Marshall Street, between London Road and St George's Road, where there were two opposed crescents of about forty houses no wider than about 14 ft each. Many houses were smaller, some in back-to-back groups (figs 7, 9, 130 and 131). The City did not retrieve the situation until after 1800 when a number of the Hedgers' houses were pulled down and replaced with larger and more durable buildings, as survive in part on St George's Circus itself.[99] Meanwhile Albion Mill, a steam-powered flour mill and London's first great purpose-built factory, had been built just south of Blackfriars Bridge in 1783–6, to designs by Samuel Wyatt. The mill was destroyed by fire in 1791, arson being suspected though never proven, as it had put millers out of work and become a powerful and unpopular symbol of the Industrial Revolution (fig. 132).[100]

132 'Conflagration!' Millers on Blackfriars Bridge celebrate the destruction by fire in 1791 of Albion Mill, built 1783–6, Samuel Wyatt, architect. Etching by Samuel Collings, 1791 (BM).

133   Nos 51 and 53 Tower Bridge Road, Bermondsey, houses of 1780–85. This was part of what was built as a highly various row of twenty-one five- or six-room houses for tradespeople. There were originally front gardens to what was then Bermondsey New Road. No. 53 incorporates a central chimneystack. Photographed 2000 (EH, AA004707).

The aptly named Hedgers illustrate the ambivalence of 'improvement' when highly capitalistic speculative development coincided with limited demand for big houses. Large profits from speculations of small houses tended to come about only through the deliberate provision of numerous poor buildings. This exploitative degradation was assuredly not what John Gwynn had intended, but in the absence of enthusiasm for St George's Fields from the well-to-do it was what the market provided. There were other unintended consequences of improvement, just as far removed from what Gwynn or the City might have considered 'conformable', but less disreputable and more traditional. The undeveloped southern margins of Bermondsey, though not strictly part of St George's Fields, were very much influenced by developments there. By 1773 Bermondsey

New Road (since 1902 the southern part of Tower Bridge Road) had been formed to link Bermondsey Street and the Old and New Kent Roads. Between 1780 and 1791 a row of twenty-one brick houses was built on the north-west side of the new road on land that was part of the West Estate (figs 98 and 133). These houses were set well back behind ample front gardens, that is they were conceived with amenity in mind, though there was a tanyard to the rear. They were not large, comprising five or six rooms each behind fronts of about 16 ft, save for two 30 ft-front houses to the south. Nor were they a 'terrace', rather they were built to a number of different patterns singly, or in pairs, twos and threes, design and production intertwined. Early occupants remain unknown, but speculative development of this nature would not have been aiming to house other than artisans or tradespeople. A central portion of the row survives as Nos 41–53 Tower Bridge Road, front gardens shortened by road widening and otherwise covered in shops, the upper storeys empty or drastically rebuilt. Nevertheless, it can be seen that the central chimneystack endured, alongside other arrangements, probably including rear-staircase plans, with some of the small back rooms lacking heating. It is also evident that front-wall brickwork, fenestration and rooflines all varied. There was disunity in both elevations and layouts.[101] This acceptance of variety and the undisciplined melding of the new and the old, the decent and the humble, the polite and the vernacular, gardens in front, tanyard behind, characterised Southwark and Bermondsey through the seventeenth and eighteenth centuries, from Jacob's Island to Colombo Street, Mayflower Street and Crosby Row. Its expression in the 1780s was a last gasp of an improvisational artisan approach to housebuilding that was neither emulative nor exploitative. The first occupants of these houses would have been as likely as their social superiors to have wanted pleasant gardens and clean air, less likely, perhaps, to have been concerned with architectural conformity.

Improvement was coming to Bermondsey in other guises. Road widening on Bermondsey Street and Snowsfields in 1787–8 involved much demolition, and in 1789 George Gwilt, Surveyor to the County of Surrey and District Surveyor for the Parish of St George, Southwark, drew up plans for the West Estate for a substantial development on fields to the south and east. Grand planning in the form of a semi-hexagonal layout was rejected in favour of a more linear arrangement that permitted a larger number of small (17 ft-front) houses, but this too came to nought.[102] However, from about 1790 development of a much higher standard did take off between Bermondsey and St George's Fields. On the south side of the New Kent Road, just a few yards from the Bermondsey New Road corner, was the Paragon, an architecturally innovative crescent of large semi-detached houses, built in 1789–90 to designs by Michael Searles for the Rolls Estate, and followed by the more modest Union Crescent. These crescents have gone, but an adjoining terrace (formerly Dover Place) survives at Nos 154–70 New Kent Road, a row of nine ten-room houses with 20 ft fronts and front-staircase layouts, not for multiple occupation, but to allow full-width rear bow windows overlooking the fields to the south (figs 123 and 134). These developments were an entirely new presence in the area. Viewed beside their neighbouring predecessors on Bermondsey New Road, they would have seemed majestically uniform and extraordinarily alien.[103] They were followed by other comparably high-status,

planned and consciously suburban developments on the West and Rolls estates, at West Square, from 1791, and Surrey Square, from 1796, both set back from main roads on the south or open side.[104]

While these and other attempts to gentrify the district were under way in the 1790s, St George's Fields was coming into its own as Southwark's new-style depository for London's unwanted. The Lambeth Asylum for Girls and the Magdalen Hospital had been the first of numerous pioneering institutions to find the newly accessible fields a congenial site on the metropolitan margins, ideally suited to intentions that combined the cleansing and control of both individuals and the city at large. The existing prisons were supplemented by the Surrey County Gaol and Sessions House, built in 1791–8 to designs by Gwilt, across Blackman Street from the King's Bench Prison. Nearby, other approaches to social reform through incarceration were introduced. The Philanthropic Society, founded in 1788 to take criminal children and the children of convicts off the streets, established the Philanthropic Reform, building houses and workshops on a triangular plot just south of St George's Circus from 1793 (fig. 131). On Borough Road in 1799 Joseph Lancaster founded the school where he introduced his system for educating as many as 1,000 children in one space through the use of child monitors, subsequently promulgated through the British and Foreign Schools Society. The Asylum for the Deaf and Dumb, the country's first school for the deaf, was set up in 1792, near the present-day junction of New Kent Road and Old Kent Road. Towards Lambeth, the Dog and Duck, finally suppressed in 1799, was taken over to be the School for the Indigent Blind, which moved to new buildings between St George's Circus and the Philanthropic Reform in 1811–12 to make way for the new Bethlehem Royal Hospital (Bedlam), which asylum building survives as the Imperial War Museum.[105] The phased replacement of a pleasure garden with a school for the blind then a lunatic asylum says much about the nature of late Georgian improvement in south London. By 1810 all common rights still existing on St George's Fields had been extinguished and a battery of new institutions, for orphans, prostitutes, urchins, convicts, the disabled and the lunatic, stretched from Lambeth to Bermondsey, amid rows of new houses, many of which were packed together in mean and airless courts.

It was at the Lambeth end of this emerging and bizarre no-man's-land of suburban amenity, ready-made slums and institutional decant that William Blake, artist, poet, hosier's son, Dissenting heir to the Muggletonians, political radical and artisan prophet, lived from late 1790 or early 1791 until late 1800. With his wife Catherine he

134   Nos 154–70 New Kent Road (formerly Dover Place), a uniform row of ten-room houses of *c.*1790, a short distance away from the Tower Bridge Road houses (fig. 133), but speculative development of a wholly different order. Photographed 2003 (EH, AA033433).

moved from Soho into No. 13 Hercules Buildings, just west of the Refuge for Orphan Girls (fig. 131). Hercules Buildings were demolished in 1918, but maps and views indicate a row of twenty-four three-storey brick buildings, probably built in the 1780s, the fronts looking across the fields towards the Thames and Westminster Bridge, with variable fenestration incorporating bay windows, tripartite sashes and even Serliana (fig. 135). Records of Blake's house indicate a rear-staircase layout, with a basement and two rooms on each level, in a substantial home of eight rooms. Architecturally Hercules Buildings seem to lie somewhere in the murky middle ground between the humble irregularity of Bermondsey New Road and the imposing uniformity of New Kent Road. Though hardly fashionable, these were good big houses with amenities and some pretensions to gentility, in erst-

while rural surroundings that were rapidly becoming urban.[106] Just beyond the north end of the road there were pleasure gardens that, by 1796, were falling into ruin and being suppressed for being disorderly and the resort of 'democratic shopmen'.[107]

Blake's reference to 'Lambeth beneath the poplar trees' in his *Songs of Innocence* of 1789 suggests that his move was a retreat from Soho to something more pastoral, and it was in Lambeth that Blake enjoyed 'the most creative and productive period in his life'.[108] However, during the early 1790s Blake's outlook darkened. There were, of course, many contributory factors, not least events in France, but it is as if to chronicle the gap between the Lambeth he sought and the Lambeth he found that among his *Songs of Experience* of 1794 was 'London':

I wander thro' each charter'd street,
Near where the charter'd Thames does flow
And mark in every face I meet
Marks of weakness, marks of woe.

In every cry of every Man,
In every Infant's cry of fear,
In every voice: in every ban,
The mind-forg'd manacles I hear.

How the Chimney-sweepers cry
Every black'ning Church appalls;
And the hapless Soldier's sigh
Runs in blood down Palace walls.

But most thro' midnight streets I hear
How the youthful Harlot's curse
Blasts the new born Infant's tear,
And blights with plagues the Marriage hearse.[109]

Blake was a product of his London artisan origins. Like many others of similar background he experienced a loss of agency, a fracturing of his ability to engage with or form the world. He had no illusions about the nature of 'improvement', understanding it as it was understood in the City and by Gwynn, as the sublimation and ordering (chartering) of urban space as property for commerce. But for Blake commerce and 'improvement' were symptomatic of decline, not progress. Some of his anger at what London was becoming would have been rooted

135   Hercules Buildings, near Lambeth on the west side of St George's Fields, probably built in the 1780s. William Blake lived here between 1790/91 and 1800. Drawing by Frank Lewis Emanuel, 1914. Demolished 1918 (LMA).

in what he was witnessing close to hand in and around St George's Fields.

In the name of improvement uniformity was extinguishing variety, and standardisation was displacing invention. The activities of the Hedgers and the like gave small houses a bad name, and anomie was no longer anachronistic. The 1790s were a pivot point, not in that change was absolute – it never is – but in that change was sufficient for fundamental perceptions and attitudes to be shifted. After 1800 the possibility that ordinary people might provide themselves with modest but respectable housing was gradually forgotten, and the timber houses of Jacob's Island became themselves the signifiers of the squalor into which they had lately fallen. Just as those people who could not be controlled were swept into peripheral reforming institutions, so buildings that were not 'conformable' had to be cleared away.

136 Kingsland Road, showing the Fox Public House as rebuilt in 1790, with Nos 362–70, also of 1790, and Kingsland Crescent, built 1792–3, in a view of 1852 depicting early nineteenth-century topography. Watercolour by C. H. Matthews (HAD).

Chapter 5

WASTE AND PLACE:
MILE END ROAD, KINGSLAND ROAD
AND AMBIVALENCE AT THE MARGINS

Certain parts of these extremities of the town are, however, exposed to a great
nuisance; the air is poisoned by the emanation from brick-kilns, exactly like carrion,
to such a degree, as to excite nausea, and the utmost disgust [. . .]. As soon as we got
beyond the sight and the smell of bricks the country appeared to great advantage.

Louis Simond[1]

St George's Fields, described in the previous chapter, have brought into view London's marginal spaces, the places that began the eighteenth century as lands outside the city and ended it as inhabited parts of the great wen. But St George's Fields were not typical in that they were a vast open area, planned works on which were intended to facilitate urban expansion. Crucially, the area's roads were new. Elsewhere the edge was more fragmentary, and its transformation more gradual and unpremeditated. Long-established roads and the ribbon development they attracted offer more typical insights, typical both in terms of the nature of development, and in that they were those then open to road travellers. Simond's disgust with the urban fringes was certainly not new in 1810. Indeed things had perhaps rather changed for the better by then. A century earlier it had been said: 'everybody knows that for a mile or two about this City, the [highways] and the ditches hard by are commonly so full of nastiness and stinking dirt, that oftentimes many persons who have occasion to go in or come out of town, are forced to stop their noses to avoid the ill-smell occasioned by it.'[2] Eighteenth-century London's outer parts were not shanty towns, but semi-agricultural semi-industrial chaos; 'graziers, cow-keepers, hog-keepers, brickmakers, scavengers, night-men, nursery- and market-gardeners monopolised most of the land round London.'[3] Into the nineteenth century an abrupt edge separated densely populated suburbs from open space. Peripheral roadsides were not only or even necessarily

unpleasant; they were also convenient. Within the city sites fronting onto larger roads were thought desirable (fig. 27). On the margins and beyond many very substantial houses were placed right on major roadways to make the most of speedy access to the heart of the capital.

This chapter considers two of the principal roads that led into and out of London's industrial suburbs – Mile End Road to the east and Kingsland Road to the north. As a dual case study it juxtaposes two very different kinds of ribbon development on roadside land designated waste.[4] Mile End Road had many sixteenth- and seventeenth-century buildings in an established settlement with a number of large houses and well-to-do residents. Kingsland Road began the eighteenth century as a virtual blank slate in terms of buildings, adjacent land used for antisocial purposes, from brickmaking to an isolation hospital for venereal disease. From these different starting-points, there was, by the end of the century, a transformation, even transferral, albeit ambiguous, whereby the retreat became overspill, and the overspill became a retreat. Throughout, marginality made for the absence of clear identity. The forms of houses in these places amply illustrate this ambivalence, with vernacular and polite traditions convergent, making for telling comparisons and exemplifying contrasting aspects of London's growth. While in the ever-expanding West End concerted efforts were being made to develop large landholdings with regular and uniform housing for the

161

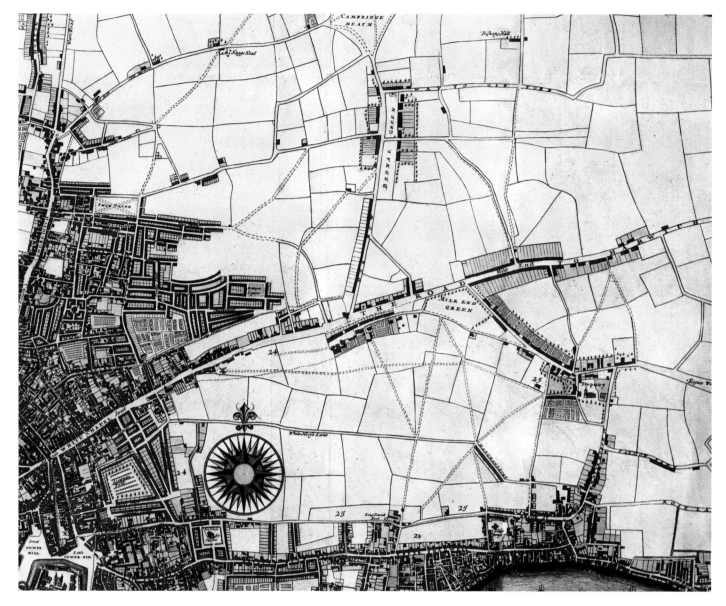

137 London's eastern fringes and Mile End Old Town, around 'Mile End Green', c.1690 (from Richard Morden and Philip Lea, *London, Westminster and Southwark*, ed. 1700, GL).

'middling sort', London's growth was not everywhere so coherent. Mile End Road and Kingsland Road provide insights into the uneven fringes of expansion.

Mile End Road

DEVELOPMENT TO 1760

Concentration on the insalubrious in these prefatory remarks is harsh on historic Mile End Road. Early eighteenth-century Mile End Old Town was, after all, 'built

with many good Houses, inhabited with divers sea Captains and Commanders of Ships. [. . .] It used also to serve for Country Retirement to Citizens and other wealthy Men.'[5] However, the intention here is not to reconstruct the halcyon days of the seventeenth- and early eighteenth-century resort, but to look at some less exalted roadside aspects of early Mile End, to explore how the district where Boswell's walk across London in 1763 concluded came around that time to be an integral part of the metropolis rather than a place apart.

Mile End Road was the main road linking London and Essex, and the hamlet of Mile End Old Town had a name that spoke both of historic distance from London and of a linear understanding of the intervening space. The mile-long common, manorial waste that had stretched from Whitechapel to the medieval parish church of St Dunstan, Stepney, had been reduced to half that length by eastwards growth from the City by the beginning of the seventeenth century. Stow had written:

> both the sides of the streete bee pestered with Cottages and Allies, even up to White chappel church: and almost halfe a mile beyond it, into the common field: all which ought to lye open & free for all men. But this common field, I say, being sometime the beauty of this City on that part, is so incroched upon by building of filthy Cottages, and with other purprestures, inclosures and Laystalles (notwithstanding all proclaimations [sic] and Acts of Parliament made to the contrary) that in some places it scarce remaineth

a sufficient high way for the meeting of Carriages and droves of Cattell, much less is there any faire, pleasant or wholsome way for people to walke on foot: which is no small blemish to so famous a city, to have so unsavery and unseemly an entry or passage thereunto.[6]

By 1700 there was virtual contiguity between Whitechapel and Mile End Old Town, 'the road to Harwich' being much built up (fig. 137). Whitechapel itself was one of London's poorest districts in the late seventeenth century, and largely timber built.[7] Yet the wealthier local inhabitants had found the wherewithal for an architecturally ambitious rebuilding of the parish church of St Mary Matselon in 1672–3, and the newly built-up area south-west of the church included good brick houses of the 1680s, as on Braham Street (figs 17 and 35). Further east, on the south side of the road and beyond straggling outlying houses close to Fieldgate Street, a self-explanatory reminder of marginality,

138   Mile End Old Town around Mile End Green in the 1740s (from John Rocque, *Plan of the Cities of London and Westminster and Borough of Southwark*, 1746).

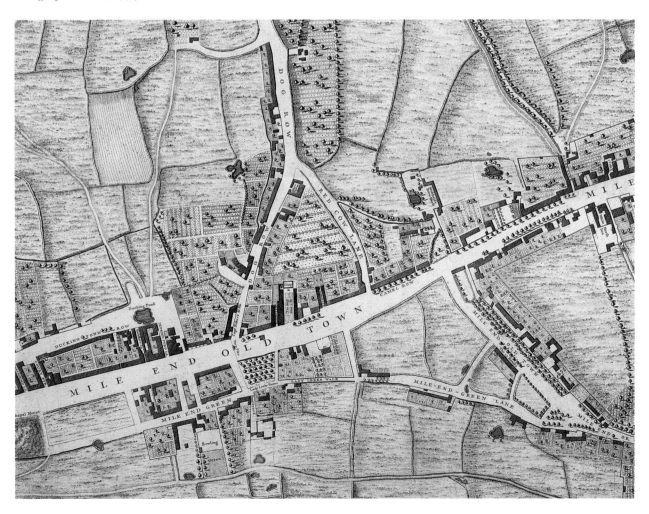

139   No. 37 Stepney Green. In the years around 1700 Mile End Old Town was outside London and a resort for merchants and mariners of means. This house was newly built in 1694. Early occupants included Mary Gayer, widow of the East India Company governor of Bombay. Photographed 1997 (EH, BB98/03153).

there were open fields, a windmill and the remains of Whitechapel Mount, a civil-war fortification. There had long been more continuous development on the north side of the road. The late seventeenth-century creation of Mile End New Town, which led to its being constituted a separate hamlet in 1690, but which was in reality outwards growth from Spitalfields, made the hinterland to the north of the main road wholly part of the built-up metropolis.[8] The orderly but humble streets of Mile End New Town extended almost out to Dog Row

(Cambridge Heath Road) (figs 17 and 26), where long-standing ribbon development of waste extended northwards towards Bethnal Green. At the junction with Dog Row was the turnpike, later Mile End Gate, effectively marking the point at which one left or entered London.

Mile End Old Town, concentrated to the east and north of the remaining waste known as Mile End Green, was a place of marked gentility in the late seventeenth century and the early eighteenth, with many large mansions, some old, more new, not only facing the green,

140   Nos 169–77 Mile End Road, a row of seventeenth-century timber houses with central chimneystacks. Photographed shortly before demolition in 1902 for the building of Stepney Green Underground Station (EH, BB95/555).

but also along the wide road to and from London, as at No. 131 Mile End Road (figs 138 and 143).[9] This settlement away from but close to London was a pleasure and retirement retreat for City and maritime people of means. Residents of Mile End Green included influential merchants and affluent mariners. Among the former was Maurice Thompson, 'the greatest colonial merchant of his day',[10] who gained political eminence during the Commonwealth when he lived on the green in a medieval mansion known as King John's Court or Palace. Among the latter were Admiral Sir John Berry and Captain Arnold Browne, whose land on the east side of the green was developed by his sons, Arnold and Robert, and others in the years up to 1700, most notably with the house that survives as No. 37 Stepney Green (fig. 139).[11]

However, as in any other part of the metropolis at this time, gentility in Mile End Old Town was not exclusive of other kinds of habitation. The area had a broad social mix, and this diversity was manifest in great architectural variety. On the west side of the green, directly across from the mansions, there was a late seventeenth-century row known as 'the thirteen houses', each with a frontage of only about 15 ft. On the main road seventeenth-century development included Nos 169–77 Mile End Road (fig. 140). The Black Boy at No. 169 was one of

numerous hostelries on the road, about one in eight of the approximately four hundred houses in the hamlet having had victuallers' licences. A bit further east No. 195 Mile End Road was a more modest timber house of around 1700 that survived into the 1940s (fig. 141).[12]

By 1700 the retirees resident on Mile End Road included many humble people. The north side of the road east of Dog Row and facing the green was built up with a clutch of almshouses, in sequential courts off the main road. These included the architecturally imposing group of 1695 administered by Trinity House and still standing (fig. 31), with the Skinners' Company Almshouses of 1698 and the Vintners' Company Almshouses of 1676 to either side. At the east end of the town was Bancroft's Almshouses, founded by the Drapers' Company in 1727, to either side of which some of those beyond retirement were interred in Sephardic Jewish burial grounds, the oldest to the west of 1657 being the first Jewish burial ground to be established in London after the Resettlement. In 1697 and 1761 two Ashkenazi Jewish burial grounds were also laid out in the vicinity.[13]

There was no discernible loss of heterogeneity in the area's developments up to 1750, but this is not to say there were no changes. Fitzhugh House, a mansion as large as any in the locality, was built around 1738 for the widow of an East India Captain, William Fitzhugh, at the east end of a mixed cluster of buildings on the south side of the road near the turnpike, freestanding and set well back in large grounds with curving forecourt walls (fig. 138).[14] By this date there had been straws in the speculative building wind that blew east from London. Just east of the group mislabelled by the surveyor John Rocque as Camel Row, was Ireland Row (Nos 107–13 Mile End Road), a short but substantial terrace of around 1717 that housed 'middling sort' merchants and mariners in rear-staircase-plan houses (figs 138, 142 and 143).[15] Further east, on the plot immediately east of the large

143 (*facing page*)   Reconstructed plans of houses on Mile End Road.

141 (*left*)   No. 195 Mile End Road, a small timber house of *c*.1700. Photographed 1928. Demolished (EH, AP292).

142 (*below*)   Ireland Row, Nos 107–13 Mile End Road, four 20 ft-wide eight-room houses of *c*.1717 first occupied by merchants and mariners. Photographed 2002 (EH, AA033067).

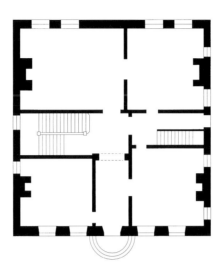

131 MILE END ROAD
GROUND FLOOR
c. 1700 (dem.)

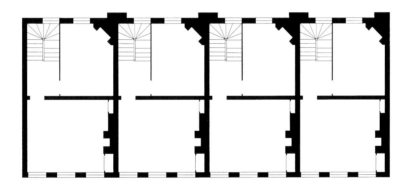

IRELAND ROW
107-113 MILE END ROAD
FIRST FLOOR
c. 1717

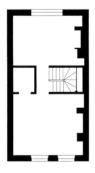

94 MILE END ROAD
FIRST FLOOR
1763

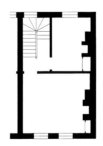

88 MILE END ROAD
FIRST FLOOR
1764 to 1765 (dem.)

1 0   5   10   15   20 metres

5 0   30   60 feet

house at No. 131, an even bigger late seventeenth-century mansion was replaced on a more forward line by a row of three houses, built in 1741–2 by Thomas Andrews, a local bricklayer. Two of these were substantial double-fronted twelve-room houses that survive as Nos 133–9 Mile End Road, having internal joinery that is notably conservative in London houses of such size from the 1740s. Early occupants of this unusual and apparently difficult to market speculation included Rebecca Brandon, the widow of a Sephardic merchant, and Captain Matthew Court.[16] Together these buildings illustrate the road's continuing but shifting gentility through the first half of the century.[17] High-quality speculations of small numbers of substantial houses were in the ascendant, with freestanding mansions becoming more of a rarity, pointing to incipient though far from rampant urbanisation.

Humbler building traditions also endured. Just southeast of Fitzhugh House, on a corner of the green where Jubilee Street (formerly Mutton Lane) now meets Redman's Road (formerly Mile End Green Lane), was a group of early eighteenth-century buildings that included what survived into the twentieth century as Nos 212–15 Jubilee Street, small houses that were probably timber built behind brick fronts (figs 138 and 144).[18] The rest of the east side of Jubilee Street was developed in 1758–61, with numerous small houses, some at least timber built. On the east side of the green, development extended southwards in 1745 in the shape of Mapp's Row (fig. 145), a speculation by Charles Mapp, a wealthy quill or pen seller, a tax collector and Dissenter. Despite their height and regular façade, these were modest four-room timber houses, not, it seems, aimed at captains.[19]

The face of Mile End Road was further complicated by the mid-eighteenth century as manufacturing, retailing and further institutional use spread out from Whitechapel. The Anchor Brewery grew up behind Ireland Row, and in the 1750s the London Hospital was built on remaining open frontage on the Whitechapel side of the turnpike. Mile End Old Town was ceasing to

144   Nos 212–15 Jubilee Street, early eighteenth-century brick-fronted two-storey houses built on the waste at Mile End Green. Photographed 1928. Demolished (EH, AP 290).

145 Mapp's Row, Stepney Green, timber houses of 1745, each only 17 ft by 14 ft, indicating one-room plans. Photographed in the early twentieth century. Demolished (EH).

be a distinct settlement, becoming increasingly identifiable as urban sprawl. However, while many gaps on Mile End Road had been filled by 1760, the road frontage east of Fitzhugh House had stayed open (fig. 138).[20]

LATE EIGHTEENTH-CENTURY DEVELOPMENT

This last substantial piece of Mile End Green, the pentagon bounded by Mile End Road, Stepney Green, Redman's Road and Jubilee Street, was part of a large wedge of waste that had been enclosed by Dr John Nicholson as early as 1694. It was not until after 1760 that Ebenezer Mussell, to whom this part of Nicholson's enclosure had been demised, began to give sixty-one-year building leases of plots along Mile End Road.[21] By 1770 the whole Mile End Road frontage had been continuously developed with thirty-seven brick houses, Nos 82–124 Mile End Road. These came to be known as Assembly Row, after the Assembly Room that was built in 1766 behind Nos 112–24 Mile End Road as a communal space for local courts and political dining clubs.[22] By the 1790s Assembly Passage linked through to Redman's Road, which had also been built up after 1760, following the death of Captain John Redman (figs 148 and 150).[23]

The development of Assembly Row in the 1760s ran broadly from west to east, suggesting that its builders saw it as growth from London rather than as expansion of Mile End Old Town. This dense and extensive speculative development is, accordingly perhaps, different to what has been encountered heretofore on Mile End Road. The houses are not so readily classifiable as being either grand or humble. In their number and in their relatively narrow plots they accept that the common had become part of a metropolitan street, but they are sufficiently ambitious in their scale to indicate that the gentility and amenity of Mile End Old Town was not being abandoned, something the building of the Assembly Room confirms. The implication here of a single intent is misleading. This was not a coherent speculation, but a gradual and accretive development by numerous builders that, within its parts, reveals changing social and architectural attitudes.

To the west Nos 82 and 84 survive as a large mirrored pair of three-bay three-storey and garret houses, looking stylistically earlier than the other houses in Assembly Row with segment-headed windows and blind openings over the entrances. Yet they are not as early as they look, having been built in 1761–2.[24] The large site that became No. 86 Mile End Road was taken by John Curtis, a wine merchant, who opened the Bunch of

146 The mixed group that is the earlier houses of Assembly Row, at Nos 90–98 Mile End Road, houses of 1763–6 with the empty site of Captain Cook's house at No. 88, to the right. Photographed 2002 (EH, AA033062).

Grapes here in 1762–3, using a large piece of land behind as business premises for Curtis's Wine Vaults.[25]

Beyond the access road to Curtis's yard Nos 88–92 Mile End Road were built together in 1764–5 in a three-house speculation by John and George Sawyer (figs 143, 146 and 147). These were relatively modest three-storey brick houses, each having only a 15 ft front. But with eight rooms each they were clearly not aimed at the same market as was Mapp's Row. They had raised ground floors, some marble chimneypieces, and the rear-staircase layout that had long since become standard in London's 'middling sort' speculations, albeit with 'old-fashioned' closed-string turned-baluster stairs.[26] Nos 90 and 92 survive, but No. 88, demolished in 1958, had the greater fame for having been the home of Captain James Cook (1728–79) from when it was new, his widow Elizabeth continuing here after his death until 1787. In 1765 Cook was not yet a captain and had yet to make the voyages for which he achieved fame. He was a labourer's son who had apprenticed himself to a ship owner in Whitby then enlisted in the Navy in 1755 (see chapter 8). He acquired a reputation for navigational compe-

tence and in 1759 was given command of a survey vessel as 'marine surveyor of the coast of Newfoundland and Labrador'. Spending winter months in England preparing his surveys for publication, he married Elizabeth Batts, the daughter of a Wapping publican, in December 1762. About two years later they moved from the much less genteel mariners' district of Shadwell into the new house at No. 88 Mile End Road.[27] No. 90 was taken by David Witherspoon, a baker, who had a bakehouse to the rear. It is reasonable to surmise that he sold bread from a shop in the house.

No. 94 Mile End Road, slightly broader with a 16 ft front, but originally lower for not having a raised ground floor, had been built a little earlier than Nos 88–92; George Potter, a bricklayer from South Ockendon, Essex, put up the house in 1763, initially perhaps for his own occupation (figs 143 and 146). No. 96, another singleton with a 16 ft front and even lower storey heights, went up in 1765–6, to be occupied by Joseph Norton, a 'gentleman'. These houses provide fascinating evidence of singularities in approaches to house design. Like Nos 88–92 both have eight rooms, though with rather more

147 (*right*) Captain Cook's House at No. 88 Mile End Road. With eight small rooms behind a 15 ft frontage (see fig. 143), this was comfortable but far from grand accommodation for Cook and his wife Elizabeth from 1765 when he was relatively little travelled and not yet a captain. No. 90, next door to the left, was a baker's premises. Photographed 1950. Demolished 1958 (EH, BB50/821).

space. No. 94 has an asymmetrical two-window front, something that makes it distinctive in the whole group. No. 96 has a more regular three-bay front, but the windows are closely spaced, producing proportions that seem more 'old fashioned' than those of neighbouring houses. Neither of these houses was given a rear-staircase plan. No. 94 has a central-staircase layout with a narrow lightwell (fig. 143), an arrangement typically associated with the late seventeenth century (see chapter 2). No. 96 had a central chimneystack and, given the absence of staircase fenestration in its back wall, was probably arranged according to a 'Moxon' plan, otherwise unknown in London north of the Thames at such a late date.[28]

Further along the row Nos 98–106 Mile End Road were first built in 1764–5, perhaps a single development on a 100 ft frontage, centred on a 27 ft-front property at No. 102, with two-bay 18 ft-front houses in pairs to

148 (*below*) Mile End Old Town, showing the extent of development on Mile End Green in the 1790s (from Richard Horwood, *Plan of London*, 1799).

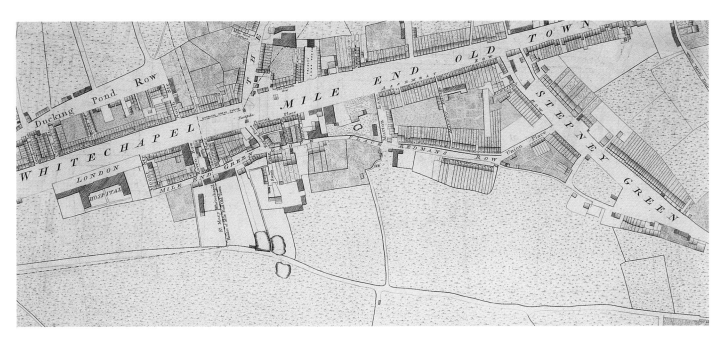

149 The later houses of Assembly Row at Nos 112–24 Mile End Road, a uniform row of 1766–8. Photographed 2002 (EH, AA033064).

either side, all probably having at least eight rooms and rear-staircase plans. No. 104 was taken by Captain John Harris. Nos 108 and 110 followed in 1766 with the Assembly Room beyond, John Fenn of Greenwich being a builder. The uniform terrace of seven houses in front of the Assembly Room at Nos 112–24 Mile End Road was up by 1768, Joseph Rowland, a West End carpenter, joining with Fenn in a building partnership (fig. 149). These were better eight-room houses, each with a 20 ft three-bay front, raised ground floors and, it appears, rear-staircase layouts; at least one more captain was in residence by 1769. The row originally turned eastwards to Stepney Green, off which Rowland also built some much smaller houses facing a court in 1768–9 (fig. 148). Further south, completion of what was known as Rowland's Row followed from 1785.[29]

The houses of Assembly Row, all built in a line within a narrow date range and all broadly comparable in scale, contain distinctive variety in form. For the most part the houses conform to the central London higher-status standards of the regular front and the rear-staircase plan. However, the non-standard features of Nos 94 and 96 from the early part of the development seem to be conservative perpetuation of traditional housebuilding practice, where fashion was less likely to override functionality. The asymmetry and close spacing of the window openings at Nos 94 and 96 contrast sharply with the regular march of evenly spaced windows to the east. As development progressed eastwards and away from London, scale and regularity increased, the higher specifications of the later houses perhaps indicating that to some degree speculation here took off. It is interesting to note that the builder of No. 94 was from Essex, and perhaps, therefore, not steeped in West End practice as Joseph Rowland, the builder of the uniform terrace at Nos 112–24, would have been.

These differences signify more than the simple vagaries of piecemeal development. They also point to aspects of the changing character of Mile End Old Town. The earlier houses at the west end of Assembly Row seem to have been more commercially oriented than the rest of the development, incorporating a public house and related wine vaults at No. 86 and a bakery at No. 90. That the adjoining houses at Nos 94 and 96 were conservative in architectural terms does not necessarily mean that they too were used for shops, rather that they were conceived from within an artisan culture oriented as much to shopkeeping as to gentility. With Cook's house they were among the smaller houses in the Assembly Row group, though far from mean, having eight rooms each and incorporating ornamental finish, that is marble chimneypieces and staircases with turned balusters. They can be linked to at least one 'gentleman'. It has been calculated that as much as half of Mile End Old Town's late eighteenth-century population were of 'middling sort' or higher status, and that in this prosperous district in 1780 only 44 per cent of houses had five or fewer rooms.[30]

As speculative development these eight-room houses were aimed at a 'middling sort' rather than an artisan market, but at its lower end, where there were overt links to trade origins. James Cook was a man on the way up in 1764–5, bettering himself from his previously humble address. His move from Shadwell reveals both aspirations and limitations at a crucial early point in his career. He chose to come to the traditional locus of prestigious sea captains' homes, but to a new house of less than prodigious dimensions when compared with the houses of other local captains, though, of course, vastly spacious when compared with life on board ship. Cook's move is revealing of more than his own circumstances, also illustrating social convergence whereby architecture was becoming less explicit as a guide to status. Mile End Old Town was in transition, changing from being a select marine quarter and heading towards a lower status as respectable London overspill. With neighbours who were a wine merchant, a baker and an Essex builder, as well as one who styled himself a gentleman, the Cooks were part of a group of new residents in Mile End who were evidently neither 'sea captains' nor 'wealthy men'. Here, the tradesman, the artisan and the mariner aimed to achieve gentility in a district that had already seen its most fashionable days. It is worth noting finally that these occupants of Assembly Row are from just those

150   London's eastern fringes showing Mile End Road to the east and Kingsland Road to the north, *c.*1790 (from John Stockdale, *A New Plan of London*, 1797, GL).

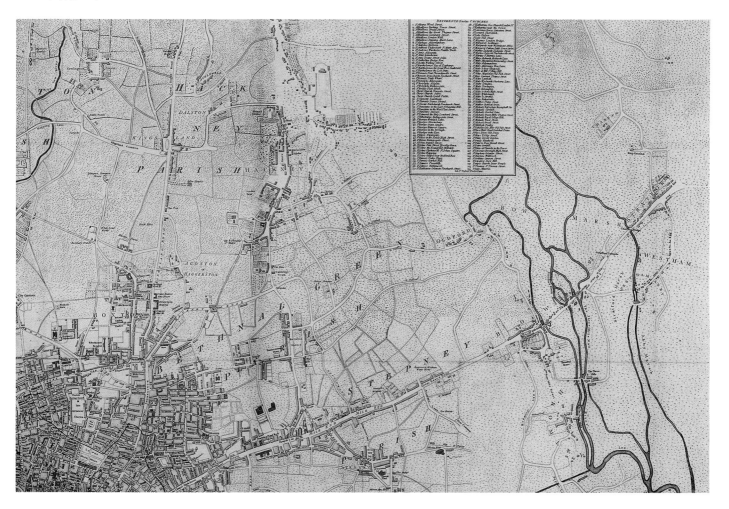

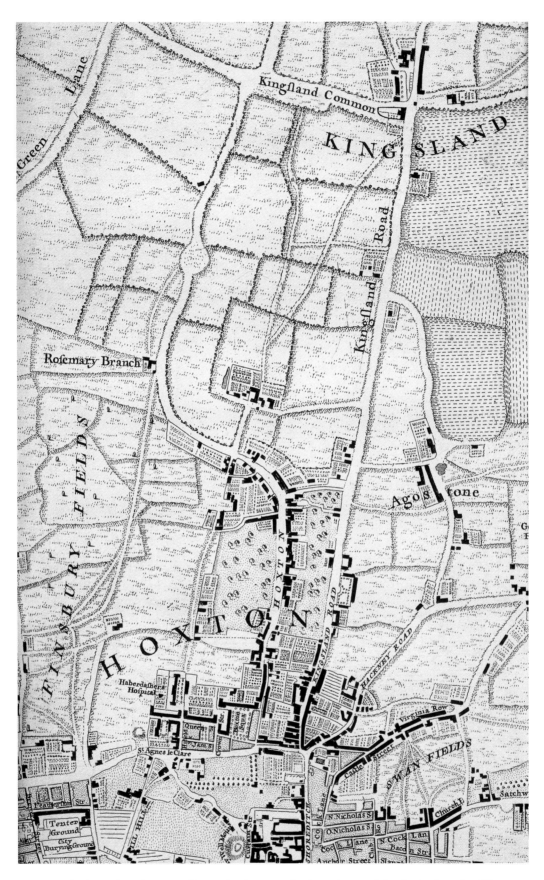

151   Kingsland Road in the 1740s (from John Rocque, *An Exact Survey of the City's of London, Westminster* [. . .] *and the Country near Ten Miles Round,* 1746).

levels of society that most strongly supported John Wilkes, who held politically important meetings with Middlesex electors and others in the neighbouring Assembly Room in 1768–72.[31]

The residents of Assembly Row may have been on the up, living in an area that still had many desirable houses, but the future of Mile End was not to go their way. The smaller houses of Rowland's Row, built on the west side of Stepney Green in the 1780s (fig. 148), were mirrored to the west by Barnes Place, comparable houses of 1782–4, built by John Barnes, a Whitechapel brick-layer who established himself as a major developer in the area. His heir Thomas Barnes built streets of small two-storey terrace houses in the early nineteenth century that took Mile End further down the social scale and housed neither captains nor much by way of either architectural aspiration or variety (see chapter 9).[32]

152   The Geffrye Museum, formerly the Ironmongers' Company almshouses of 1712, at the Shoreditch end of Kingsland Road. Photographed 2002 (EH, AA033086).

Kingsland Road

The second and longer part of this chapter is devoted to Kingsland Road, to which the observation by Louis Simond with which it opened might well have re-ferred.[33] Kingsland Road was part of Ermine Street, the main route north from Roman London, and it remained a major road in the Middle Ages. In 1713 the Stamford Hill turnpike trust was established to administer what was sometimes known as the Great North Road as a toll road, from Shoreditch, where it left London, to Enfield. A tollgate at the hamlet of Kingsland was the first to the north of London. In the early eighteenth century, when the road was 'exceedingly thronged',[34] with more car-riage traffic than any other road round London, there were scarcely any buildings along its margins between the upper reaches of Shoreditch (just east of Hoxton) and Kingsland (fig. 151).[35]

To the south Shoreditch was a populous and impov-erished district, dominated by the silk industry until the early nineteenth century (fig. 72). There was another exceptional concentration of almoners at the south end of Kingsland Road where, on the east side, the former Ironmongers' Company almshouses of 1712 survive as the Geffrye Museum (fig. 152). Beyond, save for Bourne's Framework Knitters' Almshouses of 1734, there were no buildings on the east side of the road as far as the Fox Public House, established in 1727, which stood on its own just south of Haggerston Lane; further north was the equally solitary Lamb Inn.[36] Immediately south-west of the Kingsland tollgate on the west side of the road there was a lock hospital for those afflicted with venereal disease, considered communicable by other than only sexual contact, and so removed from the town. Founded in the sixteenth century, and owned and main-tained by St Bartholomew's Hospital, this hospital closed in 1760, though its chapel continued to serve the local population.[37] Kingsland Road thus ran through the part of the parish of Hackney that was closest to London, but that remained one of its least peopled places. Settlements at Stoke Newington and Hackney were as remote in fact and in character as was London proper.

The land flanking Kingsland Road was not idle, providing vital support to the metropolis as brickfields and market gardens. Such use could be lucrative provid-ing a disincentive to development. Housebuilding was one of the capital's biggest industrial sectors, and the significant costs of transporting bricks made brickmak-ing close to the city economically crucial. Since the seventeenth century land along Kingsland Road had been given over to use as clay pits for brickmaking; Daniel Lysons noted that 'vast quantities' of bricks and tiles had been made around Kingsland by 1795 (fig. 153).[38] The landscape would have been as much industrial as pastoral, punctuated by piles of topsoil, drying hacks, clamps for firing the bricks, tile kilns, and ephemeral shed-like constructions (fig. 154).[39] Even more casual use was not documented, though, as Dorothy George noted, 'Hogs were kept in large numbers on the outskirts and fed on the garbage of the town [. . .] and in the brickfields vagrants lived and slept, cooking their food at the kilns.'[40]

Following closure of the lock hospital, Kingsland itself was growing more than Hackney's other hamlets in the 1760s and 1770s, when its rate-paying population more

153 Much of Kingsland Road remained open land in the eighteenth century. Brickmaking and market gardening are shown here on the west side of Kingsland Road in a painting of 1852 depicting earlier topography. Opposite stands Acton Place (Nos 268–98), built soon after 1808. Watercolour by C. H. Matthews (LMA).

154 A depiction of brickmaking, c.1800, showing a typical 'gang' of men, women and children working together moulding bricks, an improvised thatched cover keeping both sun and rain off the unmade bricks (from Pyne, i, 1803).

than doubled, and so building along the road that separated it from London might be anticipated, particularly following an Act in 1768 that provided for widening of the road at Shoreditch. However, the widening was not carried through until 1799. This delay and continuing insalubrity may have deterred concerted development. Into the 1780s Kingsland's growth was predominantly to the north, away from London. The less desirable character of the land along Kingsland Road to the south seems confirmed by the building in 1776–7 of the Shoreditch Workhouse, on the road near the north end of Hoxton. The value of the land for brickmaking would also have countered any temptation to sell for housebuilding. The economic equation in this respect did shift; between 1778 and 1798 rents for brickfields trebled, but this may have been an effect of as much as an impediment to local housebuilding.[41]

Speculative housebuilding on Kingsland Road did begin in 1758, and gradual development followed in piecemeal stages through the 1770s and 1780s (figs 150 and 155). With a run of about thirty mostly small houses for artisans and labourers, a strip of waste came to be what in 1790 was the first built-up stretch of frontage that one came to on travelling north from Shoreditch once past the workhouse. Beyond was an innovative and ambitiously conceived, but haltingly realised, speculation of the 1770s at Kingsland Place. Kingsland Crescent, a unified classical composition of thirty houses, followed on to the south in 1792–3. These buildings repay closer investigation.

KINGSLAND WASTE: BUILDERS, OCCUPANTS
AND ARCHITECTURE

In 1750 the land on which Nos 374–438 Kingsland Road now stand was the southern part of a long strip or verge of manorial waste ground, lying behind a causeway that ran alongside the highway. Thomas Upsdell, a brickmaker from Norton Folgate (between Spitalfields and Shoreditch), who may have been renting adjoining land for brickmaking, had been 'granted' this common land by 1758 when he built Upsdell's Row (Nos 430–36), four houses near its north end. By 1770 Upsdell had effectively enclosed the land, appropriating it with a lease from Francis John Tyssen, who held the manor (see chapter 3). Enclosure of the waste may have been a matter of policy for the trustees responsible for the turnpike; in 1763 they were filling in the roadside ditch further north and planning to put up a fence on the footway.[42]

In the early 1770s Upsdell lived in a house to the east amid the brickfields, at the end of a drive on the site of what became Swan Lane (later Richmond Road). He may have died in or shortly before 1774, when his son Peter, then described as a 'gentleman', took a new ninety-nine-year lease of the waste at a negligible rent of £2 a year, renegotiated a year later to take in the roadside causeway.[43] Peter Upsdell held on to the waste and profited from its further development in the 1770s, but he had ambitions beyond continuing his father's brickmaking business and marginal housebuilding. He was described as being of Hackney in 1774, but a year later, when he mortgaged his lease on the waste, he was described not only as a gentleman, but also as a surveyor, of Islington. His background in brickmaking had led to more 'professional' involvement in housebuilding. Such mobility from a building trade to the status of surveyor was entirely normal, and in itself is not necessarily indicative of a rise in status. More telling of ambition is Upsdell's situation in 1779, when he was living and working as a surveyor in Soho, holding property in Marylebone and remortgaging his Kingsland Road property. He was deeply in debt, owing more than £1,000. In March 1780 Upsdell, now described as a builder, had left Soho, bankrupt. After his venture into West End property speculation had foundered, his Kingsland Road property was assigned to John Elkins, a Mayfair bricklayer and brickmaker.[44] In 1785 Elkins turned his attention to Kingsland Waste, paying off Upsdell's mortgages and setting up his own, while undertaking to finish development of the frontage that had been largely built up since 1770. Upsdell recovered, practising as a surveyor in Soho, Westminster and Holborn from 1786, and living in Soho from then until 1797. He was still active in 1817.[45]

This land tenure underlay the development of the waste, undertaken by these people and their tenants, erratically and in small parcels. Many of the first-phase houses went up in the 1770s and were thus part of a London-wide building boom. Upsdell's financial difficulties and other slowing down in the development process at Kingsland Waste around 1780 reflect a general downturn in the market.[46] The northern part of the waste remained largely undeveloped, and its single eighteenth-century pair of houses is treated separately hereafter (fig. 155).

The earliest development on Kingsland Waste was Upsdell's Row of 1758 (fig. 157). The 'row' was four approximately 16ft-square houses at Nos 430–36, each originally comprising only three rooms (fig. 156), set back behind the causeway, on the strip of waste where it was only 20ft deep (fig. 155). All the houses further south as far as No. 388 always fronted onto the forward building line, all being built after the encroachment

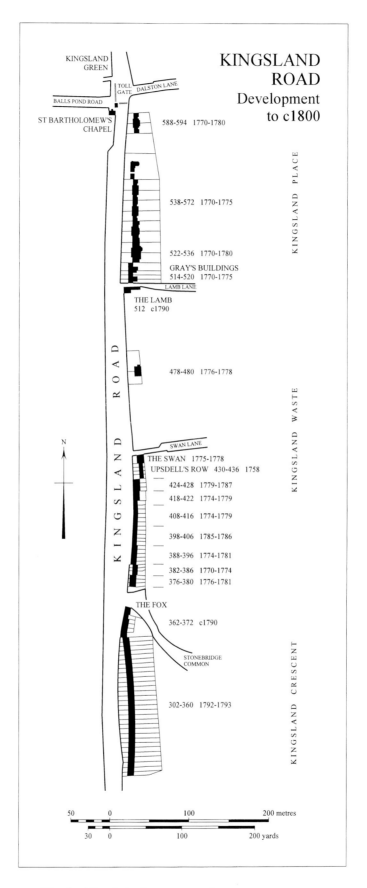

155   Kingsland Road, development to *c.*1800.

156 (*facing page*)   Reconstructed plans of houses on Kingsland Road.

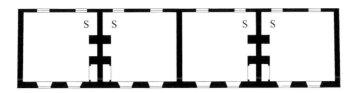

UPSDELL'S ROW
430-436 KINGSLAND ROAD
FIRST FLOOR
1758 (part dem.)

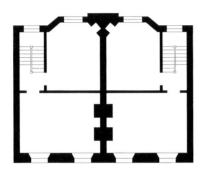

KINGSLAND PLACE
540-542 KINGSLAND ROAD
FIRST FLOOR
1770 to 1775

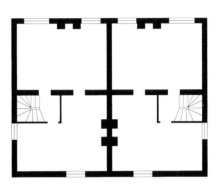

478-480 KINGSLAND ROAD
FIRST FLOOR
1776 to 1778

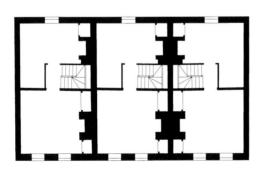

376-380 KINGSLAND ROAD
FIRST FLOOR
1776 to 1781

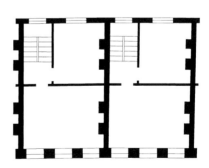

KINGSLAND CRESCENT
336-338 KINGSLAND ROAD
FIRST FLOOR
1792 to 1793

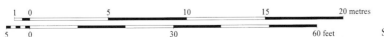

| 1 | 0 | 5 | 10 | 15 | 20 metres |
| 5 | 0 | | 30 | | 60 feet |

S = FORMER STAIR POSITION

157 Nos 430–38 Kingsland Road, formerly 'Upsdell's Row', of 1758, and the Swan Public House. Only No. 436 survives from the first development when it was one of four 16 ft-square three-room houses. Photographed 1999 (EH, BB99/11003).

across the causeway in 1774–5. Of Upsdell's Row only No. 436 survives, bearing a stone panel in its front wall, inscribed 'Upsdells Row 1758' (fig. 158). The house now has three full storeys, the upper storey being a rebuilding of a garret. The datestone is between the first-floor windows, which retain their original tall proportions in a symmetrically fenestrated two-bay front.

From at least 1770 one of the Upsdell's Row cottages, probably No. 436, was occupied by Thomas Summers, a scavenger. Scavenging, or the removing of household rubbish and street dirt, was closely linked to brick-making, as bricks incorporated 'spanish', that is rubbish including excrement and ash. Perhaps Thomas Upsdell built the short row to house Summers and other core members of his brickmaking workforce. These would

158 The inscribed stone panel on the front wall of No. 436 Kingsland Road. Photographed 1999 (EH, MF99/01466/17).

have been few, most brickmaking labour being casual, seasonal and unskilled.[47]

In 1775, following the elder Upsdell's death, the site of No. 438, then a stable and garden, was taken by Summers, together with his own house, at an annual rent of £13 8s on a thirty-year lease, a substantial sum that shows that Summers was no mere street cleaner, more likely a cleaning contractor. By 1778 he had put up a large building at No. 438 to be the Swan Public House, wholly rebuilt in the nineteenth century (fig. 157). Though apparently not having roots in a building trade, Summers was himself being described as a surveyor in 1779 when he held leases of all of Upsdell's Row as well as adjoining properties to the south. The latter, Nos 418–28 Kingsland Road, had been developed by 1787 as larger houses, probably all two rooms deep with three full storeys, one for Summers himself at No. 420, built in 1779–80 with a stable (not a coach-house) adjoining on the site of No. 422 (fig. 159). Summers's career evidently followed that of Peter Upsdell into speculative building; from scavenger to surveyor within a decade represents a notable rise, social mobility outside the traditional hierarchies of artisan production.[48]

Further south Nos 408–16 Kingsland Road were built in 1774–9 as a row of five three-room houses, seemingly put up by Hugh Byrne, a Covent Garden bricklayer, who may previously have worked with Peter Upsdell in the West End (figs 155 and 159). The 75 ft frontage south of this at Nos 398–406 was the last on this part of the waste to be developed, John Elkins building five one-room-plan houses like those adjoining to the north in 1785–6. Five more 15 ft-wide houses had been built at Nos 388–96 by 1781, starting in 1774, when a house at No. 388 leased to David Grantham, a Buckinghamshire carpenter, was up and occupied by John Gracey, a gardener. These houses were larger than those to the north, perhaps being two rooms deep; Nos 382–96 were the only houses on the waste given the amenity of privies at the ends of their gardens.[49]

At the south end of the waste Thomas Upsdell had sublet the site of Nos 374–86 to Mark Milliken, a Bermondsey carpenter, in 1770. By 1774 a short row of three houses, perhaps built by Milliken, possibly with Upsdell, stood at its north end on the approximately 45 ft-wide site of Nos 382–6, their fronts set back from the present building line behind the causeway (fig. 155). These houses were probably two rooms deep. Another group of three houses, at Nos 376–80, was joined to the earlier group in 1776–81, but further forward to align with the contemporary buildings further north. This group may have been built by Thomas Lake, a Hackney brickmaker, with Thomas Brown, a carpenter.[50] The houses of 1770–74 at Nos 382–6 have gone, replaced on the forward building line. Nos 376–80 survive, altered around 1840 when No. 374 was added to the south and Nos 376 and 378 were refronted (fig. 160). No. 380 remains a surprisingly intact building of 1776–81.

The southern part of Kingsland Waste was thus solidly built up by 1787, with what must have appeared a motley array of houses. Elsewhere Kingsland Road still remained largely undeveloped, excepting Kingsland Place to the north (see below and fig. 155). Thomas Upsdell's first encroachment onto the waste in 1758 set the tone for its development – entrepreneurial, but modestly so. He later took the whole strip of land in one parcel, but seems to have had no interest in managing coherent development. Nevertheless, it was probably envisaged from the outset that the whole frontage would become built up. All the building plots were narrow fronted and therefore urban in nature, the builders having varied backgrounds, though most if not all were accustomed to operating in an urban context. The row

was surrounded by fields, but in terms of the space given to each house it might as well have been in the town. In spite of a surprising predominance of long (ninety-nine-year) leases, nothing very ambitious was attempted. Instead this was typical small-scale artisan speculation. With the cost of building a single house being more than most artisans earned in a year, and credit not easily come by, the houses on the waste went up in groups of three to five. Some of these small groups may have taken several years to complete, with a hiatus around 1780 when the market was slow. There would have been cash-flow problems, though perhaps not for Elkins, hailing from Mayfair and evidently a bigger operator.

Peter Upsdell's rise, fall and recovery typifies the lives of countless small building entrepreneurs, buffeted by the vagaries of economic cycles and housing demand. Many other late eighteenth-century London artisans travelled similar journeys, as exemplified by Simon Place, the Westminster baker and father of Francis Place, who went from journeyman, to 'gentleman', to ruin.[51] The

159 Nos 412–22 Kingsland Road. The house at No. 420 was built in 1779–80 by Thomas Summers, a scavenger and surveyor, for himself. The smaller 16 ft-square three-room houses at Nos 414 and 416 also have their origins in the late 1770s. Photographed 1999 (EH, BB99/11000).

160 (*above*) Nos 374–84 Kingsland Road, of which Nos 376–80 are altered six-room buildings of 1776–81. Photographed 1999 (EH, BB99/10993).

161 (*right*) No. 380 Kingsland Road, the stairs of 1776–81 at first-floor level. They combine an 'old-fashioned' closed string with stick balusters, and are cased with plain-panelled partitions to the L-plan back rooms, leaving a narrow lightwell beside the party wall. Photographed 1999 (EH, BB99/10988).

Upsdells' story and its sequel are more unusual for the way they clearly outline how brickmakers became housebuilders, and how aspiring artisans made low-status peripheral development and higher-status West End development interdependent. Upsdell moved from his roots on Kingsland Road to Soho, where he failed, bringing Elkins to Kingsland Road from Mayfair (and perhaps also Byrne from Covent Garden) to finish the modest development that Upsdell's father had started. Some of the same people who were developing the West End were also building three-room houses amid brickfields. As businessmen they knew that different markets demanded different products. Amid this Thomas Summers, the local scavenger, became a speculating surveyor, moving from a three-room house to one with at least six rooms and a stable. Upsdell and Summers were not so much 'gentlemen in the building line' as 'builders in the gentlemen line'.[52] The other artisans who are documented as having built on the waste were a mix of those with local roots and newcomers, some from far away, perhaps simply coming to build and move on, as many of the names are not known to recur in a local context.

As to who lived on Kingsland Waste, little can be discovered about those whose names appear in ratebooks and land-tax assessments before 1800, and the intelligibility and completeness of these sources are not such as to enable the systematic placing of individuals in particular houses. Architectural scale and character, along with what is known about rents, suggest that the houses would have been lived in by artisans, many no doubt in the brickmaking and gardening trades. The three- or four-room houses at Nos 398–406 were built to generate rents of £8 a year each, affordable for an established and regularly employed tradesman, but a stretch for a bricklayer's labourer who, even in full employment, would struggle to earn £30 in a year. Summers's £13 8s annual rent for No. 436 with the adjoining site for No. 438 would have excluded all but a few highly successful artisans (see chapter 1).

This, of course, assumes single occupancy. Census data from 1811 show that the houses along the waste were then nearly all in single occupancy, suggesting that they always had been; the exceptions were three of the somewhat larger houses, at Nos 386, 390 and 392, which housed two or three families in each. The three- or four-room houses further north had eight or fewer occupants, the absence of overcrowding indicating a degree of respectability. Householders at the south end of the waste ranged from a bank clerk in No. 376 to labourers in Nos 386–92. A baker, John Spears, was in No. 378, where his family had been since the 1790s; Ann Armitage, a widow, had been in No. 380 for a similar time, and lived there with one other female in 1811. There were those who were makers – of combs and dresses, as well as a warehouseman, a chandler, a leather curer, a carpenter (at No. 416), a bricklayer, a nurse, a milkman and gardeners. The bigger houses at Nos 420–28 all housed bank clerks. Upsdell's Row (Nos 430–36) housed a stonemason, a shoe maker, a coach maker, and John Rowley, a gardener (in No. 436).[53] The long occupancies of Spears and Armitage at Nos 378 and 380 were exceptions. Short-term occupancy was the norm in the houses along Kingsland Waste, insecurity of tenure being characteristic of lower-status housing. This was a fluid 'community', probably incorporating many recent immigrants to London, much as it has latterly. Many commercial activities would have been undertaken within the houses from the outset, though there were few 'shops' in the

modern sense. Before about 1830 there was no built-up hinterland for them to serve.

Ranging in size from three to eight rooms each, the late eighteenth-century houses of Kingsland Waste would have been vastly preferable housing to much of what would have been available nearby in Shoreditch or Spitalfields (see chapter 3). Such intermediate eighteenth-century housing rarely survives, and is now exceptional in the area, though it would not have been when new. Nearby there were, until the 1970s, late eighteenth-century groups on Hoxton Street that were closely comparable with the houses of Kingsland Waste.[54] On Kingsland Road itself the Geffrye Museum provides a kind of a reminder, albeit exceptionally coherent, of the equivalent scale of much early eighteenth-century housing (fig. 152). Upsdell's Row shows the one-room plan occurring in conjunction with elements of an awareness of polite appearances. Regular fenestration with tall first-floor windows not only provided the internal amenity of well-lit bedrooms with views across fields, but also pointed to a desire to make an outward impression that comprehended regularity. These were not furtive squatters' cottages, but, as the datestone confirms, a proudly proclaimed brickmaker's speculation, prominently situated on its own beside London's busiest approach road.

But the extent of such vanity should not be exaggerated. Nos 376–80 Kingsland Road were three larger houses, the vernacular character of which is manifest in many qualities. This was one of several groups of houses built in odd numbers on the waste. In building a group of three or five, the economy or classical rationality of mirrored pairing could not be systematically applied. Building in threes, a reflection of what these builders could afford to undertake, inevitably resulted in asymmetry. Further, the window positions in the two-bay front at No. 380 are not centred to the whole house, but rather to the open floor area of the rooms, an approach that, in taking internal arrangements rather than external appearances as primary, is more vernacular than polite (fig. 156). Disengagement from fashionable architectural practice can also be seen internally. There is a two-room central-staircase plan, with the staircase between the central partition and the rear chimneystack, lit by a narrow lightwell, a compressed and even later version of the layout of No. 94 Mile End Road, itself a seemingly late deployment of an ostensibly seventeenth-century type. These houses are not related to large high-status central-staircase houses of the period, as at the Adelphi, where the staircases were full-width intermediate cells. The staircase at No. 380 is simply a rectangle taken out of the back room (fig. 161). It is conservative in its forms, though the stick balusters it has were widespread in many higher-status late eighteenth-century houses, perhaps representing not so much a change in fashion as an acceptance into greater prominence of a thinned-down version of what had long been low-cost joinery.

Size and politeness were not necessarily linked. There is front-elevation asymmetry at No. 380 and No. 420, but not at the smaller houses at Nos 416 and 436 (figs 156–60). No. 416 was put up by a central London builder, and No. 436 by a local brickmaker with aspirations. No. 420 may show the scavenger-cum-surveyor Summers disregarding the exigencies of classical proportionality in his own larger house. While No. 380 does incorporate simple classical ornament in its internal joinery, it is so far from emulating higher-status house-building in both plan and elevation that its design can be understood only as knowingly indifferent to fashion. In houses that were not intended for occupants likely to have been overly concerned with polite appearances, builders who had not been conditioned by a market bearing such concerns had little reason not to adhere to customary or vernacular practice. Away from the realm of functionality, aspects of the classical could be and were readily adopted for surface ornament.

KINGSLAND PLACE AND SEMI-DETACHMENT

While the waste was being developed, something very different was happening to the north. Kingsland Place was built in the 1770s as the first extension of the hamlet of Kingsland towards London (figs 155 and 162). When the lock hospital closed in 1760, a strip of land opposite that had for many years been let as meadow was part of the property owned by St Bartholomew's Hospital, which was governed through the Corporation of London. In 1767 George Wyatt, 'carpenter', and Edward Gray, 'bricklayer', were given a sixty-one-year building lease of this land, having approached the hospital with a scheme for its development. They undertook to spend at least £2,000 erecting 'substantial' brick buildings within two years, but failed to meet this commitment. By July 1771 only foundations had been laid. Having 'been often admonished' and censured for being 'very negligent' by the hospital, they were threatened with a lawsuit if progress was not rapid. Some houses were up by October 1772, and thirteen had been built by 1775, Wyatt and Gray (by then designated 'surveyor' and 'builder' respectively) having spent a 'much larger sum' than they had initially intended.[55]

George Wyatt (d. 1790) may or may not have been a member of the Wyatt architectural dynasty. He was certainly a successful builder, becoming Surveyor of Paving in the City of London and a parliamentary witness for new building legislation in the 1770s (see chapter 9), as well as being one of the Corporation's Common Councillors. He had a timber wharf at Bankside, where, in the 1780s, he was one of the proprietors, along with its architect Samuel Wyatt, of Albion Mill (see chapter 4), adjoining which he lived.[56] His co-speculator, Edward Gray (died 1798), was no simple bricklayer. He had extensive brickfields near what is now King's Cross, and was also involved in high-profile developments, in his case in the West End, where he lived in the 1770s. He was Sir Robert Taylor's 'usual builder' in the 1760s and in 1771–5 he worked with both Sir William Chambers, who reproached him for the 'infamous' quality of his bricks, at Melbourne House (The Albany) and with Robert Adam at No. 20 St James's Square.[57] At Kingsland Wyatt and Gray were working in association with other established tradesmen of standing, spreading the costs and risks of the development by subletting house plots, as was usual in larger speculations. These associates included Thomas Poynder, a City bricklayer who worked at Uxbridge House in the 1780s and extensively for the East India Company in the years around 1800; Daniel and William Pinder, the latter a City mason; and John Horobin, a West End mason who was bankrupt by 1779.[58]

The thirteen houses that were built in the early 1770s were a single large freestanding house on the site of No. 572 (demolished), three almost but not strictly 'semi-detached' pairs that survive at Nos 540–66, Gray's Buildings, a row of four smaller houses on the sites of Nos 514–20 (demolished), and either the intervening pair at Nos 524–30, or the isolated pair at Nos 590 and 592 (figs 155, 156 and 162). The plot to the north of No. 572 remained empty, and the final semi-detached pair at either Nos 590 and 592 or Nos 524–30 was probably added in the late 1770s. Among the first occupants of Kingsland Place were John Box, a City corn factor, in No. 556, and Robert Campbell, a Westminster merchant, tenant of both Nos 540 and 542.[59]

Though only partially realised, this was an ambitious development, largely comprising linked pairs of substantial 40 ft-front properties. Clearly Wyatt and Gray had second thoughts about the commercial viability of the commitment made in 1767, perhaps owing to the failure to implement the Act of 1768 for road widening at Shoreditch. When they did get on with building, they left part of the land vacant and mixed house types in an irregular fashion that is unlikely to be what was initially intended. Nevertheless, the 'semi-detached' pairs of houses that survive are, and doubtless were always meant to be, dominant in this imposing group. Their regularity

162 Kingsland Place, showing Nos 530–66 Kingsland Road. This once imposingly regular group of houses of the 1770s was built in 'semi-detached' pairs with linked coach-house blocks by George Wyatt and Edward Gray, from designs perhaps emanating from the ideas of George Dance junior. Front gardens were built over with shops in the late nineteenth century. Photographed 1999 (EH, BB99/11225).

163 Nos 550–54 Kingsland Road, one of the Kingsland Place pairs of the early 1770s, showing the recessed entrance bays with oculus (round) and lunette (half-round) openings. Photographed 1999 (EH, BB99/11224).

suggests that the original scheme might have envisaged the whole frontage developed with eight pairs of houses, larger and smaller houses perhaps being substituted to give the speculation greater marketing flexibility.

Five pairs of the 1770s survive at Kingsland Place. The core of each pair is an almost cubic and carefully proportioned four-bay block, the footprints of the houses proper being less extensive than might be supposed (figs 156 and 163). Two-storey coach-house blocks, much rebuilt, flanked the houses, linking the adjoining pairs. Four of the five pairs, with Nos 540 and 542 as the exception, have or had recessed outer entrance and staircase bays, reinforcing the appearance of semi-detachment to what is strictly a continuous row, the northern pair excepted. To front and back these outer bays are or were articulated with what were termed 'fancy' fanlights and oculi below lunettes, to light the upper-storey staircase landings, classical flourishes that subtly set off the otherwise stark simplicity of the fronts, set back behind forecourt gardens.[60] Some variability in the elevations of the group probably reflects the involvement of different tradesmen on different sites and a breakdown from intended uniformity. There were eight rooms to each of the paired houses, with Portland stone and marble chimneypieces, as well as classical plaster enrichments in some of the parlours.

The quasi-semi-detached row was a fashionable innovation in the late eighteenth century on London's margins, insinuating greater gentility than a mere terrace, without obliging the waste of frontage that detachment entailed. Kingsland Place seems to stand at the beginning of the architectural exploration of the possibilities of semi-detached houses in series.[61] There had been isolated developments of this nature in the late seventeenth century and the early eighteenth, but the 'semi' in series does not really take off as a suburban house type until after 1800, in developments that follow on from Kingsland Place and its immediate successors, as at Michael Searles's Paragons on New Kent Road and Blackheath of 1788 onwards. Single semi-detached pairs had long been widespread, at differing social levels. The conceptual jump at Kingsland Place was seriation. Its particular innovative twist lies in the way that semi-linkage was used to blur the distinction between isolation and connection, carried through with real finesse in the articulation of the entrance bays. This was a milestone towards 'that lusty bastard, that misshapen key to the English suburb – the semi-detached house', expressing the 'equivocal blend of dependence and independence [that] is the essence of suburban architecture.'[62]

Perhaps George Wyatt was the architect of Kingsland Place, and he did call himself a 'surveyor' in the 1770s.

However, his accomplishments have otherwise come down only as those of a builder. Emanuel Crouch, Surveyor to St Bartholomew's Hospital from 1768 to 1778, had a supervisory role in respect of the completion of Wyatt and Gray's contract, but there is no evidence that he was involved with the design. He appears otherwise to have been even more of an architectural cipher than was Wyatt. Wyatt had strong City connections, as did Poynder and Pinder, and both Wyatt and Gray worked with the period's leading architects in other places. Given the innovative nature and architectural quality of Kingsland Place, which may have been designed as early as 1767–8, it is not unreasonable to look for the involvement, perhaps at one remove, of an architect. As Clerk of the City Works from 1768 George Dance junior would have had close dealings with Wyatt, as well as with St Bartholomew's Hospital, to the surveyorship of which he succeeded in 1778. Among Dance's many accomplishments was comparable innovation in the laying out of town houses in and around London, as in America Square, Minories and the adjoining Crescent and Circus (1767–74), unexecuted schemes for St George's Fields (1769–85), Finsbury Square (1769–92) and the layout of the Camden estate in Kentish Town (c.1790).[63] Given Dance's connections and his known and analogous inventiveness within classical canons in similar contexts, it may be that he was responsible for the ideas behind the semi-detached treatment and articulation of Kingsland Place, though this can be advanced only speculatively. Summerson has written about the origins of the semi-detached house in series as a widespread suburban type, acknowledging that he lacked evidence for pioneering models. Kingsland Place helps fill this gap.[64]

Moving south, the first development on the northern part of the long strip of manorial waste between Kingsland Place and Upsdell's Row was a single pair of houses which survives as Nos 478 and 480 Kingsland Road (figs 155 and 164). This pair was built in 1776–8 following the acquisition of a somewhat wider plot in a fifty-four-year lease to John Faulkner (alternatively Faulconer), perhaps identifiable as a bricklayer.[65] Kingsland Place was then newly built, and much other housebuilding was under way to the south along the waste. Of the first occupants, John Barrow and Samuel Taylor, no more than their names are known, but No. 480 was taken in 1780 by Thomas Hollingshead, a victualler who later occupied the Lamb Inn to the north.[66]

This pair of houses was freestanding amid brickfields, midway along Faulkner's plot and at its back, away from the road. There were front gardens with room to the sides for yards and outbuildings. The original entrance

164 Nos 478 and 480 Kingsland Road, a pair of houses of 1776–8 built by John Faulkner, topographically and typologically halfway between the houses of Kingsland Waste and Kingsland Place. Photographed 1999 (EH, BB99/11005).

positions at the outer ends of the fronts endure, and, despite much alteration, it seems clear that the entrances dictated off-centre positions for single window bays on each house. There is ample width for two-window fronts, but it is unlikely that had such ever existed they would have been separately replaced by different single-window fronts. The mirrored houses have a distinctive plan (fig. 156). Each house probably had two big rooms on each floor, those to the front on the upper storeys being L-shaped and heated from the party wall, those to the rear being large rectangles heated from the back. The staircases are, or were, sited in the forward half of each house, against the outer walls and the brick internal partition. From the front door of No. 478 a hallway leads to the base of the original staircase, much of which survives, being of traditional form, with closed strings, the

lower flights having turned column-on-vase balusters, and the upper flights stick balusters.

Isolated semi-detached pairs of houses were common around eighteenth-century London. Some were high-status buildings, designed for well-to-do commuters and having integrated coach-houses. Others were humbler pairs, built as such simply because two houses would often have been the limit of artisan speculation (see chapters 4, 6 and 7). Nos 478 and 480 Kingsland Road have none of the classical refinement of Kingsland Place, nor are they much like earlier purpose-built commuter pairs in outlying settlements further north such as Stoke Newington or Tottenham.[67] They are not, however, modest houses, each having six big rooms and 21 ft fronts. Flank-wall windows indicate that adjoining buildings were not envisaged; Faulkner's plot amid open fields might easily have been more densely developed. Given the temporal and spatial proximity to Kingsland Place, it appears that Faulkner was imitating the polite semi-detached house type, but freely adapting it from vernacular precedent.

This conjunction warrants closer scrutiny. There are no known close parallels for the plan (fig. 156). Unconstrained by the conventions of narrow town-house plots, it seems equally unaffected by rural building practice. The unconventional back-wall chimneystacks may reflect the large size of the houses in a vernacular context; the outer ends of the back rooms might have been thought too remote from a party-wall stack. The siting of the staircases is also unusual. The rear-staircase layout used a good deal of floor space for circulation, something embraced elsewhere as a signal of conspicuous consumption. Here the unforced compression of the staircase, giving tight, and therefore low-status, circulation, reflects vernacular practice in narrower houses, as at No. 380 Kingsland Road or No. 94 Mile End Road. Perhaps the stairs were placed to the front of centre, leaving bigger rooms to the back, because the backs overlooked fields while the fronts overlooked a busy road. Such an interpretation seems confirmed by the siting of the houses at the back of their plot, and indications that, despite the stacks, the back wall was more amply fenestrated than the front.[68]

The size of the houses, the disposition of spaces with attention to prospect and amenity, and the reflected proximity of Kingsland Place do imply some aim at gentility. However, the layout and the unproportional front point to the dominance of vernacular functionality. Minimum space was used for circulation, and single-window fronts were deemed sufficient given the availability of light from the flank walls. Internal detail can be similarly evaluated. In high-status stylistic terms, the mouldings of the staircase are typical of the early eighteenth century, their appearance in the 1770s indicating conservative disengagement from fashion.

While Nos 478 and 480 Kingsland Road seem in their particular form to be something of a one-off, buildings of similarly mixed character do survive elsewhere (see chapters 4, 6 and 7). The acceptance of aspects of fashionable form that brought amenity in conjunction with the absence of others that did not should not be interpreted as arising from clumsiness. It is more likely a result of selective emulation. The adoption of high-status practices would not have been universally understood as standardising, as something that needed to be taken on holistically rather than partially.

This pair of houses is engagingly intermediate, conforming with none of the contemporary buildings in the vicinity, though reflecting aspects of what was happening in both higher- and lower-status houses. Those at whom Faulkner was aiming his speculation would have needed to have been unconcerned with fashion, yet able to afford a large house, a seemingly peculiar convergence. Faulkner's likely market might have been locally based prosperous artisans with links to the surrounding brickmaking or gardening economy rather than commuters. There were no coach-houses, and Hollingshead did work locally.[69] The site, the builder, the houses and, very probably, the first occupants were between positions, neither 'middling' nor artisan, neither in the town nor in the country.

★ ★ ★

165 From Kingsland Waste to Kingsland Crescent, with the Fox Public House (as rebuilt in 1881) between. Photographed 1999 (EH, BB99/11006).

The development of the Kingsland Road frontage immediately south of the waste is the last element in this story, and the more interesting for knowledge of what preceded it to the north (figs 155 and 165). From around 1770 the tenant of the Fox Public House was William Brooks, followed from about 1780 by his widow Elizabeth, who also leased a substantial triangle of land to the south. She had the Fox rebuilt in 1790, about when five houses at Nos 362–70 Kingsland Road were also built (fig. 136). Elizabeth Brooks lived at No. 362, which may explain its distinctiveness, the tall first-floor *piano nobile* carrying relieving arches as if to create a visual stop in a prominent position.[70]

The scale and ambition of development here changed radically in 1792–3 when Kingsland Crescent (Nos 302–60 Kingsland Road) was built on Brooks's land to the south.[71] When she remarried in 1794 the property settlement was mediated by James Carr (*c.*1742–1821), an architect based in Clerkenwell. He had been responsible for the rebuilding of the church of St James, Clerkenwell, in 1788–92, and had put up his own speculative terrace at Newcastle Place, Clerkenwell, around 1793.[72] Perhaps Carr was the architect of the crescent.

Kingsland Crescent originally comprised thirty three-bay houses, the whole symmetrically composed with entrance positions radiating away from the centre (figs 136, 155, 156, 165 and 166).[73] The speculation attracted City-based professionals. In 1811 the houses were single-family homes for two to ten people, households predominantly headed by insurance, ship, wine and stock brokers, bank clerks and 'gentlemen'. There were two schools. John Sheldrake, a carpenter and exceptional in the crescent for being an artisan, lived at the south end in No. 302. Sheldrake may have been related to Richard Sheldrick, a carpenter active in numerous local speculations around 1800, whose success can be gauged by the fact that he had an address at Kingsland Place. Sheldrick was a leading developer of the last open frontage on the waste, building much of Warwick Place, later Nos 440–72 Kingsland Road, in 1802–8. These were small houses with 16 ft fronts that mixed labouring, artisan, professional and even genteel occupancy when new.[74]

In the local context and given the tone set at the waste, Kingsland Crescent was an astonishing speculation. This single long run of uniformly conceived houses was as ambitious in its scale as Kingsland Place had been twenty years earlier. This time, however, there are no coach-houses, the terrace having nothing of the suburban about it and making no apologies for its urban appearance. The shallow sweep of the crescent is obvi-

166   Kingsland Crescent, built in 1792–3, perhaps to designs by James Carr. Photographed 1999 (EH, BB99/11221).

ously inspired by high-status town planning elsewhere, ultimately deriving from Bath's Royal Crescent of 1766 via Dance's introduction of the form to London in 1767 at the Minories. The frontages were not significantly greater than those of the waste, but with ten rooms each the houses were bigger. In terms of the connotations of outward appearance, they carried utterly different signification. In its grandeur Kingsland Crescent stands alone between the waste and Shoreditch; the outbreak of war in 1793 perhaps put paid to any possible imitations.

The gap between Shoreditch and Kingsland was all but bridged by Acton Place (Nos 266–98 Kingsland Road), semi-detached pairs of large houses, built soon after 1808 (fig. 153). Though a generation later than

Kingsland Place, this was even then an early example of semi-detached housing in series. Here the pairs are wholly separate without linking blocks, though recessed entrance bays do seem to reflect the earlier development.[75] The ribbon that was Kingsland Road was cut by the Regent's Canal in 1819, irrevocably altering the character of development between Shoreditch and Kingsland. Yet there was not a wholesale shift towards the industrial and away from the residential, and later housing developments, as in De Beauvoir Town, reflect the suburban dialogue between the vernacular and the polite that had started here in the late eighteenth century. Tensions between the urban and the rural, the classical and the traditional, had become more self-conscious in the formal idioms of the Romantic and the Picturesque.

Conclusions

The eighteenth-century buildings of Mile End Road and Kingsland Road are intelligible as separate objects, but looked at together in and across their local contexts they reveal more. In terms of patterns of speculative development and building cycles, what happened in these places was in many ways typical. Stop-start development without estate planning tended to lead to the cheek-by-jowl juxtapositions of different kinds of housing that characterised these roads. On Mile End Road there was a long seventeenth- and early eighteenth-century period of mixed and sporadic development through which an aura of pastoral desirability endured. In the 1760s new building shifted towards urban density leading to further infilling and subsequently to decline. On Kingsland Road Thomas Upsdell's diminutive row of artisans' houses of 1758 stood alone until the 1770s, when there was over-reaching ambition in Kingsland Place and much humbler development of the waste, both of which fizzled with the downturn in the building market that lasted to the mid-1780s. Things picked up thereafter with the revival of upmarket aspirations at Kingsland Crescent, after which the outbreak of war in 1793 and consequent difficult finance killed off much speculative building. Another burst of activity after 1802 filled in gaps modestly, extending towards London more imposingly at Acton Place.[76]

In the early eighteenth-century retreat of Mile End Old Town wooden cottages faced big mansions without causing wealth to flee. Rather it is the gradually emergent regularity of Assembly Row in the 1760s that seems symptomatic of the area's fall from grace into sprawl.

Late eighteenth-century Kingsland Road presents a different opposition. The elegance, symmetry and proportionality of Kingsland Place and Kingsland Crescent contrast sharply with the irregularity of what was being built in between along Kingsland Waste at much the same time; the former developments seem to have aspired to being beacons of a new suburban light in what was otherwise an architecturally benighted district.

Distinctions between classes of housing emerge most clearly at the cusps of the transitions on each road. In terms of plot width and room size Nos 94 and 96 Mile End Road do not differ greatly from the slightly later buildings to either side. Similarly Nos 376–80 Kingsland Road, among the larger houses along the waste, are not substantially smaller than the houses of Kingsland Crescent. Yet in each case there are significant differences. Some houses were not given rear-staircase plans or regular classical elevations. This variability is not merely to do with design habits, but has also to do with manners of living. Where much of Assembly Row and Kingsland Crescent were thoroughgoing emulative expressions of the ascendance of the polite, Nos 94 and 96 Mile End Road and the houses at the waste were not.

As important as the intrinsic properties of houses in this polite-vernacular interface were external qualities such as surrounding space, whether yards, gardens or greens, and linkages, whether none, semi- or row-like. Perhaps most significant of all were spaces and linkages in relation to the town. On Mile End Road until the 1760s the town was something to be kept at arm's length. Similarly, on the Kingsland Road the politeness of the houses built before 1790 increased with their distance from London. Kingsland Crescent broke this pattern and instead of the suburban semi-autonomy that the pairs of Kingsland Place promised, presented classicism for a drone-like collectivity unambiguously dependent on the urbanity of London. Where land tenure had dictated the set-back frontages of the waste, the other developments (including Faulkner's) chose to create distance between the road and the houses as an amenity, the front garden being a crucial element of the suburban character of the houses. Kingsland Place seems to pass on the semi-detached idiom to Faulkner's isolated and eccentric pair, an important reminder, like Captain Cook and Peter Upsdell, that these were times and places of great social mobility, and that there can be no clean line separating the artisan from the gentleman. In seriating pairs of semi-detached houses Kingsland Place was, in fact, classicising a marginal and vernacular building form. The vernacular also informed the polite. Differing classes of houses were architecturally interdependent and cultural transmission was not a one-way street.

Relative coherence in Assembly Row, Kingsland Place and Kingsland Crescent is predicated not only in an understanding of classicism, but much more crucially in greater capitalisation. A few developers had financial backing beyond that available to most aspiring builders. This is not to say that the speculations of Kingsland Waste were not capitalist in nature, simply that they were small. The development of Kingsland Waste between 1758 and 1787 represents the waning of vernacular traditions in London that had long been an expression of the small artisan builder's ability to participate in a capitalist economy. The small houses of 1802–8 at Warwick Place were put up in larger and more uniform groups. The very different kinds of eighteenth-century houses on Mile End Road and Kingsland Road therefore reflect an argument that was less about architectural style than about control over the economics of housebuilding, about who was to live where and in what manner of house.

For centuries up to about 1800 the edge-of-town suburb in east and north London had been low-rent overspill. More desirable places were beyond in separate settlements. That the margins of the town might be marketed as desirable commuter retreats was a new phenomenon and a kind of compromise. The meaning and nature of the suburban was changing (see chapter 7). In the late eighteenth century it would not have been evident that London's outward growth would not continue to be as it always had been – uncontrolled and undesirable. On one level developments on Mile End Road and Kingsland Road are obviously to do with London's expansion, land ownership and land value, fashion, and the growing willingness of the professional classes to live out of London and commute. St George's Fields (see chapter 4) pointed to another direction from which to view the changing aspect of London's margins, that is as part of a pervasive campaign of improvement that began in earnest in the 1760s, aiming to bring order and regularity to a city that had grown to seem frighteningly out of control (see chapter 9). In these terms both Mile End Road and Kingsland Road were battlegrounds, with Assembly Row representing a defeat for old-style gentility, and Kingsland Crescent a victory for new-style improvement, at highly significant points in the mid-1760s and early 1790s. A capital with a disorderly built environment was thought to be dangerous. Routes into and out of the city were crucial for circulation, access, release and visual impact. At a time when enclosure was the general means of bringing land under control, the open highway was a place of crime and disorder, and a potent locus of fear. Mile End Road and Kingsland Road were principal routes into and out of London, and their tollgates were literally gateways to the metropolis. In 1766 John Gwynn argued against building along main roads, to allow clear separation between the city and each of its surrounding 'villages', within each of which he hoped for uniformity.[77] It was just too late for Mile End, but two years later came the Act for widening (clearing) the Shoreditch end of the otherwise largely open Kingsland Road.

The transformation of Kingsland Road through house development in the late eighteenth century was a shift from disorder to order, from clay pits, scavengers and waste to a grand classical crescent for insurance brokers, by way of an uncompleted experiment in high-status suburban housing, all in the space of about twenty-five years. Kingsland Place came about through a major City institution in the 1770s, putting large houses within railed plots immediately inside a tollgate, ordering the local environment without broaching the separation from London that Gwynn desired. That this attempt fell so short of its intended coherence, leaving such a prominent signpost to the metropolis to be overshadowed by the haphazard vernacular buildings of Kingsland Waste, would have seemed an affront to Gwynn, Dance and others of a similar mindset. What had risen up on the waste might have been perceived as something of a thrown gauntlet. It is as if with the building of Kingsland Crescent in 1792–3 the vernacular houses were surrounded, locked into politeness and thereby subdued. The long-awaited clearance and widening of Kingsland Road at Shoreditch in 1799 was more deliberate improvement.

The best attempts of eighteenth-century and later improvers notwithstanding, vernacular heterogeneity has reasserted its primacy on Mile End Road and Kingsland Road. The alterations, rebuildings and conversions that have disfigured the classical purity of Kingsland Place and Kingsland Crescent may be losses in terms of 'taste', but as denials of standardisation they need not be regarded so negatively. 'Heritage' in these places might appropriately be identified in the architecturally erratic, modestly commercial, tenurially transient qualities of Kingsland Waste. Next to this the aspirations of the grander developments to either side appear as short-lived aberrations.

Chapter 6

THE MILITARY·INDUSTRIAL SATELLITE: SHIPBUILDING AND HOUSEBUILDING FROM DEPTFORD TO WOOLWICH

> we came to Deptford, where I think the first House in the Town, like many others, is accounted a Conveniency for his Majesties Water-Rats, when residing upon Land, to Cool their Tails in, when we came a little further into the Town, we might easily discern, by the built [*sic*] of the Houses, what Amphibeous sort of Creatures chiefly Inhabited this part of the Kingdom.
>
> Edward [Ned] Ward[1]

From Shadwell to Rotherhithe, Thames-side London has so far made cameo appearances (see chapters 2 and 4), sufficient to indicate that riverside localities had unifying qualities in the eighteenth century, prominent among which were their 'amphibious' populations – mariners, artisans and labourers whose livelihoods depended on the sea. Much of this work was land-based industry, with shipbuilding and military connections being especially important. As riparian industry spread eastwards, it formed a link to previously remote places (figs 7 and 211), and perceptions of what was or was not London changed. Thus Defoe related in the 1720s, 'the Town of Deptford, and the Streets of Redriff, or Rotherhith (as they write it) are effectually joyn'd, and the Buildings daily increasing; so that Deptford is no more a separated Town, but is become a Part of the great Mass, and infinitely full of People also.'[2] He was not the first to perceive this connection. Prodigious growth and flourishing religious Nonconformity had meant that Deptford and neighbouring Greenwich had been two of the first settlements to benefit from the Act of 1711 for building new churches in the metropolis (see chapter 1). Such leads justify treating these places as being of, if not strictly in, London in the eighteenth century.

Deptford was unlike Shadwell or Rotherhithe, or anywhere else more integrally part of London, in that its riverside industry was dominated by a military installation, a naval dockyard, an early industrial facility at the

heart of the rise of British seapower. Downstream along the south bank of the river, the state had other important sites. From 1694 a former royal palace at Greenwich was transformed to be a royal hospital, a vast almshouse for naval pensioners. Beyond Greenwich the next settlement was Woolwich, where there was another important naval dockyard, alongside other military establishments. Greenwich was not a centre of shipbuilding, and in other important respects it was significantly unlike Deptford and Woolwich. However, in considering ordinary domestic eighteenth-century architecture, these three places, each then a large 'town' in its own right, can be treated together as having been a single major conurbation, a military-industrial satellite, neither suburbs (in so much as that word implies commuting or overflow) nor independent towns. Deptford, Greenwich and Woolwich were linked to and economically dependent on London, but they were not simply part of the decanting of industry and the poor into the capital's peripheries. They had a distinct collective identity as vital and self-sustaining maritime places.

Unusually for the time, the local economies of Deptford and Woolwich were built on wage labour. These were industrial towns where everything revolved round work in the yards. It would be anachronistic to imagine a cowed Lowry-esque proletariat in breeches; the shipbuilding artisan populations that walked to work in the dockyards were characteristically skilled, literate,

---

167 (*facing page*)   No. 62 Deptford High Street, a plain-panelled staircase partition in a house of 1790–91 that John Ashford, carpenter, built for himself (see figs 184 and 195). Photographed 1997 (EH, BB97/1583).

Dissenting, democratised and distinctly independent-minded. Deptford and Woolwich (though not Greenwich) were socially and culturally homogeneous with few of a status above that of artisans. That much was like Bethnal Green, but compared with the weavers the shipwrights were aristocrats. Domestic architecture was accordingly different. There is, for instance, no evidence for purpose-built multi-occupied tenement houses in the shipbuilding towns. In these places the vernacular housebuilding idiom had more in common with that of Southwark and Bermondsey, but without the cramping consequences of proximity to the City. Here developments in housebuilding reflect a confident and prospering artisan culture that was squeezed at the end of the eighteenth century, as economic relationships changed and middle-class and working-class identities emerged. This chapter probes into this, beginning with brief accounts of the three riverside settlements and further exploration of the significance of the naval dockyards. There follows closer study and differentiation of early and late eighteenth-century housebuilding and occupancy in Deptford, where more smaller eighteenth-century houses survive, leading to description of physical aspects of the architecture of houses across the wider area.[3]

Deptford, Greenwich and Woolwich

Deptford, the largest part of the military-industrial satellite, and closest to London, is about 3 miles south-east of London Bridge, just off most eighteenth-century maps of London (figs 6, 9, 168 and 211). It is separated from Greenwich by a tributary of the Thames, the northernmost part of which is known as Deptford Creek. Deptford began as two distinct settlements, a small riverside fishing port, where there was some shipbuilding by the fifteenth century, and, well to the south, around what became Deptford Broadway, another hamlet on the road that linked London and Dover, beside the northernmost crossing of the creek (the 'deep ford').[4]

Between 1513 and 1520 Henry VIII established a dockyard on Deptford's riverfront, for building and maintaining his ships. This royal naval dockyard grew to be a defining presence. As the dockyard grew, so did Deptford. By the 1680s the two hamlets had merged to be a single 'town', much the most substantial and densely built of any of the settlements around London, a distinction retained into the nineteenth century. Around 1703 John Evelyn recorded that 'By the increase of Buildings may be seene, that the Towne is in 80 years

become neare as big as Bristoll.'[5] This was not hyberbole; Deptford's population had risen rapidly to around 10,000 from about 4,200 in 1664 and 6,600 in 1676, making it in its own right truly one of England's larger towns. The rate of growth slowed in the eighteenth century, the population in 1801 being calculated as 15,548.[6] While large, Deptford was not a regional centre with its own hinterland and markets, but a satellite of the metropolis.

Riverside and maritime Deptford was richly described by Ned Ward in 1700:

> The Ladies that chiefly Inhabit these Cabbins, were the Wives of Marriners, whose Husbands were some gone to the East-Indies, and some to the West, some Northward, some Southward, leaving their Disconsolate Spouses, to make Tryal of their Vertue, and live upon Publick Credit till their return [. . .]. Many Shops we observ'd open in the Streets, but a Brandy-Bottle, and a Quatern, a Butcher mending of a Canvas Doublet, a few Apples in a Cabbage-Net, a Peel-full of Deptford Cheesecakes, an old Waste-Coat, a Thrum Cap, and a pair of Yarn Mittings, were the chief Shows that they made of their Commodities, every House being distinguish'd by either the Sign of the Ship, the Anchor, the Three Marriners, Boatswain, and Call, or something relating to the Sea. [. . .] The Town's without Necessaries; they've Butchers without Meat, Ale-houses without Drink, Houses without Furniture, and Shops without Trade; Captains without Commission, Wives without Husbands, Whores without Smocks, a Church without Religion, and Hospitals without Charity.[7]

While picturesque, this is neither a reliable nor a complete representation of Deptford. It omits the industry. Many more men lived inland, the male workforce of the naval dockyard ranging from about 700 to about 1,400 in the course of the eighteenth century. About one in three Deptford families was directly dependent on employment in the naval dockyard. There were also smaller private shipbuilding yards, and many more were indirectly dependent on the shipbuilding economy.[8] The quoted passage is also a view from 1700. In the course of the eighteenth century much changed, not least in relation to commodities. As will become clear, the houses did not remain without furniture.

Greenwich was close by, 'contiguous' according to Defoe.[9] It was not much smaller than Deptford, having a population that was rising similarly rapidly, from about 2,600 in 1664 to 4,600 in 1676, then from about 6,000 to about 14,000 in the course of the eighteenth century (figs 168 and 169).[10] However, Greenwich has a very dif-

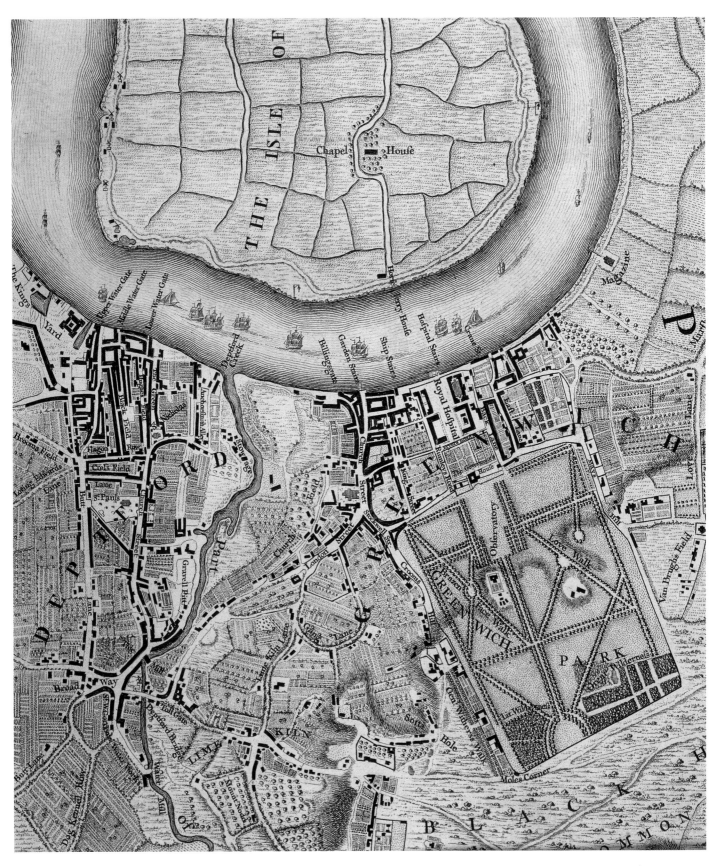

168   Deptford and Greenwich in the 1740s (from John Rocque, *An Exact Survey of the City's of London, Westminster [. . .] and the Country near Ten Miles Round*, 1746).

169 A view from Greenwich Park in 1729, showing the Queen's House and Greenwich Hospital at the foot of the hill, with the towns of Greenwich and Deptford beyond, and London in the distance. Detail of a painting by Robert Griffier (Belton House, Brownlow Collection, The National Trust).

ferent history, centring on the riverside site east of the medieval village. This was a royal outpost from the early fifteenth century and a favourite palace and park of the Tudor monarchs through the sixteenth century. The royal palace faded in importance through the vicissitudes of the seventeenth century, but the site was renascent from 1694, when Queen Mary gave it for the establishment of the charitable foundation that was the Royal Hospital for Seamen, or Greenwich Hospital. Adaptation and rebuilding to house naval pensioners in Britain's grandest ensemble of Baroque buildings continued until 1751.[11]

Greenwich was dominated by its majestic pile, whether as a palace or as a home for pensioners. In the sixteenth century the presence of the Court meant that many other fine houses were built in the town. There were also, of course, many smaller and humbler houses in what had otherwise been and remained a base for fishing and working seamen. The spine of the early town was Church Street, linking the parish church (rebuilt in 1711–14) and the Thames. By the late seventeenth century the town west of the palace was mirrored by dense development to the east beyond the royal grounds. The departure of the Court did not halt growth, but it probably exacerbated poverty, and the degree to which the attention of the visitor to Greenwich was drawn to

the humble. In 1700 Ned Ward 'took Notice of several Good Houses on the Left Hand, which look'd like Habitations fit for Christians to Live in; but in some parts of the Town the Huts were no bigger than Wig-wams, scarce big enough for a Cuckold and his Wife, to lye at length, without puting [*sic*] their Head or their Heeles in the Chimney Corner.'[12] Yet through the eighteenth century Greenwich remained distinctly genteel, still characterised by 'the lustre of its inhabitants',[13] now based more in military commissions and commerce than in courtliness. It was a place of resort that has retained much of what then made it attractive. The town grew southwards and uphill away from the river, and many fine seventeenth- and eighteenth-century houses still look over the former royal hunting ground that became Greenwich Park, as on Croom's Hill and Maze Hill. Where more modest houses survive, it is on lower ground, where the views are less good. Filling up gradually through the century, Greenwich Hospital housed upwards of 2,000 pensioners from 1770, carrying considerable servicing implications for the rest of Greenwich. The pensioners were let loose into the town, and many of their families lodged there. Despite the architectural glories, enduring gentility and the sublime open space of the park, there were sordid and raffish sides to eighteenth-century Greenwich. Not only were there

170 Woolwich in the 1740s (from John Rocque, *An Exact Survey of the City's of London, West-minster [. . .] and the Country near Ten Miles Round*, 1746).

all the pensioners, whose death rates meant rapid satu-ration of successive designated burial grounds. In the river there were convict hulks and, for three-day spells at Easter and Whitsun, Greenwich was a holiday resort for many thousands of London's apprentices, journey-men and servant girls, all in their finest clothes, in the park by day and the town by night for Greenwich Fair, the debauched excesses of which were notorious.[14]

A prolonged campaign to enlarge Greenwich Hospital and create a *cordon sanitaire* between the naval premises and the town resulted in the razing and redevelopment of much of the town centre in the later Georgian period, while related initiatives led to the fabrication of a local identity rooted in maritime heroism.[15] Little pre-nineteenth-century fabric survives in the old town. There are a few late seventeenth-century buildings on Church Street, and some small eighteenth-century houses are to be found to the south-west, as well as on the east side of the royal precinct.

East of Greenwich there were open marshes. On Greenwich Peninsula the Board of Ordnance built a gunpowder magazine in 1694–5, a source of anxiety to local inhabitants not removed until the 1760s. There was little else until a tide mill was formed on the east side of the peninsula in 1801–3.[16] Beyond lay Woolwich, where Henry VIII had established another royal ship-building yard in 1513 (fig. 170). East of this naval dockyard and the town there was a major ropeyard and Woolwich Warren. This land had been used as a depot for military stores from the sixteenth century. Fortified and adapted for manufacturing ammunition in the late

seventeenth century, the Warren remained a relatively small employer until the end of the eighteenth century, when massive expansion began. In 1805 the site became the Royal Arsenal, Britain's principal ordnance factory.[17]

In 1665, when Samuel Pepys, Clerk of the Acts to the Navy Board, decamped to Woolwich to escape the plague, the town had only about 1,150 people, many fewer than either Deptford or Greenwich. By 1800 Woolwich had burgeoned to hold a population of about 10,000.[18] Like its big sister upriver, Woolwich was over-whelmingly populated by artisans and labourers. Even more than Deptford it was 'wholly taken up by, and in a manner raised from, the yards, and public works, erected there for the public service'.[19] The naval dockyard and related ropeyard together employed from about 500 to about 1,400 men through the eighteenth century, at times paid a third more than their peers in other naval dockyards because Woolwich was thought such an unhealthy place to live.[20] Early on there was relative prosperity; in 1664 Deptford, Greenwich and Woolwich all had few inhabitants who were too poor to pay hearth tax.[21] But the rapidly growing population of Woolwich thereafter included many poor immigrants who had difficulty finding steady work.[22] Particularly narrow economic and low rating bases meant acute poverty and serious problems with social maintenance at times of low employment in the royal establishments.[23]

The town of Woolwich was compact but essentially linear, running along the river between and behind the dockyard and the Warren, with continuous development along the south side of the High Street by the 1670s.

171   Woolwich from the Thames in 1739. Engraving by Samuel and Nathaniel Buck (EH, BB86/3871).

The parish church was rebuilt on the high ground south-east of the dockyard in 1727–39 (fig. 171), by when alleys were filling up the central riverside, an area that declined into squalor and later came to be notori- ous as the 'Dusthole'. More open ribbon development of houses extended westwards opposite the dockyard on Church Street, not moving further inland until the end of the century (figs 170 and 172).[24] Very little of the early

172   Woolwich Royal Naval Dockyard in 1790. Painting by Nicholas Pocock (© National Maritime Museum, London).

173 Deptford Royal Naval Dockyard in 1752, showing *HMS Buckingham* on the stocks. The building with a shaped gable that is behind the quayside crane is the Master Shipwright's House of 1708, within the dockyard and still extant. Painting by John Cleveley the Elder, who was himself a shipwright (© National Maritime Museum, London).

town of Woolwich survives. There are some distinctive industrial and administrative buildings on the former dockyard and Arsenal sites, but evidence of the town's housing from before 1800 is scarce.

The Naval Dockyards

The naval dockyards at Deptford and Woolwich, alongside those away from London at Chatham, Sheerness, Portsmouth and Plymouth, were the nation's greatest industrial establishments in the seventeenth and eighteenth centuries, and important agents in the world's political economy. Deptford and Woolwich together built more men-of-war and merchant vessels than anywhere else in Europe in the seventeenth century, but receded in importance in relation to Chatham, Portsmouth and Plymouth in the eighteenth century. It was the scale of the naval dockyards as industrial enterprises that made Deptford and Woolwich atypical early

modern towns, unusual in their economic base, population mix and housing density, more so because they were so close to London. Without the dockyards, Deptford and Woolwich would have remained straggly riverside hamlets until London grew to meet them. With them they became substantial 'towns', albeit defined by their function as military-industrial service facilities for maritime trade, largely generated by London.[25]

Important determinants in the size and growth of Deptford and Woolwich were the labour-intensive nature of shipbuilding, and the relative security of employment in the dockyards, though wages were often much in arrears. There were concentrations of skilled artisans, workers in wood, technically sophisticated and in close contact with power and fashion. Late seventeenth-century ships built in these dockyards were fitted out above decks with ornamental carving of the highest quality. There was familiarity with and fluency in a Baroque figural and foliate ornamental vocabulary; it was as a ships' carver in Deptford that Evelyn, who

199

lived at Sayes Court, Deptford's manor house, 'discovered' Grinling Gibbons (1648–1721).[26] There were objections to the lavishness of ships, and later ornament was less figural and more architectural, as in balustraded balconies (fig. 173). Through the eighteenth century ships got bigger, and proportionally lighter, yet the shape and constituent parts of a ship of 1800 were much as they had been in 1600, while surface ornament and fitting out had altered with fashion. In anticipating the discussion of houses, it is worth registering that in formal terms shipbuilding was a conservative trade in which functionality and fashion remained distinct.[27]

Deptford and Woolwich were home to hundreds of shipwrights, each dockyard employing four hundred or more from that trade alone during wartime in the eighteenth century. The shipwrights owned their own tools and worked in gangs with elected 'team leaders'; their skills extended to complex draughting, and literacy was the norm. Each dockyard also employed dozens of house carpenters, and as many joiners. Wage rates were not exceptionally high, but the continuity of the work was important, and apprenticeships were both highly sought after and carefully limited. There was great and cultivated continuity of custom and practice. While the dockyards might have been havens for virtuosi, they were not for the virtuous, being notorious for corruption, jobbery and theft. Skilled workers were not easily replaced, and were thus able to command pay increases, particularly during wars. Difficult labour relations were endemic. Communication between and organisation across the naval dockyards was such as to enable effective combined strike action on numerous occasions.[28] With mid-eighteenth-century workforces of about 1,000 and annual wage bills of substantially more than £20,000 for each naval dockyard, considerable spending power was fed into the towns of Deptford and Woolwich, even allowing for usury and late payment. Those in work did not live uncomfortably. Shipwrights were paid 2s 6d to 3 shillings a day, and labourers a shilling to 1s 6d a day around 1740, about when a three-room house in a partially surviving row on Tanner's Hill in Deptford (see below) was sold for £35, indicating a likely annual rent of around £2 10s, affordable for any regular dockyard labourer.[29] When work was short in the naval dockyards, it was sought elsewhere, anywhere from the private shipbuilding yards to helping with harvests. Artisans who built ships in the dockyards also built houses in the town. The above-decks fitting out of ships was, in many essentials, little different to the building of a timber house (fig. 174): 'a Ship consists of divers Apartments, which may also be termed Stories, as well as in House-building.'[30]

An important by-product of the dockyards was waste timber, customarily used as payment in kind in vast volumes. Varying estimates all hold that the greater part of timber brought into the dockyards came out as what was known as 'chips'. It was asserted at the time that many of these 'chips' found their way into the fabric of local houses. Through the eighteenth century the Admiralty's attempts to abolish what it saw as an expensive perk, and what the workforce regarded as part of basic pay, were a constant source of grievance. 'Chips' were also the source of the expression 'a chip on the shoulder' as representing resentment against authority.[31]

When she visited Deptford in 1786, Sophie von la Roche was struck by the dockyard men,

> seeing the carpenters go out through the gate for lunch, each carrying his ration of wood on his shoulder, while a number carried a large net full of shavings. A nice sight indeed, this crowd of family fathers with their domestic provision of tinder going to their midday soup, weary from their labours and honest toil. God! How small a portion of these six million guineas they help to earn, falls to their lot! They were mostly fine-looking fellows; many of them with the eye of a mathematician, still making calculations. In them I saw embodied the fine English schools, where the citizen's son, like the son of the aristocrat, is taught all kinds of mathematics and really good Latin. I am sure many of them will be reading the papers this evening and talking of the common welfare [. . .]. The respect with which our coachman had to treat these working-people, not being allowed to turn in the narrow street until they had passed, gave me time to consider and contemplate them.[32]

What she saw, and what others have since described, were people who were keenly conscious that their skills combined with solidarity gave them dignity, power and independence, as well, crucially, as mutual responsibilities. Unwillingness to bend to authority was underpinned by intolerance of individualism. Collectivism was not simply a function of labour relations, but extended into the daily life of the town. In the 1750s shipwrights in Deptford, Woolwich and Chatham combined to form a retail society or food co-operative.[33] Even in the context of London's increasingly radicalised artisan class, the shipwrights were exceptionally well organised; in 1793 they formed the St Helena Benefit Society, an early trade union. However, the naval dockyards in Deptford and Woolwich had long since been in obvious decline relative to other naval dockyards. Awareness of this and the proximity of the alternatives presented by the metropolis no doubt brought additional pressures to bear on the skill-based solidarity of these inward-looking dockyard communities in the late eighteenth century. In the 1770s Admiralty pressure for changes in working practices at all the naval dockyards increased, with growing criminalization of petty transgressions, and Lord Sandwich's attempt to impose 'task work', that is restructuring of the self-elected working groups and the abolition of existing rates of pay. In 1775 this was resisted in what was perhaps the most serious strike of the century, one, it has been argued, that may have compromised the effectiveness of the British response to the American rebellion. Troops were sent to Woolwich, while Deptford was the only yard to keep working. Nationally the changes were rescinded, but 'task work' did stick at Deptford and Woolwich.

After the 1790s, when food prices rose by 90 per cent, hunger overrode defiance, and efficiency won out over liberty. Another wartime attempt at reform, spearheaded by Samuel Bentham (1757–1831) in the newly devised post of Inspector General of Naval Works, was more rigorous.[34] Bentham's mechanising and administrative initiatives not only succeeded in finally doing away with 'chips' in 1801, they also fundamentally altered the social topography of the dockyard towns, making shipbuilding less labour-intensive and more flexible, to conform with a doctrine of individual responsibility that left no place for collectivist traditions. On top of all this there was globalisation to contend with, as Indian-made teak ships reduced the Admiralty's dependence on English shipwrights. By 1815, before the advent of metal ships, the

174   Captain John Bentinck and his son William in a ship's cabin in 1775. Some of the carpenters and joiners who built such floating domestic spaces also built houses in Deptford and Woolwich. Painting by Mason Chamberlin (© National Maritime Museum, London).

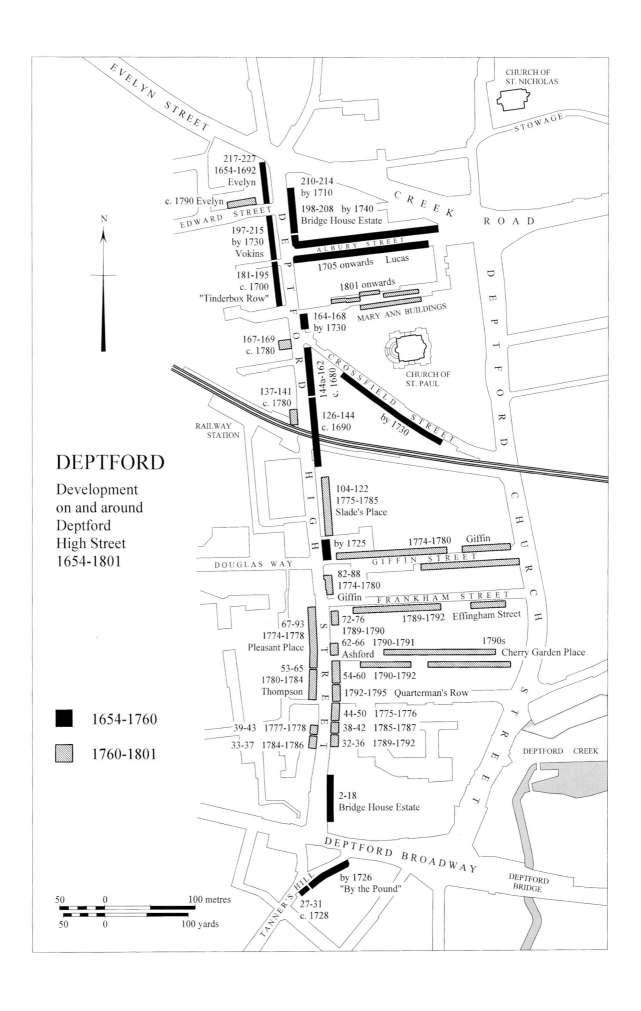

CHURCH OF
ST. NICHOLAS

STOWAGE

EVELYN STREET

217-227
1654-1692
Evelyn

c. 1790 Evelyn

EDWARD STREET

210-214
by 1710

198-208 by 1740
Bridge House Estate

CREEK

ROAD

197-215
by 1730
Vokins

ALBURY STREET

1705 onwards Lucas

181-195
c. 1700
"Tinderbox Row"

1801 onwards

MARY ANN BUILDINGS

164-168
by 1730

167-169
c. 1780

CHURCH OF
ST. PAUL

CROSSFIELD STREET

144a-162 c. 1680

137-141
c. 1780

126-144
c. 1690

by 1730

RAILWAY
STATION

DEPTFORD

Development
on and around
Deptford
High Street
1654-1801

104-122
1775-1785
Slade's Place

HIGH

by 1725

1774-1780 Giffin

GIFFIN STREET

DOUGLAS WAY

82-88
1774-1780
Giffin

FRANKHAM STREET

67-93
1774-1778
Pleasant Place

STREET

72-76
1789-1790

1789-1792 Effingham Street

CHURCH

62-66 1790-1791
Ashford

1790s
Cherry Garden Place

53-65
1780-1784
Thompson

54-60 1790-1792

1792-1795 Quarterman's Row

STREET

44-50 1775-1776

39-43 1777-1778

38-42 1785-1787

33-37 1784-1786

32-36 1789-1792

■ 1654-1760

▨ 1760-1801

2-18
Bridge House Estate

DEPTFORD BROADWAY

DEPTFORD CREEK

DEPTFORD
BRIDGE

TANNER'S HILL

by 1726
"By the Pound"

27-31
c. 1728

50   0   100 metres

50   0   100 yards

power, prosperity, customs and social structures of the dockyard shipwrights and other artisans had been decisively broken. What has been called a 'republic of wood' had been defeated, its denizens proletarianised.[35]

Builders and Occupants:
Early Eighteenth-century Deptford

Too few small eighteenth-century houses survive in Greenwich or Woolwich to warrant exposition of local development patterns. As Deptford retains more early houses, it is here considered in more detail. The early houses of what was the most densely populated part of Deptford, near the river, have gone, with the sole exception of the substantial former Master Shipwright's House within the former dockyard (fig. 173). Most of the eighteenth-century survivals are inland, along the road that became Deptford High Street, known as Butt Lane until 1825. Well into the seventeenth century this was little more than a track through market-garden fields linking the distinct riverside and Broadway hamlets.[36] Here the maritime merged with the agricultural, and houses of varying sizes were incoherently mixed. Until about 1770 the road retained some rusticity, built up at its north end and sparsely developed near the Broadway, with open land to the centre. The Broadway continued as a place of shops and inns, with the town pound to the south-west at the foot of Tanner's Hill (figs 168 and 175).[37]

Inland Deptford in the early eighteenth century had some notable architectural highlights. The parish church of St Nicholas stood to the east, having been rebuilt with local funds in 1696–8 to designs by Charley Stanton, the Southwark carpenter who had also rebuilt St Mary Magdalene, Bermondsey, the already derivative design of which he repeated in Deptford to provide another centralised auditory with a chaste Tuscan interior (see chapters 1 and 4). East of Butt Lane was Union Street (latterly Albury Street and mislabelled 'Crossfield Lane' by Rocque), ambitiously laid out and developed from 1705 by Thomas Lucas, a local bricklayer, who lived in one of the Butt Lane corner houses. He oversaw the building of some forty substantial brick houses, granting ninety-nine-year building leases that were extensively mortgaged via dockyard contacts. Remarkably, conditions on the leases imposed outward architectural uniformity (figs 176, 194 and 204). Early occupants included affluent sea captains, shipwrights and a dancing master.[38] Further south were the stupendous and full-blooded Baroque Church of St Paul and its extraordinary triangle-plan rectory, both designed by Thomas Archer for

176   Nos 34 and 36 Albury Street, Deptford, part of Thomas Lucas's precociously regular development of 1705 onwards. Photographed 1997 (EH, BB97/01642).

the Commissioners of the Act of 1711, and built from 1713 to 1730, their imposing architectural presence underscored by surrounding open space, as well as by contrast with surrounding buildings (fig. 177).[39] Evelyn's manor house at Sayes Court, nearer the naval dockyard to the north-west (fig. 180), was replaced with a workhouse in the 1720s, a different symptom of the growth and social shifts that came with industrialisation.[40]

Among Deptford's houses those on Albury Street were highly atypical. The north end of Butt Lane, the west side of which was at the margin of Evelyn's Sayes Court estate, was built up from 1654 onwards, largely in timber, in piecemeal stages, house plots having varying frontages, usually about 15 ft. Early lessees and occupants included Edward Ledger and Nathaniel Pile, both shipwrights.[41] Albury Street aside, the most coherent devel-

175 (facing page)   Deptford, indicating development on and around Deptford High Street, 1654–1801.

177 The Church of St Paul, Deptford, and its rectory, of 1713–30, Thomas Archer, architect. The view also shows timber houses on Butt Lane (Deptford High Street), to the left in the foreground, and Crossfield Street, to the right in the distance. Anonymous engraving, c.1740 (GL).

opment in the vicinity was probably Tinderbox Row, fourteen timber houses of around 1700, each probably having three 15 ft-square rooms, and following the lead set on Evelyn's land in 1654 in being set back behind small forecourts (figs 175 and 178).[42] Rapidly increasing density in this area is revealed by the early eighteenth-century introduction of a housing form that was more widespread in parts of Deptford closer to the river, that is the use of narrow plots for twin front/back houses (see

178 Tinderbox Row, timber houses of c.1700 on the site of Nos 179–95 Deptford High Street, as painted in 1841. Demolished 1843 (by permission of the British Library, Add. MS 16945, f. 17).

below). Across Butt Lane and further south there was a continuous run of more than twenty three- or four-room late seventeenth-century brick houses. Two of these, built around 1680 by Joseph Hall, a Greenwich potter, were adapted around 1692 to be a Quaker Meeting House. Another house of similar date survives as No. 150 Deptford High Street (figs 179, 194 and 196). At the south end of the group was the Congregational Meeting House of 1702.[43] Much further south across the Broadway was an early row known as 'By the Pound' (latterly Nos 1–25 Tanner's Hill). Thirteen predominantly small timber properties were present by 1726, with three three-room timber houses that survive as Nos 27–31 Tanner's Hill being added around 1728. There was rebuilding and enlargement of many of the earlier properties in this row from the 1720s to the 1750s, for occupation by dockyard artisans, labourers, gardeners and a fisherman (figs 188, 193, 194, 196 and 207).[44]

Deptford's early eighteenth-century housebuilders were a diverse range of prospering artisans, based either in the naval dockyard or in other local trades. As elsewhere, those who became builders were most commonly carpenters, apparently acquiring small freeholds before building modest speculations, though the evidence relating to tenure and the costs of land, houses and rents is thin. Probate inventories of the household goods of two property-owning house carpenters, William Baker (d. 1732) and John Timms (d. 1736), indicate that Deptford's early eighteenth-century builders were, like

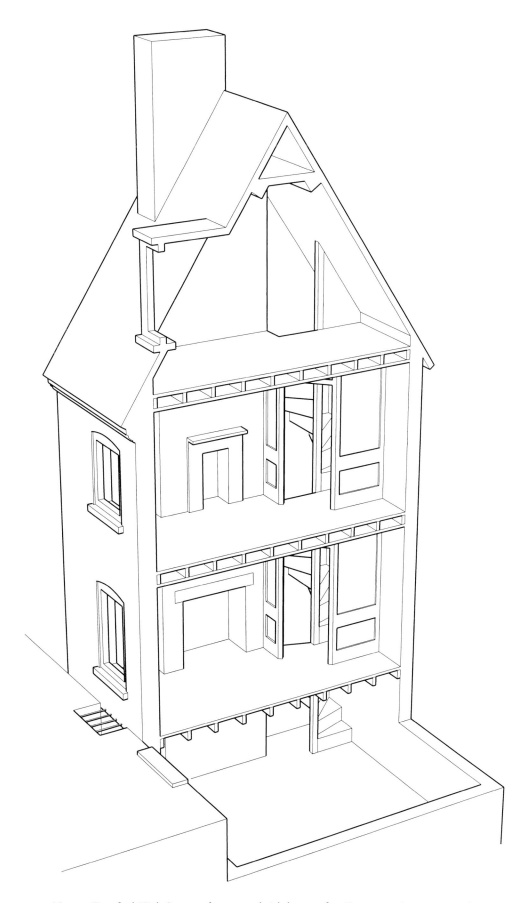

179 No. 150 Deptford High Street, a four-room brick house of *c.*1680, perspective reconstruction.

those of Bethnal Green, moderately affluent and well housed in local terms, literate and in possession of luxury goods, perhaps even cosmopolitan, but not magnates. Baker on Butt Lane and Timms on Church Street both occupied houses of six rooms with closets, seemingly in two storeys and garrets, with their yards and workshops adjoining. Baker owned a tea table, Delftware, a writing slate, '6 bound books and some pamphlets', a clock, two looking glasses, and, in his 'best bedchamber', '18 pictures with glass' and '10 India pictures'. Timms's home incorporated a room that was a 'counting house', with a writing desk, a bookcase, twelve books and pamphlets. He too had a tea table, a looking glass and numerous pictures. Even with possessions of this nature, the household goods left by these men were worth only about £50 each, greater wealth residing in small property holdings.[45]

Butt Lane's other rate-payers were probably, like Baker, living in the houses for which they paid rates. There were 120 rated properties in 1744, virtually all houses. The trades of sixty rate-payers have been identified, of whom fifty-one were paid for working in the naval dockyard, twenty-seven as shipwrights. Among the other sixty rate-payers, there were twenty who were women, at least half of whom were widows.[46] This suggests that in the 1740s a quarter or more of Butt Lane's householders were shipwrights, and that about half or more were dependent on the naval dockyard for income. Deptford's artisans were not the workshop-based class found elsewhere, and Butt Lane was not a commercial street until the nineteenth century. Many of the houses were just that, probably incorporating neither workshops nor shops.

A more particular impression of Butt Lane's occupancy in the early eighteenth century can be conveyed through another specific example that also illustrates the local ascendancy of artisan-entrepreneurs. Thomas Lewis (d. 1732) was a dockyard caulker who, with his wife Sarah, owned and lived in a well-furnished four-room brick house with a wash-house and a yard, among scattered dwellings midway along Butt Lane on the east side, about 200 ft south of the Congregational Meeting House (figs 168 and 175). His 'parlour' furnishings included a tea table, Delftware and two framed pictures, and the 'kitchen' incorporated a looking glass, two small glass sconces and a large oval table. There were thirty-one prints on the staircase, fifty-one cups in 'the chamber', and his working tools were in the 'garret'. Inventories do not necessarily record items in the spaces where they had been used, but Lewis seems to have had so much material culture that clutter was spilling out; '27 old bound books' and many kitchen implements including a chocolate mill were in his wash-house. Yet Lewis's household goods were altogether worth only about £23. Abutting his house to the north were two more brick houses sharing a 31 ft frontage. In 1744 these were occupied by James Mollinson and John Smallpiece, both shipwrights. Sarah Lewis appears to have been the daughter of William Baker, the aforementioned house carpenter, who lived a short distance to the south in his rather larger house. Baker's sister Mary was married to John Sewer, whose family owned larger tracts of Deptford, including much of Butt Lane and property near the pound.[47]

A sample of fifty-six inventories from Deptford spanning the period 1687 to 1762 is sufficient to indicate that respectability and comfort, as manifest in possessions ranging from good fabric to birdcages, were widespread, even in small houses, and particularly where there were maritime links. However, it must be recalled that those who had their possessions documented were more likely to have been those with more possessions. Ned Ward's 'Houses without Furniture' and 'Huts [. . .] no bigger than Wig-wams' are important reminders that there was humble housing of which no other accounts survive. The inventory sample also shows that, the biggest houses aside, there was no strong correlation between house size and the value of possessions, as well as that the household goods for which a Deptford artisan might have expected to have to find space increased considerably through the first half of the eighteenth century. Those inventories exhibited at the Prerogative Court of Canterbury suggest that Deptford's population was cosmopolitan and literate; Rochester inventories provide a humbler corrective. Books are linked closely with the skilled trades that were mostly maritime in nature.[48]

The inventories of John Anthony (d. 1690), a waterman, George Humphreys (d. 1710) and Robert Brown (d. 1711), both cobblers, and Thomas Beard (d. 1743), a glazier, describe homes of working Deptford people without evident links to the dockyard or the sea. Each home of three or four rooms was described as containing a sparse array of goods of less than £15 in value (excluding stock in trade). With the exception of a few looking glasses, what was noted was straightforwardly utilitarian, just chairs, beds, tables and cooking utensils, in rooms without functional designations other than kitchen, chamber or shop.[49]

Inventories of mariners and dockyard workers present a different picture, tending to describe homes with many more objects, but of no greater overall size or wealth.[50] Josiah Mansfield was a merchant seaman who, in 1725, left his widow Anne a four-room Deptford home for which they paid £5 yearly rent. Among goods worth only £9 7s 3d, they had a number of Indian objects,

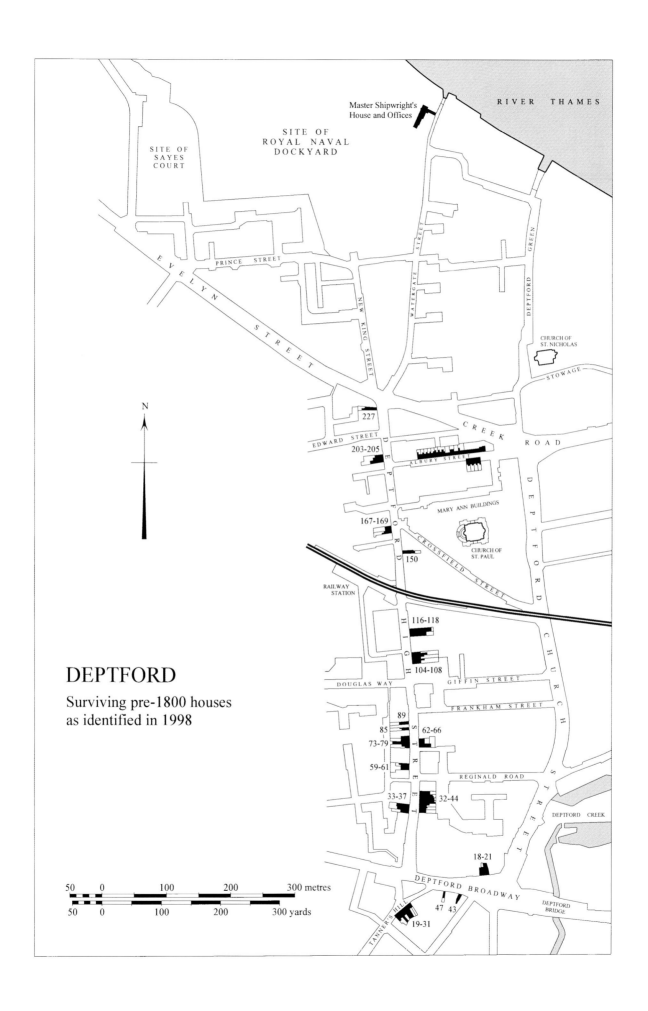

RIVER THAMES

Master Shipwright's
House and Offices

SITE OF
ROYAL NAVAL
DOCKYARD

SITE OF
SAYES
COURT

DEPTFORD GREEN

CHURCH OF
ST. NICHOLAS

PRINCE STREET

EVELYN STREET

NEW KING STREET

WATERGATE STREET

STOWAGE

N

CREEK ROAD

227

EDWARD STREET

203-205

ALBURY STREET

DEPTFORD

MARY ANN BUILDINGS

DEPTFORD ROAD

167-169

CROSSFIELD STREET

CHURCH OF
ST. PAUL

150

RAILWAY
STATION

CHURCH STREET

116-118

HIGH

104-108

DEPTFORD
==============

DEPTFORD

Surviving pre-1800 houses
as identified in 1998

DOUGLAS WAY

GIFFIN STREET

FRANKHAM STREET

89

85

62-66

73-79

STREET

59-61

REGINALD ROAD

33-37

32-44

DEPTFORD CREEK

18-21

DEPTFORD BROADWAY

DEPTFORD
BRIDGE

47 43

TANNER'S HILL

19-31

50	0		100	200	300 metres
50	0		100	200	300 yards

including books, pictures and, in a designated 'parlour' that was probably on the ground floor, a tea table. Joseph and Sarah Herring had a two-room home. He too was a merchant seaman, owed wages by the East India Company when the inventory was taken in 1728. Money owing excepted, the Herrings' whole estate was worth £9 11s 9d. Their 'lower room' had cooking utensils, tables and chairs, as well as India pictures, other small prints and a large looking glass. Upstairs the 'chamber' contained two beds, a walnut chest of drawers, trunks, chests and four old chairs. It also had other less purely functional objects, including prints on the walls, another smaller looking glass, an 'India' cabinet, a model ship, a tea board and teaware. In such small households rooms were of necessity flexibly used, so single-purpose designations to rooms may be misleading. The Mansfields and the Herrings were not wealthy people, yet both households contained objects indicative of new kinds of consumption. That they can not have had the space in which to display these objects discretely and that access to the Herrings' upper 'chamber'/parlour can have been only via the 'kitchen'/dining room are revealing signs of tensions and overlaps between vernacular and polite cultures.[51] Over-furnished multi-purpose rooms are recurrent in Deptford inventories by the 1740s. William and Margaret Vening died within a week of each other in 1757, William being owed for work in the naval dockyard. The 'kitchen' in their three-room home had a 'clawfoot dining table', books and Delftware, and their 'back chamber' had a bed along with '2 chinese paper prints', '16 small glazed prints', a coffee mill and more Delftware.[52] Emulative consumption was becoming increasingly usual in this worldly maritime milieu, but it was neither universal nor thoroughgoing. At this period conspicuous consumption for the sake of comfort and respectability might have tended more to reinforce than to undermine Deptford's strong artisan identity.

Builders and Occupants:
Late Eighteenth-century Deptford

Independent Deptford's greatest growth took place in the years up to 1730. There followed a mid-century period of relative stasis, after which there was a substantial if episodic housing boom, with hundreds of new houses being built between 1770 and 1792, of which about seventy were in Butt Lane. These houses, the great majority being brick, have a higher survival rate (figs 175 and 180). They are of great interest for what they show about both continuity and discontinuity in relation to earlier development.

A few new streets were laid out, with some outside money being invested. To the north, on the Sayes Court estate, the Evelyn family enabled development again. King's Yard Row, on what became Prince Street, was built in 1770–72 during enlargement of the dockyard (fig. 181). This was an orderly range of nearly forty brick houses, deep enough to suggest that, above cellars, they had six rooms each.[53] In 1774–80 Giffin Street was created by Thomas Giffin, a Southwark builder, in partnership with Robert Clark, a Greenwich merchant. This was the most ambitious housebuilding project in Deptford since Albury Street, but the houses were more modest, and the scheme was only partially realised, as fifty-eight three-storey six-room houses with 15 ft frontages.[54]

On Butt Lane the grandest late eighteenth-century development was Slade's Place (Nos 104–22 Deptford High Street), ten almost regular houses in what would conventionally be termed a terrace (figs 182, 195 and 196), built between 1775 and 1785 by Mary Lacy (1740–95), an extraordinary person. Exceptionally for an eighteenth-century woman she independently acquired and practised a building-trade skill. She did this through subterfuge; other female 'builders' of the time became such through inheritance or marriage. Born with a self-confessed 'restless and intractable disposition',[55] she left home aged nineteen disguised as a man, and went to sea, finding a place on a ship as a carpenter's apprentice. Ashore after the Seven Years War she gained and completed a shipwright's apprenticeship in Portsmouth Naval Dockyard in 1770, only for 'arthritis' to force her to reveal that she was a woman in 1771. In a notable instance of compassionate flexibility she was granted an Admiralty pension. She moved to Deptford from where she published her autobiography in 1773 under the name Mary Slade, ostensibly gained through marriage, but perhaps in fact adopted to pass as related to Elizabeth Slade, with whom she lived in the biggest of the houses she built at Slade's Place. Their house had a 30 ft front and huge gardens. Most of the other houses had only 18 ft frontages, but even this was substantial in Deptford. The whole group had three full storeys and raised ground floors, front gardens and views across fields to London. First occupants included a captain, a clergyman and a 'gentleman'.[56]

Elsewhere along Butt Lane there were smaller developments by local builders, gradual and fragmentary infilling of open frontages. John Thompson was a dockyard carpenter who developed property as he rose in status. From 1787 to 1794 he was Master House Carpenter at the Naval Dockyard, but in 1777 he had been simply a 'carpenter and broker', then in 1781 a 'surveyor'.

Between 1780 and 1784 he headed a consortium of tradesmen who developed a 108 ft frontage with seven houses that became Nos 53–65 Deptford High Street, a central 18 ft-wide three-storey property flanked by smaller 15 ft-wide two-storey houses.[57] Across the road, and in part replacing what had been William Baker's house, Nos 32–60 Deptford High Street were six- and eight-room 16 ft-front houses built in threes and fours between 1775 and 1792, seemingly for occupation by artisans or tradespeople (figs 183, 195, 202 and 206). Five much smaller 'cottages' were squeezed in as Quarterman's Row in 1792–5, all but one of the first rate-payers being women. Three houses at Nos 62–6 Deptford High Street were built in 1790–91 by John Ashford, another carpenter, who took the larger house at No. 62 for himself (figs 167, 184 and 195).[58] With eight rooms each, the two smaller houses adjoining were, like Nos 32–50, substantially larger than houses from Deptford's earlier small speculations (fig. 196).

There was also rebuilding and the enlargement of older properties, timber being replaced with brick, and front/back pairs with larger single houses. At Nos 203 and 205 Deptford High Street two pairs of small early eighteenth-century front/back timber houses built by and for dockyard shipwrights were separately replaced in 1774–5 and 1775–6 with single six- and eight-room houses of different form, the larger and earlier one at No. 205 incorporating a shop, first occupied by John Creasy, a tea dealer (figs 185 and 195). By the 1770s even labourers were tea drinkers, a fact that itself gives the lie to any simple equation of emulative consumption with gentility, but Creasy's arrival is a sign of wider transformations in Deptford. At No. 227 Deptford High Street another front/back pair that had been occupied by dockyard artisans was replaced in 1791–2, providing another eight-room shophouse for Thomas Palmer, a baker (figs 195 and 205).[59] Like Creasy, Palmer represents shifting fortunes. He was not just a baker and a shopkeeper, but also a landlord with other property in Deptford.[60] Late Georgian refronting, if not complete rebuilding, was also apparently widespread nearer the river, along both Deptford Green and Watergate Street (figs 186 and 187).

Deptford's late eighteenth-century housing boom was not like that of Bermondsey. It was not part of London's outward growth; Deptford remained beyond the commuter belt, still a satellite rather than a suburb. The new houses appear in greater measure to reflect local factors. The replacement and enlargement of older houses suggests that the boom was not simply about housing units. It was at least in part to do with the scale of available housing. Economic insecurity might have combined

181   King's Yard Row, houses of 1770–72 on the site of Nos 2–46 Prince Street, Deptford, those more distant retaining door hoods. Photographed 1946. Demolished (LMA).

182   Slade's Place (Nos 104–22 Deptford High Street), showing houses built in 1775–85 by Mary Lacy (alias Slade), the 'seaman', turned shipwright, turned housebuilder, at Nos 104–8, 116 and 118, with the site of her own house at No. 110 between. Photographed 1999 (EH, BB99/11290).

with prosperity as a motor for housing development. There would have been growing awareness of Deptford's decline in naval importance, while, with the advent of 'task work' in the 1770s, shipwrights were obliged to reform their working lives. Perceptions of the future may have altered and cultural continuity been disrupted by

183   No. 36 Deptford High Street, an eight-room brick house of 1789– 92, perspective reconstruction.

184 (*above*)   Nos 62–6 Deptford High Street, built 1790–91 by John Ashford, carpenter. The larger house was for himself, Nos 64 and 66 being a pair of smaller houses, though even these had eight rooms each. Photographed 1998 (EH, BB98/03024).

185 (*right*)   Nos 203 and 205 Deptford High Street, the former built in 1775–6, the latter in 1774–5 as a large eight-room shophouse first occupied by John Creasy, a tea dealer. Photographed 1998 (EH, AA98/01692).

individuals seeking new economic footholds. Social diversification included the transfer of prospering local people to a wider range of enterprise and into better housing. John Thompson was one of a number of shipwrights and other dockyard artisans found relabelling themselves. Another was Gilbert Ferguson, a shipwright for whom the four-room house at No. 152 Deptford High Street was substantially extended in 1765–70. He moved into an even larger new house at the south end of Slade's Place in 1776–7, and was later designated a surveyor.[61] Mary Lacy shifted her endeavours from

186   Deptford Green from the tower of the Church of St Nicholas, showing the variety of Deptford's townscape. Photographed *c.*1900. All demolished (EH, BB98/05029).

187 Watergate Street, Deptford, with a good turnout for the photographer. Many of the houses appear to have been refronted or rebuilt in brick in the later Georgian period. Photographed 1911. All demolished (LMA).

dockyard work to property development, not for artisans, but for a professional and genteel market. Her reasons for doing so were exceptional, but her choice of this route for her energies was not. Investment in bigger houses, either for oneself or as speculations, might have become increasingly attractive as a hedge against decline and insecurity.

Of course there were still many who had no option but to live in small houses, and these were not all old. At the end of the century there was a distinct falling off in the quality of the houses being built on and around Butt Lane, as was the case much more widely in the 1790s as builders found finance increasingly difficult. The instance of Quarterman's Row has already been mentioned. The south side of Effingham Street (Frankham Street) was developed in 1789–92 and Cherry Garden Place (Hales Street) was built up gradually through the

1790s with together more than a hundred houses, all smaller than those that had preceded along Giffin Street (fig. 175). John Thompson had taken a strip of land south of Albury Street in 1777, but he sold it on and it remained open until 1801, from when even meaner two-room cottages with fronts of 10–12 ft were put up as Mary Ann Buildings.[62]

Late eighteenth-century developments in Deptford show a merging of artisan investment and self-improvement with activity on the part of a wide range of traders, shopkeepers, professionals and gentry. Deptford was becoming less monocultural as prosperity brought diversification in the local economy. By 1800 shops had started to appear on Butt Lane as it became a spine for numerous side streets and began to transform itself into a High Street. In the early nineteenth century Deptford was less than ever a desirable suburban retreat. It was

188 Nos 19–31 Tanner's Hill, Deptford, timber-framed houses of c.1728 and thereabouts. Photographed 1998 (EH, AA98/01656).

189 Nos 111 and 112 Woolwich High Street, early eighteenth-century three-room timber-framed houses. Photographed 2000 (EH, AA004701).

densely populated and unsuited to picturesque or sylvan development. One step behind the upward mobility for some there was a downward shift for others. Independent artificers were being replaced with tractable and impecunious workers. Such early nineteenth-century development as there was around Butt Lane was of small, low-grade housing in interstitial courts.

House Construction

From Deptford to Woolwich, as in riparian east London and Southwark, timber house construction endured well into the eighteenth century, remaining the norm below all but the highest social levels. In Deptford in 1700 'their Dens were chiefly Wood, all of one form, as if they were oblig'd by Act of Parliament, to all Build after the same Model.'[63] Of this wooden housing there is little surviving witness, though Nos 19–31 Tanner's Hill still stand, as do Nos 111 and 112 Woolwich High Street, similar houses on a closely analogous site that faced that town's cage and stocks at the junction with Bell Water Gate (figs 170, 188, 189 194 and 196). There are also numerous early views of comparable buildings long since demolished (figs 177, 178, 186, 187 and 190).[64] Unlike Southwark and Bermondsey, Deptford, Greenwich and Woolwich remained untouched by London's late eighteenth-century building-control legislation, yet they seem to mirror the inner districts in that timber fell out of use fairly comprehensively after around 1760, brick having become gradually less exceptional over the preceding century. That most surviving early houses in Deptford, Greenwich and Woolwich are brick built is, of course, an unrepresentative reflection of the differential survival rates of large and small, brick and timber. Brick was not, however, as uncommon as it was in Southwark. There were brickfields in Deptford from at least the sixteenth century and, with potteries across the area, there is no evidence that any roofing material other than plain tiles or pantiles was used before the nineteenth century.[65] Brown stock bricks that were probably locally made are found widely in surviving buildings, from Albury Street to Slade's Place (figs 176, 182 and 204), in the latter case being used in a relatively grand development at a time when finer stock bricks from north Kent were available. This evidence of economy is a reminder that while at one level the endurance of timber house-building is a reflection of artisan conservatism and continuity, it is more fundamentally representative of material factors. The shift away from timber construction, which coincides with the decline in the shipwrights' 'republic of wood', probably reflects changes in

190   Church Street, Greenwich. Photographed *c.*1900. Demolished (EH, BB029363).

availability and cost more than it does either legislation or cultural emulation.

Timber houses that were designedly brick fronted are known in London districts where such construction might be understood as a compromise reaction to legislation. But this was a common eighteenth-century approach to housebuilding outside London. Beyond the reach of the Acts it must be indicative of concern for outward appearances, at the same time seeming to confirm that timber building did remain more economical. Significantly perhaps, evidence for such houses in the area covered by this chapter comes only from relatively high-status Greenwich. No. 24 Royal Hill survives from what was built as a freestanding pair on the semi-rural southern margins of Greenwich in the early eighteenth century (figs 191 and 194). It retains its original asymmetrical brick front, and evidence that it was originally timber-built behind. The three houses at Nos 4–8 Feathers Place are a similar small speculation of 1744, just north of Greenwich Park on the east side of the former palace precinct, probably put up as infill on a densely built road that had many large houses (figs 192 and 194). They too have a brown-brick front wall,

and appear originally to have been timber-built behind.

In the timber houses that do survive little structural wood is visible. There is insufficient basis for general conclusions as to the nature of house carpentry in this context, but there are interesting pointers. Nos 27–31 Tanner's Hill, Deptford, is a single build of around 1728 with framing that, though largely concealed, appears to be intact above the ground floor and of regular scantling. Low-cost construction is evident in the use of quarter-round wall plates, also present in the back wall of the closely comparable house at No. 111 Woolwich High Street. No. 24 Royal Hill retains the thin stud-and-brace partition that was all that separated it from its pair, as well as rough rafters, some clearly re-used, others made from halved thin branches. More extensive is the evidence from Nos 23 and 25 Tanner's Hill, Deptford, an unequal pair that was wholly timber framed when built sometime around 1750 (figs 193 and 194). The timber here is interesting not only for what it reveals about low-status housebuilding practice, but also in relation to the proximity of a naval dockyard. The front, back and north flank walls have been rebuilt, but the south flank and party walls and the roof retain framing that is particu-

215

sidered in the context of metropolitan attempts to regularise internal timber construction, such as the specified scantlings for structural timbers in the Rebuilding Act of 1667, or recommended practice in early carpenters' manuals, the framing in No. 23 Tanner's Hill is from another world, one where the principles of architectural order that tend to underpin understandings of both rural vernacular house construction and polite town houses were known but unattainable, and thus met with nonchalance. Surprisingly, given this crudity of construction and evidence that the rooms were ceiled and otherwise lined out, the party-wall framing was originally open to view in No. 23, the smaller of the two houses. On the first floor there was a simple black painted skirting,[68] a classical *coup de grâce* on an improvised sub-vernacular piece of architectural design.

★   ★   ★

191   No. 24 Royal Hill, Greenwich, to centre, the surviving right half of an early eighteenth-century pair of brick-fronted five-room timber houses. Photographed 1998 (EH, BB98/02673).

192   Nos 4–8 Feathers Place, Greenwich, built in 1744 as three five-room brick-fronted timber houses. Photographed 2000 (EH, BB000817).

larly informative. There is much re-used timber. Where economy counted and conservatism permitted it, the re-use of building materials was entirely usual.[66] In a mix of cheap softwoods, one beam has been identified as Baltic larch, a wood not generally encountered in English houses, though other documented buildings are invariably either earlier or bigger.[67] The party wall or cross frame as seen on the first floor in No. 23 Tanner's Hill comprises two frames made with thin rough-sawn and waney softwood studs and 'dado' rails. There are substantial tension braces across the lower corners of each frame, to triangulate the assembly and support the rails, an unconventional construction repeated in the formerly external south flank wall of No. 25. These braces have cleanly sawn outward faces, but their inward faces are waney edge timber. They vary greatly in depth and curvature, and are fixed to the endposts of the panels by long wrought-iron nails. At first glance braces of this size might suggest an early build date. However, they are not typical of earlier timber framing in either form or fixing, nor are they likely to be re-used pieces of house timber. Perhaps they were 'chips' from the dockyard. Other details illustrate the low quality of the construction. There are quarter-round beams, the rounded faces hidden within the flooring, and lower-grade studs in the garret incorporate what looks like sapling wood. Con-

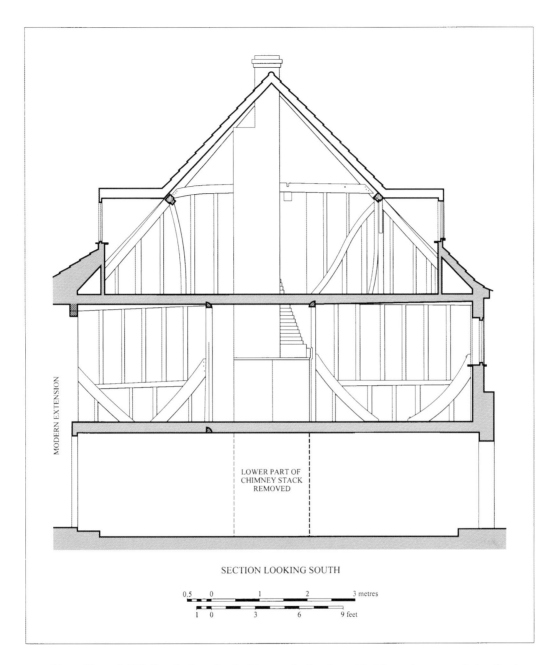

MODERN EXTENSION

LOWER PART OF
CHIMNEY STACK
REMOVED

SECTION LOOKING SOUTH

0.5   0   1   2   3 metres

1   0   3   6   9 feet

193   No. 23 Tanner's Hill, Deptford, section looking south, showing mid-eighteenth-century timber framing.

House Plans

The 'one form' to which Ned Ward referred in 1700 was probably the basic one-room-plan house, three rooms in two storeys and a garret. Sparse survival, early views and rateable values suggest that such houses were widely built in both Deptford and Woolwich from at least the mid-seventeenth century until the mid-eighteenth. Late medieval antecedents were probably typically one-room-and-garret dwellings.[69] By 1664 the semi-

metropolitan 'new towns' of Deptford, Greenwich and Woolwich had many small new houses, but few with only one hearth compared with most other towns in Kent. High proportions of the houses in Deptford and Woolwich had two to four hearths, while 'royal' Greenwich had an unusually high percentage of houses with five or more hearths.[70]

Surviving examples of the one-room plan all have roughly square footprints with sides of 13 ft to 16 ft, and rear-stair compartments framed against side-wall chim-

217

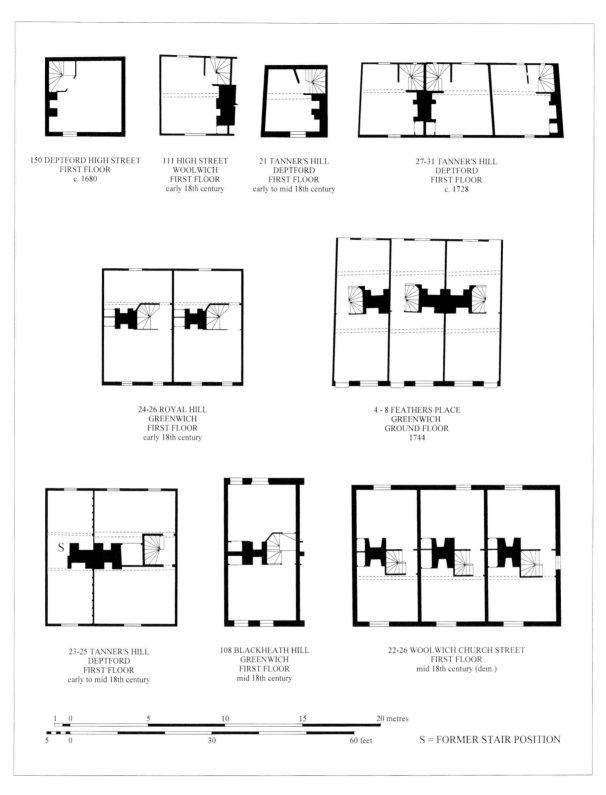

150 DEPTFORD HIGH STREET
FIRST FLOOR
c. 1680

111 HIGH STREET
WOOLWICH
FIRST FLOOR
early 18th century

21 TANNER'S HILL
DEPTFORD
FIRST FLOOR
early to mid 18th century

27-31 TANNER'S HILL
DEPTFORD
FIRST FLOOR
c. 1728

24-26 ROYAL HILL
GREENWICH
FIRST FLOOR
early 18th century

4 - 8 FEATHERS PLACE
GREENWICH
GROUND FLOOR
1744

23-25 TANNER'S HILL
DEPTFORD
FIRST FLOOR
early to mid 18th century

108 BLACKHEATH HILL
GREENWICH
FIRST FLOOR
mid 18th century

22-26 WOOLWICH CHURCH STREET
FIRST FLOOR
mid 18th century (dem.)

1 0   5   10   15   20 metres

5   0   30   60 feet   S = FORMER STAIR POSITION

194a and b (*above and facing page*)   Reconstructed plans of late seventeenth- and early to mid-eighteenth-century houses in Deptford, Greenwich and Woolwich.

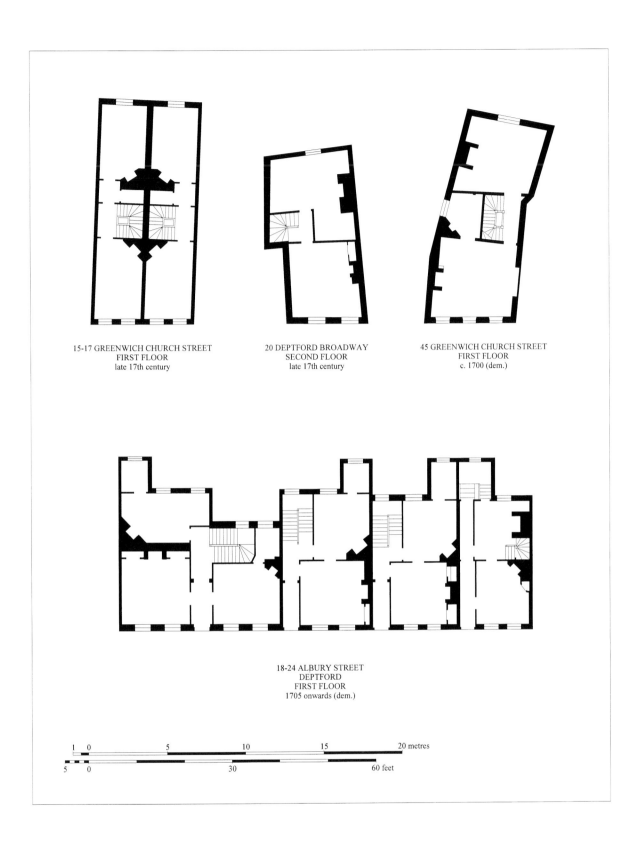

15-17 GREENWICH CHURCH STREET
FIRST FLOOR
late 17th century

20 DEPTFORD BROADWAY
SECOND FLOOR
late 17th century

45 GREENWICH CHURCH STREET
FIRST FLOOR
c. 1700 (dem.)

18-24 ALBURY STREET
DEPTFORD
FIRST FLOOR
1705 onwards (dem.)

1   0   5   10   15   20 metres

5   0   30   60 feet

195 (*following page*)   Reconstructed plans of late eighteenth-century houses in Deptford and Greenwich.

196 (*page 221*)   Reconstructed sections of Deptford houses.

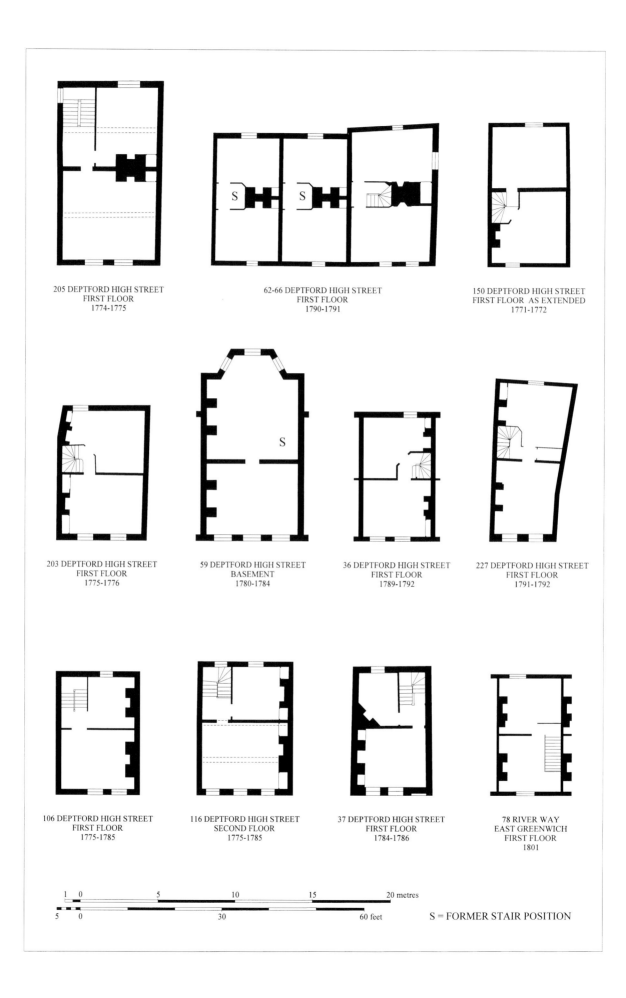

205 DEPTFORD HIGH STREET
FIRST FLOOR
1774-1775

62-66 DEPTFORD HIGH STREET
FIRST FLOOR
1790-1791

150 DEPTFORD HIGH STREET
FIRST FLOOR AS EXTENDED
1771-1772

203 DEPTFORD HIGH STREET
FIRST FLOOR
1775-1776

59 DEPTFORD HIGH STREET
BASEMENT
1780-1784

36 DEPTFORD HIGH STREET
FIRST FLOOR
1789-1792

227 DEPTFORD HIGH STREET
FIRST FLOOR
1791-1792

106 DEPTFORD HIGH STREET
FIRST FLOOR
1775-1785

116 DEPTFORD HIGH STREET
SECOND FLOOR
1775-1785

37 DEPTFORD HIGH STREET
FIRST FLOOR
1784-1786

78 RIVER WAY
EAST GREENWICH
FIRST FLOOR
1801

1 0   5   10   15   20 metres

5 0   30   60 feet

S = FORMER STAIR POSITION

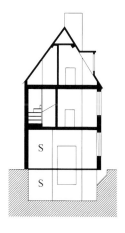

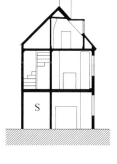

31 TANNER'S HILL
c1728

152 DEPTFORD HIGH STREET
c1680

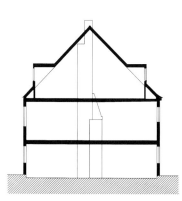

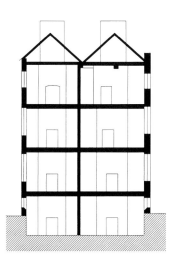

23 TANNER'S HILL
early to mid 18th century

116 DEPTFORD HIGH STREET
1775-1785

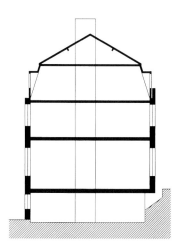

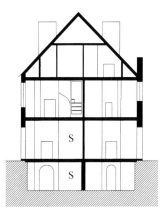

64 DEPTFORD HIGH STREET
1790-1791

36 DEPTFORD HIGH STREET
1789-1792

S = FORMER STAIR POSITION

neystacks (figs 179, 188, 189 194 and 196). Landing doors are angled to maximise living space (fig. 207), and the rear-stair position means that the chimneys rise or rose in front of the ridge. This distinctive external feature means that views of demolished buildings can be compared with rateable values to point to further examples of the type for which there are no plans (fig. 178). There is no evidence for the front-staircase tenement layout found in more central and less prosperous districts.

Such three- or four-room houses were built singly, in pairs, threes, long rows or as front/back pairs. Mention has already been made of the latter, an interesting reflection of density, widespread in Deptford in the early eighteenth century, but not traced elsewhere. On or behind narrow town-house plots, two houses were built one in front of the other, contiguous but separately occupied, with side-passage access, each with a one-room plan. Examples at the north end of Butt Lane have been cited, but most of these pairs were nearer the river; there was a run of eleven pairs in Hughes Fields.[71]

As noted above, many of the early occupants of these and other one-room-plan houses would have been mariners, shipwrights and other dockyard artisans. For such people three-room houses were good accommodation at the beginning of the eighteenth century, especially given that there was no need for workshops, nor yet possessions or social habits such as to necessitate numerous rooms. As in Bethnal Green and Southwark, the vertical one-room-plan house was not just a reflection of urban density. It was frequently built in circumstances where other options were possible, on deep plots, sometimes set back from the road, and sometimes given cellars. It was no more a product of expensive land than it was of population density. Nor is there evidence that it is explicable here in relation to purpose-built multiple occupation or workshop use. In an artisan culture it was a traditional and respectable house type, departures from which would have been either unaffordable or pointless. Two-room plans in houses of four or fewer rooms would have meant unnecessarily dark interiors and saved little climbing of stairs. Any emulative virtue afforded by horizontal circulation would, if perceived at all, have seemed far less worth acquiring than tea, silk or literature.

Yet one-room-plan housing appears not to have formed part of any of Deptford's housing developments of the 1770s and 1780s, and the front/back one-room-plan pairs seem not to have survived beyond 1800. The traditional house type had apparently become less acceptable. The spread of possessions and prosperity meant that it lost respectability in the late eighteenth century. From the 1790s smaller one-room-plan developments in places like Quarterman's Row and Mary Ann Buildings were clearly for inferior habitation. As in other towns one-room-plan houses continued to be built widely in Deptford, Greenwich and Woolwich well into the nineteenth century, but in mean clusters that were never anything but poor housing.

To follow, once again, the house-plan typology set out in chapter 2, a consideration of two-room-plan houses should start with those having a central chimneystack (figs 194 and 195). This layout was current, indeed widespread, in Deptford, Greenwich and Woolwich throughout the eighteenth century, most notably and widely in the form codified by Moxon (fig. 44). From Deptford there are many recorded examples, most now demolished,[72] perhaps in large part because central chimneys impeded adaptation for open circulation, for shops and otherwise. A number have survived, some being oddities that depart from the Moxon standard. Nos 23 and 25 Tanner's Hill are narrow and wide variants of the more usual layout, the larger house being particularly eccentric. In the large purpose-built shophouse built for the tea dealer Creasy at No. 205 Deptford High Street in 1774–5, a central chimney was combined with a showy rear staircase, as in the virtually contemporary house at No. 27 Crosby Row, Bermondsey (fig. 123). Nos 62–6 Deptford High Street of 1790–91 are more typical, and evidence of how long the appeal of this layout endured.[73] Even in his own somewhat larger house, the carpenter Ashford kept the basic Moxon layout, with a dogleg staircase rather than the winder stair that narrower fronts forced (fig. 167). These staircases would have been lit by borrowed light, ample if a door is open. This might explain the rear stair in Creasy's deeper house.

In Greenwich the freestanding pair from which No. 24 Royal Hill survives was virtually identical with Ashford's pair in plan and scale, but from more than half a century earlier. It is a measure of the town's growth that this urban double-pile layout was here deployed in largely open surroundings. All these houses were so small that even with winder staircases it was impossible for the back rooms to be regular. Nos 4–8 Feathers Place of 1744 are, like No. 23 Tanner's Hill, so narrow as to have no room for closets. Here the ground- and first-floor back rooms were under a separate lean-to roof, the taller main range being one room deep with staircases and chimneystacks in line at its back. This variant seems to point to two-room layouts being conceived as simple extension from one-room traditions. The central-chimneystack layout thrived in the late eighteenth-century inland spread of Greenwich to the south. Nos 62, 64 and 74–8 Royal Hill (fig. 197), Nos 55 and 57 Greenwich South Street, and Nos 106 and 108 Blackheath Hill are small brick speculations that are analogous in layout to the earlier buildings on Royal Hill. It has been shown that houses like these went up at much the same time on the margins of Bermondsey, in close proximity to Michael Searles's more sophisticated conceits; here too Searles was active, laying out Gloucester Circus between Royal Hill and Croom's Hill from 1791.[74] Tradition and innovation converged on the same ground.

In Woolwich houses with central chimneystacks were once numerous, but most have gone. Kingsman Street, running inland from the dockyard, had a long row of late eighteenth-century houses much like those on Royal Hill.[75] Nos 121–3 Woolwich High Street survive, retaining the form if not the fabric of their eighteenth-century origins as three of a group that was four (fig. 198).[76] At what was the westernmost end of Woolwich in the mid-eighteenth century, opposite the dockyard, stood Nos 18–26 Woolwich Church Street (figs 170, 172, 194 and 199).[77] Nos 22–6 were five-room houses, like the Feathers Place houses in Greenwich in having chimneystacks that rose behind a one-room-deep main block, the back rooms being roofed as lower rear wings. Here the stairs projected into the front rooms. Further east, opposite later extension of the dockyard, were Nos 146–68 Woolwich Church Street, a terrace of eleven houses of around 1800 that also incorporated central chimneystacks (fig. 200).

All these examples of the central-chimneystack plan have been presented to emphasise that, though long since abandoned in fashionable London, this traditional house plan was standard in this locality right through and even beyond the eighteenth century. It continued to be built in a range of sizes, with variety of staircase provision being a rough guide to the diversity of means of those for whom it was built. The enduring popularity of this layout is a distinctive characteristic of settlements along and near the south bank of the Thames (see chapters 4, 7 and 8). It is not paralleled on the north side of the river, but is reflected further east in Kent. While it seems that the Thames was a cultural barrier, the relative ease of water-borne communications in the period goes a long way to explaining why the vernacular housebuilding traditions of the London riverside, from Bermondsey downstream, retained stronger affinities with those of the towns of the north and east Kent coasts, from Gravesend and Chatham round to Deal and Dover, than they did with non-riparian parts of London.

This does not explain why this plan remained popular in these places. Indeed builders from south of the Thames have been found working north of the river. There were also deeper cultural factors at work. Moxon's *Mechanick Exercises* remained sufficiently well known

197   Nos 74–8 Royal Hill, Greenwich, late eighteenth-century brick houses with central-chimneystack layouts. Photographed 2000 (EH, BB000820).

198   Nos 121–3 Woolwich High Street, eighteenth-century houses with central-chimneystack layouts, much rebuilt in the late twentieth century. Photographed 2000 (EH, AA004702).

199 Nos 18–26 Woolwich Church Street, mid-eighteenth-century houses with central-chimneystack layouts. Photographed 1928. Demolished *c.*1960 (EH, R37).

through the Georgian period for Peter Nicholson to decide to update it in 1812, but this does not mean that dog-eared century-old copies were being thumbed by south London carpenters in the 1790s. The plan might

200 Nos 146–68 Woolwich Church Street, a terrace of *c.*1800 incorporating central chimneystacks. Photographed 1951. Demolished (LMA).

seem to suit commercial use as it provides clear separation between front and back, shop and domestic spaces. However, many of the documented examples were originally houses without shops, and if such a rationale lay behind its use it would be odd that shopkeepers elsewhere did not hang on to it. Similarly, the cellular nature of the plan could be understood as having suited multiple occupation and subletting, perhaps granting a greater measure of privacy to each room, but documentation of any such instances of designed multiple occupation has not been found. Perhaps the central stack was, or, more importantly, was perceived to be, a cheap way of building, though the cost differences seem unlikely to have been other than marginal (see chapter 2).

There are not convenient functional or material explanations for the longevity of the central-chimneystack plan south of the Thames. It seems rather to be an enduring local habit that may simply be a reflection of the strength of the area's artisan identity and the proportionally weak influence here of emulative culture emanating from the West End. As prospering artisans became increasingly able to build themselves houses of more than four rooms, which practicality dictated had to be two rooms deep, the traditional central-chimneystack layout was a more likely choice than a genteel import in districts where artisans were socially dominant. Without habituation to the virtues of interconnecting suites, there would have been less impulse to avoid the greater separation of rooms.

The central-staircase plan that was the norm in better town houses in late seventeenth-century London recurs in mirrored pairs of houses in Greenwich, as it does in Bermondsey, from the late seventeenth century to the mid-eighteenth. A narrow late seventeenth-century version survives at Nos 15 and 17 Church Street (fig. 194), as does a much wider variant in a substantial free-standing pair of around 1730 at Nos 47 and 49 Maze Hill. No. 45 Greenwich Church Street (demolished 2000) and No. 20 Deptford Broadway are relatively large houses, the former evidently designed to incorporate a shop. Both have eccentric variations on the central-staircase plan that place framed-newel stairs on the side away from the chimneys, perhaps to accommodate a

third heated room in one case, and an irregular plot in the other.[78]

In the late eighteenth century a different kind of central-staircase plan was used lower down the social scale, in smaller and narrower houses where winder staircases were framed against the rear stacks, as at Nos 32–44, 203 and 227 Deptford High Street (figs 195 and 205). This layout is distinctive for the way that it makes the most of available floor space, essentially just adding a room to a traditional one-room plan, as indeed happened at No. 150 Deptford High Street in 1771–2. However, it meant the ground-floor front room had to be crossed before going upstairs. This is not the case at Ceylon Place (Nos 70–84 River Way) of 1801, houses from a new century and a new kind of industrial world (figs 195 and 201). This neat brick row of eight two-storey 'cottages' was 'workers' housing' in a planned industrial development in the middle of nowhere – a part of Greenwich marshes that had been known as Bugsby's Hole. The place was redesignated 'New East Greenwich' and the

201   Ceylon Place, Nos 70–84 River Way, 'New East Greenwich', an industrialised row, built in 1801 to house workers at a new tide mill. Photographed 2002 (EH, AA033078).

202 Nos 32–44 Deptford High Street, a row of eight-room brick houses of 1775–92, broadly vernacular in form and originally occupied by artisans and tradespeople. Photographed 1998 (EH, AA98/01663).

houses built for the families of those manning the substantial new tide mill.[79]

The rear-staircase plan was introduced to Deptford from 1705 in the largely eight-room houses of Albury Street, though not uniformly. It has been said that this genteel street 'was like a testing ground for compact urban plans'.[80] This overlooks truly compact options, but given the external regularity of the street the variety of its internal layouts is striking (figs 176, 194 and 204).[81] The rear-staircase plan seems not to have appeared on Butt Lane until 1775, in Slade's Place (fig. 195). At Nos 33–7 Deptford High Street of 1784–6 the rear-stair position in 17 ft fronts forced very small back rooms and angle fireplaces. Stair windows were sometimes absent, all these houses remaining small enough for the stairs to be lit by borrowed light. It is significant that even the smaller rear-staircase-plan houses seem to have attracted genteel occupants, unlike the central-staircase-plan houses of equivalent size. The relative absence of the rear-staircase plan from Deptford in the late eighteenth century seems to be due to the type's attractions having lain in the kind of gentility to which the area was neither suited nor overly given.

Precedent was strong in Deptford, Greenwich and Woolwich, but house planning was enormously varied and underwent major change in the late eighteenth century. A traditional preference for vertical living in a small number of rooms receded in favour of more rooms and horizontal movement, though not decisively towards the fluidity of the rear-staircase plan. The well-established central-chimneystack layout endured because artisan culture thrived. At the same time other variations of two-room layouts were widespread. There was probably greater diversity of plan form in this area's smaller houses in the late eighteenth century than there had been either fifty years earlier or would be fifty years later; it was a time of great upheaval.

Surfaces and Classicism

Construction and plan form are revealing aspects of developments in domestic architecture, but for most people the qualities that make houses noticeable reside in visible surfaces, so it is on surfaces that conscious architectural statements tend to be made. In Deptford

203 Nos 33–7 Deptford High Street, eight-room brick houses of 1784–6 immediately across the road, comparable in scale but broadly polite in form and originally occupied by some of Deptford's more genteel inhabitants. Photographed 1998 (EH, AA98/01676).

and Woolwich one-room-plan timber houses had boarded or plastered single-bay fronts; in Greenwich rather more houses seem to have been given brick fronts. Survivors invariably have altered ground floors, but it is obvious that the combination of a door and a window on the ground floor under a single window dictated uneven façade rhythms, even in long rows (figs 178 and 188). First-floor windows tend not to be centred on each house, but on axes that probably lined through with the original ground-floor windows, placement that results in better light near the fireplaces, where people would sit (fig. 194). Such functional asymmetry in elevations was a centuries-long characteristic of vernacular housing. In an early attempt to mitigate this, Albury Street has blind windows over its doors, evidence that an impression of regularity mattered (figs 176 and 204). However, in Deptford this was an anomaly. On the whole insouciant vernacular asymmetry transferred to brick building and to two-bay fronts. The longer and taller the row, the less irregular it looked (figs 179, 181–3, 191–2 and 199–201). The front walls of the area's smaller late eighteenth-century brick houses are strikingly various in their window-to-wall proportions and fenestration rhythms,

reflecting tensions between a classically dictated search for symmetry and the constraints of size and economy. Resolution of regularity with the local idiom in the late row at Nos 146–68 Woolwich Church Street results in a disconcertingly large solid to void ratio.

Rooflines clash glaringly even where adjoining buildings were built together or nearly so (figs 184–6). More than a century after the Rebuilding Act of 1667 had established the principle of regular heights in the City, it remained an alien notion only 3 miles away. The gable front endured here and there, and prominent late eighteenth-century roofs show the continuation of traditional practice, with parapets, as at Nos 32–44 Deptford High Street, seeming distinctly half-baked gestures to classical fashion (figs 181, 197 and 202). The contemporary houses across the road at Nos 33–7 Deptford High Street came closer to demure regularity, hiding their roofs, using the blind-window ploy, and squeezing three window bays into 17 ft fronts to create steady if not proportional articulation that this time prefers void over solid (fig. 203).

Classicism was a feature of house fronts, but more usually as ornament rather than system. As with ship-

205   No. 227 Deptford High Street, the first-floor back room in a house rebuilt in 1791–2 for Thomas Palmer, a baker, retaining a clothes closet with a peg rail, a moulded fireplace mantelpiece and a plain-panelled staircase partition. Photographed 1998 (EH, BB98/02927).

building and the interiors evinced by inventories, the incorporation of fashion was not about form but about surfaces, the conspicuous consumption of a pictorial overlay. There are richly carved doorcase consoles on Albury Street (figs 176 and 204), some so lavish as to reflect the presence of both expert ships' carvers and acquisitive competitiveness. Such embellishment was once more widely found,[82] and simpler classical door and eaves ornament was common in the early eighteenth century (fig. 178).

Most interiors in the area's surviving smaller early houses have been radically altered. There are, however, fragments. Staircases are informative, for their position, form and, occasionally, ornamentation. There are several partial survivals of winder staircases. The newel post in No. 27 Tanner's Hill carries a sawn cyma-recta and cavetto bracket, showing that even in such confined spaces classical ornament was deemed appropriate. Framed-newel stairs gave greater scope for display, as in No. 20 Deptford Broadway and No. 45 Greenwich

204 (facing page)   Albury Street, Deptford, showing its classical regularity and doorcase detail, which is indicative of the presence in Deptford of skilled ships' carvers. Photographed 2003 (EH, AA033754).

206   No. 36 Deptford High Street, the garret in an eight-room house of 1789–92. Photographed 1998 (EH, BB98/02941).

Church Street, relatively large houses given robust or-namental balusters. The rearward staircase at No. 205 Deptford High Street of 1774–5 has a closed string, column-on-vase balusters and other detailing that in higher-status housing would generally be thought to be earlier.

Plain panelling is sometimes found lining walls, more often as partitions or defining a staircase compartment, even in houses from the last decades of the eighteenth century (figs 167 and 205). Fitted closets beside chimney breasts were standard. Even more humbly, there are plank-and-muntin partitions and plank doors on upper storeys and in cellars, in houses from as late as the 1770s.

Several moulded mantel shelves survive, with almost identical cyma-recta over cyma-reversa profiles in houses from around 1728 and 1792 (figs 205–7), evidence, if such is needed, that in this context mouldings are unreliable dating tools. Given plainness of finish otherwise, it is as if a particularly bold flourish was expected above upper-storey chamber fireplaces. No. 27 Tanner's Hill retains a ground-floor exposed brick fireplace with a cyma-stop-chamfered timber bressumer, showing that the more public lower living space was given a rougher finish, with the gentility of classicism reserved for the more private space above. This is an inversion of the 'front-stage/back-stage'[83] differentiation that has been associated with

207   No. 31 Tanner's Hill, Deptford, the first-floor room in a three-room house of *c.*1728. Photographed 1998 (EH, BB98/02671).

double-pile layouts and emulative social behaviour. It speaks instead of the older 'hall/parlour' relationship, as in the Herrings' two-room home. In these upper rooms, as in those of the buildings at No. 24 Royal Hill and Nos 4–8 Feathers Place in Greenwich, there is a conjunction of classical mantelpieces, poly-gonal partitions and exposed structural timbers; soffits of main beams have what would always have been visible pegs, and corner posts and quarter-round wall plates project into rooms. This combination of polite ornament and vernacular form does not imply misapprehension of the classical vocabulary so much as selective acquisition. There was little interest in any unified aesthetic of finish.

Fashion was understood as the application of discrete surface elements, alongside which traditional layouts and construction techniques endured.

There is little physical evidence for room use. The manner in which these houses were inhabited is best illustrated through inventories. These have indicated great flexibility, especially in smaller houses where few rooms will have had a single purpose. There was no standard name for the ground-floor front room when it was not a shop. In one-room-plan houses the ground-floor room might have served any or all domestic or commercial purposes. Among the larger inventoried houses the best room could be anywhere on the ground or first floor, a standard eighteenth-century ambiguity. From the late eighteenth century only Nos 205 and 227 Deptford High Street retain evidence for the firm separation of commercial and domestic spaces, with ground floors and basements differently divided. In inventoried two-room-plan houses, the front chamber on the first floor was usually the best. Garret chambers were sometimes unheated. Cellars were frequently absent, but where they are present in smaller houses there is often no sign of kitchen use or of design for anything other than unheated storage. The most common location for the kitchen in smaller houses was probably the back (or only) room on the ground floor. The aforementioned ground-floor fireplace in No. 27 Tanner's Hill seems to be a lone surviving reminder of what may have been a standard kitchen feature. To a large degree these households may have been dependent on outside cooking, that is cook shops. Some of the bigger late eighteenth-century houses, where there may have been servants, did have cellar kitchens. If you have to do your own cooking, a remote or unlived-in kitchen is inconvenient.

Conclusions

The three-room timber houses of Tanner's Hill and Woolwich High Street are rare survivals of what was a common form of housing in many parts of early eighteenth-century London. They should not be contrasted with the urbanity of Albury Street and read as 'rural' architecture; they are urban and vernacular. Between polite and vernacular extremes there stood a range of options, as on Royal Hill or Feathers Place. Fashionable London's ways were known, but only partially of interest. New elements were assimilated into an existing and thriving architectural system that was fundamentally based in local precedent. This was not a blind or accidental process. Conscious architectural choices were being made. The shifting social and economic sands that underlay these choices changed the area's domestic architecture in the late eighteenth century, bringing greater heterogeneity to housing from Butt Lane to Woolwich Church Street. In some respects these later houses perpetuate earlier practice, as in the many central-chimneystack houses built in the last decades of the eighteenth century in Deptford, Greenwich and Woolwich, but in other ways they introduce new approaches, principally for the sake of increased living space.

The most ambitious houses of late eighteenth-century Deptford, that is those closest to the sub-Palladian norm of speculative housing in the West End, were those of Slade's Place (figs 182, 195 and 196). When Mary Lacy began to build Slade's Place, there were scarcely any bigger houses on the street, and few anywhere else in Deptford. The houses were locally unparalleled in many of their attributes, standard though these had become in central and west London. They formed a more-or-less uniform three-storey terrace set behind front gardens, with plain, flat, brick fronts of loosely Palladian proportions. Raised ground floors enhanced the views to the west across the open fields that then remained between Deptford and London, and there were long back gardens. Internally, there were rear-staircase plans and full-height plain panelled linings, a less fashionable finish than the exteriors might indicate; at least one upper storey incorporated a rustic plank-and-muntin partition. There are other striking oddities. The fenestration of the fronts is asymmetrical, and irregular from house to house. Inside, fireplaces are set off centre, and some stair landings lacked windows. So many vernacular elements are not easily dismissed as ignorant mistakes. Even here, it seems, there was no real attempt to engage with polite precedent as a whole. Mary Lacy's building practice shows that what mattered most in this environment was the attainment of space. Amplitude, that is wide plots, two-room depths, gardens and prospects, speaks more of prosperity, if not gentility, than do the subtler attributes of symmetry and proportion.

That buildings as varied in form but comparable in scale as Nos 33–7 and Nos 32–44 Deptford High Street should be built at the same time opposite one another reflects a wider architectural irresolution. That the social standing of those who lived in each group differed says more. The urban vernacular artisan's house and the post-Barbon 'middling sort' polite terrace house met here as objectively equivalent, though subjectively far from interchangeable, options. Here and elsewhere, without regard to scale, vernacular houses were largely occupied by artisans and shopkeepers. Those with, or aspiring to, higher standing, including upwardly mobile shipwrights become gentlemen, tended not to live in such houses.

Conservatism in house design in new and industrialised towns that were radically non-traditional in their social structures makes sense. Innovative polite practices were not everywhere absorbed like water entering a sponge. Independent social attitudes were in large measure based in a sense that the past had been better, with fear of the future deriving from a changeful present. Nostalgia for a mythical *bon vieux temps* would have coexisted comfortably with imperviousness to fashion. Emulation is an expression of the collapse of traditional social relationships and of dependent conformity, so Dissenters with 'chips' on their shoulders might well not have aspired to fashionable forms of living that arose from the milieu against which their dissent was couched.[84] The rising tide of fashionable architectural form towards the end of the eighteenth century accompanied reform in the dockyards and a wider finance-driven commodification of housing. These were all parts of the breakdown of an artisan world in which vernacular architecture would have been a bulwark of identity. The squeezing of the artisan class into higher and lower social groups carried with it changes in housing forms. These changes anticipate the explicit articulation of the distinction between the working class and the middle class that permitted a more definitive separation of house types in the early nineteenth century. Late eighteenth-century houses in Deptford, Greenwich and Woolwich amply illustrate this transition, reflecting continuity and cultural complexity more subtly than is allowed by a simple division between artisan and industrialised modes of housebuilding.

Chapter 7

BETWEEN PICTURESQUE AND RESPECTABLE: URBAN-VERNACULAR ARCHITECTURE AND GENTILITY IN LONDON'S OUTLYING SETTLEMENTS

Whither will this monstrous city then extend? And where must a circumvallation or communication line of it be placed?

Daniel Defoe[1]

The narrative has begun to move away from London, and that is a strong pull. But this is a book about London, so, before roaming more widely, it is important to look at London's 'owned' hinterland, at the immediate reach of the vernacular metropolis. This is not well typified by the 'outer-urban' localities of Deptford and Woolwich. Away from the industrial river many smaller satellite settlements, from Hackney to Peckham, places now easily within 'inner' London, were not part of the city in the eighteenth century. Many of these outlying 'villages', for which the word 'suburb' is perhaps anachronistic and misleading in so far as it implies contiguity, were retreats, attracting great wealth in the person of genteel escapees, retired merchants, a few commuters, and others who preferred and could afford to put distance between themselves and metropolitan hubbub. Substantial houses of an urban nature, some of which would not have been out of place in central districts, were built for such people – as in Mile End, so elsewhere (fig. 209). But, as in all parts of London before the later eighteenth century, these places had mixed populations, also housing and attracting artisans and labourers, by no means all agricultural, many of which people would have been culturally influenced by their metropolitan counterparts. In and between these settlements there were farms, as well as the poor, with squatters' cottages situated on commons, singly or clustered (fig. 210).[2]

As in what was already then London, few small eighteenth-century houses survive in these former villages. Nevertheless, much of what does still stand is remarkable, and has been remarked on, for its vernacular qualities. These have generally been interpreted as a reflection of quasi-rural situation, taking the buildings as evidence of remoteness from the town, as if relics from quiet village greens. Such interpretations, it should by now be clear, ought not to be accepted uncritically. That large parts of London itself, especially to the east and south, continued to be dominated by vernacular architecture has not been taken into account. An awareness of London's own ordinary or vernacular housing illuminates the lesser housing of eighteenth-century London's peripheral settlements and, through it, the wider nature of these places. The vernacular was not only, or even primarily, a matter of rural presence in and around eighteenth-century London. It was also intrinsic to the metropolis as the traditional mode of urban artisan culture.

Of course, the distinguishing characteristics of the vernacular are anything but clear cut. It should not be forgotten that the polite-vernacular separation was and is a conceptual construct imposed on what was a broad continuum of material reality. Recent studies of eighteenth-century metropolitan life have recognised this, and have begun to decipher the complex relationships of 'high' and 'low' cultures. Such analysis has addressed what might be termed the genteel vernacular, a nascent Picturesque or proto-Romantic consciousness on the part of an urban elite, perhaps most famously personi-

(facing page)   Nos 112 and 114 Heath Street, Hampstead (see fig. 226), rear elevations from Stamford Close, showing late eighteenth-century extensions to early eighteenth-century three-room timber houses, that to No. 114 on the right also being timber framed. Photographed 2000 (EH, BB008996).

209 Nos 52–5 Newington Green, built 1658 in a substantial 'terrace' development of a distinctly urban and classical character in what was then a small rural settlement between Islington and Hackney, well outside London. Photographed 1996 (EH, BB96/00049).

210 A different kind of marginal habitation, a cottage 'near London'. Drawing by George Scharf, 1825 (BM).

fied by Horace Walpole, among whose aperçus was the assertion that nature abhors a straight line. From well before the middle of the eighteenth century well-to-do Londoners sought to escape from the relentless pace and growingly homogenised environments of the City and the West End, cultivating the indigenous vernacular characteristics of urban resorts like Islington and Hampstead as a palliative to the unsettling forces of the new-style metropolis. By 1790 Mary Wollstonecraft was envisaging an ideal future without cities.[3] At the centre chaos and density made heterogeneity seem threatening,

subversive or dangerous, but in quieter outlying places variability, even disorder, fell within understandings of what would then have been understood as seemliness or, in classical terms, decorum. What might now be termed local distinctiveness or, less pompously, charm was valued. In places around London the vernacular, 'with its associations of continuity, stability and permanence, was used to enhance an atmosphere of rusticity and informality, thus perpetuating an alternative environment to that of the town.'[4] This genteel vernacular sought out the pastoral not the artisanal. The rural poor were seen to partake of and evoke nature; the urban population of artisans and labourers certainly did not. However, this outlook was fundamentally relaxed and inclusive, not prescriptive, with elements that were licentious, even deliberately *déclassé*.

Another outlook shows that by 1800 gentility in the modest sense of 'middling sort' as opposed to artisan respectability was something to which great swathes of society, especially artisans and shopkeepers, aspired. The crucial ingredient in the late eighteenth- and early nineteenth-century spread of emulative behaviour to ordinary people in search of and in touch with respectability has been termed 'vernacular gentility' in a North American context, where vernacular implies everyday more than it does traditional.[5] In and beyond London an older society threw up stronger countercurrents, as have been encountered from Bethnal Green to Deptford, but the phenomenon of vernacular gentility is certainly not exclusively American. Throughout England and its cultural orbit, people with aspirations to self-advancement embraced selected aspects of politeness, manifest in architecture as what has been understood as watered-down classicism.[6] As has been seen, humbler manifestations of vernacular gentility did not spurn tradition, indeed in many ways long-standing respectability was undermined or threatened by the abandonment of tradition. Viewed from the bottom up, aspects of customary expression retained respectability long after they had been scorned from a top-down viewpoint.

The notions of the top-down genteel vernacular and bottom-up vernacular gentility are intersecting, not opposed. They hold no necessary contradiction, though ambiguity in part arises from differing use of the word vernacular on either side of the Atlantic. Both of these tendencies represent compromise or mitigation. In places around London where vernacular architecture was as much a reflection of urban as of rural traditions, and where emulation was far from being an uncritical or unmediated process, the convergence of the genteel vernacular (elite escapism) and vernacular gentility (selective emulation) does more than simply illustrate the interdependence of the vernacular and the polite. It lies at the heart of the emergence of what, since 1800, has been generally understood as the suburban.

Specifically architectural questions arise. How were London's humbler house types built in or adapted to semi-rural locations in London's environs? And how influential was this traditional urban-vernacular house-building in these peripheral environments? These issues have already been encountered, with gradually increasing relevance, from Bermondsey and Rotherhithe, to the Mile End Road and Kingsland Road, on to Deptford and Greenwich. They are posed as questions here not to underpin an argument, but as background to a tour. Introduction by means of a conceptual opposition is useful in that it provides counterpoint, but it need not compel direction. Many buildings can be fruitfully examined from either or both of these viewpoints, throwing light on discrete facets of a complex social and cultural topography. However, there are buildings that fit only awkwardly within this framework, pointing to the inadequacy of any bi-polar view, and suggesting that there was nothing deterministic in the brew. This chapter discusses houses from places outside and all round eighteenth-century London, neither large terrace houses nor squatters' cottages, but intermediate buildings. It concentrates on small houses that have qualities that make them urban in nature, not least narrow frontages. There is little evidence from within these settlements of eighteenth-century architecture that can be meaningfully classified as simply rural.[7] The material is presented in the same way as in chapter 2, as a survey or overview, by way of another anti-clockwise sweep, this time taking the outer ring road (fig. 211).

North of the Thames

A start can be made at Bethnal Green, not in the silk district, but at the green itself, away to the east of Spitalfields and north of Mile End Old Town, a place that remained surrounded by fields until the nineteenth

211   London's environs in the eighteenth century.

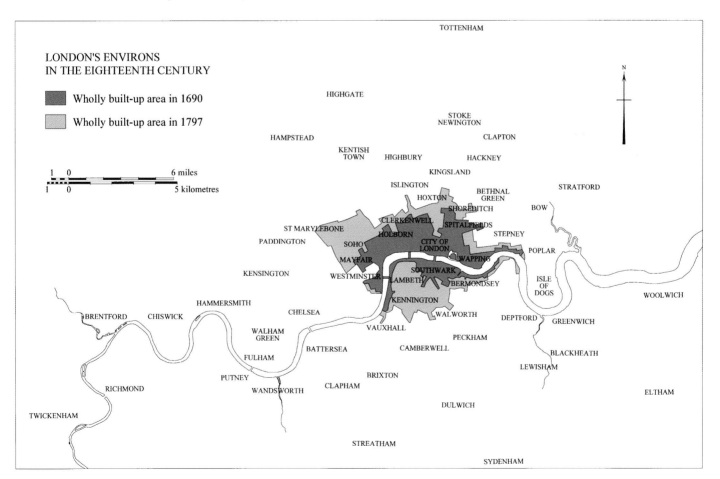

212   Nos 17–21 Old Ford Road, Bethnal Green, houses of 1753–5 built and in part lived in by Anthony Natt, a successful carpenter who retired here from the nearby silk district. Three three-bay houses were linked by lower two-bay coach-house blocks that have been raised. Photographed 2002 (EH, AA033058).

century (figs 55 and 150). Here Anthony Natt (d. 1756), the carpenter and builder who was a native of the silk district, reappears. By the 1740s Natt had become a substantial and prosperous property owner and leading light in the Carpenters' Company, and his son had become a clergyman in rural Essex (see chapter 3). Around 1748, when he would have been about sixty-five, Natt retired to the small, socially mixed and relatively bucolic settlement around the green. There he initially built two houses on the north side, on what was known as Jews' Walk; there had been an attempt to build a synagogue in the locality in 1747. In 1753–5 Natt acquired a site just to the east of these houses and built three substantial houses that survive as Nos 17–21 Old Ford Road, moving into the middle house himself (fig. 212). These were initially three-bay houses, linked by lower coach-house blocks that have been raised to make a continuous three-storey row. The houses had eight large rooms each, 22 ft fronts, raised ground floors and front gardens. This being north of the Thames, it is surprising to find that Nos 19 and 21 have central-chimneystack plans, though with rear staircases (fig. 213), the same layout used in the 1770s on Crosby Row in Bermond-

sey, and on Deptford High Street (see chapters 4 and 6), adapted to provide access to and from the coach-house from between the front and back rooms, with a lobby on the first floor. Intriguingly, No. 17 has party-wall stacks and the more standard rear-staircase plan. Despite this difference the group was strikingly regular in its overall shape and elevations. The interiors are well appointed with moulded panelling and balustraded stairs, but old-fashioned in their detailing. Set against the houses of the silk district, Natt's retirement home was generous in size and outwardly fashionable, but it was inwardly conservative – polite, but also vernacular.[8]

The road north from Bethnal Green led to Hackney, 'remarkable for the retreat of wealthy citizens'.[9] The locality had long since been a magnet for merchants by the eighteenth century, when it was also known for its nursery gardens and pleasure grounds, as well as for intellectual and Dissenting radicalism. Development was scattered around numerous hamlets, with humble commercial cores and outlying freestanding houses for wealthier inhabitants. At what was the south-west edge of the village of Hackney is No. 4 Sylvester Path, latterly tucked away under the shadow of the Hackney Empire

213 (facing page)   Reconstructed plans of houses from London's northern outlying settlements.

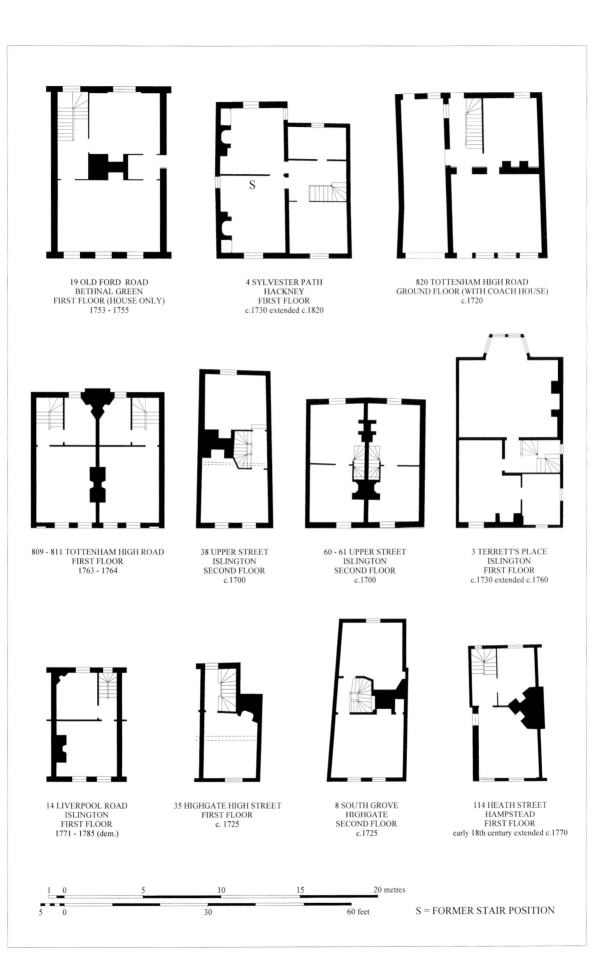

19 OLD FORD ROAD
BETHNAL GREEN
FIRST FLOOR (HOUSE ONLY)
1753 - 1755

4 SYLVESTER PATH
HACKNEY
FIRST FLOOR
c.1730 extended c.1820

820 TOTTENHAM HIGH ROAD
GROUND FLOOR (WITH COACH HOUSE)
c.1720

809 - 811 TOTTENHAM HIGH ROAD
FIRST FLOOR
1763 - 1764

38 UPPER STREET
ISLINGTON
SECOND FLOOR
c.1700

60 - 61 UPPER STREET
ISLINGTON
SECOND FLOOR
c.1700

3 TERRETT'S PLACE
ISLINGTON
FIRST FLOOR
c.1730 extended c.1760

14 LIVERPOOL ROAD
ISLINGTON
FIRST FLOOR
1771 - 1785 (dem.)

35 HIGHGATE HIGH STREET
FIRST FLOOR
c. 1725

8 SOUTH GROVE
HIGHGATE
SECOND FLOOR
c.1725

114 HEATH STREET
HAMPSTEAD
FIRST FLOOR
early 18th century extended c.1770

1 0   5   10   15   20 metres

5   0   30   60 feet

S = FORMER STAIR POSITION

214   Nos 2–6 Park Lane, Tottenham, Nos 2 and 4 to the right being a pair of three-room houses of the 1690s. Photographed 1949. No. 6, once probably a similar pair, has since been demolished (EH, BB49/3439).

215   Nos 818–22 Tottenham High Road, No. 820 to the centre being a central-chimneystack house of *c.*1720, built singly with a coach-house attached, and probably always incorporating a shop. Photographed 2001 (EH, AA033165).

theatre. This house of around 1730, originally four rooms in two storeys with cellars, stood among a mixed and marginal group, without a prominent front and with almshouses and the Ship Inn nearby. At the beginning of the nineteenth century large-scale speculations extended Hackney to the west and south with terraces of houses for middle-class habitation, while pre-existing road frontages towards London on Broadway Market and Cambridge Heath Road were built up with small working-class houses. The owner of the four-room house on Sylvester Path aimed to associate it with the former not the latter. It was almost doubled in size around 1820, with the removal of a confined central staircase, and the addition of an unheated new block largely devoted to entrance and circulation (fig. 213), simultaneous refacing giving the house a homogeneous entrance front in what had become a continuous row. Improvement here had more to do with appearances than with increasing living space. The vernacular house could no longer be accepted as respectable.[10]

Moving across to the Great North Road at Kingsland and turning to travel several miles further north along what was already an all but continuously built-up street, one comes to Tottenham. In the early eighteenth century this relatively far-flung place housed many wealthy Londoners. Tottenham's distinction was its position on such an important road. Development was strung out in a long line. Some affluent commuters had very big houses, many of them highly fashionable in their architecture, but there were other kinds of houses here too. The face of Tottenham High Road was hugely varied; few of the many timber-built and small-scale buildings now survive. Nos 2–6 Park Lane (fig. 214), just off the High Road facing Tottenham Hotspur's White Hart Lane football ground, once had many counterparts on the main road. Nos 2 and 4 survive as an altered pair of three-room houses, said to date from the 1690s, with winder staircases and timber framing to the rear, each house plan being about 15 ft square. Nearby No. 820 Tottenham High Road is a much larger brick house of around 1720, built singly with its own two-storey coach-house (figs 213 and 215). With an original side entrance from the former coach-house, the building has perhaps always incorporated a shop, and may have been a 'self build' rather than a speculation. It has three window bays squeezed into an asymmetrical 20 ft-wide façade, and is an early instance of the central-chimneystack and rear-staircase layout used by Natt and south of the Thames. Across the road Nos 809 and 811 Tottenham High Road are a small mirrored pair of 1763–4, conservative in appearance and detailing, but with blind windows for the sake of regularity in the façade, and rear-staircase

layouts in 14 ft-wide plots that forced very cramped back rooms (fig. 213). Further south, where development was less dense, Charlton House at No. 581 Tottenham High Road is an unusual mid-eighteenth-century building, broad fronted and one room deep with rear-wall chimneystacks to what is a variant of the traditional rural kitchen-hall-parlour layout, with a large brick oven at the service end suggesting there might have been a bakery here. Out here there were all kinds of intermediate possibilities that variously combined the vernacular and the polite.[11]

Within London's more immediate orbit, Islington was a large linear settlement at the beginning of the other, more westerly, Great North Road, extending so far south as almost to meet London's outwards growth by the eighteenth century (figs 6 and 7), but retaining a distinctly separate identity. There were many inns and, given the convenient access to London, some large houses. Islington was an 'extensive and opulent village, and remarkable for the sweetness of the air, which brings many citizens to lodge in it, for their health, and contributes chiefly to the increase of new buildings.'[12] Its population rose from something around 2,000 at the beginning of the century, to 10,212 in 1801, increase parallel with that of Woolwich (see chapter 6), but in a place that was very differently peopled, with a disproportionately large number of the wealthy.[13]

Some of Islington's less wealthy inhabitants were concentrated in Hedge Row, on the west side of the High Street, along what became part of Upper Street, alongside and south of Islington Green. There were tradespeople living here by the beginning of the seventeenth century, and, fronting a main thoroughfare, many of the properties would have maintained commercial use, shops or otherwise.[14] Elements of the early row do survive, showing its modest scale and vernacular irregularity. At Nos 37 and 38 Upper Street there are two houses of late seventeenth- or early eighteenth-century origins, similar, but not a pair, that at No. 38 having a central-chimneystack layout, the stack being so massive and the stair so spacious in a 15 ft-wide plot that between them they completely divide the house (figs 213 and 216). Panelled stair partitions bisect stop-chamfered ceiling beams, yet the first-floor front room has a classical cornice. A bit further north, and facing the green, Nos 60 and 61 Upper Street were built as a mirrored pair of six-room houses in the same period, each only about 12 ft wide (figs 213 and 217).

Islington's commercial identity was based on much more than a busy thoroughfare. It remained a centre of dairy farming and it was a spa. There were a great many minor spas all around London throughout the long eigh-

216 Nos 37 and 38 Upper Street, Islington, showing the backs of houses of *c.*1700 in what was known as Hedge Row, where many humble commercial properties were concentrated. Photographed 2000 (EH, BB000364).

217 Nos 60 and 61 Upper Street, Islington, a small mirrored pair of *c.*1700, the garrets having been made a full storey and the shared central chimneystacks having been cut down. There were gables to the rear. Photographed 2001 (EH, AA033129).

teenth century. The taking of waters was generally thought of as 'medicinal', but this was, of course, a hope more than a reality. Living in a city where untreated water was generally undrinkable (even children drank beer), the lure of nearby places where 'natural' water could be consumed was strong, invested with significance, and by no means restricted to an elite. The medicinal value of Islington's spring waters was promoted from 1683, initially and most famously at Sadler's Wells, alongside a music house adjoining the New River. Other spas followed, with tea gardens and other recreational resorts, all flourishing through the eighteenth century in the open land between Clerkenwell and Islington. These places attracted huge numbers of visitors, with a great social mix, proximity to London making access possible for those who could not afford to visit more remote resorts. Hogarth's 'The Four Times of Day' series of 1738, depicting the comedy and chaos of London's streets, moves from Covent Garden and St Giles to Sadler's Wells, before returning to the centre, the green scene of Islington contrasting greatly with the densely built-up inner areas, but no less a part of Hogarth's dysfunctional London. Deliberately perpetuated, Islington's rustic environment was a sustained rich mix. Vernacular character was in part pastoral, a reflection of enduring separation from the metropolis, in part due to the survival of older buildings, in part due to qualities cultivated as appropriate to a retreat, but it was also in part a reflection of the presence of ordinary people, artisans and labourers, both as locally resident and as visitors.[15]

Small speculations extended Islington and replaced earlier buildings, with more than six hundred new houses being built in the quarter century to 1732. There was a new burst of growth at the end of the century, with another six hundred houses or more going up in the 1780s and 1790s. Many of these houses were polite in character, following the standardising influences of higher-status London developments. However, this was not the West End, and development was not sufficiently planned or coherent as to hide away lesser buildings. Vernacular character was not eradicated. Along Upper Street there was enormous variety in the shapes, sizes and materials of houses through the eighteenth century.[16] Just off Upper Street is No. 3 Terrett's Place, a small house of around 1730, largely timber-framed, and grandly extended from three rooms to nine around 1760, the new back rooms having canted bay windows that looked over fields, and a marvellous and dramatically out-scale Rococo chimneypiece (fig. 213). Elsewhere the house remained much more plainly finished, gaining a plank-and-muntin partition to create a ground-floor entrance passage. Fashion and rusticity coincided here

218 Nos 51–61 Cross Street, Nos 53–9 being a four-house carpenter's speculation completed in 1785. Photographed 2000 (EH, AA004689).

inside one erstwhile small house.[17] Off the other side of Upper Street late eighteenth-century stencilled Gothick wall decoration in No. 53 Cross Street is a rare survival of a cheap alternative to wallpaper, evocative of the still semi-rural retreat, and evidence of the penetration of genteel vernacular tastes (figs 218 and 219). This ten-room house, part of a four-house speculation completed in 1785, adjoins an earlier and taller house at No. 61 which was a retreat for William Hyde, the magistrate who ordered out the militia during the Gordon Riots in 1780, and whose West End house then came under seige.

The building of new roads to intersect with Islington at the Angel (latterly Pentonville Road, completed in 1756 as part of the New Road that extended from Marylebone, and its eastward continuation, City Road, completed in 1761) created a new east–west axis and improved links with London. From the mid-1760s to the end of the century land along the New Road west of Islington High Street that was owned by Henry Penton was gradually developed. A relatively regular grid of streets forming the new district of Pentonville resulted. There were houses of varying sizes and shapes, some large, but most single fronted and arranged in terraces, many probably designed to be marketed to prosperous tradespeople aspiring to greater gentility away from London. The mix, including some smaller houses, can still be seen behind market stalls on Chapel Street. At its east end, where Pentonville met old Islington, stood Nowell's Buildings, Nos 2–28 Liverpool Road, built from 1771 to 1785 by Thomas Nowell and demolished in 2000. These were modest five-room houses with 15 ft frontages, outwardly regular as a row with three-storey

219 No. 53 Cross Street, Islington, late eighteenth-century stencilled Gothick wall decoration. Photographed 2000 (EH, AA000229).

fronts, but with each house asymmetrically fenestrated. There were plat bands in the two-storey back walls, plain panelled and plank-and-muntin partitions, and confined dogleg stairs in rear-staircase layouts (fig. 213). This development is another illustration of the late eighteenth-century merging of humble vernacular building traditions with urban standardisation, encountered in other marginal districts in earlier chapters.[19]

As Islington and London continued to grow and to merge, vernacular character came to seem unsustainable. By 1827 a sense of loss had emerged.

Thy fields, fair Islington! begin to bear
Unwelcome buildings, and unseemly piles;
The streets are spreading, and the Lord knows
    where

243

220   Townsend's Yard, Highgate, eighteenth-century timber houses off Highgate High Street. Photographed shortly before demolition *c.*1890 (HLSI).

Improvement's hand will spare the neighb'ring
   stiles,
The rural blandishments of Maiden Lane
Are every day becoming less and less,
While kilns and lime roads force us to complain
Of Nuisances time only can suppress.
A few more years, and Copenhagen House
Shall cease to charm the tailor and the snob;
And where attornies' clerks in smoke carouse,
Regardless wholly of tomorrow's job,
Some Claremont Row, or Prospect Place shall
   rise,
Or terrace, p'rhaps misnomer'd Paradise![20]

Continuing out of London from Islington, the medieval Great North Road led uphill to Highgate, defined by its altitude (high) and its transitional position as a place between places (gate), connecting the metropolis with points north. Highgate had many fine houses for aristocratic inhabitants from at least the late sixteenth century, its principal attraction at that time and for long after being healthy air above and away from London. But Highgate served travellers as much as it did the rich. It was not so much a resort as an attractively sited place to stop on the way to or from London, good connections and ambiguity of situation being essential qualities.[21]

The heart of the early village was on the London side of the 'gate', around the High Street and Pond Square, which latterly dry polygon was formerly the village green. Elevation meant limited water supply, so early development clustered around the ponds on the green, giving the place some urban density. There were always small houses and inns amid the bigger houses, in greater concentrations along the High Street. By 1664 there were 161 houses in Highgate, suggesting a population in the order of about 1,000. Late seventeenth- and early eighteenth-century developments included irregular encroachments onto the green, and the impressively coherent and precociously 'suburban' group at Nos 1–6 The Grove, three large semi-detached pairs of houses of

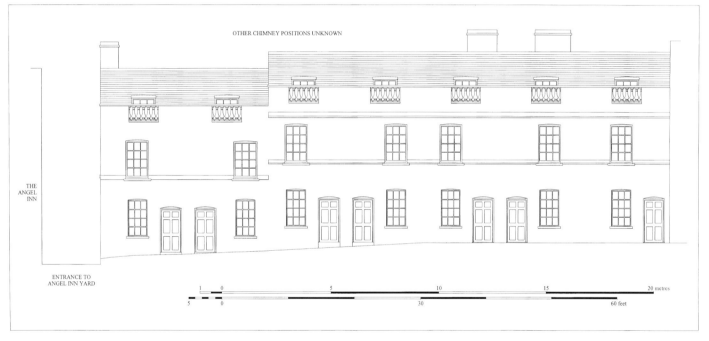

OTHER CHIMNEY POSITIONS UNKNOWN

THE
ANGEL
INN

ENTRANCE TO
ANGEL INN YARD

221 (*top*) Watch-House Row, Nos 43–59 Highgate High Street, piecemeal development on the village green, with the Angel Inn and No. 2 South Grove visible behind the carts. Photographed in the late nineteenth century (HLSI).

222 (*above*) Nos 2–7 South Grove, Highgate, a reconstruction of the front of the Angel Inn's seven-unit shops and lodgings range of the 1720s.

223 (*right*) Nos 33 and 35 Highgate High Street and the Angel Inn, the former being a refronted three-unit shops and lodgings range of the 1720s, originally analogous to Nos 2–7 South Grove. Photographed 2000 (EH, BB009459).

around 1680. Highgate's reputation for air and views held through the eighteenth century, with the rich if not the aristocratic still widely present. A straggly spread of smaller houses also continued, the roadside nature of the place making it a commercial centre as well as a select settlement. By 1841 Highgate had grown, though not spectacularly, to have a population of 4,302.[22]

Eighteenth-century Highgate thus mixed metropolitan affluence – views, air, landscapes and fine residences, with roadside chaos – travellers, inns, provisioning and highway robbery. For genteel travellers reaching London from the north, Highgate was a kind of proscenium or curtain raiser at the threshold to the great metropolis, the theatre of all that was fashionable: 'When we came upon Highgate hill and had a view of London, I was all life and joy.'[23] This was an exciting but transitional place. Road travel in the eighteenth century was slow, dirty and uncomfortable, so many heading for London would have stopped for a night in Highgate rather than descend into the capital in the dark along a road that was dangerous for both its ruts and its thieves. Coaching inns here and elsewhere around the perimeter of London allowed well-to-do travellers to collect themselves, so as to be able to arrive in the city the following morning refreshed and suitably dressed. This would have been an important factor in the social dynamics of Highgate.

A handful of Highgate's smaller early buildings do survive. Though much rebuilt, Nos 43–67 Highgate High Street (formerly Watch-House Row) are the successors to humble first developments arising from seventeenth-century piecemeal enclosures encroaching onto the north side of the village green (fig. 221). No. 59 Highgate High Street endures as a two-storey two-bay house on a plot about 17 ft wide, first enclosed in 1685. Adjoining properties were closely comparable before rebuilding. Some of these low and proportionally wide buildings may have comprised no more than two rooms. Originally timber framed, some were given brick fronts in the late Georgian period. Across the High Street there were back alleys by the seventeenth century, along which many small timber houses were built during the eighteenth century. Among these was Townsend's Yard (fig. 220), named after a local family of bricklayers and builders. Though some of these houses may have had no more than two rooms, they would have started as decent dwellings for artisans or labourers. These back places were also home to some isolated eighteenth-century buildings of a more rural nature, good brick houses, as surviving at No. 36A Highgate High Street, as well as some tiny single-storey thatched cottages that are long gone. Further from the centre of Highgate many other small houses stood amid mixed linear development.

Bigger houses were scattered, and on the whole rather more isolated.[24]

In Highgate, as in other outlying settlements, the polite and the vernacular were interdependent metropolitan outlooks, not uncommunicative town and country neighbours. Beyond Watch-House Row stood the Angel Inn, just visible behind the carts in the late nineteenth-century view (fig. 221). Present as a coaching inn from at least 1610, the Angel has a plum corner site at the heart of the village on the crest of the hill. It is not the inn itself that is of prime interest here, but dependent properties. The nearby building with a balustraded parapet, latterly No. 2 South Grove, was the endmost part of a seven-unit range of coaching-inn lodgings and lock-up shops (fig. 222). A shorter but otherwise comparable three-unit range extended down the High Street on the other side of the Angel Inn, both groups having been built in the 1720s by James Crompton, senior and junior, innholders and carpenters (figs 213 and 223). Each of the ten separate units may originally have comprised no more than four rooms, each about 12 ft square, with large chimneystacks and disproportionately spacious and impressive staircases behind.[25] Adjoining at one end was No. 8 South Grove, a three-storey central-chimneystack-plan house with a 15 ft front and an ornamental open-well stair. This house may also have been built by or for the Cromptons in the 1720s (fig. 213). A short way down the hill from the Angel, a slope graced with some very fine houses further on, are Nos 17–21 High Street, three larger houses of 1733, uniform save for an integral extra bay on No. 17 that was designed to include a shop.[26] These buildings speak of the architecturally conservative and commercial aspects of the locality, while also suggesting fluid boundaries to house types, occupancy, polite living, domesticity and commerce.

The Angel Inn lodging ranges were not built as houses, but they are germane to an understanding of humble domestic architecture in eighteenth-century Highgate and beyond. This was a neatly flexible speculation, providing overnight accommodation for travellers, separated from and above lettable ground-floor lock-up shops and cellar storage, all achieved by enclosing a yard. In early eighteenth-century Highgate compact cellular accommodation and fashionable appearance were both appropriate. The small rooms would have sufficed for a single overnight stay for all but the grandest of travellers, while the roomy staircases, it might have been thought, would have attracted a better class of customer. In this context space for public circulation mattered more than private floor space. Similarly, the balustraded parapet panels were a loud and prominent

246

statement of gentility, clearly intended to be seen from a distance, across the village green and ponds, standing as if railings at the crest of the hill from which London could be viewed, and perhaps consciously echoing the balustraded balconies of London's late seventeenth-century galleried inns.

These buildings are fascinating evidence of early eighteenth-century architectural improvisation. Traditional approaches to domestic building overlaid with embellishments of a fashionably classical nature are generally seen as characteristically provincial, a dilution of what London had to offer. Yet such architecture was also widespread within and around London, and not simply a function of misapprehension. Until the late eighteenth century the vernacular could be seen, even by the most sophisticated cultural consumers, as fitting to place and purpose. Highgate was such a place, and a coaching inn such a purpose.

Within fifty years the shops and lodgings had failed to pay their way. Sold off in lots in 1769, they were adapted to humble occupancy alongside shop use. Some of the vertical four-room units were used as shophouses without significant enlargement, but most of the units were soon found to be too small, some being knocked together, others rebuilt or extended. It is significant that it was ordinary tradespeople, not high-status occupants, who found the need for more room. This is indicative of the limitations of the original lodgings-range architecture, but it might also reflect growing expectations of privacy and domestic space.

A more westerly spoke out of London leads to Hampstead, less arterial than Highgate. Already in the seventeenth century Hampstead had a social mix that was more that of the town than that of the countryside, though disproportionately wealthy, with nearly as many 'houses' (sixty-eight) as 'cottages' (seventy-eight) noted in a parliamentary survey of 1646. The proximity of London, hillside eminence and an associated reputation for pure air fuelled growth, particularly after 1698 when Hampstead's wells were successfully promoted. Throughout the eighteenth century Hampstead was a resort, a favoured place for summer retreat or retirement. For a time at the beginning of the century the town boomed, the appeal of its waters bringing a flood of visitors, and much new development. After about a decade of fashionable exclusivity Hampstead rapidly became less select; it was found to be accessible to ordinary people, including 'so many loose women in vamped-up old clothes to catch the City apprentices, that modest company are ashamed to appear'.[27] By the 1720s, when Defoe exaggeratedly claimed that Hampstead 'is risen from a little Country Village, to a city',[28] the boom had tailed

off. Housebuilding had been, and remained, piecemeal encroachment rather than coherent estate development, most speculations being no more than two houses at a time. Small houses went up alongside more conspicuous large properties, many of the smaller houses scattered amid the bigger ones, some of which were built to be lodging houses for visitors.[29]

Hampstead's eighteenth-century character was determined by the proximity of London, but it was not urban *per se*, more what has been characterised as 'a hilltop *urbs in rure*'.[30] Defoe's further hyperbolic claim that Hampstead 'grew suddenly populous, and the concourse of people was incredible'[31] may have derived from an impression given by hordes of day-trippers. The resident population of the town has been estimated as only about 1,300 in 1720, rising to about 4,300 in 1801. There were about five hundred houses and cottages by 1762, many more than there had been a century previously, but hardly a 'city'. Hampstead was, like Highgate, one of the more substantial of London's eighteenth-century satellites, but nowhere near as populous as many urban parishes or the riparian industrial satellites of Deptford and Woolwich.[32]

Hampstead High Street is oriented towards London, and its early houses are continuous, predominantly large, with wide fronts and three storeys. Here and elsewhere, most prominently on Church Row, Hampstead's fashionable eighteenth-century houses were often timber behind brick fronts; internally they were far from standardised.[33] To the north, Heath Street, which name was not used until the nineteenth century, was a continuation of the High Street, leading less invitingly to the bleak heath and places beyond. It hosted an uneven array of modest buildings, largely timber, in what was not a rural village, but a place of artisans, workshops and shops, a newly established end of the town, low in status though not exclusively so in what was a very mixed place. This character remains evident in narrow frontages, and in the survival of a number of early two-storey buildings, often refronted in brick (fig. 224). On the west side Golden Yard has its origins in a cottage and forge, built shortly before 1662 by Thomas Goulding, a blacksmith. The area to the west from Holly Hill to The Mount had some late seventeenth-century development of a modest character, many cottages being scaled up in eighteenth-century redevelopment to provide larger houses and stabling. Some small new houses made gestures to outward fashionable regularity, but with little rigour (fig. 225). Across Heath Street and towards the north the town spread around New End in the years either side of 1700.[34] Nos 112 and 114 Heath Street were part of this early eighteenth-century urbanisation (figs 213 and 226),

224 Nos 70–84 Heath Street, showing the modest scale of this working end of eighteenth-century Hampstead. Photographed 2000 (EH, BB008989).

being closely analogous to artisan houses in London, each about 15 ft square with three rooms, timber built save for a brick north wall where the building was exposed to and visible from the heath.

In the late eighteenth century 'Hampstead consolidated its position as a select residential town and summer station for some of London's wealthier professional and mercantile classes.'[35] Though no longer a spa, the town continued to be renowned for its healthy air, though it too was visited by the Gordon Riots. Below the highest social levels there was decline, with many houses being subdivided, inns closing and other small houses standing empty. A rating assessment of 1774 shows that about one in five houses in the Heath Street area was empty.[36] Nevertheless, around this time Nos 112 and 114 Heath Street were separately extended (figs 208 and 213). The layout that arose from the extension of No. 114 was the standard rear-staircase plan, with rooms divided by both ovolo-moulded panelling and plank-and-muntin partitions. The three-room house had been rendered not just more spacious, but also more respectable in the language of London's higher-status speculative housing.

Artists and writers were among Hampstead's many visitors through the eighteenth century, and the town's scenic qualities were exploited from at least the 1740s, with a contrived emphasis on pastoral gentility that admitted the existence of shepherds, though not of blacksmiths. As elsewhere round London a proto-Picturesque sensibility does appear to have taken an early hold here.[37] But this should not allow Hampstead's vernacular building traditions to be understood as rural. Rather, in this peculiar sub-metropolitan context, they should be associated with urban artisan development, even where aspects of gentility intrude, as they did everywhere. It was not until after 1800 that Hampstead came to be considered a literary, artistic and intellectual centre. Even then growth was very mixed in quality and status, much speculative development around 1800 being aimed at the poor; in 1815 there were 'hundreds of mean houses and alleys' in Hampstead.[38] A century later, many densely built courts were cleared, as they were in

Highgate. Hampstead's surviving smaller houses still evoked insalubrity in the 1930s when Stamford Close, the yard from which the backs of Nos 112 and 114 Heath Street are visible (fig. 208), was described as 'a miserable dark square – a black spot'.[39] Since then perceptions have changed radically, and such spots have come to represent an important aspect of what continues to make Hampstead 'select'.

Much of what goes for Hampstead might also be said of the 'shabby genteel suburb'[40] that was Chelsea, a place with an even longer pedigree as a fashionable retreat. In a parish that had a population of about 12,000 by 1800 there were once many humble eighteenth-century buildings. Here, in parallel with another Thames-side resort at Greenwich, there was also a very grand 'sheltered housing' complex in the shape of a royal hospital, Chelsea's being founded in 1682 to provide for hundreds of disabled soldiers. Barbonesque speculative terraces with rear-staircase plans had arrived by 1700, but, in streets further away from London and running back from and behind the Thames frontage that has become Cheyne Walk, there were also short rows of more modest two-storey brick houses (fig. 227). All but comprehensive redevelopment in Chelsea appears to have left no opportunity for analysis of the latter through surviving buildings.[41] Royal Kensington also had some such houses, but they too have gone.[42]

Around these and other more westerly settlements, market and nursery gardening was a significant presence. The parish of Fulham had no populous centre but was, like Hackney, several scattered hamlets.[43] Gardening was dominant, orchards displacing arable in the late seventeenth century. Rural buildings were joined by large fashionable houses in their own grounds in the eighteenth century as the cultural orbit of the metropolis extended. One notable property owner in the hamlet at Walham Green, the place latterly better known as Fulham Broadway, was Bartholomew Rocque, 'an eminent Florist', landscape gardener and the brother of the surveyor John Rocque. In 1749 he celebrated the locality in verse:

Hail, happy Isle, and happier Walham Green,
Where all that's fair and beautiful are seen!
Where wanton zephyrs court the ambient air,
And sweets ambrosial banish every care;
Where thought nor trouble social joy molest,
Nor vain solicitude can banish rest.
Peaceful and happy, here I reign serene,
Perplexity defy, and smile at spleen;
Belles, beaux, and statesmen, all around me shine,
All own me their supreme, me constitute divine,

225 (*facing page bottom left*) Nos 23 and 24 Holly Mount, Hampstead, a pair of small mid-eighteenth-century houses, only one room deep but given fronts that aim at loose proportionality. Photographed 2000 (EH, BB009004).

226 (*facing page bottom right*) Nos 112 and 114 Heath Street, Hampstead, having origins as early eighteenth-century three-room timber houses, like those being built in the capital's artisan districts. Photographed 2000 (EH, BB008999).

All wait my pleasure, own my awful nod,
and change the humble gard'ner to the god.[44]

Where there were neither waters nor prospects, gentility was attracted by tranquillity. A simple and socially diverse agricultural place was idealised through urbane yearnings, the serenity of Fulham's rural scene contrasted with metropolitan 'spleen'. Of standing buildings there is, as for Chelsea, little to say. A small two-cell eighteenth-century house that might just have been an admissible part of Rocque's Arcadian idyll does survive at the back of Nos 17 and 19 Jerdan Place, at the heart of what was Walham Green. Early nineteenth-century wrap-round additions were part of the area's wider suburbanisation (fig. 228). However, evidence of other buildings long since demolished tends to give the lie to Rocque's paean, indicating that eighteenth-century Fulham had intermediate kinds of houses between the rural vernacular and the wholly genteel. Nos 1–3 Jerdan Place were much more urban in appearance, being an early eighteenth-century row of three-room brick cottages, three full storeys tall.[45] Just behind on Vanston Place there was a comparably urban pair (fig. 229).

Hammersmith, back on the Thames, had a larger population. When Defoe visited in the 1720s, it 'was formerly a long scattering place, full of gardeners' grounds, with here and there an old house of some bulk: I say, in this village we see now not only a wood of great houses and palaces, but a noble square built as it were in the middle of several handsome streets, as if the village seemed inclined to grow up into a city.'[46] Again the word 'city' needs to be taken with a grain of salt, but there were buildings with the flavour of the town. Among subsequent substantial developments was Hammersmith Terrace, sixteen three- and four-storey houses of around 1755 designed to be seen from the river, and presenting a remarkably irregular face to the street (fig. 230). There were many humbler developments, often single houses or pairs, but sometimes more extensive, as at Nos 65–79 Queen Street (latterly Queen Caroline Street, by Hammersmith Broadway), a row of eight three-room brick houses probably datable to the early eighteenth century. These houses also had irregular fronts, with small upper-storey openings that may have lit front staircases on the sides away from the entrances (fig. 231).[47]

Following the north bank of the Thames further west past Chiswick and Brentford leads to Twickenham, across the river from Richmond, all places a long way from London proper in the eighteenth century, but touched, even stamped on, by metropolitan gentility. While Chiswick was distinctive for its villas, there were also speculatively built rows. By contrast the houses around

228   Nos 17 and 19 Jerdan Place, Fulham Broadway, showing a two-cell eighteenth-century building that survives from the rural hamlet of Walham Green, under a hipped roof and engulfed by nineteenth-century additions. Photographed 1999 (EH, BB99/09851).

229   A pair of brick-fronted timber houses on Vanston Place, Walham Green, Fulham, probably late seventeenth century, laid out with central-chimneystack plans. Photographed c.1900. Demolished (EH, BB001527).

227 (*facing page*)   Nos 55–9 Milman's Street, Chelsea, houses of c.1700. Photographed c.1910. Demolished (EH, BB013038).

230   Hammersmith Terrace, houses of *c*.1755, designed to be seen from the Thames, leaving staircases rising against irregularly fenestrated entrance elevations to the road. Photographed 1914 (EH,
AA63/7520).

231   Nos 65–79 Queen Street, Hammersmith, a row of eight early eighteenth-century three-room
houses, perhaps also having front staircases. Photographed in the early twentieth century. Demolished (EH, George Trotman).

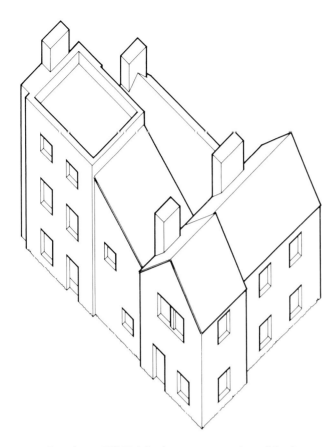

232 Strawberry Hill, Twickenham, reconstruction of the former coachman's house of 1698 as it stood when acquired by Horace Walpole in 1747, as viewed from the garden with early eighteenth-century back additions to the fore.

the informal square that is the Butts in Brentford were highly irregular in scale and form. In Richmond a royal palace had brought Tudor courtliness, as in Greenwich. Compensation for the departure of royalty came with the discovery of mineral wells in 1696. Developments around Richmond Green at the beginning of the eighteenth century were strikingly urban in character, with several Barbonesque terraces, but there were also some more uneven groups made up of small speculations, and humbler buildings stood behind. Both Richmond and Twickenham had their rustic riverside villa retreats, but these were scattered amid irregular smaller houses, the forms of which were sometimes typically urban, sometimes typically rural, and sometimes incapable of such categorisation.[48]

Horace Walpole's Strawberry Hill in Twickenham epitomises these ambiguities and the roots of the genteel vernacular mentality. His famously Gothic house began as 'Chopp'd Straw Hall', an asymmetrical and wholly vernacular six-room coachman's house of 1698. When

Walpole, the twenty-nine-year old son of the nation's greatest politician, took it on in 1747, it had a most unprepossessing appearance, having already been irregularly extended for genteel use (fig. 232). As Lady Townshend remarked, 'Jesus, what a house.'[49] Its irregularity charmed Walpole, and helped to direct his subsequent energies in opportunistic and piecemeal enlargement. For him this humble vernacular building was 'the prettiest bauble you ever saw', a 'little plaything-house . . . set in enamelled meadows, with filigree hedges.'[50]

South of the Thames

Crossing the Thames at Richmond, the circuit can continue, heading back towards the east and briefly surveying a few outlying southern districts. These were not essentially different to places north of the river in that the proximity of London had similar effects on social and architectural mix, but transport links were poorer and there were different local building traditions.

Wandsworth was not a resort, but an industrial place on the banks of the river Wandle close to its outflow into the Thames. Here Dutch and French refugees settled, chiefly employed as dyers, hatters and metal-workers. By the end of the eighteenth century as many as five hundred people were employed in local factories and mills.[51] There is little left of the former small-scale heterogeneity of the High Street. An exceptionally regular pair from a once larger group of mid-eighteenth-century houses survives at what was the west end of the settlement, at the foot of West Hill, as Nos 140 and 142 High Street (fig. 233).[52] Downstream was Battersea, also industrial in the eighteenth century, but now bereft of small early buildings. Recorded before their late twentieth-century demolition, Nos 89–101 Battersea High Street appear to have begun as an early to mid-eighteenth-century row of seven three-room houses (fig. 236).[53] Closer in, Lambeth is another riverside district that housed many artisans and labourers where no early houses survive, though a number of small seventeenth- and eighteenth-century houses comparable in character with those of Bermondsey had been photographed by the early twentieth century (fig. 234).[54] In the absence of more substantial evidence it is given short shrift here (for Lambeth Marsh, see chapter 4).

Back out and inland, Clapham was 'situate upon a fine Rising; whence is a pleasant Prospect over the River Thames.'[55] Towards the end of the seventeenth century it gained popularity as a well-heeled retreat, to which the elderly Samuel Pepys retired in 1700. There are

233 Nos 140 and 142 Wandsworth High Street, mid-eighteenth-century double-fronted one-room-deep houses from the western margins of what was an industrial settlement in the eighteenth century. Photographed 2002 (EH, AA033091).

still relics of this early settlement, many of them on and close to the stretch of road known as Old Town. An early eighteenth-century house at Nos 13 and 14 The Pavement, perhaps timber framed originally, looked out to the open common south-west of the village. Its double-fronted double-pile plan with two central chimneystacks had been used by London gentry for large but compact houses through the seventeenth century (fig. 236). After about 1760, when the common was drained, levelled and planted, Clapham enjoyed prodigious growth, and virtuous association with the religious and political high-mindedness of the district's eponymous 'Sect', a model proto-middle-class-suburban community. Clapham's best late eighteenth-century residences were strung along the edges of the common, large villas with green prospects. Away from these fashionable addresses, Nos 13 and 14 The Pavement had already been divided and adapted to shop use before 1800, when, incidentally, the building was owned by the distinguished architect Samuel Pepys Cockerell.[56]

Further from the common, Nos 120–42 Clapham High Street provide more telling evidence of what was happening at the margins of local gentrification (figs 235 and 236). This row of ten two-bay houses with 17 ft fronts was built in 1771, when the road was not a high street, just a sparsely developed and busy route that linked Clapham to London. A home here would have been convenient for the town, but less sought after than one facing the common. The row was given amenities, being set well back from the road with front gardens and raised ground floors. It was unified with a stone cornice, and articulated by two extra bays that may have had open ground floors, permitting access to the backs for the horses, chaises or coaches essential for connection with London. Yet the houses were surprisingly humble, originally only one room deep, comprising four rooms each, and probably timber framed at the back. Gentility here was skin deep. As Clapham grew and rapidly gained in cachet, the houses were knocked together and substantially enlarged, the modest speculation of 1771 perhaps having come before the area's fashionable character had reached a critical mass. By 1815 the ten houses had become five, all with rear extensions. From the 1780s William Prescott, Colonel Commandant of the Clapham Volunteers, lived in Nos 138–42, three properties made into a single house with a 50 ft frontage, and massively extended around 1800 with a full-height canted bay that looked across open fields (fig. 236). Next door at Nos 134 and 136 one of the early houses and one of the extra bays was the much smaller five- or six-room home of Elizabeth Cook (1741–1835), the Wapping publican's daughter who had married Captain James Cook (see chapter 5). She stayed in Mile End after her husband's death in Hawaii in 1779, moving in 1788 to more fashionable Clapham, where she stayed until her death. She was a devout Methodist and was perhaps attracted by Clapham's renown as a centre of Evangelism. It is fascinating to find that a wealthy widow of humble origins but surpassing associative fame chose to move to this district, yet into such a humble property. Three of her sons and her only daughter had died before she settled in Clapham, and her remaining two sons died in 1793 and 1794. Thereafter she may not have been quite alone, the house perhaps also being occupied by her sister. More surprisingly, from 1807 to 1827 her cousin Admiral Isaac Smith, who is said to have been the first European to set foot on the continent of Australia, also seems to have occupied the house. Modest extension to double the size of the original building might date from his arrival, though it may be earlier, as in 1792 it was reported that Elizabeth Cook 'lives in high style at Clapham and keeps a footman.'[57] Even so, the enlarged house was only about 25 ft by 30 ft on plan rising only two full storeys. It is entirely possible that Elizabeth Cook and others with similarly vernacular gentility found no contradiction between this house and 'high style'.[58]

Eighteenth-century Peckham was another resort: 'It's all holiday at Peckham!' is a catch-phrase the origins of which have been linked to Oliver Goldsmith, a Peckham resident in the mid-eighteenth century, when he eked out a living as a teacher before achieving literary success. The title of Edward Jerningham's play of 1799, *The Peckham Frolic or Nell Gwynn*, says as much as Nell's legendary Peckham sojourn itself to confirm this reputation. Peckham was like Clapham in being on top of a

235 (*right*)   Nos 136–42 Clapham High Street, part of a row of ten one-room-deep houses of 1771, knocked together and extended from the 1780s for Colonel William Prescott and for Elizabeth Cook, the widow of Captain James Cook. Photographed 2000 (EH, MF000195/4).

234   Nos 20–3 Lambeth High Street, one-room-plan early eighteenth-century houses in what was then Lambeth's 'Back Lane'. Photographed 1923. Demolished (NMR, AF35).

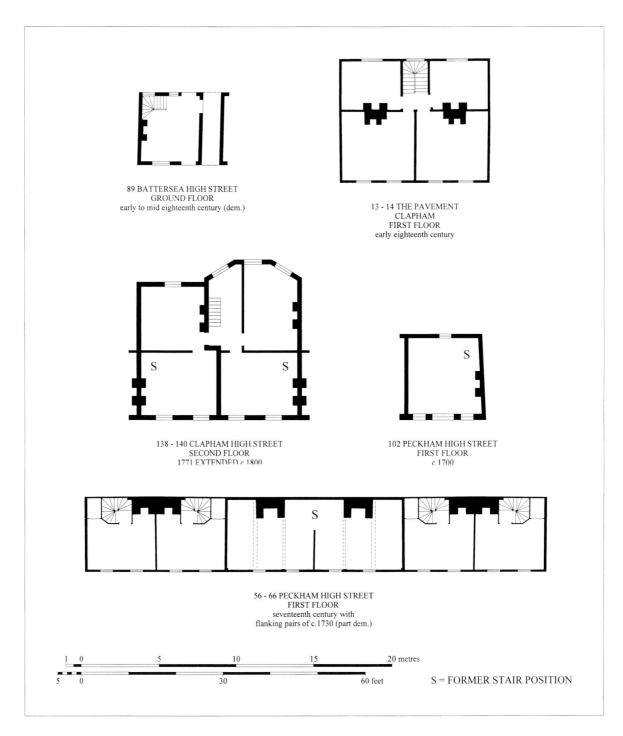

89 BATTERSEA HIGH STREET
GROUND FLOOR
early to mid eighteenth century (dem.)

13 - 14 THE PAVEMENT
CLAPHAM
FIRST FLOOR
early eighteenth century

138 - 140 CLAPHAM HIGH STREET
SECOND FLOOR
1771 EXTENDED c 1800

102 PECKHAM HIGH STREET
FIRST FLOOR
c 1700

56 - 66 PECKHAM HIGH STREET
FIRST FLOOR
seventeenth century with
flanking pairs of c.1730 (part dem.)

1 0   5   10   15   20 metres

5 0   30   60 feet   S = FORMER STAIR POSITION

236a and b (*above and facing page*)   Reconstructed plans of houses from London's southern outlying settlements.

gentle rise that offered prospects of London, not as dramatic as those from the northern heights, but appreciable none the less. In terms of population Peckham was little more than a village, growing from about 600 people around 1700 to about 1,700 around 1800.[59] However, lying beyond Bermondsey and market gardens, it was just 2 miles south-east of London Bridge, and thus one of the nearest settlements to London to be untouched by the commercial hustle of a major through road. Peckham was an accessible retreat from the city, and comparisons with Islington or Hampstead are not out of place.

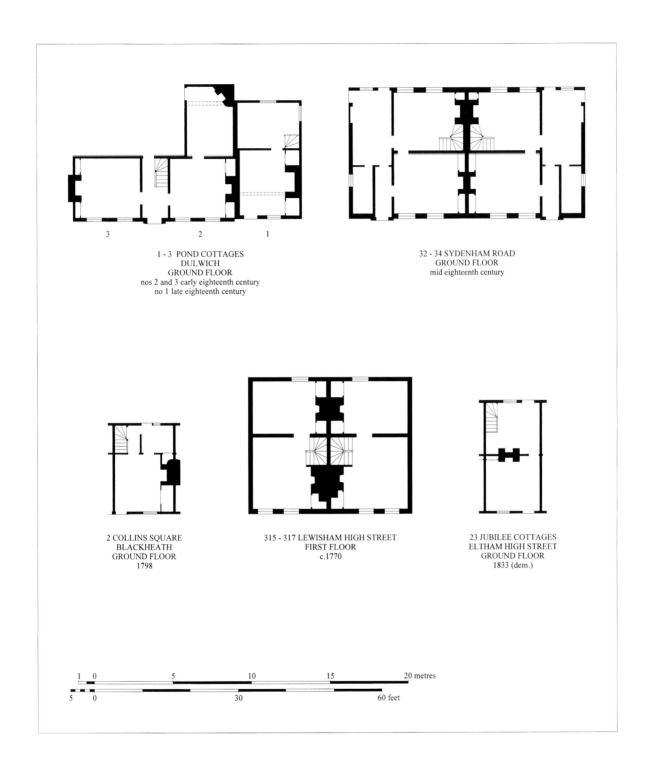

1 - 3 POND COTTAGES
DULWICH
GROUND FLOOR
nos 2 and 3 early eighteenth century
no 1 late eighteenth century

32 - 34 SYDENHAM ROAD
GROUND FLOOR
mid eighteenth century

2 COLLINS SQUARE
BLACKHEATH
GROUND FLOOR
1798

315 - 317 LEWISHAM HIGH STREET
FIRST FLOOR
c.1770

23 JUBILEE COTTAGES
ELTHAM HIGH STREET
GROUND FLOOR
1833 (dem.)

1   0   5   10   15   20 metres

5   0   30   60 feet

Developed around a crossroads, most of Peckham's early houses were irregularly strung along the east–west road that has become the High Street. Many of these were large houses, some of a decidedly urbane architectural character. For Defoe, Peckham was a pleasant village with 'some of the finest dwellings about Lon-don'.[60] The finer houses were not so much primary residences as lodges for well-to-do courtiers or merchants; none survive. There were also numerous public houses and a theatre that all contributed to a cosmopolitan and leisure-based local ambience, socially mixed and as licentious in its architecture as in its activities. New building

257

237 Nos 100–08 Peckham High Street, the smaller buildings being one-room-plan timber-framed houses of *c.*1700. Photographed 1928 (EH, AP 314).

came through a process of piecemeal encroachment; there were no major estate holdings, and large-scale speculative development arrived only after 1800. Peckham's religious life was notably Nonconformist, with the large Hanover Chapel occupying a prominent position on the south-west corner of the crossroads.[61]

The largest of Peckham's houses was that rebuilt in 1672 by Sir Thomas Bond (d. 1685), a Restoration courtier and one of the West End developers of the area that included Bond Street. With a deep plot on the north-west corner of the crossroads, Bond's large U-plan house (demolished in 1797) was set well back amid ornamental formal gardens of French inspiration. The gardens and the prospects of London were admired by John Evelyn, and later by Defoe: 'a beautiful prospect, terminated by a view of St Paul's and the Tower of London. The beauties of this prospect were greatly increased by the masts of the ships being seen over the trees as far as Greenwich.'[62] There were some short terraces of substantial Barbonesque houses on the village's eastern fringes, as endure at Nos 4–10 Queen's Road.

Among numerous smaller groups of eighteenth-century brick houses, there were three central-chimneystack-plan houses at Nos 68–72 Peckham High Street just east of the crossroads. Much else along the High Street was timber built, ranging from a late medieval Wealden house that survived until about 1850 to irregular groups of small houses.[63] East of the crossroads the Peckham Theatre, a wooden playhouse that attracted performers and companies of renown, stood on the south side of the High Street by the 1770s, behind Nos 98–104 Peckham High Street, a much rebuilt group of one-room-plan houses of around 1700 (figs 236 and 237).[64]

Nos 58–62 Peckham High Street are two surviving early timber buildings that were formerly part of a larger group (figs 239 and 240). Set well back from the present line of the High Street, these houses were on the south-west corner of Peckham's large open crossroads, immediately opposite a gate lodge at the south end of the main axis of what had been Thomas Bond's gardens. To their east was the Hanover Chapel; to their west was Basing Manor House, a substantial property of seventeenth-century or earlier origins.[65] At the centre of the formerly three-part group, Nos 60 and 62 form a low four-bay range with origins as a seventeenth-century double-fronted single-pile house, distinctive for having back-wall chimneystacks (fig. 236). No. 58 is a taller building, the last survivor from two mirrored pairs of three-storey houses built around 1730 on either side of the earlier building in what appears to have been a single specula-tion. These houses were also only one room deep, the rooms being about 15 ft square, each house presumably comprising two chambers over living and cooking space, probably with single-storey lean-to rear outshuts (fig. 242). Again the houses were given back-wall chim-neystacks, beside which there were tight twin-newel staircases and closets across the back in an unusual but eminently rational layout. In No. 58 there is a single turned baluster on the first floor and the second-floor room retains original joinery including a robustly moulded chimneypiece mantel (fig. 241). From the front windows of this upper room there are views in which St Paul's cathedral is still prominent. It is significant that the composition and proportions of the façades of these houses were made carefully classical, even Palladian, and intriguing that three of the four occupants in 1755 and again in 1774 were women. The size and location of these houses would have made them ideal repositories for the mistresses of rich men. Commercial use had come in by the 1830s, but from some time around 1800 until the 1860s Richard Wallis, a music teacher, lived in No. 58.[66]

These pairs were unusual houses for which no close parallels are known. Cheap timber construction, a layout devised around limited accommodation and confined circulation, and back-wall chimneys, a predilection that was perhaps inherited from local rural vernacular prac-tice, combine unexpectedly with elements of the polite in façade design and internal finish. Most striking in houses of this scale from such an open site is the pres-ence of a full third storey, which must relate to the prospects for which the locality was noted. In Peckham a small house with a view could perhaps be fashionable in a way that the same building might not have been in central London. Gentility and smallness of scale, classi-cism and timber-frame construction were not neces-sarily mutually exclusive. The exploitation of a view of the City of London from these houses captures the essentially Picturesque ambivalence of the interac-tion between the urban and the rural in these London retreats.

Eighteenth-century Peckham's heterogeneous and undisciplined mix of houses – timber with brick and small with big – contrasts markedly with the well-

238   Commercial Way, Peckham, a row of early nineteenth-century timber houses. Photographed 1945. Demolished (EH).

chronicled, middle-class, commuter-based suburban development of the wider Camberwell area with brick and stucco terraces and villas in the classical idiom after 1800.[67] Even so, a terrace of timber houses that appears to have had central- or back-wall-chimneystack layouts was put up on Commercial Way on the north side of Peckham soon after 1800 (fig. 238), an instance of the tenacity of timber if not of tradition difficult to match so close to London. As Peckham became a suburb where vernacular gentility (respectability) counted more than the genteel vernacular (escape), so the values attached to its attractions and its public buildings changed. In 1822 the Peckham Theatre closed and the site was redevel-oped as a boys' school. Peckham Fair was abolished in 1826.[68]

Dulwich and Streatham were also places of retreat, spas with 'waters' and attendant entertainments, further out than Peckham, but low down in the recreational hierarchy because close enough to London that 'common people' could walk there and back on a Sunday, 'which makes the better sort also decline the place; the crowd on those days being both unruly and unmannerly.'[69] The heart of Dulwich retains some of its eighteenth-century aspect, with great variety in its streetscape. There are still some eighteenth-century timber houses, both large and small, including a group associated with local brickmaking at Pond Cottages that overlooked clay pits towards London (figs 236 and 243). A double-fronted early-eighteenth-century house that was timber built behind a proud and polite brick façade originally comprised only five rooms, each about 14 ft

239 Nos 54–62 Peckham High Street, the long low building at Nos 60 and 62 having seventeenth-century origins, the somewhat taller one at No. 58 being the last survivor of two flanking pairs of three-storey timber houses built c.1730. Photographed 1999 (EH, BB99/00122).

240 Nos 56–66 Peckham High Street, showing the two three-storey pairs of c.1730. Photographed 1928 (EH, AP 313).

square. Later Georgian timber and brick houses adjoining are smaller.

A bit further south, Sydenham Wells was another minor spa from the late seventeenth century, the attraction shifting, as elsewhere, from the medicinal to the recreational. Little of this period remains, but at Nos 32 and 34 Sydenham Road there is a pretty survival from the mid-eighteenth century (figs 236 and 244). This semi-detached pair has a brick screen front, enlivened by entrance bays with Gibbs-surround doorcases and swan-necked parapets, but with irregular window positioning in keeping with the vernacular form of everything behind the façade. The houses have seven rooms each, with ground-floor kitchens in the service outshuts behind the entrances. The main block has central staircases laid out in the way favoured in late eighteenth-century Deptford, but doglegged with columnar balusters. This seems to be an artisan speculation souped up with a fashionable façade and ornamental trim.[70]

In the more easterly locales of Blackheath, Lewisham and Eltham, no more than small settlements in the eighteenth century, houses of vernacular form that have been understood as rustic reminders of Kent can be related to urban building practice. Blackheath in the 1790s was more a hamlet than a village. Development of a large frontage facing the notoriously lawless open heath was then initiated by John Collins, a substantial local landowner and the son of a Greenwich joiner with naval connections who had been a leading builder in the area. The result was very varied, with most of the frontages on Tranquil Vale given substantial but conservatively designed brick buildings. Adjoining groups of smaller timber houses were built in 1798, seemingly by Henry Blow, a carpenter, most facing an alley that has become known as Collins Square. One row of three houses survives (figs 236, 245 and 246). Evidently built for occupation by artisans, these houses were laid out with ground-floor kitchen/living rooms in front of winder staircases and unheated service spaces. On the upper storeys there were two rooms in each house, those to the rear unheated. It should be recalled that Michael Searles's majestic suburban development at The Paragon is contemporary and just a short hop away, a very different part of the taming of the heath.[71]

Lewisham was essentially linear, with a great mix of buildings along its lengthy High Street. Opposite the parish church, largely rebuilt in the 1770s, there was a

241 (left)   No. 58 Peckham High Street, second-floor room, view to the back wall showing the early eighteenth-century closet, stairs and fireplace all in line. Photographed 1999 (EH, BB99/00131).

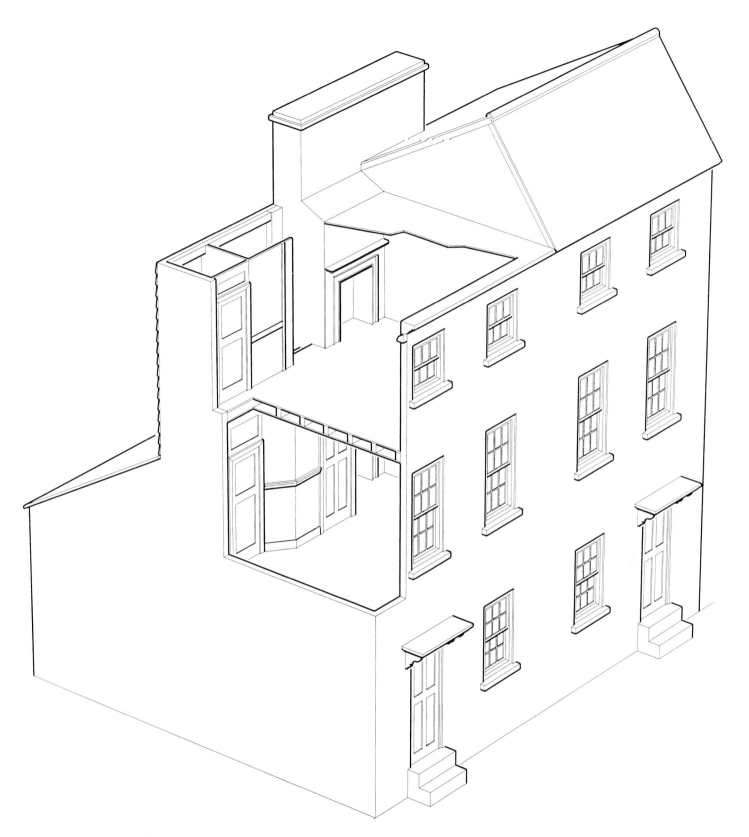

242 Nos 56 and 58 Peckham High Street, perspective reconstruction.

243   Pond Cottages, Dulwich, an early eighteenth-century double-fronted five-room house with later and smaller timber and brick houses adjoining, all built in association with local brick-making. Photographed 2000 (EH, BB009673).

244   Nos 32 and 34 Sydenham Road, a mid-eighteenth-century semi-detached pair from a minor spa, houses of vernacular form with lively classical entrance bays. Photographed 1960 (LLSA).

245   Collins Square, Blackheath, three four-room timber houses from a larger group built in
1798. Photographed 1943 (LMA).

246   No. 3 Collins Square, Blackheath, the ground-floor interior from the front wall, showing
doorways to the service room and staircase. Photographed 1957 (LLSA).

247 (*above*) Nos 315 and 317 Lewisham High Street, a brick-built pair of six-room houses of *c*.1770, opposite the parish church. Photographed 2000 (EH, BB000821).

248 (*left*) No. 1 Sherard Street, Eltham, a mid-eighteenth-century central-chimneystack timber house. Photographed by Philip Norman in the early twentieth century. Demolished (EH, BB99/06765).

miscellaneous group, including a late medieval jettied range that may have been a guildhall, demolished in the late nineteenth century. Just south of this were Nos 315 and 317 Lewisham High Street, a mirrored pair of around 1770 that has much in common with houses in nearby Deptford (figs 236 and 247) (see chapter 6). Like the grander pair from Sydenham, these six-room double-pile brick houses were given central-staircase layouts of the type that seems to grow out of one-room-plan tradi-tions, asymmetrically fenestrated fronts and columnar balusters on tightly wound close-string dogleg staircases. As a pair they seem to be another artisan's speculation, manifesting the now familiar late eighteenth-century combination of enduring vernacular form with some sub-fashionable detail.[72] In Eltham there were long rows of two-room brick houses, behind the High Street on Pound Place, and larger timber houses with central chimneystacks (fig. 248). Jubilee Cottages, just off the High Street, a six-house row of 1833 that was outwardly comparable with the row on Commercial Way, Peckham (figs 236 and 238), were another reminder of the prevalence and longevity of this layout and timber construction south of the Thames.[73]

Conclusions

This anti-clockwise jaunt round London has thrown up a great muddle of smaller eighteenth-century houses, enormously varied, but having much in common with contemporary smaller housing of the proximate metropolis. Much of what has been seen as the meeting of urban and rural architectural traditions in these buildings can, through another prism, be understood as the working through of two opposed but equally urban forces, the polite and the vernacular, or the fashionable and the traditional. However, boundaries between all these conceptual categories were probably no clearer at the time than they are now, no more for architectural form than for social class.

Distinctions have been drawn between what was introduced as the genteel vernacular, understood as Picturesque sensibilities on the part of an elite that could entertain the possibility of slumming it within a low-status context provided it was understood as rural, and vernacular gentility, understood as rising artisan to 'middling sort' respectability. It is sometimes clear that one of these forces is more in evidence than the other, but sometimes there is no such clarity. There were overlaps and ambiguities; architecture does not, of course, invariably express cultural dynamics neatly, and smaller eighteenth-century buildings in London's outlying settlements were not a product of Picturesque consciousness any more than they were of rural isolation. What does emerge, however, is that the urban vernacular was a powerful presence in and between the Picturesque and the respectable. The intermediate, hybrid or negotiated character of the buildings considered in this chapter arises from proximity to London and from wider ambivalence in terms of imagined barriers between the polite and the vernacular.

It would be misleading to suggest that artisan aspects of the vernacular were cultivated as fashionable in the eighteenth century. Walpole's odes to 'rural' Strawberry Hill made no play of the prosaic coachman for whom his house had first been built. Rusticity was about milkmaids and shepherds, not about carpenters and brickmakers. Yet, just as Walpole's first forays into the Gothic style were wholly unarchaeological, so Romantic openness to what was reassuringly familiar in the vernacular did not trouble to differentiate between the architecture of the peasant and that of the hat maker. There was not reverse emulation, but amid all the interdependence of these mixed milieux the genteel vernacular on its downward search did bump inadvertently into vernacular gentility on its way up. Urban vernacular houses were not overtly incorporated into rising notions of the Picturesque in London's environs. They were, however, accommodated into what were considered desirable *genii loci* in a way that was not paralleled within London. The nurturing of mixed eighteenth-century built environments in what are now (but were not then) suburbs, from Islington to Blackheath, is distinct from what happened in central London, where, from the standpoints of 'taste' and 'wealth', the vernacular was ignored and then largely purged. The polite/vernacular mix in fact characterised the whole city. Outlying places presented, and still present, this in unthreatening microcosms.

From Pentonville to The Paragon, large-scale speculative building took hold in these outlying districts in the late eighteenth century, mixing in with already convergent cultural forces in the creation of places that are recognisable as indubitably suburban in a modern sense. After 1800 the interweaving of the polite and the vernacular became much more overt in conscious Picturesque revivalism, from Camberwell to Nash's Park Villages East and West, on to De Beauvoir Town in Hackney.[74] One reason this happened in this way was that at the centre urban-vernacular architecture was being eradicated through improvement or urban renewal. The imposition of rationality on the metropolitan built environment brought standardisation and caused the decline of vernacular traditions, simultaneously encouraging those who could afford it to look outside the city for the antitheses of rationality and standardisation in just such traditions. Once the vernacular as a mode of urban building had been cleansed of troubling connotations, it could be appropriated and reinvented as a conceptually rural branch of the polite.[75]

Chapter 8

ALONG THE COAST AND ACROSS THE SEA: REFLECTIONS OF THE VERNACULAR METROPOLIS

Not only that, I mean to shew
How grand a place is Whitby now.
See how they all in pride abound
Their houses are all sashed around
Houses were low and poor compent
Of two times twenty shillings rent
Built up with mortar, lime and lath,
With outside white and inside black,
And by the winds blown from the hills
Made all the houses smoke like kilns.
Some thought their habitations good
In little houses built of wood,
If not with paint, daubed round with prime
They thought they looked most wondrous fine,
But now like Yarmouth it is said
They've changed white herrings into red.

John Twisleton,
a late eighteenth-century Whitby barber and poet[1]

This is a book about London, but it is about an aspect of London with wide resonance. Urban-vernacular houses analogous to those built in eighteenth-century London were built in towns throughout England and beyond, notably along the Atlantic coast in North America. From Deal to Philadelphia, such buildings are known and valued where they survive, but others have remained obscure. They all deserve further study, both particular and comparative, though this is not the place

249 *(facing page)* The house (centre) in Grape Lane, Whitby, where (Captain) James Cook lived from 1746 as an apprentice to the ship owner John Walker in what was then a prosperous ship-building town. The plaque indicates a build date of 1688, but there appears to have been a refronting since. Perhaps the one-room-deep building started as a mirrored pair of four-room houses, with the round windows indicating front-staircase layouts. Photographed 1945 (EH, A45/5235).

for proper accounts of buildings from towns other than London. It is, however, appropriate to bring other places to the fore briefly because houses of this nature have rarely been related to evidence from London. So this chapter is a net cast wide. As a net, it touches only the surface of that which it catches. Through a few vignettes of towns in eighteenth-century England and North America, the aim is to raise questions about the relationship of London's vernacular architecture to that of other places.

There has been much valuable synthesis of architectural developments in eighteenth-century provincial English towns, but the comparative significance of London has generally been invoked only in terms of the spread of fashion, politeness or emulation.[2] Buildings that, if considered at all, have been understood as semi-rural, pre-urban or simply late, debased or declining vernacular, and therefore as purely local or provincial – in contrast to the more assertive polite or classical buildings that are well understood as reflecting metropolitan culture – might offer new insights if related to less familiar aspects of a heterogeneous metropolis. This is not to diminish what is truly local, nor to suggest one-way traffic; the insights might apply to the metropolis as much as to the provinces. Nor is it to suggest that artisans, labourers, mariners and other working people around England looked to their peers in London for an architectural lead. The point, rather, is that small houses built for occupation by artisans and others in eighteenth-century English-speaking towns away from London can be understood in relation to comparable houses in what was then the world's greatest industrial and maritime city, as well as in purely local terms. As much as London was the centre of England's aristocratic and 'middling sort' worlds, so it was of its artisan world. It should not be assumed that the transmission of architectural ideas happened only in the contexts of genteel or print culture. Of the numerous towns with large artisan and maritime populations, many had small houses of a distinctive character, neither polite nor rural, much as was the case in London. Some of England's larger towns of the eighteenth century have lost as high or higher proportions of their early small houses as has London; Birmingham and Manchester were by 1800 only beginning the industrialisation that was to make them great. Nevertheless, there are some remnants and there is some evidence of what has gone. More survives in other places where subsequent growth has not been so all-encompassing. In some towns, small eighteenth-century housing survives much better than it does in London.

Houses in Some Maritime Towns

Given the relative ease of waterborne communication as against land links in the eighteenth century, it is appropriate to start this exploration by travelling out from London along the Thames to England's eastern coasts. The narrative has already begun to follow the Thames into Kent, reaching out via naval dockyards from Deptford as far as Woolwich (see chapter 6). Outside the reach of the London Building Acts in Kent and Surrey, timber stayed in favour as a building material well into the nineteenth century (see chapter 7). Further along the Thames estuary on the Kent side, Gravesend was the first main stop outside London, beyond which, near the mouth of the tributary Medway, are Rochester and Chatham, the latter the site of another important naval dockyard in the seventeenth and eighteenth centuries. Gravesend was rebuilt after a major fire in 1727, much

of the new High Street being timber built, outwardly regular but internally varied (fig. 250).[3] Rochester, a much earlier cathedral town, grew towards Chatham in the eighteenth century, timber houses on the linking High Street diverging greatly in scale and form. Some smaller two- or three-room 15 ft-square survivors seem closely comparable with contemporary houses in Deptford and Woolwich (fig. 251). On Chatham New Road, there were numerous eighteenth-century brick central-chimneystack houses, this plan form enduring here into the nineteenth century at Ordnance Terrace, where timber framing was still used behind brick fronts, and where Charles Dickens lived as a boy while his father worked in the naval dockyard.[4]

Leaving the Thames estuary and turning round the coast to the south leads to Deal, an important and fascinating eighteenth-century maritime town where virtually all ships travelling between London and points overseas stopped. Deal was a chartered port from 1699 with a naval provisioning yard from 1703. It was also a flourishing centre of boatbuilding, less formal marine provisioning, and smuggling. Deal's Middle Street retains an astonishingly large and varied group of modest late seventeenth- and eighteenth-century urban houses, said to have been built for habitation by sea pilots, mariners, traders and victuallers (fig. 252). Emphasis has been given to the long and picturesque street's low-life reputation for smuggling and debauchery. In spite of, because of or regardless of this, many of its small one-room-plan houses are finished to a high standard. Some of the houses are clearly informed by the vernacular architecture of the Netherlands, not least in a proliferation of shaped gables, and others are closely comparable in form with houses documented in Deptford and Greenwich; Nos 2–7 Exchange Street of 1788 appear to replicate the unusual form of Nos 4–8 Feathers Place, Greenwich, of 1744 (see chapter 6).[5] In Dover, too, the central-chimneystack layout endured, and in nearby Folkestone there were long rows of approximately 15 ft-square three-room houses on North Street, probably built in the early eighteenth century, being very like houses of that date in Deptford.[6]

Great Yarmouth, northwards up the east coast, had much in common with Deal, though the buildings under consideration here were predominantly slightly earlier. Yarmouth was a fishing town, its prosperity based on herrings, though coal ships supplying London and the timber trade were also important. In a confined and densely populated town, most working people lived in the 'Rows', a remarkable concentration of small urban houses in a tight ladder of narrow alleys. By 1784 there were 156 Rows with 2,500 houses for 12,608 people.

250 (*above left*) Nos 76–82 Gravesend High Street, mid-eighteenth-century timber shophouses in a Thames-side town. Their regular 15 ft-wide fronts disguised varied internal layouts, including both central-chimneystack and central-staircase plans. Photographed 1972 (EH, BB72/3356).

251 (*above right*) Nos 342 and 344 Rochester High Street. In the eighteenth century Rochester grew from the vicinity of these houses to meet the naval dockyard town of Chatham. These buildings resemble those of the other Kentish dockyard towns of Deptford and Woolwich. Photographed 1943 (EH, B43/2571).

252 (*right*) Middle Street, Deal, showing a pair of the numerous small eighteenth-century houses in this maritime town. Photographed by V. J. Torr, 1947 (EH, VJT 31).

Yarmouth's Rows were virtually all cleared by the 1950s following war damage, but much valuable recording was done in the interval between bombs and bulldozers. The timber, flint and brick houses were largely one room on plan, many about 15 ft square, comprising two to four rooms. In buildings said to date from the early seventeenth century until around 1700, there were front staircases lit by small, sometimes oval, windows. This feature was described as 'the real "hall-mark"' of Yarmouth's small houses, but it can now be understood as anything but local.[7] Paralleled in contemporary

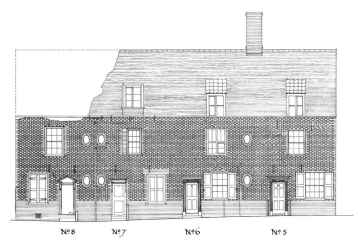

FRONT ELEVATIONS FROM ROW 101

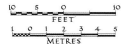

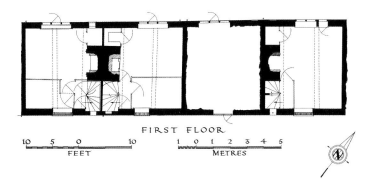

FIRST FLOOR

253 Nos 5–8 Row 101, Great Yarmouth, front elevation and first-floor plan as recorded c.1950. These three-room houses of c.1700 were part of a densely populated fishing town housed in 'Rows'. The front-staircase layout and fenestration echo contemporary housing in London (see fig. 33) (EH, Ministry of Works Drawing 582/15).

London's smaller houses, it appears to indicate design for multiple occupation (fig. 253) (see chapters 2 and 3). East Anglia had been a significant destination for Dutch immigration since the sixteenth century, and Yarmouth's houses also had what have been understood as Netherlandish links, as in the use of decorative wall anchors, that is iron ties from internal timber beams to brick walls.[8] Further up the coast was the cloth and whaling port of Hull, a great and cosmopolitan centre of commerce and shipbuilding in the eighteenth century, and, like Yarmouth, 'exceeding close built' and 'extraordinary populous'.[9] Until the 1770s Hull grew in piecemeal manner with a great variety of small one-room-plan houses, many in courts and alleys; in that decade dock

building began to transform the town and it spread outwards more rapidly.[10]

Whitby was another east-coast port with a concentration of shipbuilders and ship owners as well as a substantial artisan population. The coal trade that ran essentially between Newcastle and London, along with whaling and government transport during wartime, made eighteenth-century Whitby a prosperous town, England's seventh largest port by tonnage of shipping, the links of which with east London are memorialised through the Wapping riverside public house, the Prospect of Whitby. A reminder that Whitby's coastal trade was human as well as carboniferous comes with the return to these pages of Captain Cook (see chapters 5 and 7). In 1746 the young James Cook was apprenticed to John Walker, a Whitby ship owner with whom he took up residence in Grape Lane, in a house, evidently built in 1688, that has hallmark small, round

254 Nos 1–5 Linskill Square, Whitby, not, in fact, a square, but a court of two opposed rows. These well-appointed three-room houses were laid out in the late eighteenth century in the yard of a large house, the name deriving from John Linskill, an influential ship's master and Quaker. Inside there are partitions in front of rear staircases and small unheated bed enclosures, as at No. 74 Bermondsey Street (see figs 115, 116 and 123). Photographed 1994 (EH, AA94/4044).

255   King Street, Portsea, Portsmouth, late eighteenth-century houses in a suburb developed to house artisans and others dependent on the adjoining naval dockyard. Photographed 1943 (EH, AA022199).

windows (fig. 249). There were many smaller dwellings in Whitby, the town's prosperity in the late eighteenth century leading wealthier inhabitants to move away from the centre, leaving the backs of early plots to be filled with court developments (fig. 254). As Twisleton's poem records, Whitby's earlier timber houses were being replaced in brick, but his 'grand' is a relative term, and many of the new houses had only two to four rooms. Nevertheless, these houses were not only 'all sashed around', they were also well finished internally, with classically moulded joinery like that recorded in equivalent houses in Deptford. As in Deptford, these buildings would have housed shipwrights and mariners.[11]

On the south coast, Portsmouth was the naval town *par excellence*. Its eighteenth-century suburb of Portsea was built alongside the great naval dockyard to house dockyard workers and associated tradespeople, growing to have a population of 4,419 in its own right by 1801, living in numerous rows of small houses that have since been swept away. Artisan culture here was analogous with what is described above as characterising Deptford and Woolwich, excepting the influence of the proximity of London. Portsea's mid- to late eighteenth-century development was similarly led by speculating dockyard workers, who, with their independent and self-sufficient traditions, built their own Church of St George in 1753–4, using the same cross-in-rectangle auditory internal arrangement that had been used in Poplar, Whitechapel, Bermondsey and Deptford. Movement between the dockyard towns was common and, against any perception of isolation, it should be remembered that throughout the eighteenth century naval dockyard workers were capable of organising effective strikes on a national basis. Houses were put up piecemeal on Portsea's narrow streets, with little architectural unity or coherent planning, largely in brick, with frontages of 11 ft to 15 ft. Again, central-chimneystack layouts were in use until at least the 1790s (fig. 255).[12]

More could be added regarding the south-west and the west, most notably in relation to the great Georgian ports of Bristol and Liverpool, sophisticated and heterogeneous commercial towns, both much rebuilt, but both having had substantial eighteenth-century artisan and maritime populations in small houses, in courts, tenements and elsewhere. Continuing survey-based studies of these towns are likely to provide interesting comparative evidence.[13] In the meantime this journey round the coast speeds past these places to go as far from London as possible while remaining in England, to the largely eighteenth-century, largely stone-built and genteel port of Whitehaven in Cumbria, a well-studied town that can, given its relative remoteness, provide an

271

256　The east side of Selwood Road, Frome, Somerset, small houses of the 1690s in what was an industrial suburb of a cloth-manufacturing town. Photographed 1979 (EH, BB83/258).

indicative measure of the pervasive extent of London's relevance within eighteenth-century England. In White-haven the one-room plan suffered the same decline in status at the end of the eighteenth century that it did in London. In single-fronted double-pile houses there was a variety of central-staircase layouts, but by the later eighteenth century the rear-staircase plan had become widespread, reflecting what, even here, has been interpreted as decline in the regional character of domestic architecture and rising conformity with standardising national norms.[14] The central-chimneystack plan appears to have been absent from eighteenth-century White-haven, as it evidently was from inland and comparably genteel Stamford, where one-room, central-staircase and rear-staircase plans were also all present. In contrast, all three of the basic single-fronted double-pile layouts were in use in more socially mixed eighteenth-century towns as far apart as Poole, Norwich and York.[15]

In ranging across all England it is important to distinguish between English and English speaking. There are, of course, other important cultural traditions in the British Isles. However, for the sake of brevity, this overview does not attempt to embrace Scottish or Irish houses. There may well be fruitful lines of enquiry in exploring the ways these traditions might have intersected, as, for example, in the question of design for multiple occupation and the use of front staircases in Edinburgh's tenement blocks or 'lands' (see chapter 2).

Houses in Some Industrial Towns

Not all artisan settlements were maritime, and inland eighteenth-century towns invariably had some small houses, in large groupings where industry so dictated. Much manufacturing remained scattered and essentially rural, as on the Shropshire coalfields, in Lancashire and Yorkshire's textile industries, and in metalworking in and around Sheffield, but urban concentrations of artisans did occur widely, as in Exeter, Bath, Banbury, Norwich and Leeds, to name diverse places not discussed further. There was great variance between the small houses of particular places, and not just in terms of differences in locally available building materials. Local distinctiveness had deeper regional vernacular roots, but, as with the maritime towns, there are sometimes qualities in smaller houses that resonate with evidence from London, suggesting a shared imperviousness to the tide of the polite.[16] A few instances of notable industrial towns will serve present purposes.

The Trinity area of Frome in Somerset was a substantial industrial suburb, built up in the period 1670 to 1725.[17] Prosperity based in cloth manufacturing led to intensive speculative development to provide numerous small houses for weavers and other artisans. Generally built of stone rubble, most of these houses had variants of one-room layouts, often being less than 20 ft square and comprising only two or three rooms, yet sometimes having good decorative finish (fig. 256). Similar houses continued to be built as infill in the area through the eighteenth century.[18] Though not unlike many contemporary London houses in form, close similarities with London's weavers' houses are not evident.

Eighteenth-century Birmingham was a workshop-based metalworking town that was neither technologically nor socially stagnant just because it did not develop to become factory based. With manufacturing concentrated on guns, jewellery and other luxury or 'toy' metal products, Birmingham was strongly linked to and aware of the London market. It had a rapidly growing population and more than 10,000 houses were built during the century. From early on much artisan housing was fitted in behind larger houses or around small courts, and generally comprised singly occupied small brick houses of two or three rooms, with integral or adjoining workshops and warehouses. Growing densities had led to these courts being arrayed in back-to-back groups by the 1770s; even so disposed, however, many three-room 15 ft-square houses were originally perfectly respectable, only later coming to be slums.[19]

Manchester was different, and not just for its part in the development of the factory system of manufacturing. Cotton-cloth manufacture had become a significant local industry by the seventeenth century, and despite great expansion it remained largely unmechanised and domestically based until the end of the eighteenth. Prodigious growth in population, from about 22,000 in 1773 to about 75,000 in 1801, necessitated the building of some 6,500 houses in the same period. By 1800 many two-room dwellings had come to be very densely packed together, setting the scene for Friedrich Engels's coruscating description in his *Condition of the Working Classes in England* (1844). There were also numerous late eighteenth-century three-storey houses with upper-storey or cellar weaving workshops, concentrated in what has become known as the Northern Quarter, where there are still a few survivors (fig. 257). Generally, but not invariably two rooms deep, these houses were not built in large speculations, but in ones and twos. In a place and at a time when any houses built for single occupation were quickly being divided and becoming overcrowded, it could be that some were designed for multiple occupation. Whether this was so or not, their forms can be related to those of tenement housing that had long been current in London's silk district. Manchester also had some two-storey workshop houses, providing a mix not unlike that of late eighteenth-century Bethnal Green (see chapter 3).[20]

It was not just in London that weaving remained resistant to restructuring in factories in the early nineteenth

257 No. 36 Back Turner Street, Manchester, a house with a top-storey workshop and a separate and once well-lit cellar dwelling. Perhaps datable to the 1760s, before mechanised cotton weaving was firmly established, it has workshop fenestration that resembles that in contemporary weavers' workshop tenements in London's silk district. Photographed 2000 (EH, AA006123).

century. Domestically based handloom weaving endured much more widely. Houses with long windows designed to incorporate workshops are widespread, often, though not necessarily, linked to weaving. In Yorkshire's woollen-cloth-producing areas, hundreds of late eighteenth- and early nineteenth-century houses built in small speculations incorporated upper-storey workshops with long mullioned windows.[21] In the silk industry, from Macclesfield and elsewhere in east Cheshire to Leek in Staffordshire, numerous brick 'garret houses' were built in the first decades of the nineteenth century, with large upper-storey windows for the weaving workshops. Often in terraces, these houses were unlike the contemporary two-storey weavers' 'cottages' of Bethnal Green and more like their forerunners in having three storeys, typically with 15 ft fronts, but with two-room layouts to provide four-room dwellings below the work-

258 Paradise Street, Macclesfield, early-nineteenth-century silk-weaving 'garret houses' that bear comparison with London's earlier workshop houses. Photographed 1989 (EH, BB88/671).

shops (fig. 258).[22] The development of housing in Georgian London's silk district needs to be related to the housing of textile industries elsewhere, as well as to an acknowledgement of the widespread endurance through the nineteenth century of domestic workshop production. The progressivist understanding of the development of manufacturing from 'proto-industrial' domestic rural roots into factories in towns can be re-interrogated with a greater awareness of the architecture of London's domestic industry.

★   ★   ★

Across the Atlantic

'Things are regarded as peculiarly American, because all their antecedents, phases, and particulars are by now far better known in America than in Europe. Thus English or Continental precedent is often disregarded because not familiar.'[23] So Nikolaus Pevsner long ago admonished a kind of historical amnesia that has not been cured. In some respects it has deepened. His comment should help the reader to make what might seem a huge geographical and mental leap across the Atlantic, serving as a reminder that the gulf may not be so great. The admonition can be applied to urban-vernacular houses as much as it can to churches, in relation to which Pevsner elsewhere made a similar point in saying of the artisan dockyard church of St George, Portsea, that 'It must strike American visitors as a greeting from New England.'[24] The original direction of travel was, of course, the other way round.

A broader American understanding of the term 'vernacular' is broached in terms of the concept of 'vernacular gentility' in chapter 7. In a way that is not true in England, almost any American building – indeed almost any aspect of American culture – can be and has been interpreted in terms of the 'vernacular'. So, in turning to North America in the eighteenth century, one should pause first to consider some origins for that breadth of understanding. The first critical salient is the well-travelled Atlantic, a place that had its own culture. The sea was the home of a 'London-centred international nautical proletariat'.[25] Maritime transmission was not only of immigrants, slaves, tobacco, sugar or tea, but also of discrete outlooks and ideas, from many sections of many different societies that looked at each other across the Atlantic and blended on the ships that it carried.[26]

The melting pot that was the Atlantic notwithstanding, it hardly needs to be stressed that English precedent is at the heart of the development of towns in North America in the eighteenth century. Numerous towns along the Atlantic coast can perhaps be regarded as relating to London in much the same way as did such English ports as Whitby, except that they were further away. English emigrants to America, many of whom were artisans, might be expected to have taken with them the vernacular customs and cultures of English artisans, manifest, not least, in a search for liberty and simplicity. Politeness was in the ascendant in eighteenth-century England, but its roots were in a dominant section of society, the established and prospering members of which would not, as a rule, have been inclined to leave for the hardships of a new country. For many, of course, emigration offered an open road to gentility where other routes were full of obstructions. The American path to politeness that has been characterised as vernacular gentility may have been relatively open, but for most it was a long haul from a humble starting-point, and many of its travellers will have carried within themselves ambivalence about fashion and emulative behaviour. The road metaphor is misleadingly linear, but it is perhaps permissible in this context because the convergence of vernacular and polite viewpoints in the 'new world' would have lacked many of the oppositional currents of eighteenth-century London. Where London's artisans might have perceived themselves as a rearguard attached

to an old culture, American artisans were seeking a better life in a new place, with fewer barriers to mobility, and fewer undertones of coercion. The horizons of such emigrants might have been more imaginative than nostalgic.[27]

A great deal has been written about North American vernacular architecture, much of it looking penetratively, both squarely and obliquely, at social and cultural contexts, often bridging the polite-vernacular divide that plagues English architectural history. Indeed the Chesapeake is the nest of the study of buildings through an avowedly 'material culture' approach, an important scholarly heritage on which this study as a whole draws. However, all that is intended in bringing America into this book about London is that the potential for deeper consideration of links between American buildings and London's own eighteenth-century urban-vernacular architecture be emphasised.[28]

In the laying out of houses in eighteenth-century 'English' North America, in both towns and the countryside, there was great diversity, but brick as opposed to timber continued to be a signifier of wealth, and anything more than one room deep in plan was rare until after 1750. A high proportion of all pre-revolutionary houses had only one room on each of one, two or three storeys. The highest-quality houses in eighteenth-century North America were no more than equivalent in size and finish to houses in London's middle-range speculative developments or minor English country houses. Plan form in later eighteenth-century double-pile town houses was very variable, there being no settled standards, even on a regional basis. Both rear- and central-staircase layouts were widely popular into the nineteenth century. Urban central-chimneystack plans seem to be all but unknown in eighteenth-century North America, though the layout has been recorded in a short row of houses from late seventeenth-century Jamestown, as well as in the Dutch context of early eighteenth-century New York. Uniform speculations of large numbers of town houses did not occur until well after the revolution: Charles Bulfinch's Tontine Crescent, Boston, of 1793–4, was the first real American 'terrace', a term little used where such developments continue to be called rowhouses. From Marblehead, Massachusetts, to Charleston, South Carolina, eighteenth-century houses and development patterns along the Atlantic seaboard seem to have more in common with those of the commercial and maritime world of Bermondsey than with those of the elite and fashionable world of Westminster. In North America standardisation and more general urban systematisation were essentially early nineteenth-century phenomena.[29]

In the Quaker colony of Pennsylvania, William Penn had founded Philadelphia in 1682. Though the new town was given a grid layout, there was no uniformity of house form before 1800. Philadelphia grew from being a small settlement of about 2,000 people around 1700 to have a population of about 70,000 in 1800, making it the fifth largest English-speaking town, and not much smaller than Manchester, Liverpool or Birmingham. It was the new nation's capital in the 1790s, before when there were no more than relatively humble row developments. Given the emerging scale of the city and its rational grid base, the absence of standardisation through large-scale speculations is all the more remarkable when set against what was happening in London, and is indicative of both economic limitations and local horizons. For artisan and shopkeeping immigrants, there were great opportunities for wealth creation and upward movement into a landowning elite. Yet many such early Philadelphians lived in two-storey one-room-plan houses, often brick, sometimes timber. In the maritime (shipbuilding and port) part of the town called Southwark, most of the houses had one-room plans. Philadelphia did have some larger houses, but taken as a whole its early domestic architecture is strikingly modest (figs 259–61). As in Deptford or Whitby, the small houses were far from mean, having well-appointed interiors with much ornamental joinery.[30]

Baltimore was another important port in which there was huge growth in the later decades of the eighteenth century, its population rising to about 26,500 in 1800, when about half of the town's buildings were timber; this balance was to change, as legislation in 1799 banned wooden construction. As in Philadelphia and Boston, there were no real terraces before the 1790s, after which rear- and central-staircase layouts were both used in newly ambitious speculative developments. Freestanding or in rows, houses built for artisans, tradespeople and mariners tended to be of two storeys, often with only one room per storey. Smaller houses had only one full storey, sometimes accommodating the city's large free black population, many of whom relied on maritime employment (fig. 262).[31]

Other American towns could be invoked, but enough has been said to emphasise the need for compara-

262   Wolf Street, Fells Point, Baltimore, late eighteenth-century two-room timber houses from another important early North American port. Photographed by Bernard Herman in the 1990s.

tive study that recognises the importance of urban-vernacular traditions that crossed the Atlantic. Given its overwhelming pre-eminence among eighteenth-century English towns, it would be perverse to deny the centrality of London to any such study. Of course, it is a paradox to speak of the spread of any vernacular, if vernacular is understood as meaning local and indigenous. Whether it is called vernacular or not, there is more to the analysis of common ground across eighteenth-century English-speaking urban society in relation to domestic architecture than the tracking of the spread and permutations of emulative gentility. Polite culture was not the only trans-regional unifying force with a base in London. It is necessary to make these points because important facets of the eighteenth-century metropolis have been obscured. Earlier chapters have drawn some of these out, but without directly addressing how they came to be obscured. To make up that deficit, the next chapter returns to London.

259, 260 and 261 (*facing page top, bottom left and bottom right, respectively*)   Drinker's Court, Fitzwater Street and League Street, Southwark, Philadelphia. Eighteenth-century houses from what was the fifth-largest English-speaking town in 1800, much settlement having been by English artisans. Drinker's Court photographed *c.*1900 (City of Philadelphia Historical Commission); Fitzwater Street and League Street photographed by Bernard Herman in the 1990s.

263   Chapel Grove, Somers Town, a uniform row of *c.*1820, two-room houses inserted between the backs of terraces on Chalton and Willsted streets (see fig. 267) in a post-improvement suburb. Photographed 1927. Demolished (LMA).

Chapter 9

'DESPICABLE COTTAGES': IMPROVEMENT AND ARTISAN ECLIPSE

– like an entrance into a large city, after a distant prospect. Remotely, we see nothing but spires of temples, and turrets of palaces, and imagine it the residence of splendor [*sic*], grandeur, and magnificence; but, when we have passed the gates, we find it perplexed with narrow passages, disgraced with despicable cottages, embarassed [*sic*] with obstructions, and clouded with smoke.

Samuel Johnson, as quoted by John Gwynn[1]

If eighteenth-century urban-vernacular houses can be found so widely, it might again be asked, what makes those in London so special as to warrant book-length exposition? The answer to this is that much of their significance resides not in the buildings *per se*, but in what they reveal about eighteenth-century London, a city celebrated as a cauldron of cultural modernity that has disproportionately large importance for understanding the world since the eighteenth century. That such buildings existed in eighteenth-century London says something about the first great 'modern' city, something either previously unknown or assumed to be true without adequate exploration, that is that there was an enduring vernacular side to its domestic architecture. This and consequent mix both colour and complicate understandings of London's modernity. Further, indications that vernacular houses came no longer to be built in London around the end of the century suggest something perhaps always understood, but not given much attention in relation to ordinary domestic architecture. There was a price to be paid for modernisation; it was a trade-off. This chapter addresses this second point. It is about the demise of London's urban vernacular.

In and around east and south London, from Bethnal Green to St George's Fields, Kingsland Road to Deptford, Islington to Clapham, local and variable – that is vernacular – housebuilding traditions that were expressions of the ordinary artisan's ability to participate independently in an industrialising capitalist economy endured through the eighteenth century. Artisan housing culture was strongly informed by precedent, but was otherwise generally unsystematic, though accepting of classicism as an *ad hoc* overlay. Improvisation from the base of precedent was rooted in an integration of design and production that depended on the transmission of trade skills through apprenticeship. Standardisation was neither avoided nor sought, but between small-scale speculative developments undertaken by different groups of skilled artisans it remained unlikely. This Georgian London, the vernacular metropolis, has been largely swept away and forgotten. The evidence pieced together in the preceding chapters has attempted to bring it back to the fore. It is now possible to take a step back to look at what happened to it, by recalling some of the social and economic factors that contributed to the decline of artisans as a distinct social class (see chapter 1), by focusing on 'improvement', particularly legislation and changes, consequential and otherwise, in the nature of speculative building, and by dipping a toe into the waters of the housebuilding scene after 1800, just enough to show how it differed.

Improvement

Urban and social improvement, understood as the implementation of the rational and utilitarian ideas of the English Enlightenment (see chapter 1), has been repeatedly mentioned. However, the topic has not yet been directly addressed, either as a phenomenon or in relation to housebuilding. Before going into specifics, therefore, a general characterisation is due. Improvement was not new in the eighteenth century, the word having long served to signify faith in a panacea for the woes of the public sphere.[2] Though rooted in a long tradition of idealistic and progressive thinking, London's late eighteenth-century urban improvements were less about the extension of enlightened gentility than they were pragmatic avoidance of chaos. They were largely a top-down reaction to glaring and grotesque mid-century social disasters, both real (high mortality) and perceived (rampant criminality). They arose from and addressed uncontrolled growth and commercial congestion, that is the impacts of industrialisation and the intensification of capitalism, of which improvement is always an essential aspect. Some initiatives certainly helped the poor, particularly as regards medicine and sanitation; free public dispensaries were introduced and mortality rates were significantly reduced (see chapter 1). Improvement was thus beneficent, but it was also controlling, or, to follow Michel Foucault, 'policing', in the sense of the word that was then current that pertained to any domain of state regulation. For the most part new interventions arose from the enlightened self-interest of dominant groups; attempts to contain poverty were conceived to benefit the wealthy by reducing the insecurities and impediments that obstructed the free circulation of commerce and capital. Late eighteenth-century urban regeneration was about removing disorder, much of it seen as being manifest in poor roads and poor buildings. Much was achieved, but as invariably happens, many fundamental problems were displaced rather than solved.

These points need to be made if a Panglossian view is to be avoided, but it is just as important to temper cynicism and to emphasise that improvement and the Enlightenment underpinning it were not parts of a repressive conspiracy.[3] Real benefits and the degree to which they filtered down should not be underestimated. Yet neither the motives nor the success or failure of the improvers is the core issue here. This is not an evaluation of the new voices, rather an attempt to listen to older muted voices. In considering how improvement was experienced by London's humbler housebuilders, it is important to remember that, well beyond the degree to which improvement might in fact have been about control and cultural cleansing, the social and economic changes through which it was manifest would have been perceived by many Londoners, notably artisans, as reflecting or threatening a loss of agency and identity (see chapter 1).

There was major physical reordering in London. A capital with a disorderly built environment was vulner-

able, dangerous and inefficient. Improvements were not primarily about houses, except in so far as some were in the way, but more about roads and bridges, crucial for access, circulation and egress. Georgian urban renewal can be tracked back to Westminster Bridge, which opened in 1750. Associated new roads across London's south side were in place by 1760 (see chapter 4), and to the north major new roads, the New Road (Marylebone, Euston and Pentonville roads) of 1756 and the City Road of 1761, formed an outer bypass and West End/City link, all these roads opening up large tracts of land to profitable development. This and other growth prompted the highly reactive Corporation of London to realise that, 'unless proper measures should be taken to make the city of London more airy and commodious for the mercantile and genteel part of its inhabitants, [. . .] the estates in the city would inevitably be ruined.'[4] In 1757–62 London Bridge was part rebuilt, houses thereon being removed, and Southwark Fair, nothing if not disorderly, was abolished. In 1760 the City gained road-widening powers; quarters deemed unsavoury were cleared and the old City gates, save Newgate, were dismantled. Blackfriars Bridge was built in the 1760s (see chapter 4), and the last, southerly part of Fleet Ditch was covered, with associated new roads in place by 1771.

New roads and bridges changed London, but roads and bridges were not, as such, new. What has been taken as more emblematically marking the beginning of 'a new era'[5] was the Westminster Paving Act of 1762,[6] seminal for taking responsibility for paving away from individual property owners, and for providing for the enforced removal of manifold encroachments on streets. The City Paving Act of 1766 and other related Acts followed, together bringing major changes to the appearance and cleanliness of the public spaces that were London's streets. Stone slabs replaced cobbles or pebbles in principal roads and projecting street signs were removed, this particular loss of identity leading to the beginnings of house numbering. These Acts ostensibly dealt with dirt, but disorderliness was as much the target of concern. They imposed a degree of conformity if not uniformity on householders, and extended the scope of the public sphere at the expense of individual liberty, and not without controversy. The Paving Acts were an important step away from acceptance of the vernacular in an urban context, leading to the creation of unprecedentedly ordered and polite public spaces.[7]

If, however, this analysis is to engage with houses it must lift its gaze from the gutter. Architecturally, the late Georgian era of improvement had been foreshadowed by Wren, Evelyn and other exponents of the classical who believed that architectural regularity and harmonic proportion were symbols of good order and good government, conducive to a stable society, and so more necessary in urban than rural situations.[8] Late eighteenth-century improvers echoed these ideals, but with more determined pragmatism. In *Georgian London*, Summerson's chapter 'The spirit and practice of "improvement"' begins with a discussion of John Gwynn (1713–1786). Gwynn has already been encountered, deploring Southwark (see chapter 4) and in the epigraph to this chapter. A friend of Samuel Johnson and James Boswell, who thought him 'a fine, lively, rattling fellow',[9] Gwynn came to be an architect late in life, rising from having been a carpenter (fig. 264). Significantly, he was not a Londoner but a Midlands reformer, a pioneer improver and extender of the 'publick good'; his *London and Westminster Improved* of 1766 was an ultimately prophetic manifesto setting out an ambitious agenda for ridding London's built environment of chaos. Gwynn supposed that visitors found London to be 'nothing more than a confused heap, an irregular, slovenly, ill-digested composition, of all that is absurd and ungraceful'.[10] He especially reproved 'the practice of erecting irregular groups of houses at the extremities of the town'.[11] For him Bath was exemplary, that testing ground for innovation providing the only instance of a British town wherein he was prepared to admit there was sufficient regularity and elegance, though he did also praise the newly paved and lit streets of Westminster, which were 'not only made safe and commodious, but elegant and magnificent'.[12] Gwynn proposed public intervention to bring about substantial redevelopments of large parts of the City and West End, involving, *inter alia*, obliteration of the artisan suburbs of St Margaret, Westminster, and Southwark near London Bridge, and major clearances for extensive street widening in Soho and St Giles. He addressed the problems of rehousing the poor and social segregation with a call for upwards cultural homogenisation (emulation) and an invocation of the convergence of the self-interest of the wealthy and the public good that is the essence of the rhetoric of improvement:

> In settling a plan of large streets for the dwellings of the rich, it will be found necessary to allot smaller spaces contiguous, for the habitations of useful and laborious people, whose dependance [*sic*] on their superiors requires such a distribution; and by adhering to this principal [*sic*] a political advantage will result to the nation; as this intercourse stimulates their industry, improves their morals by example, and prevents any particular part from being the habitation of the indigent alone, to the great detriment of private property.[13]

264   Anonymous, *John Gwynn*, c. 1770. Gwynn, a minor architect, was influential as the author of *London and Westminster Improved* (1766), a manifesto of polite urban renewal (National Portrait Gallery, London).

However, Gwynn's was a knowingly impossibilist agenda. He knew the nature of the game and anticipated that 'the old cry of private property and the infringment [*sic*] on liberty will be objected.'[14] Needless to say, his schemes were not implemented. He was, nevertheless, highly influential, sowing the seed for the 'Metropolitan Improvements' of half a century later, and, as Summerson put it, he 'crystallizes a point of view'.[15]

Without attempting to provide a history of late eighteenth-century architectural improvement, mention must also be made of the leading role of one other figure encountered above. George Dance junior was a chief agent of urban improvement as Clerk of the City Works from 1768 (see chapters 4 and 5). Housebuilding schemes aside, he was responsible for Newgate Prison, a highly symbolic edifice that was rebuilt in 1768–75 (only to be gutted in 1780 in the Gordon Riots) to radical and forbidding designs that seem to indicate a hope that architecture itself might help deter crime. Dance later became involved with the protracted discussions for reforming the Port of London that ran through the 1790s. He was also an accomplished portraitist, who knew and drew

Gwynn and Boswell. The protagonists of urban improvement, while perhaps not properly characterised as conspirators, did talk to each other.

After the widespread social unrest of the 1760s and the Gordon Riots, London was remarkably stable, a change perhaps in part directly attributable to the improvements of the 1760s and 1770s. However, the American and then French revolutions provided unsettling examples of where enlightened thinking might lead if too avidly pursued. Improvement became more overtly defensive, with deeper infringement of traditional liberties that earlier initiatives had not seriously confronted. Urban barracks were built in the 1790s amid fears of revolution, and, with the establishment by Patrick Colquhoun of the Marine Police in 1798, Foucaultian 'policing' became policing. This force patrolled the Thames to protect property in the port and aimed to control the population of the eastern suburbs, perceptions of which places Colquhoun was instrumental in transforming (see chapter 1). From 1799 east London's great enclosed docks were dug and fortified in the most extensively radical reconstruction of London's infrastructure since the post-Fire rebuilding of the City. The river was the imperial capital's most crucial and vulnerable artery, and merchants had long been complaining of the loss of large sums through the theft of goods still on the river. The docks were built to bring the port 'economy, security and dispatch',[16] and, long before Haussmann, more than a thousand houses in those areas where Colquhoun had identified criminality were cleared in the process.[17] At the end of the war years the 'Metropolitan Improvements' that centred on the formation of Regent Street served to separate and thereby to protect wealthier West End enclaves from Soho and points east. These were just some of the manifestations of wider cultural shifts, much of the architectural history of which lies in the development of institutional building types such as prisons, schools, hospitals and workhouses.[18] Other ramifications of related changes are described in the case studies, ranging from the institutionalisation of St George's Fields to Samuel Bentham's administrative and mechanising reforms in the naval dockyards (see chapters 4 and 6).

The Building Acts

In terms of the wider world of housebuilding in London, the most important components of the late eighteenth-century campaign of improvement were the Building Acts of 1764, 1772 and 1774. There had been no significant new building act legislation in London since 1724, when London had been widely defined to include outlying parishes (see chapter 2). The Act of 1764 covered the same area and was not so much a step forward as a consolidating measure and a reaction to frequent fires in 'timber' parts of London, 123 houses having been destroyed in two separate fires in Shadwell in 1763.[19] New emphasis was given to the need for all new houses to be built of stone or brick 'both in the forefront, and back front thereof'.[20] Significantly, there was also new provision for the certification of new buildings through affidavits to be issued by surveyors.

The Act of 1772 was petitioned for by a building trades' consortium led by the City companies seeking simplification and tightening up of the legislation. Their leading witness was the City-based George Wyatt (see chapter 5), appearing as 'a Builder'. Wyatt, who deplored 'the Latitude left open' to other builders, was himself a leading 'improver' as the City's Surveyor of Paving and a Common Councillor in the 1770s.[21] The Act permitted the new class of certifying surveyors to enforce existing provisions through the imposition of penalties, relying on common informers. It also introduced new measures relating to ruinous structures which could be construed as presenting a danger to passers-by, extending a provision first made in the Act of 1760 that had given the City of London road widening powers.[22] This permitted parish overseers or churchwardens to notify property owners that such ruinous structures should be taken down, and, if no action was taken, to take them down themselves or put up a protective hoard without prior recourse to the courts, the costs to be passed on to the owners. Retrospectively unexceptionable, at the time this was a draconian imposition of a public duty to keep private property in good repair.[23] It may explain some late eighteenth-century refrontings in such places as Bethnal Green that were clearly not undertaken for reasons of fashion (see chapter 3).

This Act did not last. Within two years a new petition was submitted to Parliament by Robert Taylor and James Adam, joint architects to the Office of Works, 'in behalf of the Builders of London and Westminster'.[24] It can be taken that they were speaking for those with whom they dealt, big operators like Wyatt or Edward Gray, Taylor's 'usual builder' (see chapter 5), people the scale of whose operations necessitated forms of remote control. They would not have been representing the views of the much more numerous but less influential artisan builders who built a few houses at a time here and there. The principal complaint was that penalties were being unjustly and inconsistently imposed, because of the dependence on informers. The London Building Act of 1774, said to have been drafted by George Dance junior with Taylor,

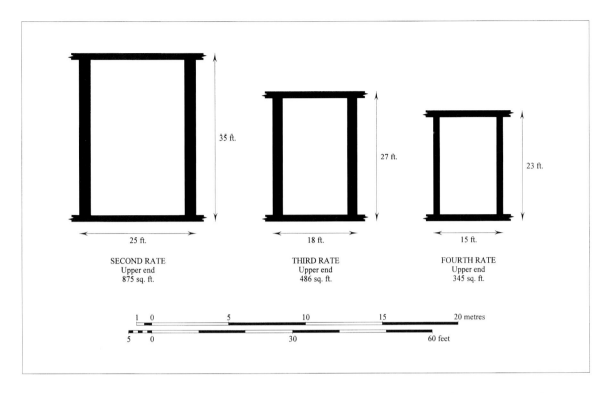

265 Diagram of ground-floor house-plan sizes and wall thicknesses at the upper limits of the three smaller house rates made law in the London Building Act of 1774: first rate = more than 900 square feet on plan (with a 25 ft front, a depth of at least 37 ft), or more than £850 in value; second rate = more than 500 square feet on plan (with a 25 ft front, a depth of no more than 35 ft), or more than £300 in value; third rate = more than 350 square feet on plan (with an 18 ft front, a depth of no more than 27 ft), or more than £150 in value; fourth rate = anything smaller on plan, and of less value.

was comprehensively consolidating. It was a belt and braces attempt to crack once and for all continuing disregard for the Building Acts, particularly in respect of timber construction. It complained that even since 1772 'wooden buildings have been erected on the tops and other parts of houses'.[25] Even without this testimony, enough evidence of the continuation of timber building has been advanced to illustrate what the Act was directed against. The concern was not just to remove the threat of fire from those humbler properties that were still being timber built. Fires that started in 'despicable cottages' might spread. The Act laid much emphasis on the importance of brick party walls as impermeable fire breaks, though this was not new other than in its details.

The greater significance of the Act of 1774 lay in its sounder provisions for enforcement and in its rates. Dependence on informers was escaped by putting enforcement of the Act into the hands of new statutory District Surveyors who were to be appointed by magistrates, charging all builders fees for their services on a scale calibrated in terms of newly defined rates, certifying new buildings and imposing penalties for breach of

the terms of the Act. Since the invention of the 'sorts' of the City Rebuilding Act of 1667 (fig. 27), there had been no attempt at the stratification of house types in London, and so enforced standardisation had made little impact on housebuilding outside the City. The Act of 1774 identified seven 'rates or classes' of building and laid out standards for each, including minimum wall thicknesses that varied in accordance with size. Only the first four rates pertained to houses. The definitions of the rates were based on the size of the ground-floor footprint and value; height was a determinant only in buildings other than houses, a point sometimes overlooked. First-rate houses were the largest; few of the houses mentioned in this book would have been larger than third rate. Smaller two-room-plan houses and virtually all one-room-plan houses would have been fourth rate (figs 265 and 266). Value, which, of course, varied in relation to location, could override categorisation by size, making certainty in the retrospective application of the rates elusive.

Surer enforcement is what made the Act durable (the next major London Building Act was not until 1844), and is the key to the Act's importance. It was given teeth.

Though only gradually arrived at, stepwise through the three Acts, the earnestness of the policing was new. Nearly two centuries of bans on timber building had been only moderately successful, because they had not been rigorously enforced. That the Act of 1774 may thereby have helped to prevent the spread of fires would represent real improvement, and not only in terms of the safeguarding of property. However, the actual reach of enforcement should not be overestimated. The relatively small number of certificates issued through District Surveyors suggests that even after 1774 many new buildings may not, in fact, have been certified.[26] Nevertheless, seriousness about enforcement had wider implications. Where the Act of 1667 had conceived its 'sorts' largely in relation to streetscape, as a matter of amenity, 'rates' were introduced in 1774 in large part because proper enforcement had to be paid for, necessitating a scale for fees, explaining the link between the rates and value. Policing depended on stratification, and thereby led to standardisation.

The Act was standardising in that its provisions 'tended to create optimum types'.[27] Speculators were nudged towards building up to the upper limit of each of the lower rate brackets, to avoid having to use extra bricks in thicker walls and pay extra fees. The second, third and fourth rate upper ends thus became 'standards', but there was no bottom end for the fourth rate, and one-room-plan houses well below the threshold for fourth rate continued to be built (see below). Summerson misleadingly claimed that the Act 'laid down minimum standards for working-class urban housing'.[28] Apart from stipulating brick walls of minimum thicknesses, it did not. It was not a housing Act, having nothing to say about overcrowding or sanitation, nor did it address matters of planning such as the width of streets or the heights of buildings thereon, as the Act of 1667 had. What was imposed in 1774 was orderliness in much the same vein as the Paving Acts, requiring the removal of projections, and that the alignments of streets should be followed. Fire-preventive provision for the placing of timber window frames behind brick reveals affected the appearance of house fronts, and there were perhaps other incidental impacts on domestic architecture. Other fire-preventive stipulations, requiring that divided ground-floor occupancies or horizontally adjoining rooms in different ownership (the inns of court excepted) be separated by brick walls, may have tended to work against design for multiple occupation. The Adam brothers' Robert Street 'chambers' of 1768–74 (see chapter 2) were not imitated, and new, designed tenement housing does seem to be absent from London for the period that the Act of 1774 was in force. Another factor in this area

might have been awareness that extra storeys could have pushed the value of a house that was small on plan into a higher rate, making it better for a builder to use up the whole plan 'allocation' than to build tall, something that might have had an impact on the design of housing in the silk district (see chapter 3).

Like the Paving Acts, the Building Acts thus extended the public sphere into areas that had previously been deemed private, taking the standardising impulse deeply into a housebuilding milieu that had not previously been so structured. More than a hundred years after it had first been introduced to metropolitan house design, rational conformity had not penetrated far. To reach further it had to be encoded and enforced. Custom would not just fall over, it had to be pushed.

Improvement did not otherwise impact directly on housebuilding. Not only did the Building Acts not concern themselves with housing for the poor, nor did much else, workhouses excepted. Late eighteenth-century improvement addressed the street and house construction for the sake of the 'public good', but there was no housing reform. The point of improvement was, as Dorothy George put it, 'removing nuisances of all kinds, including dilapidated hovels and their inhabitants. Civic pride had its share in expensive rebuilding schemes, but hardly humanity.'[29]

Builders and Standardisation

Building control legislation had been around for centuries. There were other important ways in which the world changed for builders. Indeed, specific instances of improvement were reactions to rapid change through growth as much as they were instruments of change. The underlying, continuous and intensifying forces of industrialisation and capitalism brought standardisation by other routes. These can be summarily presented, without in-depth exploration of the complexities of the building process and the links between property owners and builders that are discussed elsewhere.[30] In London capitalist production had taken a hold in speculative housebuilding in the late seventeenth century, as primarily personified by Nicholas Barbon (see chapter 2). However, economies of scale and standardisation remained exceptional away from higher-status developments. Through the eighteenth century London's housebuilding industry had space for, was perhaps even characterised by, artisan engagement and production within a capitalist framework. There was great continuity, but changing practices did spread, and the benefits of standardisation for the producer gradually

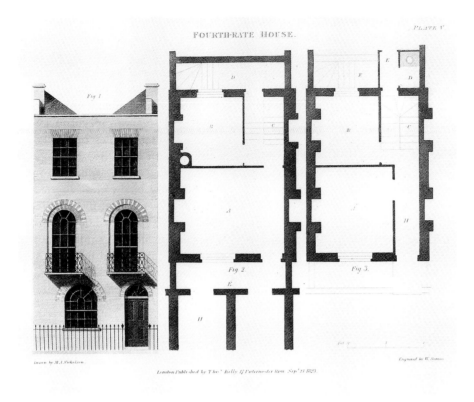

266 A pattern-book fourth-rate house, about 16 ft by 20 ft on plan (from Nicholson, i, 1823). By 1800 such houses were invariably given rear-staircase plans (by permission of the British Library, 558*b.21).

percolated down to smaller operators. At the end of the century the balance altered significantly, industrialisation transforming the building of humble houses in London. The nature of the construction industry did not change fundamentally, but there was a critical shift whereby the forces of capitalist building production unleashed in the late seventeenth century became all but universal.

After the stagnant decades around the middle of the century the building cycle had returned to full swings, rising very sharply in the 1760s and again in the late 1780s, with troughs around 1770 and 1782. During the ups, speculative development may have become more than previously an end in itself as a wealth generator; improvement and its spin-offs perhaps came to be understood as routes to quick riches.[31] Against this background things tightened up in many ways that tended to lead to standardisation. On larger estate developments, late eighteenth-century landowners were generally wiser and more closely in control than their predecessors had been, effectively enforcing the terms of building agreements as contracts. Many good early eighteenth-century streets had been highly variable, even when street fronts were unified (figs 118, 123, 176, 194 and 204), as differ-

ent builders took small parcels or sold on unfinished house carcasses. By the late eighteenth century it was less usual for builders to sell such shells, more likely that they would complete the fitting-out, tending to greater uniformity. There was also industrialisation of supply, as with ready-sawn imported Baltic timber. The complexity of the Act of 1774 and the prospect and costs of its enforcement must have presented problems for artisan builders operating on a small scale. This and the standardisation that the Act anyway encouraged might have led to greater use of price books and pattern books (fig. 266). Even small operations needed increasingly to be paper based. This tended to divorce design from production, further reinforcing standardisation. The role of carpenters as designers diminished, as that of architects or surveyors grew, the spreading use of the pattern books that told carpenters how to perform the basics of their trade both reflecting and causing growing alienation from skill based in apprenticeship. London's more ambitious housebuilders, whether themselves acting as 'architects' or not, would have been able to learn lessons from the organisation of major road- and canal-building projects, as well as from the successes, and failures, of such as the Adam brothers. These builders would have been affected by the kind of reasoning exemplified by the Yorkshire architect John Carr. He consciously standardised his own architectural designs, simplifying components to a core of forms that could be variably repeated in a process that has been interpreted as a reflection of wider industrialisation.[32]

In the London housebuilding world of the end of the eighteenth century, James Burton (1761–1837) was the greatest master of mass production, and 'the most enterprising and successful London builder of his time'.[33] Having arrived in London from Scotland, he started building houses in Southwark in 1785, soon moving across the river to become, *pace* Barbon, 'the first captain of the building industry'.[34] Burton probably generated his own designs, industrialising the production of joinery and ironwork and making his own bricks. He built 922 houses on the Foundling Hospital and Bedford estates between 1792 and 1803, of which 379 (41 per cent) were fourth rate. He was also a magistrate in Kent and a leading member of the Bricklayers' Company, thereby helping to produce the price books that set wage rates.[35]

Despite all the standardising forces, Burton was exceptional. There was no concentration of housebuilding into large undertakings. In 1775 nearly 77 per cent of London builders built five or fewer houses in the year, only 9 per cent erected more than ten. This did not change markedly over the next half century; in 1825 equivalent figures were 74 per cent and 7 per cent. But such statistics say nothing of the nature of production. The implied continuity disguises great change, not just in terms of the standardising conditions already described, but also in the identity of the undertakers, both the builders and their workforces, and, critically, in how they were paid. Towards the end of the eighteenth century, even in small enterprises that did not involve surveyors, speculative housebuilding was increasingly being controlled by 'master builders' (contractors) rather than by single-trade-based artisans working in consort. 'Work-for-work' or barter arrangements had been given up by around 1810. Master builders at any time, place or level were significant capitalists who, in pursuit of profit, would not have felt constrained to respect traditional trade-based artisan hierarchy, that is master, journeyman and apprentice, in the make-up of their workforces. The gradual and protracted breakdown of the apprenticeship system meant that the people engaged to build lower-status houses were more and more likely to be formally unskilled and working as wage labourers rather than as journeymen or apprentices. The grievances of the increasingly 'proletarianised' carpenters' trade came to a head in a London-wide strike of over 4,000 journeyman carpenters in 1787–9.[36]

Different systems of paying for building work, by the day (direct labour or a journeyman's pay from a master), 'measure and value' (by the piece or a master's pay from a builder/contractor), or 'by the great' (a builder/contractor's single contract for a whole job), coexisted in speculative housebuilding in London through the eighteenth century. Larger speculators working 'by the great' through building leases or agreements usually spread their risk with several separate contracts across different trades working on a 'measure and value' basis. At the end of the century 'by the great' contracting evidently spread to the humbler end of the industry, with 'measure and value' payment squeezed out of the picture as workforces were paid directly. This shift from payment by measure or piece to time-based payment is fundamental in the transition from the artisan to the worker, and was paralleled by comparable changes in other industries, not least silk weaving and shipbuilding (see chapters 3 and 6). For artisan masters the 'measure and value' system, whereby the price of their work was determined afterwards, declined in favour of 'tenders' or advance estimation, turning them into contractors. For journeymen day rates, which had come to represent piece rates via price books, were also a measure of artisan production. These fell out of favour as contractors preferred and were prepared to pay slightly more for hourly time-based rates, turning journeymen into wage labourers. This transformation intensified after 1793 when inflation brought about a marked decline in the real wages of those, that is artisans, on piece rates or their equivalents.[37]

These changes in the way in which building work was paid for suppressed variety and favoured standardisation. If a producer was paid for the thing he made, variation was not a great problem from the employer's standpoint, provided the product made was suitable. If, however, he was paid for the time spent making the thing, any departure from a predetermined and efficiently devised standard tended to reduce surplus value and be to the employer's disadvantage. The shift from houses built by artisan masters, journeymen and apprentices, to houses built by contractors, subcontractors and building labourers, cut the scope for production based in precedent or tradition, with attendant vernacular improvisation. Production had rather to be paper based and standardised, with a sometimes relatively unskilled workforce being paid by time to meet a contract. The Building Acts notwithstanding, good building at the level of houses for ordinary people was compromised.

★　★　★

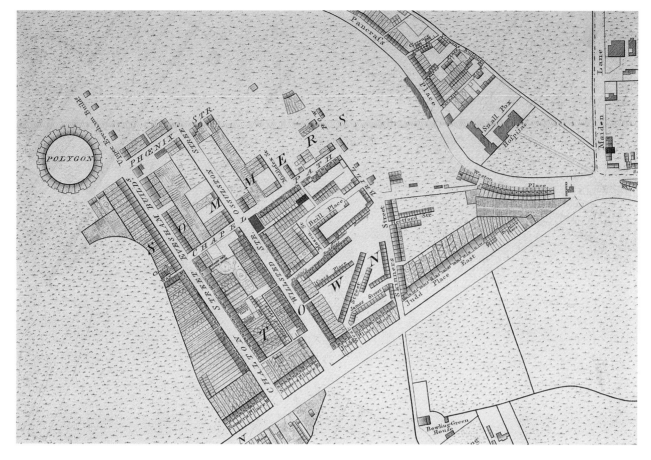

267 Somers Town, as surveyed in 1794, the area east of Willsted and Ossulston Streets and north of what is now Euston Road having become the site of the British Library (from Richard Horwood, *Plan of London*, 1799).

Crisis

Following the outbreak of war with France in February 1793, interest rates rose and many builders were bankrupted. With credit in short supply, both small and large operators struggled, though James Burton did thrive, supported by the estates that were depending on him, and bailing out those working under him. Inflation meant that land costs rocketed, tending to make those builders who were still active put up smaller houses, in denser groupings. With much tighter margins, sites had to be intensively developed if smaller operators were to survive.

In her *Building Capitalism* (1992), Linda Clarke used the development of Somers Town from 1786 onwards to illustrate the demise of artisan production and the emergence of contractor production. A short summary of her extensive case study will help to fill out a view of the changing situation.[38] Situated on the north side of the New Road (Euston Road), Somers Town was initially away from the town on land that had been opened up

to development by the formation of the New Road (figs 7, 9 and 267). Land on the other side of the road to the south was where Burton was active from 1792 and contiguity with London followed soon after 1800. Like nearby Pentonville, Somers Town was begun with the objective of attracting 'middling sort' habitation, but things quickly deteriorated. Lord Somers's principal leaseholder was Jacob Leroux (d. 1799), a brickmaker and a magistrate, and thereby, like David Wilmot in Bethnal Green, in a position to control the building process while himself acting as a developer. An insight into Leroux's methods is gained from Charles Dibdin's *Musical Tour* of 1788, which alleged that Leroux, 'architect, brickmaker, and trading-justice [. . .] with a dastardly speciousness for which a Hyena might envy him, promised me a license in the name of several magistrates *who opposed the motion*, and [. . .] erected the skeleton of a building which was blown down by the first high wind after the licence was refused.'[39]

By fair means or foul, a regular grid of streets was laid out, incorporating many fourth-rate but mid-size

268 The Polygon, Somers Town, Jacob Leroux, architect and developer. Begun in 1792, the Polygon was, in effect, a circle of sixteen outward facing 'semi-detached' pairs of 18 ft-front houses, linked by entrance bays and all enclosed within a square. In 1797 Mary Wollstonecraft lived and died at No. 29 The Polygon. Drawn by 'Swains', 1850. Demolished in the 1870s.

houses, most of the lesser ones being of three storeys with fronts of 15 ft. In the late 1780s Leroux entered into building agreements with both traditional artisan builders and high-volume 'contract builders'; these men ranged from William Latham, a bricklayer, who built three houses in 1786 (one for himself), to George Davidson, a 'labourer' or unarticled (non-apprenticed) carpenter, who in 1787 undertook to build twenty houses within six months. Somers Town was enlivened from 1792 by its intended high point, a Polygon (figs 267 and 268), the building of which was begun by Job Hoare, a carpenter, who ambitiously undertook to build the thirty-two large houses within eighteen months, but failed to complete, falling bankrupt in 1794. Davidson too had been bankrupted, and, external influences aside, it had become clear that humbler housing was needed, if only to house the local building workforce. Willsted Court, a uniform row of sixteen two-room houses, each no more than 12 ft square, had been inserted in what had been laid out as gardens between the two main roads that ran off the New Road. In the later 1790s Somers Town hit the rocks. As was the case all over London buildings were left unfinished, half the houses certified

in 1797 had to be rebuilt, and 'many carcasses of houses were sold for less than the value of the materials.'[40]

Gathered together as witnesses to the sharp transformations wrought by this wartime crisis of speculative housebuilding, Somers Town's population was notably mixed. Alongside many labourers and traders, there was an influx of French refugees, and there were, as well, some of those at whom the development had first been aimed, professionals, spiced by a group of writers, artists and radicals. Anti-urban Mary Wollstonecraft lived with comparably iconoclastic William Godwin at No. 29 The Polygon after their marriage in 1797. There their daughter, later to achieve fame as Mary Shelley, was born, as her mother died.[41]

All round London building activity resumed in 1802. In Somers Town quick profits were possible: 'any person who could obtain the means became builders – carpenters, retired publicans, persons working in leather, haymakers, or even keepers of private houses for the reception of lunatics, each contrived to raise his house or houses and every street was lengthened in its turn.'[42] This commodification of housing led to short-view, short-life and largely unrestricted development. New contracts were for the building of a dozen or more houses at a time, not two or three, even though many of the contracts were to small operators. Small-scale building by artisan builders had disappeared, and development was poor in quality and high in density, with further courts being inserted between the larger houses, as at Chapel Grove, immediately north of Willsted Court (fig. 263). It was easy for anybody moving into house-building to make money building poor houses, as the Hedgers had earlier shown south of the Thames on St George's Fields (see chapter 4).

Intensification of speculative development and the collapse of artisan independence were two sides of the same process. Throughout London people from widely varying backgrounds engaged in housebuilding, the costs of which had marginalised many traditional practitioners. Trade-based artisans were more quickly squeezed out of entrepreneurial opportunities than in less highly capitalised industries. What had begun with Barbon had reached down to the lowest levels, where 'speculative housebuilders introduced a more dynamic mode of organisation, analogous to factory production, and jeopardised an element of stability derived from craft producers, replacing it with aggressive competition, unsold houses, risk and uncertainty.'[43]

The demise of artisan production in housebuilding around 1800 is a significant marker in the process of class transformation that everywhere eventually pushed artisans into the middle or working classes.[44]

After 1800

This study has 1800 as its end date, and it should now be evident that there are good reasons for this, quite apart from the neatness of round numbers. However, any cut-off is more or less arbitrary, and it would be precipitate to drop the narrative without a bridge into the nineteenth century. The decades since the 1720s had been a relatively quiescent period in London's expansion. After 1800 there was a return to rapid growth, more than ever, with population increases of more than 100,000 each

269   London housebuilding by volume from the 1790s to 1819 (based on evidence derived from Richard Horwood's maps, adapted from Laxton, 1999).

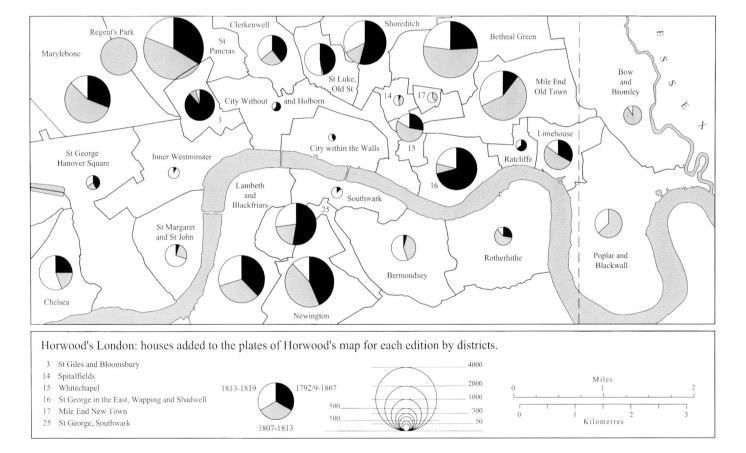

Horwood's London: houses added to the plates of Horwood's map for each edition by districts.

3   St Giles and Bloomsbury
14   Spitalfields
15   Whitechapel
16   St George in the East, Wapping and Shadwell
17   Mile End New Town
25   St George, Southwark

1813-1819   1792/9-1807

1807-1813

decade in the early nineteenth century bringing great pressures. Despite the continuation of war up to 1815, housebuilding boomed. Estimates based on Richard Horwood's maps and census data suggest that in the period 1799 to 1819 around 30,000 houses were built in London, of which about two-thirds were in parishes to the south and east, where the new enclosed docks were both displacing old houses and attracting new labour (fig. 269). The character of areas considered in earlier chapters, Bethnal Green, Mile End Old Town and Bermondsey, was also changing quickly, yet comparatively stealthily in so much as most of the extensive speculative development was not coherently planned by large estates. Nevertheless, what was produced did have coherence through relative uniformity. Even where there were small developments, residential mix had fled. Gwynn's notion that the houses of the labouring classes might be contained and 'managed' by wealthier neighbours proved naïvely optimistic. Instead social segregation increased, improved transport making it easier for the better off to retreat from poor districts. The anarchic tendencies of free-wheeling capitalism were mitigated through the emergence of an hierarchical understanding of the metropolis as a whole (see chapter 2). The parts of London where vernacular traditions had endured through the eighteenth century were being transformed through the building of innumerable 'modest grey bare streets' (fig. 93).[45]

Such developers as the Bethnal Green tallow chandler Saunderson Turner Sturtevant (see chapter 3) provided 'instant slums' (fig. 69), in many cases for those displaced by improvements, whether dock building, road widening or otherwise. The clearance of cheap timber housing and its replacement in brick raised rents, reducing the affordability of space, and, living standards having declined in the late eighteenth century, people were forced into smaller dwellings. Despite huge population growth, in some places early nineteenth-century building outstripped demand, as contract builders needed to keep their capital at work and their workforces active. Intensive site development of a kind that had not been typical in the eighteenth century continued, as the financial pressures on smaller speculative builders did not lift. By 1815 this kind of building could be characterised:

> the principle of speculation is to take large tracts of ground by the acre, and crowd as many streets and lanes into it as they can, in order to create so many feet lineal (of frontage) to underlet for building; and the fruit of speculation is the sale of the increased ground rents. The houses therefore are of the meanest sort, are built of the worst and slightest materials and,

but for their dependence on each other for support, would, many of them, not stand the term of their leases.[46]

The resulting developments were what middle-class improvers came to label slums, the first recorded use of which word dates from 1812. Little survives, much being cleared even before the end of the nineteenth century, but particulars of London's early nineteenth-century slums have been widely if diffusely chronicled. As Bethnal Green grew eastwards beyond the silk district to merge with the growth of Mile End Old Town in the years around 1810, rows of 10ft-square two-room houses were built on interstitial back streets. But this was by no means just an east London phenomenon. Rows and rows of comparably puny houses, sometimes in back-to-back groups, went up in the first quarter of the nineteenth century all across London, from Knightsbridge, to Bloomsbury, to Poplar (figs 263 and 270).[47] Such small houses, invariably densely built, were widespread in areas built up after 1800, far more so than they had been in areas developed before 1800. Poor housing, slighter than anything documented here, was indubitably built in the eighteenth century, but far less widely or systematically. Where there is documentation of eighteenth-century courts, the houses are less mean. Problems stemmed not so much from the nature of the earlier houses, as from overcrowding and decay. Changes in the building industry aside, the greater rate of population growth after 1800 is obviously another important part of any explanation for dense development.

There was also infilling in the older parts of the town. Just east of Clerkenwell Green off Aylesbury Street was Aylesbury Place, a court of twenty-nine houses of around 1820 squeezed into an already densely built area, each only two rooms in 12ft squares (fig. 271). Almost a century earlier, in 1726–8, Bishop's Court had been built just to the east, ten three-storey six-room houses, each about 15ft by 23ft, more living space thus taking up less land (fig. 272).[48] Housing density can not be judged from maps alone. Even if the earlier buildings were designed for multiple occupation, with each storey intended as a home, such a two-room tenement would have offered appreciably more space (about 350 square feet) than there was in the whole of the later two-storey two-room houses (about 290 square feet). Where there was dense development in the eighteenth century, people tended to be stacked up rather than packed in. Though less spacious, the lower and later buildings would have provided greater privacy. A preference for privacy over intimacy as regards neighbours would have been a value judgement that most individuals would not have been free to

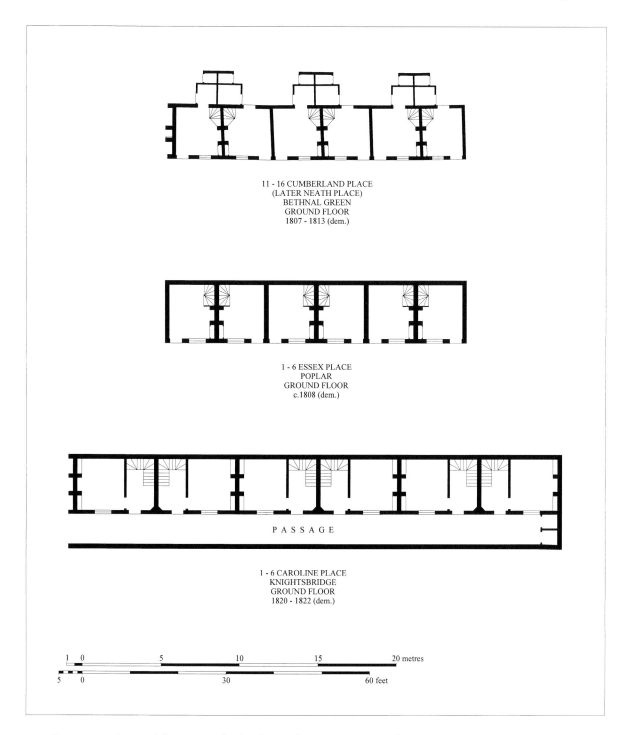

11 - 16 CUMBERLAND PLACE
(LATER NEATH PLACE)
BETHNAL GREEN
GROUND FLOOR
1807 - 1813 (dem.)

1 - 6 ESSEX PLACE
POPLAR
GROUND FLOOR
c.1808 (dem.)

PASSAGE

1 - 6 CAROLINE PLACE
KNIGHTSBRIDGE
GROUND FLOOR
1820 - 1822 (dem.)

| 1 | 0 | | 5 | 10 | 15 | | 20 metres |
| 5 | 0 | | | 30 | | 60 feet | |

270   Reconstructed ground-floor plans of early nineteenth-century two-room houses.

make for themselves. The unasked-for trade-off appears to have been privacy and separation over living space. Of course, without information about occupancy, the like of which is rarely traceable for the earlier period, it is not possible to be sure that one is comparing like with like. The contrast is fair, however, as representing typical court developments from both periods, both of which came to be condemned by the end of the nineteenth century.

It would be misleading to suggest that all early nineteenth-century 'fourth-rate' speculative housing was so poor. While one-room-plan houses had lost respectabil-

271 and 272 (*facing page*)   Aylesbury Place, Clerkenwell, *c.*1820, and Bishop's Court, Clerkenwell, 1726–8. These adjoining court developments of a century apart are typical of their periods, the two-storey early nineteenth-century houses providing about 290 square feet of living space in two rooms, while each storey of the three-storey, early eighteenth-century houses comprised about 350 square feet of living space, also in two rooms. Photographed 1906. Demolished *c.*1910 (LMA).

ity, the two-room rear-staircase plan spread through eastern and southern suburbs in fourth-rate developments that were eminently decent. These aimed at those striving for 'vernacular gentility', as on the Mercers' Company Estate in Stepney, in places such as York Square (fig. 273), where politeness and amenity went hand in hand in rows developed by the Barnes family, whose building activities had begun on the Mile End Road in the 1780s (see chapter 5). Peter Nicholson (1765–1844), a cabinetmaker who had turned to publishing handbooks for carpenters and joiners in the 1790s before practising as an architect, and who had updated Moxon's

Mechanical Exercises in 1811, published his own *New Practical Builder and Workman's Companion* in 1823 with what have become the classic illustrations of 'standard' designs for houses to fit the rates set by the Act of 1774 (fig. 266). Clearly fourth-rate houses were not necessarily all that small. Writing in the 1830s, J. C. Loudon described such fourth-rate houses as that drawn by Nicholson, that is with eight rooms in three storeys and cellars, as 'mostly occupied by the families of respectable artisans'; smaller houses, he explained, were 'built principally for the occupation of mechanics, in suburbs of London, in inferior situations'.[49] In eastern and southern suburbs

fourth-rate housing, both good and bad, quickly came to be subdivided, as with the two-storey weavers' 'cottages' in the silk district (see chapter 3). By the 1850s rows of two-storey model dwellings in Mile End New Town were being designed as cottage flats, with double entrances, and taller purpose-built tenements returned to favour in the late nineteenth-century East End.[50]

The rear-staircase plan came down the social ladder to achieve virtual ubiquity in nineteenth-century London. Other traditional options better suited to narrow frontages had died out.[51] Deeply rooted and pervasive tendencies to standardisation apart, there are no clear reasons for this. As John Papworth put it in 1857, 'Why our dwelling houses in London are built after one plan, viz., an entrance passage, a front room, a smaller back room, and a staircase by its side, is a mystery to many besides myself.'[52] It was not legislative or functional imperative, and seems only readily comprehensible as a symptom of much deeper cultural shifts, part emulation perhaps, but also part enervation, through market forces.

Standardisation begot monotony, and the prettiness achieved at York Square is also misleading. The huge early nineteenth-century expansion of east London was unplanned and uncoordinated, yet:

> monotony is the observer's first impression: rows upon rows of houses, all of one size and all of one colour: the grimy dun of London stocks. The little houses squat in their lines, without basement or area; the transition from street to home is made without any ceremony beyond a doorstep. Nearly all are of two storeys, and nearly all observe the basic Georgian propriety: that a parapet should make it impossible, from the front, to see what form of roof construction has been used. This conventional parapet intensifies the feeling of monotony, for in every street, the flat roofline parallels and echoes the lines of roadway and pavement.[53]

Standardisation and monotony do not themselves make for bad housing. It is important to differentiate between architecture and housing provision. Francis Place (1771–1854), artisan tailor and radical reformer, thought the London of the 1820s much improved over that of his childhood, with many 'miscreant neighbourhoods' where there had been tall four-storey tenements destroyed, and east London made brick rather than timber, with wider streets and 'superior' children. Describing Walworth in 1832, he wrote: 'Many of these streets are inhabited by very poor people – but neither the streets nor the houses are by any means so dirty as were the narrow streets and lanes which have been

destroyed to make way for modern improvements – nor do they stink as such places used to do.'[54] In 1828 Edwin Chadwick also thought London's artisans better off than they had been in the eighteenth century: 'their houses are better constructed, they have acquired some notions that fresh air is conducive to health, and the streets where they reside are less filthy and pestilential than formerly.'[55] Until about 1830 the new buildings seemed to be thought better than the old ones, but comparisons were between what was then new with what had become old. Set against the rookeries of mid-eighteenth-century St Giles, the new suburb of Walworth was a clear advance. In that regard there was undoubtedly improvement in the housing that was available. But, save for brick replacing timber, there is not clear testimony that the new buildings were in themselves either more commodious or otherwise inherently superior to their predecessors. A decade later Chadwick's great report of 1842 on the sanitary condition of Britain's labouring population noted that many of the newer dwellings were poorly built and without basic amenities. His fellow campaigner for improved housing, Hector Gavin, found in his *Sanitary Ramblings* of 1848 that the eighteenth-century tenements of London's silk district were not as bad as its early nineteenth-century courts (see chapter 3). The writings of these and other reformers, from Charles Dickens to Henry Mayhew, to George Godwin in *The Builder*, do not reinforce an impression that a golden age of housing improvement had just passed. Many of the early nineteenth-century buildings had exhausted their short lives by 1850.

Conclusions

Comparisons of this nature across periods need extensive quantitative study that is beyond the scope of this book. Questions as fundamental as whether housing did or did not improve will remain endlessly debatable. But that artisan housing in London changed in the years around 1800 does seem clear. Where there had been variety, there was uniformity. Politeness and respectability had spread and perhaps, as Place seemed confident, there had been 'moral' improvements. At the same time

273 (*facing page*) York Square, Stepney. These polite and highly standardised fourth-rate houses, built on the Mercer's Company Estate in 1823–5, were laid out with rear-staircase plans in 16 ft frontages and the external amenities of an open square and the Queen's Head Public House on the corner (EH, GLC Drawings Collection 96/7430).

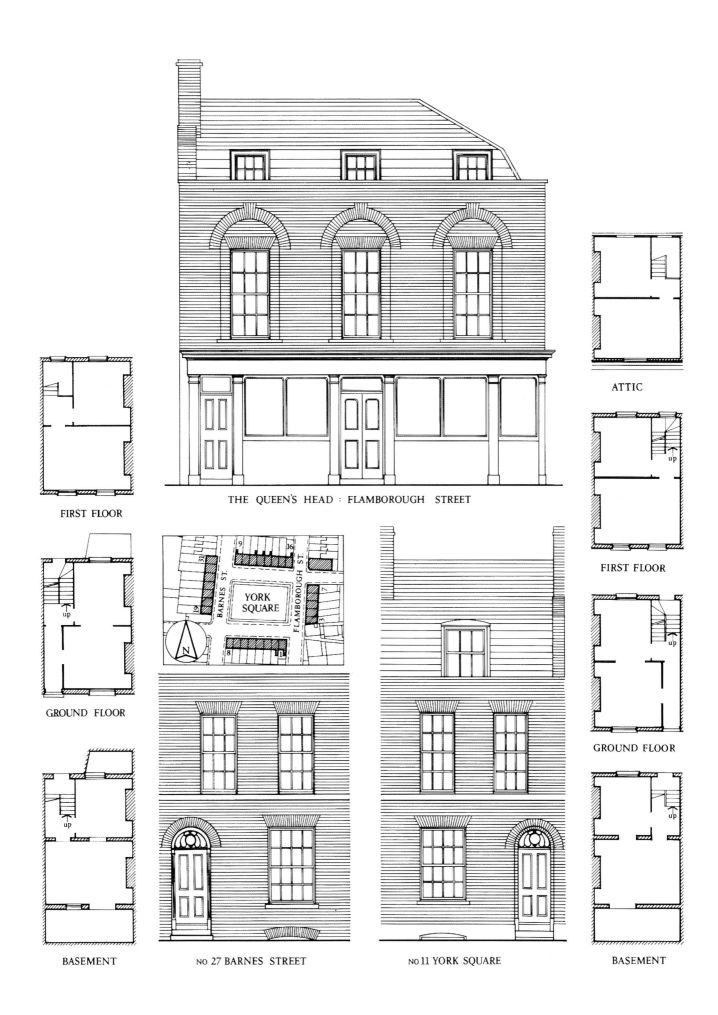

FIRST FLOOR

GROUND FLOOR

BASEMENT

THE QUEEN'S HEAD : FLAMBOROUGH STREET

YORK SQUARE

NO 27 BARNES STREET

NO 11 YORK SQUARE

ATTIC

FIRST FLOOR

GROUND FLOOR

BASEMENT

there was a decline in the quality of housebuilding and the engagement of ordinary artisans in determining the nature of their own houses had decreased, part of a much broader cultural decline, the negation of agency and identity among a large part of London's population.

In the late eighteenth century commodification and consumption were homogenising and levelling forces, more seductive than repressive, status increasingly being defined through the market. If a person is able to buy something, that person can be considered equal to anyone else who can buy that thing. However, against this grain many insecure artisans did continue to define themselves through production rather than consumption, and to look back rather than forward (see chapter 1). Discontinuities should not be overemphasised. The case studies in preceding chapters reveal great ambivalence. Changes in the silk district, on St George's Fields, on Kingsland Road and in Deptford were partial, compromising and negotiated. Improvement and industrialisation did not simply carry the day, and the urban vernacular did not just roll over and die in the face of the emulative juggernaut of the polite. Its eradication had to be policed through legislation and squeezed through a financial crisis.

Chapter 10

A LIVING TRADITION?
CONCLUDING REMARKS

by their diversity of frontings [London buildings] do declare a freedome of our
subjects, that what they acquire by industry may be bestowed at pleasure; not obliged
to build so for the will of princes: whereas the citizens of Paris are so forced to
uniformity.

Anonymous author of *Gallus Castratus*[1]

This proud assertion of a link between London's architectural diversity and political freedom comes from 1659, at the *Paradise Lost* end of the Interregnum. A hundred years later an enlightened consensus was emerging that urban growth should be 'conformable', even if this meant suppressing some freedoms.[2] However, seventeenth-century concepts of liberty were deeply embedded in English society, and they had not everywhere been rendered utilitarian. Architecture that was neither 'conformable' nor even legal remained a living presence throughout the eighteenth century in London, maintaining expression through a continuing 'diversity of frontings'.

The houses discussed in this book provide evidence that in places London's eighteenth-century domestic architecture was resistant to fashion, less polite than vernacular, in varying degrees laggardly, negotiated, hybrid or indifferent. This was not a political statement, but nor was it solely attributable to economic imperatives. It can be evaluated as a reflection of identity, essentially though not simply that of class or status, and linked to the perceptions of a 'paradise lost' that characterised the world view of many, particularly artisans, in eighteenth-century London. Defensive preoccupation with identity was very much tied up with retrospective or nostalgic notions of freedoms lost, yearnings for the imagined simplicities of an earlier time. It tended therefore to be expressed through cultural conservatism, which coexisted happily alongside political radicalism. At the beginning of the nineteenth century, as at the beginning of the twenty-first, technological change was driving people into a

maw of consumptive and emulative standardisation, against which peristalsis there was little articulate counter-movement other than oppositional denial.

But London's eighteenth-century domestic architecture does not speak of clear ideologies or epistemologies. Links between architecture and identity must be made cautiously, and not over-valued. There are always those, crucial to social change, who ignore the shackles of prescriptive and proscriptive identity, and there are also always those who remain blithely unaware that they are shackled. In eighteenth-century London any moderately ambitious speculative builder accepted and exploited fashion, if only to avoid bankruptcy. Vernacular architecture survived as an option for the least ambitious among those who built houses, artisans building for themselves or their peers, not the poor who did not build. In such hands the absence of fashion may sometimes have been conscious avoidance; otherwise it may merely be the absence of fashion, though even then it is not without meaning.

With these caveats it can, nevertheless, be concluded that there are clear reasons why the architectural expression of artisan identity that can be traced right through the eighteenth century disappeared in early nineteenth-century London. This was the period during which London artisans were themselves either managing to retain their 'precarious gentility', through upward mobility into the middle class, or, more often, to lose it through downward mobility into the working class. The loss of agency was manifest in relation to housebuilding by the mid-nineteenth century, when the term 'artisan housing' came to denote something imposed from above: middle-class beneficence in the shape of model dwellings and legislative reform. In the meantime much of the eighteenth-century city had been replaced and forgotten. Thousands of small seventeenth- and eighteenth-century houses were cleared in early nineteenth-century improvements, from dock building in the East End, to road building in the West End, with mixed commercial, institutional and road works in Southwark. There followed in the 1830s and 1840s the exposure by social reformers of insalubrious 'slums', further metropolitan improvements and, not least, redevelopment for the railways. For Chadwick, Gavin, Dickens and Mayhew, much of the eighteenth-century vernacular metropolis had already gone, and many of the problems they addressed arose directly from the nature and density of early nineteenth-century housing. Where there were old houses they rarely saw beyond decay.[3]

As the variety of vernacular housing disappeared from London, so it came to be missed. There were aesthetic reactions against the uniformity that improvement had brought. What came to be labelled the 'Black Act' of 1774 'contributed largely to what the later Georgians and early Victorians conceived to be the inexpressible monotony of the typical London street.'[4] Writing in 1847, Disraeli blamed the Act for 'all those flat, dull spiritless streets, all resembling each other, like a large family of plain children'.[5]

By the 1840s anti-classical and neo-vernacular outlooks had long since emerged. While smaller houses had become more uniform, bigger houses had become less so, through the Picturesque taste, early aspects of which are here characterised as a 'genteel vernacular', strongly metropolitan and proto-suburban. The reaction against uniformity that led to consciously Picturesque suburban variety in London has elsewhere been traced from plans of 1794 for semi-detached houses masquerading as villas on the Eyre Estate, St John's Wood, through to Nash's villa suburbs at Park Villages East and West in the 1820s. Nash's first Park Village designs of 1823 sought to maximise variety, introducing consciously rustic neo-vernacular elements in small 'village' houses, though the market dictated that the houses built were rather larger, and rather less vernacular.[6] By the mid-nineteenth century the amorphous and architecturally undisciplined Old English taste had emerged from these Picturesque beginnings. Thereafter the more urbane neo-vernacular Domestic Revival or Queen Anne style was hugely popular in the 1870s, as in Chelsea and in the new London suburb of Bedford Park. The sources for these revivals were not, of course, the kind of buildings discussed in this book, but the Queen Anne aesthetic was

sympathetic to the appearance and materials of London before the 'Black Act', emphasising the virtues of variety and irregularity. The informal use of classicism in London's speculative brick houses of the seventeenth century and the early eighteenth was understood in the late nineteenth as being vernacular in a way that has needed recently to be reaffirmed. But all this was seemingly little more than *de haut en bas* playfulness. It has been generally understood that the nineteenth century killed off vernacular architecture 'and put a romantic image in its place'.[7]

The architecture and the image are perhaps not so cleanly separable. The romantic image can itself be projected back to suggest that nineteenth-century vernacular revivals may have had some roots in the wreckage of London's eighteenth-century independent artisan culture wherein vernacular architecture had survived. Vernacular and artisan outlooks found continuous if mutated expression, in opposition not only to classicism, but also to capitalism and industrialisation. Vernacular revivals might therefore be understood, to some degree, as representing survival rather than revival, if not of specific architectural forms, then of underlying attitudes to domestic architecture. Conventional awareness of the growing separation of design and production, of mind and hand, in the century from 1750 to 1850 is of a straightforward decline, associated with the industrial revolution, the rise of the architectural profession and general contracting, but this terrain is full of myth and easily over-simplified. There were many complicating factors. Architects were not necessarily divorced from production; some influential late eighteenth-century improvers, such as John Gwynn, and neo-classicists, such as William Chambers, did not regard the 'mechanical' as base, but as part of an ideally unified building process. On the other side of the coin *The Artizan: A Monthly Journal of the Operative Arts*, first published in 1843, drew on artisan radicalism going back to the 1790s; artisan identity in relation to 'art' production had not been wholly suppressed.[8]

Looming large here are the great and hugely influential architectural writers of the nineteenth century who linked architecture, artisans and morality, making connections that had not been made in the eighteenth century. From his *Contrasts* of 1836 onwards Augustus Welby Northmore Pugin, the son of a French refugee and draughtsman who had worked extensively beside Nash, is hard to dissociate from the pictorial and polemical power of his Gothic-fuelled Catholicism and medievalism. However, Pugin's reactionary nostalgia does seem prefigured in the proud attitudes of determinedly Protestant and post-medieval artisans. Like any good Luddite, Pugin was concerned with the preservation of skill. He saw clearly the consequences of, and criticised the spread of, general contracting in building, and he was certainly not the first, though he was perhaps the most vociferous, to put honesty of construction before appearance. His mythologisation of 'medieval' craftsmen resembles the 'golden age' nostalgia of eighteenth-century artisans and, more specifically, the Gothic tastes of such as William Blake.[9]

John Ruskin took similar views, but from a higher vantage point, more as a revelation than as an inheritance. Developing his thought from a nature-loving Romantic base to a piercing deprecation of capitalist and industrial society, mediated by contact with Thomas Carlyle, Cromwell's first sympathetic biographer, Ruskin respected the independent building artisan as a source of good design, advising architects to work in masons' yards. For Ruskin in the 1850s Gothic architecture was moral, true and democratic because it involved 'the liberty of the workman'.[10] From the late 1850s onwards William Morris was an even more overt champion of the 'craftsman', a retrospectively romantic redesignation of the artisan. Morris's heroes were medieval: 'the village carpenter, smith, mason, what not – "a common fellow," whose common everyday labour fashioned works that are to-day the wonder and despair of many a hard-working "cultivated" architect.'[11] Despite embracing Marx, his concern for art over-rode his interest in the more recent successors of these 'craftsmen'. Though utopian, Morris was motivated by an awareness that vernacular architecture could bring and had brought good building into the lives of ordinary people. His associate and fellow socialist Philip Webb believed architectural design need not be Gothic or any other 'style', but simply 'good building'. As an architect, Webb insisted on full control, as a good artisan master would, so that design could emerge from construction and materials, as part of, not a determinant of production. Morris and Webb did not need to look back five hundred years. It had not been so long ago that a measure of 'good building' had moved out of the reach of ordinary people.

This is not intended to suggest that the surviving humbler houses of eighteenth-century London inspired the great minds that led to and championed the Arts and Crafts movement. Indeed, these theorists would have seen such buildings as symptomatic of decline. Many of the houses of the kind that they might have seen – and there were more standing then than now – would already have been refronted and otherwise altered so as to have lost any visual charm. The point, rather, is that an eighteenth-century vernacular and anti-classical outlook characterised by primitivist conservatism and

commitment to the integration of design and production, which had endured among London artisans and been manifest in the houses that are the subject of this book, had found new expression through these writers. The link is cultural, not intellectual, one of outlook rather than one of ideology. These nineteenth-century writers may have seen the origins of their thinking in literary Romanticism more than in artisan culture, but Blake exemplified how in London these could be allied.

An exception to the disclaimer regarding direct influence from the eighteenth-century vernacular metropolis can be made for the architect, designer and writer Charles Robert Ashbee. As a young man, he gave himself to east London, living there from 1886, studying Ruskin with working men. In 1888 Ashbee established the Guild of Handicraft, which combined anti-industrial nostalgia with a philanthropic and socialist mission. The guild moved to Mile End in 1891. From this base in 1894 Ashbee established the Committee for the Survey of the Memorials of Greater London, out of which grew the Survey of London. The subject of its first publication was

274   Nos 72 and 73 Cheyne Walk, Chelsea, Arts and Crafts movement artists' studio houses of 1896–7, C. R. Ashbee, architect. These 'workshop' houses reflect Ashbee's intimate knowledge of London's urban vernacular, particularly in the East End. Photographed 1903. Destroyed 1941 (EH, BB65/1682).

275   Dombey House, Dickens Estate, Wolseley Street, Jacob's Island, Bermondsey. This typical London County Council housing of the interwar period shows the picturesque redeployment of a simple eighteenth-century vernacular architectural vocabulary, usage common in areas where its sources had been most widespread. Photographed 2002 (EH, AA033073).

the Trinity Hospital almshouses on the Mile End Road (fig. 31), saved from demolition as 'An Object Lesson in National History'. In his own architectural design Ashbee sought to sustain and reflect local character through his antiquarian knowledge of 'Old London'. Nos 72 and 73 Cheyne Walk, Chelsea, were tall free-style brick artists' studio houses of 1896–7 (fig. 274). With upper-storey 'workshops', principally lit from the back, architectural form here seems to echo that of the silk district's eighteenth-century weavers' tenements, as well as a real or imagined 'genteel vernacular' Chelsea. In the highly varied group of houses of which this pair formed a part, Ashbee 'seemed to be flaunting town house proprieties deliberately, to be slumming. [. . .] It was almost as if he wanted to hide the hand of a single architect behind the appearance of some anonymous building process.'[12]

From 1893 onwards other architects steeped in Ruskin and Morris worked in the Housing of the Working Classes Branch of the London County Council, and there explored Arts and Crafts approaches

276   Houses of 2000 in Schoolbank Road, Greenwich Millennium Village, 'masterplan' architect Ralph Erskine, twenty-first-century London's neo-vernacular small rowhouses. Photographed 2002 (EH, AA032626).

277 (*above*) and 278 (*right*)   Deptford High Street and Brick Lane in 2003, both with markets, parts of the continuing vernacular metropolis (EH, AA033468 and AA033438).

to urban working-class housing, consciously using archi-tecture as a tool for social reform. From the large build-ings of the Boundary Street estate in Bethnal Green to numerous suburban cottage estates, they reacted against the uniformity of nineteenth-century working-class housing, attempting through artful means to reintroduce informal variety, to suggest accident and natural growth, in the hope that this would allow or inculcate a sense of separate identity and individuality.[13] The radicalism and inventiveness of the early initiatives settled into greater predictability and a new kind of standardisation in the LCC's neo-Georgian housing estates of the 1920s and 1930s. From Spitalfields to Bermondsey and Deptford, and much more widely, early twentieth-century slum clearance programmes were replacing nineteenth-century housing and remnants of earlier buildings by harking back to picturesque aspects of the eighteenth century (fig. 275).

Nikolaus Pevsner made it a commonplace that Modernism, with its social commitment, its collectivism and its moralistic emphases on truth to materials and form following function, had roots in Arts and Crafts traditions.[14] However, the ideals of good building and vernacular individualism were often lost in twentieth-century approaches to housing, and more evident in architecture that resisted the dominance of Modernist doctrine. Elements of vernacular traditions have remained capable of serving opposing architectural styles and ideologies. Indeed, as has been said, 'eclecticism is the vernacular of sophisticated societies'.[15] Late twentieth-century shifts included the rise of architectural conservation, in a radical rejection of improvement through bad building. Disregard for perceptions of identity and agency rooted in the familiar built environment, whether understood as historic or not, had consequences that gave architectural conservation mass support. Changes in the balance of public and private in house-building and home ownership permitted broad-based vernacular individualism, if not good building, to be reasserted, and class identity was as fluid as it had been in the years around 1800.

Urban-vernacular architecture can now be identified in disparate locations. It is detectable in major planned improvements, as in the rows of small dwellings in the social housing of the Greenwich Millennium Village, with steep roofs, asymmetrical fronts, adaptable interiors and, remarkably, central 'chimneystacks' (fig. 276). Through adaptive re-use it also remains present, in fragile and heterogeneous form, on Brick Lane, Kingsland Road and Deptford High Street, richly faceted and increasingly rare shopping 'high streets' with thriving markets, in architectural environments that have roots in the eighteenth century, with later elements randomly intermixed (figs 277 and 278). These places have been havens of urban vitality, where long-term poverty and the absence of planned improvement have left the 'conformable' notably absent. Heavily, casually and continuously rebuilt, altered and converted, they have been, and have depended on being, in healthy states of flux – contingent and vivacious, with immense and genuine cultural diversity.

To bring the vernacular into play as an irrepressible and continuous historical force, autochthonous tradition endlessly resurfacing, is not to regret the sometimes genuine improvements that have diminished its sway, nor to forget that preoccupation with the loss of vernacular identity characterised twentieth-century Fascism. Awareness of the vernacular as an omnipresent force that resists homogenisation should inform any understanding of the historic environment. The enduring qualities that characterise places where remnants of London's eighteenth-century vernacular survive have troubled influential aesthetes and improvers from Deptford's own John Evelyn onwards. They are diametrically opposed to many qualities that have often been marshalled to buttress historic value. They are not, however, at odds with a re-radicalised approach to conservation that engages with heritage as everyday social environments rather than simply as art or artefacts. As the anonymous essayist responsible for *Gallus Castratus* witnessed, 'diversity of frontings' was for some a positive factor at the heart of London's character in Evelyn's time. The vernacular and the polite have always coexisted in London, where improvers have rarely been all that rigorous or systematic. Fragmentary though the evidence is, it is still possible to find an empirical base for a study of the eighteenth-century vernacular metropolis. The legacy of these fragments is substantial, and salutary.

Abbreviations

BL   British Library, London

BM   British Museum, London

CKS   Centre for Kentish Studies, Maidstone, Kent

CLRO   Corporation of London Records Office, London

CLSA   Camden Local Studies and Archives, London

DNB   *Dictionary of National Biography: Compact edition, complete text* (Oxford, 1975)

EH   English Heritage

GL   Guildhall Library, Corporation of London

GLC   Greater London Council

GLHL   Greenwich Local History Library, London

HAD   London Borough of Hackney Archives Department

H-H   Hand-in-Hand Insurance policy registers (at GL)

HLSI   Highgate Literary and Scientific Institution, London

LT   Land Tax assessments (in various collections)

LCC   London County Council

LLSA   Lewisham Local Studies and Archives, London

LPL   Lambeth Palace Library, London

LMA   London Metropolitan Archives

MDR   Middlesex Deeds Registry (held at LMA)

MiD   Museum in Docklands Library and Archive, London

NA   The National Archives, Kew

NMM   National Maritime Museum, Greenwich, London

NMR   National Monuments Record, Swindon

OS   Ordnance Survey maps

RB   Ratebooks (in various collections)

RCAHMS   Royal Commission on the Ancient and Historical Monuments of Scotland

RCHM(E)   Royal Commission on the Historical Monuments of England

SBH   St Bartholomew's Hospital Archives, London

SLSL   Southwark Local Studies Library, London

SoL   Survey of London publications, 1896–

THLHL   Tower Hamlets Local History Library and Archives, London

VCH   Victoria Histories of the Counties of England publications, 1899–

WA   City of Westminster Archives Centre, London

Notes

INTRODUCTION

1 M. Dorothy George, *London Life in the Eighteenth Century* [1925], reprint (New York, 1964), p. 155.

2 Raphael Samuel, *Island Stories: Unravelling Britain, theatres of memory*, ii (Guildford, 1998), pp. 367–8.

3 Fernand Braudel, *Capitalism and Material Life 1400–1800* [1967], trans. Miriam Kochan (London, 1973), pp. 192–3.

4 Johan Huizinga, *The Waning of the Middle Ages* [1924], reprint (New York, 1954), p. 335.

5 For important exceptions, see Neil Burton, ed., *Georgian Vernacular*, papers given at a Georgian Group Symposium, 28 October 1995 (Tonbridge, 1996); and Nicholas Cooper, 'Display, status and the vernacular tradition', *Vernacular Architecture*, xxxiii (2002), pp. 28–33. Even Matthew Johnson, who has so ably questioned many of the assumptions of vernacular studies, and who has himself warned of the need to avoid Whiggish pathways, has equated the eighteenth century with the polite, stressing the need to trace the origins of 'the Georgian order', without considering the endurance of the traditional. See Matthew Johnson, *An Archaeology of Capitalism* (Oxford, 1996), p. 202.

6 Michela Rosso, '*Georgian London* revisited', *London Journal*, xxvi/2 (2001), pp. 35–50; Alan Powers, 'John Summerson and modernism', in Louise Campbell, ed., *Twentieth-century Architecture and its Histories*, Society of Architectural Historians of Great Britain (Otley, 2000), pp. 153–75; Elizabeth McKellar, 'Popularism versus professionalism: John Summerson and the twentieth-century creation of "the Georgian"', in Barbara Arciszewska and Elizabeth McKellar, eds, *Articulating British Classicism: New approaches to eighteenth-century architecture* (Aldershot, forthcoming).

7 John Summerson, *Georgian London* [1945], ed. Howard Colvin (London 2003), preface. p. xi.

8 John Landers, *Death and the Metropolis: Studies in the demographic history of London 1670–1830* (Cambridge, 1993), p. 54.

9 See especially Dan Cruickshank and Neil Burton, *Life in the Georgian City* (London, 1990); and Elizabeth McKellar, *The Birth of Modern London: The development and design of the city 1660–1720* (Manchester, 1999a).

10 Walter Benjamin, *The Arcades Project* [1927–40], trans. Howard Eiland and Kevin McLaughlin (London, 1999), p. 842.

11 Miles Ogborn, *Spaces of Modernity: London's geographies, 1680–1780* (London, 1998), p. 36.

12 I am grateful to Paul Barnwell for help with Latin nuance.

13 Paul Oliver, ed., *Encyclopaedia of Vernacular Architecture of the World*, 3 vols (Cambridge, 1997), i, p. xxi.

14 Jill Lever and John Harris, *Illustrated Dictionary of Architecture 800–1914* (London, 1993), p. 42.

15 Eric Mercer, *English Vernacular Houses: A study of traditional farmhouses and cottages* (London, 1975), p. 1.

16 See Albert E. Richardson and H. Donaldson Eberlein, *The Smaller English House of the Later Renaissance, 1660–1830: An account of its design, plan and details* (London, 1925); and Harry Forrester, *The Smaller Queen Anne and Georgian House, 1700 to 1840* (Chelmsford, 1964).

17 For an important acknowledgement of this, see Bob Machin, 'The lost cottages of England: An essay on impermanent building in post-medieval England', typescript, Vernacular Architecture Group, 1997.

18 See Eric Mercer, 'The unfulfilled wider implications of vernacular architecture studies', *Vernacular Architecture*, xxviii (1997), pp. 9–12; Matthew Johnson, 'Vernacular architecture: The loss of innocence', *Vernacular Architecture*, xxviii (1997), pp. 13–19; Bob Meeson, 'Archaeological evidence and analysis: A case study from Staffordshire', *Vernacular Architecture*, xxxii (2001), pp. 1–15; and Sarah Pearson and Bob Meeson, eds, *Vernacular Buildings in a Changing World: Understanding, recording and conservation*, Council for British Archaeology Research Report 126 (York, 2001), esp. Pearson, 'Exploring the issues: Changing attitudes to understanding and recording', pp. 3–10.

19 Alice T. Friedman, 'The way you do the things you do: Writing the history of houses and housing', *Journal of the Society of Architectural Historians*, lviii/3 (September 1999), pp. 406–13.

20 See Catherine Belsey, 'Classicism and cultural dissonance', in Lucy Gent, ed., *Albion's Classicism: The visual arts in Britain, 1550–1660* (London, 1995), pp. 427–42; David Lowenthal, *The Past is a Foreign Country* (Cambridge, 1985).

1 THE VERNACULAR METROPOLIS

1. James Boswell, *London Journal 1762–1763*, ed. Frederick Pottle (London, 1950), p. 153.
2. Daniel Defoe, *A Tour through the Whole Island of Great Britain* [1724–6], ed. Pat Rogers (London, 1971), p. 286.
3. Jeremy Boulton, 'London 1540–1700', in Peter Clark, ed., *The Cambridge Urban History of Britain*, ii: *1540–1840* (Cambridge, 2000), p. 316; Leonard Schwarz, 'London 1700–1840', in Clark, ed., ibid., p. 642. The estimate of density is based on the population figures used here, on maps, and on figures for 1996 from www.demographia.com.
4. E. A. Wrigley, 'A simple model of London's importance in changing English society and economy 1650–1750', in P. Abrams and E. A. Wrigley, eds, *Towns in Societies: Essays in economic history and historical sociology* (Cambridge, 1978), pp. 215–43; E. Anthony Wrigley, 'Urban growth and agricultural change: England and the Continent in the early modern period', in Peter Borsay, ed., *The Eighteenth-century Town: A Reader in English Urban History 1688–1820* (Harlow, 1990), pp. 41–7.
5. M. Dorothy George, *London Life in the Eighteenth Century* [1925], reprint (New York, 1964), pp. 412–14; Craig Spence, *London in the 1690s: A social atlas* (Loughborough, 2000), p. 65; David Barnett, *London, Hub of the Industrial Revolution: A revisionary history 1775–1825* (London, 1998), p. 117; Paul Laxton, 'The evidence of Richard Horwood's maps for residential building in London, 1799–1819', *London Journal*, xxiv/1 (1999), pp. 1–22.
6. In London 'no less than forty-three thousand new houses were built between 1762 and 1779': Johann Wilhelm von Archenholz, *A Picture of England*, i (London, 1789), p. 121.
7. Fernand Braudel, *Capitalism and Material Life 1400–1800* [1967], trans. Miriam Kochan (London, 1973), pp. 430–36.
8. Leonard Schwarz, *London in the Age of Industrialisation: Entrepreneurs, labour force and living conditions, 1700–1850* (Cambridge, 1992); A. L. Beier, 'Engine of manufacture: The trades of London', in Beier and Roger Finlay, eds, *London, 1500–1700: The making of the metropolis* (Harlow, 1986), pp. 141–8; Peter Earle, *The Making of the English Middle Class: Business, society and family life in London, 1660–1730* (London, 1989a), pp. 18–25; Richard Rodger, *Housing in Urban Britain, 1780–1914* (Cambridge, 1995), p. 18.
9. Schwarz, 1992, pp. 34, 197, 206–7; Maxine Berg, *The Age of Manufactures, 1700–1820: Industry, innovation and work in Britain* (London, 2/1994).
10. Schwarz, 1992, pp. 7–9, 60, 254; Barnett, 1998, pp. 28–31; Tim Meldrum, *Domestic Service and Gender 1660–1750: Life and work in the London household* (Harlow, 2000); Hoh-Cheung Mui and Lorna H. Mui, *Shops and Shopkeeping in Eighteenth-century England* (London, 1989), pp. 40 and 109.
11. Valerie Pearl, 'Change and stability in seventeenth-century London', *London Journal*, v/1 (May 1979), pp. 3–34; Schwarz, 1992, *passim*.
12. Neil McKendrick, John Brewer and J. H. Plumb, *The Birth of a Consumer Society: The commercialization of eighteenth-century England* (London, 1982); Lorna Weatherill, *Consumer Behaviour and Material Culture in Britain, 1660–1760* (London, 1988); John Brewer and Roy Porter, eds, *Consumption and the World of Goods* (London, 1994); John Brewer, *The Pleasures of the Imagination: English culture in the eighteenth century* (London, 1997); Peter Borsay, *The English Urban Renaissance: Culture and society in the provincial town, 1660–1760* (Oxford, 1989); Richard L. Bushman, *The Refinement of America: Persons, houses, cities* (New York, 1992).
13. McKendrick, in McKendrick, Brewer and Plumb, eds, 1982, p. 27.
14. Plumb, in ibid., p. 323.
15. Weatherill, 1988, pp. 44, 47–50. However, few households of the poorer half of the population were inventoried; see Tom Arkell, 'Interpreting probate inventories', in Arkell, Nesta Evans and Nigel Goose, eds, *When Death Do Us Part: Understanding and interpreting the probate records of early modern England* (Oxford, 2000), pp. 72–102.
16. As quoted in McKendrick, Brewer and Plumb, eds, 1982, facing p. 1.
17. Jan de Vries, 'Between purchasing power and the world of goods: Understanding the household economy in early modern Europe', in Brewer and Porter, eds, 1994, pp. 85–132.
18. Jules Lubbock, *The Tyranny of Taste: The politics of architecture and design in Britain, 1550–1960* (London, 1995), pp. 3–12.
19. Borsay, 1989, *passim*; Bushman, 1992, *passim*.
20. Colin Campbell, 'Understanding traditional and modern patterns of consumption in eighteenth-century England: A character-action approach', and Lorna Weatherill, 'The meaning of consumer behaviour in late-seventeenth- and early-eighteenth-century England', in Brewer and Porter, eds, 1994, pp. 40–57 and 206–27.
21. Earle, 1989; Peter Earle, *A City Full of People: Men and women of London 1650–1750* (London, 1994); David Cannadine, *Class in Britain* (London, 1998), pp. 24–56.
22. Schwarz, 1992, p. 57.
23. Daniel Defoe, *Review*, 25 June 1709, widely quoted, not least accessibly in Terry Deary, *Horrible Histories: The gorgeous Georgians* (London, 1998), pp. 29–34.
24. Wrigley, in Abrams and Wrigley, eds, 1978, p. 221.
25. George, 1925, ed. 1964, pp. 156–7, 210.
26. George Rudé, *Hanoverian London 1714–1808* (London, 1971), p. 83.
27. Schwarz, 1992, p. 6.
28. As quoted by George, 1925, ed. 1964, p. 157.
29. Peter Earle, 'The middling sort in London', in Jonathan Barry and Christopher Brooks, eds, *The Middling Sort of People: Culture, society and politics in England, 1550–1800* (Cambridge, 1994), pp. 141–58; Edmund M. Green, 'The taxonomy of occupations in late-eighteenth-century Westminster', in Penelope J. Corfield and Derek Keene,

eds, *Work in Towns 850–1850* (Leicester, 1990), pp. 164–81; Mui and Mui, 1989, pp. 169, 205.

30 As quoted in Donald Woodward, *Men at Work: Labourers and building craftsmen in the towns of northern England, 1450–1750* (Cambridge, 1995), p. 93.

31 Pierre-Jean Grosley, *A Tour to London* (London, 1772), p. 78.

32 Adam Smith, *An Inquiry into the Nature and Causes of the Wealth of Nations*, i (London, 1776), as quoted by Linda Clarke, *Building Capitalism: Historical change & the labour process in the production of the built environment* (London, 1992), p. 77.

33 John Rule, *The Experience of Labour in Eighteenth-century Industry* (London, 1981), p. 62; see also Joan Lane, *Apprenticeship in England, 1600–1914* (London, 1996), and, for an emphasis on the adaptability of both individuals and trade guilds in the seventeenth century, Joseph P. Ward, *Metropolitan Communities: Trade guilds, identity and change in early modern London* (Stanford, Calif., 1997).

34 R. Campbell, *The London Tradesman* (London, 1747, facs. Newton Abbot, 1969), as quoted by Schwarz, 1992, p. 181.

35 Christopher Brooks, 'Apprenticeship, social mobility and the middling sort, 1550–1800', in Barry and Brooks, eds, 1994, pp. 52–83.

36 Peter Earle, 'The female labour market in London in the late seventeenth and early eighteenth centuries', *Economic History Review*, 2nd series, xlii/3 (1989b), pp. 328–53; Maxine Berg, 'Women's work, mechanisation and the early phases of industrialisation in England', in Patrick Joyce, ed., *The Historical Meanings of Work* (Cambridge, 1987), pp. 64–98; Spence, 2000, p. 77; Meldrum, 2000, *passim*; Richard Grassby, *Kinship and Capitalism: Marriage, family and business in the English speaking world, 1570–1740* (Cambridge, 2001), pp. 312–16.

37 Anon., *Low-life: Or, One half of the world knows not how the other half live* (London, c.1750), p. 102.

38 William C. Baer, 'Housing the poor and mechanick class in seventeenth-century London', *London Journal*, xxv/2 (2000), pp. 18–19.

39 Stephen Porter, *The Great Plague* (Stroud, 1999); George, 1925, ed. 1964, pp. 109–53; John Landers, *Death and the Metropolis* (Cambridge, 1993), pp. 48–9; Peter Linebaugh, *The London Hanged: Crime and civil society in the eighteenth century* (London, 1991), p. 349.

40 Patrick Colquhoun, *A Treatise on the Police of the Metropolis* (London, 1796), *The State of Indigence and the Situation of the Casual Poor in the Metropolis Explained* (London, 1799) and his *Treatise on the Commerce and Police of the River Thames* (London, 1800). Colquhoun is discussed by Schwarz, 1992, p. 9, appendix 1; Linebaugh, 1991, pp. 421–30; and in John Marriott and Masaie Matsumura, eds, *The Metropolitan Poor: Semi-factual accounts, 1795–1910* (London, 1999), pp. xv–xix.

41 Jeremy Boulton, 'Wage labour in seventeenth-century London', *Economic History Review*, 2nd series, xlix/2 (1996), pp. 268–90; L. D. Schwarz, 'Occupations and incomes in late eighteenth-century east London', *East London Papers*, xiv/1 (April 1972), pp. 87–100; Elizabeth Waterman Gilboy, *Wages in Eighteenth Century England* (Cambridge, Mass., 1934), pp. 14, 109, 255–7; R. Campbell, 1747, *passim*.

42 Schwarz, 1992, pp. 158–73; Linebaugh, 1991, *passim*; Peter D'Sena, 'Perquisites and casual labour on the London wharfside in the eighteenth century', *London Journal*, xiv/2 (1989), pp. 131–47.

43 George, 1925, ed. 1964, p. 169.

44 Anon., *Low-life*, c.1750, p. 58.

45 George, 1925, ed. 1964, p. 170. Anon., *Low-life*, c.1750, p. 33: 'The Wives and *Servant Girls* of Mechanicks and Day-Labourers, who live in Courts and Alleys, where one Cock supplies the whole Neighbourhood with Water, taking the Advantage before other People are up, to fill their Tubs and Pans' [emphasis added].

46 George, 1925, ed. 1964, pp. 284–307; C. Campbell, 1994, pp. 40–41; Jonathan Rose, *The Intellectual Life of the British Working Classes* (London, 2001), pp. 1–39, 62–3; Roy Porter, *London: A social history* (London, 1994), pp. 181–2; Peter Clark and R. A. Houston, 'Culture and leisure 1700–1840', in Clark, ed., 2000, pp. 599–601; James R. Farr, 'Cultural analysis and early modern artisans', in Geoffrey Crossick, ed., *The Artisan and the European Town, 1500–1900* (Aldershot, 1997), pp. 56–74.

47 Green, in Corfield and Keene, eds, 1990, p. 165.

48 Vanessa Harding, 'Controlling a complex metropolis, 1650–1750: Politics, parishes and powers', *London Journal*, xxvi/1 (2001), p. 34.

49 Rudé, 1971, p. 224.

50 Ibid., pp. 163–253; Brewer, in McKendrick, Brewer and Plumb, 1982, pp. 197–262; C. R. Dobson, *Masters and Journeymen: A prehistory of industrial relations, 1717–1800* (Guildford, 1980); Linebaugh, 1991, *passim*.

51 Rudé, 1971, p. 211.

52 Schwarz, 1992, p. 209.

53 Michael Berlin, '"Broken all in pieces": Artisans and the regulation of workmanship in early modern London', in Crossick, eds, 1997, pp. 75–91; see also Giorgio Riello, 'The shaping of a family trade: The Cordwainers' Company in eighteenth-century London', in Ian Anders Gadd and Patrick Wallis, ed., *Guilds, Society and Economy in London, 1450–1800* (London, 2002), pp. 141–59.

54 David R. Green, *From Artisans to Paupers: Economic change and poverty in London, 1790–1870* (Aldershot, 1995), pp. 87–91; Edward P. Thompson, *The Making of the English Working Class* (Harmondsworth, 1968); Iorwerth J. Prothero, *Artisans and Politics in Early Nineteenth-century London: John Gast and his times* (Folkestone, 1979).

55 Plumb, in McKendrick, Brewer and Plumb, 1982, p. 332.

56 George, 1925, ed. 1964, pp. 1–61, 312–22; Roy Porter, *Enlightenment: Britain and the creation of the modern world* (London, 2000), pp. 381–2; H. T. Dickinson, 'Radical culture', in Celina Fox, ed., *London – World City 1800–1840* (London, 1992), pp. 209–11; Pamela Sharpe, 'Population and society 1700–1840', and Leonard Schwarz, 'London 1700–1840', in Clark, ed., 2000, pp. 521, 671; Eileen Yeo and Edward P. Thompson, *The Unknown Mayhew* (New York, 1971).

57 Joseph Addison, *The Spectator*, no. 403 (12 June 1712).

58 John Fielding, *A Description of the Cities of London and Westminster* (London, 1776), pp. 28–9.

59 Archenholz, 1789, p. 122.

60 Louis Simond, *An American in Regency England: The journal of a tour in 1810–1811*, ed. Christopher Hibbert (London, 1968), p. 32.

61 Tobias Smollett, *The Expedition of Humphry Clinker* [1771], intr. and notes by L. Rice-Oxley (Oxford, 1925, repr. 1967), p. 104.

62 L. D. Schwarz, 'Social class and social geography: The middle classes in London at the end of the eighteenth century', in Borsay, ed., 1990, pp. 315–37.

63 Boswell, as quoted by George, 1925, ed. 1964, p. 68.

64 J. Richardson, *Recollections [. . .] of the Last Half-century* [1856], as quoted by George, 1925, ed. 1964, p. 343.

65 James Peller Malcolm, *Londinium Redivivum: Or, An ancient history and modern description of London*, 4 vols (London, 1803–7), i, p. 5.

66 Defoe, 1724–6, ed. 1971, p. 306.

67 Spence, 2000, p. 2.

68 Malcolm, 1803–7, iii, p. 477; see Michael H. Port, ed., *The Commissions for Building Fifty New Churches: The minute books, 1711–27: A calendar* (London, 1986); William Palin, 'The conception and siting of the "Stepney Churches": A study of the relationship between the churches of the "Fifty Churches" commission and their surroundings in the parish of St Dunstan's, Stepney', MA thesis, Courtauld Institute of Art, University of London, 1998.

69 This applies to the Broadway Chapel, Westminster, of the 1630s, to the Poplar and Shadwell Chapels of the 1650s, and to the later rebuildings of St Mary Matselon, Whitechapel, St Mary Magdalene, Bermondsey, and St Nicholas, Deptford. See Peter Guillery, 'The Broadway Chapel: A forgotten exemplar', *London Topographical Record*, xxvi (1990), pp. 97–133; see also Keith Thomas, 'English Protestantism and classical art', in Lucy Gent, ed., *Albion's Classicism: The visual arts in Britain, 1550–1660* (London, 1995), pp. 221–38.

70 SoL, iii, 1912, v, 1914, xxix–xxxvi, 1960–70; for a brief summary, see Francis Sheppard, *London: A history* (Oxford, 1998), pp. 175–85.

71 William Petty, as quoted in George, 1925, ed. 1964, p. 64.

72 Elizabeth McKellar, *The Birth of Modern London* (Manchester, 1999a); see also Miles Ogborn, *Spaces of Modernity* (London, 1998); Cynthia Wall, *The Literary and Cultural Spaces of Restoration London* (Cambridge, 1998).

73 John Strype, *A Survey of the Cities of London and Westminster, etc* (London, 1720), book iv, p. 75; see also R. Malcolm Smuts, 'The court and its neighbourhood: Royal policy and urban growth in the early Stuart West End', *Journal of British Studies*, xxx/2 (April 1991), pp. 117–49; Jeremy Boulton, 'The poor among the rich: Paupers and the parish in the West End, 1600–1724', in Paul Griffiths and Mark S. R. Jenner, eds, *Londinopolis: Essays in the cultural and social history of early modern London* (Manchester, 2000), pp. 197–225.

74 SoL: xxiii, 1951; xxxiii–iv, 1966; xxxix, 1977; xl, 1980.

75 Spence, 2000, p. 65.

76 Braudel, 1973, p. 391.

77 Stella Tillyard, *Aristocrats* (London, 1995), p. 169.

78 John Stow, *A Survey of London* [1598], ed. Charles Lethbridge Kingsford (London, 1908), ii, pp. 69–91.

79 M. J. Power, 'East London housing in the seventeenth century', in Peter Clark and Paul Slack, eds, *Crisis and Order in English Towns 1500–1700: Essays in urban history* (London, 1972), p. 241; M. J. Power, 'The social topography of Restoration London', in Beier and Finlay, eds, 1986, pp. 199–224; M. J. Power, 'The East and West in early-modern London', in E. W. Ives, R. J. Knecht and J. J. Scarisbrick, eds, *Wealth and Power in Tudor England* (London, 1978), pp. 167–85; M. J. Power, 'The east London working community in the seventeenth century', in Corfield and Keene, eds, 1990, pp. 103–20; Norman G. Brett-James, *The Growth of Stuart London* (London, 1935); SoL, xliii, 1994, pp. 388–93; Spence, 2000, p. 56.

80 Michael J. Power, 'Shadwell: The development of a London suburban community in the seventeenth century', *London Journal*, iv/1 (1978), pp. 29–46.

81 SoL, viii, 1922, xxvii, 1957.

82 George, 1925, ed. 1964, p. 413.

83 Defoe, 1724–6, ed. 1971, p. 178.

84 Strype, 1720, book iv, p. 27.

85 Defoe, 1724–6, ed. 1971, p. 287.

86 McKellar, 1999a, p. 181.

87 Defoe, 1724–6, ed. 1971, p. 338. See VCH: v, 1976; vi, 1980; viii, 1985; ix, 1989; x, 1995. See also Chris Miele, 'From aristocratic ideal to middle-class idyll: 1690–1840', in Andrew Saint, intr., *London Suburbs* (London, 1999), pp. 31–59; Elizabeth McKellar, 'Peripheral visions: Alternative aspects and rural presences in mid-eighteenth-century London', *Art History*, xxii/4 (November 1999b), pp. 495–513.

88 John Entick, *A New and Accurate History and Survey of London, Westminster, Southwark, and Places Adjacent*, iii (London, 1766), p. 443.

89 John Summerson, *Georgian London* [1945], ed. Howard Colvin (London, 2003), p. 318.

90 Francis Sheppard, Victor Belcher and Philip Cottrell, 'The Middlesex and Yorkshire Deeds Registries and the study of building fluctuations', *London Journal*, v/2 (1979), pp. 176–217.

91 Ibid., pp. 182–8.

92 George, 1925, ed. 1964, p. 65.

93 Thomas Milne, *Land Use Map of London and Environs in 1800*, London Topographical Society facsimile, nos 118 and 119 (1975–6).

94 Malcolm, 1803–7, iii, p. 500; see also Peter Ackroyd, *London: The biography* (London, 2000), pp. 131–43.

95 Schwarz, in Borsay, ed., 1990, p. 319.

96 Schwarz, 1972, pp. 87–100.

97 Malcolm, 1803–7, iv, pp. 565–6.

98 Henry Fielding, *An Enquiry into the Causes of the Late Increase in Robbers* (London, 1751), p. 75.

99 George, 1925, ed. 1964, pp. 81–5; Linebaugh, 1991, pp. 107–10, 149–50; Millicent Rose, *The East End of London* (London, 1951), pp. 58–61.

100 Dr Willan's 'Reports on diseases in London', March 1800, in T. A. Murray, *Remarks on the Situation of the Poor in the Metropolis* (London, 1801), as quoted by George, 1925, ed. 1964, pp. 86–7.

101 Ibid., p. 87.

102 Isaac Ware, *A Complete Body of Architecture* (London, 1756), p. 347.

103 James Peller Malcolm, *Anecdotes of the Manners and Customs of London during the Eighteenth Century* (London, 1808), p. 486.

104 Anon., *Low-life*, *c.*1750, p. 2.

105 Malcolm, 1808, p. 485.

106 Dan Cruickshank and Neil Burton, *Life in the Georgian City* (London, 1990), pp. 30–33, 60–63.

107 George, 1925, ed. 1964, p. 73.

108 Traditional, as transcribed by George Cruikshank, *Scraps and Sketches* (London, 1828).

109 Grosley, 1772, p. 76.

110 Kathryn Morrison, *The Workhouse: A study of poor-law buildings in England* (Swindon, 1999), pp. 13–16; Elaine Murphy, 'The metropolitan pauper farms 1722–1834', *London Journal*, xxvii/1 (2002), pp. 1–18; Jeremy Boulton, '"It is extreme necessity that makes me do this": Some "survival strategies" of pauper households in London's West End during the early eighteenth century', *International Review of Social History*, xlv, suppl. 8 (2000), pp. 47–69.

111 For this and much of what follows, see Landers, 1993.

112 Ronald Paulson, *Hogarth*, iii: *Art and Politics 1750–1764* (Cambridge, 1993), pp. 17–26.

113 Earle, 1994, p. 166.

114 Power, in Beier and Finlay, eds, 1986, *passim*; Power, in Ives, Knecht and Scarisbrick, eds, 1978, *passim*.

115 Power, in Clark and Slack, ed., 1972, pp. 253–4; Power, in Ives, Knecht and Scarisbrick, eds, 1978, pp. 170–71; Baer, 2000, pp. 23–4; Spence, 2000, pp. 56, 101–2.

116 Edward Hatton, *A New View of London; Or, An ample account of that city* (London, 1708), p. iv.

117 Roger Finlay and Beatrice Shearer, 'Population growth and suburban expansion', in Beier and Finlay, eds, 1986, p. 47; Spence, 2000, p. 65; Earle, 1989a, p. 213.

118 Adam Smith, as quoted by Schwarz, in Borsay, eds, 1990, p. 325.

119 Earle, 1989a, pp. 212–18; Wrigley, in Abrams and Wrigley, eds, 1978, George, 1925, ed. 1964, pp. 412–14.

120 Simond, ed., 1968, p. 36.

121 Baer, 2000, *passim*.

122 Fielding, 1751, p. 92; William Maitland, *The History of London* (London, 1739), p. 532; Spence, 2000, pp. 67–71; Earle, 1994, pp. 168–9.

123 George, 1925, ed. 1964, pp. 92, 96; Rudé, 1971, pp. 87–8; Dobson, 1980, p. 113.

124 Spence, 2000, p. 72; Earle, 1989a, p. 209; Earle, 1994, pp. 168–9; George, 1925, ed. 1964, p. 91.

125 Rudé, 1971, p. 226.

2 'THE MULTIPLICITY OF HUMAN HABITATIONS'

1 Speaking on 5 July 1763, as recorded by James Boswell, *The Life of Samuel Johnson* [1791], in *Boswell's Life of Johnson, together with Boswell's Journal of a Tour to the Hebrides and Johnson's Diary of a Journey into North Wales*, ed. George Birkbeck Hill, rev. and enlarged by L. F. Powell, 6 vols (Oxford, 1934–50), i, pp. 421–2.

2 C. R. J. Currie, 'Time and chance: Modelling the attrition of old houses', *Vernacular Architecture*, xix (1988), pp. 1–9.

3 John Schofield, ed., *The London Surveys of Ralph Treswell*, London Topographical Society Publication 135 (London, 1987); John Schofield, *Medieval London Houses* (London, 1995); John Schofield, 'Urban housing in England, 1400–1600', in David Gaimster and Paul Stamper, edS, *The Age of Transition: The archaeology of English culture 1400–1600* (Oxford, 1997), pp. 127–44; Nicholas Cooper, *Houses of the Gentry, 1480–1680* (New Haven and London, 1999).

4 C. C. Knowles and P. H. Pitt, *The History of Building Regulation in London: 1189–1972* (London, 1972), pp. 12–25; Norman G. Brett-James, *The Growth of Stuart London* (London, 1935), pp. 67–126; Frank Kelsall, unpublished notes on legal restrictions on building in London; Stephen Porter, *The Great Fire of London* (Stroud, 1996), p. 17; Jeremy Boulton, 'Wage labour in seventeenth-century London', *Economic History Review*, 2nd series, xlix/2 (1996), p. 270; Jules Lubbock, *The Tyranny of Taste: The politics of architecture and design in Britain, 1550–1960* (London, 1995), pp. 25–9.

5 Roger H. Leech, 'The prospect from Rugman's Row: The row house in late sixteenth- and early seventeenth-century London', *Archaeological Journal*, cliii (1996), pp. 201–42.

6 NMR, investigator's record card.

7 Summerson aside, see Brett-James, 1935, pp. 151–86; SoL, iii, 1912; SoL, xxxvi, 1970; Lubbock, 1995, pp. 29–36; McKellar, 1999a, pp. 191–8.

8 Philip Norman, 'London buildings photographed, 1860–1870', *London Topographical Record*, ii (1903), p. 39; OS, 1875.

9 Leech, 1996, p. 225; for the Hoop and Grapes, see NMR, GLC Drawings Collection 96/6881–9 and 7827–30.

10 SoL, xxxvi, 1970, pp. 266–70; R. Malcolm Smuts, 'The court and its neighbourhood', *Journal of British Studies*, xxx/2 (April 1991), pp. 117–49; M. J. Power, 'The East and West in early modern London', in Ives, Knecht and Scarisbrick, eds, 1978, p. 170.

11 I am grateful to Elizabeth McKellar and Sarah Pearson for sharing thoughts on this subject.

12 M. J. Power, 'East London housing in the seventeenth century', in Clark and Slack, eds, 1972, pp. 237–62; Power, 'Shadwell', *London Journal*, iv/1 (1978), pp. 29–46.

13 NA, C5/422/117.

14 MiD, Shadwell portfolio, undated cutting.

15 For other late seventeenth-century timber houses in Shadwell, see RCHM(E), v, 1930, p. 100, with investigators' record cards in the NMR; there is a view of a late

seventeenth-century house at the north end of Old Gravel Lane in the NMR's Gerald Cobb Collection (BB99/06770).

16 BL, Crace Plans, portfolio XVI/24: 'A correct ground plan of the dreadful fire at Ratcliff'.

17 RCHM(E), v, 1930, pp. 57, 100; SoL, xliii, 1994, pp. 55–61, 111–13, plates 2–5.

18 RCHM(E), v, 1930, p. 9, and investigator's record card in the NMR; VCH, xi, 1998, pp. 101–3, plate 24.

19 For the Great Fire and its aftermath, see Porter, 1996, *passim*.

20 Lubbock, 1995, p 38.

21 19 Car. II, cap. 8.

22 Porter, 1996, pp. 105–15.

23 John Evelyn, 'An account of architects and architecture', preface to his translation of Roland Fréart, *A Parallel of the Antient Architecture with the Modern* (London, 1707), p. 5.

24 Letter from Nicholas Hawksmoor to Dr George Clarke in 1715, as quoted by Kerry Downes, *Hawksmoor* (London, 1959), pp. 241–2. As this comment implies, the Act of 1667 had not put a stop to the spread of large fires in the City. In 1715 a fire near the Thames destroyed 120 houses and the Custom House, all brick built since 1666. I am grateful to Stephen Porter for this point.

25 Porter, 1996, pp. 116–80; Frank Kelsall, unpublished lectures and personal communication.

26 Frank Kelsall, 'A note on the building', *Post-medieval Archaeology*, x (1976), pp. 158–9; RCHM(E), iv, 1929, p. 162, and investigator's record card in the NMR.

27 NMR, GLC Drawings Collection, 96/9476.

28 Joseph Moxon, *Mechanick Exercises: Or, The doctrine of handy-works* (London, 2/1693–4), p. 147.

29 Brian Hobley, John Schofield *et al.*, 'Excavations in the City of London: First interim report, 1974–1975', *Antiquaries Journal*, lvii (1977), pp. 39, 41.

30 Guildhall MS 8269; I am grateful to Frank Kelsall for this reference.

31 RCHM(E), 1929, p. 59; Simon Bradley and Nikolaus Pevsner, *The Buildings of England, London*, i: *The City of London* (London, 1997), p. 621.

32 William C. Baer, 'Housing the poor and mechanick class in seventeenth-century London', *London Journal*, xxv/2 (2000), pp. 13–39.

33 McKellar, 1999a, *passim*.

34 Ibid., pp. 57–113; Dan Cruickshank and Neil Burton, *Life in the Georgian City* (London, 1990), pp. 111–23; James Ayres, *Building the Georgian City* (London, 1998).

35 John Summerson, *Georgian London* (London, 1945, rev. 7/1988), p. 53. See also John Summerson, *Georgian London* [1945], ed. Howard Colvin (London, 2003), pp. 24, 28, 64, 405.

36 McKellar, 1999a, p. 89.

37 Ibid., pp. 138–87; Howard M. Colvin, *A Biographical Dictionary of British Architects 1600–1840* (London, 3/1995), pp. 21–8.

38 Ralph Hyde, intr., *The A to Z of Restoration London*, London Topographical Society Publication no. 145 (London, 1992).

39 Charles Robert Ashbee, *The Trinity Hospital in Mile End:*

An object lesson in national history, first monograph of the Committee for the Survey of the Memorials of Greater London (London, 1896); RCHM(E), 1930, pp. 54–5; SoL, xliii, 1994, p. 187.

40 THLHL, TH94; Essex Record Office, D/DL/TI/804; RCHM(E), 1930, p. 100, and investigators' record cards in the NMR.

41 'Wooden London: Lingerings of the past', *The Builder* (17 September 1859), p. 609.

42 Hyde, intr., 1992; RCHM(E), 1930, p. 99, and investigators' record cards in the NMR; NMR, GLC Drawings Collection 96/7266.

43 Pierre Le Muet, *The Art of Fair Building* [1623], trans. Robert Pricke (London, 1670), pp. 4–6.

44 I am grateful to Chris Ellmers for sharing this information arising from his research on Clerkenwell.

45 SoL, Clerkenwell South, forthcoming.

46 RCHM(E), ii, 1925, p. 63, and investigator's record card in the NMR.

47 NMR, photograph AA50/7726; SoL, xx, 1940, p. 121; Simon Bradley and Nikolaus Pevsner, *The Buildings of England, London*, vi: *Westminster* (London, 2003), pp. 38, 361.

48 Francis Sheppard, *London: A history* (Oxford, 1998), p. 181.

49 John Strype, as quoted in SoL, xxxiv, 1966, p. 374.

50 Ibid., pp. 374–7, plate 55.

51 SoL, xxxi, 1963, p. 53, plate 123.

52 Ibid., pp. 165–6, and supporting ratebook notes in the NMR.

53 SoL, xxxiii, 1966, pp. 196–7, plate 9.

54 Isobel Watson, *Westminster and Pimlico Past: A visual history* (London, 1993), pp. 81–4, 104.

55 Schofield, in Gaimster and Stamper, ed., 1997, p. 139; RCHM(E), 1939; RCHM(E), 1959; NMR, reference collection, measured drawings of Lamb Building, Middle Temple; RCHM(E), v, 1930, pp. 36–7; Neil Burton, *The Geffrye Almshouses* (London, 1979); SoL, xviii, 1937, pp. 109-110; NMR, GLC Drawings Collection, 96/3889-90

56 Use of the word 'tenement' in the eighteenth century was ambiguous, sometimes referring to what would now be termed a house. The word is used in this book to indicate what might otherwise be called flats or apartments.

57 Le Muet, trans. 1670, p. 5; Françoise Boudon *et al.*, *Système de l'architecture urbaine: Le Quartier des Halles à Paris* (Paris, 1977), pp. 70–101; David Garrioch, *Neighbourhood and Community in Paris, 1740–1790* (Cambridge, 1986), pp. 221–5.

58 RCAHMS, 1951, pp. lxvi–lxxi, 71–85; John Gifford, Colin McWilliam and David Walker, *The Buildings of Scotland: Edinburgh* (Harmondsworth, 1984), pp. 59–60, 194–8, 205–7; Miles Glendinning, Ranald MacInnes and Aonghus MacKechnie, *A History of Scottish Architecture: From the Renaissance to the present day* (Edinburgh, 1996), pp. 62–4, 135–7.

59 John Gwynn, *London and Westminster Improved* (London, 1766), p. 129.

60 Stephen Primatt, *The City and Country Purchaser and*

Builder [1667], reissued by William Leybourne (London, 3/1680), p. 141.

61 Ibid., p. 141.

62 Ibid., pp. 80–136.

63 I am grateful to Nicholas Cooper for sharing his thoughts on this layout. See also Cooper, 1999, pp. 149–50; Matthew Johnson, *Housing Culture: Traditional architecture in an English landscape* (London, 1993).

64 John Summerson, ed., *The Walpole Society*, xl: *The Book of Architecture of John Thorpe in Sir John Soane's Museum* (Glasgow, 1966), pp. 27, 46, plate 6.

65 Schofield, ed., 1987, pp. 138–9; Leech, 1996, pp. 218–24; Alan Thompson, Francis Grew and John Schofield, 'Excavations at Aldgate, 1974', *Post-medieval Archaeology*, xviii (1984), pp. 1–33; McKellar, 1999a, pp. 164–8; RCHM(E), 1929, p. 162, and investigator's record card in the NMR.

66 CLRO, Plans of City Lands and Bridge House Properties, 2 vols, *c.*1680–*c.*1720; BL, Crace Collection, Plans of City Properties, portfolio IX/145, 188 and 207; SoL, xliii, 1994, p. 73; RCHM(E), 1930, p. 100, and NMR investigator's record card for Nos 68–72 Limehouse Causeway.

67 Primatt, 3/1680, pp. 95–7. His rear-staircase layout example (fig. 42c) is different in size and its costs can not be meaningfully compared with those of alternative layouts.

68 Moxon, 2/1693–4, preface.

69 Ibid., p. 115.

70 Ibid., p. 129, plate 10.

71 Ibid., p. 145; see also Eileen Harris, *British Architectural Books and Writers, 1556–1785* (Cambridge, 1990), pp. 325–6; McKellar, 1999a, pp. 143–6, 160–63; Ayres, 1998, pp. 1, 13; T. M. Russell, ed., *The Encyclopaedic Dictionary in the Eighteenth Century*, iii: *The Builder's Dictionary* (Cambridge, 1997), pp. 1–4.

72 Nicholas Barbon, *An Apology for the Builder* (London, 1685); see also Nicholas Cooper, 'Display, status and the vernacular tradition', *Vernacular Architecture*, xxxiii (2002), pp. 28–33.

73 A. F. Kelsall, 'The London house plan in the later 17th century', *Post-medieval Archaeology*, viii (1974), pp. 80–91; Schofield, in Gaimster and Stamper, eds, 1997, p. 139; Bradley and Pevsner, 1997, pp. 70, 417; examples are illustrated in Alison Maguire with Howard Colvin, eds, 'A collection of seventeenth-century architectural plans', *Architectural History*, xxxv (1992), pp. 140–82, fig. 29; SoL, xx, 1940, pp. 118–21; R. Meischke *et al.*, *Huizen in Nederland: Amsterdam* (Amsterdam, 1995), pp. 278–302; SoL, Clerkenwell South, forthcoming.

74 I am grateful to Kathryn Morrison for sharing thoughts arising from an English Heritage national survey of shops; see also McKellar, 1999a, pp. 128, 163–4; CLRO, Plans of City Lands and Bridge House Properties, 2 vols, *c.*1680–*c.*1720; BL, Crace Plans, Portfolio IX/125, 139, 141, 144, 197; SoL, The Charterhouse, forthcoming; LMA, ACC/1876/D1/904; Hoh-Cheung Mui and Lorna H. Mui, *Shops and Shopkeeping in Eighteenth-century England* (London, 1989).

75 John Summerson, *Georgian London* (London, 1945), p. 34.

76 Summerson, 7/1988, p. 31.

77 Roger North, *Of Building* [*c.*1690], ed. Howard M. Colvin and John Newman (Oxford, 1981), p. 69.

78 Moxon, 2/1693–4, p. 147.

79 Kelsall, 1974, pp. 88–9; McKellar, 1999a, pp. 160, 162, 169–71; SoL: xxix–xxxiv, 1960–6; xxxix, 1977; and xl, 1980.

80 SoL, Clerkenwell South, forthcoming.

81 Summerson, 7/1988, p. 45.

82 'Small street houses', *The Builder* (16 September 1843), p. 391.

83 Meischke *et al.*, 1995, *passim*; Le Muet, trans. 1670, plate 23.

84 Tim Meldrum, 'Domestic service, privacy and eighteenth-century metropolitan households', *Urban History*, xxvi/1 (1999), pp. 27–39, summarised in his *Domestic Service and Gender 1660–1750* (Harlow, 2000), pp. 76–83. For an approach that does not heed these cautions, see Christoph Heyl, 'We are not at Home: Protecting domestic privacy in post-fire middle-class London', *London Journal*, xxvii/2 (2002), pp. 12–33.

85 Dan Cruickshank, *A Guide to the Georgian Buildings of Britain & Ireland* (London, 1985), pp. 23–35; Cruickshank and Burton, 1990, pp. 123–31; McKellar, 1999a, pp. 155–87; Andrew Byrne, *London's Georgian Houses* (London, 1986); Elizabeth McKellar, 'The city and the country: The urban vernacular in late seventeenth and early eighteenth century London', in Burton, ed., 1996, pp. 10–18.

86 Knowles and Pitt, 1972, pp. 37–9; Ayres, 1998, pp. 148, 230–31; Cruickshank and Burton, 1990, pp. 99–104.

87 Isaac Ware, *A Complete Body of Architecture* (London, 1756), pp. 345–7; see also Cruickshank and Burton, 1990, pp. 51–60.

88 Peter Earle, *The Making of the English Middle Class* (London, 1989a), p. 211.

89 Summerson, 1945, ed. 2003, p. 58.

90 Harris, 1990, *passim*; David T. Yeomans, 'Early carpenters' manuals 1592–1820', *Construction History*, ii (1986), pp. 13–33; T. M. Russell, ed., 1997.

91 R. Campbell, *The London Tradesman* (London, 1747, facs. Newton Abbot, 1969), p. 159. See also James W. P. Campbell, 'The carpentry trade in seventeenth-century London', *Georgian Group Journal*, xii (2002), pp. 215–37.

92 Campbell, 1747, facs. 1969, p. 160.

93 Ayres, 1998, pp. 1–16, 133; Colvin, 3/1995, pp. 21–7; McKellar, 1999a, pp. 138–54; Cruickshank and Burton, 1990, p. 218; Christopher William Chalklin, *The Provincial Towns of Georgian England: A study of the building process, 1740–1820* (London, 1974), pp. 188–203.

94 McKellar, 1999a, pp. 93–137; Ayres, 1998, pp. 1–16; Linda Clarke, *Building Capitalism* (London, 1992), pp. 48–73.

95 Campbell, 1747, facs. 1969, p. 158.

96 Dan Cruickshank and Peter Wyld, *London: The art of Georgian building* (London, 1975).

97 James Peller Malcolm, *Anecdotes of the Manners and Customs of London during the Eighteenth Century* (London, 1808), p. 465.

98   Pierre-Jean Grosley, *A Tour to London* (London, 1772), p. 76.

99   Ibid., pp. 76–7.

100 Alan Cox, 'A vital component: Stock bricks in Georgian London', *Construction History*, xiii (1997), pp. 57–66; Blake Tyson, 'Transportation and the supply of construction materials: An aspect of traditional building management', *Vernacular Architecture*, xxix (1998), pp. 63–81.

101 Bob Machin, 'The lost cottages of England', unpublished typescript, Vernacular Architecture Group, 1997.

102 David Yeomans, 'Structural carpentry in London building', in Hermione Hobhouse and Ann Saunders, eds, *Good and Proper Materials: The fabric of London since the Great Fire*, London Topographical Society (London, 1989), pp. 38–47; David Yeomans, '18c timber construction', *Architect's Journal* (10 July 1991), pp. 51–6.

103 I am grateful to Alan Cox for passing on this information, derived from research by Robin Lucas.

104 Millicent Rose, *The East End of London* (London, 1951), pp. 20–22, 55–8.

105 Colvin, 3/1995, pp. 751–2; Bradley and Pevsner, 2003, p. 513.

106 Grosley, 1772, p. 77.

107 James Peller Malcolm, *Londinium Redivivum* (London, 1803–7), iii, p. 477.

108 Borsay, *The English Urban Renaissance* (Oxford, 1989), p. 290.

109 Lubbock, 1995, pp. 87–178; Catherine Belsey, 'Classicism and cultural dissonance', in Gent, ed., 1995, pp. 427–42; Colin Campbell, 'Understanding traditional and modern patterns of consumption in eighteenth-century England: A character-action approach', and Lorna Weatherill, 'The meaning of consumer behaviour in late-seventeenth- and early-eighteenth century England', both in Brewer and Porter, eds, 1994, pp. 40–57, 206–27; Cooper, 2002, p. 33. See also James Ayres, *Domestic Interiors: The British tradition 1500-1800* (London, 2003).

110 Frank Kelsall, unpublished report on No. 8 New Bond Street, 2001.

111 Comment on the Foundling Estate in 1818, as quoted by Alan Cox, 'In darkest London: Slums in the capital', unpublished typescript of a talk delivered at the Victorian Society conference 'The Victorian underworld', 24 November 2001; see also Giles Worsley, 'Inigo Jones and the origins of the London mews', *Architectural History*, xliv (2001), pp. 88–95.

112 See, for example, SoL, xxxi, 1963, pp. 203–6.

113 SoL, xxxix, 1977, p. 86; SoL, xl, 1980, p. 85, with supporting notes in the NMR from LMA, TC/StG/1; SoL, unarchived survey notes and drawings, c.1990; EH, London Region casework files and photographs; Neil Burton, *Georgian Stairs* (London, 2001), p. 25.

114 SoL, xxxix, 1977, pp. 84–9.

115 WA, RB (St George, Hanover Square).

116 SoL, xxxix, 1977, pp. 108–11.

117 SoL, xxxi, 1963, p. 299; SoL, xxxii, 1963, p. 528.

118 Cruickshank and Burton, 1990, pp. 118, 130, 236–54; Cruickshank, 1985, pp. 47–8; Richard Garnier, 'Speculative housing in 1750s London', *Georgian Group Journal*, xii (2002), pp. 163–214; NMR, GLC Drawings Collection 96/1788; Andrew Saint, intr., *London Suburbs* (London, 1999), p. 43.

119 SoL, xxxi, 1963, supporting ratebook notes.

120 Similar and earlier accommodation has been recorded nearby at No. 68 Dean Street. See David Bieda, 'Soho Masochism', *The Georgian: The magazine of the Georgian Group* (Spring 2003), pp. 23–5.

3   ANOTHER GEORGIAN SPITALFIELDS

1   Verse from 1773, as quoted by John Rule, 'The property of skill in the period of manufacture', in Patrick Joyce, ed., 1987, p. 109.

2   Millicent Rose, *The East End of London* (London, 1951), pp. 44–5.

3   SoL, xxvii, 1957.

4   Mark Girouard, Dan Cruickshank, Raphael Samuel *et al.*, *The Saving of Spitalfields* (London, 1989).

5   Edward P. Thompson, *The Making of the English Working Class* (Harmondsworth, 1968), p. 13.

6   This chapter is based on an English Heritage survey report issued in July 2000. Particular thanks are due to Andrew Byrne, then of the Spitalfields Historic Buildings Trust, for first drawing attention to some of the buildings discussed here. The survey report is a detailed account, with entries on each of the buildings investigated. With supporting material it may be consulted through the NMR (see appendix).

7   Daniel Defoe, *A Tour through the Whole Island of Great Britain* [1724–6], ed. Pat Rogers (London, 1971), p. 298.

8   VCH, xi, 1998, pp. 94–5; *Commons' Journals*, xvi/10 (March 1710/11), p. 542, and xxiv (10 January 1742/3), p. 369.

9   For more detail, see VCH, xi, 1998, pp. 88, 92, 95, 104–9, 156–62, 172, and the survey report in the NMR.

10 Edward Hatton, *A New View of London* (London, 1708), p. 37.

11 Roger Finlay and Beatrice Shearer, 'Population growth and suburban expansion', in Beier and Finlay, eds, 1986, pp. 43–7; David Barnett, *London, Hub of the Industrial Revolution* (London, 1998), p. 117; Leonard Schwarz, *London in the Age of Industrialisation* (Cambridge, 1992), pp. 35–8, 202–7.

12 VCH, xi, 1998, pp. 178–82; M. Dorothy George, *London Life in the Eighteenth Century* [1925], reprint (New York, 1964), pp. 176–95; N. K. A. Rothstein, 'The silk industry in London, 1702–1766', University of London, MA thesis, 1961; Richard Grassby, *Kinship and Capitalism* (Cambridge, 2001), p. 313.

13 THLHL, LT (BG197-251, 1745–1824); VCH, xi, 1998, pp. 92–3, 177; N. K. A. Rothstein, 'Huguenots in the English silk industry in the eighteenth century', in Irene Scouloudi, ed., *Huguenots in Britain and their French Background 1550–1800* (London, 1987), pp. 125–40.

14 *Commons' Journals*, xxiv (3 March 1742/3), p. 448.

15 L. D. Schwarz, 'Occupations and incomes in late eighteenth-century east London', *East London Papers*, xiv (April 1972), p. 93.

16 Edward Church, a Spitalfields solicitor, as quoted in J. H. Clapham, 'The Spitalfields Acts, 1773–1824', *Economic Journal*, xxvi (1916), p. 466.

17 Rothstein, 1987, p. 136.

18 Peter Linebaugh, *The London Hanged* (London, 1991), p. 263.

19 Eileen Yeo and Edward P. Thompson, *The Unknown Mayhew* (New York, 1971), pp. 105–6; *The Builder* (23 April 1853), p. 337; Clapham, 1916, pp. 465–6; Rose, 1951, pp. 103–4.

20 George, 1925, ed. 1964, pp. 188–92.

21 Linebaugh, 1991, p. 256.

22 George, 1925, ed. 1964, pp. 180, 193; SoL, xxvii, 1957, p. 6; VCH, xi, 1998, pp. 18, 177.

23 VCH, xi, 1998, pp. 94–5; Francis Sheppard, Victor Belcher and Philip Cottrell, 'The Middlesex and Yorkshire Deeds Registries and the study of building fluctuations', *London Journal*, v/2 (1979), pp. 176–217.

24 George, 1925, ed. 1964, pp. 192–5; Linebaugh, 1991, pp. 270–71.

25 The Shelburne Papers, University of Michigan, as quoted by Linebaugh, 1991, p. 274.

26 Linebaugh, 1991, pp. 277–83; VCH, xi, 1998, p. 178; G. F. Vale, *Old Bethnal Green* (London, 1934), pp. 36–7.

27 13 Geo. III, cap. 68; Clapham, 1916, pp. 459–71; VCH, xi, 1998, p. 95.

28 George, 1925, ed. 1964, pp. 103–7; Rose, 1951, p. 159; Linebaugh, 1991, pp. 408–9; VCH, xi, 1998, pp. 178–9; Schwarz, 1992, p. 207; Schwarz, 1972, pp. 92–3; Hoh-Chueng Mui and Lorna H. Mui, *Shops and Shopkeeping in Eighteenth-century England* (London, 1989), pp. 111–18; Paul Laxton, 'The evidence of Richard Horwood's maps for residential building in London, 1799–1819', *London Journal*, xxiv/1 (1999), pp. 1–22.

29 Stephen Wilson, as quoted by Clapham, 1916, pp. 464, 469. Wilson also pointed out that the Acts worked against mechanical improvements like the Jacquard loom, as masters had to pay the same piece rates whether labour-saving appliances were used or not; ibid., p. 466. See also Natalie Rothstein, 'The introduction of the Jacquard loom to Great Britain', in Veronika Gervers, ed., *Studies in Textile History* (Toronto, 1977), pp. 281–304. For the Streatham mill see an unpublished report by Andrew Saint, EH, London historical research file, Lambeth, 44.

30 Hector Gavin, *Sanitary Ramblings: Being sketches and illustrations of Bethnal Green. A type of the condition of the metropolis and other large towns* (London, 1848); Yeo and Thompson, 1971, pp. 104–15; *The Builder* (23 April, 28 May and 4 June 1853), pp. 257–8, 337–8, 360; Rose, 1951, pp. 163–7; VCH, xi, 1998, pp. 124–5, 178–9; SoL, xxvii, 1957, p. 8; David R. Green, *From Artisans to Paupers* (Aldershot, 1995), pp. 158–9; Maxine Berg, *The Age of Manufactures, 1700-1820* (London, 2/1994), pp. 219–20, 228, 244.

31 SoL, xxvii, 1957, p. 252; VCH, xi, 1998, pp. 125, 131; *The Builder* (28 January 1871), p. 69; Arthur Morrison, *A Child of the Jago* (London, 1896, reprinted 1966); Susan Beattie, *A Revolution in London Housing: LCC housing architects and their work, 1893–1914* (London, 1980), pp. 17–19.

32 *The Builder* (28 January 1871), p. 69.

33 VCH, xi, 1998, pp. 181–2, 190; Rose, 1951, p. 104; Raphael Samuel, *Theatres of Memory*, i: *Past and present in contemporary culture* (London, 1994), p. 355.

34 Information kindly supplied by Frank Kelsall.

35 VCH, xi, 1998, pp. 104–6, 162.

36 NA, PROB 3/18/267. In bringing forward inventories, the usual caveats about their usefulness in reconstructing house form need to be applied. It is sometimes unclear whether one is dealing with a house or merely a household; rooms may be left out, and spatial relationships are often ambiguous. See Tom Arkell, 'Interpreting probate inventories', in Arkell, Evans and Goose, eds, pp. 2000, 72–102.

37 THLHL, BG 257; TH 2891, 2893, 2906; LMA, MDR 1719/6/270–71; 1728/2/181 and 446; 1737/5/216; 1771/1/20; 1793/7/57; GL, H-H, MS 8674/20, 38214–16; MS 8674/21, 39383–4, 40013; MS 8674/121, 38214, 39383; MS 8674/144, 40013, 95811, 97666; 8675/3, 97211, 97721; GL, MS 21742/2; NA, PROB 6/118; VCH, 1998, pp. 92, 193.

38 THLHL, LT; MDR 1737/5/215–16; 1793/7/57.

39 MDR 1728/2/124, 181; THLHL, TH 2895; GL, MS 21742/2; SoL, xxvii, 1957, pp. 89, 184, 214, 279.

40 Elizabeth McKellar, *The Birth of Modern London* (Manchester, 1999a), pp. 71, 75–6; Stephen Porter, *The Great Fire of London* (Stroud, 1996), pp. 112, 168; Valerie Pearl, 'Change and stability in seventeenth-century London', *London Journal*, v/1 (May 1979), pp. 8–15; B. W. E. Alford and T. C. Barker, *A History of the Carpenters' Company* (London, 1968); M. J. Power, 'East London housing in the seventeenth century', in Clark and Slack, ed., 1972, 237–62.

41 NA, PROB 3/36/1124; MDR 1737/5/215, 1771/ 3/126.

42 VCH, xi, 1998, pp. 106, 178; MDR 1741/4/77.

43 MDR 1723/6/276; GL, H-H, MS 8674/20, 38214.

44 McKellar, 1999a, pp. 61, 81–9, 103–4; Dan Cruickshank and Neil Burton, *Life in the Georgian City* (London, 1990), pp. 115–17, 209–20.

45 MDR 1767/9/309; GL, MS 21742/2; VCH, xi, 1998, p. 107.

46 THLHL, LT; TH 2229; LMA, MR/B/R/1; VCH, xi, 1998, p. 97.

47 VCH, xi, 1998, pp. 92, 114; Schwarz, 1992, pp. 204, 221. Wilmot Street was redeveloped from 1868 by Sidney Waterlow's Improved Industrial Dwellings Company, to provide, ironically, tall rows of tenements laid out with staircases to the front. I am grateful to Charles O'Brien for this information.

48 Anon., *Low-life* (London, c.1750), p. 97.

49 LMA, MR/B/R/1 and 3; VCH, xi, 1998, pp. 88, 92, 193; George Rudé, *Hanoverian London 1714–1808* (London, 1971), pp. 131–2; Vale, 1934, pp. 31–4; George, 1925, ed. 1964, p. 191.

50 THLHL, LT; TH 2906 and 7970.

51 As quoted in VCH, xi, 1998, p. 124.

52 Report of the Select Committee on Building Regulations (1842), x, p. 1009, as quoted by Enid Gauldie, *Cruel Habitations: A history of working-class housing 1780–1918* (London, 1974), p. 91; see also Gavin, 1848, p. 67.

53 VCH, xi, 1998, p. 177; Rothstein, 1961, *passim*; Berg, 2/1994, pp. 219-20; Clapham, 1916, pp. 461–2; SoL, xxvii, 1957, *passim*.

54 Gavin, 1848, p. 67.

55 *Commons' Journals*, xxiv (3 March 1742/3), p. 448.

56 *Commons' Journals*, xxiv (10 January 1742/3), p. 369; George, 1925, ed. 1964, pp. 412–14; VCH, xi, 1998, pp. 94–5.

57 *Commons' Journals*, xvi (10 March 1710/11), p. 542.

58 MDR 1728/2/446, 1745/2/255; NA, PROB 3/51/31; THLHL, TH 2887; Cruickshank and Burton, 1990, p. 219.

59 *The Builder* (28 May 1853), p. 337.

60 I am grateful to Natalie Rothstein for this information.

61 George, 1925, ed. 1964, pp. 179–85; Schwarz, 1972, pp. 87–100.

62 *Commons' Journals*, xxix (2 and 9 February 1763), pp. 425, 446.

63 George, 1925, ed. 1964, p. 186.

64 Daniel Lysons, *The Environs of London etc*, 4 vols (London, 1792–6), ii, p. 28.

65 George, 1925, ed. 1964, pp. 103–7; Rose, 1951, p. 159.

66 A report of 1817 by the Society for Preventing Contagious Fever, as cited by George, 1925, ed. 1964, p. 192.

67 James Peller Malcolm, *Londinium Redivivum* (1803–7), iii, p. 386.

68 George, 1925, ed. 1964, p. 194.

69 I am grateful to Natalie Rothstein for this point.

70 For an extensive demonstration of the value of inventories in this regard, see Ursula Priestley and P. J. Corfield, 'Rooms and room use in Norwich housing, 1580–1730', *Post-medieval Archaeology*, xvi (1982), pp. 93–123.

71 NA, PROB 3/34/46.

72 NA, PROB 3/39/65.

73 NA, PROB 3/51/5.

74 GL, Sun Fire Insurance policy registers, MS 11936: 253, 377892; 259, 388489; 261, 389095; 285, 430804; 290, 441187; and 303, 462590. THLHL, LT.

75 GL, Sun Fire Insurance policy register, MS 11936: 253, 376260. NMR, GLC Drawings Collection 96/2766.

76 THLHL, copy of NA, HO 107/694, census of 1841.

77 SoL, xxvii, 1957, *passim*; Nikolaus Pevsner, *The Buildings of England: London except [. . .]*, ii (Harmondsworth, 1952), p. 70.

78 THLHL, LT; TH 2891; MDR 1719/6/270–71; 1728/2/181 and 446; 1771/1/20; GL, H-H, MS 8674/20, 38214–16, 3 February 1718/19; MS 8674/21, 39383–4, 40013, 3 September and 29 December 1719; MS 8674/121, 38214, 39383, 16 December 1778; MS 8674/144, 40013, 95811, 97666; MS 8675/3, 97211, 97721; for Nos 7 and 9 Granby Street, see NMR, GLC Drawings Collection 96/3765.

79 SoL, xliii, 1994, pp. 284–6; Colum Giles, 'The historic warehouses of Liverpool', unpublished RCHME report, 1998.

80 Nearby Austin Street had similar houses of similar date. See RCHM(E), v, 1930, p. 9 and investigator's record card in the NMR.

81 THLHL, TH 2906; LT.

82 Information kindly supplied by Andrew Byrne.

83 SoL, xxvii, 1957, p. 276 (demolished).

84 Ibid., p. 82; I am grateful to Dan Cruickshank for having drawn this building to my attention.

85 For case studies, see Julian Harrap, 'Nos 5 and 7 Elder Street', *The Saving of Spitalfields* (London, 1989), pp. 103–15; and (on No. 15 Elder Street) Cruickshank and Burton, 1990, pp. 209–20.

86 There are scattered instances of front staircases from more genteel contexts around eighteenth-century London. Some very substantial Mayfair houses have entrance-hall staircases up to the *piano nobile*. They occur also in some terraces as in Colebrooke Row, Islington, Hammersmith Terrace (fig. 230), Warren Street, Gower Street or on the New Kent Road, Southwark (figs 123 and 134), where desires for unimpeded views from the backs led to the deployment of front staircases. But these higher-status houses do not have winder staircases, nor, except at Hammersmith where the 'backs' facing the river are primary, are the proportions of the fronts compromised. I am grateful to Neil Burton for information about some of these examples.

87 I am grateful to Maryannick Chalabi, Nadine Halitim-Dubois and Olivier Zeller for information about weavers' housing in Lyons.

88 Gavin, 1848, p. 34.

89 SoL, xxvii, 1957, pp. 81–7, 198.

90 Ibid., p. 198.

91 THLHL, TH 2906; LT; LMA, MR/B/R/3, Nos 123–4, 15 June 1778; GL, H-H, MS 8674/121, 82794, 83085; SoL, xxvii, 1957, pp. 111–12.

92 Though probably later, these houses might have been built as early as around 1766 by Samuel Coombes, a Spitalfields carpenter. See MDR 1766/6/183–4, 1766/7/236, 1808/5/780; THLHL, LT; LMA, MR/B/R/1; NA, E140/21/3; VCH, xi, 1998, p. 108.

93 MDR 1719/6/271, 1754/2/299, 1771/6/42–3 and 86, 1776/6/240–41, 1777/5/525, 1779/4/189; THLHL, LT; BG 257; TH 2893 and 2906; copy of NA, HO 107/694, census of 1841; Huguenot Society Publications, xxiii: *The Registers of the French Church, Threadneedle Street, London* (London, 1906), iii, pp. 290, 352, and iv, p. 163; VCH, xi, 1998, pp. 105–6, 160. I am grateful to Jim Howett for drawing the watercolour of 1914 to my attention.

94 NMR, GLC Drawings Collection 96/1886 and 2095; Gavin, 1848, pp. 66–7.

95 *The Builder* (28 January 1871), p. 69.

96 C. C. Knowles and P. H. Pitt, *The History of Building Regulation in London: 1189–1972* (London, 1972), p. 52; 14 Geo. III, cap. 78, section LXX.

97 I am grateful to Dan Cruickshank for sharing his thoughts on this subject.

98 THLHL, BG 257; LT; LPL, MS 27250/15; RCHM(E), v, 1930, p. 9 with investigator's record card in the NMR; LMA, photograph F2307, 1944.

99 It may be doubted that 1778 is the date of its making, but there is separate evidence to indicate that the building is of that date. Further, the plaque shows no signs of having been altered or reset, the second and third numerals are identical and not like the first, and a reading of 1718 makes little sense on a site first developed in 1720.

100 David Garrioch, *Neighbourhood and Community in Paris, 1740–1790* (Cambridge, 1986), pp. 16–55, 205–60; Arlette Farge, *Fragile Lives: Violence, Power and Solidarity in Eighteenth-Century Paris* (Cambridge, 1993), pp. 9–20. For the faubourg Saint-Antoine's dense courts of artisan tenements, see Dominique Hervier, Marie-Agnès Férault and Françoise Boudon, *Le Faubourg Saint-Antoine: Un double visage*, Cahiers du patrimoine no. 51, éditions de l'Inventaire (Paris, 1998). I am grateful to Keith Falconer for this last reference.

101 Farge, 1993, p. 16.

102 Andrew Ballantyne, 'Joseph Gandy and the politics of rustic charm', in Arciszewska and McKellar, eds, *Articulating British Classicism: New approaches to eighteenth-century architecture* (Aldershot, forthcoming). For the very different early nineteenth-century transformation of weavers' housing in Lyons, see Josette Barre, *La Colline de la Croix-Rousse* (Lyons, 2001), pp. 44–78; and Pierre Cayez, *Métiers Jacquard et Hauts Forneaux aux Origines de l'Industrie Lyonnaise* (Lyons, 1978)

4 ACROSS LONDON BRIDGE

1 *Aesop's Fables*, trans. V. S. Vernon Jones (London, 1912, ed. 1979), p. 89.

2 John Gwynn, *London and Westminster Improved* (London, 1766), p. 8.

3 For the history of medieval Southwark up to the mid-sixteenth century, see Martha Carlin, *Medieval Southwark* (London, 1996). The story is taken on a century, with the focus on Southwark's people, in Jeremy Boulton, *Neighbourhood and Society: A London suburb in the seventeenth century* (Cambridge, 1987). There has been no synthetic history of eighteenth-century Southwark, though the Survey of London has published volumes on Bankside, the South Bank and St George's Fields. See SoL, xxii, 1950; SoL, xxiii, 1951; and SoL, xxv, 1955. See also VCH, ii, 1905, and iv, 1912.

4 Daniel Defoe, *A Tour through the Whole Island of Great Britain* [1724–6], ed. Pat Rogers (London, 1971), p. 178.

5 Boulton, 1987, pp. 19–21; M. Dorothy George, *London Life in the Eighteenth Century* [1925], reprint (New York, 1964), p. 414; E. Anthony Wrigley, 'Urban growth and agricultural change: England and the Continent in the early modern period', in Borsay, ed., 1990, p. 42.

6 Carlin, 1996, p. 254.

7 Ibid., pp. 53, 186; Boulton, 1987, pp. 71–3, 97, 153, 184–7,

204; VCH, iv, 1912, pp. 128–9; David J. Johnson, *Southwark and the City* (Oxford, 1969), pp. 305–17.

8 SoL, xxii, 1950, and xxv (1955); Carlin, 1996, pp. 19, 22, 255; Boulton, 1987, pp. 167, 193–4.

9 Boulton, 1987, pp. 85, 115, 172–4, 192; see also Carlin, 1996, pp. 58–9, 254; VCH, iv, 1912, p. 128; George, 1925, ed. 1964, p. 346.

10 VCH, iv, 1912, pp. 133–4; George, 1925, ed. 1964, p. 75; Leonard Reilly and Geoff Marshall, *The Story of Bankside: From the River Thames to St George's Circus* (London, 2001), pp. 13–32.

11 Boulton, 1987, pp. 179–82, 194–219; Montague S. Giuseppi, 'The parliamentary surveys relating to Southwark', *Surrey Archaeological Collections*, xiv (1899), pp. 42–71; VCH, iv, 1912, p. 144.

12 Stephen Porter, *The Great Fire of London* (Stroud, 1996), p. 155; Leonard Reilly, *Southwark: An illustrated history* (London, 1998), p. 15.

13 See chapter 1, n. 69, and SoL, xxii, 1950, pp. 79, 93, 101–4; Robert Wilkinson, *Londina illustrata*, 2 vols (London, 1819–25), i, pp. 135–9.

14 SoL, xxiii, 1951, p. 78; Graham Gibberd, *On Lambeth Marsh: The South Bank and Waterloo* (London, 1992). For Lambeth, the early housing of which riverside settlement has left no standing trace (fig. 234), see VCH, iv, 1912, pp. 50–64; SoL, xxiii, 1951; and Stephen Croad, *Liquid History: the Thames through time* (London, 2003), pp. 77-85.

15 John Strype, *A Survey of the Cities of London and Westminster, etc* (London, 1720), book iv, p. 27.

16 Reilly and Marshall, 2001, pp. 48–51; Peter Thorold, *The London Rich: The creation of a great city, from 1666 to the present* (London, 1999), pp. 102–8.

17 Carlin, 1996, pp. 119–27, 256; see also Johnson, 1969, p. 317; Francis Sheppard, *London: A history* (Oxford, 1998), pp. 114, 188, 191.

18 Boulton, 1987, pp. 98, 227–31, 262–74, 291–4.

19 This account of Bermondsey and subsequent interpretations of houses are heavily dependent on 'Georgian Bermondsey', an unpublished EH Architectural Investigation report, researched and written by Joanna Smith in 2001.

20 VCH, iv, 1912, pp. 84–5.

21 Strype, 1720, iv, p. 5.

22 Carlin, 1996, pp. 31, 47.

23 Ibid., pp. 44–5, 178, 185–6; VCH, ii, 1905, pp. 330–41; VCH, iv, 1912, p. 18.

24 BL, Add. MS 35684, f. 24, anonymous undated letter (*c.*1755) in Sheldon Papers, ii, papers relating to Thomas Steavons.

25 Daniel Lysons, *The Environs of London, etc*, 4 vols (London, 1792–6), i, p. 547.

26 Reilly, 1998, p. 28.

27 John Burridge, *The Tanner's Key to a New System of Tanning Sole Leather* (London, 1824), as quoted by R. J. Hartlidge, 'The development of industries in London south of the Thames 1750 to 1850', thesis, University of London, 1955, unpaginated.

28 BL, MS Egerton Charter 325–6.

29 As cited by Hartlidge, 1955.

30 NA, PROB 3/20/213 and 3/38/23.

31 As quoted by Eileen Yeo and Edward P. Thompson, *The Unknown Mayhew* (New York, 1971), p. 452.

32 Thomas Pennant, *Some Account of London* (London, 2/1791), pp. 56–7.

33 VCH, ii, 1905, pp. 359–63; David R. Green, *From Artisans to Paupers* (Aldershot, 1995), p. 130.

34 NA, PROB 3/34/9.

35 George, 1925, ed. 1964, p. 414.

36 James West (1703–72) inherited the estate through marriage to Sarah Steavons, who held it until her death in 1799 (SLSL, West papers).

37 SoL, xxii, 1950, pp. 31–3.

38 This radical and secretive sect scorned permanent places of worship, but had a vigorous publishing policy, its small membership consisting almost entirely of tradespeople, many of them women. See Christopher Hill, Barry Reay and William Lamont, *The World of the Muggletonians* (London, 1983).

39 VCH, ii, 1905, p. 19; Walter Wilson, *The History and Antiquities of Dissenting Churches and Meeting Houses*, 4 vols (London, 1808–14), iv, pp. 279, 285.

40 VCH, iv, 1912, p. 86.

41 These houses were all cleared in the twentieth century.

42 Donald Murray Connan, *History of the Public Health Department in Bermondsey* (London, 1935), pp. 58–9; Neil Jackson, 'Built to sell', in Colin Cunningham and James Anderson, ed., *The Hidden Iceberg of Architectural History*, Papers from the Annual Symposium of the Society of Architectural Historians of Great Britain (London, 1998), p. 89.

43 Lysons, 1792–6, i, p. 547.

44 Frank Keyse, *Thomas Keyse and the Bermondsey Spa* (Aberystwyth, 1986).

45 G. W. Phillips, *The History and Antiquities of the Parish of Bermondsey* (London, 1841), p. 47.

46 Charles Dickens, *Oliver Twist* [1837–9], reprint (London, 1994), p. 468.

47 Ibid., p. 469; see also Thomas Beames, *The Rookeries of London: Past, present and prospective* (London, 1850), pp. 85–102; *The Builder* (21 April 1855), p. 183; Matthew Hillier, 'A history of Jacob's Island', typescript, SLSL, 1997, unpaginated.

48 Schnebbelie's original watercolour is in the Guildhall Library, London, as are several watercolours of 1828 by J. C. Buckler that show Jacob's Island in a relatively attractive light.

49 GL, MS 11,936/224–5; RCHM(E), v, 1930, p. 8; SLSL, Hillier, 1997, *passim*.

50 F.B., 'The autobiography of a Bermondsey boy', in Sidney Gutman, ed., *Seven Years' Harvest: An anthology of the Bermondsey Book 1923–1930* (London, 1934), p. 305.

51 VCH, iv, 1912, pp. 144–5; SoL, xxv, 1955, p. 24.

52 *The Builder* (29 October 1853), p. 661; SoL, xxv, 1955, pp. 22–5; BL, Crace Views, 34/73; Peter Marcan, *Visions of Southwark* (London, 1997), p. 84.

53 Kevin Wooldridge, 'The archaeology of 151–153 Bermondsey Street, London', Pre-Construct Archaeology, pre-publication typescript, 2002; BL, Add MS 24433/163, drawing by J. C. Buckler, 29 June 1820.

54 *The Builder* (29 October 1853), pp. 673–5; J. F. C. Phillips, *Shepherd's London* (London, 1976), pp. 84–5.

55 Strype, 1720, iv, p. 28.

56 Peter Earle, *A City Full of People* (London, 1994), p. 11.

57 RCHM(E), v, 1930, p. 68, and investigator's card in the NMR; SoL, xxii, 1950, pp. 125–6, and SoL survey notes in the NMR. Lean-to rear outshuts and ground-floor partitions have been interpreted as additions.

58 See J. P. Emslie's drawing of Queen's Court (latterly Lafone Street), reproduced in Peter Marcan, *Bermondsey and Rotherhithe Perceived* (London, 1998), p. 88; *The Builder* (7 August 1858), pp. 530–31; NMR, Gerald Cobb Collection, engraving of Long Lane, BB99/06771; RCHM(E), v, 1930, p. 8; LMA, photographs.

59 The adjoining building at No. 78 has seventeenth-century origins, but it has been rebuilt since the eighteenth century, and raised with a boarded leatherworking loft.

60 SLSL, RB (St Mary Magdalene, Bermondsey, Poor Rates).

61 SLSL, RB; GL, MS 11936/263.

62 Strype, 1720, iv, p. 28.

63 SoL, xxii, 1950, p. 81.

64 NMR, GLC Drawings Collection 96/2309; LMA, photographs.

65 SLSL, West Estate papers, box 37, sales particulars, 1821; RCHM(E), v, 1930, p. 7.

66 It stood until around 1960. See B. H. St. J. O'Neil, 'Bridge House, 64 George Row, Bermondsey', *Antiquaries Journal*, xxxii (1952), pp. 192–7; RCHM(E), v, 1930, p. 8; NMR, reference collection; SLSL, Hillier, 1997.

67 LMA, photographs.

68 Connan, 1935, p. 55.

69 NMR, measured drawing 1946/20 and reference collection; GLC Drawings Collection 96/1452–5, 2718, 3320–22, 3389, 4705, 7579; LMA, photographs.

70 SoL, xxii, 1950, pp. 111–12; RCHM(E), v, 1930, p. 68.

71 Gibberd, 1992, pp. 2 and 5.

72 SoL, xxii, 1950, pp. 22–3, and SoL survey notes in the NMR.

73 Dan Cruickshank and Neil Burton, *Life in the Georgian City* (London, 1990), pp. 72–3.

74 John Schofield, ed., 1987, *The London Surveys of Ralph Treswell* (London, 1987), pp. 138–9.

75 Wooldridge, 2002, pp. 5–7.

76 BL, Egerton Charter 325–6. I am grateful to Malcolm Airs and Frank Kelsall for bringing these documents to my attention.

77 See n. 69 above.

78 LMA, HI/ST/E67/39/14. There were other mid- to late eighteenth-century central-chimneystack-plan houses on Grange Walk and on Newington Butts (NMR, reference collection).

79 SoL, xxii, 1950, pp. 9–30; RCHM(E), v, 1930, p. 68; NMR, GLC Drawings Collection 96/1673 and 1681; EH, London historical research file, Southwark 3.

80 SoL, xxii, 1950, pp. 61–2; NMR, GLC Drawings Collection 96/7557.

81 SoL, xxii, 1950, p. 92; RCHM(E), v, 1930, p. 68; NMR, GLC Drawings Collection, 96/3637; R. Meischke *et al.*, *Huizen in Nederland: Amsterdam* (Amsterdam, 1995), pp. 177–300.

82 SLSL, West Estate papers, box 37, sales particulars, 1821.

83 NMR, GLC Drawings Collection 96/7540.

84 NMR, GLC Drawings Collection 96/3389, 4705.

85 It is unclear whether the back room was originally heated from the central stack, or from a party-wall stack that may be an alteration. The builder and first occupants remain unknown, but from 1777 Gabriel Arnold Rogers, a bricklayer, was resident at No. 21 or the house adjoining to the south. He was involved with house-building in Walworth, and may have been a builder here. See SLSL, RB; SLSL photographs; GL, Sun Fire Insurance policy registers, MS 11936/254, 274, 298, 303, 336; LMA, photographs.

86 SoL, xxv, 1955, p. 49.

87 Defoe, 1724–6, ed. 1971, p. 287.

88 SoL, xxv, 1955, pp. 11–13, 39–41, 49, 52–3; Reilly and Marshall, 2001, p. 36.

89 Gwynn, 1766, p. 10.

90 A contemporary description quoted in SoL, xxv, 1955, p. 42.

91 Ibid., pp. 41–4.

92 Crosby was a popular reformer who had refused to back Press Warrants in 1770 and who was imprisoned for printing parliamentary debates in 1771. Bridge, road and obelisk had all been the responsibility of Robert Mylne, who won a competition, in preference to Gwynn among others, to become surveyor to the Blackfriars Bridge Committee. See *DNB*; John Summerson, *Georgian London* [1945], ed. Howard Colvin (London, 2003), pp. 121–3, 328–9; Roger Woodley, '"A very mortifying situation": Robert Mylne's struggle to get paid for Blackfriars Bridge', *Architectural History*, xliii (2000), pp. 172–86.

93 SoL, xxv, 1955, p. 45.

94 Ibid., p. 52.

95 Carlin, 1996, note 6.

96 SoL, xxiii, 1951, pp. 72–3; VCH, iv, 1912, p. 64; Gibberd, 1992, pp. 38, 130–31; Michael Phillips, 'Reconstructing William Blake's lost studio: No. 13 Hercules Buildings, Lambeth', *British Art Journal*, ii/1 (2000), p. 45.

97 SoL, xxv, 1955, pp. 66–8; Miles Ogborn, *Spaces of Modernity* (London, 1998), pp. 39–74; Howard M. Colvin, *A Biographical Dictionary of British Architects 1600–1840* (London, 3/1995), p. 548.

98 The Gordon Riots continued longest in Bermondsey, where 'Catholic' houses on East Lane were destroyed. John Fielding's house was among those attacked elsewhere. See George Rudé, *Hanoverian London 1714–1808* (London, 1971), pp. 224–6; Peter Linebaugh, *The London Hanged* (London, 1991), pp. 333–70; SoL, xxv, 1955, pp. 19–20; Reilly and Marshall, 2001, pp. 35–40, 66–71.

99 SoL, xxv, 1955, pp. 52–4; George, 1925, ed. 1964, p. 81; Reilly and Marshall, 2001, pp. 42–6; CLRO, 47.A.3,

Plan of the City's Estate, St George's Field, 1788; OS, 1872.

100 Timothy Shaw, 'A blaze for the London mob: The burning of the Albion Mills', *Country Life* (29 December 1966), pp. 1722–4; A. W. Skempton, 'Samuel Wyatt and the Albion Mill', *Architectural History*, xiv (1971), pp. 53–73. For an incisive analysis of Collings's etching (fig. 132), see B. E. Maidment, *Reading Popular Prints, 1790–1870* (Manchester, 1996), pp. 27–52.

101 SLSL, RB; SLSL, West Estate papers, sales particulars, 1879; survey of estate, 1819; NA, IR 58/78037. Access to the interiors has not been possible.

102 SLSL, West Estate papers, box 38.

103 SoL, xxv, 1955, pp. 117–19. I am grateful to Gary Elliott of the Elliott Wood Partnership for permitting adaptive re-use of his survey plan.

104 One of those given building leases at West Square was James Hedger, evidently capable of upping his game where circumstances dictated. See SoL, xxv, 1955, p. 63.

105 Ibid., pp. 20–21, 68–70, 76–8; VCH, iv, 1912, p. 162; Malcolm Seaborne, *The English School: Its architecture and organization, 1370–1870* (London, 1971), pp. 136–42; Dell Upton, 'Lancasterian schools, republican citizenship, and the spatial imagination in early nineteenth-century America', *Journal of the Society of Architectural Historians*, lv/3 (1996), pp. 238–51.

106 Documentation of Hercules Buildings provides no clear evidence of the build date. See SoL, xxiii, 1951, p. 72 and SoL notes in the NMR; Robin Hamlyn and Michael Phillips, eds, *William Blake* (Norwich, 2000), pp. 98–102, 144–5, 152–4; Phillips, 2000, pp. 43–8; Edward P. Thompson, *Witness against the Beast: William Blake and the moral law* (New York, 1994); Kathleen Raine, *William Blake's Fourfold London* (London, 1993).

107 David V. Erdman, *Blake: Prophet against Empire* (New York, 3/1977), p. 289. It was in a local tavern that Colonel Edward Despard was arrested in 1802 at a meeting of some forty artisans and labourers attempting to organise a revolutionary republican army. See Peter Linebaugh and Marcus Rediker, *The Many-headed Hydra: Sailors, slaves, commoners and the hidden history of the revolutionary Atlantic* (London, 2000), pp. 248–76.

108 Phillips, 2000, p. 43.

109 William Blake, 'London', *Songs of Experience* (London, 1794), plate 46.

5 WASTE AND PLACE

1 Louis Simond, *An American in Regency England: The journal of a tour in 1810–1811*, ed. Christopher Hibbert (London, 1968), p. 143.

2 *Proposals for Establishing a Charitable Fund in the City of London* (1706), as quoted by M. Dorothy George, *London Life in the Eighteenth Century* [1925], reprint (New York, 1964), p. 97.

3 George, 1925, ed. 1964, p. 97.

4 Among the definitions of 'waste' in *The Shorter Oxford English Dictionary* is: 'A piece of land not cultivated or

used for any purpose, and producing little or no herbage or wood. In legal use [specifically] a piece of such land not in any man's occupation, but lying common.'

5 John Strype, *A Survey of the Cities of London and Westminster, etc* (London, 1720), iv, p. 47.

6 John Stow, *A Survey of London* [1598], ed. Charles Lethbridge Kingsford, 2 vols (London, 1908), ii, p. 72; see also Holinshed's *Chronicle* (1587), as quoted by George, 1925, ed. 1964, p. 72.

7 *The Builder* (17 September 1859), p. 609.

8 SoL, xxvii, 1957.

9 The surviving fragments of the green, extending southeast towards the parish church, were designated Stepney Green by the end of the eighteenth century. The account of Mile End Old Town here owes a great deal to Isobel Watson and to Derek Morris. See Isobel Watson, 'From West Heath to Stepney Green: Building development in Mile End Old Town, 1660–1820', *London Topographical Record*, xxvii (1995), pp. 231–56, and Derek Morris, *Mile End Old Town 1740–1780: A social history of an early modern suburb*, East London History Society (London, 2002), as well as unpublished work by the latter. For No. 131 Mile End Road, see RCHM(E), v, 1930, p. 98, and investigators' record cards in the NMR; NMR, GLC Drawings Collection 96/7412–5 and reference collection.

10 Robert Brenner, *Merchants and Revolution: Commercial change, political conflict, and London's overseas traders, 1550–1653* (Cambridge, 1993), p. 115.

11 Watson, 1995, pp. 235–42; RCHM(E), v, 1930, pp. 98–9; G. W. Hill and W. H. Frere, ed., *Memorials of Stepney Parish* (Guildford, 1891), p. 189; the NMR, GLC Drawings Collection 96/1323. For the younger Arnold Browne's unsuccessful career as a property speculator and associate of Nicholas Barbon, see Elizabeth McKellar, *The Birth of Modern London* (Manchester, 1999a), pp. 67–8.

12 Watson, 1995, pp. 238–44; RCHM(E), v, 1930, p. 98, and investigator's record card in the NMR; LMA, photograph 72355.

13 Information kindly supplied by Sharman Kadish; see Bernard Susser, ed., *Alderney Road Jewish Cemetery: London E1, 1697–1953* (London, 1997); Morris, 2002, p. 60.

14 Derek Morris, 'Fitzhugh House, Mile End Old Town, Stepney 1738–1849', *London Topographical Society Newsletter* (May 1999), pp. 10–11.

15 Watson, 1995, p. 244; information kindly supplied by the Spitalfields Trust, including plans by Gus Alexander, architects, 1990.

16 EH, London historical research file, Tower Hamlets 98; Watson, 1995, p. 249; Morris, 2002, p. 15; information, including unpublished research by Isobel Watson, kindly supplied by the Spitalfields Trust, Todd Longstaffe-Gowan and Tim Knox.

17 There are other much less regular early eighteenth-century survivors at Nos 29–35 Stepney Green. For Roland House, No. 29 Stepney Green, see Watson, 1995, pp. 244–5, and NMR, RCHM(E) Measured Drawings 1947/436.

18 RCHM(E), v, 1930, p. 99, and investigator's record card in the NMR. No. 19 Redman's Road may be a larger survivor from the east end of this group, a three-storey house with a narrow window bay over its entrance, perhaps indicating a front-staircase layout.

19 Watson, 1995, pp. 250–51; Morris, 2002, pp. 14–15 and 99.

20 Watson, 1995, pp. 232–4, 248–51; Morris, 2002, p. 43.

21 Watson, 1995, pp. 248–51; Morris, 2002, p. 15.

22 The Assembly Room perhaps stood over stabling, and there was a bowling green adjoining. See Watson, 1995, p. 238; Morris, 2002, p. 95.

23 The specifics of construction dates, early occupancy and other details in this and the following paragraphs on Assembly Row are taken from a database compiled by Derek Morris and based on his research into land tax assessments, the MDR, insurance registers and other sources. See Derek Morris, 'Land tax assessments for Mile End Old Town, 1741–90', *London Topographical Society Newsletter* (November 2000), pp. 5–7, and Morris, 2002, pp. 15 and 16.

24 A third similar house at No. 80 was demolished in the late twentieth century. Department of the Environment, List of Buildings of Special Architectural or Historic Interest, 1973.

25 The front building has been replaced, but the site including the yard behind continued as the Curtis Distillery Company Ltd until 1958. Watson, 1995, p. 249; Tom Ridge, 'Central Stepney History Walk', typescript, THLHL, 1998.

26 NMR, GLC Drawings Collection 96/3168.

27 *DNB*.

28 The chimneystack was removed some time after 1983. See LMA, photograph 83/3348. Inspection of the interior of No. 96 has not been possible.

29 Watson, 1995, pp. 249–50; Morris, 2002, p. 15.

30 Morris, 2002, p. 13.

31 Ibid., pp. 96–7.

32 Watson, 1995, pp. 250–52.

33 This account of Kingsland Road is based on an EH survey report of 1999; for a short version, see Peter Guillery, 'Waste and Place: Late-18th-century development on Kingsland Road', *Hackney History*, vi (2000), pp. 19–38. For the road's broader history, see 'Panorama – Kingsland Road', a guide and CD-ROM produced in 2001 by Hackney Building Exploratory.

34 Daniel Defoe, *A Tour through the Whole Island of Great Britain* [1724–6], ed. Pat Rogers (London, 1971), p. 438.

35 VCH, x, 1995, pp. 4–5; David Mander, 'One for the roads: Highways in Hackney before 1872', *Hackney History*, ii (1996b), pp. 9–16.

36 VCH, x, 1995, p. 12; David Mander, ed., *The London Borough of Hackney in Old Photographs* (Gloucester, 1989); Chris Miele, 'From aristocratic ideal to middle-class idyll: 1690–1840', in Saint, intr., 1999, pp. 35–6.

37 Robert Wilkinson, *Londina illustrata*, 2 vols (London, 1819–25), i, pp. 123–4.

38 As quoted in VCH, x, 1995, p. 96; Thomas Milne, *Land Use Map of London and Environs in 1800*, London

Topographical Society, Nos 118 and 119 (London, 1975–6).

39 Alan Cox, 'A vital component: Stock bricks in Georgian London', *Construction History*, xiii (1997), pp. 57–66; Linda Clarke, *Building Capitalism* (London, 1992), pp. 94–101.

40 George, 1925, ed. 1964, p. 97.

41 VCH, x, 1995, pp. 13, 28–30, 96; 8 Geo. III c.33; David Mander, *More Light, More Power: An illustrated history of Shoreditch* (London, 1996a), pp. 52–3.

42 HAD, M515; RB/LT (Poor Rate and Land Tax Assessment Books, St John, Hackney); MDR 1774/3/36, 1774/4/150, 1775/2/219; VCH, x, 1995, p. 40; SBH, Journal 1757–70, HA 1/13, 305.

43 MDR 1774/3/36; 1774/4/151; 1775/2/193 and 219; HAD, D/F/TYS/66; VCH, x, 1995, pp. 30, 75–6, 88.

44 MDR 1775/2/220, 1776/4/433, 1779/3/237, 1779/5/88, 1780/2/391–3; SoL, xl, 1980, pp. 173, 318; SoL, xxxii, 1963, p. 368.

45 MDR 1785/2/180; SoL, xxiv, 1952, p. 31; SoL, xxxiv, 1966, p. 393; Howard M. Colvin, *A Biographical Dictionary of British Architects 1600–1840* (London, 3/1995), p. 1002.

46 Francis Sheppard, Victor Belcher and Philip Cottrell, 'The Middlesex and Yorkshire Deeds Registries and the study of building fluctuations', *London Journal*, v/2 (1979), pp. 176–217.

47 HAD, RB/LT; Dan Cruickshank and Neil Burton, *Life in the Georgian City* (London, 1990), p. 15; Henry Mayhew, 'Of the dustmen of London', in *London Labour and the London Poor* [1850], Victor Neuburg, ed. (Harmondsworth), 1985, pp. 218–29; Cox, 1997, pp. 57–66.

48 HAD, RB/LT; MDR 1775/2/219, 1776/4/433, 1779/3/240–41, 1779/5/88; GL, MS 11936/273, Sun Fire Insurance policy register 410910, 9 March 1779; HAD, Starling's *Map of the Parish of St John, Hackney*, 1831; West Hackney Tithe Map, 1843.

49 HAD, RB/LT; MDR, 1775/5/482, 1779/3/238–9, 1785/2/180; LMA, MR/B/R/3, Register of Surveyors' Affidavits and Certificates, 1776–84, Nos 155–7, 14 September 1779; HAD, D/F/TYS/66.

50 HAD, RB/LT; MDR 1774/4/150–51; 1778/5/159; 1779/2/442.

51 Mary Thale, ed., *The Autobiography of Francis Place 1771–1854* (Cambridge, 1972), pp. 22–34.

52 With apologies to Isobel Watson; see her *Gentlemen in the Building Line: The development of South Hackney* (London, 1989).

53 HAD, RB/LT; HAD, P/J/MISC/II, 1811.

54 Examples stood at Nos 75–83 and 167–223 Hoxton Street; see HAD, P 6525; EH, London historical research file, Hackney 5; NMR, GLC Drawings Collection 96/8304; LMA photographs.

55 SBH, Journal 1757–70, HA 1/13, pp. 179, 194–5, 200, 206, 501, 528, 601; Journal 1770–86, HA 1/14, pp. 76, 301; SBH, Deeds 2521, 2974.

56 Colvin, 3/1995, p. 1106; SoL, xxii, 1950, p. 65.

57 Marcus Binney, *Sir Robert Taylor: From Rococo to Neo-*

Classicism (London, 1984), pp. 61–2, 71, 79; SoL, xxix, 1960, p. 164; SoL, xxxii, 1963, p. 369; SoL, Clerkenwell North, forthcoming.

58 SBH Deeds, 2521, 2539, 2602, 2640–42, 2974; SoL, xxxvii, 1973, p. 60; SoL, xliv, 1994, pp. 656, 659.

59 SBH, Deeds, as in n. 58.

60 Ibid. For forecourt gardens on main roads, see Todd Longstaffe-Gowan, *The London Town Garden, 1700–1840* (London, 2001), pp. 58–63.

61 As early as Kingsland Place are Nos 123–33 Kennington Road of 1773–5, which lacked coach-houses, having linked two-storey entrance bays. See Miele, 1999, pp. 48–9.

62 Saint, intr., *London Suburbs* (London, 1999), p. 15.

63 Colvin, 3/1995, pp. 288–92.

64 John Summerson, 'The beginnings of an early Victorian suburb', *London Topographical Record*, xxvii (1995), pp. 1–48.

65 A bricklayer with this name was involved with the Adelphi Theatre in the early nineteenth century. See SoL, xxxvi, 1970, p. 245.

66 The Lamb Inn shifted around in the eighteenth century. After 1746 it moved back from the road to a property in Upsdell's brickfields, moving again around 1790 to a new building at No. 512 Kingsland Road, having been displaced by a new farmhouse in 1787–9 (fig. 150). The building of the latter is a reminder that even in the late 1780s urban encroachment was not considered imminent: the farmhouse remained surrounded by fields until the 1820s. See MDR 1794/3/501–2, 1805/5/121, 1808/2/670; HAD, RB/LT; HAD, D/F/TYS/66; D/F/RHO/8; estate map, c.1821; VCH, 1995, pp. 88–9.

67 For example Nos 169–83 Stoke Newington Church Street of 1714 and Nos 808 and 810 Tottenham High Road of around 1720.

68 On attitudes to views, prospects and aspects, front and back, see Longstaffe-Gowan, 2001, pp. 63–72.

69 An outbuilding attached to No. 480 is identified as a chaise house, but not before the 1820s, and there was no equivalent for No. 478 (fig. 155). It may have been more like the stable that adjoined Summers's house on the waste than like the two-storey coach-houses of Kingsland Place. See HAD, RB/LT; HAD, D/F/TYS/66.

70 HAD, RB/LT; HAD, M1137–8, D/F/TYS/66, P/J/MISC/II, 1811; MDR, 1794/3/501–2; 1794/4/615.

71 HAD, M4267/8; MDR 1792/8/544.

72 HAD, M1139; MDR 1808/3/24; Colvin, 3/1995, pp. 216–17; NMR, reference collection B43/812. SoL, Clerkenwell South, forthcoming.

73 HAD, P/J/MISC/II; OS, 1914.

74 HAD, RB/LT; MDR, 1806/4/144–5, 1806/8/256, 1807/1/8, 1807/2/532–4, 1808/4/40, 1809/6/731; HAD, M403, P/J/MISC/I and II, 1811.

75 VCH, x, 1995, pp. 14, 85; HAD, estate map, c.1821.

76 Sheppard, Belcher and Cottrell, 1979, pp. 182–93.

77 John Gwynn, *London and Westminster Improved* (London, 1766), pp. x and 14.

6 THE MILITARY-INDUSTRIAL SATELLITE

1 Edward [Ned] Ward, *A Frolick to Horn-Fair: With a walk from Cuckold's-point thro' Deptford and Greenwich* (London, 1700), pp. 13–14.

2 Daniel Defoe, *A Tour thro' London about the Year 1725*, ed. Mayson M. Beeton and E. Beresford Chancellor (London, 1929), p. 3.

3 The discussion of Deptford here is largely derived from 'Deptford houses: 1650 to 1800', an RCHME report of 1998, based on a survey in which Bernard Herman of the University of Delaware was a partner. A shortened version of this report has been published. See Peter Guillery and Bernard Herman, 'Deptford houses: 1650 to 1800', *Vernacular Architecture*, xxx (1999), pp. 58–84.

4 For an authoritative summary of the early history of Deptford, see Christopher Phillpotts, 'Deptford Creek: Archaeological desk-based assessment', report for the London Borough of Lewisham, Creekside Project, August 1997.

5 BL, Evelyn Papers, Map of Deptford in 1623, as copied and annotated by John Evelyn, *c*.1703.

6 Duncan Harrington, ed., *Kent Hearth Tax Assessment, Lady Day 1664*, British Record Society, Hearth Tax Series II (London, 2000), pp. xxx–xxxii; C. W. Chalklin, 'The towns', in Alan Armstrong, ed., *The Economy of Kent, 1640–1914* (Woodbridge, 1995), Appendix IIIA; B. R. Leftwich, 'The parish of St Nicholas, Deptford', *Ecclesiological Society Transactions*, i/4 (1941), p. 224; E. Anthony Wrigley, 'Urban growth and agricultural change', in Borsay, ed., 1990, p. 42; Freda Neale, 'Deptford 1745', typescript, LLSA, 1992, unpaginated; Daniel Lysons, *The Environs of London etc*, i/2 (London, 2/1811), p. 458.

7 Ward, 1700, pp. 14–15.

8 M. Oppenheim, 'Maritime history', in VCH, ii, 1926, pp. 340–78; Philip MacDougall, 'The Royal Dockyards of Woolwich and Deptford', in Robert Carr, ed., *Dockland: An illustrated historical survey of life and work in east London* (London, 1986), p. 125; Neale, 1992.

9 Daniel Defoe, *A Tour through the Whole Island of Great Britain* [1724–6], ed. Pat Rogers (London, 1971), p. 294.

10 Harrington, ed., 2000, pp. xxx–xxxii; Chalklin, in Armstrong, ed., 1995, Appendix IIIA; Michael Egan, 'The population of Greenwich in the seventeenth century', *Journal of the Greenwich Historical Society*, ii/3 (2000), pp. 83–8; Daniel Lysons, *The Environs of London etc* (London, 2/1811), i/2, pp. 532–3.

11 John Bold *et al.*, *Greenwich: An architectural history of the Royal Hospital for Seamen and the Queen's House* (London, 2000).

12 Ward, 1700, p. 15.

13 Defoe, 1724–6, ed. 1971, p. 114.

14 Bold *et al.*, 2000, pp. 24–5; M. Dorothy George, *London Life in the Eighteenth Century* [1925], reprint (New York, 1964), p. 170.

15 Bold *et al.*, 2000, pp. 105, 187–93, 207–14; Neil Rhind, 'Joseph Kay: An architect for Greenwich', *Journal of the Greenwich Historical Society*, i/6 (1997), pp. 180–99; Joanna Smith, 'Completing Greenwich Hospital: Joseph Kay, E. H. Locker, and "the general plan of improvements"', *Journal of the Greenwich Historical Society*, ii/4 (2001), pp. 109–19; Joanna Smith, 'Moving statues and Maritime Greenwich', *Journal of the Greenwich Historical Society*, ii/5 (2002), pp. 136–45.

16 Mary Mills, *Greenwich Marsh: The 300 Years before the Dome* (London, 1999), pp. 17–41.

17 O. F. G. Hogg, *The Royal Arsenal: Its background, origin and subsequent history* (London, 1963).

18 Harrington, ed., 2000, pp. xxx–xxxii; Lysons, 2/1811, i/2, p. 592.

19 Defoe, 1724–6, ed. 1971, p. 116.

20 VCH, ii, 1926, pp. 367–78; MacDougall, 1986, p. 125.

21 Harrington, ed., 2000, pp. xxx–lvi, xciii–cii.

22 Immigration was not only from the countryside. The wider area's overseas immigrants included many Huguenots, many Irish, and some of African origin who had escaped slavery. Two of the latter gained subsequent renown. Olaudah Equiano (1745–97) lived on Maze Hill, and Ignatius Sancho (1729–80) was brought up as a servant at Montague House near the south-west corner of Greenwich Park. See Olaudah Equiano, *The Interesting Narrative of the Life of Olaudah Equiano, or Gustavus Vassa the African* (London, 1789); and Ignatius Sancho, *Letters of the Late Ignatius Sancho* (London, 1782).

23 I am grateful to Julian Watson for this point.

24 GLHL, View of Woolwich in 1662 by Jonas Moore, engr. C. Matthews, 1842; John Barker, 'An accurate plan of the town of Woolwich, etc', 1749.

25 Jonathan G. Coad, *The Royal Dockyards, 1690–1850* (London, 1989); VCH, ii, 1926, pp. 340–78; MacDougall, 1986, pp. 111–26.

26 David Esterly, *Grinling Gibbons and the Art of Carving* (London, 1998), pp. 16–34. In 1698 Tsar Peter the Great stayed at (and famously trashed) Sayes Court, while learning about shipbuilding. See also NMM, Van de Velde drawings, 2 vols; Brian Lavery and Simon Stephens, *Ships' Models* (London, 1995).

27 This can be seen in the ship models on display at the NMM, Greenwich, as well as in exhibits at Chatham and Portsmouth dockyards.

28 VCH, ii, 1926, pp. 340–78; Roger Knight, 'From impressment to task work: Strikes and disruption in the Royal Dockyards, 1688–1788', in Kenneth Lunn and Ann Day, eds, *History of Work and Labour Relations in the Royal Dockyards* (London, 1999), pp. 1–20; Roger Morriss, *The Royal Dockyards during the Revolutionary and Napoleonic Wars* (Leicester, 1983), pp. 99, 101, 108; Peter Linebaugh, *The London Hanged* (London, 1991), pp. 374–6, 381.

29 Knight, 1999, p. 4; LLSA, A85/4.

30 William Sutherland, *The Ship-builder's Assistant* (London, 1711), p. 64. I am grateful to Ann Coats for information about dockyard-town interchange, with particular reference to Portsmouth. For an unusually well-documented example of skills transfer, also significant as an instance of emigration to America by an early eighteenth-century dockyard artisan, a well-trodden path, see John B. Wastrom, 'John Drew's Memorandum Book

31 (1707–1722): The artisan intellectual and the rise of the Renaissance architectural style in New England', MA thesis, Boston University, 1996. I am grateful to Bernard Herman for this reference; see also Knight, 1999, p. 5.

31 VCH, ii, 1926, p. 340–78; Knight, 1999, pp. 6–13; Linebaugh, 1991, p. 381; Philip Banbury, *Shipbuilders of the Thames and Medway* (Newton Abbot, 1971), pp. 52, 74.

32 Sophie von la Roche, *Sophie in London, 1786: Being the Diary of Sophie von la Roche*, trans. Clare Williams (London, 1933), p. 253.

33 The reported presence of Thomas Paine (1737–1809), the author of *Rights of Man*, as the keeper of a stay-maker's shop on Woolwich High Street in 1757–8 or 1766–7 is an anecdotal reflection of local radicalism, even if apocryphal. See BL, 'A collection of prints chiefly relating to Deptford, Greenwich and Woolwich', cutting No. 14, 1833; *DNB*.

34 Samuel, younger brother of Jeremy Bentham, had been an apprentice shipwright at Woolwich from 1770. Unsuccessful as a practitioner, he went abroad and became a manager of a dockyard in Russia. See Ian R. Christie, *The Benthams in Russia, 1780–1791* (Oxford, 1993); Coad, 1989, pp. 29–33; Roger Morriss, 'Samuel Bentham and the management of the Royal Dockyards, 1796–1807', *Bulletin of the Institute of Historical Research*, liv/130 (November 1981), pp.226-40; VCH, ii, 1926, pp. 340–78; Linebaugh, 1991, pp. 371–401; Carolyn C. Cooper, 'The Portsmouth System of Manufacture', *Technology and Culture*, xxv/2 (1984), pp. 182–225; William J. Ashworth, '"System of terror": Samuel Bentham, accountability and dockyard reform during the Napoleonic Wars', *Social History*, xxiii/1 (January. 1998), pp. 63–79; *DNB*.

35 Resistance did not entirely evaporate. John Gast, a Deptford shipwright, gained prominence from 1818 as an early trade-union leader. Knight, 1999, pp. 1–20; Roger Morriss, 'Government and community: The changing context of labour relations, 1770–1830', in Lunn and Day, eds, 1999, pp. 21–40; Philip MacDougall, 'The changing nature of the dockyard dispute, 1790–1840', in Lunn and Day, eds, 1999, pp. 55–6; Stuart Rankin, 'The shipwrights: From craft guild to trade union', in Stuart Rankin, ed., *Shipbuilding on the Thames and Thames-built Ships* (London, 2000), pp. 74–86; Iorwerth J. Prothero, *Artisans and Politics in Early Nineteenth-century London: John Gast and his times* (Folkestone, 1979), pp. 3–50.

36 BL, Evelyn Papers, Map of Deptford in 1623, as copied and annotated by John Evelyn, *c.*1703.

37 LLSA, RB (St Paul, Deptford).

38 Anthony Quiney, 'Thomas Lucas, bricklayer, 1662–1736', *Archaeological Journal*, cxxxvi (1979), pp. 269–80.

39 For the siting of the Commissioners' churches, see William Palin, 'The conception and siting of the "Stepney Churches"', MA thesis, Courtauld Institute of Art, University of London, 1998; for the rectory, see Paul Jeffery, 'Thomas Archer's Deptford rectory: A reconstruction', *Georgian Group Journal*, iii (1993), pp. 32–42.

40 Lysons, 2/1811, i/2, p. 454; Jess Steele, *Turning the Tide: The history of everyday Deptford* (London, 1993), pp. 36, 57–8.

41 BL MSS, Evelyn Papers, E27–9, 33, 40, Abstracts of Deptford leases; BL, Joel Gascoyne, 'Plan of the Manor of Sayes Court in Deptford', 1692; LLSA, RB; LMA, 0/267/1, John Dugleby, 'A Map of an Estate belonging to Fredk Evelyn Esq. in Deptford', 1777; G. B. G. Bull, 'John Evelyn and his Deptford', *Transactions – Lewisham Local History Society* (1966).

42 LLSA, RB; LLSA, A96/18/12; Thankfull Sturdee, *Reminiscences of Old Deptford* (Greenwich, 1895), p. 57.

43 LLSA, RB; LLSA, PH 79/9271; Friends' House Library, Property Records, Deptford Meeting House.

44 LLSA, RB; LLSA, PT 86/527/93, A85/4, A96/18/24; Neale, 1992.

45 LLSA, RB; NA, PROB 3/32/126 and 35/83.

46 LLSA, RB; Neale, 1992.

47 LLSA, RB; LLSA, A97/21/M81–2, A96/18/23; GLHL, misc. deeds; NA, PROB 3/31/162; CKS, DRB/PW38; Neale, 1992; Phillpotts, 1997, p. 36.

48 For more analysis of the inventories, see the RCHME survey report. The inventories are: CKS, DRA/Pi 23/13 and 17; DRB/Pi 1/10A, 2/28 and 33, 3/44A, 46A, 68 and 84, 4/4, 51, 109 and 144, 5/71, 6/18, 8/8, 11/1 and 14, 17/27, 21/30, 24/26 and 44, 25/4, 53/1A, 57/9A; NA, PROB 3/18/84, 97 and 255, 20/203, 22/53 and 66, 23/24, 24/152, 25/51 and 138, 27/175, 28/167, 29/162 and 177, 29/215, 30/95, 31/162, 32/126, 35/83, 38/120, 39/12 and 61, 40/95, 41/11, 42/93, 47/36 and 50, 51/33, 55/3, 56/20 and 33.

49 CKS, DRA/Pi 23/13, DRB/Pi 4/4, 24/26, 25/4.

50 Lorna Weatherill's much wider studies of English inventories between 1675 and 1725 show that 25 per cent of mariners owned utensils for hot drinks, and 48 per cent pictures, as against 3 and 0 per cent for carpenters, and 2 and 2 per cent for weavers. In the 1720s 57 per cent of all London inventories included utensils for hot drinks, and 78 per cent pictures. See Weatherill, *Consumer Behaviour and Material Culture in Britain* (London, 1988), tables 3.3 and 8.4. Divergence between urban and rural inventories has been invoked as evidence for the topographical limits to emulation. See Carl B. Estabrook, *Urbane and Rustic England: Cultural ties and social spheres in the provinces 1660–1780* (Manchester, 1998), pp. 128–63.

51 NA, PROB 3/25/138 and 3/27/175; I am grateful to Bernard Herman for insights into the interpretation of these inventories.

52 NA, PROB 3/56/20.

53 LLSA, RB; LLSA, A88/8/10, 1777 map.

54 LLSA, RB; LLSA, A97/21/M69–70 and 73–4.

55 Mary Slade, *The History of the Female Shipwright: To whom the Government has granted a superannuated pension of twenty pounds per annum, during her life. Written by herself* (London, 1773), preface.

56 LLSA, RB; LLSA, A96/18/22–3; Suzanne J. Stark, *Female Tars: Women aboard ship in the age of sail* (London, 1998), pp. 123–67; Peter Guillery, 'The further adventures of

Mary Lacy', *Georgian Group Journal*, x (2000a), pp. 61–9; Richard Hewlings, 'Women in the building trades, 1600–1850: A preliminary list', *Georgian Group Journal*, x (2000), pp. 70–83.

57 LLSA, RB; LLSA, A96/18/19, 21, 27; GL, MS 11936, 253/377760, 258/385363 and 290/440200; Morriss, 1983, p. 158.

58 LLSA, RB; LLSA, A89/3, MS, Frederick Ashford, 'Views of Deptford', *c*.1860.

59 LLSA, RB; *Post Office Directories*; Neil McKendrick, John Brewer and J. H. Plumb, *The Birth of a Consumer Society* (London, 1982), p. 28.

60 GL, MS 11936, 292/445188.

61 LLSA, RB; *Post Office Directories*.

62 LLSA, RB; CLRO, Comptroller's Bridge House Plans 48.c.14, 48.e.3, 53, 57A, 202.23, 202.72 and 205.24.

63 Ward, 1700, p. 14.

64 For more examples in Greenwich, see RCHM(E), v, 1930, p. 42, and investigators' record cards in the NMR.

65 Phillpotts, 1997, p. 41; Steele, 1993, p. 34.

66 The prevalence of the re-use of materials in vernacular buildings has been inadequately addressed. For an exception, dealing with the stone-building context of Cumbria, see Blake Tyson, 'Management attitudes towards reusing materials in traditional Cumbrian buildings', *Vernacular Architecture*, xxxi (2000), pp. 32–44.

67 Information kindly provided by Steve Jones (the identification having been made by Jo Darrah, formerly of the Victoria & Albert Museum, London) and Cathy Groves of the University of Sheffield. See James W. P. Campbell, 'The carpentry trade in seventeenth-century London', *Georgian Group Journal*, xii (2002), p. 225.

68 Information kindly provided by Steve Jones.

69 BL, Evelyn Papers, Map of Deptford in 1623, as copied and annotated by John Evelyn, *c*.1703; J. H. Harvey, 'Four fifteenth-century London plans', *London Topographical Record*, xx (1952), pp. 1–8; P. E. Jones, 'Four fifteenth-century London plans', *London Topographical Record*, xxiii (1972), pp. 35–41.

70 Harrington, ed., 2000, pp. xxx–xxxii; Ian Roy, 'Greenwich and the Civil War', *Transactions of the Greenwich and Lewisham Antiquarian Society*, x/1 (1985), p. 13.

71 LLSA, RB; GLHL, RB (St Nicholas, Deptford); Jones, 1972, pp. 35–41.

72 For Nos 109 and 111 Deptford Church Street, Nos 14–26 Edward Street, and Nos 216–22 and 323–77 Evelyn Street, see NMR, GLC Drawings Collection 96/1845, 7001 and 7338, and LMA photographs; for Nos 164–8 Deptford High Street, see LLSA, Ashford, *c*.1860; for Nos 12 and 16 Crossfield Street, see *Architect's Journal* (21 March 1973), p. 657; for Nos 146 and 148 Watergate Street, see Jones, 1972, pp. 35–41.

73 The last standing chimneystack in this group, at No. 62, was removed in 2000.

74 NMR, GLC Drawings Collection 96/10660; RCHM(E), v, 1930, pp. 43 and 51, with investigators' record cards in the NMR.

75 LMA and GLHL photographs.

76 LMA, photograph 71/10771.

77 RCHM(E), v, 1930, p. 112, with investigator's record card in the NMR; NMR, GLC Drawings Collection, 96/1936; LMA, photographs.

78 NMR, GLC Drawings Collection 96/7340. For less recently demolished examples, see RCHM(E), v, 1930, pp. 42–3, and investigators' record cards in the NMR.

79 Mills, 1999, pp. 34–43; EH, London historical research file, Greenwich 75.

80 Dan Cruickshank, *A Guide to the Georgian Buildings of Britain & Ireland* (London, 1985), p. 45.

81 NMR, GLC Drawings Collection 96/6918. Short rows of rear-staircase-plan houses were also built in early eighteenth-century Greenwich. See RCHM(E), v, 1930, pp. 42–3, with investigators' record cards in the NMR.

82 Some houses on Watergate Street, Deptford, had comparable ornament. NMR, reference collection, photograph of 1911; LMA, photograph 3277C.

83 Weatherill, 1988, p. 9.

84 For the acceptance of social differentiation as a limiting factor on the spread of the polite, see Nicholas Cooper, 'Display, status and the vernacular tradition', *Vernacular Architecture*, xxxiii (2002), pp. 28–33.

7   BETWEEN PICTURESQUE AND RESPECTABLE

1   Daniel Defoe, *A Tour through the Whole Island of Great Britain* [1724–6], ed. Pat Rogers (London, 1971), p. 288.

2   Summerson wrote of 'Greater Georgian London' in terms of 'the suburbia of prosperity, of the townsman's search for a country foothold', in contrast to 'the draggled, straggling suburbia which is the poverty fringe of the town'; John Summerson, *Georgian London* [1945] ed. Howard Colvin (London, 2003), p. 318. For an overview of the shift from seventeenth-century retreats to early nineteenth-century suburbs around London, see Chris Miele, 'From aristocratic ideas to middle-class idyll: 1690–1840', in Saint, intr., 1999, pp. 31–59.

3   Mary Wollstonecraft, *A Vindication of the Rights of Men* [1790], *A Vindication of the Rights of Woman, and Hints* [1792], both ed. Sylvana Tomaselli (Cambridge, 1995).

4   Elizabeth McKellar, 'Peripheral visions: Alternative aspects and rural presences in mid-eighteenth-century London', *Art History*, xxii/4 (November 1999b), p. 508; see also Elizabeth McKellar, *Landscapes of London: The metropolitan environs, 1660–1830*, forthcoming; Carl B. Estabrook, *Urbane and Rustic England* (Manchester, 1998), pp. 245–75; Jules Lubbock, *The Tyranny of Taste* (London, 1995), p. 178; Peter Borsay, *The English Urban Renaissance* (Oxford, 1989), p. 315.

5   Richard L. Bushman, *The Refinement of America* (New York, 1992); see also Henry Glassie, *Vernacular Architecture* (Bloomington, Ind., 2000)

6   Borsay, 1989, *passim*; John Brewer, *The Pleasures of the Imagination* (London, 1997).

7   For metropolitan influence on rural form in larger buildings, see Elizabeth McKellar, *The Birth of Modern London* (Manchester, 1999a), pp. 180–83; and Miele, 1999, pp. 36–7.

8   VCH, xi, 1998, p. 97; NMR, GLC Drawings Collection 96/5231–2 and 6539–40.

9   Defoe, 1724–6, ed. 1971, p. 337.

10 VCH, x, 1995, pp. 18–22; Isobel Watson, *Gentlemen in the Building Line* (London, 1989), pp. 16–34.

11 RCHM(E), 1937, with investigators' record cards in the NMR; NMR, reference collection; London Borough of Haringey Conservation Department, photographs and unpublished survey by the Cambridge Historic Buildings Group, 1999; information kindly supplied by Anthony Baggs and Steve Gould; VCH, v, 1976, pp. 310–16; Miele, 1999, p. 40.

12 John Entick, *A New and Accurate History and Survey of London*, iii (London, 1766), p. 444.

13 VCH, viii, 1985, pp. 1–16.

14 Ibid., p. 14.

15 McKellar, 1999b, pp. 497–504.

16 See Thomas Hosmer Shepherd's views of Upper Street in 1841–2 in GL.

17 Duncan Wilson *et al.*, 'Recent work at 3 Terrett's Place: An early-eighteenth-century house in Islington', *ASCHB Transactions*, xv (1990), pp. 25–30; Andrew Byrne *London's Georgian Houses* (London, 1986), pp. 186–7.

18 Martin King, 'A late eighteenth century wall stencil at 53 Cross Street, Islington', MA dissertation, Royal College of Art and Victoria and Albert Museum, London, 1995.

19 Nowell also replaced five timber houses in Hedge Row in brick in 1779; Miele, pp. 44–7; VCH, viii, 1985, p. 15; SoL, Clerkenwell North, forthcoming.

20 A. G. Holmes, 'Islington 1827', *Table Book* (London, 1827), as quoted by King, 1995, p. 34.

21 This account of Highgate is derived from that in Peter Guillery, 'On the road to London: Coaching-inn lodgings in Highgate', *Georgian Group Journal*, xi (2001), pp. 203–19.

22 VCH, vi, 1980, pp. 122–39.

23 James Boswell, *London Journal 1762–1763*, ed. Frederick Pottle (London, 1950), entry for 19 November 1762, p. 43.

24 SoL, xvii, 1936, pp. 19–26, 41–5, 105–6, 109–11, plates 32–3 and 87–9; John Rocque, *An Exact Survey of the City's of London, Westminster [. . .] and the Country near Ten Miles Round* (London, 1746); CLSA, 'Thompson's plan of the parish of St Pancras', 1801, and Highgate Digest, typescript, part 1; HLSI, late nineteenth-century photographs and notes; RCHM(E), iv, 1925, p. 90, and investigators' record cards in the NMR; VCH, vi, 1980, pp. 125–9; John Richardson, *Highgate: Its history since the 15th century* (Chatham, Kent, 1983), pp. 124–6, 150, 154–5, 176, 231; John Richardson, *Highgate Past* (London, 1989), p. 87; LMA, photograph 72749; NMR, reference collection.

25 For a more extensive and referenced account of these buildings, see Guillery, 2001, pp. 203–19.

26 SoL, xvii, 1936, pp. 19–30, plates 15–18, 23; VCH, vi, 1980, p. 127.

27 John Macky, *A Journey through England*, 1709, as quoted in VCH, ix, 1989, p. 11.

28 Defoe, 1724–6, ed. 1971, p. 339.

29 F. M. L. Thompson, *Hampstead: Building a borough, 1650–1964* (London, 1974), pp. 18–23; VCH, ix, 1989, pp. 9–11.

30 McKellar, 1999b, pp. 504.

31 Defoe, 1724–6, ed. 1971, p. 339.

32 VCH, ix, 1989, pp. 9–13; Thompson, 1974, pp. 23–4; Daniel Lysons, *The Environs of London etc* (London, 1792–6), ii, p. 592.

33 RCHM(E), ii, 1925, p. 42; Miele, 1999, p. 39.

34 VCH, xi, 1989, pp. 17, 19, 21–3; CLSA, photographs and Hampstead manorial map and fieldbook, 1762; LMA, photograph 16380, 1951; NMR, GLC Drawings Collection 96/5288.

35 Thompson, 1974, p. 26.

36 CLSA, RB (St John, Hampstead, Poor Rate), 1774.

37 McKellar, 1999b, pp. 504–11.

38 Contemporary comment as quoted by Christopher Wade, *The Streets of Hampstead* (London, 3/2000), p. 11; see also VCH, xi, 1989, pp. 11–13; Thompson, 1974, p. 28.

39 As quoted by Wade, 3/2000, p. 47.

40 Summerson [1945], ed. 2003, p. 3.

41 SoL, iv, 1913, pp. 9, 45.

42 SoL, xlii, 1986, pp. 30, 77–80.

43 This account of Fulham is derived from an EH report on Nos 17 and 19 Jerdan Place (see Appendix), researched and written by Jonathan Clarke.

44 From the *London Magazine* (June 1749), as quoted by Thomas Faulkner, *An Historical and Topographical Account of Fulham: Including the hamlet of Hammersmith* (London, 1813), p. 328.

45 Charles James Fèret, *Fulham Old and New: Being an exhaustive history of the ancient parish of Fulham*, ii (London, 1900).

46 Defoe, 1724–6, ed. 1971, p. 347.

47 SoL, vi, 1915, pp. 35, 92, plate 31; RCHM(E), ii, 1925, pp. 38–9, and investigators' record cards in the NMR; NMR, reference collection; Miele, 1999, p. 38.

48 RCHM(E), 1937, and investigators' record cards in the NMR; NMR, reference collection; John Cloake, *Richmond Past: A visual history of Richmond, Kew, Petersham and Ham* (London, 1991); Donald Simpson, *Twickenham Past: A visual history of Twickenham and Whitton* (London, 1993).

49 As quoted in Joseph Mordaunt Crook, 'Strawberry Hill revisited', *Country Life* (7 June 1973), p. 1598.

50 Horace Walpole, letter to Henry Seymour Conway, 8 June 1747, in Wilmarth Sheldon Lewis, ed., *The Yale Edition of Horace Walpole's Correspondence*, xxxvii (London, 1974), pp. 269–70; see Peter Guillery and Michael Snodin, 'Strawberry Hill: Building and site', *Architectural History*, xxxviii (1995), pp. 102–28.

51 VCH, iv, 1912, pp. 108–10.

52 RCHM(E), ii, 1925, pp. 98–9, and investigators' record cards in the NMR.

53 NMR, GLC Drawings Collection 96/1318.

54 RCHM(E), ii, 1925, p. 86; SoL, xxiii, 1951; NMR, reference collection; LMA photographs.

55 John Strype, *A Survey of the Cities of London and Westminster, etc* (London, 1720), book vi, p. 79.

56 VCH, iv, 1912, pp. 36–41; RCHM(E), ii, 1925, p. 98, and investigators' record cards in the NMR; Eric E. F. Smith, *Clapham* (London, 1976), p. 49; Nicholas Cooper, *Houses of the Gentry, 1480–1680* (New Haven and London, 1999), pp. 142–3, 170–72; Surrey Record Office, LT, as noted by GLC historians; Andrew Saint, intr., *London Suburbs* (London, 1999), pp. 14–15.

57 A friend of Mrs Cook's, as quoted by Smith, 1976, p. 84.

58 Minet Library, Lambeth Archives: Daniel Gould, 'A plan of Clapham and its vicinity', 1815; H. N. Batten, 'A plan of Clapham with the common and its environs', 1827; Clapham Tithe Map and Awards, 1838. See also OS, 1874; Clapham Antiquarian Society, *Occasional Sheet*, No. 108 (Jan 1957); *DNB*.

59 William Harnett Blanch, *Ye Parish of Camerwell* (London, 1875), pp. 78, 148–9, 231; W. W. Marshall, 'Peckham Town', unpublished and undated typescript in his possession.

60 Defoe, 1724–6, ed. 1971, p. 176.

61 Harold James Dyos, *Victorian Suburb: A study of the growth of Camberwell* (Leicester, 1966); Blanch, 1875, pp. 230–32; VCH, iv, 1912, pp. 25, 35.

62 As quoted by Blanch, 1875, p. 31.

63 RCHM(E), v, 1930, p. 11, and investigators' record cards in the NMR; Blanch, 1875, pp. 311, 350; John D. Beasley, ed., *Peckham and Nunhead*, Archive Photographs Series (Stroud, 1995), pp. 16–19, 30–31; Stephen Humphrey, *Britain in Old Photographs: Camberwell, Dulwich and Peckham* (Stroud, 1996), pp. 77, 79; LMA photographs 4447c and F999–1002, 1912 and 1942; NMR, GLC Drawings Collection 96/4764–5, 7676.

64 W. W. Marshall, 'Brief history of the Peckham theatre', unpublished and undated typescript in his possession.

65 Blanch, 1875, pp. 332–3; Beasley, ed., 1995, p. 18.

66 RCHM(E), v, 1930, p. 11, and investigator's record card in the NMR; LMA, SKCS/332–41, Surrey and Kent Commissioners of Sewers Rate Books, 1723–75; SLSL, Ratebooks for the Parish of St Giles, Camberwell, 1774–1855; *Post Office Directory*; LMA, photographs 58/3614–15.

67 Dyos, 1966, pp. 30–42.

68 Marshall, see n. 64.

69 Defoe, 1724–6, ed. 1971, p. 166.

70 NMR, GLC Drawings Collection 96/1567 and SoL survey notes.

71 Neil Rhind, *Blackheath Village and Environs, 1790–1970*, i: *The Village and Blackheath Vale* (London, 1976), pp. 87–8, 108–9; Neil Rhind, *The Heath* (London, 1987), p. 65; John Bold *et al.*, *Greenwich* (London, 2000), p. 226; NMR, SoL survey notes; LMA photographs.

72 RCHM(E), v, 1930, p. 52.

73 Ibid., pp. 111–12; NMR, GLC Drawings Collection 96/3880; Richard R. C. Gregory, *The Story of Royal Eltham* (Eltham, 1909), p. 289.

74 Todd Longstaffe-Gowan, *The London Town Garden* (London, 2001), pp. 235–52; Miele, 1999, pp. 55–7.

75 For rural perspectives, see Estabrook, 1998, and Andrew Ballantyne, 'Joseph Gandy and the politics of rustic charm', in Arciszewska and McKellar, eds, *Articulating British Classicism: New approaches to eighteenth-century architecture* (Aldershot, forthcoming).

8 ALONG THE COAST AND ACROSS THE SEA

1 Twistleton, as transcribed in Robert Tate Gaskin, *The Old Seaport of Whitby* (Whitby, 1909), pp. 279–80.

2 Christopher William Chalklin, *The Provincial Towns of Georgian England: A study of the building process, 1740–1820* (London, 1974); Peter Borsay, *The English Urban Renaissance: Culture and society in the provincial town, 1660–1770* (Oxford, 1989); Mark Girouard, *The English Town: A history of urban life* (London, 1990); Peter Borsay, 'The London connection: Cultural diffusion and the eighteenth-century provincial town', *London Journal*, xix/1 (1994), pp. 21–35.

3 NMR, Buildings Index file 39681; reference collection.

4 NMR, reference collection.

5 I am grateful to Val Horsler for first drawing my attention to Deal, to Bernard Herman and Robert Hook for co-perambulation, and to Mia Jüngskar for compiling information about the town, closer investigation of which would be particularly rewarding. See also Duncan Harrington, ed., *Kent Hearth Tax Assessment, Lady Day 1664* (London, 2000), p. xcvii.

6 B. H. St. J. O'Neil, 'North Street, Folkestone, Kent', *Antiquaries Journal*, xxix (1949), pp. 8–12.

7 B. H. St. J. O'Neil, 'Some seventeenth-century houses in Great Yarmouth', *Archaeologia*, xcv (1953), pp. 141–80. EH Press Release, 10 April 2001.

8 Ibidem.

9 Daniel Defoe, *A Tour through the Whole Island of Great Britain* [1724–6], ed. Pat Rogers (London, 1971), p. 529.

10 Chalklin, 1974, p. 129; Ivan Hall and Elisabeth Hall, *A New Picture of Georgian Hull* (York, 1978).

11 Gaskin, 1909, pp. 272–3; Girouard, 1990, p. 32; Gordon Jackson, 'Ports 1700–1840', in Clark, ed., 2000, p. 719; Gordon Jackson, *The History and Archaeology of Ports* (Tadworth, 1983), p. 28. Information deriving from field survey kindly supplied by Bernard Herman, Robert Hook and Adam Menuge.

12 Examples of the latter survive at Nos 22 and 23 Ordnance Row. See Chalklin, 1974, pp. 122–8, 188; Ann Veronica Coats, 'The oeconomy of the navy and Portsmouth: A discourse between the civilian naval administration of Portsmouth dockyard and the surrounding communities, 1650–1800', PhD thesis, University of Sussex, 2000.

13 See Roger Leech on Bristol houses and EH, Historic Environment of Liverpool Project, both forthcoming.

14 Sylvia Collier with Sarah Pearson, *Whitehaven 1660–1800* (London, 1991), pp. 85–109.

15 RCHM(E), 1977, fig. 7; RCHM(E), ii, 1970, p. 222; RCHM(E), v, 1981, pp. 134, 208–9.

16 See Barrie Trinder, 'Industrialising towns 1700–1840', in Clark, ed., 2000, pp. 805–29; Maurice Beresford, *East*

End, West End: The face of Leeds during urbanisation, 1684–1842, Thoresby Society Publications, lx/131 and lxi/132 (Leeds, 1988); Adam Fergusson, *The Sack of Bath* (Salisbury, 1973), pp. 10–13, 58; Ursula Priestley and P. J. Corfield, 'Rooms and room use in Norwich housing, 1580–1730', *Post-medieval Archaeology*, xvi (1982), pp. 93–123; VCH, x, 1972, pp. 33–8; J. G. Timmins, *Handloom Weavers' Cottages in Central Lancashire* (Lancaster, 1977); Colum Giles and Ian H. Goodall, *Yorkshire Textile Mills: The buildings of the Yorkshire textile industry, 1770–1930* (London, 1992), pp. 3–5; Barrie Trinder, *The Industrial Revolution in Shropshire* (Chichester, 3/2000), pp. 137–73; Judith Alfrey and Catherine Clarke, *The Landscape of Industry: Patterns of change in the Ironbridge Gorge* (London, 1993), pp. 169–98; Lucy Caffyn, *Workers' Housing in West Yorkshire, 1750–1920* (London, 1986), pp. 2–8; Nicola Wray et al., *'One Great Workshop': The buildings of the Sheffield metal trades* (Swindon, 2001).

17 Roger Leech, *Early Industrial Housing: The Trinity area of Frome* (London, 1981).

18 NMR, Buildings Index file 93161.

19 Chalklin, 1974, pp. 196–202; John Cattell, Sheila Ely and Barry Jones, *The Birmingham Jewellery Quarter: An architectural survey of the manufactories* (Swindon, 2002); Maxine Berg, 'Technological change in Birmingham and Sheffield in the eighteenth century', in Peter Clark and Penelope Corfield, eds, *Industry and Urbanisation in Eighteenth Century England* (Leicester, 1994), pp. 20–32; John Rule, *The Labouring Classes in Early Industrial England, 1750–1850* (London, 1986), pp. 95–6.

20 John J. Parkinson-Bailey, *Manchester: An architectural history* (Manchester, 2000), pp. 33–4; Ian Goodall and Simon Taylor, 'The Shudehill and Northern Quarter area of Manchester: "An outgrowth of accident" and "Built according to a plan"', EH, Architectural Investigation Report B/066/2001; Clare Hartwell, *Manchester* (London, 2001), pp. 9–13, 17, 227, 270.

21 Giles and Goodall, 1992, pp. 19–21; Colum Giles, 'The Yorkshire textile workshop: From cottage to factory', in Paul Barnwell, Marilyn Palmer and Malcolm Airs, eds, *The Vernacular Workshop: From craft to industry 1400–1900*, forthcoming conference proceedings.

22 Anthony Calladine and Jean Fricker, *East Cheshire Textile Mills* (London, 1993), pp. 54–5; NMR, reference collection; R. W. Brunskill, *Illustrated Handbook of Vernacular Architecture* (London, 2/1978), pp. 174–5.

23 Nikolaus Pevsner, *An Outline of European Architecture* (London, 7/1963), p. 449.

24 Nikolaus Pevsner and David Lloyd, *The Buildings of England: Hampshire and the Isle of Wight* (Harmondsworth, 1967), p. 439. I am grateful to Ann Coats for drawing my attention to these comments by Pevsner.

25 Peter Linebaugh, *The London Hanged* (London, 1991), p. 135.

26 Peter Linebaugh and Marcus Rediker, *The Many-headed Hydra: Sailors, slaves, commoners and the hidden history of the revolutionary Atlantic* (London, 2000).

27 Richard Bushman, *The Refinement of America* (New York,
1992), pp. 100–27, 193–203, 402–47. Those imaginative horizons would, however, have comprehended the nostalgic, as in James Oglethorpe's primitivist project for establishing the colony of Georgia in the 1730s, a scheme that brought together social outcasts and admired the simple housing of native Americans. See Christine Stevenson, *Medicine and Magnificence: British hospital and asylum architecture, 1660–1815* (London, 2000), p. 23.

28 In broaching connections between the vernacular architecture of eighteenth-century London and North America, I am deeply indebted to Bernard Herman, without whose insights I would have gained little purchase on transatlantic links. While holding no responsibility for its flaws, Bernard is thus effectively the joint author of what follows.

29 Bernard L. Herman, *Town House: Architecture and experience in the early American city*, forthcoming; Dell Upton, 'Vernacular domestic architecture in eighteenth-century Virginia', *Winterthur Portfolio*, xvii/2–3 c(Winterthur, 1982), pp. 95–119; Dell Upton, 'Another city: The urban cultural landscape in the early Republic', and Damie Stillman, 'City living, Federal style', in Catherine E. Hutchins, ed., *Everyday Life in the Early Republic* (Winterthur, 1994), pp. 61–117 and 137–74; Mary Ellen Hayward and Charles Belfoure, *The Baltimore Rowhouse* (New York, 1999), pp. 8–27; information about Jamestown from research by Audrey Horning via Carl Lounsbury of the Colonial Williamsburg Foundation; Roderic H. Blackburn and Ruth Piwonka, *Remembrance of Patria: Dutch arts and culture in colonial America, 1609–1776* (Albany, NY, 1988), p. 114; Brunskill, 1978, pp. 200–05.

30 Bernard Herman and Peter Guillery, 'Negotiating Classicism in Eighteenth-century Deptford and Philadelphia', in Barbara Arciszewska and Elizabeth McKellar, eds, *Articulating British Classicism: New approaches to eighteenth-century architecture* (Aldershot, forthcoming); see also John L. Cotter et al., *The Buried Past: An archaeological history of Philadelphia* (Philadelphia, 1993), pp. 30–57, 68, 162–7, 216–28. For an analysis of how housebuilding changed after 1790, see Donna J. Rilling, *Making Houses, Crafting Capitalism: Builders in Philadelphia, 1790–1850* (Philadelphia, 2001).

31 Hayward and Belfoure, 1999, pp. 8–27.

9 'DESPICABLE COTTAGES'

1 The missing first part of this simile is: 'A transition from an author's book to his conversation is too often . . .' Originally from Johnson's fourteenth Rambler essay of 5 May 1750, it is cited here because (and precisely as) it was quoted, robbed of humour, in the epigraph to John Gwynn's *London and Westminster Improved* of 1766.

2 Paul Slack, *From Reformation to Improvement: Public welfare in early modern England* (Oxford, 1999); Geoff Baldwin, 'The "public" as a rhetorical community in early modern England', in Alexandra Shepard and Phil Withington, eds, *Communities in Early Modern England:*

Networks, place, rhetoric (Manchester, 2000), pp. 199–215.

3 Roy Porter, *Enlightenment* (London, 2000), pp. xx, xxi and 486; M. Dorothy George, *London Life in the Eighteenth Century* [1925], reprint (New York, 1964), *passim*.

4 John Entick, *A New and Accurate History and Survey of London, Westminster, Southwark, and Places Adjacent*, iii (London, 1766), p. 157; see also George, 1925, ed. 1964, p. 348.

5 George, 1925, ed. 1964, p. 99.

6 2 Geo. III *c.*21.

7 George, 1925, ed. 1964, pp. 99–103, 348; Dan Cruickshank and Neil Burton, *Life in the Georgian City* (London, 1990), pp. 13–18; Miles Ogborn, *Spaces of Modernity* (London, 1998), pp. 75–115; Cynthia Wall, '"At the *Blue Boar*, over-against *Catharine*-street in the *Strand*": Forms of address in London streets', unpublished abstract of conference paper from 'The Streets of London, 1660–1870', December 1999, at the London Voluntary Sector Resource Centre, organised by Tim Hitchcock, University of Hertfordshire, and Heather Shore, University College, Northampton. For more general and theoretical discussion, see Jürgen Habermas, *The Structural Transformation of the Public Sphere: An enquiry into a category of bourgeois society* (Cambridge, Mass., 1989).

8 Jules Lubbock, *The Tyranny of Taste* (London, 1995), pp. 169–78, 207.

9 Boswell, as quoted in Howard M. Colvin, *A Biographical Dictionary of British Architects 1600–1840* (London, 3/1995), p. 441; see also *The Builder* (27 June 1863), pp. 454–7.

10 Gwynn, 1766, p. 7.

11 Ibid., p. x.

12 Ibid., pp. 14 and 17. For a less polemical view of Bath, bridging the vernacular-polite divide, see Christopher Woodward, '"In the jelly mould": Craft and commerce in 18th-century Bath', in Burton, ed., 1996, pp. 1–9.

13 Gwynn, 1766, p. viii.

14 Ibid., p. vi.

15 John Summerson, *Georgian London* [1945], ed. Howard Colvin (London, 2003), p. 120. The influence of this kind of thinking can also be seen further afield, as in Edinburgh New Town, planned in 1766, where smaller houses were incorporated in and contained by regular new developments.

16 The objectives in a 'Report of a Committee of West India Merchants', 20 December 1793, as in Sheila Lambert, ed., *House of Commons Sessional Papers of the Eighteenth Century*, cii (Wilmington, 1975), pp. 405–8.

17 SoL, xliii, 1994, pp. 247–57; Andrew Saint, 'The building art of the first industrial metropolis', in Celina Fox, ed., *London – World City 1800–1840* (London, 1992), pp. 51–4.

18 Allan Brodie, Jane Croom and James O. Davies, *English Prisons: An architectural history* (Swindon, 2002), pp. 29–53; Malcolm Seaborne, *The English School: Its architecture and organisation, 1370–1870* (London, 1971); Harriet Richardson, ed., *English Hospitals, 1660–1948* (Swindon, 1998); Christine Stevenson, *Medicine and Magnificence* (London, 2000); Kathryn Morrison, *The Workhouse: A study of poor-law buildings in England* (Swindon, 1999);

Thomas A. Markus, *Buildings and Power: Freedom and control in the origin of modern building types* (London, 1993). For rural parallels, see Andrew Ballantyne, 'Joseph Gandy and the politics of rustic charm', in Arciszewska and McKellar, eds, *Articulating British Classicism: New approaches to eighteenth-century architecture* (Aldershot, forthcoming).

19 John Entick, *A New and Accurate History and Survey of London, Westminster, Southwark, and Places Adjacent*, iii (London, 1766), pp. 228, 231, 238–9.

20 4 Geo. III *c.*14, xiv.

21 *Commons Journals*, xxxiii (29 February and 9 March 1772), pp. 538, 576.

22 33 Geo. II *c.*30.

23 12 Geo. III *c.*73, xx.

24 *Commons Journals*, xxxiv (11 February, 21 April and 11 May 1774), pp. 452, 667, 737. For Taylor's City base and connections, his deep involvement in high-status speculative housebuilding, and his conscious concern for the integration of streetscapes, see Richard Garnier, 'Speculative housing in 1750s London', *Georgian Group Journal*, xii (2002), pp. 163–214.

25 14 Geo. III *c.*78, xliii.

26 LMA, MR/B/R/2–3.

27 Summerson, 1945, ed. 2003, p. 125.

28 Ibid.

29 George, 1925, ed. 1964, p. 107.

30 For this, and for wider background to much of what follows, see Linda Clarke, *Building Capitalism* (London, 1992); James Ayres, *Building the Georgian City* (London, 1998), and Elizabeth McKellar, *The Birth of Modern London* (Manchester, 1999a).

31 Francis Sheppard, Victor Belcher and Philip Cottrell, 'The Middlesex and Yorkshire Deeds Registries and the study of building fluctuations', *London Journal*, v/2 (1979), pp. 176–217; James Anderson, 'Property finance and the building cycle in the 18th and early 19th centuries', in Colin Cunningham and James Anderson, eds, *The Hidden Iceberg of Architectural History*, Papers from the Annual Symposium of the Society of Architectural Historians of Great Britain (London, 1998), pp. 31–44.

32 McKellar, 1999a, pp. 104–37; Ayres, 1998, pp. 125–6, 133; Cruickshank and Burton, 1990, p. 117; Giles Worsley, 'Designing by numbers: John Carr and the industrialisation of architectural design', lecture delivered to the Soane Museum Study Group, London, 28 November 2001; James Ayres, 'The building crafts in an age of industrialisation', in Hentie Louw, ed., *The Place of Technology in Architectural History*, Papers from the Joint Symposium of the Society of Architectural Historians of Great Britain and the Construction History Society (London, 2001), pp. 33–40; David T. Yeomans, 'Early carpenters' manuals 1592–1820', *Construction History*, ii (1986), pp. 13–33.

33 Colvin, 3/1995, p. 199.

34 Roy Porter, *London: A social history* (London, 1994), p. 113.

35 Dana Arnold, *Re-presenting the Metropolis: Architecture, urban experience and social life in London 1800–1840* (Cambridge, 2000), p. 50; Clarke, 1992, p. 74.

36 Clarke, 1992, pp. 48, 70, 73; McKellar, 1999a, pp. 81–9, 104–10; Ayres, 1998, pp. 7–16; Summerson, 1945 ed. 2003, pp. 55, 405; David Barnett, *London, Hub of the Industrial Revolution* (London, 1998), pp. 120–22.

37 McKellar, 1999a, pp. 81–9, 104–10; Clarke, 1992, pp. 56–68, 81–2, 114, 163–5.

38 Clarke, 1992, pp. 87–190.

39 As quoted by Colvin, 3/1995, p. 611.

40 James Peller Malcolm, who lived in the locality, as quoted by Clarke, 1992, p. 157.

41 Edward Walford, *Old and New London: A narrative of its history, its people, and its Places*, v (London, 1877), p. 345; *DNB*.

42 Malcolm, as quoted by Clarke, 1992, pp. 159–60.

43 Richard Rodger, *Housing in Urban Britain, 1780–1914* (Cambridge, 1995), p. 22.

44 David R. Green, *From Artisans to Paupers* (Aldershot, 1995), and Leonard Schwarz, *London in the Age of Industrialisation* (Cambridge, 1992).

45 Paul Laxton, 'The evidence of Richard Horwood's maps for residential building in London 1799–1819', *London Journal*, xxiv/1 (1999), pp. 1–22.

46 John White, *Some Account of the Proposed Improvements of the Western Parts of London*, appx III (London, 1815), p. xxv, as quoted by Clarke, 1992, p. 154. See also Anderson, 1998, pp. 31–44; Neil Jackson, 'Built to sell: The speculative house in nineteenth-century London', in Cunningham and Anderson, eds, 1998, pp. 79–97; Schwarz, 1992, pp. 175, 234–5; Rodger, 1995, pp. 14–36, 87; Clarke, 1992, pp. 191–265.

47 For information on slums in general, I am grateful to Alan Cox for sight of his 'In darkest London: Slums in the capital', the typescript of a lecture delivered at the Victorian Society conference, 'The Victorian Underworld', 24 November 2001. See also A. S. Wohl, *The Eternal Slum: Housing and social policy in Victorian London* (London, 1977); Alan Mayne and Tim Murray, ed., *The Archaeology of Urban Landscapes: Explorations in slumland* (Cambridge, 2001). For specific instances, see Carol Bentley, 'The Brady Street scheme: Homes for the poorest Londoners in the early 20th century', *Transactions of the London and Middlesex Archaeological Society*, li (2000), pp. 189–207; SoL, xliii, 1994, pp. 188–93, 398; SoL, xlv, 2000, pp. 84–5, 99; Donald J. Olsen, *Town Planning in London: The eighteenth and nineteenth centuries* (London, 2/1982), pp. 126–32.

48 SoL, Clerkenwell South, forthcoming.

49 J. C. Loudon, *The Suburban Gardener and Villa Companion* (London, 1838), p. 35, as quoted by Jackson, 1998, p. 84.

50 For the former at Woodseer and Deal Streets, see Stefan Muthesius, *The English Terraced House* (London, 1982), p. 137, and EH, London historical research file, Tower Hamlets 193; for the latter see chapter 3, n. 47, and Rampart Street, Whitechapel, as in EH, London historical research file, Tower Hamlets 177.

51 Muthesius, 1982, pp. 79–97, 143–6.

52 John B. Papworth, 'On houses as they were, as they are, and as they ought to be', *Journal of the Society of Arts* (17 April 1857), p. 319, as quoted by Jackson, 1998, p. 85.

53 Millicent Rose, *The East End of London* (London, 1951), pp. 156–7.

54 Francis Place, *Autobiography*, as quoted by George, 1925, ed. 1964, pp. 104, 106, 354.

55 Edwin Chadwick, as quoted by George, ibid., p. 105.

10   A LIVING TRADITION?

1 From *Gallus Castratus* [1659], appended to Anon., *A Character of France* (London, 1659), p. 12, as quoted by Keith Thomas, 'English Protestantism and classical art', in Lucy Gent, ed., *Albion's Classicism: The visual arts in Britain, 1550–1660* (London, 1995), p. 225.

2 Compare John Gwynn, *London and Westminster Improved* (London, 1766), p. 12: 'In the cities of Paris, Edinburgh, Rotterdam and other places, the government takes cognizance of all publick buildings both useful and ornamental, and where any thing absurd or improper is proposed to be done the legislative seasonably prevents the intrusion of deformity in their capital, which would undoubtedly find its way if the whim and caprice of their builders was suffered to go on without this check.'

3 For appreciations of a different nineteenth-century 'vernacular metropolis', see James Winter, *London's Teeming Streets 1830–1914* (London, 1993), and Lynda Nead, *Victorian Babylon: People, streets and images in 19th-century London* (London, 2000).

4 John Summerson, *Georgian London* [1945] ed. Howard Colvin (London, 2003), p. 127.

5 Benjamin Disraeli, *Tancred; Or the New Crusade* (London, 1847), i, pp. 233–4, as quoted by Neil Jackson, 'Built to sell: The speculative house in nineteenth-century London', in Cunningham and Anderson, eds, 1998, p. 87; see also Daniel Abramson, 'Commercialization and backlash in late Georgian architecture', in Arciszewska and McKellar, eds, *Articulating British Classicism: New approaches to eighteenth-century architecture* (Aldershot, forthcoming).

6 For the 'metropolitan picturesque' in the early nineteenth century, see Todd Longstaffe-Gowan, *The London Town Garden, 1740–1840* (London, 2001), pp. 235–52; Chris Miele, 'From aristocratic ideal to middle-class idyll: 1690–1840', in Saint, intr., 1999, pp. 53–7; John Summerson, 'The beginnings of an early Victorian suburb', *London Topographical Record*, xxvii (1995), pp. 1–48; Malcolm Brown, 'St John's Wood: The Eyre Estate before 1830', *London Topographical Record*, xxvii (1995), pp. 49–68; Geoffrey Tyack, 'John Nash and the Park Village', *Georgian Group Journal*, iii (1993), pp. 68–74.

7 Anthony Quiney, 'Benevolent vernacular: Cottages and workers' housing', in Burton, ed., 1996, p. 49. For the origins of consciously 'old-fashioned' architecture in Burkean conservatism, see Andrew Ballantyne, 'Joseph Gandy and the politics of rustic charm', in Arciszewska and McKellar, eds, forthcoming. See also Reginald T. Blomfield, *A History of Renaissance Architecture in England, 1500-1800* (London, 1897); Mark Girouard, *Sweetness and Light: The Queen Anne Movement 1860–1900* (London, 1977), and J. Mordaunt Crook, *The Dilemma of Style:*

Architectural ideas from the Picturesque to the Post-modern (London, 1987).

8 Elizabeth McKellar, *The Birth of Modern London* (Manchester, 1999a), pp. 93–5; Brian Hanson, 'Mind and hand in architecture: Ideas of the artisan in English architecture from William Chambers to John Ruskin', thesis, University of Essex, 1986; Brian Hanson, *Architects and the 'Building World' from Chambers to Ruskin: Constructing authority* (Cambridge, 2003); Hentie Louw, 'The mechanisation of architectural woodwork in Britain from the late eighteenth century to the early twentieth century and its practical, social and aesthetic implications', i–iv, *Construction History*, viii (1992), pp. 21–54; ix (1993), pp. 27–50; xi (1995), pp. 51–72; xii (1996), pp. 19–40; Celina Fox, 'Art and Trade: from the Society of Arts to the Royal Academy of Arts', in Sheila O'Connell *et. al., London 1753* (London, 2003), pp. 18–27.

9 Jules Lubbock, *The Tyranny of Taste* (London, 1995), pp. 246–7. In its early stages the Gothic Revival was understood as indigenous and thus, in a sense, as vernacular. See Simon Bradley, 'The Englishness of Gothic: Theories and interpretations from William Gilpin to J. H. Parker', *Architectural History*, xlv (2002), pp. 325–46; and Michael Hall, ed., *Gothic Architecture and its Meanings 1550–1830* (Reading, 2002).

10 John Ruskin, *Lectures on Architecture and Painting* [1854], as quoted by Mark Swenarton, *Artisans and Architects: The Ruskinian tradition in architectural thought* (Basingstoke, 1989), p. 15.

11 William Morris, 'The art of the people' [1879], as reprinted in G. D. H. Cole, ed., *William Morris* (London, 1946), p. 529.

12 Alan Crawford, *C. R. Ashbee: Architect, designer and Romantic Socialist* (London, 1985), pp. 23–75, 237–59. See also Hermione Hobhouse, *London Survey'd: The work of the Survey of London 1894–1994* (Swindon, 1994), pp. 2–10; Alan Crawford, 'C. R. Ashbee in the East End', leaflet essay accompanying a temporary exhibition at the Geffrye Museum, London, 1998.

13 Susan Beattie, *A Revolution in London Housing* (London, 1980).

14 Nikolaus Pevsner, *Pioneers of the Modern Movement from William Morris to Walter Gropius* (London, 1936).

15 J. Mordaunt Crook, *The Dilemma of Style* (London, 1987), p. 11.

Appendix

LIST OF INVESTIGATED SITES WITH RELATED ARCHIVE FILE REFERENCES (REPORTS, DRAWINGS OR PHOTOGRAPHS IN THE NATIONAL MONUMENTS RECORD)

BI = Buildings Index Number

LONDON BOROUGH OF CAMDEN

Nos 70–84 (even) Heath Street, Hampstead	BI 106863
Nos 112 and 114 Heath Street, Hampstead	BI 106337
Nos 33 and 35 Highgate High Street	BI 106486
No. 59 Highgate High Street	BI 106864
Nos 2–7 South Grove, Highgate	BI 106344

CITY OF LONDON

Nos 124–6 Cheapside	BI 106865
Nos 74 and 75 Long Lane	BI 95772
No. 145 Fleet Street	BI 88600

LONDON BOROUGH OF GREENWICH

Nos 4, 6 and 8 Feathers Place, Greenwich	BI 106485
No. 17 Greenwich Church Street	BI 90832
No. 45 Greenwich Church Street	BI 95579
Nos 70–84 River Way, East Greenwich	BI 106866
No. 24 Royal Hill, Greenwich	BI 96625
No. 111 Woolwich High Street	BI 106335

LONDON BOROUGH OF HACKNEY

Nos 2–24 (even) Kingsland Road	BI 98909
Nos 302–60 (even) Kingsland Road	BI 98661
Nos 362–72 (even) Kingsland Road	BI 98662
Nos 374–80 (even) Kingsland Road	BI 98910
Nos 408–16 (even) Kingsland Road	BI 98663
Nos 420–28 (even) Kingsland Road	BI 98664
Nos 430–38 (even) Kingsland Road	BI 103195
Nos 478 and 480 Kingsland Road	BI 98911
Nos 514–94 (even) Kingsland Road	BI 98665
Nos 325 and 327 Old Street, Hoxton	BI 98920
No. 29 Pitfield Street, Hoxton	BI 98919
Nos 187–90 Shoreditch High Street	BI 98922
No. 227 Shoreditch High Street	BI 95176
Nos 169–75 (odd) Stoke Newington Church Street	BI 87757
No. 4 Sylvester Path	BI 103215

LONDON BOROUGH OF HAMMERSMITH AND FULHAM

Nos 17 and 19 Jerdan Place, Fulham	BI 98659

LONDON BOROUGH OF HARINGEY

Nos 58 and 60 Highgate High Street	BI 106368
Nos 2 and 4 Park Lane, Tottenham	BI 106867
Nos 808 and 810 Tottenham High Road	BI 87750
Nos 809 and 811 Tottenham High Road	BI 106382
No. 820 Tottenham High Road	BI 106383

LONDON BOROUGH OF ISLINGTON

Nos 53–9 (odd) Cross Street, Islington	BI 105818
Nos 12–28 (even) Liverpool Road, Islington	BI 106358
Nos 52–5 Newington Green	BI 99245
No. 3 Terrett's Place, Islington	BI 106815
No. 38 Upper Street, Islington	BI 91046
Nos 60 and 61 Upper Street, Islington	BI 106359

LONDON BOROUGH OF LAMBETH

Nos 120–42 (even) Clapham High Street	BI 106488
Nos 17 and 18 Lower Marsh, Lambeth	BI 106814
Nos 13–14 The Pavement, Clapham	BI 106487

LONDON BOROUGH OF LEWISHAM

No. 17 Albury Street, Deptford	BI 96134
No. 23 Albury Street, Deptford	BI 96130
No. 27 Albury Street, Deptford	BI 96131
No. 34 Albury Street, Deptford	BI 96132
No. 35 Albury Street, Deptford	BI 96133
No. 36 Albury Street, Deptford	BI 95956
Nos 106 and 108 Blackheath Hill, Blackheath	BI 106868
Nos 18–21 Deptford Broadway	BI 96630
No. 43 Deptford Broadway	BI 97356
No. 47 Deptford Broadway	BI 97357
No. 36 Deptford High Street	BI 96634
Nos 33–7 (odd) Deptford High Street	BI 97349
No. 59 Deptford High Street	BI 97350
Nos 62–6 (even) Deptford High Street	BI 95954
Nos 73–9 (odd) Deptford High Street	BI 97353

Nos 85 and 89 Deptford High Street	BI 97355
No. 106 Deptford High Street	BI 97351
No. 116 Deptford High Street	BI 96632
Nos 134–44 (even) Deptford High Street	BI 97354
No. 150 Deptford High Street	BI 96631
Nos 167 and 169 Deptford High Street	BI 97352
No. 203 Deptford High Street	BI 95955
No. 205 Deptford High Street	BI 97348
Nos 221–5 (odd) Deptford High Street	BI 96633
No. 227 Deptford High Street	BI 96633
Nos 315 and 317 Lewisham High Street	BI 106343
Nos 21–31 Tanner's Hill, Deptford	BI 96635

LONDON BOROUGH OF SOUTHWARK

Nos 74–8 (even) Bermondsey Street	BI 106512
No. 210 Bermondsey Street	BI 106513
Nos 31–7 Borough High Street, Southwark	BI 88074
Nos 21–7 (odd) Crosby Row, Bermondsey	BI 106514
No. 67 Grange Walk, Bermondsey	BI 106531
No. 89 Long Lane, Bermondsey	BI 106530
Nos 241–5 Long Lane, Bermondsey	BI 106807
Nos 154–70 New Kent Road	BI 97375
Nos 58–62 (even) Peckham High Street	BI 97395
Nos 98–104 (even) Peckham High Street	BI 97396
Nos 1–3 Pond Cottages, Dulwich	BI 106489
No. 5 Stoney Street, Southwark	BI 106515
Nos 41–53 (odd) Tower Bridge Road, Bermondsey	BI 106532

LONDON BOROUGH OF TOWER HAMLETS

No. 16 Bacon Street, Bethnal Green	BI 105798
No. 24 Bacon Street, Bethnal Green	BI 105805
Nos 113 and 115 Bethnal Green Road	BI 98912
Nos 122 and 130–40 (even) Bethnal Green Road	BI 105804
Nos 125 and 127 Brick Lane, Bethnal Green	BI 98916
No. 133 Brick Lane, Bethnal Green	BI 105799
No. 149 Brick Lane, Bethnal Green	BI 105800
No. 161 Brick Lane, Bethnal Green	BI 105801
Nos 190 and 192 Brick Lane, Bethnal Green	BI 105809
Nos 194–8 (even) Brick Lane, Bethnal Green	BI 105808

Nos 232–8 (even) Brick Lane, Bethnal Green	BI 105810
Nos 3–9 (odd) Cheshire Street, Bethnal Green	BI 105806
Nos 19 and 21 Cheshire Street, Bethnal Green	BI 98914
No. 46 Cheshire Street, Bethnal Green	BI 98915
Nos 3 and 5 Club Row, Bethnal Green	BI 98918
Nos 192 and 194 Hackney Road, Bethnal Green	BI 106869
No. 94 Mile End Road	BI 106384
No. 96 Mile End Road	BI 106385
Nos 107–13 (odd) Mile End Road	BI 106870
Nos 133–9 (odd) Mile End Road	BI 96994
No. 92 Narrow Street, Limehouse	BI 106809
Nos 17–21 (odd) Old Ford Road, Bethnal Green	BI 87445
Nos 4A, 5A and 6A Padbury Court, Bethnal Green	BI 98917
Nos 4–7 Puma Court, Spitalfields	BI 106529
No. 83 Redchurch Street, Bethnal Green	BI 105802
No. 87 Redchurch Street, Bethnal Green	BI 105803
No. 34 Redchurch Street, Bethnal Green	BI 103224
Nos 70–74 (even) Sclater Street, Bethnal Green	BI 98913
Nos 97 and 99 Sclater Street, Bethnal Green	BI 105796
No. 102 Sclater Street, Bethnal Green	BI 105797
No. 2 Swanfield Street, Bethnal Green	BI 105807

LONDON BOROUGH OF WANDSWORTH

No. 86 Wandsworth High Street	BI 106871
Nos 140 and 142 Wandsworth High Street	BI 87884

CITY OF WESTMINSTER

Nos 5 and 6 Avery Row, Mayfair	BI 106874
No. 101 Charing Cross Road, Soho	BI 106872
No. 19 Crown Passage, St James	BI 108820
No. 2 Derby Street, Mayfair	BI 106528
Nos 58–64 George Street, Marylebone	BI 103181
Nos 1-8 Goodwin's Court	BI 108816
No. 9 Lancashire Court, Mayfair	BI 106873
No. 4 Lower John Street, St James	BI 106527
No. 5 Meard Street, Soho	BI 106381
Nos 21–5 Newport Court, Soho	BI 106875
No. 7 Nottingham Place, Marylebone	BI 87751

Bibliography

The list below consists of published and typescript sources that have been consulted in the preparation of this book. It excludes maps, official papers and reports, items from periodicals such as newspapers or *The Builder*, and primary archive material, all of which are reflected in the notes. The sources are separated into two sections by publication date, before or after 1850. Later editions of early works appear in the first group. The items are entered alphabetically by author or editor(s), except for the publications of the RCHM(E), SoL and the VCH, which are listed chronologically under those titles in the second group.

BEFORE 1850

Anon., *Low-life: Or, One half of the world knows not how the other half live* (London, *c.*1750).

Anon., *The Book of Trades: Or Library of the useful arts* (London, 1804 and 1806).

Anon., *The Builder's Dictionary* (London, 1734).

Johann Wilhelm von Archenholz, *A Picture of England*, i (London, 1789).

Nicholas Barbon, *An Apology for the Builder* (London, 1685).

Thomas Beames, *The Rookeries of London: Past, present and prospective* (London, 1850).

James Boswell, *London Journal 1762–1763*, ed. Frederick Pottle (London, 1950).

James Boswell, *The Life of Samuel Johnson* [1791], in *Boswell's Life of Johnson, together with Boswell's Journal of a Tour to the Hebrides and Johnson's Diary of a Journey into North Wales*, ed. George Birkbeck Hill, rev. and enlarged by L. F. Powell, 6 vols (Oxford, 1934–50).

Edward Wedlake Brayley, *A Topographical History of Surrey* (London, 1841).

R. Campbell, *The London Tradesman* (London, 1747, facs. Newton Abbot, 1969).

Patrick Colquhoun, *A Treatise on the Police of the Metropolis* (London, 1796).

Patrick Colquhoun, *The State of Indigence and the Situation of the Casual Poor in the Metropolis Explained* (London, 1799).

Patrick Colquhoun, *Treatise on the Commerce and Police of the River Thames* (London, 1800).

Daniel Defoe, *A Journal of the Plague Year* [1722], ed. Louis A. Landa (Oxford, 1998).

Daniel Defoe, *A Tour thro' London about the Year 1725*, ed.

Mayson M. Beeton and E. Beresford Chancellor (London, 1929).

Daniel Defoe, *A Tour through the Whole Island of Great Britain* [1724–6], ed. Pat Rogers (London, 1971).

Charles Dickens, *Oliver Twist* [1837–9], reprint (London, 1994).

John Entick, *A New and Accurate History and Survey of London, Westminster, Southwark, and Places Adjacent*, 4 vols (London, 1766).

Olaudah Equiano, *The Interesting Narrative of the Life of Olaudah Equiano, or Gustavus Vassa the African* (London, 1789).

John Evelyn, *The Diary of John Evelyn* [*c.*1660–1706], ed. E. S. de Beer, 6 vols (Oxford, 1955).

John Evelyn, 'An account of architects and architecture', preface to his translation of Roland Fréart, *A Parallel of the Antient Architecture with the Modern* (London, 1707).

Thomas Faulkner, *An Historical and Topographical Account of Fulham: Including the hamlet of Hammersmith* (London, 1813).

Henry Fielding, *An Enquiry into the Causes of the Late Increase in Robbers* (London, 1751).

John Fielding, *A Description of the Cities of London and Westminster* (London, 1776).

Hector Gavin, *Sanitary Ramblings: Being sketches and illustrations of Bethnal Green. A type of the condition of the metropolis and other large towns* (London, 1848).

James Gibbs, *The Rules for Drawing the Several Parts of Architecture, in a more exact and easy manner than has been heretofore practised* (London, 1732).

Pierre-Jean Grosley, *A Tour to London* (London, 1772).

John Gwynn, *London and Westminster Improved* (London, 1766).

William Halfpenny, *The Builder's Pocket-Companion* (London, 1728).

William Halfpenny, *The Modern Builder's Assistant* (London, 1757).

Edward Hatton, *A New View of London: Or, An ample account of that city* (London, 1708).

Batty Langley, *The Builder's Jewel: Or, The youth's instructor, and workman's remembrancer* (London, 1741).

Pierre Le Muet, *The Art of Fair Building* [1623], trans. Robert Pricke (London, 1670).

William Leybourne, *A Platform for Purchasers, Guide for Builders, Mate for Measurers* (London, 1668).

John Claudius Loudon, *The Suburban Gardener and Villa Companion* (London, 1838).

Daniel Lysons, *The Environs of London etc*, 4 vols (London, 1792–6, 2/1811).

William Maitland, *The History of London* (London, 1739).

James Peller Malcolm, *Londinium Redivivum: Or, An ancient history and modern description of London*, 4 vols (London, 1803–7).

James Peller Malcolm, *Anecdotes of the Manners and Customs of London during the Eighteenth Century* (London, 1808).

Henry Mayhew, *London Labour and the London Poor* [1850], ed. Victor Neuburg (Harmondsworth, 1985).

Joseph Moxon, *Mechanick Exercises: Or, The doctrine of handy-works* (London, 2/1693–4, rev. 3/1700).

Mungo Murray, *A Treatise on Ship-Building and Navigation* (London, 1754).

T. A. Murray, *Remarks on the Situation of the Poor in the Metropolis* (London, 1801).

Peter Nicholson, *The New Practical Builder, and Workman's Companion*, 2 vols (London, 1823–5).

Roger North, *Of Building: Roger North's Writings on Architecture* [*c.*1690], ed. Howard M. Colvin and John Newman (Oxford, 1981).

William Pain, *Carpenter's and Joiner's Repository* (London, 1778).

Thomas Pennant, *Some Account of London* (London, 2/1791).

Samuel Pepys, *Diary* [1660–69], ed. Robert Latham and William Matthews, 11 vols (London, 1970–83).

G. W. Phillips, *The History and Antiquities of the Parish of Bermondsey* (London, 1841).

Stephen Primatt, *The City and Country Purchaser and Builder* [1667], reissued by William Leybourne (London, 3/1680).

William Henry Pyne, *Microcosm: Or, A picturesque delineation of the arts, agriculture, manufactures, &c. of Great Britain*, i (London, 1803).

Sophie von la Roche, *Sophie in London, 1786: Being the Diary of Sophie von la Roche*, trans. Clare Williams (London, 1933).

Thomas Rowlandson, *Characteristic Sketches of the Lower Orders* (London, 1820).

Ignatius Sancho, *Letters of the Late Ignatius Sancho* (London, 1782).

Louis Simond, *An American in Regency England: The journal of a tour in 1810–1811*, ed. Christopher Hibbert (London, 1968).

Mary Slade, *The History of the Female Shipwright: To whom the Government has granted a superannuated pension of twenty pounds per annum, during her life. Written by herself* (London, 1773).

Adam Smith, *An Inquiry into the Nature and Causes of the Wealth of Nations*, i (London, 1776).

J. T. Smith, *Antiquities of London and Environs* (London, 1791).

Tobias Smollett, *The Expedition of Humphry Clinker* [1771], intr. and notes by L. Rice-Oxley (Oxford, 1925, repr. 1967).

John Stow, *A Survey of London* [1598], ed. Charles Lethbridge Kingsford, 2 vols (London, 1908).

John Strype, *A Survey of the Cities of London and Westminster, etc*, 6 books (London, 1720).

William Sutherland, *The Ship-builder's Assistant* (London, 1711).

William Sutherland, *Britain's Glory: Or, Shipbuilding unveil'd* (London, 1717).

John Tallis, *London Street Views* [1838–40], intr. Peter Jackson (London, 1969).

Horace Walpole, *The Yale Edition of Horace Walpole's Correspondence*, ed. Wilmarth Sheldon Lewis, xxxvii (New Haven and London, 1974).

Edward [Ned] Ward, *A Frolick to Horn-Fair: With a walk from Cuckold's-point thro' Deptford and Greenwich* (London, 1700).

Isaac Ware, *A Complete Body of Architecture* (London, 1756).

Gebhardt Friedrich August Wendeborn, *A View of England towards the Close of the Eighteenth Century* (London, 1791).

Robert Wilkinson, *Londina illustrata*, 2 vols (London, 1819–25).

Walter Wilson, *The History and Antiquities of Dissenting Churches and Meeting Houses*, 4 vols (London, 1808–14).

Mary Wollstonecraft, *A Vindication of the Rights of Men* [1790], *A Vindication of the Rights of Woman, and Hints* [1792], both ed. Sylvana Tomaselli (Cambridge, 1995).

Henry Wotton, *The Elements of Architecture* (London, 1624).

AFTER 1850

P. Abrams and E. A. Wrigley, eds, *Towns in Societies: Essays in economic history and historical sociology* (Cambridge, 1978).

Daniel M. Abramson, 'Commercialization and backlash in late Georgian architecture', in Arciszewska and McKellar, eds, forthcoming.

Peter Ackroyd, *London: The biography* (London, 2000).

B. W. E. Alford and T. C. Barker, *A History of the Carpenters' Company* (London, 1968).

Judith Alfrey and Catherine Clarke, *The Landscape of Industry: Patterns of change in the Ironbridge Gorge* (London, 1993).

James Anderson, 'Property finance and the building cycle in the 18th and early 19th centuries', in Cunningham and Anderson, eds, 1998, pp. 31–44.

Barbara Arciszewska and Elizabeth McKellar, eds, *Articulating British Classicism: New approaches to eighteenth-century architecture* (Aldershot, forthcoming).

Tom Arkell, 'Interpreting probate inventories', in Arkell, Evans and Goose, ed., 2000, pp. 72–102.

Tom Arkell, Nesta Evans and Nigel Goose, eds, *When Death Do Us Part: Understanding and interpreting the probate records of early modern England* (Oxford, 2000).

Alan Armstrong, ed., *The Economy of Kent, 1640–1914* (Woodbridge, 1995).

Dana Arnold, 'Rationality, safety and power: The street planning of later Georgian London', *Georgian Group Journal*, v (1995), pp. 37–50.

Dana Arnold, eds, *The Metropolis and its Image: Constructing identities for London, c.1750–1950* (Oxford, 1999).

Dana Arnold, *Re-presenting the Metropolis: Architecture, urban experience and social life in London 1800–1840* (Cambridge, 2000).

Charles Robert Ashbee, *The Trinity Hospital in Mile End: An object lesson in national history*, first monograph of the Committee for the Survey of the Memorials of Greater London (London, 1896).

William J. Ashworth, '"System of terror": Samuel Bentham, accountability and dockyard reform during the Napoleonic Wars', *Social History*, xxiii/1 (Jan. 1998), pp. 63–79.

James Ayres, *Building the Georgian City* (London, 1998).

James Ayres, 'The building crafts in an age of industrialisation', in Louw, ed., 2001, pp. 33–40.

James Ayres, *Domestic Interiors: The British tradition 1500-1800* (London, 2003)

William C. Baer, 'Housing the poor and mechanick class in seventeenth-century London', *London Journal*, xxv/2 (2000), pp. 13–39.

T. M. M. Baker, *Rebuilding the City after the Great Fire* (Chichester, 2000).

Geoff Baldwin, 'The "public" as a rhetorical community in early modern England', in Shepard and Withington, eds, 2000, pp. 199–215.

Andrew Ballantyne, 'Joseph Gandy and the politics of rustic charm', in Arciszewska and McKellar, eds, forthcoming.

Philip Banbury, *Shipbuilders of the Thames and Medway* (Newton Abbot, 1971).

David Barnett, *London, Hub of the Industrial Revolution: A revisionary history 1775–1825* (London, 1998).

Paul Barnwell, Marilyn Palmer and Malcolm Airs, eds, *The Vernacular Workshop: From craft to industry 1400–1900*, forthcoming conference proceedings.

Josette Barre, *La Colline de la Croix-Rousse* (Lyons, 2001).

Jonathan Barry and Christopher Brooks, eds, *The Middling Sort of People: Culture, society and politics in England, 1550–1800* (Cambridge, 1994).

John D. Beasley, ed., *Peckham and Nunhead*, Archive Photographs Series (Stroud, 1995).

Susan Beattie, *A Revolution in London Housing: LCC housing architects and their work, 1893–1914* (London, 1980).

John Bedell, 'Archaeology and probate inventories in the study of eighteenth-century life', *Journal of Interdisciplinary History*, xxxi/2 (2000), pp. 223–245.

A. L. Beier, 'Engine of manufacture: The trades of London', in Beier and Finlay, eds, 1986, pp. 141–8.

A. L. Beier and Roger Finlay, eds, *London, 1500–1700: The making of the metropolis* (Harlow, 1986).

Catherine Belsey, 'Classicism and cultural dissonance', in Gent, ed., 1995, pp. 427–42.

Walter Benjamin, *The Arcades Project* [1927–40], trans. Howard Eiland and Kevin McLaughlin (London, 1999).

Carol Bentley, 'The Brady Street scheme: Homes for the poorest Londoners in the early 20th century', *Transactions of the London and Middlesex Archaeological Society*, li (2000), pp. 189–207.

Maurice Beresford, *East End, West End: The face of Leeds during urbanisation, 1684–1842*, Thoresby Society Publications, lx/131 and lxi/132 (Leeds, 1988).

Maxine Berg, *The Age of Manufactures 1700–1820: Industry, innovation and work in Britain* (London, 2/1994).

Maxine Berg, 'Women's work, mechanisation and the early phases of industrialisation in England', in Joyce, ed., 1987, pp. 64–98.

Maxine Berg, 'Technological change in Birmingham and Sheffield in the eighteenth century', in Clark and Corfield, eds, 1994, pp. 20–32.

Michael Berlin, '"Broken all in pieces": Artisans and the regulation of workmanship in early modern London', in Crossick, ed., 1997, pp. 75–91.

Walter Besant, *London in the Eighteenth Century* (London, 1902).

David Bindman, *Hogarth and his Times: Serious comedy* (Los Angeles, 1997).

Marcus Binney, *Sir Robert Taylor: From Rococo to Neo-Classicism* (London, 1984).

Roderic H. Blackburn and Ruth Piwonka, *Remembrance of Patria: Dutch arts and culture in colonial America, 1609–1776* (Albany, NY, 1988).

William Harnett Blanch, *Ye Parish of Camerwell* (London, 1875).

Reginald T. Blomfield, *A History of Renaissance Architecture in England, 1500-1800* (London, 1897).

John Bold *et al.*, *Greenwich: An architectural history of the Royal Hospital for Seamen and the Queen's House* (London, 2000).

Peter Borsay, *The English Urban Renaissance: Culture and society in the provincial town, 1660–1770* (Oxford, 1989).

Peter Borsay, ed., *The Eighteenth-century Town: A Reader in English Urban History 1688–1820* (Harlow, 1990).

Peter Borsay, 'The London connection: Cultural diffusion and the eighteenth-century provincial town', *London Journal*, xix/1 (1994), pp. 21–35.

Françoise Boudon *et al.*, *Système de l'architecture urbaine: Le Quartier des Halles à Paris* (Paris, 1977).

Jeremy Boulton, *Neighbourhood and Society: A London suburb in the seventeenth century* (Cambridge, 1987).

Jeremy Boulton, 'Wage labour in seventeenth-century London', *Economic History Review*, 2nd series, xlix/2 (1996), pp. 268–90.

Jeremy Boulton, '"It is extreme necessity that makes me do this": Some "survival strategies" of pauper households in London's West End during the early eighteenth century', *International Review of Social History*, xlv, suppl. 8 (2000), pp. 47–69.

Jeremy Boulton, 'London 1540–1700', in Clark, ed., 2000, pp. 315–46.

Jeremy Boulton, 'The poor among the rich: Paupers and the parish in the West End, 1600–1724', in Griffiths and Jenner, eds, 2000, pp. 197–225.

Simon Bradley, 'The Englishness of Gothic: Theories and interpretations from William Gilpin to J. H. Parker', *Architectural History*, xlv (2002), pp. 325–46.

Simon Bradley and Nikolaus Pevsner, *The Buildings of England, London, i: The City of London* (London, 1997).

Simon Bradley and Nikolaus Pevsner, *The Buildings of England, London, vi: Westminster* (London, 2003)

Fernand Braudel, *Capitalism and Material Life 1400–1800* [1967], trans. Miriam Kochan (London, 1973).

Robert Brenner, *Merchants and Revolution: Commercial change, political conflict, and London's overseas traders, 1550–1653* (Cambridge, 1993).

Norman G. Brett-James, *The Growth of Stuart London* (London, 1935).

John Brewer, *The Common People and Politics, 1750s to 1790s* (Cambridge, 1986).

John Brewer, *The Pleasures of the Imagination: English culture in the eighteenth century* (London, 1997).

John Brewer and Roy Porter, eds, *Consumption and the World of Goods* (London, 1994).

Allan Brodie, Jane Croom and James O. Davies, *English Prisons: An architectural history* (Swindon, 2002).

Christopher Brooks, 'Apprenticeship, social mobility and the middling sort, 1550–1800', in Barry and Brooks, eds, 1994, pp. 52–83.

David A. Brown, 'Domestic masonry architecture in 17th-century Virginia', *Northeast Historical Archaeology*, xxvii (1998), pp. 85–120.

Frank Brown, 'Continuity and change in the urban house: Developments in domestic space organisation in seventeenth-century London', *Comparative Studies in Society and History*, xxviii/4 (October 1986), pp. 558–90.

Malcolm Brown, 'St John's Wood: The Eyre Estate before 1830', *London Topographical Record*, xxvii (1995), pp. 49–68.

R. W. Brunskill, *Illustrated Handbook of Vernacular Architecture* (London, 2/1978).

G. B. G. Bull, 'John Evelyn and his Deptford', *Transactions – Lewisham Local History Society* (1966).

Neil Burton, *The Geffrye Almshouses* (London, 1979).

Neil Burton, ed., *Georgian Vernacular*, papers given at a Georgian Group Symposium, 28 October 1995 (Tonbridge, 1996).

Neil Burton, *Georgian Stairs* (London, 2001).

Richard L. Bushman, *The Refinement of America: Persons, houses, cities* (New York, 1992).

Andrew Byrne, *London's Georgian Houses* (London, 1986).

Lucy Caffyn, *Workers' Housing in West Yorkshire, 1750–1920* (London, 1986).

Anthony Calladine and Jean Fricker, *East Cheshire Textile Mills* (London, 1993).

Colin Campbell, 'Understanding traditional and modern patterns of consumption in eighteenth-century England: A character-action approach', in Brewer and Porter, eds, 1994, pp. 40–57.

James W. P. Campbell, 'The carpentry trade in seventeenth-century London', *Georgian Group Journal*, xii (2002), pp. 215–37.

Louise Campbell, ed., *Twentieth-century Architecture and its Histories*, Society of Architectural Historians of Great Britain (Otley, 2000).

Richard M. Candee, *Building Portsmouth: The neighborhoods & architecture of New Hampshire's oldest city* (Portsmouth, NH, 1992).

David Cannadine, *Class in Britain* (London, 1998).

Martha Carlin, *Medieval Southwark* (London, 1996).

Robert Carr, ed., *Dockland: An illustrated historical survey of life and work in east London* (London, 1986).

John Cattell, Sheila Ely and Barry Jones, *The Birmingham Jewellery Quarter: An architectural survey of the manufactories* (Swindon, 2002).

Pierre Cayez, *Métiers Jacquard et Hauts Forneaux aux Origines de l'Industrie Lyonnaise* (Lyons, 1978)

Christopher William Chalklin, *The Provincial Towns of Georgian England: A study of the building process, 1740–1820* (London, 1974).

J. A. Chartres, 'The capital's provincial eyes: London's inns in the early eighteenth century', *London Journal*, iii/1 (1977), pp. 24–39.

Bridget Cherry and Nikolaus Pevsner, *The Buildings of England, London*, iv: *North* (London, 1998).

Ian R. Christie, *The Benthams in Russia, 1780–1791* (Oxford, 1993).

J. H. Clapham, 'The Spitalfields Acts, 1773–1824', *Economic Journal*, xxvi (1916), pp. 459–71.

Peter Clark, ed., *The Transformation of English Provincial Towns* (London, 1984).

Peter Clark, ed., *The Cambridge Urban History of Britain*, ii: *1540–1840* (Cambridge, 2000).

Peter Clark and Penelope Corfield, eds, *Industry and Urbanisation in Eighteenth Century England* (Leicester, 1994).

Peter Clark and R. A. Houston, 'Culture and leisure 1700–1840', in Clark, ed., 2000, pp. 575–613

Peter Clark and Paul Slack, eds, *Crisis and Order in English Towns 1500–1700: Essays in urban history* (London, 1972).

Edward T. Clarke, *Bermondsey: Its historic memories and associations* (London, 1902).

Linda Clarke, *Building Capitalism: Historical change & the labour process in the production of the built environment* (London, 1992).

John Cloake, *Richmond Past: A visual history of Richmond, Kew, Petersham and Ham* (London, 1991).

Jonathan G. Coad, *The Royal Dockyards, 1690–1850: Architecture and engineering works of the sailing navy* (Aldershot, 1989).

Ann Veronica Coats, 'The œconomy of the navy and Portsmouth: A discourse between the civilian naval administration of Portsmouth dockyard and the surrounding communities, 1650–1800', PhD thesis, University of Sussex, 2000.

G. D. H. Cole, ed., *William Morris* (London, 1946).

Sylvia Collier with Sarah Pearson, *Whitehaven 1660–1800* (London, 1991).

Howard M. Colvin, *A Biographical Dictionary of British Architects 1600–1840* (London, 3/1995).

Donald Murray Connan, *History of the Public Health Department in Bermondsey* (London, 1935).

Carolyn C. Cooper, 'The Portsmouth System of Manufacture', *Technology and Culture*, xxv/2 (1984), pp. 182–225.

Nicholas Cooper, *Houses of the Gentry, 1480–1680* (New Haven and London, 1999).

Nicholas Cooper, 'Display, status and the vernacular tradition', *Vernacular Architecture*, xxxiii (2002), pp. 28–33.

David Cordingly, *Heroines and Harlots: Women at sea in the great age of sail* (London, 2001).

Penelope J. Corfield and Derek Keene, eds, *Work in Towns 850–1850* (Leicester, 1990).

John L. Cotter *et al.*, *The Buried Past: An archaeological history of Philadelphia* (Philadelphia, 1993).

John Coulter, *Britain in Old Photographs: Lewisham and Deptford* (Worcester, 1990, 1992 and 1997).

Alan Cox, 'A vital component: Stock bricks in Georgian London', *Construction History*, xiii (1997), pp. 57–66.

Alan Cox, 'In darkest London: Slums in the capital', unpublished typescript of a talk delivered at the Victorian Society conference 'The Victorian Underworld', 24 November 2001.

Alan Crawford, *C. R. Ashbee: Architect, designer and Romantic Socialist* (London, 1985).

Alan Crawford, 'C. R. Ashbee in the East End', leaflet essay accompanying a temporary exhibition at the Geffrye Museum, London, 1998.

Stephen Croad, *Liquid History: The Thames through time* (London, 2003)

Joseph Mordaunt Crook, 'Strawberry Hill revisited', *Country Life* (7, 14 and 21 June 1973), pp. 1598–602, 1726–30, 1794–7, 1886.

J. Mordaunt Crook, *The Dilemma of Style: Architectural ideas from the Picturesque to the Post-modern* (London, 1987).

Geoffrey Crossick, *An Artisan Elite in Victorian Society: Kentish London 1840–1880* (London, 1978).

Geoffrey Crossick, ed., *The Artisan and the European Town, 1500–1900* (Aldershot, 1997).

Dan Cruickshank, *A Guide to the Georgian Buildings of Britain & Ireland* (London, 1985).

Dan Cruickshank and Neil Burton, *Life in the Georgian City* (London, 1990).

Dan Cruickshank and Peter Wyld, *London: The art of Georgian building* (London, 1975).

Colin Cunningham and James Anderson, eds, *The Hidden Iceberg of Architectural History*, Papers from the Annual Symposium of the Society of Architectural Historians of Great Britain (London, 1998).

C. R. J. Currie, 'Time and chance: Modelling the attrition of old houses', *Vernacular Architecture*, xix (1988), pp. 1–9.

H. C. Darby, ed., *An Historical Geography of England before AD 1800* (Cambridge, 1936).

Robert C. Davis, 'Arsenal and *arsenalotti*: Workplace and community in seventeenth-century Venice', in Safley and Rosenband, eds, 1993, pp. 180–203.

Steven Denford and David Hellings, *Streets of Old Holborn* (London, 1999).

Nathan Dews, *History of Deptford* (London, 1884).

H. T. Dickinson, 'Radical culture', in Fox, ed., 1992, pp. 209–24.

C. R. Dobson, *Masters and Journeymen: A prehistory of industrial relations, 1717–1800* (Guildford, 1980).

Kerry Downes, *Hawksmoor* (London, 1959).

H. H. Drake, ed., *Hasted's History of Kent* (London, 1886).

Peter D'Sena, 'Perquisites and casual labour on the London wharfside in the eighteenth century', *London Journal*, xiv/2 (1989), pp. 131–47.

A. J. Dunkin, *History of the County of Kent: Deptford* (London, 1877).

Harold James Dyos, *Victorian Suburb: A study of the growth of Camberwell* (Leicester, 1966).

Peter Earle, *The Making of the English Middle Class: Business, society and family life in London, 1660–1730* (London, 1989a).

Peter Earle, 'The female labour market in London in the late seventeenth and early eighteenth centuries', *Economic History Review*, 2nd series, xlii/3 (1989b), pp. 328–53.

Peter Earle, *A City Full of People: Men and women of London 1650–1750* (London, 1994).

Peter Earle, 'The middling sort in London', in Barry and Brooks, ed., 1994, pp. 141–58.

Michael Egan, 'The population of Greenwich in the seventeenth century', *Journal of the Greenwich Historical Society*, ii/3 (2000), pp. 83–8.

English Heritage, *Georgian Joinery, 1660–1840: The history, design and conservation of interior woodwork in Georgian houses* (London, 1993).

English Heritage, *London Terrace Houses 1660–1860: A guide to alterations and extensions* (London, 1996).

David V. Erdman, *Blake: Prophet against empire* (New York, 3/1977).

Carl B. Estabrook, *Urbane and Rustic England: Cultural ties and social spheres in the provinces 1660–1780* (Manchester, 1998).

David Esterly, *Grinling Gibbons and the Art of Carving* (London, 1998).

Arlette Farge, *Fragile Lives: Violence, power and solidarity in eighteenth-century Paris* (Cambridge, 1993).

James R. Farr, ' Cultural analysis and early modern artisans', in Crossick, ed., 1997, pp. 56–74.

Charles James Fèret, *Fulham Old and New: Being an exhaustive history of the ancient parish of Fulham*, ii (London, 1900).

Adam Fergusson, *The Sack of Bath* (Salisbury, 1973).

Roger Finlay and Beatrice Shearer, 'Population growth and suburban expansion', in Beier and Finlay, eds, 1986, pp. 37–59.

Harry Forrester, *The Smaller Queen Anne and Georgian House, 1700 to 1840* (Chelmsford, 1964).

Celina Fox, ed., *London – World City 1800–1840* (London, 1992).

Celina Fox, 'Art and trade – from the Society of Arts to the Royal Academy of Arts', in O'Connell *et al.*, 2003, pp. 18–27.

Alice T. Friedman, 'The way you do the things you do: Writing the history of houses and housing', *Journal of the Society of Architectural Historians*, lviii/3 (September 1999), pp. 406–13.

Ian Anders Gadd and Patrick Wallis, eds, *Guilds, Society and Economy in London, 1450–1800* (London, 2002).

David Gaimster and Paul Stamper, eds, *The Age of Transition: The archaeology of English culture 1400–1600* (Oxford, 1997).

Richard Garnier, 'Speculative housing in 1750s London', *Georgian Group Journal*, xii (2002), pp. 163–214.

David Garrioch, *Neighbourhood and Community in Paris, 1740–1790* (Cambridge, 1986).

Robert Tate Gaskin, *The Old Seaport of Whitby* (Whitby, 1909).

Enid Gauldie, *Cruel Habitations: A history of working-class housing 1780–1918* (London, 1974).

Lucy Gent, ed., *Albion's Classicism: The visual arts in Britain, 1550–1660* (London, 1995).

M. Dorothy George, *English Social Life in the Eighteenth Century* (London, 1923).

M. Dorothy George, *London Life in the Eighteenth Century* [1925], reprint (New York, 1964).

Veronika Gervers, ed., *Studies in Textile History* (Toronto, 1977).

Graham Gibberd, *On Lambeth Marsh: The South Bank and Waterloo* (London, 1992).

John Gifford, Colin McWilliam and David Walker, *The Buildings of Scotland: Edinburgh* (Harmondsworth, 1984).

Elizabeth Waterman Gilboy, *Wages in Eighteenth Century England* (Cambridge, Mass., 1934).

Colum Giles, 'The historic warehouses of Liverpool', unpublished RCHME report, 1998.

Colum Giles and Ian H. Goodall, *Yorkshire Textile Mills: The buildings of the Yorkshire textile industry, 1770–1930* (London, 1992).

Colum Giles, 'The Yorkshire textile workshop: From cottage to factory', in Barnwell, Palmer and Airs, eds, forthcoming.

Mark Girouard, *Sweetness and Light: The Queen Anne Movement 1860–1900* (London, 1977).

Mark Girouard, *The English Town: A history of urban life* (London, 1990).

Mark Girouard, Dan Cruickshank, Raphael Samuel *et al.*, *The Saving of Spitalfields* (London, 1989).

Montague S. Giuseppi, 'The parliamentary surveys relating to

Southwark', *Surrey Archaeological Collections*, xiv (1899), pp. 42–71.

Henry Glassie, *Folk Housing in Middle Virginia* (Knoxville, Tenn., 1975).

Henry Glassie, *Vernacular Architecture* (Bloomington, Ind., 2000).

Miles Glendinning, Ranald MacInnes and Aonghus Mac-Kechnie, *A History of Scottish Architecture: From the Renaissance to the present day* (Edinburgh, 1996).

Ian Goodall and Simon Taylor, 'The Shudehill and Northern Quarter area of Manchester: "An outgrowth of accident" and "Built according to a plan"', English Heritage Architectural Investigation Report B/066/2001.

Richard Grassby, *Kinship and Capitalism: Marriage, family and business in the English speaking world, 1570–1740* (Cambridge, 2001).

David R. Green, *From Artisans to Paupers: Economic change and poverty in London, 1790–1870* (Aldershot, 1995).

Edmund M. Green, 'The taxonomy of occupations in late-eighteenth-century Westminster', in Corfield and Keene, eds, 1990, pp. 164–81.

Richard R. C. Gregory, *The Story of Royal Eltham* (Eltham, 1909).

Paul Griffiths and Mark S. R. Jenner, eds, *Londinopolis: Essays in the cultural and social history of early modern London* (Manchester, 2000).

Peter Guillery, 'The Broadway Chapel: A forgotten exemplar', *London Topographical Record*, xxvi (1990), pp. 97–133.

Peter Guillery, 'The further adventures of Mary Lacy', *Georgian Group Journal*, x (2000a), pp. 61–9.

Peter Guillery, 'Waste and place: Late-18th-century development on Kingsland Road', *Hackney History*, vi (2000b), pp. 19–38.

Peter Guillery, 'On the road to London: Coaching-inn lodgings in Highgate', *Georgian Group Journal*, xi (2001), pp. 203–19.

Peter Guillery and Bernard Herman, 'Deptford houses: 1650 to 1800', *Vernacular Architecture*, xxx (1999), pp. 58–84.

Peter Guillery and Michael Snodin, 'Strawberry Hill: Building and site', *Architectural History*, xxxviii (1995), pp. 102–28.

Sidney Gutman, ed., *Seven Years' Harvest: An anthology of the Bermondsey Book 1923–1930* (London, 1934).

Jürgen Habermas, *The Structural Transformation of the Public Sphere: An enquiry into a category of bourgeois society* (Cambridge, Mass., 1989).

Ivan Hall and Elisabeth Hall, *A new picture of Georgian Hull* (York, 1978).

Michael Hall, ed., *Gothic Architecture and its Meanings 1550–1830* (Reading, 2002).

Robin Hamlyn and Michael Phillips, eds, *William Blake* (Norwich, 2000).

Brian Hanson, 'Mind and hand in architecture: Ideas of the artisan in English architecture from William Chambers to John Ruskin', thesis, University of Essex, 1986.

Brian Hanson, *The Architect and the 'Building World' from Chambers to Ruskin: Constructing authority* (Cambridge, 2003).

Julienne Hanson, *Decoding Homes and Houses* (Cambridge, 1998).

Vanessa Harding, 'City, capital, and metropolis: the changing shape of seventeenth-century London', in Merritt, ed., 2001, pp. 117–43.

Vanessa Harding, 'Controlling a complex metropolis, 1650–1750: Politics, parishes and powers', *London Journal*, xxvi/1 (2001), pp. 29–37.

Julian Harrap, 'Nos 5 and 7 Elder Street', *The Saving of Spitalfields* (London, 1989), pp. 103–15.

Duncan Harrington, ed., *Kent Hearth Tax Assessment, Lady Day 1664*, British Record Society, Hearth Tax Series II (London, 2000).

Eileen Harris, *British Architectural Books and Writers, 1556–1785* (Cambridge, 1990).

Carl Harrison, 'The house that Joseph Allin built', *Transactions of the Greenwich and Lewisham Antiquarian Society*, x/4 (1988), pp. 164–78.

R. J. Hartlidge, 'The development of industries in London south of the Thames 1750 to 1850', thesis, University of London, 1955.

Clare Hartwell, *Manchester* (London, 2001).

John H. Harvey, 'Four fifteenth-century London plans', *London Topographical Record*, xx (1952), pp. 1–8.

Mary Ellen Hayward and Charles Belfoure, *The Baltimore Rowhouse* (New York, 1999).

Bernard L. Herman, *Town House: Architecture and experience in the early American city*, forthcoming.

Bernard Herman and Peter Guillery, 'Negotiating Classicism in Eighteenth-century Deptford and Philadelphia', in Arciszewska and McKellar, eds, forthcoming.

Dominique Hervier, Marie-Agnès Férault and Françoise Boudon, *Le Faubourg Saint-Antoine: Un double visage*, Cahiers du patrimoine no. 51, éditions de l'Inventaire (Paris, 1998).

Richard Hewlings, 'Women in the building trades, 1600–1850: A preliminary list', *Georgian Group Journal*, x (2000), pp. 70–83.

Christoph Heyl, 'We are not at Home: Protecting domestic privacy in post-fire middle-class London', *London Journal*, xxvii/2 (2002), pp. 12–33.

Christopher Hill, Barry Reay and William Lamont, *The World of the Muggletonians* (London, 1983).

G. W. Hill and W. H. Frere, eds, *Memorials of Stepney Parish* (Guildford, 1891).

Matthew Hillier, 'A history of Jacob's Island', typescript, SLSL, 1997.

Tim Hitchcock, 'The publicity of poverty in early eighteenth-century London', in Merritt, 2001, pp. 166–84.

Tim Hitchcock, Peter King and Pamela Sharpe, eds, *Chronicling Poverty: The voices and strategies of the English poor, 1640–1840* (London, 1997).

Hermione Hobhouse, *London Survey'd: The work of the Survey of London 1894–1994* (Swindon, 1994).

Hermione Hobhouse and Ann Saunders, eds, *Good and Proper Materials: The fabric of London since the Great Fire*, London Topographical Society (London, 1989).

Brian Hobley, John Schofield *et al.*, 'Excavations in the City of London: First interim report, 1974–1975', *Antiquaries Journal*, lvii (1977), pp. 39, 41.

O. F. G. Hogg, *The Royal Arsenal: Its background, origin and subsequent history* (London, 1963).

R. A. Houston, *Literacy in Early Modern Europe: Culture and education 1500–1800* (Harlow, 2002).

Huguenot Society Publications, xxiii: *The Registers of the French Church, Threadneedle Street, London* (London, 1906).

Johan Huizinga, *The Waning of the Middle Ages* [1924], reprint (New York, 1954).

Stephen Humphrey, *Britain in Old Photographs: Camberwell, Dulwich and Peckham* (Stroud, 1996).

Margaret R. Hunt, *The Middling Sort: Commerce, gender and the family in England, 1680–1780* (Berkeley, Calif., 1996).

Catherine E. Hutchins, ed., *Everyday Life in the Early Republic* (Winterthur, 1994).

E. W. Ives, R. J. Knecht and J. J. Scarisbrick, eds, *Wealth and Power in Tudor England* (London, 1978).

Gordon Jackson, *The History and Archaeology of Ports* (Tadworth, 1983).

Gordon Jackson, 'Ports 1700–1840', in Clark, ed., 2000, pp. 705–31.

Neil Jackson, 'Built to sell: The speculative house in nineteenth-century London', in Cunningham and Anderson, eds, 1998, pp. 79–97.

Herman Janse, *Building Amsterdam* [. . .], trans. Sue Baker (Amsterdam, 2001).

Paul Jeffery, 'Thomas Archer's Deptford rectory: A reconstruction', *Georgian Group Journal*, iii (1993), pp. 32–42.

David J. Johnson, *Southwark and the City* (Oxford, 1969).

Matthew Johnson, *Housing Culture: Traditional architecture in an English landscape* (London, 1993).

Matthew Johnson, *An Archaeology of Capitalism* (Oxford, 1996).

Matthew Johnson, 'Vernacular architecture: The loss of innocence', *Vernacular Architecture*, xxviii (1997), pp. 13–19.

P. E. Jones, 'Four fifteenth-century London plans', *London Topographical Record*, xxiii (1972), pp. 35–41.

Patrick Joyce, ed., *The Historical Meanings of Work* (Cambridge, 1987).

A. F. Kelsall, 'The London house plan in the later 17th century', *Post-medieval Archaeology*, viii (1974), pp. 80–91.

Frank Kelsall, 'A note on the building', *Post-medieval Archaeology*, x (1976), pp. 158–9.

Frank Keyse, *Thomas Keyse and the Bermondsey Spa* (Aberystwyth, 1986).

Martin King, 'A late eighteenth century wall stencil at 53 Cross Street, Islington', MA dissertation, Royal College of Art and Victoria and Albert Museum, London, 1995.

F. D. Klingender, ed., *Hogarth and English Caricature* (London, 1944).

Roger Knight, 'From impressment to task work: Strikes and disruption in the Royal Dockyards, 1688–1788', in Lunn and Day, eds, 1999, pp. 1–20.

C. C. Knowles and P. H. Pitt, *The History of Building Regulation in London: 1189–1972* (London, 1972).

Michael Laithwaite, 'Totnes houses, 1500–1800', in Clark, ed., 1984, pp. 62–98.

John Landers, *Death and the Metropolis: Studies in the demographic history of London 1670–1830* (Cambridge, 1993).

Joan Lane, *Apprenticeship in England, 1600–1914* (London, 1996).

John Langton, 'Urban growth and economic change: From the late seventeenth century to 1841', in Clark, ed., 2000, pp. 453–90.

Gabrielle M. Lanier and Bernard L. Herman, *Everyday Architecture of the Mid-Atlantic: Looking at buildings and landscapes* (Baltimore, 1997).

Brian Lavery and Simon Stephens, *Ship Models: Their purpose and development from 1650 to the present* (London, 1995).

Roderick J. Lawrence, 'Integrating architectural, social and housing history', *Urban History*, xix/1 (April 1992), pp. 39–63.

Paul Laxton, 'The evidence of Richard Horwood's maps for residential building in London, 1799–1819', *London Journal*, xxiv/1 (1999), pp. 1–22.

Roger Leech, *Early Industrial Housing: The Trinity area of Frome* (London, 1981).

Roger H. Leech, 'The prospect from Rugman's Row: The row house in late sixteenth- and early seventeenth-century London', *Archaeological Journal*, cliii (1996), pp. 201–42.

B. R. Leftwich, 'The parish of St Nicholas, Deptford', *Ecclesiological Society Transactions*, i/4 (1941), pp. 199–225.

Jill Lever and John Harris, *Illustrated Dictionary of Architecture 800–1914* (London, 1993).

Wilmarth Sheldon Lewis, *The Yale Edition of Horace Walpole's Correspondence*, xxxvii (London, 1974).

Peter Linebaugh, *The London Hanged: Crime and civil society in the eighteenth century* (London, 1991).

Peter Linebaugh and Marcus Rediker, *The Many-headed Hydra: Sailors, slaves, commoners and the hidden history of the revolutionary Atlantic* (London, 2000).

Todd Longstaffe-Gowan, *The London Town Garden, 1700–1840* (London, 2001).

Hentie Louw, 'The mechanisation of architectural woodwork in Britain from the late eighteenth to the early twentieth century and its practical, social and aesthetic implications', i-iv, *Construction History*, viii (1992), pp. 21–54; ix (1993), pp. 27-50; xi (1995), pp. 51–72; xii (1996), pp. 19–40.

Hentie Louw, ed., *The Place of Technology in Architectural History*, Papers from the Joint Symposium of the Society of Architectural Historians of Great Britain and the Construction History Society (London, 2001).

David Lowenthal, *The Past is a Foreign Country* (Cambridge, 1985).

Jules Lubbock, *The Tyranny of Taste: The politics of architecture and design in Britain, 1550–1960* (London, 1995).

Kenneth Lunn and Ann Day, eds, *History of Work and Labour Relations in the Royal Dockyards* (London, 1999).

Philip MacDougall, 'The Royal Dockyards of Woolwich and Deptford', in Carr, ed., 1986, pp. 111–26.

Philip MacDougall, 'The changing nature of the dockyard dispute, 1790–1840', in Lunn and Day, eds, 1999, pp. 41–65.

Bob Machin, 'The lost cottages of England: An essay on impermanent building in post-medieval England', typescript, Vernacular Architecture Group, 1997.

Alison Maguire with Howard Colvin, eds, 'A collection of seventeenth-century architectural plans', *Architectural History*, xxxv (1992), pp. 140–82.

B. E. Maidment, *Reading Popular Prints, 1790–1870* (Manchester, 1996).

David Mander, ed., *The London Borough of Hackney in Old Photographs* (Gloucester, 1989).

David Mander, *More Light, More Power: An illustrated history of Shoreditch* (London, 1996a).

David Mander, 'One for the roads: Highways in Hackney before 1872', *Hackney History*, ii (1996b), pp. 9–16.

Peter Marcan, *Visions of Southwark* (London, 1997).

Peter Marcan, *Bermondsey and Rotherhithe Perceived* (London, 1998).

Thomas A. Markus, *Buildings and Power: Freedom and control in the origin of modern building types* (London, 1993).

John Marriott and Masaie Matsumura, eds, *The Metropolitan Poor: Semi-factual accounts, 1795–1910* (London, 1999).

Alan Mayne and Tim Murray, eds, *The Archaeology of Urban Landscapes: Explorations in slumland* (Cambridge, 2001).

Elizabeth McKellar, 'The city and the country: The urban vernacular in late seventeenth and early eighteenth century London', in Burton, ed., 1996, pp. 10–18.

Elizabeth McKellar, *The Birth of Modern London: The development and design of the city 1660–1720* (Manchester, 1999a).

Elizabeth McKellar, 'Peripheral visions: Alternative aspects and rural presences in mid-eighteenth-century London', *Art History*, xxii/4 (November 1999b), pp. 495–513.

Elizabeth McKellar, 'Popularism versus professionalism: John Summerson and the twentieth-century creation of "the Georgian"', in Arciszewska and McKellar, eds, forthcoming.

Elizabeth McKellar, *Landscapes of London: The metropolitan environs, 1660–1830*, forthcoming.

Neil McKendrick, John Brewer and J. H. Plumb, *The Birth of a Consumer Society: The commercialization of eighteenth-century England* (London, 1982).

Bob Meeson, 'Archaeological evidence and analysis: A case study from Staffordshire', *Vernacular Architecture*, xxxii (2001), pp. 1–15.

R. Meischke *et al.*, *Huizen in Nederland: Amsterdam* (Amsterdam, 1995).

Tim Meldrum, 'Domestic service, privacy and eighteenth-century metropolitan households', *Urban History*, xxvi/1 (1999), pp. 27–39.

Tim Meldrum, *Domestic Service and Gender 1660–1750: Life and work in the London household* (Harlow, 2000).

Eric Mercer, *English Vernacular Houses: A study of traditional farmhouses and cottages* (London, 1975).

Eric Mercer, 'The unfulfilled wider implications of vernacular architecture studies', *Vernacular Architecture*, xxviii (1997), pp. 9–12.

J. F. Merritt, ed., *Imagining Early Modern London: Perceptions and portrayals of the city from Stow to Strype, 1598–1720* (Cambridge, 2001).

Christopher Miele, *Hoxton: Architecture and history over five centuries* (London, 1993).

Chris Miele, 'From aristocratic ideal to middle-class idyll: 1690–1840', in Saint, intr., 1999, pp. 31–59.

Mary Mills, *Greenwich Marsh: The 300 Years before the Dome* (London, 1999).

Derek Morris, 'Fitzhugh House, Mile End Old Town, Stepney 1738–1849', *London Topographical Society Newsletter* (May 1999), pp. 10–11.

Derek Morris, 'Land tax assessments for Mile End Old Town, 1741–90', *London Topographical Society Newsletter* (November 2000), pp. 5–7.

Derek Morris, *Mile End Old Town 1740–1780: A social history of an early modern suburb*, East London History Society (London, 2002).

Arthur Morrison, *A Child of the Jago* (London, 1896, reprinted 1966).

Kathryn Morrison, *The Workhouse: A study of poor-law buildings in England* (Swindon, 1999).

Roger Morriss, 'Samuel Bentham and the management of the Royal Dockyards, 1796–1807', *Bulletin of the Institute of Historical Research*, liv/130 (November, 1981), pp. 226–40.

Roger Morriss, *The Royal Dockyards during the Revolutionary and Napoleonic Wars* (Leicester, 1983).

Roger Morriss, 'Government and community: The changing context of labour relations, 1770–1830', in Lunn and Day, eds, 1999, pp. 21–40.

Elaine Murphy, 'The metropolitan pauper farms 1722–1834', *London Journal*, xxvii/1 (2002), pp. 1–18.

Stefan Muthesius, *The English Terraced House* (London, 1982).

Hoh-Cheung Mui and Lorna H. Mui, *Shops and Shopkeeping in Eighteenth-century England* (London, 1989).

Lynda Nead, *Victorian Babylon: People, streets and images in 19th-century London* (London, 2000).

Freda Neale, 'Deptford 1745', typescript, LLSA, 1992.

Philip Norman, 'London buildings photographed, 1860–1870', *London Topographical Record*, ii (1903), pp. 36–41.

Sheila O'Connell *et al.*, *London 1753* (London, 2003).

Miles Ogborn, *Spaces of Modernity: London's geographies, 1680–1780* (London, 1998).

Paul Oliver, ed., *Encyclopaedia of Vernacular Architecture of the World*, 3 vols (Cambridge, 1997).

Donald J. Olsen, *Town Planning in London: The eighteenth and nineteenth centuries* (London, 2/1982).

B. H. St. J. O'Neil, 'North Street, Folkestone, Kent', *Antiquaries Journal*, xxix (1949), pp. 8–12.

B. H. St. J. O'Neil, 'Bridge House, 64 George Row, Bermondsey', *Antiquaries Journal*, xxxii (1952), pp. 192–7.

B. H. St. J. O'Neil, 'Some seventeenth-century houses in Great Yarmouth', *Archaeologia*, xcv (1953), pp. 141–80.

William Palin, 'The conception and siting of the "Stepney Churches": A study of the relationship between the churches of the "Fifty Churches" commission and their surroundings in the parish of St Dunstan's, Stepney', MA thesis, Courtauld Institute of Art, University of London, 1998.

John J. Parkinson-Bailey, *Manchester: An architectural history* (Manchester, 2000).

Ronald Paulson, *Hogarth*, iii: *Art and Politics 1750–1764* (Cambridge, 1993).

Valerie Pearl, 'Change and stability in seventeenth-century London', *London Journal*, v/1 (May 1979), pp. 3–34.

Sarah Pearson, 'Exploring the issues: Changing attitudes to understanding and recording', in Pearson and Meeson, eds, 2001, pp. 3–10.

Sarah Pearson and Bob Meeson, eds, *Vernacular Buildings in a Changing World: Understanding, recording and conservation*, Council for British Archaeology Research Report 126 (York, 2001).

Margaret Pelling, 'Skirting the city? Disease, social change and divided households in the seventeenth century', in Griffiths and Jenner, eds, 2000, pp. 154–75.

Nikolaus Pevsner, *Pioneers of the Modern Movement from William Morris to Walter Gropius* (London, 1936).

Nikolaus Pevsner, *The Buildings of England: London except [. . .]*, ii (Harmondsworth, 1952).

Nikolaus Pevsner, *An Outline of European Architecture* (London, 7/1963).

Nikolaus Pevsner and David Lloyd, *The Buildings of England: Hampshire and the Isle of Wight* (Harmondsworth, 1967).

Hugh Phillips, *Mid-Georgian London: A topographical and social survey of central and western London about 1750* (London, 1964).

J. F. C. Phillips, *Shepherd's London* (London, 1976).

Michael Phillips, 'Reconstructing William Blake's lost studio: No. 13 Hercules Buildings, Lambeth', *British Art Journal*, ii/1 (2000), pp. 43–8.

Christopher Phillpotts, 'Church Street, Woolwich: Archaeological assessment', report for Woolwich Church Street Development Ltd, September 1996.

Christopher Phillpotts, 'Deptford Creek: Archaeological desk-based assessment', report for the London Borough of Lewisham, Creekside Project, August 1997.

Michael H. Port, ed., *The Commissions for Building Fifty New Churches: The minute books, 1711–27, A calendar* (London, 1986).

Roy Porter, *London: A social history* (London, 1994).

Roy Porter, *Enlightenment: Britain and the creation of the modern world* (London, 2000).

Stephen Porter, *The Great Fire of London* (Stroud, 1996).

Stephen Porter, *The Great Plague* (Stroud, 1999).

M. J. Power, 'East London housing in the seventeenth century', in Clark and Slack, eds, 1972, pp. 237–62.

M. J. Power, 'The East and West in early-modern London', in Ives, Knecht and Scarisbrick, eds, 1978, pp. 167–85.

Michael J. Power, 'Shadwell: The development of a London suburban community in the seventeenth century', *London Journal*, iv/1 (1978), pp. 29–46.

M. J. Power, 'The social topography of Restoration London', in Beier and Finlay, eds, 1986, pp. 199–224.

M. J. Power, 'The east London working community in the seventeenth century', in Corfield and Keene, eds, 1990, pp. 103–20.

Alan Powers, 'John Summerson and modernism', in Campbell, ed., 2000, pp. 153–75.

Ursula Priestley and P. J. Corfield, 'Rooms and room use in Norwich housing, 1580–1730', *Post-medieval Archaeology*, xvi (1982), pp. 93–123.

Iorwerth J. Prothero, *Artisans and Politics in Early Nineteenth-century London: John Gast and his times* (Folkestone, 1979).

Anthony Quiney, 'Thomas Lucas, bricklayer, 1662–1736', *Archaeological Journal*, cxxxvi (1979), pp. 269–80.

Anthony Quiney, 'Benevolent vernacular: Cottages and workers' housing', in Burton, ed., 1996, pp. 45–50.

Kathleen Raine, *William Blake's Fourfold London* (London, 1993).

Stuart Rankin, ed., *Shipbuilding on the Thames and Thames-built Ships* (London, 2000).

Stuart Rankin, 'The shipwrights: From craft guild to trade union', in Rankin, ed., 2000, pp. 74–86.

Steen Eiler Rasmussen, *London: The unique city* (London, 1934, rev. 1983).

T. F. Reddaway, *The Rebuilding of London after the Great Fire* (London, 1940).

Michael Reed, 'The transformation of urban space, 1700–1840', in Clark, ed., 2000, pp. 615–40.

Leonard Reilly, *Southwark: An illustrated history* (London, 1998).

Leonard Reilly and Geoff Marshall, *The Story of Bankside: From the River Thames to St George's Circus* (London, 2001).

William Rendle, *Old Southwark and its People* (London, 1878).

Neil Rhind, *Blackheath Village and Environs, 1790–1970*, i: *The Village and Blackheath Vale* (London, 1976).

Neil Rhind, *The Heath* (London, 1987).

Neil Rhind, 'Joseph Kay: An architect for Greenwich', *Journal of the Greenwich Historical Society*, i/6 (1997), pp. 180–99.

Albert E. Richardson and H. Donaldson Eberlein, *The Smaller English House of the Later Renaissance, 1660–1830: An account of its design, plan and details* (London, 1925).

Harriet Richardson, ed., *English Hospitals, 1660–1948* (Swindon, 1998).

John Richardson, *Highgate: Its history since the 15th century* (Chatham, Kent, 1983).

John Richardson, *Highgate Past* (London, 1989).

Giorgio Riello, 'The shaping of a family trade: The Cordwainers' Company in eighteenth-century London', in Gadd and Wallis, eds, 2002, pp. 141–59.

Donna J. Rilling, *Making Houses, Crafting Capitalism: Builders in Philadelphia, 1790–1850* (Philadelphia, 2001).

Richard Rodger, *Housing in Urban Britain, 1780–1914* (Cambridge, 1995).

Jonathan Rose, *The Intellectual Life of the British Working Classes* (London, 2001).

Millicent Rose, *The East End of London* (London, 1951).

Michela Rosso, '*Georgian London* revisited', *London Journal*, xxvi/2 (2001), pp. 35–50.

N. K. A. Rothstein, 'The silk industry in London, 1702–1766', University of London, MA thesis, 1961.

Natalie Rothstein, 'The introduction of the Jacquard loom to Great Britain', in Gervers, ed., 1977, pp. 281–304.

N. K. A. Rothstein, 'Huguenots in the English silk industry in the eighteenth century', in Scouloudi, ed., 1987, pp. 125–40.

Ian Roy, 'Greenwich and the Civil War', *Transactions of the Greenwich and Lewisham Antiquarian Society*, x/1 (1985), p. 13.

Royal Commission on Historical Monuments (England), *London*, ii: *West London* (London, 1925).

Royal Commission on Historical Monuments (England), *London*, iv: *The City* (London, 1929).

Royal Commission on Historical Monuments (England), *London*, v: *East London* (London, 1930).

Royal Commission on Historical Monuments (England), *Middlesex* (London, 1937).

Royal Commission on Historical Monuments (England), *An Inventory of the Historical Monuments in the City of Oxford* (London, 1939).

Royal Commission on Historical Monuments (England), *An Inventory of the Historical Monuments in the City of Cambridge*, parts I and II (London, 1959).

Royal Commission on Historical Monuments (England), *County of Dorset*, ii: *South-east, part 2* (London 1970).

Royal Commission on Historical Monuments (England), *The Town of Stamford* (London, 1977).

Royal Commission on Historical Monuments (England), *City of York*, v: *The Central Area* (London, 1981).

Royal Commission on the Ancient and Historical Monuments of Scotland, *The City of Edinburgh* (Edinburgh, 1951).

George Rudé, *Hanoverian London 1714–1808* (London, 1971).

John Rule, *The Experience of Labour in Eighteenth-century Industry* (London, 1981).

John Rule, *The Labouring Classes in Early Industrial England, 1750–1850* (London, 1986).

John Rule, 'The property of skill in the period of manufacture', in Joyce, ed., 1987, pp. 99–118.

T. M. Russell, ed., *The Encyclopaedic Dictionary in the Eighteenth Century*, iii: *The Builder's Dictionary* (Cambridge, 1997).

Thomas Max Safley and Leonard N. Rosenband, eds, *The Workplace before the Factory: Artisans and proletarians, 1500–1800* (London, 1993).

Andrew Saint, 'The building art of the first industrial metropolis', in Fox, ed., 1992, pp. 51–76.

Andrew Saint, intr., *London Suburbs* (London, 1999).

Raphael Samuel, *Theatres of Memory*, i: *Past and present in contemporary culture* (London, 1994).

Raphael Samuel, *Island Stories: Unravelling Britain, theatres of memory*, ii (Guildford, 1998).

John Schofield, ed., *The London Surveys of Ralph Treswell*, London Topographical Society Publication 135 (London, 1987).

John Schofield, *Medieval London Houses* (London, 1995).

John Schofield, 'Urban housing in England, 1400–1600', in Gaimster and Stamper, eds, 1997, pp. 127–44.

L. D. Schwarz, 'Occupations and incomes in late eighteenth-century east London', *East London Papers*, xiv/1 (April 1972), pp. 87–100.

L. D. Schwarz, 'Income distribution and social structure in London in the late eighteenth century', *Economic History Review*, 2nd series, xxxii (1979), pp. 250–59.

L. D. Schwarz, 'The standard of living in the long run: London, 1700–1860', *Economic History Review*, 2nd series, xxxviii (1985), pp. 24–38.

L. D. Schwarz, 'Social class and social geography: The middle classes in London at the end of the eighteenth century', in Borsay, ed., 1990, pp. 315–37.

Leonard Schwarz, *London in the Age of Industrialisation: Entrepreneurs, labour force and living conditions, 1700–1850* (Cambridge, 1992).

Leonard Schwarz, 'London 1700–1840', in Clark, ed., 2000, pp. 641–71.

Irene Scouloudi, ed., *Huguenots in Britain and their French Background 1550–1800* (London, 1987).

Malcolm Seaborne, *The English School: Its architecture and organization, 1370–1870* (London, 1971).

Pamela Sharpe, 'Population and society 1700–1840', in Clark, ed., 2000, pp. 491–528.

Timothy Shaw, 'A blaze for the London mob: The burning of the Albion Mills', *Country Life* (29 December 1966), pp. 1722–4.

Alexandra Shepard and Phil Withington, ed., *Communities in Early Modern England: Networks, place, rhetoric* (Manchester, 2000).

Francis Sheppard, *London: A history* (Oxford, 1998).

Francis Sheppard, Victor Belcher and Philip Cottrell, 'The Middlesex and Yorkshire Deeds Registries and the study of building fluctuations', *London Journal*, v/2 (1979), pp. 176–217.

Donald Simpson, *Twickenham Past: A visual history of Twickenham and Whitton* (London, 1993).

A. W. Skempton, 'Samuel Wyatt and the Albion Mill', *Architectural History*, xiv (1971), pp. 53–73.

Paul Slack, *From Reformation to Improvement: Public welfare in early modern England* (Oxford, 1999).

Eric E. F. Smith, *Clapham* (London, 1976).

Joanna Smith, 'Georgian Bermondsey', English Heritage Architectural Investigation report, 2001.

Joanna Smith, 'Completing Greenwich Hospital: Joseph Kay, E. H. Locker, and "the general plan of improvements"', *Journal of the Greenwich Historical Society*, ii/4 (2001), pp. 109–19.

Joanna Smith, 'Moving statues and Maritime Greenwich', *Journal of the Greenwich Historical Society*, ii/5 (2002), pp. 136–45.

R. Malcolm Smuts, 'The court and its neighbourhood: Royal policy and urban growth in the early Stuart West End', *Journal of British Studies*, xxx/2 (April 1991), pp. 117–49.

O. H. K. Spate, 'The growth of London, A.D. 1660–1800', in Darby, ed., 1936, pp. 529–48.

Craig Spence, *London in the 1690s: A social atlas* (Loughborough, 2000).

Alan Stapleton, *London Alleys, Byways & Courts* (London, 1924).

Suzanne J. Stark, *Female Tars: Women aboard ship in the age of sail* (London, 1998).

Jess Steele, *Turning the Tide: The history of everyday Deptford* (London, 1993).

Christine Stevenson, *Medicine and Magnificence: British hospital and asylum architecture, 1660–1815* (London, 2000).

Damie Stillman, 'City living, Federal style', in Hutchins, ed., 1994, pp. 137–74.

Thankfull Sturdee, *Reminiscences of Old Deptford* (Greenwich, 1895).

John Summerson, *Georgian London* (London, 1945, rev. 7/1988; ed. Howard Colvin, rev. 8/2003).

John Summerson, ed., *The Walpole Society*, xl: *The Book of Architecture of John Thorpe in Sir John Soane's Museum* (Glasgow, 1966).

John Summerson, 'The beginnings of an early Victorian suburb', *London Topographical Record*, xxvii (1995), pp. 1–48.

Laurence Gomme, ed., *Survey of London*, iii and v: *The Parish of St Giles-in-the-Fields* (London, 1912 and 1914).

Walter H. Godfrey, ed., *Survey of London*, iv: *Chelsea, part ii* (London, 1913).

London Survey Committee, *Survey of London*, vi: *The Parish of Hammersmith* (London, 1915).

James Bird and Philip Norman, eds, *Survey of London*, viii: *The Parish of St Leonard, Shoreditch* (London, 1922).

W. H. Godfrey, ed., *Survey of London*, xvii: *The Village of Highgate, The Parish of St Pancras, Part 1* (London, 1936).

George Gater and Walter H. Godfrey, eds, *Survey of London*, xviii: *The Strand (The Parish of St Martin-in-the-Fields, Part II)* (London, 1937).

George Gater and Walter H. Godfrey, *Survey of London*, xx: *Trafalgar Square and Neighbourhood (The Parish of St Martin-in-the-Fields, Part III)* (London, 1940).

Howard Roberts and Walter H. Godfrey, ed., *Survey of London*, xxii: *Bankside (The Parishes of St Saviour and Christ Church, Southwark)* (London, 1950).

Howard Roberts and Walter H. Godfrey, ed., *Survey of London*, xxiii: *South Bank and Vauxhall (The Parish of St Mary, Lambeth, Part 1)* (London, 1951).

W. H. Godfrey, ed., *Survey of London*, xxiv: *King's Cross Neighbourhood: The Parish of St Pancras, part iv* (London, 1952).

Ida Darlington, ed., *Survey of London*, xxv: *St George's Fields (The Parishes of St George the Martyr and St Mary Newington, Southwark)* (London, 1955).

F. H. W. Sheppard, ed., *Survey of London*, xxvii: *Spitalfields and Mile End New Town* (London, 1957).

F. H. W. Sheppard, ed., *Survey of London*, xxix–xxx: *The Parish of St James, Westminster: Part One, South of Piccadilly* (London, 1960).

F. H. W. Sheppard, ed., *Survey of London*, xxxi–xxxii: *The Parish of St James, Westminster, Part Two, North of Piccadilly* (London, 1963).

F. H. W. Sheppard, ed., *Survey of London*, xxxiii–xxxiv: *The Parish of St Anne, Soho* (London, 1966).

F. H. W. Sheppard, ed., *Survey of London*, xxxvi: *The Parish of St Paul, Covent Garden* (London, 1970).

F. H. W. Sheppard, ed., *Survey of London*, xxxvii: *Northern Kensington* (London, 1973).

F. H. W. Sheppard, ed., *Survey of London*, xxxix: *The Grosvenor Estate in Mayfair, Part I: General History* (London, 1977).

F. H. W. Sheppard, ed., *Survey of London*, xl: *The Grosvenor Estate in Mayfair, Part II: The Buildings* (London, 1980).

Hermione Hobhouse, ed., *Survey of London*, xlii: *Southern Kensington; Kensington Square to Earl's Court* (London, 1986).

Stephen Porter, ed., *Survey of London*, xliii–xliv: *Poplar, Blackwall and the Isle of Dogs, the Parish of All Saints, Poplar* (London, 1994).

John Greenacombe, ed., *Survey of London*, xlv: *Knightsbridge* (London, 2000).

John Greenacombe, ed., Survey of London: The Charterhouse; Clerkenwell South; Clerkenwell North; all forthcoming.

Bernard Susser, ed., *Alderney Road Jewish Cemetery: London E1, 1697–1953* (London, 1997).

K. Sutton, ed., *Up the Creek* (Deptford, 1980).

Mark Swenarton, *Artisans and Architects: The Ruskinian tradition in architectural thought* (Basingstoke, 1989).

Richard Tames, *Southwark Past* (London, 2001).

Robert Taylor, 'Population explosions and housing, 1550–1850', *Vernacular Architecture*, xxiii (1992), pp. 24–29.

Mary Thale, ed., *The Autobiography of Francis Place 1771–1854* (Cambridge, 1972).

Keith Thomas, 'English Protestantism and classical art', in Gent, ed., 1995, pp. 221–38.

Alan Thompson, Francis Grew and John Schofield, 'Excavations at Aldgate, 1974', *Post-medieval Archaeology*, xviii (1984), pp. 1–33.

Edward P. Thompson, *The Making of the English Working Class* (Harmondsworth, 1968).

Edward P. Thompson, *Witness against the Beast: William Blake and the Moral Law* (New York, 1994).

F. M. L. Thompson, *Hampstead: Building a borough, 1650–1964* (London, 1974).

Peter Thorold, *The London Rich: The creation of a great city, from 1666 to the present* (London, 1999).

Stella Tillyard, *Aristocrats* (London, 1995).

J. G. Timmins, *Handloom Weavers' Cottages in Central Lancashire* (Lancaster, 1977).

Barrie Trinder, *The Industrial Revolution in Shropshire* (Chichester, 3/2000).

Barrie Trinder, 'Industrialising towns, 1700–1840', in Clark, ed., 2000, pp. 805–29.

Geoffrey Tyack, 'John Nash and the Park Village', *Georgian Group Journal*, iii (1993), pp. 68–74.

Blake Tyson, 'Transportation and the supply of construction materials: An aspect of traditional building management', *Vernacular Architecture*, xxix (1998), pp. 63–81.

Blake Tyson, 'Management attitudes towards reusing materials in traditional Cumbrian buildings', *Vernacular Architecture*, xxxi (2000), pp. 32–44.

Dell Upton, 'Vernacular domestic architecture in eighteenth-century Virginia', *Winterthur Portfolio*, xvii/2–3 (Winterthur, 1982), pp. 95–119.

Dell Upton, 'Another city: The urban cultural landscape in the early Republic', in Hutchins, ed., 1994, pp. 61–117.

Dell Upton, 'Lancasterian schools, Republican citizenship, and the spatial imagination in early nineteenth-century America', *Journal of the Society of Architectural Historians*, lv/3 (1996), pp. 238–51.

G. F. Vale, *Old Bethnal Green* (London, 1934).

H. E. Malden, ed., *The Victoria History of the County of Surrey*, ii and iv (London, 1905 and 1912).

William Page, ed., *The Victoria History of the County of Kent*, ii (London, 1926).

R. B. Pugh, ed., *The Victoria History of the County of Oxfordshire*, x: *Banbury Hundred* (Oxford, 1972).

T. F. T. Baker, ed., *The Victoria History of the County of Middlesex*, v (Oxford, 1976).

T. F. T. Baker, ed., *The Victoria History of the County of Middlesex*, vi (Oxford, 1980).

T. F. T. Baker, ed., *The Victoria History of the County of Middlesex*, viii: *Islington and Stoke Newington Parishes* (Oxford, 1985).

T. F. T. Baker, ed., *The Victoria History of the County of Middlesex*, ix: *Hampstead and Paddington Parishes* (Oxford, 1989).

T. F. T. Baker, ed., *The Victoria History of the County of Middlesex*, x: *Hackney* (Oxford, 1995).

T. F. T. Baker, ed., *The Victoria History of the County of Middlesex*, xi: *Early Stepney with Bethnal Green* (Oxford, 1998).

Jan de Vries, 'Between purchasing power and the world of goods: Understanding the household economy in early modern Europe', in Brewer and Porter, ed., 1994, pp. 85–132.

Christopher Wade, *The Streets of Hampstead* (London, 3/2000).

Edward Walford, *Old and New London, Illustrated: A narrative of its history, its people, and its places*, 6 vols (London, 1873–8) [vols 1 and 2 by Walter Thornbury].

Cynthia Wall, *The Literary and Cultural Spaces of Restoration London* (Cambridge, 1998).

Cynthia Wall, '"At the *Blue Boar*, over-against *Catharine*-street in the *Strand*": Forms of address in London streets', abstract of conference paper, 'The Streets of London, 1660–1870', December 1999, at the London Voluntary Sector Resource Centre.

Joseph P. Ward, *Metropolitan Communities: Trade guilds, identity and change in early modern London* (Stanford, Calif., 1997).

John B. Wastrom, 'John Drew's Memorandum Book (1707–1722): The artisan intellectual and the rise of the Renaissance architectural style in New England', MA thesis, Boston University, 1996.

Isobel Watson, *Gentlemen in the Building Line: The development of South Hackney* (London, 1989).

Isobel Watson, *Westminster and Pimlico Past: A visual history* (London, 1993).

Isobel Watson, 'From West Heath to Stepney Green: Building development in Mile End Old Town, 1660–1820', *London Topographical Record*, xxvii (1995), pp. 231–56.

Julian Watson, *Woolwich Reviewed* (London, 1986).

Lorna Weatherill, *Consumer Behaviour and Material Culture in Britain, 1660–1760* (London, 1988).

Lorna Weatherill, 'The meaning of consumer behaviour in late-seventeenth- and early-eighteenth-century England', in Brewer and Porter, eds, 1994, pp. 206–27.

Ben Weinreb and Christopher Hibbert, ed., *The London Encyclopaedia* (London, 1983, rev. 1993).

Raymond Williams, *The Country and the City* (Oxford, 1973).

Duncan Wilson *et al.*, 'Recent work at 3 Terrett's Place: An early-eighteenth-century house in Islington', *ASCHB Transactions*, xv (1990), pp. 25–30.

James Winter, *London's Teeming Streets 1830–1914* (London, 1993).

A. S. Wohl, *The Eternal Slum: Housing and social policy in Victorian London* (London, 1977).

Roger Woodley, '"A very mortifying situation": Robert Mylne's struggle to get paid for Blackfriars Bridge', *Architectural History*, xliii (2000), pp. 172–86.

Christopher Woodward, '"In the jelly mould": Craft and commerce in 18th-century Bath', in Burton, ed., 1996, pp. 1–9.

Donald Woodward, *Men at Work: Labourers and building craftsmen in the towns of northern England, 1450–1750* (Cambridge, 1995).

Kevin Wooldridge, 'The archaeology of 151–153 Bermondsey Street, London', Pre-Construct Archaeology, pre-publication typescript, 2002.

Giles Worsley, 'Inigo Jones and the origins of the London mews', *Architectural History*, xliv (2001), pp. 88–95.

Giles Worsley, 'Designing by numbers: John Carr and the industrialisation of architectural design', lecture delivered to the Soane Museum Study Group, London, 28 November 2001.

Nicola Wray *et al.*, *'One Great Workshop': The buildings of the Sheffield metal trades* (Swindon, 2001).

Patrick Wright, *On Living in an Old Country: The national past in contemporary Britain* (London, 1985).

E. A. Wrigley, 'A simple model of London's importance in changing English society and economy 1650–1750', in Abrams and Wrigley, eds, 1978, pp. 215–43.

E. Anthony Wrigley, 'Urban growth and agricultural change: England and the Continent in the early modern period', in Borsay, ed., 1990, pp. 41–7.

Rebecca Yamin and Karen Bescherer Metheny, eds, *Landscape Archaeology: Reading and interpreting the American historical landscape* (Knoxville, Tenn., 1996).

Eileen Yeo and Edward P. Thompson, *The Unknown Mayhew* (New York, 1971).

David T. Yeomans, 'Early carpenters' manuals 1592–1820', *Construction History*, ii (1986), pp. 13–33.

David Yeomans, 'Structural carpentry in London building', in Hobhouse and Saunders, eds, 1989, pp. 38–47.

David Yeomans, '18C timber construction', *Architect's Journal* (10 July 1991), pp. 51–6.

Martha A. Zierden and Bernard L. Herman, 'Charleston townhouses: Archaeology, architecture, and the urban landscape, 1750–1850', in Yamin and Metheny, eds, 1996, pp. 193–227.

Illustration Credits

Index

Page numbers in *italic* refer to an illustration on that page, or to information in its caption, which may appear on an adjacent page.